# The Treasury of Precious Instructions: Essential Teachings of the Eight Practice Lineages of Tibet

## Volume 14: Chöd

## The Tsadra Foundation Series

*published by Snow Lion, an imprint of Shambhala Publications*

Tsadra Foundation is a U.S.-based nonprofit organization that contributes to the ongoing development of wisdom and compassion in Western minds by advancing the combined study and practice of Tibetan Buddhism.

Taking its inspiration from the nineteenth-century nonsectarian Tibetan Buddhist scholar and meditation master Jamgön Kongtrul Lodrö Taye, Tsadra Foundation is named after his hermitage in eastern Tibet, Tsadra Rinchen Drak. The Foundation's various program areas reflect his values of excellence in both scholarship and contemplative practice, and the recognition of their mutual complementarity.

Tsadra Foundation envisions a flourishing community of Western contemplatives and scholar-practitioners who are fully trained in the traditions of Tibetan Buddhism. It is our conviction that, grounded in wisdom and compassion, these individuals will actively enrich the world through their openness and excellence.

This publication is a part of Tsadra's Foundation's Translation Program, which aims to make authentic and authoritative texts from the Tibetan traditions available in English. The Foundation is honored to present the work of its fellows and grantees, individuals of confirmed contemplative and intellectual integrity; however their views do not necessarily reflect those of the Foundation.

Tsadra Foundation is delighted to collaborate with Shambhala Publications in making these important texts available in the English language.

# Chöd

*The Sacred Teachings on Severance*

THE TREASURY OF PRECIOUS INSTRUCTIONS:
ESSENTIAL TEACHINGS OF THE EIGHT
PRACTICE LINEAGES OF TIBET
VOLUME 14

Compiled by Jamgön Kongtrul Lodrö Taye

TRANSLATED BY
*Sarah Harding*

SNOW LION
BOULDER
2016

Snow Lion
An imprint of Shambhala Publications, Inc.
2129 13th Street
Boulder, Colorado 80302
www.shambhala.com



9 8 7 6 5 4 3 2

Printed in the United States of America

Shambhala Publications makes every effort to print on acid-free, recycled paper.

Shambhala is distributed worldwide by Penguin Random House, Inc., and its subsidiaries.

Designed by Gopa & Ted2, Inc.

LIBRARY OF CONGRESS CATALOGING-IN-PUBLICATION DATA

Names: Kong-sprul Blo-gros-mtha'-yas, 1813–1899, author. |
Harding, Sarah, 1951– translator.
Title: Chöd: The Sacred Teachings on Severance / compiled by
Jamgön Kongtrul Lodrö Taye; translated by Sarah Harding.
Description: Boulder: Snow Lion, 2016 | Series:
The Treasury of Precious Instructions: Essential Teachings of the
Eight Practice Lineages of Tibet; volume 14 | Includes bibliographical
references and index. | Translated from Tibetan.
Identifiers: LCCN 2016011239 | ISBN 9781611803723 (hardback: alk. paper)
Subjects: LCSH: Spiritual life—Tantric Buddhism. | Tantric Buddhism—Tibet
Region—Doctrines. | BISAC: RELIGION / Buddhism / Tibetan. |
RELIGION / Buddhism / Sacred Writings.
Classification: LCC BQ8938 .K6513 2016 | DDC 294.3/420423—dc23
LC record available at https://lccn.loc.gov/2016011239

# Contents

Foreword ix

Translator's Introduction xi

Technical Note xxi

*Source Scriptures and Their Commentaries*

1. Esoteric Instructions on the Noble Perfection of Wisdom 3
*Āryadeva the Brahmin*

2. The Great Bundle of Precepts 13
The Source Text of Esoteric Instruction on Severance, the Profound Perfection of Wisdom
*Machik Lapdrön*

3. Heart Essence of Profound Meaning 29
The Quintessence of All Source Texts and Esoteric Instructions on Severance, the Perfection of Wisdom
*Jamyang Gönpo*

4. Pure Honey 39
A Commentary on the Source Text of Severance, "Esoteric Instructions on the Perfection of Wisdom"
*Drung Sarupa Kunga Paljor*

5. The Great Bundle of Precepts on Severance 75
Outline and Complete Explanation
*Lord Rangjung Dorje*

6. A Hair's Tip of Wisdom 101
A Precious Treasure Trove to Enhance the Original Source Text of Severance, the Esoteric Instructions on the Perfection of Wisdom
*Machik Lapdrön and Drung Sarupa Kunga Paljor*

7. Another Bundle 123
Answers to Questions on the Esoteric Instructions of the Perfection of Wisdom
*Machik Lapdrön*

8. Vajra Play 139
Questions and Answers on the Profound Severance of Evil Object
*Machik Lapdrön*

9. The Essential Bundle 143
From the Severance of Evil Object, Esoteric Instructions on the Perfection of Wisdom
*Machik Lapdrön*

10. The Eight Common Appendices 157
*Machik Lapdrön*

11. The Eight Uncommon Appendices 171
*Machik Lapdrön*

12. The Eight Special Appendices 185
*Machik Lapdrön*

*Door-Opening Empowerments*

13. Opening the Sky Door 197
Instructions on Severance Mahāmudrā
*Rinchen Senge*

14. Object Severance Empowerment Known as Opening the Sky Door 221
*Tāranātha*

15. The Required Liturgies on the Occasion of Venerable Tāranātha's Severance Empowerment of Opening the Sky Door in the Gyaltang Tradition 233

*Instructions and Guides*

16. Practice Manual on the Profound Severance of Evil Object 247
*Karmapa Rangjung Dorje*

17. White Crystal Mirror 257
Notes on the Guru's Teaching Tradition of the Visualization Sequence for Severance Feast Activities "Endowed with All Qualities"
*Tenzin Namdak*

18. Essence of the Vital Meaning 297
A Practice Manual of Profound Object Severance
*Tāranātha*

19. Rainfall of Desirables 311
A Profound Guide on Severance Instruction
*Könchok Bang*

20. The Body Donation and Feeding Ritual Arranged as Convenient Liturgy 321
Combining Lord Rangjung Dorje's Ninefold Spirit Feast and Six Earth Lord Application with Mikyö Dorje's Single-Seat Severance Poem
*Compiled by Karma Chakme*

21. Pearl Rosary 345
A Liturgy for the Donation of the Body in Severance
*Karma Chakme*

22. Source of All Qualities 369
The Severance Feast Activities Arranged Unerringly According to the Teaching Tradition
*Karmapa Tekchok Dorje*

23. Supplication to the Long Lineage by Machik, Appended by Bengar Jampal Zangpo 421
*Bengar Jampal Zangpo*

24. Kagyu Feast Liturgy 431

25. Fulfillment Rituals of Profound Object Severance 437
*Various Authors*

26. Offering Torma to All Ḍākimas 459

27. Distillation of the Profound 471
The Way to Practice the Essence of the Vast Object Severance in a Single Sitting
*Jamgön Kongtrul*

28. Beloved Garden 483
Brief Notes on the Offering and Gift of the Body
*Jamgön Kongtrul*

29. Essence of Auspicious Renown 503
A Ritual of Offering and Supplication to All the Gurus of the Holy Dharmas of Pacification and Object Severance Together
*Jamgön Kongtrul*

Abbreviations 537

Notes 539

Bibliography 587

Index 599

# Foreword

In his vast work *The Treasury of Precious Instructions* (*gDams ngag rin po che'i mdzod*), Jamgön Kongtrul Lodrö Taye, that most eminent of Tibetan Buddhist masters, collected together all the empowerments, instructions and practices of the eight great chariots of the practice lineages. Not only that, but he himself received the complete transmissions for all the practices, accomplished them including the retreats, and preserved them in his own mindstream. He then passed on the transmissions to his own students and all who requested them.

*The Treasury of Precious Instructions* exemplifies how Jamgön Kongtrul Lodrö Taye's whole life was dedicated to teaching and spreading the dharma, whether it be sutra or mantra, *kama* or *terma*, old or new translation school, free of sectarian bias. Without his supreme efforts, many traditions of Tibetan Buddhism would have been lost.

The teachings of the Buddha have now spread throughout the Western world, and there is a growing need for major texts to be translated into English so that Western dharma students and scholars have access to these essential teachings. I was, therefore, delighted to hear that having successfully published a translation in ten volumes of Jamgön Kongtrul Lodrö Taye's *Treasury of Knowledge* (*shes bya kun khyab mdzod*), the Tsadra Foundation has embarked on a second major project, the translation of *The Treasury of Precious Instructions*, and I would like to express my gratitude to them.

May their work be of benefit to countless sentient beings.

His Holiness the Seventeenth Karmapa, Ogyen Trinley Dorje
Bodhgaya
February 21, 2016

# Translator's Introduction

The *Treasury of Precious Instructions* (*gDams ngag rin po che'i mdzod*) is the fourth of the so-called five great treasuries compiled or composed by Jamgön Kongtrul Lodrö Taye (1813–1900), who also signed as Karma Ngawang Yönten Gyatso in some of the texts herein. Kongtrul was one of the greatest Buddhist masters of Tibet. His accomplishments were so vast and varied that it is impossible to do them justice here. The reader is referred to an excellent short biography in the introduction to the first translated volume of another of his great works, *The Treasury of Knowledge*, or the lengthy *Autobiography of Jamgön Kongtrul.* Even if his achievements had consisted solely of his literary output represented in these five treasuries, it would be difficult to comprehend his level of scholarship.

Unlike *The Treasury of Knowledge*, which is Kongtrul's own composition, his other four treasuries may be considered anthologies. Kongtrul's stated mission was to collect and preserve without bias the teachings and practices of all the lineages of Tibetan Buddhism, particularly those that were in danger of disappearing. The English publication of *The Treasury of Knowledge* in ten volumes and the forthcoming translations of this *Treasury of Precious Instructions* in some eighteen volumes, of which this is the first, can attest to the success of his endeavor, perhaps even beyond what he had imagined.

*The Treasury of Precious Instructions* is, in some ways, the epitome of Kongtrul's intention. He first conceived of the project around 1870, as always in close consultation with his spiritual friend and mentor, Jamyang Khyentse Wangpo. The two of them, along with many other great masters, such as Chokgyur Dechen Lingpa and Mipam Gyatso, were active in an eclectic trend in which the preservation of the texts of Tibetan Buddhism was paramount.[1] It was with Khyentse's encouragement and collaboration that Kongtrul had created *The Treasury of Knowledge*—his incredible summation of all that was to be known—and compiled the anthologies of *The*

*Treasury of Kagyu Mantra* and *The Treasury of Precious Hidden Teachings*. This next treasury expanded the scope by aiming to collect in one place the most important instructions of *all* the main practice lineages.

Kongtrul employed a scheme for organizing the vast array of teachings that flourished, or floundered, in Tibet during his time into the Eight Great Chariots of the practice lineages (*sgrub brgyud shing rta chen po brgyad*), or eight lineages that are vehicles of attainment. This he based on a much earlier text by Sherap Özer (Skt. Prajñārasmi, 1518–1584).[2] The structure and contents of that early text indicate that the seeds of the so-called nonsectarian movement (*ris med*) of the nineteenth century in eastern Tibet had already been planted and just needed cultivation. The organizing principle of the scheme was to trace the lineages of the instructions for religious practice that had come into Tibet from India. This boiled down to eight "charioteers"—individuals who could be identified as the conduits between India and Tibet and who were therefore the sources of the practice lineages, all equally valid in terms of origin and comparable in terms of practicum. This scheme of eight practice lineages became a kind of paradigm for the nonsectarian approach championed by Kongtrul and his colleagues.[3]

*The Treasury of Precious Instructions* implements this scheme in a tangible way by collecting the crucial texts and organizing them around those eight lineages. The very structure of the *Treasury* thus stands as a statement of the nonsectarian approach. With all these teachings gathered together and set side by side—and each one authenticated by its identification with a direct lineage traced back to the source of Buddhism (India)—maintaining a sectarian attitude would be next to impossible. Or at least that must have been Kongtrul's hope. In explaining his purpose for the collection, he states:

> Generally speaking, in each of the eight great mainstream lineages of accomplishment there exists such a profound and vast range of authentic sources from the sutra and tantra traditions, and such limitless cycles of scriptures and pith instructions, that no one could compile everything.[4]

Nevertheless, he made a good start in *The Treasury of Precious Instructions*, which he kept expanding over the years until at least 1887. The woodblocks for the original printing—carved at Palpung Monastery, where Kongtrul resided in his nearby retreat center—took up ten volumes. An edition of this is currently available in twelve volumes as the Kundeling printing, published in 1971–1972.[5] With the addition of several missing texts, an expanded and altered version was published in eighteen volumes in 1979–1981 by Dilgo Khyentse. Finally, in 1999 the most complete version became available in the edition published by Shechen Monastery, which is the basis for the current translations.[6] The structure of this enhanced edition, of course, still centers on the eight lineages, as follows:

1. Nyingma (the "Ancient Tradition"), volumes 1 and 2;
2. Kadampa (the "Transmitted Precepts and Instructions Lineage"), volumes 3 and 4;
3. Lamdre (the "Path with Its Result"), volumes 5 and 6;
4. Marpa Kagyu (the "Precept Lineage of Marpa"), volumes 7 through 10;
5. Shangpa Kagyu (the "Precept Lineage of Shang"), volumes 11 and 12;
6. Zhije ("Pacification"), volume 13, and Chöd ("Severance"), volume 14;
7. Jordruk (the "Six Yogas" [of Kalāchakra]"), in volume 15; and
8. Dorje Sumgyi Nyendrup ("Approach and Accomplishment of Three Vajras," also called by its founder "Orgyenpa"), in volume 15.

Volumes 16 and 17 are devoted to various other cycles of instruction. Volume 18 comprises mainly the *Hundred Guides of Jonang* and also includes the catalog to the whole *Treasury*.

## Volume 14: Object Severance

> May One Father Dampa's Pacification of Suffering
> and One Mother Lapdrön's Severance of Evil Object—
> radical methods to sever self-fixation—be clouds of dharma
> that fill the vault of space and shelter all beings in times of
> degeneration.[7]

The sixth practice lineage of the Eight Great Chariots is Zhije, or Pacification of Suffering (*sdug bsngal zhi byed*). This lineage is traced to the Indian adept Dampa Sangye, often called Father Dampa (Pha dam pa). Severance, or Chöd (*gcod*), is considered a subsidiary of Pacification. While some aspects of the lineage can be traced to Dampa Sangye, the two systems of practice are quite separate, and there are no texts attributed to Dampa

Sangye concerning Severance practice as it developed in Tibet. The undisputed progenitor of the Severance tradition was the Tibetan woman known as Machik Lapdrön. However, as an indigenous school, Severance did not warrant separate classification within the schema of the Eight Great Chariots. It is ironic in a way that while Severance holds a unique position of pride for Tibetans because it was founded by a native Tibetan and supposedly spread to India in a reverse trajectory, that very fact keeps it as an adjunct system. Pacification of Suffering, which is rarely practiced these days, is the subject of volume 13 in *The Treasury of Precious Instructions*, while Machik's Severance is the subject of this fourteenth volume.

Machik Lapkyi Drönma (or Drolma) (Ma gcig Lab kyi sgron ma/grol ma), "The One Mother, the Light of Lap," was born in the town of Tsomer in the Lapchi region of Tibet in 1055, according to sources.[8] She was, of course, a remarkable person, rising above the oppressive limitations most women in the culture experienced and developing one of the great teaching traditions of Tibetan Buddhism. Her life of trials and accomplishments is readily available now both in Tibetan and in Western languages.[9] Of notable significance for her lineage were her connections with Dampa Sangye through her own guru Sönam Lama, direct experiences of the goddess Tārā, and realizations of the perfection of wisdom. In fact, she is often considered an emanation of the Great Mother (the perfection of wisdom), which is reflected in the appellation One Mother. During her long life of nearly a century, this one mother transmitted her realizations and practice systems to her children, grandchildren, and countless spiritual disciple-children. Though some of the teaching lines seem no longer extant, the Severance tradition continued to expand from those original disciples along a dizzying array of lineages (which will not be tackled here), until it pervaded the entire Himalayan region. Now, in the twenty-first century, the global proliferation of new texts and interpretations seems barely to have slowed down.

Almost every writer on the Severance tradition mentions this enormous proliferation of texts. A short anecdote from Jonangpa Kunga Drölchok's *Lineage Stories from the Hundred Guides* in volume 18 of this *Treasury* describes the situation as early as the sixteenth century:

> Regarding Object Severance, the only definite writings from India are the great and small poems by Āryadeva the Brahmin. These are not in the Tengyur of U-Tsang. She who was self-liberated in Tibet, the Lady Mother [Machik], greatly expanded on this. One time a Shākya geshe came to visit Rinchen Gangpa

> and found him sitting inside a four-pillared room. All around him the room was filled with stacks of cloth-bound volumes. The geshe asked, "What are all these volumes?" He replied that they were exclusively about the Severance of Machik. [The geshe] was astonished and exclaimed, "You have so many texts on Object Severance!" He replied, "If one collected in a single location all the texts on Object Severance, they would not fit in an entire valley." As this story illustrates, there are a lot![10]

So how was Jamgön Kongtrul to fit them all into a single volume of his *Treasury of Precious Instructions*? Although one can find enough information on how and why he created the *Treasury* in general, it is more difficult to understand his specific choices to include what must have been a tiny fraction of the available texts on the subject. The most apparent pattern in this "paradigm of the nonsectarian approach" is that, other than the few ancient source texts, almost all the texts included in this volume come from the Kagyu tradition, specifically the Karma Kagyu lineage and its subsects of Nedo and Zurmang. The only exceptions are the texts of Tāranātha, tracing back to the visionary Samten Özer, which may be considered the Jonangpa lineage.

Despite the success and popularity of the Severance practice, and perhaps because of its particular yogic character emphasizing the wandering lifestyle, the tradition never developed monastic institutions with successions of lineage holders like the other major traditions. Thus it was "available" to be adopted by other schools when their affiliated masters made a connection with it. For instance, there is a thriving Severance system within the Nyingma of both *kama* (original) and *terma* (rediscovered) texts. A few of the latter are in Kongtrul's *Treasury of Hidden Teachings*. The same is true for the Gelukpa school, at least since the time of Tsongkhapa (1357–1419). But it does appear that it is in the Kagyu lineage, at least since the time of the third Karmapa, Rangjung Dorje (1284–1339), where Severance was pointedly cultivated and held in such a prominent place in the roster of practices. And in the massive record of transmissions received by Jamgön Kongtrul, the comparatively short section on Severance reveals only Kagyu and Jonang transmissions, which may be another very practical reason that he chose these particular texts.[11]

In the catalog of *The Treasury of Precious Instructions*, Kongtrul organizes the contents of this volume into three major sections: first, the ancient source or "root" texts, along with a few commentaries on them; next, the required empowerments that "open the door" to effective practice; and finally, the guides—liturgies for practice and their explanations. This sequence was maintained in the Kundeling edition but for some reason was changed around in the Dilgo Khyentse and Shechen editions. Although I have relied on the most complete Shechen edition for these translations, it seemed to make more sense to follow Kongtrul's original order, indicated in the Kundeling edition's table of contents. Short introductions have been offered at the beginning of each text, so only a brief survey of the contents will be made here.

### *Source Scriptures and Their Commentaries*

Three primary source texts are provided: the "grand poem" by Āryadeva the Brahmin entitled *Esoteric Instructions on the Noble Perfection of Wisdom*; Machik's *Great Bundle of Precepts*; and *Heart Essence of Profound Meaning* by Jamyang Gönpo (b. 1196 or 1208), probably the earliest commentator in the lineage. As noted earlier, the Āryadeva poem is the only source text of Indian origin. Kunga Paljor's commentary on it and Karmapa Rangjung Dorje's commentary on the *Great Bundle* are also included. There is also a commentary on a text called *A Hair's Tip of Wisdom*, very likely a source teaching by Machik that has not been found as a separate text. Then there are two more "bundles" (*tshom*) attributed to Machik, though it seems clear that only *Another Bundle* and its attached *Vajra Play* could actually be notes by her disciples based on her teachings, while the *Essential Bundle* is someone's gloss of her teachings. Finally there are the three sets of eight *Appendices*, also collections of what might be notes on Machik's teachings but unlikely to be her direct compositions. Of these three, only *The Common Appendices* are cited in later Severance instructions and might validly be attributed to Machik.

All the texts contain remarkable material. What seems most interesting in the early texts that can safely be attributed to Machik Lapdrön is that the visualization of dismembering the body and offering it to spirits—which has become the hallmark of Severance practice—is barely and only indirectly mentioned.[12] What is taught in these earliest iterations is the fundamental view of the perfection of wisdom. Machik's particular realization of this essential Buddhist teaching came to her through understanding the idea of "evil" or "devil" (*bdud*; Skt. *māra*)[13] while reciting the Perfection of Wisdom sutras. So there is no shortage of references to devils throughout the source texts, and no question that the primary goal of these teachings is to deal with those devils, whether they are conceived of as demons, as adverse circumstances, as ego, or as ultimate evil and ignorance. Simply put, the term used to describe that process is *chöd* (*gcod*, "to sever or cut"), not in the sense of cutting up a corpse but of attaining definite resolution of one's fears and obstacles—the "object" or "field" (*yul*) to be severed—through the profound realization of emptiness and compassion. Thus we get the full title of this practice tradition: Severance of Evil Object (*bdud kyi gcod yul*). The body donation practice (*lus byin*) seems to have developed later and is considered the postmeditation activity. As Kongtrul has stated:

> [T]his unbroken tradition of ripening and liberating instructions has the sutras on the perfection of wisdom as the scriptural source of its view and the various methods which distinguish the Mantra Vehicle.[14]

### *Door-Opening Empowerments*

With the development of Mantra techniques, it became necessary for practitioners to receive the empowerment or initiation, one of the three requirements for tantric practice along with the reading transmission and the instructions. This section includes two: an authorization ritual (*rjes gnang*), similar but simpler than an empowerment (*dbang*), by Rinchen Senge; and an empowerment by Jonang Tāranātha. Both carry the signature phrase of Severance—opening the sky door—in their titles. In addition, there is a text of notations used to supplement the instructions and liturgies of Tāranātha's ritual. Many of the liturgies that are so familiar in Severance practice are included in these texts. All Severance empowerments hark back to an important mystical experience in Machik's life during an empowerment from her guru that became known as the "dharma empowerment bestowed on the mind," meaning initiation into ultimate reality.[15]

### *Instructions and Guides*

The many texts included in the section of instructions and guides are varied and not so varied, as the same beloved liturgies are used again and again in the Severance tradition. Only Karmapa Tekchok Dorje's *Source of All Qualities* attempts to actually identify their original authors. All of the fourteen texts in this section represent the later Severance tradition, which tends to emphasize the body-offering practice with its complex visualizations. Most of them are practice liturgies, supplications, healing rituals, and communal feast offerings, along with instructions on how to implement those practices. For an actual commentary, Kongtrul added his own well-known *Beloved Garden*, probably the most closely followed instruction among modern-day practitioners. With so much material collected here in this volume, it would be redundant to attempt a description of the Severance practice in this introduction. The reader should refer to Kongtrul's own overview of Severance in *The Treasury of Knowledge* as well as various Western-language publications, transcripts, and dissertations.[16] The last text in this volume is called *Essence of Auspicious Renown: A Ritual of Offering and Supplication to All the Gurus of the Holy Dharmas of Pacification and Object Severance Together*, which describes exactly what it is. This is Kongtrul's grand finale to both volume 13 on Pacification (forthcoming) and this volume 14 on Severance. His colophon in this text can stand for the whole volume:

> *The Treasury of Precious Instructions* contains the deep meaning of the essence of the Eight Great Chariots of the practice lineages unified like a priceless gem. Here, the focus was the branches of the Teachings of Pacification and Severance. It was written by Karma Ngawang Yönten Gyatso, or Gyalse Lodrö Taye, who practices the yoga of being nobody, in the retreat place Kunzang Dechen Ösal Ling at the heart of Devīkoṭi Tsādra Rinchen Drak in the upper hermitage of Palpung. May virtue increase.[17]

## ACKNOWLEDGMENTS

None of this would have happened without the initial inspiration of Kyapje Kalu Rinpoche, who started his wayward child–translators on the first project of rendering Jamgön Kongtrul's *Treasury of Knowledge* into English. That tremendous undertaking was finally completed thanks to the unflagging determination of all the translators and the generous support of the Tsadra Foundation, which averted our flagging, just in time. It is fitting and auspicious that we now advance Rinpoche's intention with the translation of another of Kongtrul's great treasuries, which contains the actual instructions that were the subject of *The Treasury of Knowledge*. Ringu Tulku Rinpoche has long envisioned such a translation of *The Treasury of Precious Instructions*, and his encouragement has provided further momentum and support. Sangye Nyenpa Rinpoche expertly conferred the needed empowerments and transmissions at Benchen Gönpa in Nepal over a two-month period in 2014. Through it all, Eric Colombel of the Tsadra Foundation has remained the steadfast benefactor. Truly I cannot adequately express my gratitude and admiration.

For this volume in particular, I am most grateful for all fellow translators, whose work constantly adds to the collective knowledge of the material. I especially appreciate those who worked on *The Treasury of Knowledge*, which, as Kalu Rinpoche had foretold, turns out to be an invaluable resource. I thank those Tibetans whom I constantly pestered for clarification (and who actually know Tibetan!), especially Lama Tenpa Gyaltsen, Ringu Tulku Rinpoche, Khenchen Thrangu Rinpoche, Gangteng Tulku Rinpoche, and Dolmakyab. Finally, I thank my editor Tracy Davis, whose propensity for precision is a perfect counterbalance to my perplexity.

# Technical Note

The anthology of Tibetan texts translated here is the fourteenth volume (Tibetan *pha*) of the Shechen edition of *The Treasury of Precious Instructions (gDams ngag rin po che'i mdzod)*. This volume is titled simply *Volume Two of Pacification and Severance* (*Zhi gcod pod gnyis pa*) or *The Branch: Severance of Evil Object* (*Yan lag bdud kyi gcod yul*). Thus it covers the practice of Severance (*gcod*), a branch or subsect of Pacification (*zhi byed*). Page numbers in curly brackets { } throughout the texts indicate the Arabic page numbers in this Shechen edition. (Cross-references found in the endnotes to the texts in this volume refer to these bracketed numbers.) Those numbers are not entirely consecutive because, as noted earlier, it was more sensible to order the texts according to the so-called Kundeling edition, which follows Jamgön Kongtrul's Palpung woodblocks.

In addition to these two editions of *The Treasury of Precious Instructions*, a newer, edited digital collection (*Dingri Volumes*) containing most of these texts was consulted, as well as any other editions of individual texts that were available to me. It was not practical to cite every mistake or variance in words, so only the most significant have been mentioned in the endnotes, where variant translations or enhanced explanations of certain passages are provided.

Throughout this book, any text found in square brackets [ ] has been added by the translator. This includes bracketed headings as well as many missing lines from familiar prayers and quotations, which were indicated by the ubiquitous "etcetera" (*la sogs pa*) and which assume that the practitioner has memorized a vast repertoire of liturgy. I hope this saves some trouble. With a few exceptions, Tibetan and Sanskrit technical terms have been rendered into English to the best of my ability. However, the range of texts, authors, historical periods, and dialects represented in this anthology is so wide that a given term cannot always be translated in the same way every time it occurs. Wherever similarity in context and meaning permits it, I have tried to maintain consistency in translation.

In the main body of the translations, Tibetan names of persons, spirits, and places appear in the phonetic system that has been developed for *The Treasury of Precious Instructions* by the translators of the Tsadra Foundation. This includes the use of the umlauted *ö* (as heard in the English *push* and *pull*). A final *e* in Tibetan words is pronounced as *ay*. In the endnotes and bibliographies, Tibetan words are transliterated according to the extended Wylie system, with the modification that the initial root letter is capitalized in proper nouns and text titles.

For Sanskrit phonetics, traditional diacritics for romanization are used with the following modifications in proper names to aid in pronunciation: *ṛi, ch, sh*, and *ṣh* rather than *ṛ, c, ś*, and *ṣ*. Mantras remain in standard diacritics. Reconstructed Sanskrit is indicated on first instance and in the endnotes with an asterisk. If a Tibetan or Sanskrit term has entered common English usage and appears in *Merriam-Webster's Collegiate Dictionary*, then it is treated as an English word (e.g., lama, chakra, mandala).

In the bibliography and endnotes, the various references from classical Indian works in the Kangyur and Tengyur are identified whenever possible according to the numbers in the Tohoku catalog (Toh.) of the Derge edition of these collections: *A Complete Catalogue of the Tibetan Buddhist Canons (Bkaḥ-ḥgyur and Bstan-ḥgyur)*, published by Tohoku Imperial University. In addition, the Lhasa Kangyur has sometimes been used, as it is found in the searchable database of the University of Vienna, Resources for Kanjur and Tanjur Studies (rKTs). Citations and references from various Tibetan masters are often located in their respective Collected Works (*gsung 'bum*) or as autonomous texts that most often may be located in the indispensable digital library at the Tibetan Buddhist Research Center (TBRC) using their catalog numbers.

The majority of the texts in this volume are liturgical practices, commentaries, rituals, or a combination of all of those. Wherever the Tibetan is written in metered verse, the translation follows roughly the same line breaks to give a sense of its rhythm. However, it is quite impossible to replicate in English the repetitive, exact meters of the monosyllabic Tibetan, which lends itself so well to chanting. Nevertheless, I hope that something of the lyrical quality comes through this cumbersome rendition that is perhaps too attached to accuracy.

# Source Scriptures and Their Commentaries

# 1. Esoteric Instructions on the Noble Perfection of Wisdom

## Āryadeva the Brahmin

This text attributed to Brahmin Āryadeva (Bram ze A rya de ba) is the single Indian source text for the Sutra tradition of Severance, which is based entirely on the perfection of wisdom. The text appears in several editions of the Tengyur, as well as in collections on Severance. It was known as the *Fifty-Verse Poem* (*Tshigs su bcad pa lnga bcu pa*), or the *Grand Poem* (*Tshigs bcad chen mo*).

There is very little information on the Brahmin Āryadeva, though it is clear that he is not the same person as Āchārya Āryadeva, the famous disciple of Nāgārjuna, since both Āryadevas often appear in the same lineage of Severance. In the many complex lines of transmission, Brahmin Āryadeva is placed variously after Nāgārjuna and Āchārya Āryadeva, after Tārā and Sukhasiddhī, and after Mañjushrī, all indicating his importance as an ancient source. In all cases, however, the direct recipient of his lineage was the Indian Dampa Sangye (d. 1117), who was his maternal nephew. It is Dampa Sangye (also called Pha dam pa, or Father Dampa) who apparently brought the text from India to Tibet, having translated it himself, and gave it to the translator Zhama to edit, as stated in the colophon. Dampa Sangye is sometimes misidentified as the great Indian scholar Kamalashīla (740–795) and even as the Ch'an patriarch Bodhidharma (c. late fourth to early fifth centuries). In any case, it is Dampa Sangye who is considered the forefather of the system of Pacification (*zhi byed*) and its subsidiary, Severance (*gcod*).

The actual lineage of Āryadeva's teaching, known as the "male Severance" (*pho gcod*), is presented in Jamgön Kongtrul's catalog of *The Treasury of Precious Instructions* as follows: "Pa Dampa Sangye gave Kyotön Shākya Yeshe and Yarlung Mara Serpo the autonomous Severance of the Sutra tradition, the meaning of Āryadeva's small *Fifty Verse* source text, as the instructions of the *Six Pieces* (*gDams ngag brul tsho drug*). Kyö gave them to his own nephew, Sönam Lama. He, then, is known to have bestowed four sections to [his disciple] Machik Lapdrön."* Many of Machik's own compositions show the influence of this source text, which had joined with her own realizations derived from her readings of the Perfection of Wisdom sutras.

---

The Sanskrit title is *Āryaprajñāpāramitā Upadeśa.*
The Tibetan is *'Phags pa shes rab kyi pha rol tu phyin pa'i man ngag.*[1]

Homage to all buddhas and bodhisattvas.

The sun and moon of your realization conquer ignorance and misconceptions,
and the moisture of your compassion matures living beings.
Lion of Speech who perfectly completes the two purposes,
I bow to you in sincere devotion with body, speech, and mind.

The essence of the subject matter is the meaning of
nondual perfection of wisdom without root,
freed from referential extremes of nihilism and eternalism.
I will explain as best I can in order to benefit beings.

Rest the three bases to be prepared directly on the word.
Recognize uncontrived, unspoiled awareness:
mind that is the root of both samsara and nirvana,
yet is not established by any causes or conditions;
unborn single cut, intrinsic emptiness.
Such realization is like cutting the root of the tree trunk:
the branches of discursive thoughts will never grow again.

**DNZ*, vol. 18, f. 19a.

Give as vast offerings to the guru and Jewels
actual and emanated appearances in your mind.
After doing prostrations and offerings,
devotedly take refuge and arouse the awakening mind.

Guard like your eyes the precepts you have taken. {3}
Do not abandon the bodhisattva precepts
even at the cost of your life.
Strive to uphold the training.[2]

Abandon the ten nonvirtues, such as killing,
and encourage others to do so as well.
Express approval of what is consistent
with abandoning killing and the others.
Merely abandoning the ten nonvirtues,
you will not discover the supreme path.

Practice the six perfections yourself,
and encourage others to do so as well.
Express approval of what is
consistent with all six perfections.

Turn away from the arising of arrogance
that results from the conduct of virtuous action
such as the six perfections.

If you do not realize that ultimate
nondual perfection is free of extremes
such as virtue/negativity, acceptance/rejection, and hope/fear,
even if you practice conditioned virtue,
you will not become liberated in this very life.

Therefore, do not reference even an atom
in all phenomena, positive or negative,
conditioned or unconditioned.

Nonetheless, wisdom that is not founded
on method will not become manifest. {4}

It is similar to the harvesting of crops
that will not grow without cultivation.

If you do not resolutely engage
in the meaning of the perfection of wisdom,
then even if you engage in generosity, ethical discipline, patience,
diligence, and meditative stability,
you are like a blind person without a cane.
How could you possibly find your way?

The meaning of the perfection of wisdom—
do not seek it elsewhere; you have it yourself.
That is the meaning of inherent great lucid clarity,
not established as an entity or with characteristics.

Meditate on recollecting the Buddha,
naturally clear of thoughts and memories,
free of all mental engagement.[3]

Outer/inner, gods/demons, samsara/nirvana,
appearance/emptiness, and so forth;
free of dualistic appearances,
Buddha's intent is unmistaken and uncontrived,
similar, for example, to the expanse of space.

The most sublime method
is to blend space and awareness.

At the times of mixing space and awareness,
things and characteristics, rejecting and accepting—
fixation on referents—are naturally cleared up.
Abide in the ultimate nature of phenomena
without subject-object dualistic fixation.

With body and mind thus uncontrived,
wherever empty sky pervades
empty direct awareness also pervades.
Rest in the extent of the great pervasive expanse.

At that time there is an experience
of awareness free of basis or root.
Awareness does not dwell anywhere
in the five senses or their objects.

Meditate without dualism in the sites
of rock houses, cemeteries,
haunted places, towns and big cities,
caves, and secluded caverns.

The meaning of the unborn taught by the guru—
practice it during the four daily activities.

If it is put into practice this way,
the blessings of the perfection of wisdom
and the realization that all phenomena are empty
will prevent obstacles from arising.
How would it be possible for emptiness
to pose a threat to emptiness?

When the empty nature of phenomena is realized, {5}
the sign or characteristic is that externally
all objects of the five sense doors—
form, sound, smell, taste, and touch—
are fully illuminated as emptiness.
Inwardly, the coarse afflictive emotions
and subtle dualistic fixation, although they arise,
are self-liberated in nonduality, beyond concern.

With that realization, abiding and arising are liberated
in the nature of phenomena,
like reaching an island of gold.

When a person's root life force is severed,
there is no need to purposefully sever
the eyes and other five sense doors.
Similarly, when the mind itself is severed at the root,
all phenomena are realized to be empty.

Since it severs the root of mind itself
and severs the five toxic emotions,
extremes of view, meditational formations,
conduct anxiety, and hopes and fears;
since it severs all inflation,
it is called *severance* by semantic explanation.

Attachment to real things with passion and aggression
is the tangible devil, so how should one sever that?

Superior, average, or inferior experiencers[4]
rest in the state of no-thought,
meditate with attention on that,
or ascertain it through examination and analysis.

For instance, like a thick forest,
a strong person,
and a sharp axe.

The apparitions of gods and demons that cause inflation
are called the intangible devil.

Set pestilence upon pestilence, directly in the flesh.
Stick the hot needle precisely there.
Go for refuge in the Three Jewels.
Put the morning star under thumb.
Reject closeness and distance toward gods and demons.
Corner the great pestilence.

In Severance, the evidence of having severed is freedom from fear.
Evidence of termination is that apparitions subside by themselves.
Evidence of turning away is fleeing in fear and terror.
Don't turn away; be like a door frame.
Don't flee, even in fear and terror.
Suppress them like a spike,
bend them down, and apply effort.
That is the supreme esoteric instruction.

Worldly gods and demons cannot bear
your meditation on nondual perfections {6}
and cause various kinds of apparitions:
manifesting, overwhelming, dreamt, and so on.

Those with superior meditative experience
rest in the nondual meaning of it all.
The average practitioners focus on that and meditate.
The inferior offer their body aggregate as food.

Afterward, an experience of direct awareness
free of any mental support will arise.

When you go to a haunted place, if gods and demons
manifest overwhelming presence, separate awareness from matter.
This body is matter, like stone;
no harm can come to it.

Mind is not an actual thing; it is like the sky.
Who harms it and who is harmed?
Thinking that, rest without despair or worry
in the nature of phenomena.
Even if you think that the gods and demons
have snatched your material body and left,
without moving from your previous place,
do not despair over anything at all.

Whatever discursive thoughts arise are devils.
They come from your own mind.
In mind, not even an atom is established
of a place from which to arise, to abide, or to go.
Buddhahood does not come after being liberated.
It is impossible to wander in samsara due to delusion.

Virtue, negativity, and all karmic action are totally pure,
pure since forever, liberated since forever, awakened since forever.
One deviates by not avoiding negativity.

Attachment to tenets is an obscuration.
Nondual self-liberation is the abiding nature.

Take refuge from within the nature of phenomena.
Arouse the aspiration and supplicate.
If obstacles arise for you,
go to a haunted place and meditate on the nondual.

In order to help other sentient beings,
with compassion as your preliminary,
know the emptiness of everything:
yourself, the patient, the evil spirit, and the disease.
Pat [the diseased area] and meditate in emptiness.
Face the reclining [patient] toward you.[5]

If thereby [the disease] is not yet pacified,
go for refuge and arouse the awakening mind in a haunted place.
Pass over [the patient] three times and meditate beyond extremes.
With a mandala, bless the sticks and stones
and confer them.

Hold the gods above to their oaths; {7}
subdue with splendor the nāgas below.
Tasks assigned to nāgas will all be accomplished.
Gods, from their abodes, will be your allies.
Nāgas without exception are bound into service.
Gurus, yidams, ḍākinīs, and dharma protectors
will watch over you as their child.

Once you have severed the tangible devils,
appearance will not rise up as your enemy.
Once you have severed the intangible devils,
male and female yakṣhas will be held under oath.[6]

That and other such benefits
that are immeasurable will occur.

The source text *Esoteric Instructions on the Noble Perfection of Wisdom* called *The Grand Poem* by Āryadeva the Brahmin is finished.

The Indian paṇḍita Dampa Rinpoche translated this himself. Zhama Lotsā received it among the ferns of Dingri and edited it.[7]

# 2. The Great Bundle of Precepts

*The Source Text of Esoteric Instruction on Severance, the Profound Perfection of Wisdom*[1]

## Machik Lapdrön

The *Great Bundle of Precepts on Severance* is considered a source text (*gzhung*) of the Severance tradition attributed to Machik Lapkyi Drönma (Ma gcig Lab kyi sgron ma, 1055–1153), also referred to as Machik Lapkyi Drolma, or Machik Lapdrön for short. She was the beloved teacher and famous founder of this lineage. According to *The Religious History of Pacification and Severance* by Khamnyön Dharma Senge (nineteenth century), it was taught in a single day to a large crowd that included three Indians who arrived instantly in Tibet by means of the practice called "swift foot" to investigate the authenticity of Machik and her increasingly popular teachings. As a woman and the originator of a "new" teaching tradition, Machik Lapdrön was under considerable suspicion and often had to prove her worth. In *Machik's Complete Explanation* she explains that the name "bundle of precepts" means that it is based on the long, middle-length, and short precepts of the Buddha Shākyamuni, which she had studied previously. In other words, she maintained that the teachings contained herein are nothing other than the authentic words (*bka'*) of the Buddha.

Such an ancient text has been reproduced many times over the years, and variations have naturally crept in. Notable alternatives in the several editions consulted here have been provided in the endnotes to enhance the range of interpretation.

Homage to the unutterable, unthinkable, unimaginable state:
basic space beyond objects, without reference.

This Great Bundle of Precepts on Severance
is written in hopes of benefiting a few.[2]

The root devilry is one's own mind.
The devil lays hold through clinging and attachment
in the cognition of whatever objects appear.
Grasping mind as an object is corruption.

Devils are classified as four:
tangible devil[3] and intangible devil,[4]
the devil of exaltation,[5] and the devil of inflation.
All are included in the devil of inflation.

Tangible devils are numerous; however,
judging the appearances that arise to our senses,
negating or affirming them, is the tangible devil.
Grasping them as definite binds us to samsara.

Form is empty of the essence of form.[6]
Do not attach to form; meditate on it as empty.
Lacking attachment to form as definite
is release from the devil of fixation on permanence.
Not meditating on emptiness mentally {8}
is definite liberation from the devil of nihilism.
The appearance of form cannot be stopped,
but without definite grasping it is lucid self-appearance.
Sound, smell, taste, tactile sensation,
mentation, and so forth are similarly released.
Mentation is the intangible devil,
but when it arises through the sense doors
it is taught as the tangible devil.
With an attitude of self-liberation,
directly cut through all that appears to the sense perceptions.
It becomes inseparable great stupidity.[7]

Intangible devils occur in this way:
good and bad sensations[8] of mental objects
that are distinguished by one's own thoughts
are revealed as the intangible devils.
Apart from being products of naturally arising mind,[9]
fixating on good gods as gods,
fixating on bad demons as demons,
and all thought-provoking mental hopes and fears
are one's own devils rising up to oneself.

From the realm of phenomena's great expanse of clarity[10]
any thoughts and memories whatsoever may arise;
for example, like the arising of waves and so on
from the unmoving ocean.
Thus a person with realization
rests on their own ground without altering it.
Liberated in space, help and harm do not occur.
Self-arisen from the space of phenomena's nature,
jealous acts and acceptance and rejection do not apply
in self-occurring mind unengaged with acceptance or rejection.

The devil of exaltation occurs in this way:
common devils and supreme devils
come from the mind of deluded cognition.[11]

In haunted places, when demons do not affect you,
arrogance arises and becomes the devil of exaltation.
When signs of blessing and ability occur,
merit and material wealth are the devil of distraction.
Wealth, fame, friends, and foes[12] are the devil of delight.
Gods and demons bestow spiritual powers;
children and relatives gather as entourage
causing joy (*dga'*) and conceit (*brod*): the devil of exaltation
(*dga' brod*).

Whatever qualities occur, whatever arises,
an attitude of nondual object and mind

does not grasp at those qualities [as the self].[13]
As with the objects in dreams,
engage without attachment to their nature.
Like the beauty produced by a lovely face, {9}
self-occurrence adorns itself—
there is no cause for arrogance.
If it does arise, fixating in deluded cognition corrupts.
This supreme conduct of nonfixation's own way[14]
fills the hearts of the wise.

Supreme devils are of two kinds:
those of the path and of the result.

The conceit of a view free of elaboration,
the conceit of a meditation in equipoise,
the conceit of conduct without thoughts,
all conceits on the path of practice,
if engaged in as objects for even a moment,
obstruct the path and are the devil's work.

View and meditation are taught only symbolically;
they certainly have nothing to do with mentation.
Without asserting any notion of a view
about the unimpeded arising of anything,
unbiased experience dawns as basic space.[15]
The supreme Severance is no view.[16]

Everything is self-occurring mind,
so a meditator does not meditate.
Whatever self-arising sensations occur,
rest serene, clear, and radiant.[17]
Serene since the meaning is unchanging,
clear because of definite realization, and
radiant since liberation is on its own ground.
For example, it is like putting butter into butter.
The meditative stability of not meditating—
that is the supreme meditation.

One's conduct is automatically self-liberated.
To do it purposefully is not to engage it.[18]
Do not grasp the arising experience through an antidote.[19]
Even if abolished,[20] when one knows it is self-occurring,
one self-liberates oneself without hindrance.
If there is particularly powerful realization,
definite conduct is uninhibited.
Do not engage conduct without realization.
The customary approach of this instruction
brings blessings of the sublime[21] and the confidence
to directly stamp down discursive thought.
As blessings gradually enter,
definite realization will arise.
This truly spoken instruction
goes beyond all spheres of engagement.[22]
It is said to be the supreme conduct of no conduct.[23]

Taking nothing at all into experience {10}
is to have taken into experience.
Experience is the intellectual experience of knowables.
In the authentic meaning, there is nothing to taste.
Apart from the unborn, there is nothing to take up.
The nature of phenomena is experienced by taking into experience.
Practice without attachment to objective reality
with the attitude of severing objective mental appearances[24]
is the supreme path of freedom, say the gurus.
The result is like a wish-fulfilling gem.[25]

The supreme devil is like this:
desiring the results of tenet systems and vehicles
of the shrāvakas, pratyekabuddhas, and such,
and the definite attainment of the three kāyas
is to have desire: the devil of conceit.

Body, speech, and mind are taught to be
by nature the resultant three kāyas.
Buddha is not accomplished apart from that.

Leaving oneself behind and searching,
even after many millions of aeons
of practicing, will not attain it.
Don't search, don't practice; rest in your nature.
The confidence of severance is to be without hope.
No hope—free of extremes of fear.
Other than the decisive cutting-off of fixation,
how could there be definite buddhahood?[26]

Devils are divided into four,
but they are included in the devil of inflation.

Becoming inflated with objective things
is taught to be the tangible devil.

Attachment and aversion to objective things,
if just realized as inflation at the root,
is like the smoke in the crevices of a wall
that subsides naturally when the hearth fire is extinguished.
Decisively cutting through inflation liberates fixation to real things.
As in cessation, appearances do not stop.
Realizing rootlessness is to cut off
the tangible devil and all definite devils.
For example, it is like a skilled illusionist
who has no attachment to [the created] appearances.
More than that, inflation [should be] decisively cut off.
Even if it is not cut off by severing it,
if rootlessness is realized it cannot take hold.
There is liberation in the expanse of the realm of phenomena.
Resolution without judgment is crucial.

The intangible devil also is included in inflation.
Afflictive emotions such as the five poisons,
fears about invisible demons,
hopes regarding unreal gods, and
all similar hopes and fears about mental objects {11}
arise from inflation and are the devil of inflation.[27]

Aggression is liberated on its own ground,
but it comes from cutting the root of inflation.
Released from the boiling and burning of hell's devil,
the mirrorlike timeless awareness is obtained.
Desire is liberated on its own ground,
but it comes from cutting the root of inflation.
Released from the hunger and thirst of the hungry ghost devil,
the discriminating timeless awareness is obtained.
Stupidity is liberated on its own ground,
but it comes from cutting the root of inflation.
Released from exploitation of the animal devil,
the timeless awareness of the realm of phenomena is obtained.
Jealousy is liberated on its own ground,
but it comes from cutting the root of inflation.
Released from the inconstancy of the human devil,
the timeless awareness of accomplishing action is obtained.
Pride is liberated on its own ground,
but it comes from cutting the root of inflation.
Released from the disputes of the devil of downfall,[28]
the timeless awareness of equality is obtained.
Inflation not decisively cut off is the five poisons,[29]
but inflation cut off is the self-liberated five awarenesses.

Thus everything is included in inflation.
Just as a lion on the high snowy peaks
has no fear or apprehension,
if you attain confidence without inflation,
the gods and demons of apparent existence cannot arise.[30]
Even if a hundred rise up, the instructions will clear them away.
If you know that they are your own apparitions,
it will certainly become a great training exercise.
Don't meditate after severing the flow of thoughts;
realizing that it is self-arising is sufficient.[31]
It is the equivalent of epidemic disease and such.
Once rootlessness is realized, this cutting off
is especially elevated above all instructions.

Even with realization, if you do not directly cut through,
it is like tossing out a tempered sharp weapon:
the view will not protect you, and you are bound by fear.[32]
The yoga that brings together view and conduct
is like the weapons carried by warriors
that vanquish all the enemy hosts.
All devils are vanquished in the space without inflation.

*Emaho!*
Devils are pacified by cutting through one's own inflation.
Awakening is actualized by realizing rootlessness.
So then rest relaxed and unaffected.[33]
Rest just so with everything. {12}

The devil of exaltation is also included in inflation.
Exaltation about common dharma and
exaltation about supreme results
come about from one's own inflation.
Definite attachment turns it into a devil.

Self-arising without attachment is not inflation.
It is said to be the adornment of dharmakāya.

Since the resultant three kāyas are oneself,
there is no need to be conceited about another.

Samsara is liberated on its own ground;
do not seek nirvana apart from that.[34]
Do not meditate purposefully on nonthought
apart from the arising of thoughts' own forms.

Since everything else is inflation,
I speak of decisively severing inflation.
Resting in refined essence is taught everywhere;
there is no recognition of the mind of refined essence.[35]

This is ascertained through example.
Yogins who have obtained the instructions

are like birds nourishing their young:
if instructions are [only] delivered by the lips,
autumn chicks will die of starvation.
One will certainly wander in samsara oneself.

Like a fine cow nourishing a small calf,
when she helps herself to a full belly
it sustains the small calves and such.
If one's own inflation is decisively cut off,
sentient beings[36] will surely become liberated.
No doubt the welfare of others will be achieved.

The great garuḍa soaring in the sky
sees the four continents effortlessly.
With no trepidation in the abyss of deep ravines,
she subdues with splendor the flocks of birds.
Likewise, when experience is decisively cut off,
the four devils are realized as rootless.
Demons and devils and such are subdued by splendor.
There is no trepidation about the three lower realms.
Engaging in cause-and-effect dharma
without a definite understanding of rootlessness
is like leaving the trunk and reaching for the branches.

Yogins who realize rootlessness
know that thoughts and memories are incidental
and engage in the dharma without rejection or acceptance.
Seeing form, they regard it as the mind's Body.
Hearing sound, they regard it as mind's Speech.
Whatever is thought is regarded as mind's Mind. {13}
Behold the meaning of no cause and effect.[37]

The method of resting, the abiding nature of meditation,
is like a statue inside the shrine room:
it has good posture and smiles,
but no thought, and no manner of thinking.
So, set one's body however is comfortable,
and with no thought, do no thinking.

No object of thought: that's exactly it![38]
Therefore rest in the state of no-thought.
Don't cut off sensations and thoughts after the fact.
As lightning bolts revert to the sky,
when conceptual thought occurs, rest just so.
Like the depths of a great ocean,
rest within an unmoving state.[39]
Circumstantial thoughts, like waves,
naturally become the realm of phenomena's nature.

Not to contrive or adulterate is the Victor's Word.
If you contrive, it is the devil of creation,
so definitely rest on your own ground.
Like a person pained by disease,
freely rest the six groups of consciousness.
Like a person who has finished their work,
rest instantly with a satisfied mind.
Like a small child not seeing its mother,
appearing though powerless—rest within that state.

Awareness carries the corpse of one's body;
cast it out in an unattached way
in haunted grounds and other frightful places.[40]
Rest mind itself[41] in the expanse of the Great Mother.
Whatever thoughts and memories consciously occur,
consider them as actual emanations of the Great Mother.
Mother's emanations[42] do not bind to samsara.
Like a simpleton with a full belly,
rest in the complete eradication of concepts.
Samsara abandoned, nirvana is certain.
*Emaho!* Effortless! Realize the intent!

Conduct is presented through analogies.[43]
Like the fierce gatekeepers, the *kinkara,*[44]
although they seem wrathful and fierce,
afflictive emotion does not arise in their being.
In the conduct of truly great yogic discipline

there is no thought of aggression or passion.
Great yogic discipline tames obstacles.
With no aggression or passion, that itself is the path.
Like fish swimming in the sea,
conduct is aimless, without fixation and attachment.[45]
Like mountain ravines cutting off the cold breezes,
attachment-aversion is traceless,[46] beyond consideration. {14}

In one's conduct toward oneself
there is no need to involve inflation or inflated objects.
Conduct yourself without fixating on yourself.
Don't you consider the enemy in a dream
as coming from yourself?
Even the spiritual powers of yidam deities
arise to the mind from the meditating mind.
Therefore, it is oneself, not another.
Other than severing[47] one's own appearances oneself,
there is no connection with others' objects, so they cannot harm,
as, for example, the poisonous snakes of India.

Results are presented by an analogy.[48]
Even though white is not established in butter,
recognizing butter confirms white.
Once butter is just recognized for sure,
there's no need to establish white elsewhere.
Similarly, although buddha is not established,
recognizing the mind confirms buddha.
Once one's mind is recognized for sure,
there's no need to establish buddha from elsewhere.

Inflation-free, rootless, victorious over all:
there is nothing else to accomplish.
With such realization devils are pacified.
Moreover it is self-occurring self-pacification.

Noncognizant stupidity in the realm of phenomena
cognized[49] as objective is deluded by grasping.

Cognition other than of a single inseparability[50]
is to cycle in the places of the three realms
and be deluded in the places of the six classes.
That is inherently deluded cognition.
Gradual vehicles of dharma that are dependent[51]
are also deluded by cognition in view, meditation, and result.
Nihilists cognize the object as absolute nothingness,[52]
eternalists cognize the object as immutability,
shrāvakas cognize objective percept-perceiver,
pratyekabuddhas cognize the emptiness of interdependence,
chittamātrins cognize reflexively aware mind,
mādhyamikas cognize freedom from elaboration,
father tantras cognize bliss-clarity energy currents,[53]
mother tantras cognize the seal of bliss-emptiness,
method and wisdom cognize nonduality,
mahāmudrā is cognition beyond intellect,
and Great Completion cognizes great atemporality.
Thus all of these cognitions
are cognitions that cognize objective [reality],
which is not the subject itself.
Without an object, there is no cognition of mind.
Any cognition is bondage by cognition.

Therefore, this noncognizant (*rig med*) stupidity {15}
the victors teach as great timeless awareness.
Ignorance (*ma rig*) is without object, so delusion is clarified.
When objective appearance is just mentally abandoned,
it is the decisive cutting-off of all inflation without exception.
Without an object what would cognition get inflated about?

If cognition is just understood as delusion,[54]
then without fixation on deluded phenomena[55]
unfixated cognition appears as anything at all,
naturally occurring without deliberation.
If such is the intent, it is ever so.

The genuine meaning, that Great Mother,
is also the ground of all samsara and nirvana.

Even the buddhas of the three times
teach[56] it as uncreated, birthless ground.

Since buddha is unconditioned,[57]
if you believe in the unborn,
then there is no creator of unborn ground.
Errors about unmade ground are severed.

Since the unmade (*ma byas*) is unconditioned,
one definitely travels the path of no making (*mi byed*).
Since appearing emptiness is not mind-made (*yid la ma byas pas*),
take the path without eternalism or nihilism.
Since nonduality[58] is not mind-made,
the devil of four perception spheres is liberated.
Cognitive obscurations are pure on their own ground.

If form and feeling, perception, and so on
are truly not mentally engaged,
they will be liberated from the place of three realms.
They will not become mixed up[59] in samsara.
If nothing at all is made in mind,
habitual patterns won't arise and the levels and paths are complete.
Mental nonengagement as the supreme path[60]
was definitely taught in the words of the Victor.
When one realizes mental nonengagement,
mental activity need not be stopped;
like a mirage it vanishes on its own ground.
The yogins with such realization
need not block carefree conduct.[61]
Whatever is done becomes the path.
Nondoing itself is the path.

Presentation of the unreal results:
three kāyas are taught as results, but
other than teaching the expedient meaning,
the marks and signs and so on
have not even an atom of definitive reality.

If real, whatever is real ultimately falls.
It does not pass to the other side of samsara.[62] {16}
The perfection of wisdom
is not real as an object of the intellect.
To the intellect, samsaric phenomena are real.
Without the realization that results are unreal,
whatever effort is made toward achieving it
will not become the attainment of freedom.

Without annihilating the mind craving dharma,
engaging in dharma with intellectual craving
becomes the support for bondage, despite being dharma.
Thus, one is cheated of the vitality of esoteric instructions.
Buddhahood is not conditional,
so how could one achieve it by conditioned effort?
Don't be mentally attached to conditioned dharma.
Don't place great hope in fabricated dharma.

Not fixating on body is the Victor's Body,
not fixating on speech is the Victor's Speech,
not fixating on mind is the Victor's Mind.
Other than lucid clarity without fixation,
do not seek elsewhere for the Victor's intent.

*Emaho!*
"Severance" means to sever conceptual thinking.
"Precepts" means unchanging in nature.
"Bundle" means teachings as a bunch of explanations.

Earnest experiential practice is taught
beyond referential objects,
free of intellectual experiential practice.

When severing in haunted places and such,
just as one who is burned by fire
is tormented [again] by that fire itself,
the instructions for suppression and severing in a place
are like cauterizing the wounds[63] by fire.

Carry the load of appearing conditions.
Understand that to carry the load is crucial.
If you don't carry the load of all phenomena,
the remedy of peace and happiness can't liberate you.

Wander in haunted places and mountain retreats.
Don't be distracted by text; the words of texts
won't convey blessings, [but] carry word-brutes.
Better to practice in haunted places.[64]

The esoteric instructions on the perfection of wisdom called *The Great Bundle of Precepts on Severance*, created by the Ḍākinī of Timeless Awareness Lapkyi Drolma, is complete.

Note: It is said that there were only eighty [people] present during the oral explanation of this source text given at the time by Drapa Haktön.[65] Early commentaries connected it with the *Verse Summary Sutra*, as can be seen in the outline and commentary by dharma lord Rangjung Dorje. Later on there were many commentaries on the source text. This and the source text created by Āryadeva the Brahmin {17} are the two wish-fulfilling jewels that seem to be like the foundation of all instructions of Severance Object.

*sarvadākalyānambhavatu*

# 3. Heart Essence of Profound Meaning

*The Quintessence of All Source Texts and Esoteric Instructions on Severance, the Perfection of Wisdom*[1]

Jamyang Gönpo

In his catalog of *The Treasury of Precious Instructions,* Jamgön Kongtrul gives the author of this text as Jamyang Gönpo ('Jam dbyangs mgon po, b. 1208 or 1196).* "Heart Essence of Profound Meaning," however, seems to be a general name referring to a whole system of teachings in the Severance tradition, and a note was added at the end of this text stating as much. Kongtrul also writes of the inception of Heart Essence written down by Samten Özer of Gyaltang after a visionary experience of Machik Lapdrön, which later became known as the direct lineage of the Gyaltang system. A collection of texts transmitted by Samten Özer, however, is differently entitled *Cycle of Profound Severance of Evil (bDud gcod zab mo'i skor),* and this is not among them.

In a rare collection of ancient works on Severance entitled *Practices of the Severance Collection and So Forth* (*gCod tshogs kyi lag len sogs*) from Limi Monastery, this same text is signed "the Shākya monk, holder of the vajra, Prajñāsambhava," a Sanskrit translation of Jamyang Gönpo's ordination name, Sherap Jungne (Shes rab 'byung gnas). The brief summary of the work is similarly signed "the Shākya monk, holder of the vajra, Mañjughoṣhanatha," translating Jamyang Gönpo. His brief biography lists eleven titles, mainly on Severance, even though his main affiliation was with the Lower Drukpa lineage. Born in the borderlands between Upper and Lower Nyang (myangs) valleys, he studied with the master Urepa (sLob dpon dBus ras pa) and Zhikpo Kunseng (Zhig po Kun seng) from the age of six. After

**DNZ,* vol. 18, f. 72a.

his mother died when he was fourteen, he entered the monastery at Serding (gSer sding) and was ordained under Lama Martön (Mar ston). His main teacher was Lorepa Wangchuk Tsöndru (Lo ras pa dBang phyugs brtson 'grus, 1187–1250).

The commentary called *The Big General Guide to Severance (gCod kyi spyi khrid chen mo)*, also under the name Mañjughoṣhanatha and available in several collections, is a commentary on this short text, greatly elaborated and inclusive. The translation has been done with reference to this commentary, as have the notes on alternative versions of the root text and the divisions into verse. The page numbers in the notes refer to the edition found in the Padma Lingpa collection.

---

Homage to the guru and mother of the buddhas.

Dharmakāya free of elaboration, unutterable, unthinkable,
unimaginable realm of space,
saṃbhogakāya fully possessing major and minor marks,
nirmāṇakāya as anything to tame anyone for their benefit:
I bow down to the consummate aspiration of emptiness and
compassion.

Mahayana dharma outshining the four devils,
neither inhibiting nor indulging samsara and nirvana, the meaning of
perfection,
making adverse conditions the path; the approach of the Lord Mother:[2]
I write of the Severance instructions that befriend adversity.[3]

[The master should be][4] realized in the words' meanings, full of loving-
kindness, endowed with eight skills,[5]
finished with personal benefit, accomplished in emptiness and
compassion, and skilled in clearing away faults.
[The disciple should] have faith, diligence, devotion, armor, fortitude,
the desire for protection, higher status, and the aspiration to excel or to
gain omniscience.

Receiving supreme empowerment, [the disciple] becomes a vessel for the profound teaching.[6]
Introduce the seeking mind itself through the path of accumulation and purification.
Fortunate ones should adhere to this path of the victorious ones
in order to sever the lack of realization, perverse realization,[7] biased realization, and doubts.

The devils are the gods, the afflictive emotions, the aggregates, and death.
The special four are tangible, intangible, exaltation, and inflation.
[Practice is in] charnel grounds, desolate valleys, temples, isolated trees, deserted houses, and so forth.
Stay in places where your mind is anxious and afraid.
At night, the terrifying gods and demons gather and thoughts abound.
This is the time to sever doubts, clear away obstructors, and enhance realization.

Those who desire omniscience go for refuge and supplicate.
With the sublime thought of enlightenment aroused, [it becomes] the path of emancipation for all beings. {18}

The resident [practitioner] is entrusted to the devil, and host and guest mix as one.
The adversary is entrusted as an escort, and one is free in a secure stronghold.
The patient is entrusted to demons and thrives in well-being without disease.
Be free of negative adverse circumstances by integrating circumstances on the path.[8]

Free the mind of self-fixation by relinquishing the body aggregate as food.
Scatter the master of self-fixation by separating body and mind.
Liberate fear on its own ground by inspecting the fearful one.
From tossing away fixation on the body as self, obstacles will arise as glory.[9]

Obstacles will subside in emptiness from the pursuit of circumstances.
Grabbing hold of evil spirits will scatter the master[10] of fearful objects.
Knowing that everything is mind will liberate on your own ground
without fixation.
Letting go at will and sending off [means that] no one can carry you off.

Whenever someone rests evenly in the meaning of the nature of
phenomena,
devils and such can't bear it and display various apparitions at that time.
Outer, inner, and secret experiential appearances manifest,
various forms show up in dreams, and unpleasant sounds echo
predictions.

When the mind becomes agitated, self-fixation emerges from objects.
Once the inner demons of your mind are tamed, the outer demons
vanish in emptiness.
If feelings of intolerance and insecurity occur, equalize and trample
them.
If fear and anxiety occur, focus intently on the thoughts.

Once apparitions increase, sever painlessly and cut off thoughts:
regret, doubts, wrong views, weariness with dharma,
disease, *duḥkha*,[11] drowsiness, and scattered practice—
as these mistaken thoughts[12] and obstacles occur, exert effort in
accomplishment.

Cornering great mistakes liberates hopes and fears on their own
ground.
Mahayana's overwhelming brilliance puts pleasure and pain in
perspective.
Putting the morning star under thumb collapses the false cave of
samsara and nirvana.[13]
Overpowering pestilence in haunted places destroys gods and demons
as illusions.[14]

If fierce apparitions are big, suppress[15] the gods and demons in place.
If they challenge you, then practice crazy yogic discipline.

If apparitions still display, delight in illness and be happy to die.[16]
Hold them by the hook of a compassionate mind that benefits all. {19}

Know that the times and signs[17] of termination occur in actuality, visionary experience, and dreams,
arising to oneself outwardly, inwardly, and secretly.
If you rest in one-pointed meditative stability within emptiness,
no doubt the delusion of samsara and nirvana will be distinguished in unity.[18]

If there are no signs of uprising in the preliminaries, remove the anticipation of uprising.
If there are no signs of suppressing in the main practice, turn your back on anger and desire.
If there is no evidence of termination at the conclusion, remove the anticipation of evidence.
The hopes and fears of a desiring mind are devils, which the wise reject.

Helpers and harmers are subdued by gentle and fierce conduct.
Make aspirations to establish them in enlightenment through various means.

Desiring the attainment of omniscient buddhahood for oneself and others,
fortunate ones rely on this path of emancipation.

This idea that it is hard to give up long-familiarized habitual patterns
is the single cause that gives rise to the variety of duḥkha in existence.

Here in this charnel ground of collected aggregates and elements of the support and supported,
sever [mental] motion in this place of fluctuating thoughts and memories.

The yogin who has actualized the meaning of empowerment[19] and introduction

[should practice] Severance until this devil of discursive thought
is cut off.

The nature of phenomena primordially possesses incidental stains.
View, meditation, and conduct conquer them in analysis through
ground, path, and result.[20]

When phenomena's nature is ascertained, harmful thoughts abound.
Thoughts about the various objective appearances of knowables come
and go.

Without the courage of realization and the experiences of meditation,
equalizing and subjugating by engaging circumstances does not occur
and you regress.

Cut through the trunk of thought-provocation with the axe of view,
meditation, and action,
and all the leaves of mental events and concepts will be systemically
stopped.

As the warm rays of sunlight overcome all humidity and gloom,
the dawning of timeless awareness removes flaws and you traverse the
stages of grounds and paths.

[There are three methods:] natural nonconceptuality, the transformer's
ability to relinquish through remedies,[21]
and the knowledge to make offerings with the awakening mind of
emptiness and compassion.[22]

Devils and spirits cannot lead you to the lower realms.
Since toxic emotions give rise to the duḥkha of existence, overcome
them. {20}

The place is this haunted charnel ground of channels and elements
collected in one's own body,
where all afflictive emotion spirits abide as in a dwelling.

Light rays of luminous timeless awareness of realization expand.
Until they banish the darkness of ignorance, keep severing.

Whenever afflictive emotions arise, grasp them with the remedy
through view, meditation, and action,
and at that time be totally victorious over devils.

Just as the unpleasant taste of poison in food will rise up,
afflictions of anger and passion will rise up under the influence of
practice.

Unless one has attained tolerance of dharma, the path evinces terrifying
conditions.
Regret, wrong views, doubts, and annoyance with dharma will surface.

When afflictive emotions arise, oppose them with method and wisdom.
Realization of emptiness, transformation methods, and offerings are the
supreme remedies.

The unbearable net of afflictive emotions in the ocean of existence
is best conquered by the equal taste of timeless awareness, the supreme
measure.

With faith, compassion, comprehension, and the vital points of
instruction,
yogis and yoginis practice Severance for the purpose of attaining
emancipation.

Intense sickness, duḥkha, and toxicity are everyone's devils.
They rob the life force of attaining freedom if suchness is not realized.

The support that produces all happiness and sadness, faults and
qualities, samsara and nirvana,
is the abode of four elements, afflictions, winds, phlegm, bile, and
aggregates.

When sickness and duḥkha arise in body, speech, and mind,
you are tormented by painful discordant adverse conditions.

The support for sickness and duḥkha and every fault and problem
is body and mind; if those two are separated, liberation is assured.[23]

Snakes cannot bear a threatening finger pointed at them.
Whoever meditates on the meaning of emptiness quells the sickness spirit and it flees.

Whenever you are afflicted by intense sickness and duḥkha,
you become discouraged and lack confidence, and then give up and become blocked.

Vigor increases with mental heroism, experience, and realization.
The arsenal of view and conduct of acute confidence conquers the devil's hordes.

Sickness and duḥkha subside from the profound integration of method and wisdom.
Free of faults, qualities increase like the waxing moon.

With the confidence of realization, the force of experience, education, {21}
courage, magnanimity, determination, path,[24] vigor, and yogic conduct,

sever the devils of various worldly adversities such as
sickness, corpse spirit-contamination, the eight concerns, and attachment and aversion.

Sever the places that give rise to afflictive emotions such as
one's own house, area, city, country, monastery, and so forth.

The duration is long or short, straightforward time, or until awakening;
[practice] for as long as joy and sorrow, obstacles, and adversities arise.

Integrate sickness, spirits, violation-contamination, the eight concerns, happiness and sadness, and so forth
by meditating on their lack of intrinsic nature and knowing them as karma.

As sickness, duḥkha, and so on become more blatant than before,
various discords occur, such as outer and inner adverse conditions.

When you doubt cause and effect, the instructions, and the spiritual friend,
and fear circumstances, the conditions of the path wear you down.

Since it is nonexistent, how is this appearance of a bad spirit hurting me?
Vanquish this unreal delusion of an enemy with a mental antidote.

When this devil of attachment and aggression, the afflictions of existence, is finished off,
it opens the coffers of all qualities, the source of joy and well-being.

Recognize dreams through diligent accumulation and purification, and intentional conditioning.
When under control, refine, increase, and then meditate on lucid clarity.

Drawing up energy currents and consciousness is the path of transference.
The arising of lucid clarity from subtle and coarse melting sequences is the *bardo* practice.

Physical diseases and various mental problems occur when gods and demons are agitated.
Meditate on emptiness and giving various gifts [of the body] with the courage of possessing the remedies.

Karmic causes and the conditions of afflictive emotion produce all sickness.
Expel them by channel and vital wind methods and yogic exercise visualizations.

Depression, pervasive duḥkha, and lethargy are mental problems. {22}
Meditate on methods and interdependence; do energy-current and yogic exercise visualizations.

Boundless devotion, vast compassion, and reversing and taking on
adverse conditions
become the enhancement of all qualities.

Whoever grasps this supreme Object Severance, the victors' intent,
finds the treasure of the path to freedom and vast, immeasurable
qualities.

Profound and vast, this precious holy teaching that benefits everyone
is especially elevated in its adherents, tenets, continuity, harmony, and
renunciations.

Uphold this priceless precious teaching with devotion,
like someone who grasps the value when finding a real gem.

Through the arrangement of this Severance source text *Heart Essence of Profound Meaning*, distilled from the huge ocean of manifold and profound [teachings], may all migrators realize the meaning of severance in consummating Object Severance and attain the supreme mother perfection, the totally pure space of phenomena.

This completes the esoteric instruction pertaining to Severance of Evil Object, the intention of the perfection of wisdom, the personal advice of the gurus and adepts, the esoteric instructions pertaining to Severance of Evil Object called *Heart Essence of Profound Meaning*, a teaching difficult to find in the world.[25]

Note: This is the root of most of the later instructions. There are many commentaries and guidebooks and such.

# 4. Pure Honey

## *A Commentary on the Source Text of Severance, "Esoteric Instructions on the Perfection of Wisdom"*[1]

### Drung Sarupa Kunga Paljor

The author of *Pure Honey*, the commentary to Āryadeva's *Grand Poem* (see chapter 1), is named in the colophon as Kunga Paljor. Tashi Chöpel's *Record of Teachings Received* gives his full name as Drung Sarupa Kunga Paljor (Drung Sa ru pa Kun dga' dpal 'byor) and states that Kongtrul received the cycle of empowerments and transmissions of all the source scriptures directly from Machik Lapdrön in a visionary experience.[*] "Drung" may indicate the Trungpa lineage, and "Saru" appears to be a place name, since in Kongtrul's catalog his immediate predecessor in the lineage of transmission of Āryadeva's text is called the Great Adept of Saru, Sönam Paljor.[†] The latter was active in the fifteenth century, which gives us an approximate date for Kunga Paljor. He is quoted from an unknown source in *Collected Histories of the Glorious Zurmang Kagyu* to support the theory that Severance is based on the teachings of buddha nature (*sugatagarbha*) as well as those of the perfection of wisdom, despite his own classification of it as a middle-turning teaching in *Pure Honey*.[‡] Other than this, and that according to Kongtrul he also authored the commentary to an important text attributed to Machik called *A Hair's Tip of Wisdom* (see chapter 6), not much information has been discovered. Yet these two commentaries together provide important supplemental

[*] Tashi Chöpel, *Record of Teachings Received*, p. 778.
[†] Sa ru grub chen bSod nams dpal 'byor, *DNZ*, vol. 18, f. 71b.
[‡] *Collected Histories of the Glorious Zurmang Kagyu*, p. 542.

material to the source texts of Severance collected in *The Treasury of Precious Instructions*.

---

*namo gurave*

*Pure Honey* is a brief commentary on *Esoteric Instructions on the Perfection of Wisdom*, the source text on Severance by Āryadeva the Brahmin.

Homage to the sovereign of speech, the awakening being, the great being Mañjushrī, Lion of Speech.[2]

The mandala of omniscience free of the two veils' eclipse
is pervaded to the sky's limits by the light of compassion,
while warm rays of awakened activity dry up the ocean of samsara.
The victors and their heirs dispel the darkness of ignorance,
and the precious lineage of precepts is the jewel of the sky.
The yogin born from the swamp of existence
fully opens [to them] the thousand-petaled lotus of faith.
As the anthers of happiness and delight manifest,
the banquet of pure nectar is dispensed
to all who aspire to it with the six feet of the perfections
and the superior wings of faith and diligence.
This elixir of the source's meaning will fully satisfy.

The commentary to this treatise will be explained using the fivefold rubric [of treatise composition].[3]

## I. The Master by Whom It Was Composed

Blessed by his special deity {25}, Mañjushrī, Lion of Speech, he fully integrated the source textual traditions of both Noble Nāgārjuna and Master Asaṅga. Thus he became learned in scripture and reasoning and possessed sublime absorption. Endowed with these three qualities for undertaking a treatise, Brahmin Āryadeva created it.

## II. How It Is Classified and on What Word It Is Based

In general, of the two vehicles, greater and lesser, this belongs to the Great Vehicle.[4] Of course, the ultimate meaning to understand in both Sutra and Mantra is the perfection of wisdom. So while it is based on all sections of the sutras and tantras, this treatise was composed in particular based on the sutras of the middle Word, the Turning of the Wheel of the Dharma on the Absence of Characteristics, comprised of the seventeen mothers and sons and so forth.[5]

## III. The Reason for Its Composition

Some intelligent folks can see that the three realms of cyclic existence are the nature of suffering, and they would like to practice the perfection of wisdom, which is the means to liberate themselves and all others from it. But having little time and meager diligence, they cannot realize the meaning of the Mother. {26} Even if they study the Mother's hidden meaning [in commentaries] such as *Ornament of Clear Realization*,[6] it is hard for the meaning to arise in their mindstreams. This was composed so that they could realize the perfection of wisdom with little effort.

Accepted by mighty Mañjushrī, Lion of Speech, [Āryadeva] understands that kind of method and has the destined transmission (*bka' bab*) of the blessing, so he possesses the ability to realize that meaning.

## IV. The Source of the Name

There are many ways to assign a name: according to meaning, example, size of the source text, individual, place, time, and function. Of those, this takes its name from the meaning. The meaning that is expressed is the perfection of wisdom. The means of expression is this text that teaches it.

## V. Presentation of the Text from Beginning to End

This is summarized in three points: the introduction, the main text, and the colophon.

### A. Introduction

The first has three parts: the title, the homage, and the promise to explain.

#### 1. The Title

The Sanskrit title *Āryaprajñāpāramitā Upadeśanāma* is translated into Tibetan as *'Phags pa shes rab kyi pha rol tu phyin pa'i man ngag zhes bya ba* (*Esoteric Instructions on the Noble Perfection of Wisdom*). To explain that [in detail]: Since it is elevated above the grounds of the three realms, it is *ārya*. The attainment of lucid appearance in the realm of phenomena by the timeless awareness of individual reflective awareness is the wisdom of realizing the ultimate: *prajñā*. Not to fall into the two extremes of existence or peace on the path of emptiness and compassion united is to arrive at the other side, which is *pāramitā*. The easy way to realize that meaning with little effort and immediate benefit is through esoteric instructions, which is *upadeśa*. The language used to indicate the name of this source text is "the so-called," which is *nāma*.

In addition, there is the salutation of the translator [and] scholar: *"Homage to all buddhas and bodhisattvas."* This accumulates merit in relation to the excellent mother and accomplishes one's wishes exactly as they are intended.

#### 2. The Homage {27}

*The sun and moon of your realization conquer ignorance and misconceptions,*
*and the moisture of your compassion matures living beings.*
*Lion of Speech who perfectly completes the two purposes,*
*I bow to you in sincere devotion with body, speech, and mind.*

The one who bows here is the one who was inspired to compose this text.

What he is bowing to is unconditioned dharmakāya spontaneously present and abiding in one's own continuum. That is, to Mañjushrī, Lion of Speech, whose realization of the self-reflective awareness of timeless awareness is like the sun and moon. With that compelling power, both the cognitive obscuration from habitual patterns of ignorance and the emotional obscuration from misconceptions of imputations have been eliminated, so he has the excellent qualities of achieving personal benefit. The timeless awareness of knowledge manifests the awakened activity of loving and compassionate deeds, like rainfall ripening the grain. Thus he has the excellent qualities of achieving the benefit of others.

The manner of bowing is with the motivation of uncontrived faith, in sincere devotion with body, speech, and mind.

The purpose of bowing is that since Mañjushrī is both main guru and special deity, bowing to him establishes the two benefits effortlessly.

### 3. The Promise to Explain

*The essence of the subject matter is the meaning of*
*nondual perfection of wisdom without root,*
*freed from referential extremes of nihilism and eternalism.*
*I will explain as best I can in order to benefit beings.*

Āryadeva is the one explaining. He will explain the perfection of wisdom, the ultimate essence of the subject matter that is expressed through the media of the twelve divisions [of rhetorical exposition] of excellent speech[7] or the Three Precious Collections (Tripiṭaka). That meaning is revealed as being without ego-clinging, the root of cyclic existence, and as the nonarisen [nature] of deluded conceptions of dualistic fixation. It is explained through the unmistaken word-meanings that go beyond the referent objects of the eight extremes. As was taught [by Nāgārjuna]:

He who taught interdependent arising,
which is without cessation and without birth,
without end and without permanence,
without coming and without going,
without division and without unity in meaning;
the peace of the total pacification of elaboration: {28}
I bow to the perfect Buddha,
sublime among speakers.[8]

The purpose of the explanation is that bodhisattvas, right from the time of being beginners, do whatever they can for the sake of others. Therefore, this also is for the benefit of beings.

Furthermore, of the three usages of *perfection of wisdom*—as text, path, and meaning—it is the last one that is the result to be accomplished: the nondual timeless awareness of awakened mind. However, the path that accomplishes it and the texts that teach it are both expressed by the term *perfection of wisdom*. It is as Master Dignāga stated:

> Perfection of wisdom is nondual
> timeless awareness that is the One Thus Gone.
> The texts and path bear that name
> because they have that goal as their purpose.[9]

As the medium, this text is able to teach the meaning of the subject matter. Furthermore, the word-meanings unmistakably connect the subject matter with the medium. That teaching can cause the followers to realize the meaning to be understood, which is the purpose. And once it is realized, putting it into practice results in the attainment of awakening, the purpose of purposes. Being thus endowed with four features is the defining characteristic of an excellent treatise.[10]

### B. The Main Text

This has three parts: a brief presentation, an extensive explanation, and a final statement.

#### 1. Brief Presentation

This has three parts: the method to rest body, speech, and mind in equipoise; the abiding nature of mind; and presentation of the benefits of such realization.

##### a. The Method to Rest Body, Speech, and Mind in Equipoise

> *Rest the three bases to be prepared directly on the word.*

This is an uncommon method of realizing the perfection of wisdom. It is the esoteric instruction for meditation on the absorptions, based on the teachings of the many enumerations of meditative absorption from the Mother [texts]. The three bases to prepare are body, speech, and mind. "Word" means the perfection of wisdom, the nature of the three doors to liberation.[11] {29} Rest right upon that.

In addition to that, one may purify the habitual patterns of the six classes of beings. It is taught in the secret [Mantra texts] and so on that one has the habitual patterns of the six classes and once they ripen in one's body they exist there as the root letters of the six classes. *Tri* is at the sole of the feet, *pre* in the perineum, *du* at the navel, *nṛi* at the heart, *su* at the throat, and *a* at the crown of the head.[12] The habitual patterns that are based on those supports are absorbed in stages from the bottom up, and, through the blending of basic space and awareness, delusion is purified and one realizes emptiness. At the time of applying such instructions to the pupil, do the refuge and aspiration to awakening described below as the preliminary to start with.

### b. Presentation of the Abiding Nature of the Mind[13]

*Recognize uncontrived, unspoiled awareness:*
*mind that is the root of both samsara and nirvana,*
*yet is not established by any causes or conditions;*
*unborn single cut, intrinsic emptiness.*

Whoever relies on that method and recognizes this awareness as the mind, which is the root of both samsara and nirvana, severs all imputations of existence, nonexistence, and so forth. Once mind is ascertained, the whole of samsara and nirvana is ascertained. As Saraha has said:

Mind itself alone is the seed of everything.
It emanates samsara and nirvana.
It bestows the fruits of our desires.
Homage to the wish-fulfilling jewel of the mind.[14]

Therefore that mind does not arise from causes, nor is it generated by conditions. It is not established as any shape or color. As it is unborn, the single cut that frees from foundation and root is intrinsic emptiness. All phenomena are also not beyond that, which is the abiding nature.

### c. The Benefits of Such Realization

*Such realization is like cutting the root of the tree trunk:*
*the branches of discursive thoughts will never grow again.*

Once the foundational root of the mind is cut, one will not return to samsara again. {30} Once the continuity of deluded thoughts is interrupted, total liberation is attained.

The practice of blending basic space and awareness is presented extensively below. This method is unknown in other textual traditions, but since it is the especially profound feature of this instruction, it was revealed at the beginning.

## 2. Extensive Explanation

This has three parts, which are presentations on the initial cause: arousing the mind of supreme awakening; the actual instructions on the practice of the path; and the results of having practiced.

### a. The Initial Cause: Arousing the Mind of Supreme Awakening

The first has three parts: presentations on the preliminaries, the main part, and the precepts of arousing the awakening mind.

#### i. The Preliminary of Arousing the Awakening Mind

> *Give as vast offerings to the guru and Jewels*
> *actual and emanated appearances in your mind.*

This presents the master's activities. Set up whatever supports and offerings there are. Then imagine in front of you the Great Mother with her children: the buddhas and bodhisattvas of the ten directions and the three times. Above her imagine the lineage gurus and below her the glorious protector guardians all around. Invoke their presence and without mental grasping make the three kinds of offerings—actual material, mentally emanated immaterial offerings, and the appearances of mind objects—as much as you can.

#### ii. The Main Part

> *After doing prostrations and offerings,*
> *devotedly take refuge and arouse the awakening mind.*

This presents the disciple's activities. Prostrate to the guru and Jewels and present whatever offerings you have. Then go for refuge with a devoted mind and take the vows of individual liberation and the bodhisattva vows of arousing the mind. Then the above instructions can be applied.

### iii. The Precepts [of the Mind of Enlightenment]

> *Guard like your eyes the precepts you have taken.*[15]
> *Do not abandon the bodhisattva precepts*
> *even at the cost of your life.*
> *Strive to uphold the training.*[16]

Similarly, it says in *Entering the Way of the Bodhisattva:*

> The children of the Victor who thus
> hold steady to the awakening mind
> must always strive energetically {31}
> never to stray from the training.[17]

And:

> In view of that, I will act with devotion
> according to whatever oaths I have made.
> For if I do not apply myself from now on,
> I will sink lower and lower.[18]

As it is taught here, know the benefits of upholding the precepts and the drawbacks of not upholding them. Do not transgress them even at the cost of your life and guard them like your eyeballs. The precepts to guard were taught at great length by Noble Asaṅga in *Bodhisattva Stages*[19] and its meaning similarly [summarized] in Master Chandragomin's source text *The Twenty [Verses on Bodhisattva] Vows*[20] and others.

## b. The Actual Instructions on the Practice of the Path

This has five parts: presentations on method, the path that must go first; wisdom, which must be practiced; the actual meaning of the perfection of wisdom; the semantic explanation and derivation of *severance*; and elimination of inconsistencies with that.[21]

### i. Method, the Path That Must Go First

This has six parts: the presentation of abandoning the ten nonvirtues oneself and for others; presentation of the path, the six perfections; eliminating the arrogant mind inconsistent with that; the faults of not realizing the meaning of the middle free of extremes; eliminating the poison of reference points; and exemplifying the reason for the five perfections of method as the preliminaries.

### A) Abandoning the Ten Nonvirtues Oneself and for Others

This has three[22] parts: abandoning the ten nonvirtues oneself and encouraging others, rejoicing in others' abandonment of nonvirtue and expressing approval, and just abandoning the ten nonvirtues by itself will not liberate.

### 1) Abandoning the Ten Nonvirtues Oneself and Encouraging Others

> *Abandon the ten nonvirtues, such as killing,*
> *and encourage others to do so as well.*

All the definite paths of methods are subsumed into three: first avoiding negative actions, in the middle avoiding virtue, and in the end avoiding everything.

Negative action (*sdig pa*) refers to the three physical nonvirtues of killing, taking what is not given, and sexual misconduct; the four verbal nonvirtues of verbal abuse, idle chatter, {32} lying, and slander; and the three mental nonvirtues of covetousness, maliciousness, and wrong view. Motivated by the three poisons, engaging in those ten to a greater, middling, or lesser degree has the *fully ripened result* of being born as a hell being, deprived spirit, or animal, respectively.

*The results that conform with the cause* are twofold: *the [resultant] experiences that conform with the cause* are that even if one is born as a human being, one will have a short life span (due to killing), experience material impoverishment (due to stealing), have numerous enemies (due to adultery), experience much ridicule (due to lying), be separated from loved ones (due to slander), hear unpleasantness (due to harsh speech), have one's words not honored (due to chatter), have one's hopes crushed (due to covetousness), have many fears (due to maliciousness), and fixate on negative views (due to wrong view).[23]

*[Resultant] actions that conform with the cause* are that one will desire to repeat whichever of those nonvirtues one is accustomed to, continually producing the seeds of suffering.

The *dominant results,* or the results caused by the person,[24] are to take birth in an area with little vitality;[25] abundant frost and hail; dust storms; bad smells; irregular terrain; salty land; reversed seasons; crops that are meager, stinky, and small;[26] or where there is no harvest at all.

If one understands these things, one will abandon them oneself and also cause others to abandon them as well. The precepts of refuge and the vows of individual liberation are to abandon harming others and its basis—namely, the seven physical and verbal nonvirtues that harm others and the three mental [nonvirtues] that are the bases of those.

### 2) Rejoicing in Others' Abandonment of Nonvirtue and Expressing Approval

> *Express approval of what is consistent*
> *with abandoning killing and the others.*

If one does that, one's own merit increases and others are matured.

### 3) Just Abandoning the Ten Nonvirtues by Itself Will Not Liberate

> *Merely abandoning the ten nonvirtues,*
> *you will not discover the supreme path.*

There are two paths: the ascendant path of gods and humans and the liberation path of awakening. {33} Abandoning the ten nonvirtuous actions and practicing the ten virtuous actions will not enable one to attain more than just the state of gods and humans of the desire realm. Moreover, through the cultivation of causal meditative stability (*bsam gtan*) of equilibrium (*snyoms 'jug*), the particular results produced by meditative stability are birth as a god in the four meditative stabilities in the form realm and the four formless realms of infinite perception.[27] This is called nontransferring karmic action.[28]

### B) Presentation of the Path: The Six Perfections

This has two parts: practicing the six perfections oneself and encouraging others, and expressing approval of what is consistent with that.

#### 1) Practicing the Six Perfections Oneself and Encouraging Others

*Practice the six perfections yourself,*
*and encourage others to do so as well.*

If the five practices of generosity through meditative absorption lack wisdom, they do not deserve the name "perfections" because that is still a dissipating path. Therefore, wisdom is preeminent in the path of awakening, which is liberation. If wisdom is present, then the other five, generosity and so forth, may be called "perfections." Then the bodhisattva path is complete. One is personally engaged in it while one is also encouraging others to do so by means of the four methods of attraction: generosity, pleasant speech, appropriate behavior, and [teaching] suitable content.

#### 2) Expressing Approval of What Is Consistent with That

*Express approval of what is*
*consistent with all six perfections.*

This is the method to purify one's own mindstream and mature others. In addition to not harming others, the precepts of arousing the awakening mind aim to accomplish their welfare as much as possible. That is the essence of the bodhisattva vows. Eight topics on practicing the six perfections are presented in another place.[29]

### C) Eliminating Arrogance Inconsistent with That

*Turn away from the arising of arrogance*
*that results from the conduct of virtuous action*
*such as the six perfections.*

This presents turning away from virtue in the middle. Actually, the virtue of the two accumulations in unity is not contradictory to the path of awakening. {34}[However,] focusing just on higher status in this life and the state of gods and humans in the next life, and engaging in the virtue of wishing to excel, are hindrances to awakening. Therefore turn away from that. Also, the arising of arrogance is the devil of exaltation, so abandon it.

### D) The Faults of Not Realizing the Meaning of the Middle Free of Extremes

*If you do not realize that ultimate*
*nondual perfection is free of extremes*
*such as virtue/negativity, acceptance/rejection, and hope/fear,*
*even if you practice conditioned virtue,*
*you will not become liberated in this very life.*

This presents finally turning away from everything, both high and low. The ultimate is free of all dualistic clinging to dual phenomena such as subject and object and so forth. Until that is realized, no matter how much virtue is enacted, one will not attain liberation. Therefore, to know that all dual phenomena, such as accepting virtue and rejecting negativity, or hoping for nirvana and fearing samsara, are not ultimately established as truly existent is to turn away from everything.

### E) Eliminating the Poison of Reference Points

*Therefore, do not reference even an atom*
*in all phenomena, positive or negative,*
*conditioned or unconditioned.*

Relatively, all of these phenomena of samsara and nirvana that appear as mental objects are nothing but dependently arisen. In reality, not even an atom of true existence is referenced. That is emptiness beyond intellect. Noble Nāgārjuna said:

Whatever is interdependently arisen,
that is held to be emptiness.[30]

Therefore, emptiness and the view and even the ultimate just have no frame of reference. As Shāntideva says:

> The habit of real entities will disappear
> when you get used to the habit of emptiness.
> Through getting used to saying "nothing whatsoever,"
> that too will gradually disappear.[31]

### F) Exemplifying the Reason for the Five Perfections of Method as the Preliminaries

> *Nonetheless, wisdom that is not founded*
> *on method will not become manifest.*
> *It is similar to the harvesting of crops* {35}
> *that will not grow without cultivation.*

Turning away from everything in the end only means being free from fixation. It [does not mean] that one does not accomplish the virtue of the unity of the two accumulations. The ground is the unity of the two truths, the path is the unity of the two accumulations, and the result is the unity of the two kāyas. Based on arousing the relative [awakening] mind, the accumulation of merit as the method serves as the substantial cause[32] and the accumulation of timeless awareness serves as the cooperative condition for the qualities of the ten stages to arise and finally the attainment of the form kāyas. Based on the arousing of the ultimate awakening mind, the accumulation of timeless awareness as wisdom serves as the substantial cause and the accumulation of merit serves as the cooperative condition for the qualities of the five paths to arise and finally the attainment of the dharmakāya.

One can understand this from the example of worldly crop cultivation and autumn harvest. The two definite paths—this definite path of method and the wisdom that will [be explained] below—should be taken into practice in unity.

### ii. Wisdom, Which Must Be Practiced

This is presented in eight parts: without the perfection of wisdom, the five alone will not accomplish the path; not an external condition since one has it oneself; meditation on recollecting the Buddha; the actual enlightened intention of the Buddha; the method to realize that; the place to practice; the method of practice; and the benefits of such practice.

### A) Without the Perfection of Wisdom, the Five Alone Will Not Accomplish the Path

*If you do not resolutely engage*
*in the meaning of the perfection of wisdom,*
*then even if you engage in generosity, ethical discipline, patience,*
*diligence, and meditative stability,*
*you are like a blind person without a cane.*
*How could you possibly find your way?*

Since the five other perfections—generosity and so on—are just the accumulation of merit, without the eyes of wisdom they will not become the path of unity [of the two accumulations] and one will not arrive at the city of great freedom.

### B) Not an External Condition Since One Has It Oneself

*The meaning of the perfection of wisdom—*

{36} It appears that this line of verse was out of order, according to the note. This source text should have fifty quatrains, and since there must be an extra line, it could well be this. However, since it contributes some meaning that is helpful to understand, it was left.[33]

*do not seek it elsewhere; you have it yourself.*
*That is the meaning of inherent great lucid clarity,*
*not established as an entity or with characteristics.*

You may wonder whether you have the ability to find such sublime perfection of wisdom. Since the phenomenal nature (*chos nyid*) of one's own mind is free of all obscuring covers, it is precisely its very own lucid clarity [that's the thing]. The sutra says:

Mind is no-mind;
the inherent nature of mind is lucid clarity.[34]

And from Lord Maitreya:

> The inherent nature of mind is lucid clarity
> that, like space, is unchanging.
> Adventitious stains, such as desire that comes of improper
> thoughts,
> do not change it into afflictive emotions.[35]

### C) Meditation on Recollecting the Buddha

> *Meditate on recollecting the Buddha,*
> *naturally clear*[36] *of thoughts and memories,*
> *free of all mental engagement.*

The path to actualize that lucid clarity is taught in the Mother:

> With no mental activity, not remembering anything,
> that is recollection of the Buddha, dharma, and sangha.[37]

The method to cultivate that is the blending of space and awareness described below.

### D) The Actual Enlightened Intent of the Buddha

> *Outer/inner, gods/demons, samsara/nirvana,*
> *appearance/emptiness, and so forth;*
> *free of dualistic appearances,*
> *Buddha's intent is unmistaken and uncontrived,*
> *similar, for example, to the expanse of space.*

In that way, the meaning of cultivating the recollection of the Buddha is [to realize] that freedom from all dualistic fixation is the Buddha's intent. It goes beyond falling into limits and partiality, and all thoughts of characteristics. It is like the expanse of space, the inherent nature of the realm of phenomena. That, then, is the special method for an ordinary person to experience the Buddha's intent in practice.

### E) The Method to Realize That

This has four parts: blending space and awareness, the results of blending space and awareness, {37} the actual method for blending space and awareness, and the reason for blending space and awareness.

#### 1) Blending Space and Awareness

> *The most sublime method*
> *is to blend space and awareness.*

This is the method to actualize the meaning of the perfection of wisdom right now. The sublime special feature of this teaching, not well known in other traditions, is the blending of space and awareness. This is the reason: The two—space and awareness—made out to be subject and object, result in dualistic fixation. The entire confusion of samsara comes from that. The ultimate result of meditating on blending space and awareness as the path is that, presently, space and awareness become totally pure and the consciousness groups are transformed [in] awareness. Then the three kāyas are attained after the fourfold timeless awareness mixes inseparably. Thus it is profound in having the threefold relationship of ground, path, and result, in keeping with the path of Secret Mantra.

#### 2) The Results of Blending Space and Awareness

> *At the times of mixing space and awareness,*
> *things and characteristics, rejecting and accepting—*
> *fixation on referents—are naturally cleared up.*
> *Abide in the ultimate nature of phenomena*
> *without subject-object dualistic fixation.*

When the result is actualized, the power of mixing space and awareness clears away (*sangs*) the fixation of all dual phenomena and then expands (*rgyas*) the phenomenal nature of nondual timeless awareness.[38] Now, at the time of meditating, one can rest in a concordant experience.

### 3) The Actual Method for Blending Space and Awareness

*With body and mind thus uncontrived,*
*wherever empty sky pervades*
*empty*[39] *direct awareness also pervades.*
*Rest in the extent of the great pervasive expanse.*

When the instructions are bestowed on the disciples, the blending of space is based on the three bases to prepare that were presented before. The energy of direct awareness (*rig rtsal*) blends into space. The aspects of physical tension, verbal restraint, and mental focus should all be relaxed. With body and mind uncontrived, wherever the sky pervades, direct awareness also pervades. Wherever direct awareness pervades, dharmakāya pervades.[40] {38} Rest evenly in the state of the great pervasive expanse of dharmakāya. Whether or not one continues practice with Opening the Sky Door[41] does not matter: rest evenly in the state of knowing that space and awareness are inseparable since forever.

### 4) The Reason for Blending Space and Awareness

*At that time there is an experience*
*of awareness free of basis or root.*
*Awareness does not dwell anywhere*
*in the five senses or their objects.*

After one rests in inseparable space-awareness, all phenomena are realized to be the essential awareness of one's own mind, yet the essence of that very awareness is not established and is without basis and free of a root. At that time, awareness—the five sense organs such as eyes and so on, and the five objects such as form and so on—have no frame of reference whatsoever. As it says in the *Heart of the Perfection of Wisdom*, "no eyes, no ears . . ." and so on.[42] In that very state, the view is of the unborn, empty, and nonexistent inherent nature. The meditation is on the great pervasive expanse. The integration on the path is the threefold abiding, arising, and liberating. The conduct is to conquer fear directly. The result is the perfection of buddha. In terms of gods, that is the stainless pure god. In terms of absorptions, it is the absorption of suchness. In terms of recitation, it is the recitation of the genuine meaning. So it is taught.

### F) The Place to Practice

*Meditate without dualism in the sites*
*of rock houses,*[43] *cemeteries,*
*haunted places, towns and big cities,*
*caves, and secluded caverns.*[44]

Abandon distracting fears and meditate in those kinds of places in order to savor the bliss of meditative stability. The removal of obstructors and enhancement of practice will happen automatically through meditation in the nonduality of the problem and its remedy and the nonduality of the regional spirits and the yogin.

### G) The Method of Practice

The actual method of how to practice has two parts: what teaching to practice and the method by which to practice it.

#### 1) What Teaching to Practice

*The meaning of the unborn taught by the guru—*

#### 2) The Method by Which to Practice {39}

*practice it during the four daily activities.*

Blend the subsequent attainment of equipoise with daily activities by maintaining mindful awareness constantly.

### H) The Benefits of Such Practice

*If it is put into practice this way,*
*the blessings of the perfection of wisdom*
*and the realization that all phenomena are empty*
*will prevent obstacles from arising.*
*How would it be possible for emptiness*
*to pose a threat to emptiness?*[45]

You may wonder whether or not obstacles will come when you meditate in that way in the secluded places mentioned above. There are two reasons that they won't come: First, as it says in the *Verse Summary [on the Perfection of Wisdom]*:

> When a mother with many children becomes sick,
> they will all feel anxious and tend to her.
> Similarly, the buddhas of the world realms in the ten directions
> bring intention to this perfection of wisdom, their mother.[46]

That is the Mother's blessing. And:

> Whenever those experts who fully possess the aspiration
> view the sublime meaning of the perfection of wisdom, day
> or night,
> at that time their minds move through space like a bird.
> How could negative companions take advantage?[47]

Thus the power of the yogin's realization that all phenomena are the sky-like nature of the three doors of liberation prevents the onslaught of obstacles. From the *Mother*:

> Emptiness cannot take advantage of emptiness. So too for signlessness and wishlessness. External space cannot disturb inner space.[48]

This completes the two sections of definite method and definite wisdom.

### iii. The Actual Meaning of the Perfection of Wisdom

This has three parts: the essence of realization, evidence of warmth, and the meaning of the example.

#### A) The Essence of Realization

> *When the empty nature of phenomena is realized,*
> *the sign or characteristic is that externally*[49]

*all objects of the five sense doors—*
*form, sound, smell, taste, and touch—*
*are fully illuminated as emptiness.*
*Inwardly, the coarse afflictive emotions*
*and subtle dualistic fixation, although they arise,* {40}
*are self-liberated in nonduality,*[50] *beyond concern.*

When the realization of the inseparability of space and awareness—the meaning of the empty nature of phenomena—arises in one's mindstream, the perceiver's five sense-organ consciousnesses and their five objects of form and so on, including all phenomena, arise as emptiness. Although occasionally coarse afflictive emotions arise due to the old habitual patterns of confusion, they will be liberated upon arising. Therefore, one will not act on those afflictive emotions and accumulate karma. And although something like dualistic fixation appears, it is unable to fulfill the function of dualistic fixation, so it is subtle and occurs beyond any concern of hopes and fears. It states in the *Sutra of Skill in the Methods of the Great Secret*:

> Noble child, it is like this: Seeds that have been severely affected by fire have not completely lost their color, yet do not have the chance to sprout. Similarly, afflictive emotions in bodhisattvas, if they are severely affected by emptiness and signlessness and wishlessness and selflessness and the perfection of wisdom, then even if [those bodhisattvas] completely engage in all the joys of the sense pleasures as they desire, they will not completely grasp all-consuming afflictive emotion which would cause them to fall back. They do not completely lose the color of buddha.[51]

### B) The Evidence of Warmth

*With that realization, abiding and arising are liberated*
*in the nature of phenomena,*
*like reaching an island of gold.*

When one rests within the ocean-like state of realization of the nature of phenomena, even though thoughts come and go like rain, whatever arises will be naturally liberated. No other remedy is needed. Everything arising as the nature of phenomena is like being on an island of precious gold where it is impossible to find [ordinary] dirt and rock: one does not find a bad thought.

### C) The Meaning of the Example

*When a person's root life force is severed,*
*there is no need to purposefully sever*
*the eyes and other five sense doors.*
*Similarly, when the mind itself is severed at the root,*
*all phenomena are realized to be empty.*

It was said in the brief presentation section above {41} that the mind is the root of both samsara and nirvana. Severing the foundational root [of mind], like cutting the tree trunk from the root, was taught as the single cut of the unborn. This verse has the same significance, so it is easy to understand the meaning of the example. In this case, which draws from *The Bundle of Precepts*,[52] being without fixation on body, speech, and mind is the Victor's Body, Speech, and Mind. These two—the teaching of appearance, sound, and awareness as the mind's Body, Speech, and Mind, and the explanation in highest Secret Mantra (*uttaratantra*) that the essence of mantric vows is the sacred pledge of vajra Body, Speech, and Mind that protects one from fixation on attributes—should be understood as the same vital point. This is the custom of integrating [practice] on the path right from the start as a beginner in Mantra. Here the particular intent is that it [refers to] the qualities of realization.

### iv. The Semantic Explanation and Derivation of *Severance*

*Since it severs the root of mind itself,*
*and severs the five toxic emotions,*
*extremes of view, meditational formations,*[53]
*conduct anxiety, and hopes and fears;*
*since it severs all inflation*[54]
*it is called* severance *by semantic explanation.*

The main problem with mind is fixation on the self. It says in the *Verse Summary*:

> Greatly severed the views of all sentient beings.[55]

And:

> Severance of the five poisons of desire and the others, fixation on extreme views, mental engagement in meditation, anxiety of conduct, and the attachment of hopes and fears about results—to sever attachment one must exhaust attachment to everything.[56]

Severance of whatever is inconsistent with the path of generosity and so on is taught in tantra:

> The bodhisattva's generosity severs migration to deprived spirits. Poverty and likewise all afflictive emotions are severed. The four devils, such as inflation, which are the cause of suffering, are all severed.

And in tantra: "The Great Vehicle severs suffering."[57]

Those [quotes] mean that the name *severance* was attributed from the influence of the perfection of wisdom. There is a meaningful connection with the name that is derived from teachings in the sutras and tantras. {42} It is not as if it is random or without scriptural source.

### v. Elimination of Adversities on the Path

This has three presentations: identifying the two devils and the way to sever them, the reason that devils occur, and the way to subdue devils.

#### A) Identifying the Two Devils and the Way to Sever Them

This has seven parts: the tangible devil, the intangible devil, signs of severing,[58] evidence of termination, the times of turning away, the method to not turn away, and instruction on spike-like suppression.

#### 1) The Tangible Devil

This has two parts: the object to be severed and the instructions to sever it.

### a) The Object to Be Severed

> *Attachment to real things with passion and aggression*
> *is the tangible devil, so how should one sever that?*[59]

The five desirable objects such as form are tangible. When our minds are attached and attracted to them, the three or five poisons arise. That is the devil that severs the life force of liberation.[60] Also, the tangible devil is the objective aspect and the intangible devil is the afflictive emotions that arise in the mind. Therefore, those two devils have a common ground.

### b) The Instructions to Sever It

This has three parts: the individual's characteristics, actual instructions, and size.

#### i) The Individual's Characteristics

> *Superior, average, or inferior experiencers*

#### ii) Actual Instructions

This has three parts: superior capability, average capability, and inferior capability.

##### (A) Superior Capability

> *rest in the state of no-thought,*

##### (B) Average Capability

> *meditate with attention on that,*

##### (C) Inferior Capability

> *or ascertain it through examination and analysis.*

Those of superior capability realize all objective appearance as emptiness and thus rest within the state of recollecting Buddha. Those of average capability know objective appearance to be mind, and so they meditate with attention on the mind. Those of inferior capability ascertain, through the eight examples of illusion and so forth, that objective appearance is without intrinsic nature. They train without attachment and aversion arising.

### iii) Size

> *For instance, like a dense forest,* {43}
> *a strong person,*
> *and a sharp axe.*

The object to be severed is immense and numerous, so in that way it is like a dense forest. The one cutting it down has experience and realization, like a strong person. The profound instructions of Severance are like a sharp axe. Therefore, if one exerts oneself, even a small remedy can conquer a sizable problem.

## 2) The Intangible Devil

This has two parts: identifying the devil to sever and the instructions to sever it.

### a) Identifying the Devil to Sever

> *The apparitions of gods and demons that cause inflation*
> *are called the intangible devil.*

Of the inner devil of afflictive emotions and the outer devil of gods and demons, the former was discussed above. In presenting that outer devil here, the devil of inflation is revealed incidentally.

### b) The Instructions to Sever It

This has six parts: setting pestilence directly upon pestilence, sticking the hot needle precisely, the dharma to practice, putting the morning star under thumb, rejecting closeness or distance toward both gods and demons, and cornering the great pestilence.

### i) Setting Pestilence Directly upon Pestilence[61]

*Set pestilence upon pestilence, directly in the flesh.*

### ii) Sticking the Hot Needle Precisely

*Stick the hot needle precisely there.*[62]

These [refer to] the mountain cycle.[63] Of the three practice skills, the first is to be skilled in the bases to prepare, as has been presented.

### iii) The Dharma to Practice

*Go for refuge in the Three Jewels.*

The definite practice of wisdom is meditation on recollecting the Buddha, which is refuge. Meditation on blending space and awareness in part of the meditation session is the actual main practice.

### iv) Putting the Morning Star under Thumb

*Put the morning star under thumb.*[64]

If the body is the house of devils, the mind is what outshines them. This is presented by means of an aphorism.

### v) Rejecting Closeness or Distance toward Both Gods and Demons

*Reject closeness and distance toward gods and demons.*

The training is to meditate in the nonduality of rejections and remedies. {44}

### vi) Cornering the Great Pestilence

*Corner the great pestilence.*

This presents the focus on the extremes of outer, inner, and secret, and so on, at the time of uprisings.[65]

### 3) Evidence of Severing

> *In Severance,[66] the evidence of having severed is freedom from fear.*

Those refer to the evidence of warmth of attaining confidence in practice.

### 4) Evidence of Termination

> *Evidence of termination is that apparitions subside by themselves.*

This refers to teachings on common, special, and excellent evidence of termination. Apparitions and uprising signs and so forth are appended below, which is the middle practice skill of laying down the path.

### 5) The Times of Turning Away

> *Evidence of turning away is fleeing in fear and terror.*

This presents the changes wrought by one's own and others' gods and demons and so forth: the causes of turning away.

### 6) The Method to Not Turn Away

> *Don't turn away; be like a door frame.*
> *Don't flee, even in fear and terror.*

Whatever frightening appearances occur, finish the task with a willingness to die.

### 7) Instruction on Spike-Like Suppression

> *Suppress them like a spike,*
> *bend them down, and apply effort.*
> *That is the supreme esoteric instruction.*

This is the special method to turn obstacles into spiritual powers by tackling adverse factors head on.

These have been the final practice skills of the concluding severance. The method of severing two devils is finished.

### B) The Reason That Devils Occur

This has three parts: identifying devils, instructions for severing them, and signs of uprising.

#### 1) Identifying Devils

> *Worldly gods and demons cannot bear*
> *your meditation on nondual perfections*
> *and cause various kinds of apparitions:*
> *manifesting, overwhelming, dreamt, and so on.*

Unable to bear the brilliance of your meditation on the profound path, apparitions come. It is not that they would not rise up without your doing a fierce visualization. Furthermore, various apparitions that obscure mental functions and outer, inner, and secret uprisings that occur are included in this vital [category]. {45}

#### 2) Instructions for Severing Them

This has three parts: superior, average, and inferior capability.

##### a) Superior Capability

> *Those with superior meditative experience*
> *rest in the nondual meaning of it all.*[67]

##### b) Average Capability

> *The average practitioners focus on that and meditate.*

### c) Inferior Capability

*The inferior offer their body aggregate as food.*[68]

That which is to be severed are those three [kinds of] apparitions. That which severs them is practice through the three integrations on the path. That is, the superior practitioner does not reference any duality between the yogin and the gods and demons displaying apparitions. The average practitioner focuses the mind on blending inseparably. The inferior practitioner offers the body aggregate as food, which will be presented below.

### 3)[69] Signs of Uprising

*Afterward, an experience of direct awareness*
*free of any mental support will arise.*

That presents the manner in which uprising signs occur for an average yogin. Inferior ones must rely on the evidence of termination.

### C) The Way to Subdue Devils

This has two parts: identifying devils and instructions for severing them.

### 1) Identifying Devils

*When you go to a haunted place, if gods and demons*
*manifest overwhelming presence, separate awareness from matter.*

### 2) Instructions for Severing Them

This has three parts: completely severing inflation of the body, completely severing inflation of the mind, and thoughts emanating as devils.

### a) Completely Severing Inflation of the Body

*This body is matter, like stone;*
*no harm can come to it.*[70]

### b) Completely Severing Inflation of the Mind

*Mind is not an actual thing; it is like the sky.*
*Who harms it and who is harmed?*
*Thinking that, rest without despair or worry*
*in the nature of phenomena.*
*Even if you think that the gods and demons*
*have snatched your material body and left,*
*without moving from your previous place,*
*do not despair over anything at all.*

This is the practice for those of average and inferior capabilities, but everything is needed for the main practice of the mountain cycle.

### c) Thoughts Emanating as Devils

*Whatever discursive thoughts arise are devils.*
*They come from your own mind.*
*In mind, not even an atom is established*
*of a place from which to arise, to abide, or to go.*
*Buddhahood does not come after being liberated.*
*It is impossible to wander in samsara due to delusion.*

All deluded thought is the devil of inflation. {46} Since it is the mind's own energy, when one realizes freedom from the extremes of arising, ceasing, and abiding, then no essence of liberation and delusion is established. Without basis and free of roots—it is totally resolved.

That concludes the presentation on all the instructions for practice. The details of the mountain cycle can be learned from my composition "Space Diamond"[71] and other sources.

## c. Results: The Stages of Having Practiced the Path[72]

This has five parts:[73] the supreme result, eliminating deviances, revealing obscurations, revealing the abiding nature, and presenting the common results.

### i. The Supreme Result

*Virtue, negativity, and all karmic action are totally pure,*
*pure since forever, liberated since forever, awakened since forever.*

At first, when one enters the path, one trains in accepting and rejecting so that the power of virtue increases and negativity gradually decreases until finally the qualities of the five paths and ten stages are complete. Then all karmic actions are totally pure: forever pure in the absence of examination and renunciation, forever liberated in excellent realization, forever awakened in the excellent two purposes. Again: the abiding nature of the primordially pure ground, the refining methods of the primordially pure path, and the way of arising of the resulting primordial awakening.

### ii. Eliminating Deviances

*One deviates by not avoiding negativity.*

Since one does not obtain the result without renouncing emotional obscurations, that would be a deviation.

### iii. Revealing Obscurations

*Attachment to tenets is an obscuration.*

Fixation on the three spheres and fixation on all tenets and views is revealed as cognitive obscuration.

### iv. Revealing the Abiding Nature

*Nondual self-liberation is the abiding nature.*

Once the two obscurations are eliminated, the ultimate abiding nature is realized. All misconceptions are severed in those three results.[74]

### v. Presenting the Common Results

This has six parts: general preliminaries of the practice, the dharma to practice, instructions for clearing up one's own obstacles, methods to clear up others' obstacles, the removal rite, and general results of practicing the perfection of wisdom. {47}

### A) General Preliminaries of the Practice

*Take refuge from within the nature of phenomena.*

### B) The Dharma to Practice

*Arouse the aspiration and supplicate.*

As well as entering the path, meditating on the path, going to a haunted place, and going for refuge at the start of a session, one should also meditate on both ultimate refuge and the awakening mind in the main part.

### C) Instructions for Clearing Up One's Own Obstacles

*If obstacles arise for you,*
*go to a haunted place and meditate on the nondual.*

Whichever of three kinds of obstacles happens to the yogin who meditates on the path—whether it is afflictive emotion, illness, or evil spirits—meditate in the nonduality of the problem and its remedy in order to increase diligence. Practicing each of the path-integrations in conjunction with the five paths yields fifteen paths.

### D) Methods to Clear Up Others' Obstacles

*In order to help other sentient beings,*
*with compassion as your preliminary,*
*know the emptiness of everything:*
*yourself, the patient, the evil spirit, and the disease.*
*Pat*[75] *[the diseased area] and meditate in emptiness.*
*Face the reclining [patient] toward you.*[76]

If the need arises to help someone who is afflicted by disease and evil spirits, first meditate on love and compassion as the preliminary, and know that all four [factors]—oneself, the patient, the evil spirit, and the disease—are emptiness. Then pat the diseased area with your hand. Face the head of the reclining patient toward you or face the head toward the place where fierce gods and demons dwell, lying down. This is known as Wandering Severance.[77]

## E) The Removal Rite

*If thereby [the disease] is not yet pacified,*
*go for refuge and arouse the awakening mind in a haunted place.*
*Pass over [the patient] three times and meditate beyond extremes.*
*With a mandala, bless the sticks and stones*
*and confer them.*

If the yogin and the patient are together, then do refuge, arouse the awakening mind, supplicate, and do many feast offerings. Then step over the patient three times and perform whatever tantric conduct is appropriate. If the disciple is staying somewhere else, {48} then during the feast offering bless the stones and confer them, then give the command for protection.[78] Here, for a disciple keeping strict mountain retreat, there is also the custom of [bestowing] life-force empowerment for gods and demons. The implementation of this is taught elsewhere.

All these here depend upon the lack of hindrances in attaining the results on the stages, and thus present the incidental results.

## F) General Results of Practicing the Perfection of Wisdom

This has three parts: temporary results of severing in isolated haunts, ultimate results of having severed the four devils through meditation on the meaning of the nature of phenomena, and the benefits accruing from both.

### 1) Temporary Results of Severing in Isolated Haunts

*Hold the gods above to their oaths;*
*subdue with splendor the nāgas below.*
*Tasks assigned to nāgas will all be accomplished.*
*Gods, from their abodes, will be your allies.*
*Nāgas without exception are bound into service.*
*Gurus, yidams, ḍākinīs, and dharma protectors*
*will watch over you as their child.*

Through meditation on the meaning of the perfection of wisdom, the three toxic afflictive emotions in one's mindstream are brought under control in the nature of phenomena. All living beings, in whom those three poisons abound, are thereby also brought under control and held under oath to accomplish one's activities. The gods are chiefly [afflicted by] desire, and the nāgas are chiefly [afflicted by] aggression and stupidity. All others are included in those two. In the past, in the presence of the Conqueror, the four retinues [of nuns, monks, laymen, and laywomen] and the glorious protector guardians promised to guard the doctrine of the Mother. Likewise, gods and nāgas must be made to guard and protect and befriend, and so too the three roots will protect with loving affection.

### 2) Ultimate Results of Having Severed the Four Devils through Meditation on the Meaning of the Nature of Phenomena

> *Once you have severed the tangible devils,*
> *appearance will not rise up as your enemy.*
> *Once you have severed the intangible devils,*
> *male and female yakṣhas*[79] *will be held under oath.*[80]

With the direct realization that objective appearances are not truly existent (*bden med*), the afflictive emotions that depend upon objects will not arise. {49} That is the elimination of emotional obscuration; it is the path of seeing and the first stage. By the purification of afflictive emotion inwardly, all phenomena, both outer and inner, are conquered and one is liberated from the fixation on the three spheres [of subject, object, and act]. That is the elimination of cognitive obscuration; it is the consummation of the ten stages and five paths.

### 3) The Benefits Accruing from Both

> *That and other such benefits*[81]
> *that are immeasurable will occur.*

Through proper practice of the ten virtues on the paths of higher status and gods and humans, and the six perfections on the path of awakened liberation, the temporary result will be to possess the seven qualities of the higher realms.[82] Ultimately, [through the attainment of] actual complete awakening, the two purposes will happen effortlessly and spontaneously, and so on, as explained in all the sutras of Mahayana. The immeasurable branches of the fruition cannot be described here.

The extensive explanation is finished.[83]

### 3. Final Statement

> *"The Grand Poem on the Meaning of Perfection of Wisdom."*
> *Instructions by Āryadeva the Brahmin.*

This *Fifty Verses* source text of esoteric instructions on how to practice the meaning of the perfection of wisdom is the intended meaning of the source text, *Perfection of Wisdom in One Hundred Thousand Lines*, and the profound vital points of the path perfection of wisdom, such as the *Ornament of Clear Realization*. It reveals the vast meaning of the six perfections and so forth, and the profound vital points, such as the blending of space and awareness, and so forth. Since the path that can bring an individual to actual, complete awakening has been fully revealed, {50} it is complete. Thus it was taught. All the points of the source text are now finished.

## C. Colophon

> *The Indian paṇḍita Dampa Rinpoche translated this himself.*[84]
> *Zhama Lotsā received it and edited it.*[85]

The name "Dampa Rinpoche" refers to Kamalashīla. It says in the *Eulogy to the Eighty Great Adepts*:

> Expert in grammar, logic, scripture, reasoning, and esoteric
> instruction,
> possessing the spiritual power of an awareness-holder's longevity,
> the one called Kāmāla,
> to that supreme one I pay homage.[86]

On his third visit to Tibet, in Dingri,[87] he gave this source text to Kyotön Kuche,[88] and then the Lady Mother, emanation of the goddess of the Ganges,[89] spread it far and wide. However, the intended meaning of the source text was taught in whatever way appropriate according to the individual's potential. Other than that, the fully complete bestowal of the word-meanings of the source is said not to have occurred after Khugom Chöseng.[90] Then gradually the lineage came down to Zalmo Drakpa,[91] who for the sake of the Nyang prince Rinchen Sal[92] apparently wrote the commentary on the source text's meaning and many diverse notes. My lama adjusted it to a middle-length commentary, and I wrote both an extensive and an abridged version.

The effort of the enlightened activity in writing this
not only fulfills the ḍākinī's undeceiving prophecy
but also completely fulfills the intentions of the guru.
That was my totally pure noble thought. {51}

By that truth, and by the suns of merit of the four kinds of individuals
in the ten directions and three times
having utterly arisen in the sky of the pure realm of phenomena,
may the mental darkness of infinite beings clear away.

Until I also enter the ocean of the all-knowing,
may the rivers of joy and bliss of two accumulations swell,
and possessing the glorious nectar of two purposes,
may all beings without exception be satisfied by this wealth.[93]

# 5. The Great Bundle of Precepts on Severance

*Outline and Complete Explanation*

## Lord Rangjung Dorje[1]

The third Karmapa, Rangjung Dorje (1284–1339), was one of the earliest and most important figures in the Severance tradition. His many works on Severance are considered authoritative in the Kagyu lineage, and he may have been the first to incorporate the term *mahāmudrā* as part of the descriptive title of Severance, thus bringing it into the Kagyu fold.* The text translated here—his commentary and structural outline for *The Great Bundle of Precepts on Severance*—appears in *The Treasury* under the simple title *Outline*, although it also contains a commentary as a separate text, bearing the Sanskrit name *ṭīkā*, usually translated into Tibetan as "complete explanation" (*rnam par bshad pa*). It is unusual and quite edifying for a Tibetan author to actually separate out the outline from the commentary, although it does present a few extra problems of consistency. Nevertheless, Rangjung Dorje's work exhibits his usual precision and brilliance. The text is also found in his collected works. The words in parentheses after the headings in the *Outline* were included by Rangjung Dorje to indicate the beginning word(s) of each verse, and they are repeated in the commentary. However, due to the differences between Tibetan and English grammar, it was not always possible to keep them exactly as they appear at the very beginning of each verse in the translation.

*See Sorensen, "Mahāmudrā Chöd? Rangjung Dorje's Commentary on the Great Speech Chapter of Machik Labdrön" for this argument and for another translation of this text.

**Outline**

Homage to the perfection of wisdom.

There are three parts to this *Great Bundle of Precepts on Severance of Evil*:

I. Introduction
  A. Homage (beginning with "unutterable")
  B. Presentation of the name (Severance)
  C. Brief explanation (a few)
II. The source text
  A. Brief presentation (devils)
  B. Extensive explanation
    1. The particular four devils
      a. Tangible devil
        i. Identifying that devils come from oneself (tangible)
        ii. Ascertaining their essential emptiness (form)
      b. Intangible devil
        i. Identifying the sensations (intangible)
        ii. Natural liberation as realization dawns (realm of phenomena)
      c. Devil of exaltation
        i. Brief presentation (exaltation)
        ii. Extensive explanation {55}
          A) Common
            1) If attached to qualities, it is a path devil (haunted places, demons)
            2) Taught to be like a dream (qualities)
          B) Supreme
            1) The path as devil if not understood
              a) Identifying the devil
                i) Brief presentation (supreme)
                ii) Extensive explanation (free from elaboration)
              b) Liberation if understood as symbolic
                i) No view or viewed in the self-arisen (view and meditation)
                ii) No meditation or meditator (everything)
                iii) If one holds the view, one's conduct will automatically be one's play (one's conduct)
                iv) Experience is beyond intellect (experience)

2) Mental fabrication as devil
a) Having desire is the devil of result (supreme)
b) If realized to be oneself, nothing to accomplish (body, speech, and mind)
d. Devil of inflation
i. Brief presentation (devils)
ii. Extensive explanation {56}
A) The tangible devil is included in inflation
1) Things not held in the view are taught as the devil (objective things)
2) Knowing they are rootless liberates everything (objective things)
B) The intangible devil is included in inflation
1) Identifying five devils that come from the root devil of inflation (intangible)
2) Realization of five timeless awarenesses and emancipation from six classes if inflation is liberated (aggression)
3) Example of fearlessness (thus)
4) Even with realization, it is bondage if not severed (even with realization)
5) Becoming buddha once inflation is severed (*emaho*)
C) The devil of exaltation is included in inflation
1) Common
a) If attached to spiritual powers, it's a devil (exaltation)
b) If not attached, it's an ornament (without attachment)
2) Supreme
a) Excitement as a devil (three kāyas)
b) Not inflation if understood (samsara's own ground)
2. Ascertaining by example
a. Explanation of examples
i. Bondage if not carried into one's being (through example)
ii. Benefiting others if one realizes it oneself (fine cow)
b. View
i. Realizing that devils are rootless (great garuḍa)
ii. Cutting through by knowing that (rootless)
c. Meditation
i. Examples of nonthought (method of resting)

ii. Resting freely uncontrived (contrive or adulterate)
iii. Transcending misery through knowing thoughts and memories are not validly existent (intrinsic awareness)[2]

d. Conduct
i. Yogic discipline free of afflictive emotion (conduct)
ii. Everything as an ally through mastering conduct (one's conduct)

e. Results
i. Realizing the meaning, no [result] to establish (results) {57}
ii. You are buddha for sure (inflation)

3. Presentation without example

a. Deluded cognition
i. Naturally deluded (noncognizant)
ii. Deluded regarding tenets (single inseparability)

b. Ignorance, timeless awareness
i. Stupidity transformed into timeless awareness (therefore)
ii. Whatever arises is naturally occurring (cognition)

c. Unmade ground
i. Not made by buddha (genuine meaning)
ii. Not realized by fixation[3] (unmade unconditioned)

d. The path of no making
i. Realizing the four perception spheres are invalid (unmade)
ii. Liberation from samsara through realizing the meaning (form and feeling)

e. Unreal results
i. The expedient method for the small-minded (unreal)
ii. Something established as real is meaningless (if real)
iii. If mind is not liberated, it is meaningless (of dharma)
iv. Realizing nonfixation reveals body, speech, and mind (on body)

III. Conclusion

A. The meaning of the name (*emaho*)

B. Experience
1. Experience free of intellect (earnestly)
2. Special instructions (haunted places)
3. If the load is carried, it is the view (appearing conditions)
4. The importance of wandering in haunted places (haunted places)

The condensed meaning of *The Great Bundle* is complete.

### Complete Explanation of Severance (*gCod kyi ṭīkā*)

Homage to the perfection of wisdom;
total pacification of elaboration, unconditioned peace
transcended to the heart of unimpeded compassion,
flawless and copious like blooming lotuses:
I bow to the Mighty Sage and bodhisattvas who love beings.

A gathering of letters and names from ineffable space,
emanated as the speech treasury of eighty-four thousand, {58}
all essentialized in the perfection of wisdom practice:
I compose the letters of the severance of conceptual thought.

The explanations of whatever treatises and instruction anthologies there are from the Word of the Victor and the bodhisattvas and their immeasurable emanations who came to the world are all included in the greater or lesser vehicles. This text is from the Great Vehicle. Of the two intentions of the sutras and the tantras, this is the ultimate: the perfection of wisdom. Of the two ways to take that into practice—training thoroughly and ascertaining the lack of the eight extreme conceptual constructs[4] by means of scripture and reasoning and the way to destroy the illusion of valid appearance of form and so on based on interior attention—plus the enhancement of both of those by the nondual mixing of subject and object: this is the instruction of Severance, the perfection of wisdom. It has two parts: the story of how it emerged and the actual instructions. The first, which concerns the three types of lineage transmission and the stories of Machik and others, can be learned elsewhere. The second has three sections: the instructions of the sugata precept lineage, the instructions of the blessing-empowerment lineage, and the instructions of the prophecy lineage. Of those three, the first consists of Machik's own personal experiences that were written down in four [versions]: (1) Outer: the peaceful *Great Bundle of Precepts*, which is explained extensively; (2) Inner: pointing-out instruction found in the *Appendices* (*Le lag*); (3) Meaning: teachings culled from *The Steps of Vital Points* (*gNad them*); and (4) Secret: translating to the symbols of the symbol-dharma. All of those are found most exquisitely in this *Great Bundle of Precepts*, which has three parts: the introduction, the main text, and the conclusion.

## I. Introduction

### A. Homage

The first two lines present the homage, beginning with *the unutterable.* {59} The meaning that is taught here is freedom from conceptual extremes. What is made manifest by the noble ones, the principle of the total pacification of all elaborations, cannot be expressed. Since ordinary individuals are incapable of figuring it out by thinking, it goes beyond subject and object. This is an homage to the perfection of wisdom itself, the principle that is separate from anything covered over and obscured by a frame of reference. Therefore this is no different from:

> Unutterable, unthinkable, inexpressible perfection of wisdom,
> unborn, unending, the very essence of space,
> experienced in the timeless awareness of one's reflexive cognition:
> Homage to the mother of the buddhas of three times.[5]

### B. Presentation of the Name

"Bundle of Precepts on Severance . . ." is the first mention of the title.

### C. Brief Explanation

The five lines beginning with *in hopes of benefiting a few* . . . represent the promise to explain [the text] and the brief presentation. The root of all phenomena is that they are not truly existent. To come to that realization requires the elimination of the two obscurations. The root that causes obscuration is conceptual thought from the all-base [proliferating] into twice deluded and thrice deluded concepts. The attachment and clinging that comes from cognizing the valid existence of form and other objects becomes the devil that obscures their ultimate invalidity. Mind is empty since forever and inherently lucid clarity. Abiding in that is no different from the timeless awareness of a buddha. Therefore it states in a sutra:

> If mind is realized, it is buddha. Therefore, meditate well with the idea that you won't seek elsewhere for the Buddha.

## II. The Source Text

### A. Brief Presentation {60}

What are the devils that obscure the mind, which is self-aware, lucid dharmakāya? They are tangible, intangible, exaltation, and inflation, but all four come from the root inflation.

### B. Extensive Explanation

There are three parts to the extensive explanation: (1) presenting the four devils to beginners and then practicing; (2) engaging in invalid existence by means of example; and (3) presenting the practice without example. Those will also be connected with the five paths.

#### 1. The Particular Four Devils

##### a. The Tangible Devil

###### i. Identifying That Devils Come from Oneself (four lines beginning with *tangible*)

This refers to all that appears directly to the sense organs, such as forms and so on, and the negation and affirmation of them that binds us to samsara.

###### ii. Ascertaining Their Essential Emptiness (sixteen lines beginning with *form*)

When appearances of forms and so on are established [as real], apprehending their essential nature as empty and [so] designating them are again establishing [them as real]. Scripture says, "Form is emptiness." The Conqueror ascertained the emptiness of everything from form up to omniscience. Through meditation on the invalidity of form and such, the fixation on permanent things is abandoned. By not mentally engaging even in that emptiness, one is free of the conventional designations of nihilism. In this kind of lack of valid existence, even though the mere appearances of form and so on cannot be stopped, the realization of form's lack of intrinsic existence is the perfection of wisdom. Meditating like that is the supreme path. It states in the *Noble [Perfection of Wisdom]*:

> As for form, it is free of the very essence of form. Similarly, feeling, perception, formation, and consciousness {61} are free of the very essence of consciousness and so on.[6]

Letting discursive thought stop on its own is the meditation. Discursive thought is the intangible devil; however, the clinging by the deluded mind that becomes obstinate reification is the tangible devil. Therefore, it is said of these, "Transform them into the timeless awareness of the realm of phenomena."

### b. The Intangible Devil

#### i. Identifying the Sensations (nine lines beginning with *intangible*)

This refers to "the good and bad sensations arising from the mentation consciousness." Those, however, will be naturally liberated if they are realized.

#### ii. Natural Liberation as Realization Dawns (ten lines beginning with *realm of phenomena's great expanse*)

Thoughts are like waves [arising] from the basic space of mind itself,[7] but it is said that they will be liberated by resting evenly within lucid reflective awareness without accepting or rejecting, as was explained before.

### c. The Devil of Exaltation

#### i. Brief Presentation (three lines beginning with *exaltation*)

The devil of exaltation comes of your own cognition being deluded about the two devils, common and supreme.

#### ii. Extensive Explanation has Two Parts: Common and Supreme

##### A) Common

##### 1) If Attached to Qualities, It Is a Path Devil (eight lines beginning with *haunted places*)

Having taken into experience the instructions of the guru, you may develop an arrogant mind from integrating on the path the uprisings of minor demons. Also, distractions and other obstructions to awakening may occur. These are all taught to be devils.

### 2) Taught to Be Like a Dream (eleven lines beginning with *qualities*)

This presents the lack of validity of the antidote as well, once the problem of the aforementioned devils is cleared up. {62} Whatever minor common qualities have developed, remain unattached by means of the attitude of wisdom which eradicates the nonduality of object and mind. As in a dream or the water filling the hands of a beautiful girl, all positive aspects and so forth are just your own discursive thoughts. Do not develop an arrogant mind. In the same way, understand whatever forms of suffering there are and once you understand, sever them directly.

Up to this point the instructions for the enhancement to the practice on the path of accumulation have been presented.

### B) Supreme

This has two parts: presenting the path as devil if not understood and presenting mental fabrication as the devil.

### 1) The Path as Devil if Not Understood
### a) Identifying the Devil
### i) Brief Presentation (in two lines)
### ii) Extensive Explanation (in six lines)

"Supreme" means the view free from elaboration, the meditation in equipoise, conduct without discursive thought, and holding the experience aspect in practice. If you do not know that object and mind are nondual, then there is fixation and it does not become the special path that brings about the realization of nonself.

### b) Liberation if Understood as Symbolic
### i) No View or Viewed in the Self-Arisen (six lines beginning with *view and meditation*)

There are limitless specialized explanations on view and meditation for certain individuals who have sharp faculties. However, ultimately it comes down to mental nonactivity (*yid la byar med*). Therefore, to abandon obstinate reification and apply the seal of invalidity to appearances of unimpeded energy is the supreme Severance. A similar sentiment is stated in the *Extensive* [*Sutra*] from "Do not mentally engage form" up through "knowledge of all aspects."[8] Therefore mental nonengagement (*yid la mi byed pa*) is taught. {63}

### ii) No Meditation or Meditator (ten lines from *everything is self-occurring*)

Everything that was mentioned above and so on is all one's own mind, and so there is no meditation involving deliberate antidotes. "Clear, serene" and so on [mean that] although there are particular meditative stabilities, the examples of water and butter and so on demonstrate that the meditation object and the meditator are not two.

### iii) If One Holds the View, One's Conduct Will Automatically Be One's Play (sixteen[9] lines beginning with *one's conduct*)

Conduct that is purposefully engaged for the sake of invalid existence is no conduct, and experienced appearances won't be held with antidotes of obstinate reification because if you do not understand self-liberation, it is bondage. Even if the applied antidote does self-liberate—since really there is nothing at all to prevent it—nevertheless do not engage in conduct without realization. According to this approach, directly severing afflictive emotions and other thoughts by powerful antidotes and applying the seal of invalid existence to the severing consciousness is taught as the supreme conduct.

### iv) Experience Is Beyond Intellect (ten lines beginning with *experience*)

This gives the instructions for severing deviations of the path. Since the root of devilry is to have a frame of reference, referential meditation is not the meditation of the perfection of wisdom. But how can that be? To be free of a meditation object and a meditator is the epitome of isolation from all fixation. When you rest without fixation [on perceived] appearances and [perceiving] mind, a range of experiences occur, but they are annihilated as fictitious. If you were to meditate with subject and object for a million aeons or whatever, it would not be the path of suchness. But one split second of realizing invalid existence brings all devils liberation on their own ground. It is for this reason that one relies on an excellent guru. {64}

**2) Mental Fabrication as Devil**

**a) Having Desire Is the Devil of Result (five lines beginning with *supreme*)**

The signs of warmth on the path of the three vehicles and the desire for results and all fixations are devils.

**b) If [Realized] to Be Oneself, Nothing to Accomplish (eleven lines beginning with *body, speech, and mind*)**

To be liberated from having hopes and fears regarding the above-mentioned causes and results and so forth, you must realize that your own body, speech, and mind are the three kāyas. Therefore, buddhahood is not accomplished from anything else. As Master Nāropa explained, "It is taught that all phenomena abide in mind; that mind itself is the root of phenomena." If you do not come to the realization of mind itself as such, practicing for aeons will not bring attainment. Buddhahood will not be accomplished anywhere apart from cutting through all fixation on the selfhood of phenomena and persons, without any hopes for the path and results.

**d. The Devil of Inflation**

**i. Brief Presentation**

The two lines beginning with *devils are divided into four* are easy to understand.

**ii. Extensive Explanation**

This has three parts: the tangible devil is included in inflation, the intangible devil is included in inflation, and the devil of exaltation is included in inflation.

**A) The Tangible Devil Is Included in Inflation**

**1) Things Not Held in the View Are Taught as the Devil (two lines beginning with *objective fixation*)**[10]

Attachment to the objects of deluded sensory consciousness, such as white-red, object-subject, is said to become the tangible devil.

### 2) Knowing They Are Rootless [Liberates Everything] (fifteen lines beginning with *objective things*)

As mentioned above, when you realize as inflation any concepts composed of dualistic fixation, you realize coarse apprehended objects without fixation. {65} Severing that inflation cuts off the four devils. For example, when the fire inside is extinguished, the smoke in the crevices of the wall naturally subsides. Furthermore, like cessation or the nirvanic peace of the shrāvakas, mere objective appearances are not stopped. The objects of form and so on continue to appear, but their essence remains the empty nature of phenomena. Like a rainbow in the sky, the appearance has no nature of its own. Just so, the noble ones see this as totally obvious, while ordinary individuals know it is so if they examine and investigate by means of scripture and reason. In the *Heart Sutra* it is explained, "Form is empty; emptiness is form." For example, it is like a skilled illusionist in whom thoughts of attachment to the created illusions do not occur. Therefore, other than realizing that the four devils that come from inner inflation are not truly existent, it is not that the dualistic intellect has something to sever. The realization that things and fixations are rootless means that form and so on are liberated in their own ground. That is the perfection of wisdom. Therefore it is said, "Rest within the state free of dualistic fixation."

### B) The Intangible Devil Is Included in Inflation

### 1) Identifying Five Devils That Come from the Root Devil of Inflation (six lines beginning with *intangible*)

The five poisons and so forth that become hopes and fears are devils of inflation.

### 2) Realization of Five Timeless Awarenesses and Emancipation from Six Classes if Inflation Is Liberated (twenty-two lines beginning with *aggression is liberated on its own ground*)

Again, as with the explanation in the section on the inclusion of the tangible in inflation, knowing that conceptual thought is without basis liberates the five afflictions in their own ground. Once the sufferings of the six types of beings are purified in their own ground, the five afflictions become the five timeless awarenesses. {66} To expand upon that: taking the afflictive emotion of aggression as the cause, the suffering of hell will be experienced. Since that is inflation, based on the realization that it is without basis, the mirror-like timeless awareness will be obtained. The same can be applied to the other triads: desire, hungry ghosts, and discriminating timeless awareness; stupidity, animals, and the timeless awareness of the realm of phenomena; jealousy, gods and humans, and the timeless awareness of accomplishing action; pride, demigods, and the timeless awareness of equality. Therefore it is said, "Inflation liberated on its own ground is the perfection of wisdom."

### 3) Example of Fearlessness (thirteen lines beginning with *thus*)[11]

This is a special instruction. Since all conceptual thought is a devil, you sever it. For example, just as a lion that lives in the snow mountain ranges has no hesitation or apprehension, annihilate inflation and rest evenly within the state of the absence of valid existence. No outer or inner obstacles whatsoever will arise. But in case they do, they will certainly become a training exercise, because they are your own apparitions. Now you may wonder whether the cutting-off of thoughts and concepts is not meditation. It is not like that. Through the cutting-off of whatever arises as not validly existent, even the lesser vehicle and so forth are eclipsed; what need to mention disease and spirits and so forth? Therefore, this severance that is free of root is especially elevated.

### 4) Even with Realization, It Is Bondage if Not Severed (seven lines beginning with *even with realization*)

So for individuals who may have the realization of the meaning of the lack of valid existence as explained above, yet have not taken the unity of view and meditation into their experience, {67} it is no different from having fixation on objects. For example, it is like an untempered sword. Devils are vanquished by taking into experience the unity of view and conduct. For example, it is like a great being who knows the skills of a warrior that vanquishes hosts of enemies. This is taught in the *Verse Summary*: in the part starting with "For example, like a great man who is skilled and endowed with qualities" up through "gets away safely and again comes back home." That provides the analogy, and the explanation is: "Similarly, at that time the skilled bodhisattva generates great compassion for the sentient-being realm and goes totally beyond the four devils and the two grounds."[12]

### 5) Becoming Buddha once Inflation Is Severed (four[13] lines beginning with *emaho*)

If one realizes freedom from absolutely all fixations, one becomes a buddha. As it explains in the *Verse Summary on the Perfection of Wisdom:*

> Those past lords and those present in the ten directions of the world
> became supreme physicians by training in this knowledge mantra.[14]

Rest in the lack of true existence of everything.

## C) The Devil of Exaltation Is Included in Inflation

This has two parts: common and supreme.

### 1) Common

#### a) If Attached to Spiritual Powers, It's a Devil (five lines beginning with *exaltation*)

So attachment to the signs of warmth and temporary results is itself a devil.

#### b) If Not Attached, It's an Ornament (two lines beginning with *without attachment*)

The unimpeded energy arising in the very self that is separated from dualistic fixation is an ornament. In the *Verse Summary*, there is the simile of the miracle and:

> Similarly, a skilled bodhisattva abiding in emptiness,
> gone beyond to the miracle of timeless awareness, nonabiding, {68}
> displays limitless deeds for migrators
> for millions of aeons without regret or fatigue.[15]

#### 2) Supreme
#### a) Excitement as a Devil (two lines beginning with *three kāyas*)

The three kāyas abide as an aspect of oneself. Harboring hopes and fears over any other thing is a devil.

#### b) Not Inflation if Understood (eight lines beginning with *samsara is self-liberated*)[16]

When one knows that samsara and nirvana are liberated on their own grounds and understands that thoughts and memories are not validly existent, there is no other antidote to meditate on. Therefore, it is taught to "Cut off inflation!" Furthermore, one can learn in detail about the devils' aspects in the chapter on devils from the Perfection of Wisdom sutras. Since their root is also conceptual thought, cut through that very thing and meditate.

The above concerns the path of application. Below is presented the enhancement practices of conduct in practice.

### 2. Ascertaining by Example
### a. Explanation of Examples
#### i. Bondage If Not Carried into One's Being (six lines beginning with *through example*)

People who receive this instruction and neither liberate themselves nor help others are like the example of the birds and autumn delivery. This demonstrates the attitude that "It's hard to liberate myself and others!"

#### ii. Benefiting Others if One Realizes It Oneself (six lines beginning with *fine cow*)

If the person himself or herself realizes the lack of valid existence, it automatically benefits sentient beings. Like the simile of the cow, one should realize nonself by oneself. It explains in the *Verse Summary*: {69}

> In case the notion of sentient beings and the notion of suffering
> are produced,
> thinking to help migrators and eliminate suffering,

> a bodhisattva will have fully considered self and beings.
> This is to not engage in the sublime perfection of wisdom.[17]

To achieve the authentic welfare of migrators, you must know that you are not truly existent and by the same token know that about sentient beings as well. As with sentient beings, the dharma that is the antidote for the afflictive emotions must also be understood in that way. Therefore it is also explained in the *Verse Summary*:

> However it is for the self, know it is also so for all sentient beings.
> However it is for all sentient beings, know it is also so for all dharmas.
> No thought of either nonproduction or production:
> This is to engage in the sublime perfection of wisdom.[18]

### b. View

#### i. Realizing That Devils Are Rootless (eleven lines beginning with *great garuḍa*)

In the development of the meaning of nonself, the realization of both kinds of nonself and the liberation of inflation on its own ground bring about the realization that the four devils are rootless. You attain the sign of a nonreturner and become victorious over all devils, as in the simile of the great garuḍa. Without that kind of realization, your conduct will have little meaning, as in the simile of the tree trunk.

#### ii. Cutting Through by Knowing That (six lines beginning with *rootless*)[19]

If you know that the discursive thoughts that come up are incidental and without true existence, there is liberation in the inseparability of the problem and its antidote. Then body, speech, and mind are liberated as Body, Speech, and Mind.

### c. Meditation

#### i. Examples of Nonthought (fifteen lines beginning with *method of resting*)

To rest evenly in the meaning of nonself, fully pacify all conceptual elaborations and be without thought, like a shrine-room statue. {70} Thoughts about sensations subside in the realm of the nature of phenomena like lightning. Though discursive thoughts occur, they do not move beyond the nature of phenomena, like waves in water. Rest freely without contrivance in the realm where everything is the play of timeless awareness. These methods teach the method of evenly resting.

#### ii. Resting Freely Uncontrived (nine lines beginning with *contrive* [or] *adulterate*)

Other than just resting evenly without mental engagement, to create contrivances by discursive thought is a devil. Therefore, you should rest freely without contrivance. In that sense, the similes of freely resting the six groups of consciousness are to rest like a person gripped by disease, like someone maintaining peace of mind, and like an immature child who sees its mother appear but is powerless to act.

#### iii. Transcending Misery through Knowing Thoughts and Memories Are Not Validly Existent (eleven lines beginning with *awareness*)

Your own cognition with its dualistic conceptual thinking is precisely the haunted place. Cutting through this in itself will result in cutting off all haunted places. In the case of beginners who are somewhat timid, they should do practices such as casting out the body as food without attachment, and dwell in the meaning of the perfection of wisdom. Rest without getting involved in concepts of good and bad, as in the simile of the simpleton with a full belly. Then without being afraid of memories, once you have been liberated from cyclic existence (samsara), transcendence of misery (nirvana) will be attained. Understand that the meaning of all this is to be without deliberate action. It says in the *Perfection of Wisdom*: "The perfection of wisdom is to be without thought, without mental activity" and

> Form is not wisdom, for form has no wisdom.
> Consciousness, perception, feeling, and volition—
> these are not wisdom, for these also have no wisdom.
> It is equivalent to the realm of space, indivisible.[20] {71}

### d. Conduct

#### i. Yogic Discipline Free of Afflictive Emotion (twelve lines beginning with *conduct*)

Individuals who have realized nonself, for the sake of sentient beings, display blessing conduct and the conduct on the path of severing discursive thought. Whichever of those two it is, the special characteristic of all conduct is that though there is great yogic discipline, the person's stream of being is without afflictions, like a wrathful mask. There is no fixation or attachment to the conduct, like a fish swimming in water. It is conduct without a trace of afflictive emotions, like the wind wending its way through mountain ravines. Subduing the obstacles of yogic discipline, since it is without anger or passion, is the perfection of wisdom. It says as much in the *Verse Summary*:

> At that time the devil becomes afflicted with agony,
> weary of misery, unhappy in suffering, and humbled.
> "How can I make this bodhisattva mentally despondent
> (*yid nur ba*)?"
> In order to terrify he ignites fire in all directions and hurls meteors.
>
> When those wise ones possess resolute intent,[21]
> day and night viewing the meaning of sublime perfection of
> wisdom,
> then their bodies, minds, and speech move like a bird in the sky.
> How then could the kinsmen of darkness gain purchase?[22]

#### ii. Everything as an Ally through Mastering Conduct (eleven lines beginning with *one's conduct*)

As explained before, the conduct of realized nonself must be naturally occurring conduct without the obstacle of inflation. It is not achieved by those with dualistic fixation. That is, designating with fixation is no different from delusion. In a dream, you may experience suffering, but it is your own deluded thought. Gods and so forth also depend on your own attachment to their actuality. {72} Therefore, all things good and bad are your own fixation. Your own perceptions harm you because they are the designations of dualistic reification. If you realized their lack of validity, then unrelated objective appearances would have no ability to cause harm, like the poisonous snakes of India that can do no harm in Tibet.

### e. Results

#### i. Realizing the Meaning, No Result to Establish (nine lines beginning with *results*)

When you have seen nonself in actuality, inflation is liberated on its own ground. There is no other meaning of buddha that could be established. That's because the subject (or perceiver) is realized to be the timeless awareness of the naturally occurring nature of phenomena. Thus, "Mind is no-mind; the inherent nature of mind is lucid clarity."[23] "No-mind" means unchanging and without conceptual thought according to the *Noble* [*Sutra*]. Mind is not truly existent; it is the nature of lucid clarity. Buddhahood is attained through that realization. Other than the very one who is isolated from dualistic fixation, there is no buddha that could be established. For example, if one says "butter" to a person who has already seen excellent butter extract, there is no need to establish white[24] and other aspects externally because they already have it confirmed in their mind. Similarly, an individual who has realized the two nonselves in actuality does not create the kāyas and timeless awareness or seek enlightened activity elsewhere.

#### ii. You Are Buddha for Sure (four lines beginning with *inflation-free*)[25]

As explained above, the four devils and the eighty-four thousand afflictive emotions are conquered through realization and naturally pacified.

Up to here, the conduct of the path of seeing along with its enhancement has been explained.

### 3. Presentation without Example
### a. Deluded Cognition {73}
### i. Naturally Deluded (two lines beginning with *noncognizant*)

There is no object of dualistic clinging established in the nature of phenomena. The intellect that definitely clings to mere appearance imagines various things such as being aware, that of which one is aware, and so on. Since that becomes dualistic, it is said to be deluded.

### ii. Deluded Regarding Tenets (twenty-two lines beginning with *single inseparability*)

Although the meaning of nonself is not divisible, buddhas and sentient beings occur based on awareness or lack of awareness (i.e., ignorance) of it. Thus, the delusion of ignorant dualistic fixation is said to be like water and gold and the sky.[26] Coemergent ignorance creates the condition for delusion as sentient beings. Thus, [delusion] is said to arise from not realizing that very thing and from external [sources] of erroneous ideas. There are endless wrong views, but to mention some in brief: nihilistic extremists hold that there is no cause and effect before and after and also that there is no after[life] and are thus deluded. There are those with the view of a permanent self, singular and self-contained, which is unchanging and so forth. The shrāvakas (hearers) believe that the partless atoms of the object (or percept) and indivisible moments of the subject (or perceiver) are absolute. Pratyekabuddhas (self-realizers) state that the object does not exist but the subject is absolute reality. Chittamātrins (mind only) think that both object and subject are nonexistent and that reflective awareness is absolute reality. True-image chittamātrins[27] believe that the appearing aspects, such as white, red, and so on, are true to the consciousness itself. False-image chittamātrins[28] believe that although those images are false, they are true to the consciousness of nonexistent images. However, aside from the difference in the density of delusion, it is said that these different views do not go beyond the net of conceptual thinking. Furthermore, it is said, "The mādhyamikas (centrists) are free of the eight extremes of elaboration." {74} These are the terms in use. Proponents of the father tantras of Secret Mantra believe in great bliss that arises [as] experiences of bliss-clarity based on the channels and vital winds. The mother tantrikas believe in method and wisdom, the timeless awareness of bliss-emptiness. Of the proponents of so-called mahāmudrā, the ultimate of both [those tantras], some believe it is beyond intellect, and some proponents of the Great Completion believe in even the relative truth as the nature of phenomena. There are those and other beliefs in the tenet systems. None of them will see the meaning of nonself, because they are fixated on tenets. In that vein, Telopa said:

> Through Mantravada and Pāramitā,
> Vinaya, Sutra, Abhidharma, and so forth,
> or your own scriptures and tenets,
> you will not behold the lucid clarity of mahāmudrā:
> anger and passion obscure the sight of lucid clarity.[29]

As explained there, it is not about cognizing object and subject. Since object and subject are not valid, that which is cognized and the cognizer are not two. It is the suchness of the nature of phenomena.

### b. Ignorance, Timeless Awareness

#### i. Stupidity Transformed into Timeless Awareness (six lines beginning with *therefore, noncognizant*)

If lucid clarity, the timeless awareness of the realm of phenomena, manifests seamlessly during sleep and [waking] appearances, then inflation is liberated on its own ground and the deluded appearances arise as timeless awareness. That's the real buddha.

#### ii. Whatever Arises Is Naturally Occurring (five lines beginning with *cognition*)

With the understanding that the cognizer and that which is cognized are not validly existent, fixation on subject-object is inherently pure. Deeds and beneficial activities are not enacted deliberately but happen as natural occurrences. Therefore, when such meaning as that is actualized, it is not ever manifested as reified conduct.

### c. Unmade Ground {75}

#### i. Not Made by Buddha (four lines beginning with *genuine meaning*)

The perfection of wisdom itself is also the ground of samsara and nirvana. Because it is empty since forever and nonself, it abides changelessly. Thus it is taught in the *Verse Summary*:

Those past lords and those present in the ten directions of the world
became supreme physicians by training in this knowledge mantra.
Whoever benefits and engages in the conduct with compassion,
having trained in this knowledge mantra, will become wise and touch enlightenment.
Those with conditioned happiness and those with unconditioned happiness, whichever,
all their happiness should be known as coming from this.[30]

### ii. Not Realized by Fixation (four lines beginning with *unmade*)[31]

The unconditioned, as was mentioned before, is called "ground" (*gzhi*) because it is free of the three extremes of birth, ceasing, and abiding. Therefore, sever all other errors.

### d. The Path of No Making

### i. Realizing the Four Perception Spheres Are Invalid (seven lines beginning with *unmade*)

In any case, people who see the truth of the unconditioned proceed on the path of no making. All appearances are annihilated in the lack of valid existence, so the intellect that fixates on emptiness is purified on its own ground. Since eternalism and nihilism are liberated in the lack of validity, it becomes the path of emptiness and compassion in union. Without mental engagement in appearance and nonappearance, the obscurations of the absorptions of the higher realms[32] and so on are purified on their own grounds. Then the cognitive obscuration of the path of meditation becomes pure.

### ii. Liberation from Samsara through Realizing the Meaning (thirteen lines beginning with *form and*)[33]

The aggregates such as form and so on, {76} and the elements and sense fields and so forth, are liberated as invalid, and thus you are liberated from the three realms. When you do not make anything in the mind, the two obscurations are naturally pure. This is buddhahood itself—levels and paths are completed. Mental nonengagement becomes the path. That is because it is the experiential practice of wisdom. As it states in the *Noble* [*Sutra*]:

> As all phenomena are mental nonengagement itself, the perfection of wisdom is that very mental nonengagement.[34]

Moreover, when mental movement or activity is liberated as invalid, there is no need to stop it because it is free of effort.

This above section explains just a little of the path of meditation.

### e. [Unreal] Results

#### i. The Expedient Method for the Small-Minded (five lines beginning with *unreal*)

Existence and nonexistence, birth and cessation, coming and going, eternalism and nihilism, and so forth are not truly established as real at all. The svabhāvakāya that is taught as the result and also the presentations of the three kāyas and so forth are indeed appearing for those to be tamed due to the power of aspirations. In actuality, the thirty-two excellent marks and the eighty excellent minor signs and so forth do not have even an atom of valid existence as definite appearance in addition to their abiding nature. Thus, from the *Highest Continuum*:

> Just as colors in their variety
> appear but are not the real gem,
> so appearances caused by various conditions of beings
> are not the real pervasive self.[35]

#### ii. Something Established as Real Is Meaningless (eight lines beginning with *if real*)

In the absolute sense, if kāyas and timeless awareness were separately established as real, there would be no ability to pass over samsara because the perfection of wisdom is not an action item of the intellect. Even if it could be established as the intellect or its object, since the intellect is deluded, all the effort to establish that belief {77} would not lead to the attainment of nirvana. Thus it says in the *Verse Summary:*

> The wisdom of worldly knowledge also has no outer limit.
> Whatever is the inherent nature of sentient beings also has no outer limit.

And:

> The guides have completely proclaimed, "perceptions are on this side."
> Once perception is totally annihilated, renunciation goes to the other side.[36]

### iii. If Mind Is Not Liberated, It Is Meaningless (eight lines beginning with *the mind craving dharma*)

To attain the special results that were explained above, you must be free of a craving attitude. Engaging in dharma under the power of craving is exactly the thing that binds you. Since buddhahood is unconditioned, annihilate all fixation to effortful enterprise.

### iv. Realizing Nonfixation Reveals Body, Speech, and Mind (five lines beginning with *not fixating on body*)

For the yogin, once the self has relied on the path of the six perfections, self-fixation is purified on its own ground. When perceived objects develop as kāyas and timeless awareness, it is no different from the Body, Speech, and Mind of all buddhas. So all paths are also lucid clarity without fixation. Except for the perfection of wisdom itself, there is no other place to seek the victors' enlightened intent because there is realization of being inseparable from the three kāyas.

At this point the explanation of the enhancement of the path of the perfections in connection with the five paths is finished.

## III. Conclusion

### A. The Meaning of the Name (three lines beginning with *emaho*)

The presentation that this is a bundle of explanations on unchangeability and severance of conceptual thought is easy to understand.

### B. The Method to Earnestly Take Up Experiential Practice

#### 1. [Experience] Free of Intellect (three lines beginning with *earnest*) {78}

At all times rest evenly within this very state of freedom from extremes of an objective frame of reference.

#### 2. Special Instructions (five lines beginning with *haunted places*)

When beginners practice Severance in haunted places and so on, the superior ones respond to fear and anxiety with emptiness, the average with being free of body-mind, and the inferior with casting out the body as food, and such. They should engage without fixation inwardly, and then again "out there" [those spirits] will become severed.

#### 3. If the Load Is Carried, It Is the View (four lines beginning with *appearing conditions*)

If phenomena are not carried directly onto your stream of being, you cannot be liberated by peace and happiness alone. Therefore understand that the vital point of this instruction is to carry it over and apply it to whatever conditions appear.

#### 4. The Importance of Wandering in Mountain Retreats (four lines beginning with *haunted places*)

Those individuals who receive instructions should wander to haunted places and mountain retreats and so on without attachment to the corpse of materialistic desirables. However, once you have arrived in those places, if you fail to set aside the texts and words and neglect meditation, the blessing will not enter and the words will turn you into a brute. Rather, take up practice in isolation.

The instructions that have thus been explained are the enhancement of the unity of view and conduct. To carry this unity of view and conduct from the time of being a beginner until the attainment of unsurpassable enlightenment is the profound instruction. Thus also Machik affirmed:

> Trample on the conceptual thoughts
> with the confidence of the guru's esoteric instruction.

This itself becomes the path when you can display various conducts of the realization of nonself {79} yet be without fixation. Therefore, to take into experience the unity of emptiness and compassion is crucial.

The instructions on the perfection of wisdom, the complete explanation of *The Great Bundle of Precepts on Severance of Evil Object*, was created by Rangjung Dorje with a critical intellect by applying the Mahayana sutras that are preeminent for meditators in the degenerate times.

# 6. A Hair's Tip of Wisdom

## *A Precious Treasure Trove to Enhance the Original Source Text of Severance, the Esoteric Instructions on the Perfection of Wisdom*[1]

Machik Lapdrön and Drung Sarupa Kunga Paljor

ALTHOUGH THIS TEXT is attributed to Machik Lapdrön and placed among the original texts of Severance in *The Treasury of Precious Instructions*, in fact it is a commentary on a source text, with the lines of what may have been an autonomous root text entitled *A Hair's Tip of Wisdom* found within the commentary. This root text may well have been composed by Machik, as it is similar in content and style to the other sources and retains the beauty and profundity of direct teaching. The commentary itself has no colophon. Kongtrul indicates in his records that it could be by Kunga Paljor (also called Drung Sarupa), who is the author of *Pure Honey*, the commentary to the main source text by Āryadeva the Brahmin. It is somewhat similar in style to that work. On the other hand, in *The Religious History of Pacification and Severance* it seems to be attributed to Karmapa Rangjung Dorje.* Again it is unclear, as there is no direct statement of authorship but rather an association with another text. Rangjung Dorje seems an unlikely candidate, since the text is not found among his comprehensive collected works, and stylistically it is quite different.

Sometimes the commentary seems to directly contradict the intention in the root text upon which it is commenting. For example, Machik (if she is the author) says that "the meaning . . . is introduced in oneself," while the comment on that statement advises one to request introduction or pointing-out instruction from the guru. The structural outline superimposed on what would be an inspired spontaneous teaching seems a better fit for a

*Khamnyön Dharma Senge, *Religious History of Pacification and Severance*, f. 69a.

formal treatise. Nevertheless, the comments of this deft scholar clarify and enhance the meaning of the original, and together they make a wonderful exposition on the real meaning of Severance.

---

*namo gurave*

Homage to the guru and the supreme deity Mañjushrī, Lion of Speech.

Dharmakāya great mother, perfection of wisdom,
saṃbhogakāya great bliss, assembly of five-family ḍākinīs,
nirmāṇakāya great love, exalted Tārā,
I bow to the emanation of Body, Speech, and Mind: Lapkyi Drönma.

The essential meaning of all excellent speech of the victorious ones
is ultimately the perfection of wisdom.
Its supreme esoteric instruction is the method to sever the four devils.
This is an enhancement of the original source, the amazing *Hair's Tip of Wisdom.*

This *Hair's Tip of Wisdom* has three parts: the foreword, the main text, and the conclusion.

## I. Foreword

### A. Homage

> *Homage to the mother of all.*

"Mother" because the noble ones—the shrāvakas, pratyekabuddhas, bodhisattvas, and omniscient ones—were all generated by the perfection of wisdom. {83}

It states in the *Mother*:

> Whoever desires to train in the level of a shrāvaka must train in this very perfection of wisdom.
> Whoever desires to train in the level of a pratyekabuddha must train in this very perfection of wisdom.

> Whoever desires to train in the level of a bodhisattva must train in this very perfection of wisdom.
> Whoever desires to train in the level of an omniscient one must train in this very perfection of wisdom.[2]

And Lord Maitreya says in the *Ornament of Clear Realization*:

> She guides the hearers who seek peace to utter peace through wisdom of all.
> She makes those who benefit beings accomplish the welfare of the world through wisdom of the path.
> Thoroughly possessing her, the sages proclaim the variety endowed with all aspects.
> Homage to that mother of the buddhas with the assemblies of shrāvakas and bodhisattvas.[3] {84}

**B. Commitment to Explain**

> *For one such as myself who has taken an inferior body,*
> *realizing the meaning of the mother of the victors*
> *is beyond the scope of my own cognition.*
> *Nevertheless I commit to explain this lamp of the supreme meaning.*

Saying "inferior body" here is modesty in accordance with ordinary worldly convention. Since she is an emanation of the Mother herself, she is not inferior. It states in the *Vajra Tent*:

> The illusory form[4] of a woman
> teaches dharma to the desirous.
> The woman illusion is the very buddha
> that clears away all illusions.[5]

And from *Chakrasaṃvara*:

> Of all illusions, the woman illusion is distinctively superior.[6]

All the more so here, after she has personally promised the realization of the victors' mother, to then teach that to others is the act of a buddha. It states in a sutra:

> The sages do not wash away negative actions with water.
> Beings' injuries are not healed by their hands.
> They cannot transfer their realization to others.
> They liberate by teaching the truth of the nature of phenomena.[7]

### C. Instructions on the Practice

> *Anyone with intelligence is appropriate,*
> *who forsakes samsaric phenomena*
> *and desires to obtain definite emancipation,*
> *practicing this way by means of making moral choices.*[8]

"With intelligence" is someone with a Mahayana affinity who, with thoughts of renunciation, trains in this method of obtaining emancipation and omniscience.

## II. Main Text

### A. Brief Presentation

> *Mentally relinquishing all activity,*
> *always roam in haunts and mountain retreats.*
> *Keep to secluded strongholds of confidence without inflation.* {85}
> *Observe your own mode of being.*
> *The meaning of that itself is introduced in oneself.*
> *Inspire your own mood by yourself.*

Having renounced this life's activities, request introduction [to mind's nature] and instructions from a holy guru and meditate in mountain retreats.[9]

### B. Extensive Explanation

#### 1. Teaching Meaningful Activity in the Manner of Advice

##### a. Brief Presentation

> *Engage in everything, such as the ten perfections,*
> *in accord with the significance of the three doors.*

Initially, you will not rise above cyclic existence if you are attached to enjoyments and household activities. The antidote to that is generosity and ethical discipline. The cause of reverting from an elevated state is being disheartened by the counterproductive practices of sentient beings and weariness with applying oneself to virtue for a long time. The antidote to that is patience and diligence. The cause of wasting it while not reverting is complete distraction and crazy wisdom. The antidote to that is meditative stability and wisdom. The four timeless awarenesses subsequent to the perfection of wisdom are (1) method, which is to dedicate all roots of virtue in common with everyone; (2) aspiration, which is to make various aspirations and accomplish them; (3) strength, which is never to interrupt the continuity of the perfection of the strength of meditation and discernment; and (4) timeless awareness, which is to engage in the awareness of the [first] six and to mature sentient beings.

### b. Training in the Meaning of the Ten Perfections

*Accumulate merit without bias or preference.*
*Rest at ease without presumption.*

Give generously without bias and preference toward the recipients or presumption about the results. {86}

*Practice continuously without wavering*
*and verify both words and meanings.*

Uphold every word of devoted application to ethical discipline without wavering and of the ethical discipline of constant application to continuous practice.

*Do not give free rein to the afflictive emotion*
*of hostile anger: keep it down.*

When the afflictive emotion of anger arises, bring on the antidote of patience.

*Through the diligence of the aware mind,*
*gain peaceful obedience of the corporeal body.*

Undertake diligence without attachment to physical happiness and well-being.

*If you follow for the sake of appearance, you are carried off by the devil.*
*Keep to the low ground and refine the mind itself.*

Abandon distracting places and cultivate meditative stability in isolated places.

*Conditioned virtuous roots are like donated wealth.*
*Transfer them to the treasury of the nonreferential.*

Stamp dissipating virtue with the seal of nondissipating wisdom.

*Obstacles come of giving credence to external vestiges.*[10]
*Act in the moment of recollecting anything.*

Change all appearances that you encounter to the path of awakening by using skillful methods.

*Your own qualities benefit yourself and others.*
*Engage them like a rare jewel.*

Accomplish the benefit of yourself and others through various aspirations.

*You will not cross over the pass if you have too many ideas.*
*With intention on the purpose, make up your mind.*

Roll all actions into one and develop the strength of virtue.

*Timeless awareness of realization, intentional experience:*
*become accustomed to it as your own appearance.*

Mature yourself and others by the realization of timeless awareness.

### c. Training in the Meaning of the Eightfold Path of the Noble Ones

Noble Nāgārjuna said:

> Authentic view and livelihood and effort,
> recollection, absorption, speech, results of action,[11] {87}
> and authentic thought are the eightfold path.[12]
> Meditate on them for the sake of making peace.[13]

As it says, to abandon erroneous effort is authentic effort:

> *Merit is an obstacle of dharma.*
> *It is best to give up face-saving diversions.*

Authentic livelihood:

> *Lost in prolonged begging for food,*
> *it is best to rely physically and mentally on a monastery.*

Authentic speech:

> *Lost to your own benefit in prolonged explanations,*
> *be diligent in undistracted practice.*

Authentic view:

> *All teaching of phenomena is mere symbols.*
> *Do not dwell upon books; do real practice.*

Authentic results of action:

> *Take to heart like secret words*
> *instructions that teach on the profound.*

Authentic thought:

> *Without consigning your understanding to objects,*
> *blend with your own stream of being.*

Authentic mindfulness:

> *The mind of unimpeded naturally occurring awareness—*
> *let it go free in the expanse of nonmind.*

Authentic absorption:

> *Sensations are like mist in mindful awareness;*
> *they fade away by themselves without interfering.*

Bodhisattvas dwelling on the path of meditation possess these [qualities] as they should be. Ordinary folks have a mere approximation.

### d. Instructions on the Profound Meaning

> *Vital wind with cognition is the seed of habitual patterns.*
> *Since that is the root of delusion,*
> *whatever the original causes and conditions,*
> *subsequently sever the outflow from the source.*
> *The introduction of the profound meaning*
> *depends on the speech of the holy guru.*

The mind, which is vital wind and cognition inseparable, is the abode of all habitual patterns of delusion. {88} Request the introduction on how to cut through its foundational root.

### e. Detailed Explanation of Resting in the Nonduality of Object and Mind

> *Give the gift of the awakening mind.*
> *Since everything is your own mind,*
> *apparent phenomena are not close or distant.*
> *Settle yourself in the great pervasion.*

The yogin who has obtained the pointing-out introduction rests pervasively with unmoving equanimity in space, awareness, and appearance.

Those five sections were part of the first general topic.

## 2. Teaching the Vital Points of Responsibly Integrating Practice

### a. Brief Presentation

*The sublime instruction is to sever the ties*
*to all objects which harm the mind*
*in order to blend mind and dharma, meditation and view,*
*and cut to the quick of practice,*
*and cut off all doubts about the view,*
*and take up equanimity on the path.*

The instruction is to cut ties for the sake of meditation on the path.

### b. Extensive Explanation

#### i. Identifying the Tangible Devil

*At first as an inexperienced person,*
*one errs in the distraction of loving and hating friend and foe.*
*Attachment and aversion are the devils of self-fixation.*

This presents the entanglements of tangible objects.

#### ii. The Method to Sever It

*So separation from objects is taught as severance.*

This presents the beginner's renunciation of objects.

#### iii. Identifying the Intangible Devil and the Method to Sever It

*The intangible, personified by apprehensive mind as a devil,*
*is severed by fearless confidence.*

The intangible is severed by knowing that the basic root of the entanglements of the inner mind is not established as existent.

### iv. Direct Action if Not Severed
### A) Ascertaining the Intangible Devil {89}
### 1) Direct Action

> *At the time that adverse conditions occur,*
> *it is crucial to know the vital point of taking it on.*

Act according to worldly convention toward the tangibles and do equalizing suppression of the intangibles.

### 2) An Exemplary Method to Rest without Presumption

> *It is wrong to act presumptuously with aggression and desire.*
> *Like the beasts that reside in haunted places,*
> *contemplate without presumption while in haunted places.*
> *Be without presumption, free of the inflation of helping or harming,*
> *as are foliage and boulders and such.*
> *You should understand suchness.*

Here it is saying that once you understand suchness, you rest like the beasts and boulders and so on that inhabit those haunted places. However, these days practitioners of Severance seem to say that to not employ fierce visualizations in a haunted place does not cut it. And even if somehow it does cut it, then the thieves in mountain valleys and jackals on the mountain passes and all the wild beasts would also be doing Severance [since they are in] haunted places.

This is not correct for two reasons: The yogi or yoginī is thereby equating himself or herself with deceiving thieves and wild beasts and such. And [those beings] do not know that the root of all phenomena is based on mind. Therefore, thieves and so forth do not have the practice of the perfection of wisdom, which is distinct from an evil mind. Yogis and yoginīs *do* have the practice of the perfection of wisdom, and so are [practicing] cutting in haunted places. Remember the teachings on the unimaginable benefits and blessing of the perfection of wisdom from immeasurable sutras, such as the extensive, middle, and condensed versions of the *Mother*. Thus in the *Extensive Mother*:

> Space does not disturb space. Outer space does not disturb inner space. Inner space does not disturb outer space.[14] {90}

And:

> Alternately, rest in something like space.
> As space has no conception,
> rest with openness in nonconceptuality.
> As space has no worries,
> rest relaxed without worry.
> As space has no hopes and fears,
> rest reconciled without hopes and fears.
> As space has no fixation on self,
> rest letting go of self-fixation.
> As space has no arrogant mind,
> do not be arrogant about anything.[15]

The meaning of these words is easy to understand. Their meaning is taught in the *Extensive Mother*:

> Form has the support of space; it does not transcend that support.[16]

This is further applied to all phenomena of samsara and nirvana starting from the five aggregates. And:

> Form that has the disposition of space is what is taught to all sentient beings.[17]

After applying this to the five aggregates and so on, the teaching is quite extensive. In this vein, you should rest in equanimity in the state of knowing that all phenomena are like space.

### 3) Apparitions Directly Introduced in Yourself

> *Do not pursue thoughts causing inflation.*
> *Discern external apparitions within yourself.*

Those three points conclude the discussion of the intangible devil.

### B) The Devil of Exaltation

#### 1) Identifying Common Spiritual Powers as a Devil and Severing

> *Blessings, magic, special phenomena,*
> *fame, esteem, outer and inner signs,*
> *clairvoyance, prophecies, and all common [powers]:*
> *discern the devil and keep them secret.*[18] {91}

If pride and arrogance arise about all those, since that is a devil, abandon clinging to them as supreme and understand that they are [like] illusion and dream.

#### 2) Instructions on Not Being Attached to Enjoyments

> *Discern material wealth and enjoyment as illusion*
> *and abandon the clinging of mental attachment.*

This is quite understandable. Those two points conclude the discussion of the devil of exaltation.

### C) Severance of the Devil of Inflation

#### 1) Confidence That Does Not Cling to Anything

> *Do not cling to anything at all.*
> *Do not reference even the nonreferential.*
> *If you do not reference the phenomena of apparent existence,*
> *how could you possibly reference the mind's intention?*

The *Extensive Mother*:

> [Buddha] said, "Subhuti, a frame of reference[19] is very narrow. There is no attainment in referential notions. There is no actual realization. There is no unsurpassable enlightenment." [Subhuti asked,] "If the Blessed One does not have a frame of reference, could he have attainment or actual realization or unsurpassable complete enlightenment?" The Blessed One responded, "Su-

bhuti, since there is no delusion in the realm of phenomena, being without reference is itself attainment or being without reference is itself actual realization. Being without reference is itself unsurpassable genuine complete enlightenment."[20]

### 2) Clinging Desire of Mental Phenomena Obscures the Meaning

*Whoever has asserted the unborn*
*with the conventional mind of discursiveness,*
*since it is asserted, is not the unborn;*
*the desire itself will obscure it.*
*The fool is far from that [truth].*
*Such a one does not get the meaning.*

### 3) The Reason That Buddha Is Not an Object of Mind

*Thought and cognition are deluded.*
*Buddha is not in the deluded mind.*
*How could mind and discursive thought be*
*in a buddha's self-liberated timeless awareness?* {92}
*How could there be body*[21] *and habitual patterns?*
*Not being compounded, there is no knowing.*

### 4) Resolving Mind and Thought That Does Not Contradict Demonstration by Mere Symbols

*Teachings are certainly nothing more than symbols.*

### 5) Resolution in Transcending Evaluation of the Genuine

*The genuine meaning—you say "this is it,"*
*yet it is not demonstrated and without location.*
*It transcends all reference and nonreference.*

Thus arriving at the other shore of wisdom, even the perfection of wisdom is not referenced. When engaging in the perfection of wisdom without referencing it, one sees that all phenomena are also included in that perfection of wisdom, and all those phenomena are also not referenced. Why is that? It is because in this way those phenomena and that perfection of wisdom are not two; they are not divisible into two. And why is that? Because in this way those phenomena are taught to be in the realm of phenomena without any distinction at all, and because they are taught as suchness, and because they are taught as the supremely genuine, and because all phenomena are inseparable. Thus it was taught in the *Extensive Mother.*

The meaning in those five sections is the presentation of the ultimate meaning without elaboration, no different from the intention of the reasonings of madhyamaka. It is not possible to elaborate extensively on this here.

> Clearing away the four: problem, remedy, thoughts of suchness,
> and fixation on characteristics of results;
> at that time the embodiment of space
> blooms with the flowers of characteristics.

That is to say, when one is free of fixation on the problem and fixation on the remedy and fixation on the characteristics of suchess and fixation on the characteristics of the results, then emotional and cognitive obscurations, along with all habitual tendencies, are eliminated. That is space-like dharmakāya arising as the form kāya blooming with the flowers of signs and marks. {93}

Yogis and yoginīs who are not skilled in terminology cannot ascertain the general meaning; however, they can manifest their own inherently endowed characteristics through meditating on the yogas of calm abiding and higher insight.

Lord Maitreya said:

> Without beginning, middle, or end, it is indivisible,
> nondual, free of three, stainless, and without concept.
> Realization of the inherent nature of the space of phenomena
> is seen by the yogin resting in equipoise.[22]

### 6) Not Rejecting or Accepting What Occurs Naturally

> *If it occurs automatically, whatever it is like,*
> *do not reject and do not grasp.*

For some, emptiness rises up as an enemy, so that while one is seemingly practicing generosity and so forth, one scorns the physical and verbal virtuous engagement of others. Being a layperson oneself, while seemingly exerting oneself at pretending to tread the difficult path of common virtuous roots and such, one scorns the creation of the three supports of others. While one seemingly exerts oneself at a mere six-syllable invocation, one scorns the vast study and contemplation of others. While one is seemingly diligent with mere limited virtuous roots without any connection to [actual] vows, one scorns others who keep the three ordinations and pure vows. These are all [examples] of misunderstanding the exercise of not interrupting what occurs automatically and the accomplishment of virtuous roots through two accumulations in union.

In addition to this, there is the so-called compassion rising up as the enemy. While one is seemingly unable to benefit others, enacting their welfare is refuted by the example of the little birds and autumn deliverance in *The Great Bundle*.[23] Therefore, it is said of a beginner:

> Even without the power to enact others' welfare,
> always cultivate the aspiration for it.
> Whatever you aspire to, that you'll have. {94}
> I myself have engaged that with purpose.

Thinking in that way to benefit others is the accomplishment of your own benefit through connection.

There is also the so-called cause and effect rising up as an enemy. The correct view of worldly people rests with the [idea that] karmic causes and effects are merely inevitable. But other than mere relative appearances, in fact both cause and effect are not truly existent. Not knowing that, they cling obstinately to the realness of cause and effect, which is an obstruction to the accomplishment of the path. Therefore, not falling for the three "enemies that rise up" and such, know that your innate disposition is unborn and your radiance is unimpeded. When you do not abandon the relative at all, and without any fixation on the absolute, that lack of grasping is the path of unity.

### 7) Not Pursuing Anything since Fixation Is a Devil

*Since fixated cherishing of anything is a devil,*
*recall that your body and all apparent phenomena*
*are inseparable and cast them out to the realm of space.*

In the realization of the view, since devils loom large, relinquish the fixation on tangible objects.

### 8) Severance as Symbol

*Gods, demons, and such—all objects of severance*
*should be known as symbols for training.*

Developing proficiency in practice is based on the intangible devils.

### 9) Resolution in Self-Liberation without Objectifying

*The devils of gods, nāgas, disease, plague, and anxiety,*
*since they have no real existence,*
*are your own mentally projected apparitions.*
*Liberation is certain once you relax at ease.*

This teaches that once you know that everything is mind, you can remain without mental fixation. At this point, severing the tangible devil along with the brief presentation concludes the second general section.

## 3. Teaching That Freedom from Inflation Is the Confidence of View

### a. Decisiveness in Self-Liberation without Objectivity {95}

*Other than your own decisive cutting through inflation,*
*nothing at all will happen externally.*

### b. Confidence in the Lack of Arising and Cessation

*Since ceaseless apparent existence is yourself,*
*unborn timeless awareness is comprehensive confidence.*

Those two [verses present] the decisiveness that appearance and mind are inseparable.

### 4. The Unity of Distinctiveness and Eminence
### a. Distinctive Eminent Severance

*The profound instructions on the view's meaning*
*claim realizations that are more than equal to,*
*and distinctly above, realizations of yogāchāra,*
*eminent in the basic severance of acceptance and rejection.*

As the view is nondual, it blends into the nonduality of acceptance and rejection. Since other dharma systems do not have this feature, the yoga of Severance is distinctively eminent.

### b. The Method

*Liberation from clinging to anything and*
*blending view and conduct are taught as method.*

Those objects to which normal people cling will become aids to liberation if you know this method of blending view and conduct.

### c. Meaningless If the Method Is Not Known

*Whoever has the inflation of dualistic fixation*
*and severs permanent objects with a presumptuous mind*
*is clueless and very foolish.*

This is the definitive understanding.

### d. Introducing the Method to Those Who Do Not Recognize It

*If you come to know that no-object is the method,*
*it is the esoteric instruction to introduce object as mind.*

### 5. Getting Directly to the Vital Point, Introducing the Mode of Being
### a. The Method of Resting in the Abiding Nature

*Here is the method of resting in suchness:*
*in being unimpeded and fixation free,*
*you rest naturally without contrivance.*
*Other than severing dualistic notions,*
*the devil of inflation, self-fixation, habitual patterns,* {96}
*apprehension, anxiety, hopes and fears,*
*there is nothing to do on purpose.*
*There is nothing whatsoever to pursue.*
*Relinquish fixation and rest at ease.*

Rest without contrivance in the abandonment of all purposeful effort of body, speech, or mind.

### b. Introducing the Mode of Being

*In the intentions of the buddhas of three times*
*that are without inflation, like the sky,*
*clarity and emptiness, like the sun and moon,*
*are free of the notions of self-fixation.*

This presents the unity of clarity and emptiness free of fixation as the ultimate meaning.

### 6. Teachings of Earnest Encouragement
### a. Advice of Delight

*Emaho!*
*To enter the path without myself, delightful!*
*To befriend the friend of nonfixation, delightful!*

*To stay in an unfamiliar place, delightful!*
*To keep to a hermitage without support, delightful!*
*To cut the rope of saving face, delightful!*
*To tear down the wall of conformity, delightful!*
*To be free of all fixation, delightful!*
*To rest easily in the six consciousnesses, delightful!*
*Thus, according to my words,*
*followers should train in this way.*

### b. Final Words on the Meaning of the Attributes [of This Teaching]

#### i. Upholding This Instruction

*These letters on a hair's tip of wisdom*
*condense the meaning of the essential extract of the intent.*
*Keep them in mind, noble child.*
*Hold them as sacred, noble child.*
*Speak of them as such, noble child.*
*Mix your mind with dharma, noble child.*
*Apply them in your being, noble child.*
*Be familiar with them, noble child.*
*Do not fixate on objects, noble child.*
*Cut off apprehension, noble child.*

#### ii. Decisively Cutting Acceptance and Rejection {97}

*Since it is effortless, rest within.*
*Since it abides inherently, release anger and desire.*
*Since it occurs naturally, don't take it up in mind.*
*Since it is self-liberated, don't cut it off later.*
*Since it is without causes and conditions, don't accumulate karma.*
*Since it is unborn, don't mentally cut it off.*
*Since it is unceasing, don't construct a support.*
*Since it is transparent, don't be biased.*
*Since it is all-pervasive, don't take sides.*
*Since it is oneself, don't hope for another.*
*Since it is not bondage or liberation, don't fear and hope.*
*Since it is without contrivance, stay natural.*

*Since it is without accomplishment, rest freely.*
*Since it cannot be sought, stay relaxed.*
*Since it is without meeting or parting, don't set a time.*
*Since it is without birth or death, don't hold inflation.*
*Enjoy the intention that is like illusion.*
*Be utterly certain that it is like space.*

## c. Recipients Granted Instructions

### i. Worthy Recipients

*My words are the intended meaning,*
*the quintessence of the intentions of the victors of the three times.*
*This instruction on the profound meaning is for those who*
*are of noble type and abide in the sacred,*
*are gentle by nature and graceful in conduct,*
*sensible and fearful of birth and death,*
*who follow not for the sake of words but for the meaning,*
*not for the sake of appearances but for practice,*
*are not attached to things, not meditating on emptiness,*
*not sparing one's life for the sake of the sacred,*
*and who have dedication in the profound path.*
*It is intelligent disciples such as this*
*that you awareness-holders who come after me,*
*having extracted the pith of the intent without remainder,*
*should set to meditation; they are the worthy lineage holders,*
*the intimate children of your minds.*

### ii. Unworthy Recipients

*Those who are not sensible,*
*are not afraid of birth and death, are conventional,*
*do not hold the sacred, have a presumptuous mind,*
*do not practice but are judgmental,* {98}
*hide their own flaws while examining others' flaws,*
*lack purpose and see only themselves,*
*deliver deception and are bound by clinging,*
*are filled with desire and oppressed by pride,*

*want the quintessence but shun the container,*
*gain qualities by picking low-hanging fruit,*
*cut the ties of relationships with obsequious flattery,*
*proclaim family secrets in the marketplace,*
*wave dirty rags on the tips of victory banners,*[24]
*who lay out the precious jewels,*
*and hide the precious drops as treasure—*
*do not give the teachings to such as those;*
*keep them securely hidden and secret.*

This completes the main body of the text, the extensive explanations of six general topics along with the brief presentations.

## III. Conclusion

### A. Final Instruction

*The quintessence of the intent having been extracted, the power of the instructions is brought out from the precept Perfection of Wisdom, Severance of Evil Object.*

### B. Explanation of the Title

*"A Hair's Tip of Wisdom" means that since it presents precisely the fine points of the perfection of wisdom, it is a "hair's tip." The end.*

These are the final words at the completion from beginning to end of this source text.

### C. Making the Concluding Aspiration

*May it be of benefit to many with karmic [connection].*

This unadulterated genuine teaching of the Mother [Machik] herself contains everything in the Buddhist path of the ten perfections, and all spiritual paths are included in the eightfold path of the noble ones. But since it appears to be difficult to identify these two in this source text, I have made that identification. Since these are vast spiritual paths, an extensive explanation of them was not attempted, and also not presented in *The Great*

*Bundle* and the other texts. But from the severance of the four devils on, the vital points are the same as in *The Great Bundle* and others. {99} Since this is extremely profound, realized individuals will find it easy to understand, but intellectually inferior people will not be able to understand it even when it is explained, so don't attempt a meticulous explanation.

Lapkyi Drönma, glorious lady of the realm,
lays the banquet of happiness and benefit for all.
Her teachings are deep and vast jewels of two accumulations
spreading to alleviate the poverty of beings equaling space.
May all those buffeted by the storms of temporary adverse conditions,
once aided by the fire of nondual timeless awareness,
make every tree of deluded dualistic fixation
blaze as the light of experience and realization.
May the darkness of afflictions and karma dissipate in the sky,
and the warm rays of benefit and happiness pervade the realm,
and the degenerate age and beings occur together,
and may we wield the sharp spade of the ten dharma activities.[25]
*śubham*

# 7. Another Bundle

## *Answers to Questions on the Esoteric Instructions of the Perfection of Wisdom*[1]

### Machik Lapdrön

*Another Bundle*, attributed to Machik Lapdrön, takes the form of a dialogue or question-and-answer session, perhaps written down or remembered in verse by her son Gyalwa Döndrup, who is said in several sources to be the interlocutor. In the catalog of *The Treasury of Precious Instructions,* Kongtrul traces his transmission lineage back to him. "Another" or "a further" bundle (*yang tshom*) indicates that it is another collection following *The Great Bundle.* In *The Religious History of Pacification and Severance*, Khamnyön Dharma Senge calls *Another Bundle* "the esoteric instructions on that [*Great Bundle*]."* An alternate title given in the colophon is *Another Bundle of Twenty-Five Instructions as Answers to Questions,* shortened in certain other sources to *Another Bundle of Twenty-Five.* However, one finds here twenty-eight questions, and it is not clear if this is some kind of alternate Tibetan way of counting or if the bundle tends to gain and lose questions with each reprint like a loose bunch of flowers.

This version of *Another Bundle* is also found in a collection of Severance texts called *Practices of the Severance Collection and So Forth* (*gCod tshogs kyi lag len sogs*) from Limi Monastery. Although there are many minor differences in these two editions, some of which I mention in the endnotes, the two are comparable in format. However, it is preceded in the Limi collection by another text that is indicated merely with the words "Bundle of Precepts" (*bKa' tshom*). The colophon to that text calls it "*Thirty-Five Questions and Answers on the Bundle of Precepts, the Quintessence of the Mother's*

*Khamnyön Dharma Senge, *Religious History of Pacification and Severance*, f. 68a.

*Super Secret Heart-Mind.*" It goes on to add the following: "This esoteric instruction is a word continuum. If it spreads to everyone it will be of no benefit. Keep it restricted like a mute's speech. Depend on the heirs that hold the lineage." And: "This quintessence of the heart-mind [as] questions and answers was gladly bestowed by great realized guru[s] on the Shākya monk Sangdor, and I wrote it well." This may be the same author as that of the *Heart Essence of Profound Meaning*, Jamyang Gönpo, who typically signs off as "the Shākya monk, holder of the vajra."

Although this other "Bundle of Precepts" in the Limi collection bears almost no resemblance to *The Great Bundle of Precepts* (*bKa' tshom chen mo*), it is strikingly similar to *Another Bundle* in that it is a series of questions and answers, many of which in fact are basically the same questions. Of the thirty-five questions (here correctly enumerated), twenty-six appear in *Another Bundle,* at least in content, with sometimes two questions being combined into one. Three of the responses to questions resemble sections in *The Essential Bundle* (chapter 9 in this volume), and six questions seem to be unique to this text, although parts of their answers can be found elsewhere. If this is an earlier or different "bundle," it lends more sense to the title of the present text "Another Bundle," since they are both in the same format of dialogue and may just represent two versions that were circulating in Tibet. Where Khamnyön Dharma Senge quotes Machik in *The Religious History of Pacification and Severance,* the wording is identical to the Limi "Bundle of Precepts" and not to *The Great Bundle* or *Another Bundle* in this collection. Since Khamnyön Dharma Senge was contemporary with Jamgön Kongtrul, this just indicates that both versions were available in the nineteenth century and does not confirm their relative dates. It seems likely that Machik's teachings were remembered and later recorded in many versions that were constantly shifting and reforming during nearly a millennium of transmission.

---

*Emaho!*
Homage to the nonhuman ḍākinī of timeless awareness
in the realm of immutability.

(1) How rare is it to get a human body?

When you see the bodies of other sentient beings,
they just didn't get a human body.
When you see the bodies of mere random beings,
getting a human body is barely possible.
When you compare it to other sentient beings,
it is more rare than a wheel-wielding monarch.

(2) How rare is it to practice the holy dharma?

If ignoring dharma is the standard
for all the people of peripheral lands,
then people who do practice the holy dharma
are more rare than the uḍumbara flower.

(3) What is negativity like?

People who engage in negative actions
are like little kids clutching fire
and idiots eating poison
and psychotics jumping off walls
and demonic suicides.
It produces your own sorrow.
Happiness will not occur for aeons.
You remain perpetually bound to birth and death,
engaged in actions of suffering and experiencing karma,
revolving like a waterwheel [perpetually] turning [itself].
Before the full ripening of the previous [action] runs out,
the next negative action obscures you, and so on and on. {103}
Therefore it is taught that to commit negative actions
is exceedingly stupid.

(4) What are the qualities of faith like?

Faith is like a fertile field.
Faith is like a skilled physician.
Faith is like a brave woman.
Faith is like a fine yak cow.
Faith is like an excellent sheep.

Just as all people who have those things
have everything they need and desire,
so it is with those who have faith.

(5) What is it like when faith is strong but diligence weak?

As for the faithful who have little diligence,
it is like putting shackles on a *gyiling* steed.
It is like damaged crops in a good field.
It is like forgetting to add the yeast to beer.
Since the cause exists but not the conditions,
even with great faith, there will be little purpose
and you cannot advance beyond the ordinary.

(6) What is it like when faith and diligence come together?

If you plant the crops of diligence
in the fertile field of faith,
you will attain supreme enlightenment.
Human life will have purpose.
You will have done yourself a great kindness.
You will reap the everlasting harvest. {104}

(7) What is the most sublime of all teachings?

This Great Mother Perfection of Wisdom, the spoken word of all perfect buddhas, is the most sublime of all teachings.

(8) What are the benefits of practicing that?

Whoever enters the nonreferential meaning
without calculating grounds and paths
will overwhelm all the devils.
If characteristics are not mentally engaged,
even without processing the stages of grounds and paths,
you will dwell in the space of the Great Mother.
Once the meaning of that Great Mother is realized,
the disease of striving will be quelled.

Being free of striving,
holding the pedigree of the buddhas of three times,
you will dwell on the ground of the unborn.[2]
In the nonreferential, unthinkable, ineffable,
uncontrived, unborn, unobstructed state,
intrinsic nature is lucid clarity.
The birth mother of the buddhas of the three times
is just that and nothing else.
To dwell within that state
is to dwell in the space of the Great Mother.
[Not to dwell in the space of the Great Mother,][3]
although performing characterized virtuous acts,
is to remain a long time in cyclic existence
and not attain the ground of no birth and death.

(9) How does one rest in a nonreferential state? What is a so-called devil?[4]

To be without any mental engagement at all
is to rest within a nonreferential state.
If, in that sense of freedom from mental engagement,
you do not contrive with reference to aggression and passion,
it is definite nonreferential meditation.

In the presentations of the various devils
there are the tangible devil, the intangible devil,
the devil of exaltation, and the devil of inflation.
They come from you yourself and then harm you,
like the saliva of a silkworm.[5]

(10) What is the tangible devil?

The eye organ is tangible[6] in form.
Pleasant or unpleasant forms by nature cause
dualistic clinging of attachment and aggression: the devil. {105}
Since the very mind of dualistic fixation
is not established with essential base or root,
if you rest in the rootless state,
the tangibility of form is overcome

and again becomes timeless awareness itself.
Form is neither binding nor liberating.[7]
Apply the above to the ears and the other organs.
This is the teaching of the tangible devil.
It should be known as an external devil.

Without an objective appearance of actual things,
when you are gripped by a malicious mood,
have mental desire without an object,
languish through lack of instructions,
feel a sense of your own superiority,[8]
indulge in a jealous temperament,
or engage gods and demons in your mind,
even though there is no actual tangible appearance,
these [states] harm and interrupt the mind
and are therefore devils that occur without being tangible.

(11) How should one practice to overwhelm the devils?

*Emaho!*
In these vital points of my instruction,
whatever movement occurs, whatever arises,
if you do not do anything about it on purpose,
all the intangible devils are overwhelmed.
The occurrence of mental objects is a devil:
to fixate on apprehending is to welcome them.
Don't fixate on apprehension, noble child.
Don't block sensations, noble child.
Don't contrive body and mind, noble child.
Don't entertain speculation, noble child.
If you maintain practice in that way,
all the devils will be overwhelmed.

(12) How are thoughts of devils conquered? How is the thread of inflation severed?

To rejoice in something and become elated over it
without maintaining the lack of reference

is not the meaning of the perfections.
You have gone over to the devil's power.
Such is the devil that is each of us,
abiding in a mere [belief in] intrinsic nature.[9]
But since intrinsic nature is not established in oneself,
by the same token a devil will not be established.
If your fixations are overwhelmed {106}
by the nature of phenomena without basis or root,
then all devils are overwhelmed
and all misery will be transcended.
Exaltation is pure in its own ground of the unborn.
Fixation on "I" is liberated in its own ground of no clinging.
Conceptual thought is empty of its own intrinsic nature.
Consider it so, noble child.
If you know that you yourself are dharmakāya,[10]
it is the vanquishing of the concept of devils.
So-called inflation and inflated object—
outer and inner—are all one's own inflation.
The apparent existence of samsara and nirvana is one's mind.
Even the gods and demons and so forth
are also one's own inflation.
If the apparition of inflation is just interrupted,
it is unsurpassable enlightenment.
It is not to block mindfulness,
but if you know everything is merely inflation,
inflation itself[11] is incapable of grasping the dharma.
Merely resting in that incapability
will overwhelm all devils.
When mental concepts do not stir
in regard to all worldly phenomena,
it is the decisive resolution of mind.
Noble child, when you consider that,
all devils will be overwhelmed,
every effort will be dropped,
you will dwell in an effortless state,
and will abide just so.

(13) How should one frequent haunted places?

*Emaho!*
Adverse circumstances that occur directly
are difficult to turn into dharma supports.
First, with the pride of [having] the teachings,
if you just frequent haunted places and such
without falling under the influence of circumstances,
the instructions have definitely become a support.
When you fear losing your mind or body[12]
and the arising of obstacles to your life,
[you will practice diligently].[13]
Practice will guard your awareness,
and guarded awareness produces meditative experience.
When you have that kind of experience,
even though circumstances are directly encountered,
you will automatically be in control.
Circumstances act as the inspiration for dharma.
Frequenting haunted places is even more valuable. {107}
Wander in haunted places, noble child.
When you take on that kind of thinking,
apprehensive thoughts of demons and devils arising
will subside within themselves.
Without any fuss, demons will not occur
to that mind that is free of apprehension.
That is how all thoughts are stopped,
and even if a hundred do arise, they will support practice.

(14) How should one look with the view?

Since there are not two [aspects] to mind,
look in the way of not looking.
Your mind will not be seen by looking.
Not seeing in itself is the nature of phenomena.
If you see [something], it is not the nature of phenomena.
Therefore what is called "looking"
has not even an atom of existence.

(15) What is the method of resting in mind itself when one is frequenting haunted places?

*Emaho!*
Noble child,
rest the body in the way of a corpse.
Rest in the way of being ownerless.
Rest the mind in the way of the sky.
As a candle unmoved by wind,
rest in the way of clarity with no thought.
As an ocean unmoved by wind,
rest in a way serenely limpid.

Oh noble child, it is the resting of consciousness securely. It is the resting in one's own fashion without the busyness of effort. Since mind itself has no intrinsic nature, it is the resting without involvement in the fixation of meditating or not meditating. Since the unborn is free of action, it is the resting loosened by relaxation. It is the resting in deep release by releasing. Since the nature of phenomena is free of concept, it is the resting without engaging in any calculations whatsoever. Since the nature of phenomena is beyond both qualities and faults, it is resting without any thoughts of faults and qualities. Sometimes it is resting with the five sense organs hollow like a dried-up human head. Or it is resting quietly somnolent like a baby just waking from sleep. Since the nature of phenomena is without attachment, it is resting focused on the consciousness flung out in the distance, {108} as a shooting star or a person shooting an arrow. Since there is no other meaning of buddhahood than liberation from cyclic existence, it is a resting without flaws.[14] It is a resting without purpose. It is a resting in the manner of a mendicant. It is a resting in the way of having no goals from likes or dislikes. It is resting dumbfounded. Without thoughts of purposefully resting again, if you are gripped by the vital points of the instructions, however you rest and whatever you do is it. Conversely, if you don't understand ultimate rootlessness, then however you rest, it is not it. Nevertheless, train like that. Noble child, understand it in this way.[15]

(16) How should one engage in the activity methods of the conduct?

In fact there is no conduct to reference.
The appearance of circumstances is samsara's own conduct.[16]
Act like a pig without concepts
or act like a crazy person without concern.

If inflating concepts do occur,
like children butting heads,[17]
again discard them right on the spot.
Whatever circumstances appear and manifest,
recognizing their self-liberation captures them.
Don't seek only this kind of conduct—
[thinking] "this is it" is not the advice.
But do not create an elaborate narrative about it.
If you don't stand firm in mind,[18]
the devil of worldly exaltation will carry you off.
Spread the news of dharma that arouses joy.
Sing little songs about experience.
Melancholy arises while you are thinking about what to do.
Wherever you are is equable.
Rest in mental nonengagement.
Think like a gloomy person:
"I can't do anything no matter what;
no one gets anything from me."
Once you abandon all purposeful effort,
you will be liberated from all habitual patterns.

(17) What is so-called Severance?

Oh noble child,
everything is severed in mind.
Mind is severed in inflation.
There is nothing that is not included in inflation. {109}
If you just understand mere inflating,
it is like the thief in an empty house:
just recognizing him cannot capture him.
Better than blindly acting on understanding,
do not engage with purposeful meaning.
Trampling upon the unbearable is taught as severance.[19]

(18) What is the meaning of "trampling upon the unbearable"?

Lack of happiness is unbearable.
Engaging sadness is unbearable.

It is unbearable to see unbearable deities.
Casting the body to demons is unbearable.
Abandoning one's home is unbearable.
Wandering in haunted places is unbearable.
Disease and epidemics and so forth are unbearable.
If you trample upon such things,
it is the specially elevated conduct of equal taste.
Everything becomes equal in qualities.
Rejecting and accepting will lessen.
When you realize the meaning of no rejecting or accepting,
you rest within the great equanimity.

(19) How does one create blessing power for others?

First, for the outer blessing power,
singing songs of experience and little tunes
and maintaining solid behavior
arouses others' interest and blessings occur.
For the inner blessing power,
resting within the nondual unity
of one's mind and demons and sickness
brings about the blessing of pacifying suffering.
In so-called secret blessing power,
"blessing" (*byin*) means to be immutable and
"power" (*brlabs*) arises from unimpeded force.
When you rest within great effortlessness
in the nature of phenomena, once free of inflation,
blessing occurs without exertion.
Blessing that is possessed of effort
is not blessing (*byin*) and has little efficacy.
Even if it benefits others, obscurations will occur.[20]

(20) What should one do when sick?

Chop up your body and offer it as feast.
Hide concepts as treasure in the nature of phenomena.
And moreover do it many times.
Don't give rise to joy if you get better.

No matter what sickness occurs in the manifesting circumstances,
know that each one is a training exercise. {110}
If you don't know occurring circumstances as supports,
even with a lofty view, you will lose your way.
That conceit of merely mental emptiness
is the clutch of the secret devil.

(21) Will giving instructions just once work or not?

Once is good for fortunate ones with sharp minds.
They possess the karma of previous training.
Otherwise, it is crucial to persevere.
It is crucial to pursue the continuance of the genuine.
Bring the instructions inside you.
If you don't gain confidence in your understanding,
just hearing the words won't cut it.
Think about that, noble child.

(22) Nonhuman ḍākinī of timeless awareness! What is so-called buddha? How does one get there?

So-called buddha exists in this way:
Once all fixation on concepts is eliminated,
there is unborn nature, the original buddha.
The term *buddha* is applied to that.
In the presentation of how to get there,
the term *buddha* indicates
the teaching on how to abolish cyclic existence.
*Buddha* is a primitive word for the unborn.
All those of bygone generations
could not arrive at buddhahood
except by liberating fixation on its own ground.
All those who are alive now also
have no cause for getting to buddhahood
other than liberating fixation on its own ground.
All those who will come hereafter
will not ponder getting to buddhahood.
Do not pursue it for the sake of your childish mind.

Do not do it to become buddha.
Do not make the unborn a point of reference.
Do not fear cyclic existence.
Do not fixate on grasping thoughts.
Do not meditate on nonthought.
Do not fear the unborn
in the unborn primordial mind itself.
Do not hope for the unborn.
Do not strive at the practice of nonactivity
in the primordial nature of phenomena.
Do not gather through references
the infinite nature of phenomena. {111}
Do not hold thoughts of hope and fear
for nondual samsara and nirvana.
Samsara without fixation is nirvana.
Desiring nirvana is samsara.
Don't hope, don't fear, noble child.
Don't meditate, don't fixate, noble child.
Don't block, don't engage, noble child.
It says in the sutra:
"Since there is no buddha, even the name *buddha* does not exist.
The name *bodhisattva* also does not exist."[21]

(23) Queried again: "No looking, no meditating, no acting, no accomplishing"?

In fact there is nothing to see;
that person who is liberated from looking
is said to have unmistaken view.
In fact there is no object to meditate on;
that individual who is liberated from meditating
is said to have unmistaken meditation.
In fact there is no object of activity;
that one who is liberated from acting
is said to have unmistaken activity.
There is not even a speck of something to accomplish
in the fruition of the perfections;
the person who is liberated from accomplishing

is said to have the unmistaken fruition.
Once you discover meaning such as that,
you are not bound by the bonds of hope and fear;
no doubt about liberation from cyclic existence.
Like ice in the hot summer months,
though mentations are samsara's nature,
they will liberate in a mere instant.

(24) But don't altruism and good qualities arise in a buddha?

Conceptual altruism is said to be
the power of mental capability.
Buddha enacts the welfare of sentient beings
as in the example of the precious jewel:
through altruism that arises without concept.
There are unimaginable buddha qualities
in not fixating on one's own concepts.
The well-being and happiness of beings,
enjoyment of the holy dharma,
spiritual powers of attainment,
the spiritual experiences of realized ones,
the timely falling of the rain for crops—
in short, all kinds of prosperity—
are the qualities of all buddhas. {112}

(25) How should one bring about the Buddha's blessings in oneself?

Just as all the buddhas have said,
blessing will occur if you practice the meaning.
Don't think about the designations of words;
practice the real meaning, noble child.
If meaning can be gleaned from devoted interest
in the physical forms of the buddhas of the three times,
then what is there to say about actually practicing the meaning?
If realizations arise merely from the words in the sutras,
then practicing the meaning is equal to that.
[If signs arise from merely reciting the speech,
what to say of practicing the meaning?

Realize the actual meaning of the words;
don't cling to the words, noble child.][22]
Practice, noble child!
To be wise in words is not to be wise;
to be wise in meaning is to be wise.
Your own awareness dawns while thinking of the meaning.
Meaning is the realm of unborn emptiness.
Words are a method to point to that itself.
Rest in the meaning, noble child.
Practice, noble child.
Since there is no path to traverse,
rest in the basic ground, noble child.
Since there is no result to obtain,
don't be hopeful, noble child.
Since there is no fall into cyclic existence,
don't be needy, noble child.
Since there is no engaging in activity,
always stay relaxed in the three times.
The root of all phenomena will be cut
if you rest in that way without striving.
Afflictive emotions and thoughts will cease from within.
All devils will be liberated in their own unborn ground.
Samsara and nirvana are not two,
but become one in the realm of phenomena's nature.
When all the buddhas are pleased,
blessings will occur, noble child.
[Do not be riven by doubts, noble child.][23]
Uphold the lineage, noble child.
Nurture the fortunate, noble child.

(26) What is this "Severance of Evil Object"?

Since "devil" is the dharmakāya,
by recognizing that itself as mind,
rest in an uncontrived state
without meddling with mind. {113}
Then engage whatever devilish apparitions occur
while abiding in the state of the unborn.

What is taught as the severance of evil object
is this exact esoteric instruction of meaning.

(27) Will this Severance be disseminated to others or not?

It will not spread by you disseminating it.
If those who are faithful and fortunate
abide in faith, then do the teaching.
Individuals driven by circumstances[24]
will gain oral instructions with great persistence.
Since what happens after the cure is unpredictable,
don't give them the various texts.
It is crucial to examine an individual's worthiness.
[Training] for the sake of wealth is suspicious;
nevertheless you can observe their wealth,
and if they are unable to let it go,
they are definitely not fortunate and karmically endowed.
Examine carefully when making a dharma connection.
It is inappropriate to teach an unworthy student.[25]

(28) Machik, when impermanence is upon you, where will intention take you?

There is no intention within the unborn.
There is nowhere to go within the unceasing.
Still, once naturally liberated without reference—
Just *lhang nge lhan ne lham me* (vivid, quiet, radiant).

*Another Bundle of Twenty-Five Instructions as Answers to Questions.*[26]
*iti*

# 8. Vajra Play

## *Questions and Answers on the Profound Severance of Evil Object*[1]

Machik Lapdrön

*Vajra Play* is appended to *Another Bundle* in *The Treasury of Precious Instructions* but not indicated in the table of contents or in Jamgön Kongtrul's catalog. Nor is it included in other editions of *Another Bundle*. However, in the *Dingri Volumes* it appears as a separate entry, and I have followed suit here. *Vajra Play* consists of eighteen questions, with their answers delivered in short and even cryptic prose. Only a few of the questions echo those in the other collections, and this set may have a different source.

Homage to total victory over the devils' influence.

(1) Lady Mother, how would you sum up your Severance of Evil Object?

The teaching of this Object Severance is twofold: not casting out those with faith down the abyss of the lower realms, and not allowing those with wisdom to befriend samsara.

Those with faith should engage in religious activities without regard for time, be without deceit in their own minds, and maintain their sacred pledge without hypocrisy. Then they will be emancipated from samsara and the lower realms. Those with wisdom should not enter the door of tenet systems that are bad approaches, not line up the row of bad thoughts, and not be bound by the golden chains of experiences of bliss and clarity. {114} If they are possessed of wisdom, they will enter the door of Severance, the unmistaken approach, and practice meditation without minding and mental activity.

(2) How does one put it into practice?

First you need to become convinced through the view. In the middle, trust in your meditative equipoise, and in the end you'll know that all phenomena are brought into mind.

(3) In that case, are all phenomena in the lungs?[2]

Meaningless explanation, deviant meditation, disastrous desire.

(4) So then how does one meditate?

Without mental inflation or change, rest in nondual consciousness without likes or dislikes.

(5) [Please give] one reference point?[3]

Mistakes are prevented by not creating a specific focus. Just being without reference liberates fixation. I have no other flawless instruction.

(6) When afflictive emotion arises, how should one apply the antidote?

Don't block the clarity aspect and don't practice the fixation aspect. Just when devils arise is when the necessary severance should be brought to bear.

(7) Must this teaching be understood without words?

This Object Severance carries great meaning in few words and difficult realization in an easy training. It is not the realm of conceptual thought.

(8) Even though an antidote works, is there attachment to this appearance?

Again, clinging must revert naturally, arising from within. If clinging does not revert from within, then dharma becomes a big project and you might think there's something to sever, which is to be one's own devil.

(9) So how is real Severance?

Although severing, it is best without thinking, "I'm doing it, I'll do it." Just do it, flawlessly.

(10) What is the measure of realizing the evil object?

It is to be free of inflation.

(11) What is the measure of being free of inflation?

The measure of freedom from inflation is fearlessness. {115}

(12) What kinds of signs arise from practice experience?

Outwardly, there is no clinging to appearances. Inwardly, there is no entanglement in mind itself. Secretly, there will be no reference to afflictive emotions.

(13) How can one confuse basic emptiness?

Ignorant fixation arises from not understanding emptiness. That leads to cycling in the three realms and wandering in the six continuums. Then there's no way to recognize the essential nature of phenomena. It is the turmoil of fixating fixation and desirous desire.

(14) Is the realization of no fixation what they call *buddha*?

Buddhahood is blissful by nature, so it is without fixating concepts. Rest without any thoughts whatsoever in mind. Not "Now I am meditating."

(15) How much "nonthought" are we talking about?

This refers to not engaging in mind. The lack of fixation in this awareness is being called *buddha*. Meditate without squandering this mind.

(16) What is meant by the term *yogin*?

It refers to freedom from thought. Once there is freedom from the notion of self-fixation, clinging must revert by itself. If it does not arise that way in your being, even if there is talk of practicing dharma, it wouldn't help. At first, you came alone. In the end, you will go alone. So now also you must train alone.

(17) Are all dharma teachings ascertained by understanding this Severance?

While consistent with dharma in general, it is an especially elevated instruction. Severance is the highest standard.

(18) How will just this connection with general dharma be enough?

In fact it is the destruction of delusion. If hope is destroyed, there is freedom from gods. If fear is destroyed, there is freedom from demons. If delusion is destroyed, it is freedom from demons.

The answers to questions called *Vajra Play* is perfectly complete.

# 9. The Essential Bundle

*From the Severance of Evil Object, Esoteric Instructions on the Perfection of Wisdom*[1]

Machik Lapdrön

The *Essential Bundle* is the third of the "bundles," attributed everywhere to Machik Lapdrön, and might be considered the innermost or secret version, as indicated by the word "essence" (*nying*). However, it seems rather to be a summation and a systematic presentation of what is in the other bundles; the title might have been translated as "The Essence of the Bundles." Unlike the other two, it has a structural outline and uses scriptural citations to back up the main points. It even cites Machik herself, using the respectful "Lady Mother" (*ma jo mo*), which would be a highly unusual way for Machik to refer to herself. It appears, therefore, to be written by someone else, perhaps an early commentator such as Jamyang Gönpo.

I pay homage and go for refuge to the mother of the victors.

These teachings by the Lady Mother Lapkyi Drolma, the emanation form that reveals the intention of the perfection of wisdom, have five parts: (1) the preliminary instructions; (2) the instructions to recognize mind; (3) the blessing, instructions to separate mind and body; (4) the meditation, resting in the abiding nature; and (5) the view, not getting lost in the devil's domain.

## I. Preliminary Instructions

This has ten parts: refuge, arousing the aspiration, taking vows, supplicating, prostrating, making vast offerings, special refuge along with prayers, confessing negative actions, rejoicing, and dedicating those to unsurpassable enlightenment.

## II. Instructions to Recognize Mind

Whence came this wandering through the three realms as the six continuums since beginningless samsara until now? It came from three [causes]: not recognizing oneself, not grasping the guru's instructions, and one's own meager effort in discipline. Furthermore, if you just let go of awareness and do not strive in the guru's instructions henceforth, you will not be released from the great suffering of samsaric existence. Therefore, to create confidence and willfully take control, you should be inspired by faith and diligence and, without giving in to the power of indifference and lassitude for even a moment, listen to and internalize the instructions of the holy guru and all the profound scripture of the victorious ones and then practice them. {117} To practice, you must meditate on the precious awakening mind. For that, you first must identify just exactly what the mind is. That has two presentations: recognizing mind and the methods of resting in it.

### A. Recognizing Mind

That mind of awakening did not arise from a cause in the first place, nor was it generated by conditions in the middle, and in the end it is without birth, destruction, and transition. Since it is free of all recognizable essence, it is impossible to demonstrate any particular characteristic [of mind]. Natural clarity without concepts about that clarity, it is unconditional meaning. You must know that it is only this in itself. Thus, from the *Great Mother*: "Mind is unchanging and without conceptual thought."[2] And: "Mind is not mind; the nature of mind is lucid clarity."[3]

### B. Methods of Resting

This presentation has seven parts: resting uncontrived, uncorrupted, unchanging, undistracted, in its own fashion, on its own ground, and in the native state.

### 1. Resting Uncontrived

Intrinsic awareness (*rig pa*) is the awakened mind that has been present since forever. Release by relaxing consciousness (*shes pa*) in its own fashion directly upon the nature of phenomena. Buoyant (*bol le*), loose (*shig ge*), lucid (*gsal le*), crisp (*yer re*), spreading unbounded (*phyogs med du gdal le*), pervading unrestricted (*ris med du khyab be*),[4] brilliant (*sing nge*), spacious (*phyal le*), joyful and transparent (*dga' yal le*)—rest clear and blissful (*bde sang nge ba*) without losing your mind in any thought whatsoever.

### 2. Resting without Corruption by Conceptual Thought

This is to rest your mind in an uncontrived state without any mental engagement at all. This means not to engage mentally in any likes and dislikes, pleasure and pain, hot and cold, food and drink, enemies and friends, self and others, clinging to desirables, or samsara and nirvana. Thus it states in the *Mother:* {118}

> By having no mental engagement in form up through no mental engagement in total omniscience, one will not become mixed up with the desire realm, and not become mixed up with the form realm, and not become mixed up with the formless realm.[5]

### 3. Resting Unchanged by References

It is to rest your mind uncontrolled (*khres se*) without inflation, unmoved by anything at all. "There being no obscuration of mind, there is no fear. Having completely passed beyond all error, they perfectly transcend all misery."[6]

### 4. Resting Undistracted by the Objects of the Six Consciousness Groups

Within a state of no-thought, mind's nature is clear, pristine, and blissful. Rest continuously in the sky-like nature without any distraction from thoughts about good and bad objects. Again, it says in the *Mother*, "All phenomena have the support of space; they do not transcend that support."[7]

### 5. Resting in the Suchness of Its Own Fashion

It is to rest consciousness without support in the state that is bliss, empty, and clear without losing it to mind's thoughts and memories. Again, from the *Mother*: "Since the perfection of wisdom is equality, all phenomena are equal."[8]

### 6. Engaged on Its Own Ground, Not Entertaining Notions

It is to rest in the meaning of totally nonreferential mind, open and alert (*hri ge*) in the state just as it is: the primordial nature of phenomena of mind itself.

### 7. Resting As Is in the Native State

It is to rest relaxed in its own fashion without effort or accomplishment in the state of great, even pervasiveness without mental perambulations in that realm of phenomena; the nature of phenomena that has always been present. It states in the *Verse Summary*: "This is inseparable, indivisible from the element of space."[9]

Thus if one knows how to rest within the recognition of mind, the expression of qualities and the experiences {119} and signs of warmth and such will occur automatically.

### III. Blessing: Instructions to Separate Body and Mind

First, go for refuge and arouse the aspiration to awaken, make vast offerings, and pray to the guru. Then quickly stand up with your two legs held together and two hands palm to palm. With the body tightly poised, and not letting consciousness wander elsewhere, contemplate body and mind in this way, thinking:

> This body consists of form like a bubble, feelings like illusions, perceptions like reflections of the moon in water, formations like mirages, and consciousness like a plantain tree. It is impermanent, suffering, impure, a leather pouch full of lymph, pus, and blood, pieces of bone, and like a net of veins and sinews and

> so on. Other than being the defining characteristic of impending impermanence, there is nothing at all of enduring stability or worthy of confidence. The mind is lucid clarity, the nature of phenomena that is naturally beyond misery. Therefore I must rest within the unborn state of mind separate from body.

[Imagine that] your mind is wholly contained within two vital drops on the soles of the feet. Then they are drawn up slithering [into one single drop] and held for a moment at the navel. Then it is drawn up to the heart, then to the top of the tongue and held there for a moment. Then vital winds and mind combine within the open cranial aperture and shoot out as far as a shooting arrow, freely passing into the vault of the sky. It is sent without attachment. Let it go loose. Send it out easily, clear and empty in natural pervasiveness. Let awareness go leaping over without support. Let it go without connections. Let consciousness go vibrating in bliss, dissolving in joy, droning in delight. {120} Awareness is empty and clear within the blending of sky and consciousness. Rest consciousness in pure clarity. The signs of holding awareness by that kind of resting are experiences of quivering, trembling, panting, agitation, jumping, being startled, speaking in various tongues, and the arising of whatever is pleasing before the guru. When experiences arise, engage continuously in that state during any of the four kinds of daily activity.

You should understand that the view is in resolving that that itself is the nature of phenomena. Meditation is to be undistracted within that state. The conduct is to know how to integrate everything in the nature of phenomena from within that state. The fruition is to realize that all phenomena are one and equal. Whatever mental attachment there is concerning sickness and suffering of the body can be integrated on the path in that way.

### IV. Meditation: Resting in the Abiding Nature

After you have obtained the guru's instructions and received the blessings, these are the places to meditate: charnel grounds, great forests, the midst of crowds, lone trees, ruins, old shrines, the middle of lakes, snow ranges, and places of great gods and demons. Once you have gone to such places, the meditation is to release consciousness that was formerly tight into relaxation, and to rest freely. Concerning this the Lady Mother [Machik] said:

> While concentrated by concentration, relax by relaxing.
> Released by release, let go freely.
> Freed by freedom, rest by resting.
> That's the resting place of meditation.[10]

Don't hold on to the body as a body. Rest buoyant and loose without hopes and fears, like cutting the rope on a sheaf of husks. Rest mind in its own fashion without fear and anxiety. Whatever appearances occur within the six groups of consciousness, rest without inflation or conceptual thought. {121} Rest without the doubts of a divided mind. This is to rest consciousness blissfully serene (*bde lhan ne*) and brilliantly lucid (*gsal sing nge*). The blessings of resting in that way are that various apparitions of vicious gods and demons will irresistibly arise, and when they arise like that, the mind grasps them. This is a sign of having the blessings. If there is agitated trembling at the occasional occurrence of apparitions, it is a sign of a distracted mind. Immediately hand over the body to those gods and demons without concern and with a mind relaxed by relaxing. Rest just so, with expanded consciousness. Rest without fear or anxiety. Rest without inflation or conceptual thought. Rest without hopes and fears. Alternatively, rest in the knowledge of the seven ways of resting in the recognition of mind [described above]. When you rest like that, experience dissolves in joy, mind relaxes in bliss, delight is droning, consciousness is vivid bliss, and mentation gives way to buoyant bliss. The consciousness of certainty dawns resplendent.

With just that, devils are cut off in the nature of phenomena, discursive thought arises as timeless awareness, the five poisons change to medicine, and bad omens betoken prosperity. Again, at the time of meditating, while you are resting within the nature of phenomena without fear and anxiety, various apparitions of gods and demons will manifest, such as thundering, droning sounds, beating, pulling, threatening, shouting various languages, displaying various forms, and throwing down mountains. At that time, no matter how the various apparitions appear, know that they are the self-appearance of mind itself. Since that itself is the inspiration for virtuous activity, do not grasp the body as the body, nor grasp the gods as gods, nor grasp the apparitions as apparitions. Turning consciousness to the ultimate nature of phenomena, without fear and anxiety, without inflation and thought, mind is released loosely in its own fashion. {122} Other than mind [feeling] happily buoyant, loose, lucid, and brilliant, mentation is without support, without connection, and you rest relaxed in flawless flexible conduct.

When you rest just so, the signs of coemergent experiences and realization are a pleasant buoyancy of mind, blissful trilling (*bde phril*) of consciousness, dissipating joy of experience (*nyams dga' yal*), vibrant bliss (*bde seng*) of body and mind, and pleasant droning (*bag dro 'ur*). You feel an ardent desire to dance, to sing, to race around without a race, and to engage in activities not done before. When you feel an unprecedented ardent desire to go to the place to give thanks to the gods and demons, it is the spontaneous release of the uninhibited consciousness.

Afterward, fall serenely into the natural state. This is the unwavering resting in release by releasing described above.

Just this much is to actualize the resolution of demons as gods.

Again, if various unpleasant things occur, such as your heart being pulled out, or [someone] saying, "Your dharma and meditation has no effect" or "You are going to die this instant," and so forth, without thinking that it is true, let consciousness go buoyant and loose. Consider them your mothers. Rest in generating a vast mind. Rest without fear and anxiety and without inflation and concepts. This is the time of genuinely cutting off wrong views.

Also it happens that various apparitions will be displayed in your dreams. These are various apparitions such as being on the verge of an avalanche from a cliff face, steep ravines, dark forests, entering a lake, great rivers, huge flames, dark tempests, collapsing mountains, many falling rocks, entering a pit, suddenly being carried off by a stag, and so forth. Again, you dream of being chased by many people, or being killed by armed men, or being smothered by many wild animals, pounded by many beasts of burden, many herds of hooved animals, or sustaining bodily harm from birds, meat flies, fish, frogs, tadpoles, {123} spiders, reptiles, horses, buffalo, and so forth. Whatever good or bad dreams come, no matter what, do not make them problematic. Know that they are the mind's deluded projections and an inspiration to meditate. Rest relaxed in the nature of phenomena without fear and anxiety, without being grasped by any recollections whatsoever, without inflation and concepts. Any good or bad dreams that occur are the apparitions of your own mind, the reflections of habitual patterns. Since there is no real existence at all in the genuine nature, in any case the apparitions will self-subside, self-purify, and self-liberate within the thoughtless mind. With mental inflation loosened, rest in empty lucid awareness. Through that, mind has bliss; consciousness is joyful and transparent, with a pleasant droning. At the time that awareness has thus become empty and clear, like the center of the pellucid sky, appearance arises without fixation. Dream-thoughts arise as the nature of phenomena.

Also, there can be despair, restlessness, anger, aversion to staying in the natural state, aversion to practicing virtue, and the mind not abiding in its own fashion due to the proliferation of many thoughts. When those occur, consciousness is distracted and the devil enters your mind. Therefore, to reverse that, recall that the mind itself *is* yourself and that the devil has no existence outside of that. Rest consciousness serenely in its own fashion within the abiding nature of mind. When you rest in that way, once mind is self-liberated within nonconceptual equipoise, consciousness is vibrant bliss, a pleasant droning, joyful and transparent. At that point, conceptual thought arises as timeless awareness.

Know that whatever sense perceptions appear in your mind—pleasant and unpleasant, fine and faulty, praiseworthy and blameworthy, good and bad, existent and nonexistent, happy and sad, {124} hostile and friendly, wealth and junk, self and other, hopes and fears, pure and defiled, fear and anxiety—whatever arises is all your own mind. When you rest within the great self-liberated, unsupported mind, everything becomes inseparable. If that much happens, all dualistic appearance will be cut off in the nondual.

Also, when you meditate as above, yidam deities will bestow prophecies, gatherings of gods and goddesses will make offerings, excellent forms of sense desirables will be displayed, all pleasantries will manifest in waking and in dreams, and various experiences and signs of warmth will occur. However, do not become joyous over their occurrence; just know that all of it is the play of phenomena's nature. Understand it as just the encouragement of the qualities of practice. Having given rise to a spacious mind in the great clarity of the nature of phenomena, rest the mind clear and brilliant without wavering within empty lucid awareness.

Thus after enhancement of the experience, awareness abides freed of root within bliss-emptiness.

Of the various appearances of the six classes of beings, various apparitions of the pleasures and pains of the three higher realms and various apparitions of the *duḥkha* of the three lower realms will appear. At that time, know that all of it is the apparition of your mind and that the essence of what never happened and never was born is by nature lucid clarity. Rest the mind directly in the natural state in its own fashion without fear, anxiety, inflation, or concept. When consciousness abides in the natural state of empty bliss, the devil of afflictive emotion is cut off in natural liberation. It states in the *Mother*:

> The son or daughter of noble family who grasps the perfection of wisdom, holds it, reads it, {125} fully comprehends it, and properly engages it in mind, even if there are gullies and abysses and rock overhangs and steep ravines, has no fear or anxiety about devils. Why is that? Because he or she is without inflation.[11]

And:

> Meditate in a nonreferential way on external emptiness.[12]

Thus, from the aspect of unimpeded appearances, whatever pleasure or pain and apparitions occur, meditate on all of them without fear and anxiety. Once you have rested in the abiding nature, then through practice all appearances will arise as the dynamic energy and ally of nature's phenomena.

In case problems occur during meditation, the two flaws of meditation are dullness and agitation. Concerning dullness, there are signs of dullness from the elements and signs of dullness from obstacles. As for the signs of dullness due to elements, when the body feels heavy and the consciousness unclear, it is a sign of the dullness of earth. If consciousness is unclear and there is shivering, it is a sign of the dullness of water. When consciousness is unclear and you feel ravenous and anxious to go, it is a sign of the dullness of wind. If you are unaware of the sluggish mind and hot and sweaty, it is a sign of the dullness of fire. So whichever of the four elements cause dullness, stand up quickly, straighten the body, put your legs together, and place your palms together at the top of your head. The outer four body elements will dissolve into the inner four elements. The outer and inner four elements will dissolve inseparably. Send the mind constantly to the sky where consciousness is without support and awareness is without object. Rest lucid and brilliant in the expanse of great intrinsic clarity without thought, and dullness will be cleared away. It states in the *Mother*:

> As earth is not in water, it is not referenced. As earth is not inside form, there is no reference. As earth is not in between form, it is not referenced.

And:

> The nature of phenomena abides in mind. {126} Space abides nowhere at all. Mind itself abides in space.

And:

> To fully meditate on space is to meditate on the perfection of wisdom.[13]

Once dullness is thus cleared away, let consciousness fall in its own fashion and rest relaxed.

Second, the signs of dullness from hungry ghosts are that mind naturally will not abide due to great drowsiness, due to muddled consciousness, or else because your heart is just not in it, and breathing becomes difficult. In that case, pray to the guru, go for refuge, and give your body and sickness and all thoughts to the demons. Strip naked and go running and jumping in scary places. Twist, rub, contract and stretch the body, and do whatever comes to mind. Afterward, with body and mind gently powerful, consciousness becomes relaxed. That is how to redress dullness.

The second fault in meditation is agitation. This is when the mind does not abide in its own fashion and consciousness flows out and in. The antidote to that is to post the guard of attentiveness. By watching the one who proliferates, you can identify that one itself as, in fact, the mind. When you suddenly recollect it, everything is set free, relaxed by relaxation, resting freely. With consciousness facing inward, rest serenely in the state without mentation and memory. If that does not calm you, then observe however much proliferation you can. Externally and internally, let it all proliferate. Letting it go like that, you know that you will not find a place where it goes again, and it goes serene.

Which is the greater fault of these two: dullness or agitation? Dullness is the greater fault. That is because dullness is predominantly stupidity, while agitation is predominantly awareness. Therefore, since it is greater to rest serene directly upon what was introduced as the abiding nature, all flaws are resolved as qualities. If it happens that consciousness radiates out to objects, since all proliferation is an aspect of agitation, it is important to grasp it with recollection. Therefore, abide within a mind free of elaboration. {127}

It is said that to engage in [thinking] "form is emptiness" or "it is not empty" is a bodhisattva's elaboration. Then, practice without wavering on the meaning of the unelaborate abiding nature. Again, when any difficult circumstances occur, the instruction is to gather all phenomena into your body, to gather body into the mind, and to let mind go in the realm of phenomena. Resting thus unmoving within the realm of phenomena, once intrinsic awareness is grasped, you go serenely to bliss. It is the birth of uncommon meditational experience. Then suffering is resolved in bliss.

In that way, when you sever all devils in the nature of phenomena and meditate, the threefold warmth will arise. In the application, external warmth is the occurrence of having no sense of the existence of the body, and the lack of disease. The sign of inner warmth is to have no sense of the movement of breath in and out, and the lack of discursive thought arising. Secretly, the bodhisattva's warmth is when the suchness of mind itself has gone serenely into the state of suchness and uninterrupted great bliss arises. Then, once the incontrovertible meaning of clarity-emptiness has arisen in your being, you easily obtain the result, total omniscience.

By practicing in that way you train in the intermediate state. The intermediate state of natural abiding is the present intermediate state. Therefore, because you are accustomed to [this practice] at this very time, all devilish obstacles will become incentives to practice or will be understood as allies of the nature of phenomena. By means of continuous practice, merely remaining unmoved within the nature of phenomena without any thoughts of good and bad is the training of the present intermediate state.

If you practice the meaning in that way, when dreaming you will know dreams to be the nature of phenomena. Then without a sense of waking up, you will remain in the vivid clarity within the nature of phenomena without elaboration. {128} That is the training of the dream intermediate state.

Following through with what you've become accustomed to in the present and continuing with practice, at the moment of death when you are gripped by sickness and are not aware of standing or sitting, before appearance is eclipsed, merely knowing that it is death and needs resolution, if you can manage [to apply it] directly upon [your meditation] experience, then you will actualize it. If you can't manage it, then mentally go for refuge and generate the aspiration for awakening. Supplicate and offer the gift of the body. From within the nature of phenomena, mind is without clinging and without attachment, without fear, anxiety, or doubts and second thoughts. Rest in the meditation experience without mental distraction, within the nature of phenomena in its own fashion. The mind dwelling serenely within the unchanging nature of phenomena without attachment and clinging or inflation about anything at all when the breath ceases is the training of the intermediate state of the moment of death.

After that, immediately after the breathing stops, the reality of the inherent abiding nature, the essence of the unborn, arises to all sentient beings. Once that is recognized, you abide within the nature of phenomena. Just by your attaining stability in that, mind holds its own ground within the sky-like realm that is naturally free of birth and cessation. Within that state, the two form kāyas enact any purpose for whoever is to be tamed. That is the training of the intermediate state of existence. It interrupts the city of the womb and bypasses cyclic existence to [arrive at] the nature of phenomena. The names given to that are: laying to rest (*ngal sos*), to pass sentence (*chad pa btang*), sigh of relief (*dbyug phyin*), the done deed (*bya ba byas*), the done action (*byed pa byas*), cessation of dissipation (*zag pa zad*), laying down the burden (*khur bor*), subsequent attainment of self and others' welfare (*rang gzhan gyi don rjes su thob*), and *arhat* (*ar han*).

These are all instructions for the meditation of resting in the abiding nature.

## V. View: Instructions on Not Getting Lost in the Devils' Domain

This has two parts: recognizing devils and cutting off the devils in the nature of phenomena by integrating.

### A. Recognizing Devils

This has two parts: {129} the root devils and the subsidiary devils.

#### 1. The Root Devils

There are four:

- the devil of the aggregates
- the devil of a child of the gods
- the devil of afflictive emotions
- the devil of the lord of death

### 2. The Subsidiary Devils

There are eighteen:

- the devil of clinging to the reality of accomplishing enlightenment
- the devil of apparitions that send obstacles
- the tangible devil of actual things
- the intangible mental devil
- the devil of straying from qualities
- the devil of a bloated mind from meditative experiences
- the devil of suspicious awareness
- the devil of subtle discursive thought
- the devil of the bloated mind of pride
- the devil of slandering envy
- the devil of dull and agitated consciousness
- the devil of sloth and indifference
- the devil of anger and hatred
- the devil of desire and wrong livelihood
- the devil of straying consciousness
- the devil of depression and despair
- the devil of obstinate reification
- the devil of murderous spirits

## B. Integrating Those Devils on the Path through the Nature of Phenomena

Those of superior scope rest within nonconceptual equipoise without fear or anxiety no matter what devils arise. Those of middling scope seek the one who has the feelings [of devils arising] and understand that devils are their own mind and rest within mind's unborn nature itself. Those of inferior scope give over the body to the dangerous obstructors and rest in nonaction within the state of mental nonrecollection. Furthermore, you should not hold the body as a body, nor hold sickness as sickness, nor hold demons as demons. Completely let go of all obstacles within the nature of phenomena. Rest by resting, release by releasing, rest gently, relax by relaxing, freed by freedom, clear and empty, buoyant and blissful, vividly clear. Rest within total mental nonaction. Thus it says in the *Verse Summary*: "The wise should know to abide in equanimity."[14]

Therefore you should abide without distraction in the meaning of the equipoised mind itself. {130} Remaining undistracted in the meaning of the abiding nature in that way will bring about the power and energy of blessing. When conferring blessings on someone like a patient, meditate without reference to demons or disease. Touching or blowing or spitting on the affected area, think that all the disease is empty. Rest mind within the state of [knowing that] nothing at all is established and there are no real things. Go for refuge, supplicate, and know the inherent way of the abiding nature.

That is how to integrate on the path by severing devils within the nature of phenomena. It is the view, the meaning of not getting lost in the devils' domain of experience by making it the domain of the nature of phenomena.

This completes the *The Essential Bundle, Root of Dharma* from *The Perfection of Wisdom, Severance of Evil Object,* a teaching by the emanation Jomo Lapkyi Drönma, liberated by the intent of the precepts of the perfection of wisdom.

# 10. The Eight Common Appendices[1]

## Machik Lapdrön

The three sets of eight appendices or "chapters" (*le lag*) are attributed to Machik Lapdrön wherever they are mentioned. Though the three are sometimes listed in different order, the specific titles given for each of the twenty-four individual appendices are nearly identical.

But that is far from the end of the story. A collection of Severance texts called *Practices of the Severance Collection and So Forth* contains an altogether different set called *The Thirteen Appendices* and a variant but still recognizable set of *The Eight Common Appendices.** This gives the impression that, as with the other three sets of teachings attributed to Machik called "Bundles" (*bKa' tshom, Yang tshom,* and *Nying tshom*), variant versions were in circulation and were not codified, perhaps even up to the time of Jamgön Kongtrul. Further research on this is required.

Karmapa Rangjung Dorje, in his commentary to *The Great Bundle of Precepts,* classifies the *Appendices* as instructions from the "sugata precept lineage" (referring to the source scriptures), consisting of Machik's own personal experiences, written in four versions of outer, inner, meaning, and secret. Of those, the *Appendices* are the inner pointing-out instructions.

*The Eight Common Appendices* is written in rather cryptic verse and contains the following headings: (1) resting uncontrived in suchness; (2) not using antidotes; (3) effort; (4) the arising of spiritual powers through practice; (5) recognizing Buddha in one life; (6) scolding that cuts off pitfalls;

* *The Thirteen Appendices* (*Le lag bcu gsum pa*) (pp. 45–57) and *The Eight Common Appendices* (pp. 58–66) in *Practices of the Severance Collection and So Forth. Gcod tshogs kyi lag len sogs: A Collection of Gcod Texts Representing the Ancient Practices of the Adepts of the Tradition.* Reproduced directly from a rare manuscript from Limi, Nepal (Bir, Himachal Pradesh, India: D. Tsondu Senghe, Bir Tibetan Society, 1985). TBRC W23390.

(7) heart essence; and (8) practical guide to the practice. One would guess that this is the original set of advice originating with Machik and recorded by disciples that did not fit into any other of the original sources, not even the bundles.

---

Homage to the holy gurus.

### I. Resting Uncontrived in Suchness[2]

Taking refuge, making vast offerings,
parting awareness from matter, applying instructions:
this nectar from the holy one's mouth
has the potential to benefit beings.
But it is the activity sphere of the fortunate;
to those of lesser fortune it is a great danger.[3]
Give the instructions appropriately[4]
to those who first serve the guru,
maintain sacred pledge, and practice diligently.

Two kinds of devils are distinguished:
tangible devils and intangible devils,
but they are none other than the devil of inflation.
If you're not embroiled in mental inflation over
appearance and then its emptiness,
all devils will be severed in the mind.
Mind subsides in the realm of the unborn.
All devils arise from the mind,
yet mind has no established essence.
Appearance and existence, gods and demons, {131}
without established essence, are liberated in their own ground.
When you realize mind's essence there,
the esoteric instruction is to give it up.
Learn from the guru's words.
Keep consciousness open and unbounded
in appearance and its emptiness.
Don't meditate directly, don't fix the mind,

rest serenely with the senses wide open.
You are your own attribute;
recognize this and apparent existence is yourself.
Like the sight of water in a mirage
that is not there when you arrive,
gods, nāgas, violation contamination, and so on
cannot exist when directly relinquished.
It is because they are your own mind,
so rest serenely without inflation.[5]
If you seek dharma by dharma, how will it be found?
Anyway the seeker is not actually established.

*Emaho!*
It is incredible to be attached and fixated
to these phenomena arising from yourself.
You not being established [means] everything is not established.
As long as the self appears, everything also appears.
Repudiating the variety does not stop it.
It's like the objects in a dream:
when you wake up they no longer appear.
Freedom from inflation is like waking from sleep.
An ignorant and philosophical mind
neglects oneself and seeks elsewhere.
To take your own mind as a demon
is to scare and sadden[6] yourself.
Designating the mind as an object is deluded.
Resting in your own ground is certain liberation.

### II. Not Using Antidotes

Request instructions of both mother and son.
Once received, stamp on devils.
Since both devils and gods have the same basis,
how is offering and rejecting even possible?
Yet this impossible phenomenon,
recognized in your own misunderstanding,
makes beings' minds Buddha Mind.
You think "impossible"—but is it possible?

Ascertain it right now.
Black and charcoal {132}
are the same and not divisible.
The yogi or yoginī who realizes that
knows buddhas and beings to be the same.
Noninflation is like the dharmakāya ocean,
and inflation is like its waves.
The yogi or yoginī who realizes that
knows inflation and noninflation to be indivisible.
Even the eighty-four thousand dharmas
are just the deception of the mind,[7]
the intellectual distinctions in profundity,
giving rise to the nine gradated vehicles.
The divisions of nine are also the mind;
aside from mind there is no dharma.
Dharma is a notion of the mind,
because if each buddha were bound to dharma,
how could there be primordial buddha?
For instance, those already arrived need no road.
Mind itself is pure since forever—
you needn't meditate on calm abiding and emptiness.
Calmness is primordially calm by nature.
Emptiness is empty—don't meditate on emptiness.
The dagger of fixation on appearance and emptiness
is extracted and you arrive in basic space.[8]
As fire cannot extinguish fire,
antidotes will not conquer concepts,
but liberation is doubtless from leaving well alone.
Like [a rope] tied on a camel's [nose],
if definite appearance were real,
it would be impossible to reverse.
If it were true that this mind exists for sure,
wouldn't all the sugatas and each of us
see that and with reasoning
proclaim mind's nature to be so?
It is impossible for a buddha to see,
as in the example of a rabbit's horns.
You are bound by attachment to mere designations,

bound before and bound even now.
Not attaining freedom, you are bound in the intermediate state.
Better not to be attached to designated phenomena
that are mere designations of apparent existence.
Lacking attachment to appearance dispels the extreme of eternalism.
Mentally not engaging with emptiness
removes the extreme of nihilism and frees hopes and fears.

*Emaho!*
Eternalism is untenable; there are no things.
Nihilism is untenable; anything appears clearly.
Naturally empty, naturally clear, certainly without agent. {133}

### III. Effort[9]

This instruction of mother and son,
this "Severance of Evil Object,"
is the heart-blood of the wise.[10]
It is the release of the mindstreams of all fortunate ones.
The danger is massive wrong view.
The enemy is the danger of pledge breaking.
The poison is prodigious ego-fixated thought.
So pay attention to the instruction's meaning.
There's nothing to see in the meaning of buddha;
think about the meaning of sentient beings.
There's nothing to meditate on in nonthought;
cut through the root of thought.
There's no saying "this is it";
rest in the merely banal.
This appearing phenomenon is just for a while.
This genuine phenomenon is beyond intellect.
Cutting off inflation revives inflation;
better to rest harmlessly when inflation occurs.
If harassed, it is like a poisonous snake.
Naturally at ease in a wide open place
without calculation is the supreme conduct.
If you don't evaluate appearance,
you have got the genuine valuation.

Calculation and miscalculation unnoticed
is the precious oral instruction.
Purposely seeking the absolute
is like separating the path and the journey.
Reifying attachment to apparent phenomena
causes conceit over mere mental emptiness.
That is to be snared by the intangible devil.
Is this not the idea that one's devils come from oneself?
Don't be attached to appearance; don't meditate on emptiness.
Don't take pleasure in competition—stay alone.
If you examine your qualities, they are faults.
Since the variety of recollections are hollow,
do not construe beliefs, all you yogins.
If you don't believe in your recollections,
dharmakāya without inflation is automatic.
Created dharma and accumulated wealth
cannot accompany you after death,
so it is smart to be certain now.
Entertaining the idea that you won't die—
if not then why make the effort? {134}

### IV. The Arising of Spiritual Powers through Practice

This instruction of mother and son,
if recited as words, is precisely words.
But if practiced, it severs all devils.
The gathering gods and demons are totally gathered.[11]
Spiritual powers come from devils and nāgas.
Devils and *gyalpo* spirits will act as patrons.
No matter what adverse circumstances occur,
taking them as supports is the supreme instruction.
The causal basis of mind is not dual.
Conceiving of two—virtue and sin—
does not apprehend the ultimate meaning.
Dividing one into two is a mistake.
Both virtue and negativity are empty by nature.
Meditating on eternal emptiness as empty now
is meaningless meditation and empty.[12]

In case [the thought of emptiness] arises from inflation,[13]
then the spirit of the instructions has deceived.
Don't meditate on emptiness; be free of identifying.
That lack of contrivance is great bliss.
To think so-called self-awareness is elsewhere—
how could self-liberation ever come from that idea?
It is the case that there is no thinking of the meaning.
Awareness is baseless and free of inflation.
When you know that the base is itself empty of essence,
base and based are nondual and equal.
Gods are the mind even as demons are the mind.
With no essence established, they are beyond mind.
As you do not see what you yourself are doing,
how could you see by mind looking at mind?
Undivided, stupid, without inflation—
that is designated as just buddha.
Without referencing beings, who is designating buddha?
There is nothing to look at in the minds of beings—
without looking, there is just buddha.
The five poisons without intrinsic nature
are designated as just timeless awareness.
Knowing them as designations, realize, transform, and meditate.[14]
Thinking and talking—big hopes.
No thought, no hope, free of inflation:
that is buddha without doubt.
Renouncing things and desiring emptiness,
those without realization are pitiful.
If there is no reference even to mere emptiness,
no need to mention fixation on things. {135}
*Emaho!*
Go to haunted grounds and wisdom springs forth.
If you relax without distraction, liberation is certain.
When the thought "fear" crosses your mind,
that inflation is a demon, so rest relaxed.
When fear arises in the mind even if relaxed,
[contemplate how] the mind is without intrinsic nature
and this body abides like earth and stone.
Examining like that, rest uncontrived.

When you meditate again and again it becomes expansive,
spontaneous presence without effort.
Whatever thoughts of good and bad occur in the mind
will definitely be liberated on their own ground without contrivance.
This is esoteric instruction for not fixating in grasping.
Inflation is the seed of cyclic existence.
Noninflation is one's own nature, self-pure,
sometimes called just buddha.

## V. Recognizing Buddha in One Lifetime[15]

The instruction received from mother and son,
this sacred teaching of severing evil object,
is different from other instructions:
others just pertain to a later time,
whereas this severs right now.
Cut off or not, you'll find out in haunted places.
Others gradually abandon discursive thinking,
whereas this assimilates it right now.
The body has abscesses and other infectious diseases
from the blessing of the absorptions.
Nāgas and other harmful spirits
must be severed directly.
All of them have arisen from inflation.
It is crucial to maintain confidence in noninflation.
At first you must have great courage.
This severing of evil objects instructs you
to remain in a happy mind state with no inflation.
All yogis and yoginīs who go to haunted places
don't instill it by meditating and meditating;
relax the mind, release the body, and let go of your fear.
Don't hold a mind of desire and accomplishment.
Be cheerful and pleasant with a happy consciousness.
Apart from integrating your own feelings,
referencing others is not being a yogin.
Buddha is just freedom from inflation. {136}
Those with an inflating mind are sentient beings.
Therefore there is nothing other than yourself.
Thereby you accomplish your own benefit yourself.

Yogis and yoginīs who don't understand the meaning
and desire severance are their own devils.
It makes sense to take up an understanding of the meaning.
All who have seen the dharma doors
never let awareness go to waste.
Whoever wastes is not practicing yoga.[16]
*Emaho!*

### VI. Scolding That Cuts Off Pitfalls

Those wise in methods of nondual unity
have taught a variety of dharmas,
but beings' own intellectual inadequacies
are like beetles tangled in wool.
In this old woman's appraisal,
practitioners are trapped by dharma.
They want liberation but are again bound.
They desire Object Severance but are bound once more.
Though there are many who desire Object Severance,
apart from desiring its renown,
what if they have no fear of birth and death?
Though many have gone to haunted places,
what if their pride is not broken?[17]
Though there are many who cut off inflating thoughts,
what if they don't abide in the primordial state?
Fear of cyclic existence is barely possible.
Though delight in giving it up arises,
attaining transcendence is barely possible.
Though there are many who abandon suffering,
to renounce pleasure is barely possible.
Though there are many who give up nonvirtue,
increasing virtue is barely possible.
Though there are many who reverse clinging,
letting go of subject-object grasping is barely possible.
Though there are many who realize the view,
freedom from extremes is barely possible.
Though there are many who meditate on nonthought,
mental nonengagement is barely possible.
Though there are many with good conduct,

vanquishing on contact is barely possible.
Though there are many who practice well,
uninterrupted practice is barely possible.
Though there are many who study a lot, {137}
cutting through assumptions is barely possible.
Though there are many with great instructions,
putting them into practice is barely possible.
Though there are many who give up nondharma,
giving up divine dharma is barely possible.
Though sometimes demons and devils are vanquished,
giving up identifying [them] is barely possible.
Though occasionally bad thoughts are vanquished,
vanquishing good thoughts is barely possible.
Though many lepers have been cured,
curing the disease of the five poisons is barely possible.
Though you may well abandon the land of your birth,
if you have not left your homeland of subject-object dualism,
wherever you stay you are like a vulture.
Though I, an old woman, explain the dharma,
I cannot rest and am unable to sleep.
Surely it's a dharma of resting in a happy mood,
but the disciples all don't believe.
Clinging to the reality of this human life,
they give dharma talks on the world of the future.
Consider the future, they say, but now
passion and aggression are strong.
So they do not believe this old woman.
The time has come to stay alone.
If it's now, they seek instructions for later.
If it's later, the passion and aggression are strong now.
Since they disbelieve, I shall stay alone.
*Emaho!*

### VII. Heart Essence

This instruction of mother and son
is written as a memo in case it benefits someone.
Give up inflating fixation on femaleness due to harm done to males by female devils.

Resolve the inflation of maleness due to harm done to females by male
devils.
Focus the mind inwardly by the nonduality of male and female.
Since being was being since forever, realize eternal being.
Since realization [comes through] examination, the agent is pacified.
Since actions done are never over, rest at ease in nonaction.
Since anything arises from within, be without passion and aggression.
Since passion and aggression are liberated in their own ground,
befriend meditation of the five sense doors.
Inflation is a momentary part;
when you realize it is so, passion is not experienced. {138}
Understanding it that way is everlasting bliss.
*Emaho!*[18]
The eighty-four thousand teachings were expounded.
But if you don't realize them as mere designations
and cling to the words, you'll be bound by attachment.
Buddha Word is banal and short-lived.
Scripture should be understood in the same way.
Esoteric instructions are without essence or root.
Meditating on calm abiding without seeing the meaning
is like covering the embers with the ashes.
If you have realized something, calling it quits and going into action
is like cutting the reins on a wild horse.
Once you see, if you remain well without distraction,
unsurpassable enlightenment is not far.
If the mind's essence will be realized,
cyclic existence in the six realms is not a problem.
Therefore, rest without conceptual analysis.
This is not an object of analysis, not the meaning.
There is no buddha other than an object of thought.[19]
Thinking there is nothing is wearisome.[20]
Fivefold afflictive emotion and timeless awareness
have a single basis in essence.
Emotion does not bind; awareness is not liberating.
They are one, not adjusted by an antidote.
Uncontrived and in its own fashion—buddha path.
Uncontrived and in its own fashion—buddha place.
The past, the future, and the present
all occur without contrivance, without ambition.

Just engaging dharma without realization
and with hope obscures the meaning.
Meditating for happiness does not cut off inflation.
If there's hope, even hope for buddhahood is a devil.
If there's fear, fear of hell is also a devil.
Not to renounce yourself is to delude yourself.
Do not hate others; others are your own mind's children.
*Emaho!*
When you focus on the patient as the demon, without duality they are inherently liberated.
By focusing on the escort[21] as the enemy, without fear you are carried to the end.
When you make path integration the condition, without discord there are no adverse circumstances.
Cutting off the possibility of bad circumstances is like having no enemies in the land.
Fixation is the devil.
Effort is the disease. {139}
Fear is the demon.
Resting is the foundation.
Whatever appears is the support.
Buddha is the sentient being.[22]
Mind itself is space.
Body is the corpse to cast out as food.
The caster is mind: rest at ease.

### VIII. Practical Guide to the Practice

To put this meaning into practice,
[the student] should have faith, diligence,
intelligence, ongoing love and compassion,
little attachment, respect for the doctrine,
and devotion to the guru.
First impart the instructions
for pointing out [mind's nature] again and again.
The preliminaries are the stages of method,
the main practice is the nature of wisdom,
and the conclusion is skillful conduct of unity.

Then to take up the practice, it says:
"Go for refuge and arouse the aspiration,
meditate on the guru, and supplicate."
Then [recite] "unspeakable, unthinkable, inexpressible . . ."
or else rest in the separation of body and awareness,
or else cast out the body as food
and rest within the state of evenness.[23]
If fear and ideas arise
about the occurrence of apparitions and such,
strengthen your awareness
and energize by *phaṭ* and so forth.
Afterward, rest in a state of nonthought.
Deluded thought self-liberated is dharmakāya.
To conclude, dedicate virtue and make aspiration prayers
with the attitude that all is like an illusion.
In between sessions, the abiding nature
gives rise to great compassion
and going for refuge and so on:
apply yourself to gathering the two accumulations.
Furthermore, when thoughts of passion and aggression
arise in connection with yourself;
remember the pointing out and relax by relaxing.
Self-liberation is great bliss.
You don't need to meditate by division into sessions;
use the reckoning of unwavering recollection.
If you can, apply the enhancements to experiences
based on the various appearing circumstances.
If they return, apply countermeasures and blend. {140}
For various unwanted [experiences], apply the training.
With the confidence of no inflation, and with no hopes and fears,
actual buddhahood is this very lifetime.

*The Eight Common Appendices* is complete.

# 11. The Eight Uncommon Appendices[1]

## Machik Lapdrön

The instructions in *The Eight Uncommon Appendices* are more practical than those in *The Common Appendices.* In general, the terms *common* (*thun mong*) and *uncommon* (*thun mong ma yin pa*) refer to teachings that are held in common with all forms of Buddhism and those that are meant exclusively for practitioners of a certain tradition, such as Secret Mantra. Perhaps here "uncommon" indicates the Severance practice itself, as this appears to be a collection of advice for dealing with particular situations that might arise for a practitioner. The eight appendices are further divided by subheadings, and thus a loose structural outline emerges. The seventh appendix contains some remarkable descriptions of what might be seen as shamanic rites of healing, which brings up the question of whether these were an integral part of the Severance taught by Machik or were incorporated from indigenous practices.

---

Homage to total victory over the devils' influence.

The instructions of the Lady Mother, these uncommon appendices, have eight parts: (1) appendix on the meaning of the name; (2) appendix presenting the vital points; (3) appendix presenting practices applied to faculties; (4) appendix presenting the clearing away of obstructions; (5) appendix presenting deviations; (6) appendix on containing inattention; (7) appendix on how to do practice when sick; and (8) appendix on enhancement at the end.

## I. The Meaning of the Name

Concerning the term *severance*, what is it that is severed?
Clinging to the body is severed, so it is severance.
The root of mind is severed, so it is severance.
Distinctions in the basic ground are severed, so it is severance.
Acceptance and rejection on the path are severed, so it is severance.
Hopes and fears about the results are severed, so it is severance.
Thoughts from everything up to everything are severed in their own ground, so it is called Severance.

## II. The Vital Points

This has four parts: (1) the vital point of setting pestilence directly upon pestilence, like the hot needle; (2) the vital point of overwhelming gods and demons, like the sun; (3) the vital point of forsaking closeness and distance toward gods and demons, like parents; and (4) the vital point of [how to cope] when obstacles accrue no matter what you do, like cornering deer.

### A. The Vital Point of Setting Pestilence Directly upon Pestilence, Like the Hot Needle

In this example, if a disease such as the pox (*rtsa 'brum*) were to erupt on certain parts of the body, one would apply the hot needle [of moxibustion] to those exact places and the disease would subside of itself. {141} Yogins need to wander in haunted retreats[2] to maintain experience. So where is it haunted? In this world it is the abodes of nāgas that are haunted, so whoever wants to *do* haunted places should go to that specific place and the yogin's own mind will [experience] emptiness simultaneously.

Alternatively, go wherever you take to be a haunted place, sit quietly [and contemplate in this way]: In general, all nonhuman beings are fierce and have great ability, but the Three Jewels have greater ferocity and power. The essence of the Three Jewels is my own root guru, who is fiercer than all the buddhas of the three times. As it is explained:

> Embodiment of all buddhas, the very essence of Vajradhara, the root of the Three Jewels . . .

And:

> Know the guru as a fiercer place than the buddhas of one hundred thousand aeons. That is because the coming of all buddhas of the aeons depends on the guru.

Meditate on your root guru upon a seat of the sun, moon, and lotus atop your head. All the lineage gurus dissolve into that guru, who then abides as the essence of all gurus. The guru has the accoutrements of an adept, holding a ḍamaru in the right hand and a khaṭvāṅga in the left, naked and wearing the six kinds of bone ornaments. Meditate on the guru who can stamp on this apparent existence and it rebounds, clearing up all obstacles and granting all spiritual powers, full of charisma. Then focus without distraction on that guru and pray:

> Precious guru, please bless me for the sake of all sentient beings. Please cause special experiences and realization to arise in my being. Please make all of my negativities, obscurations, sufferings, and obstacles subside.

Do that supplication and sit with relaxed awareness in the state of great pervasiveness. {142}

### B. The Vital Point of Overwhelming Gods and Demons, Like the Sun

In this analogy, it is like the predawn star that grows dimmer at daybreak. Then when the sun rises and the sunlight completely overwhelms it with its brilliance, it does not appear at all. In the same way, yogis and yoginīs who rest within the great pervasiveness of their own minds overwhelm all the gods and demons of spirit-appearance with the brilliance of the nature of phenomena and they cannot rise up.

### C. The Vital Point of Forsaking Closeness and Distance toward Gods and Demons, Like Parents

For example, just as you wish only happiness and not suffering for your own two parents, you should not feel closeness or distance toward gods and demons. Do not segregate good gods to venerate and bad demons to beat up. By setting aside all of samsara and nirvana and realizing self-liberation without acceptance and rejection, [you find that] gods are not helpful and demons are not harmful. Both of them are one in mind itself, which is equality. Thus it is explained in the sutra: "Since all phenomena are equality, the perfection of wisdom is equality."[3]

### D. The Vital Point of [How to Cope] When Obstacles Accrue No Matter What You Do, Like Cornering Deer

If, no matter what you do, obstacles still start up, then [you need] the vital point that is like cornering a deer.[4] In this analogy, hunters who are pursuing deer cannot catch them in the open plains no matter what they do. But if they spot a corner or edge like a cliff and then chase them there, when the deer enter that corner they will have nowhere to go and will be trapped. In haunted retreats, [spirits] might cause some harm to the yogin. When a slight sickness occurs and diverting it or giving ritual objects [as ransom][5] does not help, [try disturbing] their dwelling places: dig the earth pestilence, stir up water pestilence, cut down tree pestilence, or create a great hearth contamination.[6] Then remain right there at ease and the malicious spirits will disperse and be incapable of causing harm.

## III. Practices Applied to Faculties

{143} Individuals with superior faculties rest in the unspeakable, unthinkable, and ineffable with their bodies like corpses, voices like mutes, and minds like river stones. Apparitions are liberated as they naturally subside and purify, and the mind becomes blissfully buoyant (*bde 'bol*), pleasantly vibrating (*bag dro 'ur*), and with a passing joyful experience (*nyams dga' yal*). Afterward, special experiences and realizations occur.

Those with middling faculties know that the apparitions in haunted places are the appearances of their own minds and that mind is unborn dharmakāya. Therefore, if one knows those apparitions as ornaments—the expression or play of the mind—then even when they occur they occur as the mind's apparitions and even when appearing they are the mind's appearances. They *are*, but they are mind's apparitions. Subsiding, they subside in mind. In no sense are they different from the mind. Since mind is unborn, you can rest in that space.

Those of inferior faculties separate the mind from the body and mentally relinquish the body. When they practice with awareness unsupported and naked, once the apparitions subside, consciousness is blissfully pure or there comes a passing joyful experience. Afterward, experiences and realizations increase.

While those of superior, middling, and inferior faculties maintain practice in those ways, they should not be pleased even if the nonhuman spirits come to their assistance or the like. It is not difficult for the devil of exaltation to enter here. Whether relying again on isolation or remaining in the assembly or staying in a country village or moving among crowds of people or wherever, sanctimony and avarice and such are causes for the devil to enter, so do not indulge them. Emptiness, compassion, and guru devotion are the three things never to be without. Since staying for a long time in villages and such dissipates experiences, don't stay for a long time. Also don't go about indifferently begging alms for too long, losing control for the sake of food. {144} And don't prolong your time in the assembly. Since you might wander down the paths of distraction, words, and idle chatter, maintain your experiences in secluded mountain retreats.

While staying in mountain retreats, do not harbor covetous or fervent thoughts about animal carrion—all of these are the doings of nonhumans who are testing your love and compassion. Also don't engender covetous thoughts about the faith offerings of the locals. If they happen to occur, donate everything to feast ceremonies and the guru's projects. Though you want to settle in isolation and are inspired and joyful when first arriving in that place, once you get used to it you may not be so enthusiastic, which will cause obstacles to arise and you to move elsewhere. But if you stay put and remain enthusiastic even from the start of feeling fear and trepidation, then it is a place where virtue increases.

In this way in an isolated place, even when nonhuman spirits put your experience to the test, meditating on love and compassion brings peace. Relinquishing the body as food, as if to your mother, brings peace. Harsh activities are not preferable to gentle severance. Establish yourself and all others on the path to freedom with compassion, love, and the aspiration for enlightenment.

### IV. Clearing Away Obstructions

It is an obstruction of the practice to become inflated after curing contagious disease and tumors,[7] or lepers, murderers, transgressors, and so forth; or to sink into a dull consciousness under the pretext of some previous impurity after losing your former meditative experiences; or to experience swelling and infection of the body. Therefore, using the antidotes that were taught previously, blend whatever you have taken on with your ongoing conduct and they will quickly be pacified. When contaminations and so forth occur, rather than doing a cleansing practice, do direct subjugation[8] by [partaking of] substances mixed with the pollution of corpses and leprous substances. {145} For contraindicated directions (*phyogs ngan*) and bad astrological configurations and such, purposefully go there and do direct subjugation.

It is an obstruction of the view if you disdain the blending of space and awareness, thinking that since the unborn is primordial it is effortless, and that space and awareness are [already] mixed and blended. You should first do the seven branches and other religious activities and then mix space and awareness again and again, training your skills directly on the circumstances.

It is an obstruction of the conduct to cut through what is easily severed, such as severing demons, and make that itself sufficient without impartial training. Train your skills again and again based on what is difficult to cut: the naked arising of the thoughts based on that [easy severance].

It is an obstruction of the results to think, "This is exactly buddha" or "This is exactly the goal" after a single introduction. With a mind free of hopes and fears, within the state of the nature of phenomena, do the wide-ranging aspiration prayers of the Great Vehicle, the contributing cause of excellent enlightened activity.

## V. Deviations

This has three parts: (1) severance deviating into curative divination; (2) severance deviating into enjoyments; and (3) severance deviating into wrathful mantras.

### A. Severance Deviating into Curative Divination

Some lucid appearances will arise from your differentiating the quintessence and the residue of awareness while keeping to haunted places and maintaining practice. However, if you tell others whether or not demons will cause harm, or whether or not illness and such will be cured, everyone will hear of it and repeatedly come visiting. That is severance deviating into curative divination.

### B. Severance Deviating into Enjoyments

When exaltation, distraction, or various merits occur and it is impossible to move back and forth to haunted sites and such, your mind may be swept away by material possessions, attendants, and renown. Then meditative experiences get lost and you become involved in those ordinary enjoyments. That is known as deviating into enjoyments.

### C. Severance Deviating into Wrathful Mantras {146}

When you maintain the meditational experience, the blessings of the truth of the nature of phenomena will take you to the stage of controlling disease and spirits. Because you have blessings to bestow, all those who have been healed will broadcast it, and you will end up wandering from town to town. This causes the experiential realization to diminish and the blessings to be lost. So then you must use wrathful mantras to subdue the disease and spirits, and that is called severance deviating into wrathful mantras.

## VI. Containing Inattention

This has three parts: (1) eliminating stagnant experience; (2) collecting scatteredness; and (3) relaxing rigidity.

### A. Eliminating Stagnancy

Once you have gone to haunted places, if there are no apparitions or signs of warmth at all, your practice will be weak and the spirits will not be raised. This is stagnation.[9] The method to raise them is to corner them with meditative absorption. If that does not raise them, strip naked, wear flayed human skin, blow a human thighbone, rattle a ḍamaru, and call out to the Indian, Chinese, Nepalese, and other gods and demons by name, saying, "I'm doing Severance, so everyone gather here." First complete the accumulation of merit by giving a white torma and then a red torma; then, separating your mind from your body, give the removed flesh and blood. Complete the accumulation of wisdom by resting the mind without support in the way of space. Then even when a shimmering (*zing zing pa*) apparition does occur one time, abruptly and decisively cut through it and an exceptional experiential realization will arise.

### B. Collecting Scatteredness

Don't let the attention bifurcate, don't involve the consciousness in divisions (*kha mtshams*), and don't let consciousness wobble (*yab yob*). With your consciousness carefree, rest in the expanse (*bag phebs pa*). {147}

### C. Relaxing Rigidity

Without giving in to "meditating and meditating" and "desiring and desiring," relax with a relaxed consciousness and settle into distraction as means.

## VII. Appendix on How to Do Practice When Sick

This has four parts: (1) severing while frequenting haunted retreats; (2) balancing the four elements; (3) setting disease directly on disease; and (4) various activities.

### A. Severing While Frequenting Haunted Retreats

If you get sick, without seeking other methods go to a haunted retreat and sever thoughts of attachment to this body. Freely bestow [the body] on that spirit and say, "You and I both have this connection due to the same [former] aspirations. Therefore I now offer you this body of mine. Stay here. I have a profound aural lineage, and through my meditation on the genuine truth, I will purify the negativities of us both." Separate mind and body and rest the intellect by relaxing into the abiding nature. Whatever the sickness was, it will be mollified on its own.

To cure [another] sick person, imagine that body as big as Supreme Mountain [and say], "We three have the same immediate aspirations, so stay here and do not go elsewhere. In order to purify the negativities and obscurations of the three of us, I will meditate on the genuine truth." Give the patient's body to [the spirit] without hesitation and rest together within the abiding nature. Also, you can rub the site of the disease while in a state of emptiness, annunciating the "words of truth." Your own intrinsic awareness is empty, the sickness and spirit are also empty, the patient's body and mind are also empty, and emptiness cannot take advantage of emptiness, so [everything] has been cleared away in emptiness. Rest together directly in the abiding nature.

## B. Balancing the Four Elements

In general, the yogin afflicted with any illness {148} simply proceeds by settling directly in the practice, resting on whatever without holding on to the body as a body, and is released [from that illness]. But if you do that and do not seem to improve, [consider this:] as this body is made up of the four elements, so the illness is also generated by the four elements. If the body is sick on the outside, dissolve the external four great elements into the internal four great elements. Put whatever [part] was sick underneath (e.g., lie on that side) and like an empty house leave the body free (*khres kyis bskur*). Leave the mind without support in space, resting free (*khres se bzhag*). If the body is sick on the inside, [imagine that] these four elements inside the body lift off and dissolve into the four elements outside. Let the mind dissipate like the vanishing mist. By being at ease, [the sickness] is pacified and gone. Alternatively, the external four elements dissolve into the internal four elements, and the internal four elements dissolve into the secret *bodhichitta*. Rest mind completely free in the empty state of the unborn.

## C. Setting Disease Directly on Disease

Pacify the heat of feverish illness in fire and resolve cold illness in water. That is, if there is disease of heat, rely on whatever food and behavior exacerbates heat and think to yourself, "Now I am happy to die. Right now, death is the absolute truth. Since awakening is within the perfection of wisdom, I need to recognize it." Without attachment to this life, say *phaṭ* and separate the awareness from the material body with a whoosh, relaxing mind into relaxation without hopes or fears. Generate a vast mind. Rest awareness without mental engagement within the great pervasiveness. Rest just so (*a ma rtsi*). Rest whenever. Rest wherever you go, wherever is good. Resting in that way, you will be revived and always free from the fixation on disease. But even though you've recovered, rest unconcerned without being pleased. {149}

For cold illness, cultivate whatever ongoing conduct and food exacerbates it. Relax into relaxation, and without fixation say *phaṭ* and lie down. Separated in that way from inflation, there is nothing at all to meditate on other than that resting. Not meditating is exactly meditation. In that, even if you die it's good—you'll be liberated in the realm of phenomena. But if you don't die it's no problem—the timeless wisdom of intrinsic awareness is unimpeded. When you understand the meaning, there is nothing in mind to die, so it is the resting in wherever you go, wherever is good.

Furthermore, when you feel unhappy or the desire to leave or to cry or to be upset occurs, don't let consciousness go into its ordinary rut. Cut off the root of the subject (*mkhan po*) and recognize rootlessness, resting relaxed.

## D. Various Activities

When blessing others and so forth, do not oppose conventional reality. Meditate on love and compassion for all sick, suffering sentient beings. Go for refuge and arouse the aspiration to awaken. Supplicate the lineage gurus, invoke the truth of the yidams, and grant the blessing of pacifying all disease and spirits. On the absolute level all three—the self, the patient, and the yidam—are essentially one in the realm of emptiness, the nature of phenomena; this is to relax into that blend and rest without distraction. Just that, without thinking of previous meditation. Don't be gloomy. Do not focus on a particular reference point. Generate forbearance for the state free of thought and reference. Don't hold out hope for benefiting; don't get bloated over recovery. Allow experiences and blessings to stray. Since that is the truth of the absolute nature of phenomena, like bearing the torch that clears up the darkness, all disease will vanish on its own. It says in the *Verse Summary*:

> The blessing of the truth extinguishes the bonfire.[10]

To treat *siu*,[11] take [the affected] to a haunted place {150} and completely give over the flesh and blood to the harm-doers. The mind will be blessed in emptiness. If there is sickness, corner it with absorption. Wash the clothes in water[12] and scatter them on rocks and wood and so forth. Burn pellets[13] [from the body of] the small child and smudge the child with the smoke, curing him or her with fire. Smear on leper brains. Give [the child] the mouth excretions of a leper to drink.[14] Wrap the child in something like felt clothing that is [still] warm from a leper. Healing is certain. If you cannot take [the child] to the haunted place, accomplish it by bringing the wood and stones and so forth from the place and attaching them [to the child].[15]

To make it rain, at a spring where there are definitely nāgas, give *basuki*[16] and torma of the three whites and three sweets, and the rain will be brought forth. If it does not come, pour burned leper blood, leper brains, underwear (*dor rta*), and so on into the spring and it will come.

If enemies come to destroy the doctrine, write their clan and personal names in their filthy [clothes, etc.] and put it into an ox horn and bury it[17] in the haunted place. Call on [the yidam, etc.] as witness and to destroy [them] by this action.

To make it hail, wrap various toxic blood in the loincloth of a widow and hide it in a haunted place. Then intense cornering absorption will make it hail for sure. To protect from hail, do the visualization within the state of emptiness.

## VIII. Appendix on Enhancing Practice If You Get Stuck

If your experience does not improve even though you have tried really hard, then you have become stuck and [you need] to do enhancement practices. There are three: (1) enhancing practice by meditating on compassion for sentient beings; (2) enhancing practice by meditating on devotion to the guru; and (3) enhancing practice by directly taking on intense circumstances.

### A. Enhancing Practice by Meditating on Compassion for Sentient Beings

If you have it, first offer a torma feast to the ḍākinīs and dharma protectors. Then think:

> In general, sentient beings of the three realms of cyclic existence are pitiable. In particular, these enemies and demons that are causing me harm now are pathetic. These sentient beings have been my father and mother an incalculable number of times, {151} during which they have helped me greatly and prevented much harm, giving birth to my life, and protecting and cherishing me when I was young. Indeed, they have been tremendously kind.

Consider it again and again.

> These kindly parents of mine desire happiness, but on top of not experiencing happiness, they inevitably experience unwanted suffering. They are so wretched.

Thinking that, first meditate on dwelling in actual suffering. Even more, meditate on those involved in creating the grievous causes of suffering until you are brought to tears. Count on a rosary as you think about those sufferers, thinking "how sad" and so on one hundred eight times or more as you meditate. Resting at ease in that way, meditate for four sessions. In the end, compassion will be born in its own natural state. Through the power of that arising, all negativities and obscurations will be purified and the enhancement of virtuous activity will occur naturally. The emptiness of the abiding nature will arise in your being, and from that alone, compassion for sentient beings will arise automatically without your having to meditate.

### B. Enhancing Practice by Meditating on Devotion to the Guru

If [experience] is not increasing in your mind despite your exerting great effort on the path, it is because the guru's blessing has not entered. The reason the blessing has not entered is that strong devotion has not arisen even though you have supplicated. For this, even relentless meditation does not help. So completely leave aside all other religious activities and divide day and night into four sessions. Generate the conviction that whatever gracious root guru has benefited you through instructions and blessings is the actual Buddha. Supplicate intensely again and again through guru yoga. Devotion will be integrated and the blessings enter.

As experience and realization grow more and more, {152} sit comfortably doing practice on a comfortable seat. Firmly establish the former meditation on love, compassion, and the mind of awakening. Then meditate with extreme clarity, with yourself in your ordinary form, that above your head on a sun-moon-lotus seat is whatever gracious root guru has benefited you through instructions and blessings. Generate yearning thoughts of love. Then immeasurable light rays from the guru's heart radiate in the ten directions. The root and lineage gurus who dwell in the ten directions and three times and the hosts of deities of the yidam mandala together with the ḍākinīs and the buddhas and bodhisattvas all arrive in the form of light and dissolve indivisibly into the guru. Imagine the guru vividly present with light and dazzling brilliance as if actually there. Think that all the dharma protectors and guardians fill up all the spaces and ground so that all obstacles are banished. Mentally prostrate with intense devotion. Swear fidelity with the thought that there is no other source of hope and completely offer your body and all possessions. Supplicate:

> Precious guru, please grant me your blessing for the sake of all sentient beings. Please cause exceptionally sublime experiences and realization to be born in my being. Please pacify all of my negativities, obscurations, sufferings, and obstacles.

Cry out again and again. When yearning arises from deep within, it does not matter whether you say the words or not. The guru's heart-mind itself is a sky-like expanse from which comes a sky-like blessing. It enters one's own sky-like mind, and genuine confidence comes with the thought that doubt is not even an option. {153} Supplicate from the marrow of your bones. If you do it like that, there is no chance that the blessings won't enter. Supplicate that way for four sessions day and night. Then at the end of the sessions, imagine that the guru dissolves into light and melts into your head, blending inseparably with your own mind. Rest serenely within the great pervasive expanse of awareness. Afterward, during the four daily activities, recall just the yearning and sometimes the longing devotion. Just like that, as you sustain it again and again, devotion will be assimilated and blessings will enter. Experiences and realization will arise.

### C. Enhancing Practice by Directly Taking On Intense Circumstances

In general, just having the understanding that mind [apprehends] objects is not enough. You need to blend over and over in areas of affirming and negating and train with evenhanded effort. If you do not train that way, then just by encountering intense circumstances you will be stranded with your ordinary mind, like being abandoned by your escort when the enemy arrives. It is precisely when adverse circumstances occur that you need to take them on directly and blend mind and dharma. But just mixing them is also not enough. If you do not train with unbiased effort, nondissipating qualities will not arise indiscriminately. So directly take on various adverse circumstances and train without discrimination. If you don't do away with training that is too uptight, you will be caught up in sanctimoniousness. So you must directly sever whatever appearances occur and in conduct act upon anything, thinking as follows:

> This lack of desire for awakening has, since beginningless cyclic existence, caused me to cling to the true existence of appearance, and to make some moral choices. The problem is that their value

> has not been equalized. In the abiding nature of mind itself, birth and death, clean and dirty, enemy and friend, and so forth are not at all established. {154} I keep hanging on to establishing them and cannot let it go, so I cannot blend them. Now, you, think, "Whatever happens, let it happen."

Hurl far away the ideas of dualistic clinging and, saying *phaṭ phaṭ*, blend with whatever is dreadful and scary, training again and again until you are free of inflation.

At first, generate a heightened view in order to temper intrinsic awareness. For that, trample without hesitation or concern on enemies, children and relatives, savory or unsavory food and drink, leprosy, infectious disease, corpses, feces, and all disgusting, fearful, and horrible things. Cut the ties. Identify the faults. Reveal the flaws. Blending them in your mind without concern, relax and rest. Behave like a crazy person—crying, laughing, wailing, and such—and you will become right. Stay marginalized from human society.

Do that without keeping anything in the desiring mind and rest flawlessly without concern. As you train like that again and again, delusion will be vigorously dispatched, clinging will turn aside on its own, devotion will automatically arise, and characteristics will be self-liberated.

You may wonder whether as a result you will attain the three kāyas. Realizing that all phenomena are emptiness and then actualizing that is the dharmakāya. The arising of anything at all for the welfare of beings through the power of aspiration prayers done in that state is the nirmāṇakāya. Without your thinking specifically about the welfare of beings, the welfare of beings occurs without thinking about it. That enjoyment without duality is the saṃbhogakāya ("enjoyment body"). Realizing those three kāyas as inseparable, a single essence beyond thought and expression, is the svabhāvikadharmakāya. {155}

This concludes *The Eight Uncommon Appendices.*

# 12. The Eight Special Appendices[1]

## Machik Lapdrön

The *Eight Special Appendices* is very different in style from the other two sets. More like a guide, it is the only one that seems to present a progressive practice rather than a loose collection of topics. The first four sections are divided into subcategories that contain not only descriptions but actual liturgy to be used in the practice, as well as citations from the source teachings, inevitably the Perfection of Wisdom sutras. Indeed, this text is the only one attributed to Machik Lapdrön or any early source in which one can recognize the implementation of the practice of Severance as we have come to know it. The fact that there is only this one brings up interesting questions on the development of the Severance practice and the relationship of later liturgical texts with the "original" teachings by Machik Lapdrön and the other early masters in the lineage.

---

Homage to the mother of the victors.

There are eight parts in this appendix to the Lady Mother's instructions, *The Perfection of Wisdom, Severance of Evil Object*: (1) the entry: going for refuge and arousing the awakening mind; (2) the blessing: separating body and mind; (3) the meditation: without recollecting, mentally doing nothing; (4) the practice: casting out the body as food; (5) the view: not straying into the devils' sphere of influence; (6) the instructions for pacifying incidental obstacles of body and mind; (7) the presentation of the sacred pledges of Severance; and (8) the presentation of the results of practice.

## I. The Entry: Going for Refuge and Arousing the Awakening Mind

This has three topics: what to enter, those who enter, and how to enter.

### A. What to Enter

Enter into the unmistaken path of the genuine.

### B. Those Who Enter

Individuals of the Mahayana disposition.

### C. How to Enter

This is entering by the immeasurable two accumulations and so on from within the state of indivisible emptiness and compassion. That has two parts: going for refuge and arousing the awakening mind to open the dharma door, and going for refuge and arousing the awakening mind in ongoing meditation.

#### 1. Going for Refuge and Arousing the Awakening Mind to Open the Dharma Door

This is to perform feasts, tormas, offerings, and so forth, and to do the eight branches of going for refuge.

#### 2. Going for Refuge and Arousing the Awakening Mind in Ongoing Meditation

Generate this thought: "Since all sentient beings, headed by this spirit (*gdon*) that causes me harm, are pitiable, I must attain the state of perfect buddhahood. Therefore, I will practice virtue such as going for refuge and so forth." In that way also, it is said that if you want conviction in this vehicle, {156} cultivate equanimity toward all migrators with the belief that they are your parents.

Then meditate that in front of you is a vast and wide throne made of jewels. There is a moon mandala on top of it. Upon that, in the center, is the Great Mother Perfection of Wisdom with a body the color of refined gold. She has one face and four arms and sits in cross-legged posture. Her first right hand holds a golden five-pointed vajra and her first left hand is in the mudra of equipoise. The lower two hold a volume of the perfection of wisdom.[2] Meditate that she sits adorned with a variety of precious jewels. Meditate that below her is the Conqueror, Buddha Shākyamuni, and below him is the Lady Mother Lapkyi Drönma. She appears there smiling, her body small and white and dazzling. Below her are her son Gyalwa Döndrup and Drogön Tönyön Samdrup. They are attired as yogins, with their hair hanging down, dark complexioned, and charismatic. Meditate on them sitting there smiling. Additionally, meditate that all your root and lineage gurus are there. To the right of those gurus are the heroes and to their left is the noble shrāvaka sangha. In front of them sits an immeasurable assembly of ḍākinīs. Meditating on that, go for refuge:

> I and all sentient beings equal to the reaches of space, from this time until enlightenment, {157} go for refuge and pay homage to the Great Mother Perfection of Wisdom. We go for refuge and pay homage to the Conqueror, the Victor Shākyamuni. We go for refuge and pay homage to the Lady Machik Lapkyi Drönma. We go for refuge and pay homage to the son Gyalwa Döndrup. We go for refuge and pay homage to Drogön Tönyön Samdrup. We go for refuge and pay homage to the buddhas of the ten directions. We go for refuge and pay homage to the dharma. We go for refuge and pay homage to the sangha. We go for refuge and pay homage to the precious guru. We go for refuge and pay homage to the host of yidam deities. We go for refuge and pay homage to all the heroes and heroines.

Say that three times with devotion and faith. This is attested in the scriptures as "Having gone for refuge to the Buddha, dharma, and noble sangha."

Then, to the extent that your mind can embrace this, meditate on your own body as food with a hundred flavors, white, oily, heavy, and supple. Imagine that in your right hand is a sword of wisdom. Since one's head is the primary limb, completely sever it at the neck and offer it to the guru and Three Jewels, thinking that they accept it with great delight. Similarly, pull out the five essential inner organs and so on from the torso and offer them, thinking that they are accepted with delight. Again, imagine the pleasing offering of the lower body with the legs. Afterward, mentally let go of the guru and Jewels of refuge. Don't even conceive of your own body. Do not examine the past or anticipate the future—rest in the present moment of consciousness without any fixation whatsoever, soft and relaxed in its own fashion without contrivance.

When consciousness languishes, arouse the aspiration as before. Meditate on the guru and Jewels in front and go for refuge once, {158} offer the body, and rest upon the abiding nature of mind. One session consists of going through that process three times. In that way, do one session at twilight, one at midnight, one at dawn, one at sunrise, one at noon, and one in the afternoon, making six sessions in a twenty-four-hour day. Do not do more than that and do not do less. That is the arousing of the aspiration for supreme awakening, the going for refuge, and the accumulation of merit with the body offering as the cause. Resting afterward in the uncontrived abiding nature is the resultant accumulation of timeless awareness. Even this one practice is wholly sufficient.

## II. The Blessing: Separating Body and Mind

This has two parts: introducing the introduction and introducing the ongoing meditation.

### A. Introducing the Introduction

This has three parts: (1) the preparation: relinquishing attachment to the body; (2) the main part: separating body and mind; and (3) the conclusion: introducing mind from the realm of the nature of phenomena as being like the sky and presenting the way that experiences arise.

#### 1. Preparation: Relinquishing Attachment to the Body

Having first done the feast and torma offerings, go for refuge and arouse the awakening mind and so forth as in "Going for Refuge and Arousing the Awakening Mind to Open the Dharma Door." Then the guru offers a flower to the disciple, who stands up in front [of the guru] with legs together and the palms of the hands joined at the mid-brow. Straightening up the body, he or she first investigates this aggregate, thinking:

> This body of mine {159} is made up of thirty-two impure substances. It is a bag of pus and blood, extended by pieces of bone, with a net of sinews. Becoming attached and clinging to something like this causes the experience of suffering in cyclic existence. Now I must not be attached or clinging.

## 2. Main Part: Separating Body and Mind

Meditate that on the soles of both feet the essence of mind appears without intrinsic nature like moons reflected in water. Joining the abdomen and back, intensely compress body and mind and then draw up the lower vital wind. Like moons reflected in water, they rise up white and flowing steadily (*dkar na ra ra*). Coming through the big veins of the thighs, they steadily rise up, and then in the torso at the level of the navel the two combine into one. Focus intently on it there shimmering white and round (*dkar hri li li*). Then again rising steadily up, it comes up to the heart. Meditate that it comes up to the throat and then rises up from there clear to the cranial aperture at the crown of the head. Meditate that it is there at the cranial aperture, clear and white, the size of the eye of a medium spindle,[3] and sharply shout *phaṭ*. That sends the water moon–like [sphere] up, projecting from there into the sky as far [as it can go]. [If] you feel that [you don't want to let it] go, and that it is staying there shimmering white and round (*dkar hri le*), meditate without distraction on that.

## 3. Conclusion: Introducing Mind

Then as [the sphere] grows larger, imagine that awareness pervades wherever space pervades. Wherever awareness pervades, space pervades. Without concepts of meditating or not meditating, rest relaxed and easy in your own fashion. In that vein it is also said of this, "Equal to the realm of space [in that] it is inseparable and unfathomable."[4]

There are three kinds of experience that will arise from meditating in that way. For those of superior faculties, the experience of freedom from elaboration arises. {160} For those of average faculties, the experience of leaping over (*thod rgal*) arises. For those of inferior faculties, powerful experiences arise. Taking that into consideration, Machik said, "While concentrated by concentration, relax by relaxing. This is the single vital point of meditation."[5]

### B. Introducing the Ongoing Meditation

While going about your business in whatever way is comfortable, visualize the appearance of the essence of vital wind and mind combined, without intrinsic nature like the moon in water, meditating on it below the navel. Understand it as described above.

## III. The Meditation: Without Recollecting, Mentally Doing Nothing

Sit with your legs in vajra position, hands in the mudra of equipoise, spine straightened, neck slightly bent, and eyes focused on the tip of the nose. In mind, do not examine the past or anticipate the future. In the present consciousness, do not engage mind at all. Rest [mind] in its own fashion—buoyant, loose, blank (*had de*), undecided (*tshom me*)—free of all considerations of meditating and meditation objects. Thus it says in the scripture:

> Being without recollecting anything and without mental engagement is the recollection of the Buddha.[6]

And:

> Do not do anything in the mind. [This applies] from form up through total omniscience.[7]

And:

> "Since the perfection of wisdom is mental nonengagement, all phenomena are mental nonengagement. Since the perfection of wisdom is equality, all phenomena are equality.[8] Since the perfection of wisdom is unbornness, all phenomena are not born. Since the perfection of wisdom is unceasingness, all phenomena are without cessation." Thus the noble [buddha] Dharmodgata said to the noble bodhisattva {161} Sadāprarudita. Meditation on the perfection of wisdom itself is meditation on all phenomena.

This is the meditation for all times—going for refuge, after separating body and mind, after casting out the food, and after not losing the view in the [severance] activities of evil objects.

## IV. The Practice: Casting Out the Body as Food

From scripture: "Give away the head and limbs without hesitation."[9] This has two parts: casting out as food in general and casting out as food in particular.

### A. Casting Out as Food in General

This has three topics: (1) the preparation: meditation on compassion and love; (2) the main part: donating the body [and practicing] the six perfections; and (3) the conclusion: dedicating to unsurpassable enlightenment.

#### 1. Preparation: Meditation on Compassion and Love

Contemplate and meditate that "All sentient beings headed by this evil spirit that causes me harm are pitiable. Out of compassion I should donate this body to them." Meditate that the eighty thousand types of obstructors, headed by this harm-doer, gather before you.

#### 2. Main Part: Donating the Body and Practicing the Six Perfections

Visualize your very own body as extremely large. Meditate that the right hand holds a sword of wisdom, and totally sever [your head] at the neck and donate it. Meditate on the harm-doers and so forth who prefer flesh eating the flesh, those who like blood drinking the blood, and those who like bones sucking the bones. Then pull out the five essential inner organs and others from within the torso and donate them. Meditate that it is consumed as before. Then donate the upper torso with its arms and the lower body with legs {162}. Meditate on the harm-doers and such that like flesh eating the flesh, those that like blood drinking the blood, and those that like bones gnawing the bones. Meditate that they consume the entire body without leaving leftovers even as small as a sesame seed. After that, without examining the past or anticipating the future, rest tranquil and soft in the present consciousness without any mental engagement whatsoever. Then meditate on compassion, cast out the body as food, and rest in the abiding nature of mind. Alternating in that way, cycle through the practices to the day's peak and into night.

### 3. Conclusion: Dedicating to Unsurpassable Enlightenment

After the session is over, repeat the dedication three times:

> To the buddhas, the dharma, and the sublime assembly
> I go for refuge until I attain enlightenment.
> Through my merit of generosity and other virtues,
> may I attain awakening for the sake of migrators.

Then engage in whatever conduct suits you.

Thus the first meditation on compassion and love is the preparation; casting out the food and resting in the abiding nature is the main practice; and the dedication is the conclusion. In this way, compassion and love serve as the antidote to anger. They pacify the male spirits and the disease of intense pain (*gzer zug*). Casting out the body as food becomes the antidote of passion, pacifying the shaking disease (*ldang dub*) and female spirits. Resting in the abiding nature serves as the antidote for stupidity, pacifying nāga spirits and the disease of drowsiness (*bying can*). Moreover, casting out the body as food is the perfection of generosity; giving it away for the sake of sentient beings is morality; giving it away without hatred is patience; giving it away again and again {163} is diligence; giving it away without distraction is meditative stability; and resting afterward in the abiding nature of emptiness is the perfection of wisdom.

## B. Casting Out as Food in Particular

If, for instance, your eye is diseased, think, "Beings with eye disease are so pitiable. In order to quell all of their eye disease, I must give them my eyes." Meditating so, think that the eighty thousand kinds of obstructors appear in front of you. Give away your eyes in generosity and rest the mind without any conceptuality as before. Do the same for the hands or whatever is diseased.

## V. The View: Not Straying into the Devils' Sphere of Influence

When you practice in that way, four kinds of obstacles of gods and demons will come: the best are apparitions displaying form, middling are apparitions that emit sounds, least are apparitions of demonic oppression, and finally dream apparitions.

In [dealing with] all of those, the best practitioners rest directly upon their abiding nature. No matter what divine and demonic apparitions occur, know that they are the apparitions of your own mind, and don't engage those apparitions mentally. Rest consciousness relaxed, soft, and serene in its own fashion. All apparitions of gods and demons will naturally subside. Once self-liberated, they will rise again as a support for [realizing] the nature of phenomena.

The average practitioner separates mind and body. No matter what divine and demonic apparitions occur, suddenly separate the mind from the body, and send mind freely into space. Once consciousness has gone utterly empty, the apparitions of gods and demons will become utterly empty.

The least practitioner casts out the body as food. {164} No matter what divine and demonic apparitions occur, think, "If it is this body of mine that you desire, just take it." Completely cast out the body and relax the mind in its own fashion, resting just so. Once consciousness has gone utterly empty, the apparitions of gods and demons will become utterly empty.

In short, this is how to prevent the view from straying into the devils' sphere of influence: If you know that no matter what apparitions of gods and demons occur, they are supports for spiritual practice, then the view will not stray into the devil's sphere of influence. If you don't understand that and hold apparitions to be autonomous, the view has gone over to the devils' sphere of influence. If somehow the view does stray into the devils' sphere of influence, apply the instructions intently and ascertain the lack of intrinsic existence through discriminating wisdom.

### VI. Pacifying Incidental Obstacles of Body and Mind

These should be learned directly from the guru.

### VII. Sacred Pledges of Severance

The common sacred pledges are to abandon negativity—the ten nonvirtues—and to practice the ten virtues and the six perfections for the benefit of sentient beings. The special sacred pledges are to not perform Bön rituals, medical examination, or the beating of demons in any way or at any time.

## VIII. The Results of Practice

The immediate result is the pacification of tangible devils, intangible devils, devils of exaltation, and devils of inflation, and the release from sickness. With the mind freed from suffering, ultimately you will awaken in the nature of the three kāyas.

The Lady Machik's instruction, *The Eight Special Appendices* from *The Perfection of Wisdom, Severance of Evil Object.*
*iti*

# Door-Opening Empowerments

# 13. Opening the Sky Door

## *Instructions on Severance Mahāmudrā*[1]

### Rinchen Senge

These "instructions" (*gdams pa*) on Severance Mahāmudrā are actually meant to be performed as an authorization ritual (*rjes gnang*), as is evident in the format and stated clearly in the opening verses and colophon. An authorization is similar to an empowerment (*dbang*), though usually less complex. So in fact these are instructions on conferring the authorization, including the actual liturgies to be recited and sometimes repeated by the disciples. Perhaps this confusion is why the text was moved from its original position in the empowerment section of the Palpung blocks to the instruction section of the Shechen printing. In Kongtrul's catalog, the text is indicated by the statement "torma empowerment of the Zurmang tradition." The empowerment or blessing in this case is conferred physically using a torma (ritual sculpted dough), rather than the various other implements of initiation.

The phrase "opening the sky door" (*nam mkha' sgo 'byed*) is distinctive to the Severance tradition and refers specifically to the practice of separating consciousness from the body and sending it out the cranial aperture, a kind of transference (*'pho ba*). However, it has become a more generalized designation for a whole cycle of Severance teachings, including an enumeration of a set of ten instructions called sky-door openings. Khamnyön's *Religious History of Pacification and Severance* reports that Machik received the empowerment originally from Kyo Sakya Yeshe during the transmissions of a teaching called the *Six Pieces** and attained liberation after receiving

**Brul tsho drug.* This text, thought by modern scholars to be lost, is available in the *Dingri Volumes.*

only four of the six instructions.* Khamnyön's biography of Dampa Sangye recounts that the initiation was given by Dampa to four disciples and the instructions to Kyo Sakya Yeshe, who conferred it on Sönam Lama, who then passed it to Machik.† In any case, the term "opening the sky door" is most commonly associated with the empowerment ritual that is required before commencing the practice.

The author, Rinchen Senge (Rin chen seng ge), signs with the Sanskrit name Ratnasiṃha. It is difficult to identify this person with certainty, other than that he was active during or after the time of Rangjung Dorje (1284–1339), who is specifically mentioned in the colophon. It seems likely that he is the great preceptor of Tropu (Kagyu) Monastery (Khro phu mkhan chen Rin chen Seng ge, 13th c.), the ordination preceptor of Butön Rinchendrup (1290–1364) and also of Zurmang Khenchen Pema Namgyal.‡

Note that empowerment rituals often require the recitation of stories and instructions, and even section headings.

---

*oṃ svasti*

Body—nonfixated empty form like a water moon.
Speech—unimpeded empty sound, a divine melody.
Mind—unwavering like a vajra.
I bow to the unrivaled possessor of those.

Basic space, totally pure nature, spontaneously present,
meaning beyond the sphere of expression, thought, and utterance,
not veiled by conceptual attributes:
I pay homage to the Mother, Perfection of Wisdom.

*Khamnyön Dharma Senge, *The Religious History of Pacification and Severance,* pp. 436–37.

†Khamnyön Dharma Senge, *The Life Story of the Great Mighty Adept, Venerable Dampa Sangye,* pp. 54–55. This nineteenth-century account follows (i.e., copies) that of Gö Lotsāwa (1392–1481) in *The Blue Annals.*

‡mKhan chen Pad ma rnam rgyal, a lama of Zurmang Monastery. This tentative identification is based on the statement in his biography that he received novice vows from "Karma's Khenchen Ratna." See *mKhan chen Padma rnam rgyal gyi rnam thar* in *Collected Histories of the Glorious Zurmang Kagyu* (*Zur mang bka' brgyud chos 'byung*), p. 672.

With a mind immersed in the meaning of emptiness,
I will express, in accordance with the original sense,
the summarized meaning of the Severance practice:
the precept of the torma-blessing authorization
of the requisite empowerment of meaning.

These instructions of the precepts of Object Severance Mahāmudrā, the esoteric instructions of Opening the Sky Door, this blessed Buddha Word, has four subjects: (1) the preliminaries; (2) the preparations; (3) the main part; and (4) the conclusion

### I. Preliminaries

Adorn your residence in a graveyard sacred site or a remote place or lone tree or lake island and so forth—in short, an isolated place that facilitates experience—with the representations of Body, Speech, and Mind and arrange a mandala with five or seven heaps. Place five or three or however many tormas, whatever offerings you have, and the feast items on the shrine. That is the process for the preliminaries.

### II. Preparations

There are five: (1) generating the pledge beings; (2) invoking the awareness [beings]; (3) offering the seat and making offerings and homage; (4) offering the body as feast and supplicating; and (5) offering the torma and making offerings and praises.

### A. Generating the Pledge Beings

In some practices, there is the custom of sending out a torma to the obstructors in order to pacify obstacles. {409} But this dharma is about taking obstacles as good fortune. Therefore, since the knowledgeable practice of all the dharma lords does not [include that practice], do not do it. Then, if the disciples understand the meaning of emptiness, have them enter into it. Even if they do not understand, it would be good to do just the recitation of the *gate* mantra.[2] Then sit down on a comfortable seat and place in front of you a small drum, human-thighbone trumpet, bell, and so forth. For the sake of all sentient beings equal to the reaches of space, meditate on the meaning of emptiness, the perfection of wisdom, and say this:

> All sentient beings equal to the reaches of space—headed up by enemies, obstructors, and creditors who threaten injury to these generous patrons or to us, master and disciples with our entourage—go for refuge in the glorious guru, the epitome of Body, Speech, and Mind. We go for refuge in the Buddha. We go for refuge in the dharma. We go for refuge in the sangha. We go for refuge in the gurus of the adept lineage of Object Severance.
>
> Guru, Buddha, dharma, and the sublime assembly . . . (etc., and)
>
> Just like the lords of the three times,
> I give rise to the holy,
> the supreme, the mind of awakening
> that assuredly causes perfect awakening.
> And I uphold all the recollections. {410}
>
> May the generous patrons and so on—all sentient beings equal to the reaches of space—be endowed with happiness, be free of suffering, never be without happiness, and be free of afflictive emotions and the eight worldly concerns, which are the causes of happiness and sorrow.
>
> *oṃ svabhāva śuddāḥ sarvadharmāḥ svabhāva śuddho 'ham*
>
> Out of emptiness the Great Mother Perfection of Wisdom appears instantly on a lion and lotus-moon-sun seat in the sky in front. Her color is like refined gold. She has one face and four arms; the right hand of the first pair makes the earth-touching mudra and the left the mudra of meditative equipoise. The right hand of the lower pair holds a vajra and the left a volume [of the perfection of wisdom]. She is draped with precious ornaments, such as a crown, earrings, necklaces, armlets, bracelets, anklets, and a neckband. She sits with her legs crossed in vajra position. She has a peaceful and gentle countenance.
>
> To her right, on a lotus and sun-moon seat, is Jomo Lapkyi Drönma, white in color like a polished conch. She has one face

and two hands, holding a ḍamaru in the right and a bell at her hip in the left. Her long locks cover her back. She is fully adorned by the five bone-fragment ornaments. She gazes into space and stands with her right leg drawn up in dancing posture. In front of Jomo is Vajra Ḍākinī, with Ratna Ḍākinī to the south, Padma Ḍākinī to the west, and Karma Ḍākinī to the north. The four of them are the color of their respective directions, holding curved knives and blood-filled skull cups and adorned by the five bone ornaments. They stand in dancing posture, embracing their khaṭvāṃkas.

To the left of the Great Mother, on a lotus-moon seat, is Venerable Indian Dampa wearing the accessories of an āchārya. He has one face and two arms, rattling a joined-skull drum at the sky with his right hand and blowing a human-thighbone trumpet in his left hand. He wears a white woolen skirt on his lower body. He sits with majestic brilliance surrounded by guru adepts. {411}

Buddha Shākyamuni, the color of refined gold, is on a lotus-moon seat above the Great Mother's head. He has one face and two hands, the right one touching the earth and the left in the mudra of meditative equipoise. He sits in vajra posture, adorned by all the major and minor marks. The assemblies of buddhas, bodhisattvas, and shrāvakas of the ten directions are all around him.

White Buddha Vairochana, with the mudra of supreme awakening, is above Shākyamuni's head on a lotus-moon seat. In front of him, blue Akṣhobhya makes the mudras of earth-touching and equipoise. Yellow Ratnasambhava to the right makes the mudras of supreme generosity and equipoise. Green Amoghasiddhi to the left makes the mudras of giving refuge and equipoise. Red Amitābha in back makes the mudra of meditative absorption. All of them are in the style of the nirmāṇakāya, draped in all the ornaments and sitting in vajra posture.

All the gurus of the Severance lineage of adepts from Venerable Tārā down to your root guru are lined up around the Great Mother, starting from in front of her and proceeding to the right.

Directly in front of the legs of the Great Mother's throne and all around are the oath-bound dharma protectors: the holy wisdom beings, such as Mahākāla and Shrīdevī, and the protectors of the ten directions, such as the four great kings and so forth. Below the base of the Great Mother's seat, headed up by the gods and demons of this haunted place, are the ground masters; obedient ones of apparent existence; eight classes of gods, demigods, and spirits; lords of plague and sudden obstacles; lords and ladies of debt and liability; sorcerers; necromancers; and tutelary gods, all gathered in the space as thick as clouds, showing obeisance with their mudras to the Great Mother.

That was the generation of the pledge beings.

### B. Invoking the Awareness Beings {412}

Play the music with the ḍamaru and so forth, and burn incense.

Protector of all sentient beings without exception,
deity who conquers unbearable devils with their hosts,
you who know all things just as they are,
Great Mother and entourage, please approach this place.
*vajra samājaḥ jaḥ*

Great Mother, it is good you have come here.
We [have merit and good fortune.
Please make yourself comfortable
on this lion-lotus-moon seat
in order to enjoy my offering delights.][3]
[Please remain] right here.[4]

Just as, as soon as he was born,
the gods bathed him,
just so, with pure divine water,
I bathe your body.[5]

### C. Offering the Seat and Making Offerings and Homage

Great Mother and entourage,
Please be seated with your entourage
on this lion-lotus-moon seat
while I make offerings to you.

Imagine that when you say that, they arrive and take their seat. Then make whatever offerings are appropriate. When you say *samaya jaḥ / jaḥ hūṃ baṃ hoḥ*, think that the [awareness beings] dissolve into the pledge beings and they become inseparable. Then do the purification, cleansing, and consecration of the offerings. If you would like to do an elaborate version, then offer whatever [prayers for] the five enjoyments are appropriate, such as the "Billionfold Universe"[6] and so forth, along with the offerings of the five desirable qualities, the seven articles of royalty, and the eight auspicious symbols. Similarly for the homage, do a brief or extensive version according to your available time. For a concise offering and homage, do this:

> I present offerings of drinking water,
> washing water, incense, flowers, lamps,
> scented water, food, and music
> to the Great Mother and entourage.
>
> I present the five desirable qualities—
> form, sound, scent, taste,
> and likewise texture—
> to the Great Mother and entourage.
>
> I present the seven royal treasures—
> wheel, gem, queen, minister,
> elephant, supreme horse, and general—
> to the Great Mother and entourage.
>
> I present the offerings of eight goddesses—
> grace, garlands, song, dance,
> flowers, incense, light, and perfume—
> to the Great Mother and entourage.

At this point, set out the mandala and offer it with the verses:

> (*gang gi drin gyis . . .*)
> [I bow to the lotus feet of the vajra-endowed
> body of the guru who is like a jewel
> and through whose kindness
> great bliss arises instantly.]

(*sangs rgyas kun gyi rang bzhin sku . . .*)
[I go for refuge in the master,
the natural kāya of all buddhas.
I bow to the deities of the mandala
and the deity where my flower first landed.] {413}

(*smra bsam brjod med . . .*)
[I bow and praise the mother of the victors of three times,
unutterable, unimaginable, inexpressible perfection of wisdom,
unborn, unceasing, the very essence of space,
the domain of individual reflexive awareness.]

(*blta bas mi ngoms . . .*)
[I bow and praise the mother of the victors,
on whom one can never gaze enough,
with her one face, four arms, and color of pure gold,
sitting in vajra posture, decked in precious ornaments.]

(*zhing khams thams cad gser gyi sa gzhi la / . . .*)
[I bow and praise Mother Tārā.]
Upon the golden ground of all pure realms
[numerous precious gems are laid out,
and a rain of puṇḍarīka flowers falls.][7]

I bow to you, Lapdrön,
nonhuman ḍākinī of timeless awareness.
I bow to Dampa Rinpoche,
who guides beings by his deliberate yogic conduct.
I bow to the supreme Muni,
[sublime being of the Shākya, the Bhagavān].

(*chos sku nam mkha' lta bu . . .*)
The sky-like dharmakāya . . . (etc.)[8]

(*ston pa bla med sangs rgyas rin po che . . .*)
To the precious Buddha, supreme teacher,
[to the precious dharma, supreme refuge,
to the precious sangha, supreme guide—
we offer to the supreme precious ones.]

For short:

(*thub pa mchog la phyag 'tshal lo . . .rang rig ye shes ston mdzad pa*)
I bow and praise the great sage,
[all-knowing and supreme among the Shākyas.
I bow and praise the Indian Dampa,
who has helped beings for seven lifetimes.
I bow and praise Lapdrön,
nonhuman ḍākinī of timeless awareness.]
I bow and praise the father gurus
who show the timeless awareness of one's cognition.
I bow and praise the yidams
who definitely grant spiritual powers.
I bow and praise the holy dharma
that pacifies and is free of desire.
I bow and praise the sangha,
who have perfect relinquishment and realization.
I bow and praise the dharma protectors,
who accomplish the four activities.[9]

Then, immeasurable light rays arise from the hearts of the guru and the Great Mother. They strike your body, speech, and mind and those of all sentient beings. All negativities and obscurations exude through the soles of your feet in the form of thick black liquid sludge. Think that your body has become totally clear and limpid like a polished crystal ball, and repeat the *gate* mantra one hundred or one thousand times as appropriate.

### D. Separating the Body from Mind, Offering It as Feast, and Supplicating

Instantly, from within emptiness, awareness soars up as if coming from below, as instructed in Opening the Sky Door. That essence of intrinsic awareness shoots far out of the crown of your head and instantly transforms into Mother Jomo, red in color, holding a curved knife and skull cup. She is draped in many ornaments of precious stone and bone. Imagine that and say *phaṭ*. With the curved knife in her right hand, Mother Jomo slices off your skull at the eyebrow level. She places it upon the three skull hearthstones that are as big as Supreme Mountain. Imagine that and say *phaṭ* three times. Then when you say another *phaṭ* she chops up your body into pieces and dumps them in the skull cup. Think that your heart is set in the center as the glorious torma and the blood fills around it with red as the water torma. Utter *oṃ āḥ hūṃ* and think that it all becomes brimming elixir. {414} Say *phaṭ* seven times and imagine that Mother Jomo scoops it up by turning a skull [ladle] and draws it into the mouths of the Great Mother and the deities. Alternatively, imagine that the deities suck it up with their tongues, which are like vajra straws. Offer it to each deity seven times; three solo sessions count as one group session. Similarly, offer it to the Great Mother and so on until the dharma protectors. After that, visualize each one individually and offer to each. Then, imagine that all those sentient beings supplicate in a state of faith and devotion. Do your own extensive or concise sequence of supplications as appropriate.

### E. Offering the Torma and Making Offerings and Praises

Consecrate the first torma and offer it to the yidam deities of the mandala, Mother Jomo, and her entourage. Offer the second torma to the awareness dharma protectors. Offer the third one to the dharma protectors of the outer tantras. Offer the fourth one to the ground masters of that territory [where you are practicing]. If you did the consecration of the feast prior to the dedication of torma, then consecrate them according to the *Kagyu Feast Liturgy* (*tshogs las*). In sprinkling the first-portion feast torma (*tshogs phud gtor ma*), apply fire and wind, or else consecrate as usual. Offer to all the deities as the basis of the session, and do the offerings and praises depending on your time. There is also the practice of performing the feast offering as part of the consecration itself. If you have five [tormas], give the second one to the four ḍākinīs and the third to the outer guests. Then do the concise or extensive offering of praises as appropriate.

## III. Main Practice

> This main practice has three parts: First, altering the disciples' minds, giving refuge, and arousing the awakening mind, in order to purify their mindstreams; second, giving the vows of the eight branches, in order to endow their mindstreams with qualities; and third, the main practice blessing, in order to bless their mindstreams.

## A. Altering Their Minds, Giving Refuge, and Arousing the Awakening Mind

By your saying *phaṭ*, the essence of your own intrinsic awareness dissolves into the heart of the Great Mother in the form of Mother Jomo. Then the disciples offer a mandala and sit down in rows. The master (preceptor) explains karmic cause and effect and whatever history of these teachings is suitable.

> Giving refuge: Now then, do the liturgy, while thinking, "We go for refuge from this time forward until reaching the fruition, the essence of awakening, to the guru and Great Mother with their entourages in front in the sky." {415} Then repeat after me: Guru and Great Mother with your entourage, all of you, please think of me. I, named *so-and-so*, from now until reaching the essence and fruition of awakening, go for refuge in the Buddha, supreme among bipeds. I go for refuge in the dharmas of the Great Vehicle, peace beyond misery, supreme among those peaceful and free of desire. I go for refuge in the sangha of the Great Vehicle, who fully dwell on the great stages, supreme of all assemblies.

Say that, and explain the refuge precepts extensively or concisely as appropriate.

> Those are the methods of taking the threefold refuge, so say, "Very well" (*legs so*).
>
> Then to arouse the awakening mind, think, "I must liberate all sentient beings from the sufferings of cyclic existence and, based on the path of the six perfections, establish them in the fruition, buddhahood." Repeat after me:
>
> > Guru, Great Mother, with entourage,
> > Everyone, please listen to me.
> > I, named *so-and-so*,
> > from now until however long it takes
> > to reach the heart of awakening,
> > emulate the previous sugatas,

who aroused the mind of awakening
and undertook in proper sequence
the training of a bodhisattva;
similarly, for the sake of migrators,
I give rise to the awakening mind
and undertake in proper sequence
the training of a bodhisattva.
Those sentient beings not emancipated
I will emancipate.
Those not liberated I will liberate.
Those not reassured I will reassure,
and I will place sentient beings beyond misery.

Explain whatever precepts are appropriate.

Those are the methods of arousing the awakening mind, so say, "Very well."

## B. Giving the Vows of the Eight Branches

Second, to give the eight branches, motivated by the thought "I will take the vows of the eight branches, prostrating and so forth to the guru and Great Mother inseparable in front of me," {416} repeat:

Guru, Great Mother, and entourage,
I bow with devotion in body, speech, and mind.

If you prefer the elaborate version, then:

I bow and praise the mother of the victors,
who is beyond the realm of speech, thought, and expression.
I bow and praise the Golden One,
who has no thought of staying in cyclic existence.
I bow and praise Dampa Rinpoche,
who has helped beings for seven lifetimes.
I bow and praise Lapkyi Drönma,

nonhuman ḍākinī of timeless awareness.
I bow and praise the gurus,
who show the timeless awareness of one's awareness.
I bow and praise the yidams,
who definitely grant spiritual powers.
I bow and praise the holy dharma
which pacifies and is free of desire.
I bow and praise the sangha,
who have perfect renunciation.
I bow and praise the dharma protectors,
who cause the accomplishment of the activities.

I present vast offerings,
both actual and mentally emanated.
I confess individually whatever negative actions
I have done with body, speech, and mind.
I go for refuge until awakening
in the Buddha, dharma, and supreme assembly.
I rejoice in the roots of virtue
created throughout the three times.
Turn every wheel of dharma
for the benefit of all beings.
I request you to remain and not pass beyond misery
for the duration of cyclic existence.
I dedicate everything to awakening,
all dissipating and nondissipating virtue.

That was the method of presenting the vows of the eight branches, so say, "Very well."

## C. The Main Practice [Blessing]

Third, the main practice has three parts: First, introducing intrinsic awareness by means of separating body and mind; second, performing the blessing based on the torma; and third, the authorization and presentation of the instructions of the practice.

### 1. Introducing Intrinsic Awareness by Means of Separating Body and Mind

> First, after you all present the mandala and offerings, sit up straight with your legs in vajra position, your hands in meditative equipoise position, and your eyes looking straight ahead. Meditate for a moment. Then quickly stand up, {417} place your two legs together and your palms together above your head, and meditate like that. Think, "This body of mine is made up of thirty-two unclean substances. It is a bag of blood and pus; a net of veins and sinews; a cobbled-up sack of bone pieces; a heap of the four elements gathered together. Who could be attached to this corporeal body of flesh and blood?" Meditate in this way just until [the realization of] impermanence occurs to you. Then, meditate on that body as empty and clear like a blown-up balloon, with [the aperture at] the crown of your head open like a trumpet. At the soles of your two feet, the essence of your own awareness is two white vital drops the size of a thumb tip.

Then light frankincense and loudly play the instruments. The preceptor and all the disciples enunciate *phaṭ*.

> Imagine that the two drops at the soles of the feet travel up the calves and arrive at the two knees. (Again say *phaṭ*.) They arrive at the perineum and combine into one. (Again say *phaṭ*.) Then [the drop travels to] the navel, the heart, and the throat. (Again say *phaṭ*.) Think of it surrounded by five-colored light and projected out through the crown of the head. (Say *phaṭ* three times. The master says:) "Give up, give up, don't be attached." Imagine that the realm of space and intrinsic awareness become inseparably mixed together, and rest in a state of mental pervasiveness for as long as you can remain. (Then the master says:)
>
> That is called "separating body and mind." It is also called "opening the sky door." It is also called "raising the spear of awareness" (*rig pa mdung slong*). In this, four experiences will arise: leaping over (*thod rgal*), excitement, crying, and nonelaboration. Leaping over is intrinsic awareness with intensity. Excitement is joy. Crying is being without conscious recollection, or weariness

with cyclic existence. To be without conscious recollection is to be without elaboration and to rest in clarity-emptiness.

Then the disciples sit with their legs crossed in vajra position and hands in meditative equipoise. The master explains the four vital points according to [the description] below.

That is the introduction [of intrinsic awareness] by means of separating body and mind.

## 2. Performing the Blessing Based on the Torma

Second, [offer] the mandala.

Then the master places the torma on [the disciples'] heads and [says]: {418}

Meditate that this torma, which is no different from Buddha Vairochana and no different from Buddha Ḍākinī, dissolves into the crown of your head.

From the totally pure nature of the realm of phenomena,
the form of great timeless awareness manifests.
From the water of Buddha Vairochana's compassion,
receive the empowerment of the realm of phenomena,
the total purity of stupidity.

*kye*
Mother, nonhuman ḍākinī of timeless awareness,
when you take three steps from the center,
you are small in stature and black in color,
surrounded by a hundred thousand awareness ḍākinīs.
From the wide expanse of the space of phenomena's nature,
compassion's rain clouds cluster—*tip se tip*,
and a rain of blessings flows—*sil li li.*
Please be seated here as my crown ornament.
Once you are seated, please confer blessings.
Machikma, grant your blessing.
Machikma, grant spiritual powers.
Machikma, engender realization.

> Machikma, confer supreme empowerment.
> Machikma, clear away obstacles.
> Machikma, guide me on the path.

Say that, and:

> Meditate that your afflictive emotion of stupidity is purified and you have received the empowerment of the timeless awareness of phenomena's realm.

Similarly, touch the torma to their foreheads.

> Meditate that this torma, which is no different from Buddha Akṣhobhya and no different from Vajra Ḍākinī, dissolves into your forehead.

> From the pristine water
> of Buddha Vairochana's pure compassion,
> receive the empowerment of great mirrorlike timeless awareness,
> the total purity of anger.

> *kye*
> Mother, nonhuman ḍākinī of timeless awareness,
> when you take three steps from the east,
> you are small in stature and white in color,
> surrounded by a hundred thousand vajra ḍākinīs.
> From the wide expanse of space of phenomena's nature,
> compassion's rain clouds cluster—*tip se tip*,
> and a rain of blessings flows—*sil li li.*
> Please be seated here as my crown ornament.
> Once you are seated, please confer blessings.
> Machikma, grant your blessing.
> Machikma, grant spiritual powers.
> Machikma, engender realization.
> Machikma, confer supreme empowerment.
> Machikma, clear away obstacles.
> Machikma, guide me on the path.

Meditate that your afflictive emotion of anger is purified and you have received the empowerment of mirrorlike timeless awareness.

Again, touch the torma at the temple above the right ear.

Meditate that this torma, which is no different from Buddha Ratnasambhava and no different from Ratna Ḍākinī, dissolves into your right temple. {419}

From the pristine water
of Buddha Ratnasambhava's pure compassion,
receive the empowerment of great timeless awareness
of equanimity, the total purity of pride.

*kye*
Mother, nonhuman ḍākinī of timeless awareness,
when you take three steps from the south,
you are small in stature and yellow in color,
surrounded by a hundred thousand jewel ḍākinīs.
From the wide expanse of the space of phenomena's nature,
compassion's rain clouds cluster—*tip se tip*,
and a rain of blessings flows—*sil li li*.
Please be seated here as my crown ornament.
Once you are seated, please confer blessings.
Machikma, grant your blessing.
Machikma, grant spiritual powers.
Machikma, engender realization.
Machikma, confer supreme empowerment.
Machikma, clear away obstacles.
Machikma, guide me on the path.

Meditate that your afflictive emotion of pride is purified and you have received the empowerment of the timeless awareness of equanimity.

Again, touch the torma at the temple.

Meditate that this torma, which is no different from Buddha Amitābha and no different from Padma Ḍākinī, dissolves into your temple.

From the pristine water  
of Buddha Amitābha's pure compassion,  
receive the empowerment of great timeless awareness  
of discrimination, the total purity of desire.

*kye*  
Mother, nonhuman ḍākinī of timeless awareness,  
when you take three steps from the west,  
you are small in stature and red in color,  
surrounded by a hundred thousand lotus ḍākinīs.  
From the wide expanse of the space of phenomena's nature,  
compassion's rain clouds cluster—*tip se tip*,  
and a rain of blessings flows—*sil li li*.  
Please be seated here as my crown ornament.  
Once you are seated, please confer blessings.  
Machikma, grant your blessing.  
Machikma, grant spiritual powers.  
Machikma, engender realization.  
Machikma, confer supreme empowerment.  
Machikma, clear away obstacles.  
Machikma, guide me on the path.

Meditate that your afflictive emotion of desire is purified and you have received the empowerment of the timeless awareness of discrimination.

Then touch the torma to the temple at the left ear.

Meditate that this torma, which is no different from Buddha Amoghasiddhi and no different from Karma Ḍākinī, dissolves into your left temple.

With the pristine water  
of Buddha Amoghasiddhi's compassion,

receive the empowerment of great timeless awareness
of accomplishment, the total purity of jealousy.

*kye*
Mother, nonhuman ḍākinī of timeless awareness,
when you take three steps from the north,
you are small in stature and green in color,
surrounded by a hundred thousand action ḍākinīs.
From the wide expanse of the space of phenomena's nature,
compassion's rain clouds cluster—*tip se tip*,
and a rain of blessings flows—*sil li li*.
Please be seated here as my crown ornament.
Once you are seated, please confer blessings.
Machikma, grant your blessing.
Machikma, grant spiritual powers.
Machikma, engender realization.
Machikma, confer supreme empowerment.
Machikma, clear away obstacles.
Machikma, guide me on the path.

Meditate that your afflictive emotion of jealousy is purified and you have received the empowerment of the timeless awareness of accomplishment.

Then hold the torma on the top of the disciples' heads.

This torma upon your head is no different from the Great Mother Perfection of Wisdom with Jomo Lapkyi Drönma on her right surrounded by the hosts of ḍākinīs of the four families; Dampa Rinpoche on her left {420} surrounded by a host of one million adepts; Bhagavān Great Shākya Sage above her surrounded by assemblies of buddhas, bodhisattvas, and arhats of the past, present, and future; and the awareness protector below her surrounded by hosts of an ocean of oath-bound ones. White light comes out of all their physical forms and dissolves into the top of your head. It totally purifies the sludge of all your physical illnesses, bad spirits, negativity, and obscurations. Meditate on your body as a globe of light.

After you say that, recite the lineage supplication and the invocation of one hundred thousand ḍākinīs. Play music and burn incense. Afterward:

> Great Mother Perfection of Wisdom,
> pure as nondual space,
> dharmakāya perfection of the tenth level,
> spontaneously present unconditioned great bliss,
> may every afflictive emotion be purified
> by the pure, pristine water of timeless awareness.[

*oṃ āḥ hūṃ*
Dharmakāya Great Mother Perfection of Wisdom . . . (repeat the names of the lineage gurus) . . . , grant your blessings. Grant your blessings at this very dwelling place. Grant your blessings right now. Grant your blessings quickly. Then the Great Mother and entourage melts into light and dissolves into your body, speech, and mind. Their Minds and your minds are inseparable within the great pervasiveness. All mental proliferations of the three times are severed, so rest relaxed in your own place. That is the blessing based on the torma.

### 3. Authorization[10]

Third is the authorization. Meditate in the sites for your practice of this teaching—graveyards, lone trees, mountain ravines, lake islands, ghost towns, and haunted grounds. Cast out your body as food and supplicate with your voice. As Jomo said:

> Wandering in isolation is the vital point of place.
> Relaxing the four channels is the vital point of body.
> Singing the tunes of experience is the vital point of speech.
> Eradicating beliefs is the vital point of mind.[11] {421}

"Place" is explained as graveyards and so forth. It states in the *Two-Part [Hevajra Tantra]*:

> Lone trees, graveyards,
> abodes of the *mamo*, at night,

> or in isolated outskirts,
> there it is said to be excellent to meditate.[12]

"The vital point of the body" means to freely cast out (*khres se skyur*) the body without concern, like an empty house where the owner has died. Jomo said:

> Rest the body in the way of a corpse;
> rest in the way of being ownerless.[13]

"Singing the tunes of experience is the vital point of speech" is explained as occasionally supplicating the guru and singing little tunes of meditative experience. "The vital point of mind" means to rest in the meditative equipoise that severs all mental concepts of the three times. Lama Döndrup said:

> It is taught to rest in equipoise, buoyant, loose, amazed, and tranquil.[14]

Lama Nyen said:

> It is taught to settle the consciousness without contrivance or fabrication in its own fresh fashion and it is self-liberated.

Jomo said:

> Uncontrived mind is bliss; undisturbed water is limpid.

And:

> Transparent without love and hate,
> buoyant without trepidation,
> engaged without doing something,
> amazed without subject-object clinging.[15]

And:

> Rest the mind in the way of the sky.
> As a candle unmoved by wind,
> rest in the way of clarity with no thought.
> As an ocean unmoved by ships,
> rest in a way serenely limpid.[16]

Lord Dampa Rinpoche said:

Doing is doom.
Ruminating is ruin.
Rest in your own way
and be self-liberated.

The very mind that is resting in equipoise free of conceptual elaboration is also called the dharmakāya of inseparable ground and result. First, it is clarity unobscured by anything. In the end, there is no place to go. Brilliant, because nothing at all exists. {422} Aware, because unimpeded expression arises anywhere. First, there is no object that comes. In the middle there is no place that [something] abides. In the end, there is no object that departs. So it is freedom since forever from birth, cessation, and abiding. Although it dwells together with the phenomena of cyclic existence, it is not shrouded by them. Although the phenomena of transcendence are not accomplished, it is impossible to be apart from them. If you wonder exactly what are the characteristics of that: there is an essence, but do not hold to it; empty while appearing, it is appearing while empty; true and false do not exist at all, like the moon in water. In that sense, it says in the *Two-Part*:

Not true, not false, thus everything
is like the moon in water.
Through desire the yoginī knows.[17]

That is the instruction of the practice of the authorization.

## IV. Concluding Practices

The disciples do whatever offerings and homages they like. The master dissolves the three syllables *oṃ āḥ hūṃ* into the feast. From that, five-colored lights that are the nature of the five awarenesses dissolve into the feast substances. Offer it thinking that it is the elixir of timeless awareness and do the feast blessing and the feast serving. Sprinkle the feast and dedicate the torma. Perform the abbreviated offering and praise. Partake of the feast. Gather the leftovers, dedicate them, and throw them out. Do the dedication [of merit], the request for forbearance for omissions and additions, and the amendment. Then you, in the aspect of Mother Jomo, split off from the heart of Great Mother, and the awareness being departs. You then rest as long as you can without a frame of reference. Say whatever prayers of auspiciousness are appropriate.

This process for the authorization of the blessing precepts in the instructions of Object Severance Mahāmudrā is based on an examination of the teachings and goodness of the light rays of the speech of all the learned gurus of Object Severance, and on the great source texts of Severance, and on the goodness of obtaining the teachings of Jomo and all the others, and on the commentary (*ṭīkā*) of the second omniscient one, Rangjung Dorje.[18] It was arranged according to the practices of the gurus by the Object Severance practitioner Ratnasiṃha in order to gather all the basic practices into one place that would be easy to understand.

Let it be said here:

Many are the dharma traditions of emptiness, the Mother. {423}
An assortment has spread here in the Land of Snows
by teachers who have many theories that are not unified.
Some understand it as the empty nothingness.
Some understand it as the object of fixation on entities.
Some understand only the permanence of entities.
They are self-made scoundrels of delusion.
Without realization, a few enter into the path of delusion.
They don't do Object Severance; they teach their own dharma systems.
They don't understand practice; they make a string of concepts.
They abandon nonreferential [practice] and develop referential malicious mind.
They generate the disease of five poisons while curing the diseases of the four elements.
Without severing the root of delusion, they wander anywhere
and teach various perverse Severance anywhere in the country.
They gather an entourage of many fools and say, "This is Severance"
while teaching a malicious attitude toward the demons.
They apply noxious substances and put pressure on the gods and demons.
They destroy cliffs, cut trees, and disturb lakes for no reason,
and while fearing death in their minds say this with their mouths:
"Take me, raise him, do transgressive meditation, priest."
While anger, desire, and bad thoughts swirl inside,

they say, "You don't need anything; everything is mind."
Not understanding the ultimate nature of emptiness,
these enthroned teachers confuse a few fools.
They see them doing four empowerments of parāmitā Severance.
With no idea of the difference between Sutra and Mantra,
these rogues who fabricate their own [dharma]
will receive predictions for a long sojourn in the hell realms.

This authorization precept that accords with the sources
is for the purpose of countering them and for myself and others.
I compose this authoritative stainless Severance precept
with the net of a thousand light rays of esoteric instruction,
in accordance with the lineage teachings of the Great Mother,
Lapdrön, and so on; I forsake a desirous mind.
Guru, Great Mother, please forgive
any small contradictions and confusions.
By this virtue, may all migrators realize mahāmudrā.

May virtue increase.

# 14. Object Severance Empowerment Known as Opening the Sky Door[1]

## Tāranātha

Venerable Tāranātha (Grol ba'i mgon po, 1575–1635) was one of the great polymaths of Tibet. At the age of one year he declared himself to be the Jonang master Kunga Drölchok (1507–1566) and was formally recognized as Kunga Drölchok's reincarnation when he was four. He studied with disciples of Kunga Drölchok and received transmissions of all the schools, especially the Jonang and Shangpa lineages. He learned Sanskrit and studied with Indian yogins and scholars in Tibet, one of whom, Buddhaguptanātha, became his principal master. Tāranātha's advancement of Dolpopa's stunning philosophy of *zhentong*, or Great Madhyamaka, earned him dubious notoriety with the Gelukpa hierarchy under the fifth Dalai Lama, and his support for the rulers of Tsang, who opposed Gelukpa rule, ultimately resulted in the confiscation of Jonangpa monasteries in central Tibet and the suppression of Tāranātha's works. Nevertheless, Tāranātha remains a towering figure in Tibet for his activities and huge literary legacy.

Of that enormous output, surprisingly few of Tāranātha's texts are devoted to Severance—a total of merely fifty pages or so—and his autobiography mentions the transmission of Severance only a few times.* What connection Tāranātha did have with the practice of Severance can probably be attributed mainly to his predecessor, Kunga Drölchok. That master compiled an anthology of one hundred eight different lineage practices, *The Hundred Guides of Jonang*, of which Severance is number six. This work is reprinted in volume 18 of *The Treasury of Precious Instructions* and indeed may have been the prototype for Jamgön Kongtrul's own vast, eclectic

*Tāranātha, *Collected Works. rJe btsun Tā ra nā tha'i gsung 'bum*, vol. 1, p. 54.

collection. In any case, Kongtrul's reverence for and deep connection to Tāranātha are evident everywhere in his work. The eclectic movement (*ris med*) in eastern Tibet spearheaded by Kongtrul helped to revive the Jonang tradition and *zhentong* view. Tashi Chöpel's *Record of Teachings Received* notes that Kongtrul received the blessing empowerments of profound Severance of Evil Object in the Gyaltang tradition of the great adept Samten Özer based on Tāranātha's *Object Severance Empowerment Known as Opening the Sky Door.** Its inclusion here ensured the continuation of this lineage of Severance up to the present.[2]

---

*namo guru*

## [Preliminaries]

If you wish to confer the Object Severance known as Opening the Sky Door, arrange a mandala of a four-petaled lotus with colored heaps in the [four] directions. Upon that, on a torma stand,[3] place five round white tormas with ornaments of butter, meat, and molasses. Around the circumference, arrange whatever offering tormas you have provided. Send out the obstructor torma as usual, and then with whatever ritual is appropriate, dedicate the tormas for the exorcism of obstructors and for direction protection and the preliminary torma for the ground masters. The consecration of offerings is as usual. When refuge and arousing the awakening mind have been done as preliminaries, recite the sutra[4] as much as you can. These are the preliminaries. To summarize:

Gather well the necessities and conditions,
arrange them well, exorcise obstructors, send out torma,
consecrate offerings, give refuge, arouse the mind,
recite sutra: these are the preliminaries.

Then, purify into emptiness both the self- and front visualizations with the *svabhāva* mantra.

*Tashi Chöpel, *Record of Teachings Received,* p. 772.

Instantly out of emptiness a dharma source appears. The palace of the Blazing Graveyard is inside. In its center is a multicolored, four-petaled lotus. {363}

*oṃ buddha ḍākinī oṃ*—white buddha ḍākinī in the center with a wheel topknot.
*oṃ vajra ḍākinī hūṃ*—blue vajra ḍākinī in the east with a vajra topknot.
*oṃ ratna ḍākinī traṃ*—yellow jewel ḍākinī in the south with a jewel topknot.
*oṃ padma ḍākinī hrīḥ*—red lotus ḍākinī in the west with a lotus topknot.
*oṃ karma ḍākinī āḥ*—green action ḍākinī in the north with a crossed-vajra topknot.

They all have three eyes and hold ḍamarus, skulls, and khatvaṃgas. Their feet move into dance poses. They are adorned with all the ornaments of jewels and bones and have retinues of a hundred thousand of their own kind.

*hrīḥ mahāḍākinī oṃ āḥ hūṃ*

I appear as Machik, ḍākinī of timeless awareness, in front of the principal one, similar to her except for ringing a bell in my left hand.

Then offer incense and play the instruments. Recite, "From the palace of pure devotion . . ." to ". . . guards of the doctrine and protectors of dharma."

*oṃ guru deva ḍākinī aṅgku shajaḥ pāsha hūṃ sphoṭa baṃ ghaṇḍe hōḥ*

Light radiates from the seed syllable in the heart, and the assembly of sugatas, an ocean of victors, arrive here for the purpose of empowerment. May you be pleased by the various offerings.

Just as, as soon as he was born,
the gods bathed him,
just so, with pure divine water,

we are empowered.
*oṃ sarva tathāgata abhiṣekata samaya] śrī ye hūṃ*

Vairochana crowns the head of the buddha ḍākinī. Akṣhobhya crowns the head of the vajra ḍākinī. Ratnasambhava crowns the head of the jewel ḍākinī. Amitābha crowns the head of the lotus ḍākinī. Amoghasiddhi crowns the head of the action ḍākinī. I am Machik, ḍākinī of timeless awareness, crowned by the five families on my head.

This offering of sacred divine substance,
pleasing to the mind and without blemish,
I offer to the guru, yidam, and ḍākinī:
Please accept and grant blessings.
*oṃ guru deva ḍākinī arghaṃ pratīccha āḥ hūṃ svāhā*

Similarly, recite from "music" (*rol mo*) until *śabda*, combining this formula [with each offering]. Present the inner offering with:

*oṃ guru deva ḍākinī sarva pañca amṛta oṃ āḥ hūṃ*

If desired, recite from "In the fine wide vessel *bhandha* . . ." (*bhandha snod bzang yangs pa ru* . . .) and so forth, chanting in accordance with the tradition of Nyingma Mantra. Consecrate the tormas in accordance with the manifest iconography (*mngon rtogs*) of whatever yidam is appropriate. The first torma is offered to the guru and yidam inseparable with the torma ritual of oneself as whatever yidam. The second is for the five sets of ḍākinīs. Add *akāro* [and so on] to each of the short mantras for the deity generation above and offer it three times. The third torma for the dharma protectors is offered with their own torma rituals. The fourth is the general torma of the ḍākinīs. The fifth is offered to the ground masters with the torma feast. The sixth is dedicated to the six realms by saying *akāro* . . . six times.

Supplicate for special experiences and realizations to arise in the disciples' mindstreams. All the ritual acts of whatever was conferred on the disciples by means of the preliminary supplication to the lineage gurus should be done by you yourself by means of visualization for the self-entrance. {365} Consecrate the feast substances that were arranged [on the shrine] in accordance with the torma ritual of whatever yidam is being employed, and leave them there. To summarize:

Create deities from emptiness, invite them,
draw them in, bid them enter, seal, present the torma offering,
supplicate, self-enter, consecrate the feast:
this is a general summary of accomplishing the mandala.

Then bring in the disciples. Give them the ablution water, seat them in rows, and distribute and gather the flowers. Do the preliminary dharma explanation and lead them in the mandala offering. After this, lead them in the recitations:

> Vajra master, please heed me.
> Though your mind never leaves the realm of reality,
> you emanate in the form of Vajradhara
> for the purpose of guiding migrators.
> Please grant the profound empowerment conferral
> and turn the wheel of the dharma.
> Please turn the utterly vast,
> unsurpassable wheel of the feast.

Repeat this three times. Then master and disciples all together recite the *Heart of the Perfection of Wisdom* three times, with the averting of evil. Before this there is a custom of sending out an obstructor torma, which you can do if you wish. Then impart the refuge precepts and after that lead them in the recitation:

> All buddhas and bodhisattvas, please heed me. Master, please heed me. I, named *so-and-so*, from this time forward until such time as the essence of awakening is experienced, go for refuge in Lord Buddha, supreme among all bipeds. I go for refuge in the holy dharma that is peace and beyond misery, supreme among all freedoms from desire. I go for refuge in the noble sangha of nonreturners and bodhisattvas, supreme among all assemblies. (Repeat three times.)

Then, for the arousing of awakening mind, say, "Please heed me . . ." as above and then: {366}

> Just as in the past the tathāgatas, the conquerors, the genuine perfect buddhas, and the bodhisattvas dwelling on the high grounds aroused the unsurpassable, genuine, perfect mind of awakening, in that way I, named *so-and-so*, will also arouse the unsurpassable, genuine, perfect mind of awakening from this time forward until such time as the essence of awakening is experienced. Those sentient beings not emancipated I will emancipate. Those not liberated I will liberate. Those not reassured I will reassure. Those not completely beyond misery I will take beyond misery. (Repeat three times.)

There is, of course, a custom of reciting the arousing of the awakening mind of engagement, but it is acceptable not to do that separately. If you prefer an abridged version, do the daily confession from the *Tent*.[5] Alternatively, recite "Buddha, dharma, and supreme assembly . . . ." (*sangs rgyas chos dang tshogs kyi . . .*). That was the preliminary.

### Main Practice

> The actual Opening the Sky Door has two parts: (1) the introduction based on no thing and no elaboration and (2) the introduction based on things and with elaboration.

### 1. The Introduction Based on No Thing and No Elaboration

> You all heard the vital points of the body. Now just breathe naturally. Without any contrivance of fabricating mind, within a tranquil state, observe directly. In that essence, there is no self and other. Likewise, there is no identification of color or shape, outside or inside, body or consciousness, going or coming, and so forth. That very state that is free of arising, cessation, or abiding is itself what makes the arising of everything in samsara and nirvana possible. That precisely is what is known as the ultimate perfection of wisdom.

Thus make the introduction directly upon their abiding state.

> Again, you all, comprehend this well with attention. You must

> look at the condition of what arises to the doors of perception based on the three [aspects] of the arising, ceasing, and abiding of thought. {367} As one thought is generated, observe it and let it go.

Thus, guide them in observation. Again, say this:

> Within the state of the resting mind, when a thought arises, at that very time that it arises there is no identification. The thought arises, and without your stopping it there is a vivid quality. On that very occasion, there is no way to say, "It's like this" about the essence of anything—outside, inside, or in between; seeing, hearing, or knowing. There is also no identification in the time [that thoughts] are still. Again, when a thought vanishes, there is no frame of reference for saying, "The object came up like this," or "It stopped like this." Therefore, all these appearances that arise, abide, and cease are nothing other than just the unblocked doors of perception. This lack of identification is not something new. It is the original abiding nature, all right. Therefore, if you do not recognize it, it is the devil of thought. If you do recognize it, it is called the play of the nature of phenomena.

Thus, say such things as this to explain the introduction briefly or extensively in accordance with the mindstreams of the disciples.

> Without such realization of the abiding nature, the one who occupies this corpse is this cherishing, fixating self. So without a trace of the entangled inflation of cherishing this body, mentally cast far away all [ideas of] harm-doers and elemental spirits. Again, look directly at the essence of the very thoughts of fixated cherishing of your body and mind and say *phaṭ*. They will be transformed in basic space. *phaṭ*

### 2. The Introduction Based on Things and with Elaboration

You all have thoughts going every which way. [Imagine that they have all] gone into two white spheres of light the size of birds' eggs on the two soles of your feet. Then they wend their way upward to the perineum and stay there for a bit [combining into one]. Similarly, [the sphere] moves up through all the doors: the navel, heart, and crown of the head. It stays at the cranial aperture at the crown of the head, ready to emerge. Then say *phaṭ* to send it out and far away. That fully ripened body [that is left] is thrown out as food for the eight kinds [of gods and spirits]. {368} The lucid awareness without identification pervades evenly throughout space. Just relax into that state. *phaṭ*

Of these three imparted visualizations, in the first one the disciples sit in the full lotus posture of meditation. For the second, they squat with the buttocks barely off the ground and the two hands at the heart in the vajra-binding mudra. For the third, they stand up with the balls of the feet on the ground and the palms together on the top of their heads. For all three, the four [limbs'] muscles should be taut and the eyes should be looking up. There is also the custom of playing musical instruments at the end of each of those. At this point there is also the descent of awareness [beings].

Then the permission blessing (*rjes gnang*) of the Body mudra:

This is the ornament that indicates
the six perfections of all ḍākinīs.
Carry that ornament to sever devils.
I confer the empowerment of the six bone ornaments.
*oṃ mahāḍākinī kāya abhiṣiñca hūṃ*

Saying that, drape the six ornaments on the disciples.

The permission blessing of the Speech mantra:

This is the sound of all the ḍākinīs
severing in basic space subject-object grasping.
Utter this sound to sever devils.
I confer the empowerment of *phaṭ*, melody of Speech.
*oṃ mahāḍākinī vāka abhiṣiñca hūṃ*

Say *phaṭ* three times to blend space and awareness.

> This is the meaning of all ḍākinīs'
> ultimate emptiness and compassion.
> Meditate on this meaning to sever devils.
> The empowerment of the meaning of phenomena's nature is
> conferred.
> [*oṃ mahāḍākinī*] *citta abhiṣiñca hūṃ*

> This is the sound of all the ḍākinīs
> gaining control over the three realms.
> Uttering this sound severs devils.
> I confer empowerment with the sound of the hand drum.
> *oṃ mahāḍākinī guṇa abhiṣiñca hūṃ*

Have [the disciples] rattle the ḍamaru.

> This is the language of all ḍākinīs
> revealing apparent existence to be false.
> Translate this language to sever devils.
> I confer the empowerment of the human thighbone.
> *oṃ mahāḍākinī karma abhiṣiñca hūṃ* {369}

Have them blow the [thighbone] trumpet.

> Then the blessing, the descent of the awareness deities. Light rays radiate from the master's heart. They invoke all the buddhas and bodhisattvas in the forms of the five kinds of ḍākinīs. They come from above, below, and all directions and dissolve into all of you. Again from the master's and the front visualized [ḍākinīs'] hearts, immeasurable ḍākinīs of the five families come dancing out. They dissolve and drop into you like rainfall on the ocean.

Then with the sound of instruments, repeat many times the above mantra of the deity generation, adding to the end: *aveśaya a a*. Then say *oṃ sutra tiṣṭha vajra ye svāhā* and place the vajra on their heads and toss flowers to stabilize it. Place the vajra at their hearts and say:

The assembly of five-family ḍākinīs of the three places
perfectly enters into your hearts.
Always make them grant their blessings.
Do not talk of this method to others.

Thus bind them to secrecy.

By the offering of this flower of awareness
to the ḍākinī hosts of timeless awareness,
may the five ḍākinī families protect us
and all devil hosts be liberated in basic space.

Have them offer flowers.

*Ema!* Fortunate, noble children:
Look! Look! Look at this!
Look at this excellent mandala.
You are the family of the ḍākinīs of timeless awareness.
*he vajra paśya*

Thus, encourage them to look.

Reveal the deities to the disciples as they were created in the front visualization. Have them imagine that the five tormas on top of the mandala are Machik, the ḍākinī of timeless awareness, and the entourage of five-family ḍākinīs. Hold the utility vajra in hand, while the master and disciples all sing the supplication. {370} In the actual practice, Gyalwa Döndrup's *Supplication Stirring the Intention*[6] is used. After that, confer the torma empowerment in the usual way and then play the instruments. Then, for the spiritual powers, make sure the disciples each get pieces of the spiritual power substance from the torma. It is said, "Accomplish peaceful [powers] from the grains, enriching from butter, controlling from sugar, and destructive from meat." Afterward, do the promising, mandala, and qualities offerings as usual. To summarize those:

Dharma explanation, mandala, supplication,
obstructor torma, sutra recitation, refuge, and awakening-mind precepts,
two introductions and five permissions,

descent of deities, stabilizing,
binding, tossing flowers,
encouragement to look, revealing the deities,
supplication, torma empowerment, examination of spiritual powers,
and the concluding activities as usual.

Then do the activities from the offering of the first portions of the feast up to the giving of the leftovers torma. After that, do the hundred-syllable mantra, request for forbearance, prayer to depart, absorption of the pledge beings into oneself, aspirations, and auspiciousness prayers.

The supporting rituals, such as the feast in the source texts, were done as in the tradition of Krodhīkālī by the gurus of old. In that, they just used whatever yidam they had been accustomed to generating. As such, there was not a single definite intention. Whatever authentic deity ritual you base it on is acceptable, whether Vārāhī, Nairātmyā, or another similar deity.

This actual practice of the Severance "dharma empowerment conferred on the mind"[7] was spoken by Tāranātha according to the practices of the blessed lineage of gurus, while avoiding all the faults of additions, omissions, enigmas, conflicts, and mistakes.

*śubhaṃ. virtue. oṃ sūtra tiṣṭha vajra svāhā*

# 15. The Required Liturgies on the Occasion of Venerable Tāranātha's Severance Empowerment of Opening the Sky Door in the Gyaltang Tradition[1]

This text is characterized in the Kundeling printing of the *Treasury* as "notes on the lectures of Venerable Jonang Tāranātha," and it follows directly upon the initiation text by Tāranātha, *Object Severance Empowerment Known as Opening the Sky Door*. These notes, arranged by an unnamed compiler, fill in some of the seemingly missing parts of the empowerment ritual, such as the preliminary tormas, supplications, mantras, and other recitations.

The source of the Severance tradition that Jamgön Kongtrul inherited from Tāranātha and Kunga Drölchok is the visionary Samten Özer of Gyaltang.* Samten Özer was a recipient of both the long lineage (*ring brgyud*) of Severance, which he received on five separate occasions, and a direct lineage (*nye brgyud*) from visionary encounters with Machik Lapdrön. His remarkable experiences are recounted in *Nectar of Meaning of the Profound Severance of Evil*,† where he declares himself to be basically identical to Machik. This direct encounter engendered a lineage of teachings that became known as the Gyaltang tradition (*rgyal thang lugs*). It spread widely, particularly in the Jonang, Shangpa, and Kagyu traditions.

*rGyal thang pa bSam gtan 'od zer, who also styled himself as Man of the Charnel Ground (dur khrod pa). I have not been able to ascertain a date for him with certainty; in the long lineage that descends from him, Jonangpa Kunga Drölchok (1507–1566) is sixth in line.

†*bDud gcod zab mo don gyi nying khu* in *bDud gcod zab mo'i skor* (Darjeeling: Lama Dawa and Chopal Lama, 1974), pp. 1–22.

**Preliminaries**

Perform the obstructor torma ritual in the usual way or according to your own source text: Cleanse and purify the torma, bless it with the long mantra of the "sky treasure," and dedicate it with *akāro*. Say:

> *namo*. By the truth of the words of the Buddha, dharma, and sangha; by the truth of the words of the yidam, ḍākinīs, and dharma protectors; and by the power of my mantra, mudra, and meditative absorption, all spirits who would interfere with tonight's presentation of the empowerment of the profound method of Severance and all disrupting types of devils and obstructors: don't stay here, go away!

Expel them with the *sumbha* mantra and strike with *hūṃ* and *phaṭ*. For the common vajra protection circle, say the following mantra and meditate on the meaning of emptiness:

> *oṃ vajra rakṣa rakṣa hūṃ hūṃ hūṃ phaṭ svāhā*

For the direction protectors, cleanse, purify, and bless the torma. Invoke the guests with:

> *oṃ lokapāla saparivāra ākarṣaya jaḥ*

Dedicate the torma by adding *akāro* to that mantra.

Supplicate for desired outcomes with:

> Worldly protectors and your retinues,
> accept this torma that is offered and given.
> We yogins and our retinues . . . (etc.)

For their departure, add [*gaccha*][2] at the end of *saparivāra* . . . {166}

For the ground-master torma, cleanse, purify, and bless. Then invoke the guests with:

> *oṃ bhūmipati saparivāra ākarṣaya jaḥ*

Offer [the torma] by adding *akāro* to the end of *saparivāra* in that same mantra.

Supplicate for desired outcomes with:

> Masters of grounds and masters of places and your retinues . . . (etc.)

For their departure, add *gaccha* to the end of the mantra.

Do the blessing of the offerings as in the general highest yoga tantras and impress the thought of refuge with "Buddha, dharma, sublime assembly. . . ." Afterward, recite the *Heart Sutra* with the exorcism of evil. That is the preliminary practice.

**Main Practice**

For the main practice according to the sources, begin with the invitation:

> Gurus and Jewels, please come here
> from the mansion of pure devotion.
> Yidam deity hosts, please come here
> from the infinite palace of natural purity.
> Vajra ḍākinīs, please come here
> from the pure realm of the vajra.
> Jewel ḍākinīs, please come here
> from the pure realm of blazing jewels.
> Lotus ḍākinīs, please come here
> from the pure realm of the lotus.
> Action ḍākinīs, please come here
> from the pure realm of dragon thunder.
> Buddha ḍākinīs, please come here
> from the pure realm of the wheel.
> Mothers and ḍākinīs, please come here
> from whatever fine place you abide.
> Dharma guards and protectors, please come here
> from the palace of the precious doctrine.
> *oṃ guru deva ḍākinī* . . . (etc.), as usual

Do the torma blessing as in *Saṃvara* or *Vārāhī* or whichever of the highest yoga mother tantras is appropriate. For the first part, the ritual of the yidam torma, do your particular practice or just the generic offering:

*oṃ guru maṇḍala deva gaṇa saparivāra oṃ akāro* . . . (etc.)

The second part is as usual. For the third, if you have a special dharma protector, then do that torma ritual and add the generic offering:

*oṃ śrīvajra dharmapāla saparivāra oṃ akāro* . . . (etc.)

For those, the common [mantras]:

> *oṃ guru maṇḍala deva gaṇa pañca ḍākinī śrīvajra dharmapāla saparivāra arghaṃ* . . . (etc.) for the outer offering. {167}
>
> *oṃ āḥ hūṃ* for the inner offering.

Supplicate for desired outcomes as usual elsewhere:

> Gurus, yidams, ḍākinīs,
> and vajra dharma protectors and retinues,
> accept this torma that is offered and given.
> We yogins and our retinues . . . (etc.)

The supplication before the self-empowerment:

> *phaṭ*
> In the mansion of Akaniṣhṭha dharmadhātu,
> Great Mother Perfection of Wisdom has blessings.
>
> I supplicate the blessed one.
> Mother, I pray to you.
> I pray to the One Mother.
> Great Mother, bless me.
>
> On the mountain of Vulture's Peak,
> Buddha Shākyamuni has blessings.
> (From here on, add the four-line verse from above).

On the Five-Peak Mountain of China,
Mañjushrī Vādasiṃha has blessings.

In the pure realm Arrayed in Turquoise Petals,
Venerable Tārā has blessings.

In the infinite palace of pure bliss-emptiness,
Vajravārāhī has blessings.

In the mansion of the ḍākinī of Oḍḍiyāna,
Sukhasiddhī has blessings.

In the grass hut of India,
Āryadeva has blessings.

At Dingri Langkor of Latö,
Dampa Sangye has blessings.

In the hermitage of Rasa Panglung,[3]
Sönam Lama has blessings.

In the hermitage of Zangri Karmar,
Machik Lapdrön has blessings.

In the hermitage of Gyaltang Chuzang,
Samten Özer has blessings.

In the secluded site of Jangchup Ling,
Namkha Özer has blessings.

In the sacred sites of one hundred haunted retreats,
Shākya Özer has blessings.

In the kingdom of directionless vastness,
Delek Gyaltsen has blessings.

In the presence of the blessed guru,
Önse Chölek has blessings.

In the hermitage of Kharak Samling,
Yikdruk Shepal has blessings.

In the secluded site of Chölung Jangtse,
Venerable Drölchok has blessings. {168}

In the mansion of Draktö Dorje,
Chöku Lhawang has blessings.

In the secluded site of Chölung Demchok,
Lungrik Gyatso has blessings.

In the mansion of Takten Dorje,
Kunga Nyingpo has blessings.

In the sublime site of Chime Drupa,
Kunga Sönam has blessings.

In the secluded site blessed by Dampa,
Kunga Yeshe has blessings.

In the realm of pure dharmadhātu,
Yönten Gönpo has blessings.

In the mansion of Mokchok Dorje,
Kunga Lhundrup has blessings.

At the secluded site of Nyamtok Tarchin,
Chöying Dorje has blessings.

In the mansion of Drowa Dulwa,
Sangye Dorje has blessings.

At the sacred site of Ngedön Nyingpo,
Ngawang Trinle has blessings.

At the seat of Lungrik Mawa,
Chöpel Gyatso has blessings.

At the sanctum site of Khedrup Gyatso,
Kunga Namgyal has blessings.

In the coil of Okmin Tashi,
Jikme Wangpo has blessings.

At the sacred site blessed by ancestors,
Könchok Senge has blessings.

At the dharma school of Rikdröl Dupa,
Könchok Tenchö has blessings.

In the illusory appearance of Lhaden Gazhi,
Döndrup Gyaltsen has blessings.

Upon the seat of the crowning sun and moon,
my root guru has blessings.

In the dharma mansion in my heart,
yidam deities have blessings.

At the twenty-four sacred sites,
heroes and ḍākinīs have blessings.

In the eight great graveyards,
dharma guards and protectors have blessings.

Among participants with pure sacred pledges,
vajra siblings have blessings.

In these sacred sites with blessings,
I pray to you, bless me
to know this rare, free, and endowed life
and take to heart its grand purpose.
Bless me right now. {169}

I pray to you, bless me
to remember death and impermanence

and a sense of urgency in my being.
Bless me right now.

I pray to you, bless me
to mentally relinquish this life
and cast out the body as food.
Bless me right now.

I pray to you, bless me
to keep to haunted retreat sites
and develop love and compassion.
Bless me right now.

I pray to you, bless me
to realize the abiding nature of nonself
and cut off self-fixation at the root.
Bless me right now.

I pray to you, bless me
to pacify the four devils in their own ground
and actualize the three kāyas.
Bless me right now.

I pray to you, bless me
to bind apparent existence into service
and endow all relationships with meaning.
Bless me right now.
Bless me instantly.
Bless me right on this seat.

For the entry torma at the time of the empowerment, the *Supplication Stirring the Intention*:[4]

Mother, when your intention stirs in the east,
with the feelings of unwavering purpose,
your blue-black body radiates rays of light,
your sublime topknot sways back and forth,

the blue silk ribbons of your tiara flutter,
and your bone ornaments swing,
encircled by one hundred thousand vajra ḍākinīs—
Mother Lapdrön, I pray to you.
Dharma Lamp of Enlightenment, I pray to you.
Mistress of experiential realization, I pray to you.
Vista of clear light, I pray to you.
Ḍākinī of timeless awareness, I pray to you.
Great Mother of space, bless me.

Mother, when your intention stirs in the south,
with the feelings of equitable purpose,
your yellow body radiates rays of light,
your golden topknot sways back and forth,
the yellow silk ribbons of your tiara flutter,
and your bone ornaments swing, {170}
encircled by one hundred thousand jewel ḍākinīs—
Mother Lapdrön, I pray to you.
Dharma Lamp of Enlightenment, I pray to you.
Mistress of experiential realization, I pray to you.
Vista of clear light, I pray to you.
Ḍākinī of timeless awareness, I pray to you.
Great Mother of space, bless me.

Mother, when your intention stirs in the west,
with the feelings of flawless, pure purpose,
your red body radiates rays of light,
your coral topknot sways back and forth,
the red silk ribbons of your tiara flutter,
and your bone ornaments swing,
encircled by one hundred thousand lotus ḍākinīs—
Mother Lapdrön, I pray to you.
Dharma Lamp of Enlightenment, I pray to you.
Mistress of experiential realization, I pray to you.
Vista of clear light, I pray to you.
Ḍākinī of timeless awareness, I pray to you.
Great Mother of space, bless me.

Mother, when your intention stirs in the north,
with the feelings of irrational purpose,
your green body radiates rays of light,
your turquoise topknot sways back and forth,
the green silk ribbons of your tiara flutter,
and your bone ornaments swing,
encircled by one hundred thousand action ḍākinīs—
Mother Lapdrön, I pray to you.
Dharma Lamp of Enlightenment, I pray to you.
Mistress of experiential realization, I pray to you.
Vista of clear light, I pray to you.
Ḍākinī of timeless awareness, I pray to you.
Great Mother of space, bless me.

Mother, when your intention stirs in the center,
with the feelings of uncircumscribed purpose,
your white body radiates rays of light,
your conch topknot sways back and forth,
the white silk ribbons of your tiara flutter,
and your bone ornaments swing,
encircled by one hundred thousand buddha ḍākinīs—
Mother Lapdrön, I pray to you.
Dharma Lamp of Enlightenment, I pray to you.
Mistress of experiential realization, I pray to you.
Vista of clear light, I pray to you.
Ḍākinī of timeless awareness, I pray to you.
Great Mother of space, bless me.

Bloody arghaṃ—*khyil li li.*
Flowers of five heads—*to lo lo.*
Smoke of human fat—*chi li li.*
Melted marrow—*ya la la.*
Perfumed rakta—*khyil li li.*
Human-flesh torma—*sam se sam.*
Human-thighbone flute—*kyu ru ru.*
Human-skull drum—*tro lo lo.*
Heroes to the right—*shar ra ra.*
Symbolic language of *phaṭ—sang se sang.*

Heroines to the left—*tip se tip.* {171}
Sonorous song of *hūṃ*—*kyu ru ru.*
Dancing feet—*chem se chem.*
Flourishing hands—*shik se shik.*
Melodious songs of experience—*ur ru ru.*
Mists of blessings—*tu lu lu.*
Seasonal rains of instruction—*si li li.*

Mother Lapdrön, I pray to you.
Dharma Lamp of Enlightenment, I pray to you.
Mistress of experiential realization, I pray to you.
Vista of clear light, I pray to you.
Ḍākinī of timeless awareness, I pray to you.
Great Mother of space, bless me.

Ḍākinī of the vajra family in the east,
I pray to you with fierce faith.
Accept me with immeasurable great compassion
and bless me, your destined child.
Imbue all faithful disciples with the quintessence.

Ḍākinī of the jewel family in the south,
I pray to you with fierce faith.
Accept me with immeasurable great compassion
and bless me, your destined child.
Imbue all faithful disciples with the quintessence.

Ḍākinī of the lotus family in the west,
I pray to you with fierce faith.
Accept me with immeasurable great compassion
and bless me, your destined child.
Imbue all faithful disciples with the quintessence.

Ḍākinī of the action family in the north,
I pray to you with fierce faith.
Accept me with immeasurable great compassion
and bless me, your destined child.
Imbue all faithful disciples with the quintessence.

Ḍākinī of the buddha family in the center,
I pray to you with fierce faith.
Accept me with immeasurable great compassion
and bless me, your destined child.
Imbue all faithful disciples with the quintessence.

Afterward, do the feast offerings and so on from *Vārāhī*, *Chakrasaṃvara*, or whatever source text is appropriate. To do an extended ritual, it is excellent to practice in connection with the feast activity of Object Severance itself. For a short practice, what is here is sufficient. For the main empowerment, it is good to do the introduction (*ngo sprod*) as in the source text of the Gyaltang tradition itself; however, there is nothing of essential meaning missing from what Venerable Tāranātha has taught here. In any case, the long or short arrangement of the liturgy, from the formulation of the motivation and history of the teaching onward, should be done according to the master's discretion.

*maṅgalaṃ*

# Instructions and Guides

# 16. Practice Manual on the Profound Severance of Evil Object

## Karmapa Rangjung Dorje[1]

The third Karmapa, Rangjung Dorje (1284–1339), had a special connection with the Severance teachings and was instrumental in codifying them and bringing them into the Karma Kagyu lineage by connecting them with the mahāmudrā. He received the complete teaching cycles of Dampa Sangye at the age of eighteen (*Red Annals*) and Machik Lapdrön's Severance teachings from Lama Kunga Döndrup (Kun dga' don grub). However, in most Severance lineages and in the colophon here, he received the transmission from Lama Namtsowa ("Guru of Sky Lake"), one of his teachers at Tsurpu Monastery, whose full name was Namtso Dopa Mikyö Dorje (gNam mtsho do pa Mi bskyod rdo rje);* he was also known as Repa Sangye Nyima (Ras pa Sangs rgyas nyi ma). He heard many Severance teachings from Khambuyale's disciple Jñānajvala. Thus he is only the third in the lineage after Machik herself. Most of Rangjung Dorje's works on Severance are found in volume 11 of his collected works, with only two included here in *The Treasury of Precious Instructions.*

*namo prajñāpāramitā*
Completely quieting all conceptual elaborations,
not entering into the duality of existence and peace,
showing the middle way free of extremes,
Mother of the victors, having bowed to you,

*See *Collected Histories of the Glorious Zurmang Kagyu,* p. 376.

I write the instructions for cutting off discursive thought
in order to sever by the meaning of noninflation
the devil of dualistic clinging totally entangled
by habitual patterns since beginningless time.

There are three stages in taking up the practice of esoteric instructions in severing devils: the preliminary, the main part, and the conclusion.

## I. Preliminary

To embark, there are the esoteric instructions of going for refuge and engendering the awakening mind. With the desire to practice this, sit down cross-legged in a suitable place. Place your hands in the equipoise mudra and think, "In order to liberate all sentient beings equaling space from the suffering of cyclic existence and establish them in omniscient buddhahood, I will practice the esoteric instructions of the perfections." {175}

Meditate that in front of you in the sky there is a throne encrusted with various jewels. Upon that, on a seat of lotus and moon, is the Great Mother Perfection of Wisdom. She is the color of smelted gold with one face and four arms. Her upper right hand holds a vajra, the upper left a volume of text, and the two lower hands take the position of equipoise. She is adorned with all the precious ornaments. Meditate on the completely perfect buddha on the crown of her head, adorned with the thirty-two major excellent marks, the eighty minor exemplary marks, and the regalia of the nirmāṇakāya. Around that meditate vividly on all the buddhas and bodhisattvas, together with the root and lineage gurus and so on, inseparable from Lady Lapdrön.

### A. Common Offering and Refuge

Make offerings of flowers and so forth, and mentally emanate as many as possible. Think that you are offering exquisite forms, sounds, smells, tastes, and textures that exist in limitless infinite world realms. {176} Meditate that all sentient beings prostrate and go for refuge.

If you prefer elaboration, add the seven-branch prayer. If you don't like it, then mentally confess negativity, rejoice in merit, request the turning of the dharma wheel, supplicate for the buddhas not to transcend misery, and depend on the path of totally omniscient enlightenment. With that yearning aspiration, [recite this] three times:

> From now until attaining totally omniscient buddhahood, I and all sentient beings equaling the reaches of space go for refuge in the Great Mother, the Perfection of Wisdom. We go for refuge in the perfect genuine Buddha Shākyamuni. We go for refuge in the buddhas of the ten directions. We go for refuge in the dharma. We go for refuge in the sangha. We go for refuge in the precious guru together with the lineage. May all sentient beings be liberated from suffering and the causes of suffering and be established in great bliss.

### B. Uncommon [Method] of Offering the Body

Think of your own body as food of a hundred flavors, white and round as Supreme Mountain. First cut off the head and offer it to the guru and Jewels. Imagine that they partake of it with delight. In the same way offer all the limbs, extremities, and inner organs. Furthermore, if you like elaboration, give to the protectors of the holy dharma, the eight classes of gods and spirits, the creditors, and all the guests [invited out] of compassion and imagine that each of them gets whatever they desire in their domain. {177} Then, without reference to yourself as the offerer, the act of offering, or all the offering substances, including your body, rest in equipoise in the state of total quiescence of all elaborations. This is the ultimate going for refuge. Abiding in that is the intention of a buddha. Meditate diligently on this esoteric instruction of the entry into going for refuge and arousing the awakening mind.

## II. Main Part

This has three parts: (1) instructions for meditation without recollection[2] and mentally doing nothing, for those of superior intellect; (2) instructions for separating body and mind, for the middling; and (3) the practice of casting out the body as food and severing conceptual elaborations, for the inferior.

### A. Superior

We all have failed to cut off these inflating thoughts throughout cyclic existence without beginning. Based on thoughts fixated on rejecting and accepting samsara and nirvana, we experience the tangible objects of form, sound, smell, taste, and texture directly with our senses, and intangible positive and negative mental sensations. Without our realizing it, they become binding, and through that power they become the devils of the death lord, the afflictive emotions, and the aggregates. Fixation on exaltation based on attachment to the path's meager qualities is the devil of being a god's child. Once you understand that this has occurred from incorrect thinking about all of these, the remedy is to be without the embellishment of conceptual thought. In the ultimate sense, there is no established existence whatsoever to the harm and harming of gods and demons, self and others, and samsara and nirvana. Also, in the conventionally true sense, [these phenomena are] without concept, appearing while lacking inherent nature. As it is said, "for example, like a dream." Once you know that, meditate without thinking, without examining, without projecting, and without concentrating. {178} All the sutras and tantras say that if you abide in this, it is the Buddha's intent. That is the instruction of meditation without recollection and without mental activity.

### B. Middling

The esoteric instruction for separating body and mind has two parts, but the blessing, Opening the Sky Door, can be learned elsewhere. For the regular meditation, take a comfortable posture, or stand up, and so forth. Meditate that on the soles of your feet the essence of wind-mind is a white vital-essence drop the size of a bird's egg, appearing yet without intrinsic nature, like the moon's reflection in water. It shoots up by stages and emerges out of the crown of your head to blend with space as you utter *phaṭ*. With no discursive thought engaged in the mind, whichever of the four daily activities you are doing, do not waver from that state of nonthought.

### C. Inferior

Now, in the third there are two parts: the root is the practice of casting out the body as food, and the branches are to engage the proliferation of discursive thoughts.

### 1. The Practice of Casting Out the Body as Food

When beginners are doing the practice, if fear, anxiety, and thoughts of gods and demons arise, or if there is attachment and clinging to the body, in general cast it out as food. For this, meditate as much as the mind can manage on your body as white and round.[3] In front of you are the eight classes of spirits, creditors, and so on, headed by those nonhuman beings that cause you harm. Meditate clearly on all of them, and cultivate this intention:

> Since beginningless time I have taken innumerable bodies under the power of ignorance. They have only been meaningless. Now again this body, which is made up of thirty-two impure substances from crown to sole, will quickly disintegrate. This time I will make a gift of the body in order to realize its essence and in order that I and {179} all sentient beings equal to space will completely consummate the perfection of generosity.

Thinking that, imagine that you cut off your own head and cast it out in the midst of all those spirits. Likewise cast out and give away everything: the five solid and five hollow viscera, limbs, extremities, and so forth. "Meat lovers, eat the flesh! Blood lovers, drink the blood!" Giving to the lovers of bones, skin, feet, brains, sense organs, viscera, and so forth, imagine that they partake of it. Then rest in equipoise without referencing any of it: the recipients, the self that gives, and the body that is given. This is the practice of the bodhisattvas. It says in the *Verse Summary*:

> [Bodhisattvas] would give up their head and limbs without
>   hesitating.
> Knowing that all phenomena are empty and hollow,
> if they wish to completely give up their own flesh,
> what need to mention giving up external things at that point?[4]

This is the general practice of casting out the food. The specific practice of casting out food is to cut off whatever is occurring, such as sickness and so on, by visualizing it and casting it out many times. Afterward, rest directly in the abiding nature as described above.

## 2. The Branches

In order to clear up obstacles, such as sickness and spirits, and for enhancement, when roaming through haunted grounds, take up the practices of "Severing Delusion" (*'khrul gcod*) and those from the seventh of the *Steps of Vital Points.*[5] In going to areas of nonhuman beings' activities or their destinations, the superior individual will go at dusk without trepidation. The middling goes at noon and stays wherever it is pleasant. The inferior should carefully examine the place and then stay there. {180} In general, if fixating thoughts of self and other, gods and demons, and faults and qualities are not cut off, even if one goes to a haunted place it is of no use. Although it is certainly the case that if thoughts are severed, wherever one dwells is the same, nevertheless, having gone to those dwelling places of fierce gods and demons, [the spirits] can't bear it and become apprehensive about being made into a meal, so many apparitions will occur. Regarding those, the superior practitioner understands that they are mental apparitions and rests in their invalidity, the middling separates body from mind, and the inferior practices casting out the body as food as described above. Thus the circumstances turn into spiritual powers. When you understand that everything is a mental apparition, you attain the confidence of fearing nothing whatsoever. [But you could get] conceited about your practice due to cutting off some devils. If you become fixated on your joy and bloated mind at that time, then [it is a case of] medicine turning to poison, so do not accept or reject anything.

Now, there are four parts to the actual branches: the manner in which apparitions occur, evidence of success, the way to pacify temporary obstacles, and the instructions on not regressing.

### a. The Manner in Which Apparitions Occur

Although many are explained, they can be subsumed into three: actual, felt, and dreamed apparitions. Actual [events] are all of these: humans and so on beating you, unjustly afflicting abuse, and so on; rendering praise, veneration, or extolling your qualities, and so forth; tigers, wolves, and so forth displaying ferociousness; lightning, hail, gale winds, leprous corpses, and so on.

As for felt experiences, there is nothing that does not occur: fear, anxiety, the appearances of fire, water, wind, and earthquakes, flesh-eating cannibals, and so forth—one could not speak of them all. Also, gods and gurus and nonhumans and so forth making prophecies.

Dream apparitions are limitless and cannot be written about here. {181} In short, all of these are nothing other than the apparitions of your own mind.

### b. Evidence of Success

The immediate evidence of success is the subsiding of apparitions and a sense of well-being, clear consciousness, respectful bowing of humans and nonhumans, and so forth. The ultimate evidence of success is that although things occur, they occur as apparitions of the mind. Though there is consciousness, it is consciousness of mental apparitions. Faithful devotion to the guru and Buddha is born. Compassion for all sentient beings arises. Ultimately, when freedom from all elaboration has arisen directly in your being, it is the evidence that you have been successful.

### c. The Way to Pacify Temporary Obstacles

For superior practitioners, obstacles don't occur. For the average practitioner, they occur but disappear through the understanding that they are not truly existent. For the inferior practitioner, when you first meditate, even if humans and other beings cause obstacles to meditation through whatever good or bad means, you should recognize them and not fall under their power. If fear and so forth occur, [contemplate] what it is that is feared. Is earth feared, or water, or fire, or wind, or is space feared? If it is somehow all of those that you fear, [remember that] there is no place anywhere that all of them are absent. On the ultimate level, even the buddhas do not see anything that could harm the mind. On the relative level, how could the illusory ever harm illusion? When you rest directly in that contemplative experience, it is cleared up.

If somehow you don't have the direct experience and are beset by hopes and fears, at first do not roam in haunted retreats. Rather, apply yourself to virtuous activities. In general, obstacles are cleared up just by the casting-out of food and so forth described above.

### d. The Instructions on Not Regressing

Mere recollection suffices. Furthermore, if you hold the bad as being only bad, you regress (*ldog*). If you flee in fear of external circumstances, you regress. If you fixate on the difficulty of the temporary evidence of success, you regress. Therefore, once you know that absolutely everything is without true existence {182} and do not give in to the power of discursive thought, you will not regress. In general, everything that has not become the path of buddhahood is mistaken (*log pa*), and if it has become the path it is unmistaken.

Some people say that for suppression practices (*log non*),[6] [you should] disturb springs, cut down trees, and cause avalanches. No matter what you do about each [instance of] evil ones and such, there will be no apparitions and it only causes further sickness[7] and pain. The yogin never in any way does anything whatsoever without purpose. To do so would be to contravene the vows of a bodhisattva.

## III. Conclusion

The conclusion has two parts: the sacred pledges and the benefits. The sacred pledges in general are not to contravene the vows of individual liberation and of the bodhisattva. The temporary sacred pledges at the time of practicing Severance are no god offerings, no demon beatings, no hope for nirvana, no fear of samsara—freedom from all conceptual thought. As for the benefits, it says in the *Verse Summary*:

> Whoever makes the perfection of wisdom their protector,
> who respectfully holds and comprehends this,
> will not be afflicted by poison, weapons, fire, or water.
> Evil and devils will find no opportunity.[8]

The ultimate practice of the Object Severance of the perfection of wisdom is the combination of the work of the holy gurus and my own personal experiences, set forth by the one named Rangjung Dorje in the mountain retreat of Lhateng.

*iti*

Here is the poem:

Alas, beings at the end of time!
The meaning of this perfection
is the total quiescence of elaboration.
Do not create dualistic notions about duality.

Thus will you know the meaning of Severance.
Upon examination, it is understood this way
in three aspects of outer and inner and secret.
Outwardly, nondharma is nonvirtue:
killing, stealing what is not given,
sexual misconduct, gossip, slander, {183}
lying, harsh words, envy,
malice, wrong views—these ten nonvirtues
are abandoned in order to practice Severance daily,
and their antidotes, the ten virtues, increase.
This is held to be outer Severance.
Inwardly, the aggregates, constituents, and sense bases,
unrealized, are the devils binding you to samsara.
In order to cut them off,
realize that form is like foam,
feelings are impermanent as bubbles,
perceptions are like seeing watery mirages,
formations are similar to the plantain's pith,
consciousness is like an illusion,
sound is the nature of echoes,
smell, taste, and textures are all
the same as the dew on the grass.
That realization severs the clinging.
That is held to be inner Severance.
Secretly, the abiding ignorance,
with its neutral formations,
is taken as the root of samsara.
In order to conquer this troublemaker,
realize that the clinger, like an illusionist,
clings to the illusion-like objects.
Not lies, not truth, not both.
That very inexpressible meaning,
not meditation but familiarization,
cuts off the belief in the transitory collection.
I understand this to be the supreme Severance.
Those not knowing this meaning in this way
say, "I have the supreme instruction."
Based on the courage of a braggart,

such an individual who causes harm
to vermin and lesser ghosts
is carried off by the demon of concepts.
Some, in whom a bit of experience has arisen
based on clearing away lesser diseases and spirits,
arrogantly claim, "There is no dharma besides this."
They are possessed of wrong views.
Some, not realizing the meaning here,
speak out wrongly against Severance.
Both of these accumulate the karma of rejecting dharma.
Beings are terribly afraid of this,
as occurs in sutras, but is not told here.
Therefore, all you sublime individuals,
do not ponder the words; focus on the meaning
and straightforwardly enter the middle way. {184}
The victorious ones teach in this way.
These are the words spoken again and again
by the one with the name Rangjung Dorje.

The poem condensing the meaning of Severance is finished.

The lineage is: Genuine perfect Buddha, Mañjushrī Lion of Speech, Āryadeva, Indian Dampa, Lapdrön, Khambuyale,[9] Jñānajvala, Namtsowa,[10] and Rangjung Dorje.

*Sarvamaṅgalam*. Virtue!

# 17. White Crystal Mirror

## *Notes on the Guru's Teaching Tradition of the Visualization Sequence for Severance Feast Activities "Endowed with All Qualities"*[1]

Tenzin Namdak

White Crystal Mirror is a detailed exposition on how to put into practice the Holy Dharma Severance of Evil Object, with instructions for the visualizations of both casting out the body as food and the feast activities, written down according to the oral tradition of the fourth Trungpa Rinpoche, Kunga Namgyal. This is the first of the many texts in this collection that are particularly connected with the famous Zurmang tradition of Severance.

A sublineage of the Kagyu, the Zurmang tradition maintains a significant link to the source of that lineage, the Indian mahāsiddha Telopa. According to the *Collected Histories of the Glorious Zurmang Kagyu*, the lineage is held in common with the Karma Kagyu for thirteen generations, up through the fifth Karmapa, Dezhin Shekpa (1384–1415), before it branches off with the founder of Zurmang Monastery, Drung Mase (Drung rma se bLo gros rin chen, 1386–1423), posthumously identified as the first Garwang incarnation. But the history of the Severance transmission in particular is traced to the third Karmapa, Rangjung Dorje (1284–1339), who had received it from Namtsowa Mikyö Dorje. From him, it passed eventually to the fourth Trungpa, the great Kunga Namgyal (1567–1629), who received even more transmissions from his own father, Adro Chöpa Sangye Tashi.

It was Kunga Namgyal who codified the special Severance tradition that has been practiced at the Zurmang monasteries in eastern Tibet ever since. The *Record of Teachings Received* lists sixty-eight separate practice texts of Zurmang, the first of which is called *Brief Synopsis of Visualization Sequence for Severance Feast Activities "Endowed with All Qualities"* (*Tshogs las yon tan kun ldan gyi dmigs rim nyung ngur bsdus pa*), clearly related to the text here. *Endowed with All Qualities* appears to be the basic Zurmang Severance practice that has been enhanced by the many liturgies and explanations that followed, such as those found in this collection. It should be noted, however, that the general title *Endowed with All Qualities* (*yon tan kun ldan*) is very close to other Severance texts called *Source of All Qualities* (*yon tan kun 'byung*), such as the one in this volume compiled by the fourteenth Karmapa, Tekchok Dorje, and that even the current text is titled with the latter (*kun 'byung*) in the *Dingri Volumes*. It is not clear whether this is a mistake, or the terms *endowed with* (*ldan*) and *source of* (*'byung*) are interchangeable, or the two represent different sets of instruction. There is, however, a great deal of overlap between those two texts in this volume.

The lineage of instructions within Zurmang continues from Kunga Namgyal through seven or eight masters down to the author of this text, Bengen Tenzin Namdak (Ban rgan bsTan 'dzin rnam dag). Though he signs this work as "Old Monk" (ban rgan), he was better known as the Realized One, Tokden Tenzin Namdak. He studied with many great masters of the eighteenth century, including his root guru, the thirteenth Karmapa, Sangye Dudul Dorje (1733–1797), and continued to practice and teach until his death as a not-so-old monk of sixty-two. Details of his realizations, though unfortunately not those concerning his literary production, are recorded in his biography, *Festival of Fortunate Faith: The Life of the Hidden Buddha Tenzin Namdak*.

Tenzin Namdak reports that the inspiration and in fact the command to write this version of the Severance practice *Endowed with All Qualities* was the "supreme Garwang incarnation." In the various lineage lists, that appears to be the sixth in this important Zurmang incarnation line, named either Chökyong Namgyal or Chökyong Gyurme (or both!). After Tenzin Namdak, these instructions were passed to Lhalung Karma Desal and then to Karma Tekchok Tenpel, who was Jamgön Kongtrul's ordination preceptor as well as his source for this lineage.

All the instructions from this point on in this collection deal with the myriad specific details of visualization and liturgy for the practice of offering one's corpse as food for various "guests"—in other words, what Kongtrul has called the subsidiary or postmeditation practice. It seems that the core practice of the meaning of the Mother, Perfection of Wisdom, and the blending of intrinsic awareness and space was eclipsed over time by this more exciting ritual now identified as Severance.

Recollecting even her name liberates
from the bonds of existence and peace
and establishes one in the genuine state:
I bow to the guru, mother of the victors.

This is a synopsis of the essential esoteric instructions on how to put into practice the profound meaning of the Holy Severance of Evil Object. There are practical instructions for the visualization sequences of both casting out the body as food and the feast activities, written down according to the oral tradition of Venerable Kunga Namgyal's sequence of practice.[2] For this [project], I seek the guru ḍākinī's permission and supplicate for blessings.

Arrange the torma offerings for the feast assembly on the shrine, such as the primary torma (*phug gtor*) and so forth as described elsewhere.[3] After the elixir consecration, preliminary torma, and consecration of the offerings, the main practice is as follows:

## I. Arousing the Mind of Awakening

The aspiration is the thought "I will take up the practice of the Holy Severance of Evil Object so that I and all sentient beings equaling the reaches of space attain the state of genuine complete buddhahood." Then the actual practice is the engagement. {203} In the first case [of the aspiration], thinking that once you yourself have attained buddhahood then you will bring all beings to that state is like a sovereign; thinking that you yourself and others will attain buddhahood at the same time is like a sea captain; and wanting to establish sentient beings in the state of buddhahood first and then yourself is like a shepherd. With whichever of those attitudes is suitable to your own temperament, think, "All sentient beings, primarily the eight kinds of spirits that are here, must have happiness and be free of suffering and then attain the state of the supreme Great Mother. To that end, I will take up the practice of the profound Object Severance."

These are the eight spirits (*gdon*):

1. Hateful enemies (*sdang ba'i dgra*) are those who have a negative intention of actual inappropriate behavior, such as killing, cutting, beating, and striking you, or robbing your wealth and disputing you, or slandering and criticizing you, and so forth.

2. Harmful obstructors (*gnod pa'i bgegs*) are those who rob you of life, body, wealth, and so forth through inevident methods.

3. Interfering conditions (*bar du gcod pa'i rkyen*) are those that cause you to engage obstacles by preventing progress on the path {204} of whatever major or minor enterprise you wish to accomplish in the near or distant future.

4. Karmic spirits (*las kyi gdon*) are the very embodiment of the habitual patterns of dualistic delusion of your lack of recognition of yourself since beginningless cyclic existence until this present moment. This is the fixation on the characteristics of subject and object experienced as the various feelings of joy and sorrow in the karmic manifestations of each of the six kinds of beings. This refers to the ignorance that arises together with the continuous revolution of the wheel of twelve interdependent links, or the habitual patterns of dualistic delusion—the essence of the four devils.

5. Body spirits (*lus kyi gdon*) refer to the manifestation of diseases of wind, bile, or phlegm that circulate from the hair tips to the toenails in this flesh-and-blood body aggregate that was generated by the positive and negative habitual patterns of that dualistic delusion.

6. Spirits of place (*gnas kyi gdon*) refer to the helpful or harmful gods and demons that are the general or particular inhabitants who live in the actual place of their own abode, including their bed. Subject-object delusion manifests objectively as the external five elements. The whole world is included in them, from the four continents, Supreme Mountain, and so forth down to the individual regions, mountains, valleys, forests, graveyards, rivers, lakes, temples, stupas, and so forth.

7. Foremost are father (*pha*), who generates the seed of the body and life force, and

8. mother (*ma*), who creates the perfect interdependent causes and conditions.

So then, within that state of aroused aspiration described above, and with the pride of being the primordial dharmakāya Great Mother, clearly perfect with ornaments and accessories, strike the open end of the thighbone trumpet against the left palm. Say, "Fear not" with the first strike, "Be not afraid" with the second, and "Verily be not afraid" with the third. Imagine that all those beings hear that sound. {205} Then blow the thighbone and say *phaṭ* three times. The first time, it is the very sound of the Great Mother dharmakāya for those guests. Imagine that as soon as they hear you say, "Hey, listen!" (*kye nyon cig*), those guests stop whatever it is they were doing and listen intently. Think that when they hear you say, "Gather here!" (*'dus shig*), they start gathering with great joy, like the destitute finding refuge. Then imagine that when they hear you say, "Gather quickly" (*myur du 'dus shig*), they completely surround you like mists shrouding the mountain, like a rush of vultures converging on a carcass, like flies swarming over rotten meat, or like spectators gathering at a funeral. Imagine that after they gather like that, your father is to your right, your mother to your left, and around those two are gathered the guests of the six realms. In front and sort of below you are arrayed whichever is foremost of the spirits of place or body, and hateful enemies, harm-doers, interfering conditions, and so forth—all the kinds of guests that were described above. Imagine them being happily absorbed, without hurting one another, in a calm atmosphere of mind and body.

During daily practice, meditate that the karmic spirits surrounded by creditors are in front of you, the body spirits surrounded by harm-doers are in the middle, and the spirits of place surrounded by embodied enemies are behind. In special practices dedicated to subduing your own or others' sickness, the body spirits and entourage are in front, the spirits of place with retinue are in the middle, and the karmic spirits with retinue are behind. In the context of mountain discipline, cemeteries, and so forth, the spirits of place with retinue are in front, the body spirits with retinue are in the middle, and the karmic spirits with retinue are behind.

### II. Meditation on the Objects of Refuge

The essence of all sources of refuge is the guru inseparable from the dharmakāya Great Mother, appearing in the sky in front of you on a lion throne, lotus, and moon. {206} She is the color of refined gold, with one face and four arms. Her two right hands hold a vajra and touch the ground; her two left hands hold a volume of scripture (*pustika*) and make the mudra of equipoise. She sits with her legs in full lotus posture. Meditate on the gurus of the Kagyu lineage, the buddhas, and the bodhisattvas in the upper regions; the yidams and hosts of deities of the four tantras in the middle region; and the heroes and ḍākinīs with their retinues of dharma guards and protectors below—all clustered there like thick cloud banks.

Then you and all the various guests, led by you, contemplating sincerely from the bottoms of your hearts and not just mouthing the words, say, "All you objects of refuge, know that from this moment until reaching the essence of enlightenment, I and all these other beings filling space, whether we are ascending or descending, happy or sad, however it occurs, must actualize the attainment of your states." With that in mind, visualize yourself leading the rumble of you and all the others saying the refuge.

Then say the refuge, starting with "I and others, all sentient beings . . ." (*bdag gzhan sems can thams cad* . . .) through ". . . go for refuge in the dharmakāya, my own empty, unborn, mind" (. . . *rang sems stong pa skye ba med pa chos kyi sku la skyabs su mchi'o* ).[4] And from "Entrusting myself to the Three Jewels now and forever . . ." (*dkon mchog gsum la 'phral yun gyi blo bkal* . . .) to ". . . as body, speech, and mind enter into the genuine path of enlightenment, all the obstructions of deluded dualistic appearance, such as sickness, spirits, accidents, and obstacles, however many there are, subside into the dharmakāya expanse of lucid, clear reflective awareness. Purified, they become empty and become the expanse of great equality."[5]

### Arousing the Awakening Mind

{207} After offering the seven branches to the field of merit, think with intense longing, "I and others, all these types of guests filling space, none of whom has not been my parent, must be liberated from the ocean of samsaric suffering and be established in the state of the Great Mother, the omniscient dharmakāya. For that reason I will practice the instructions of the profound Severance and secure them all in buddhahood." Then say, "Just as the lords of the three times . . ." and so on (*ji ltar dus gsum* . . .)[6] as in the meditation liturgy, and contemplate the meaning as you say the words. Then cease the visualization of the merit field and rest.

### Assembling the Five-Tiered Refuge Sources

Meditate that a yellow syllable *trāṃ* appears within the space of three rainbow light rays in the sky in front. It dissolves and becomes a wide and vast jewel-encrusted throne. On top of that, a white *paṃ* becomes an eight-petaled white lotus. On its stamens an orange *mūṃ* becomes a sun seat, and upon that a white *āḥ* becomes the moon seat. Upon that, the white letter *hūṃ* dissolves and becomes Machik Lapkyi Drölma inseparable from the root guru. Her body color is white and so on, as described in the liturgy of the source texts. In the direction of her right ear, upon a lotus and moon, is Pa Dampa as in the sources, surrounded by an ocean of Indian and Tibetan adepts. In the direction of Machik's left ear, upon a lotus, sun, and corpse, are the five deities of Jetsunma [Vārāhī], visualized as in the source texts, surrounded by ḍākinīs of the three places. In the sky above Machik's head, on a lion throne, lotus, and moon, is the Victor Shākyamuni and a thousand buddhas. Behind, the excellent speech of the Victor, the holy dharma, is stacked up as *pustika* volumes. To the left are the eight close sons, the sixteen elders, and so forth, surrounded by the assembly of noble bodhisattvas, shrāvakas, and pratyekabuddhas with their monastic trappings and such. {208}

The Great Mother is in the space directly above Shākyamuni's head, on a lion throne and lotus-and-moon seat, with ornaments and accessories as described in the source texts. Visualize her with the buddhas of the ten directions, as found in the narrative of the *Perfection of Wisdom in One Hundred Thousand Lines*, along with the hosts of bodhisattvas, shrāvakas, and pratyekabuddhas. In the space above the Great Mother's head, on a lion throne with a lotus seat, is Vairochana, white and so forth as described in the source, along with Akṣhobhya, Ratnasambhava, Amitābha, Amoghasiddhi, and so forth, with the saṃbhogakāya regalia. To their right are the yidams of the mandala of the father tantras, such as Chakrasaṃvara, Hevajra, and Guhyasamāja, surrounded by the oceanic host of heroes, such as the hero Skull Fragment (Thod pa'i dum bu). To their left are the secret awareness ḍākinīs of the mandala of the mother tantras, such as Nairātmyā, Tārā, and Uttara, surrounded by an oceanic host of heroines, such as the heroine Ferocious Lady (Rab gtum ma). In front of them, on top of a lotus and moon, is Khadiravaṇī Tārā, her body blue-green in color, her right hand in the gesture of sublime generosity and her left holding the stem of an *utpala* at her heart, perfect in all the marks and signs.

In the back, upon a lion throne, lotus, and moon seat, in the center is dharmakāya Vajradhara, blue-black, holding in his two hands a vajra and bell crossed at his heart, sitting cross-legged in vajra position, with the regalia of a wheel-wielding monarch. Surrounding him are all the Kagyu gurus, from the gurus of the four and six precept legacies and Telo, Nāro, and so on, down to your own root guru. {209}

At the level of Machik's seat and to the right of it, upon the lotus, sun, and crossed bodies of the male and female *rudras*, are the wisdom protectors: Four Armed (Phyag bzhi pa), Black Cloaked (Ber nag can), Six Armed (Phyag drug pa), Tent Protector (Gur mgon), and so forth, surrounded by a host of other dharma protectors of the male classes. To the left of the seat, a lotus-moon-corpse seat, are places with lakes of blood, black winds, and so on, in accordance with the individual source texts. Upon the seats are the glorious goddesses Smoky Lady (Dud sol ma/Dhūmāvatī), Self-Arising Queen (Rang byung rgyal mo), Ekajaṭī, the four Retī sisters, and so forth, surrounded by a host of other dharma protectors of the female classes. At the level of their thrones is a host of harm-doers, wealth gods, and the powerful doctrine guards of worldly haughty ones as well as the powerful ones who strictly guard the doctrine, such as the seventy-two glorious protectors of the outer tantras, and so forth. They each have their individual styles, adornments, and mounts and are surrounded by multiple hosts of retinues. Meditate that they are energetically pursuing the work of guarding the doctrine.

On the ground beneath them are all the guests, primarily the spirits from before. Imagine that they are prostrating with devotion physically, verbally, and mentally and sincerely going for refuge with an attitude of obedience and servitude.

### III.[7] The Invitation of the Awareness Beings

Meditate that the five principal sources of refuge, visualized in that way, are marked on their foreheads with a white *oṃ*, on their throats with a red *āḥ*, and on their hearts with a blue *hūṃ*. Light rays radiate from those letters and strike the central figure of the Great Mother. Light rays radiate from her and strike the host of deities, evoking their mindstreams, and then gather back into the Great Mother's heart. Again light rays from the Great Mother's heart emanate above and below {210} and pervade all directions and interstices. They invoke immeasurable awareness beings from the natural pure realm of Akaniṣhṭha, such as the Great Mother, Machik, and so on, just as they were visualized, arising instantly like massing clouds. With rainbow light, incense smoke, and the sound of cymbals, think that they have arrived. Offer with, "*hūṃ* sentient beings without exception . . ." (*hūṃ / ma lus sems can* . . .), from the meditation liturgy, to ". . . Whatever makes you happy, please remain" (. . . *ci bde bar ni bzhugs su gsol*).[8] Think that the awareness beings dissolve inseparably into the pledge beings like water poured into water.

The offering goddess White Ablution Water (Khrus chab ma dkar mo) arises from both you and the offerings arrayed in front of you, grips a white vase by the stem, and bathes them and dries them with a white towel. Also various offering goddesses instantly emanate immeasurable offerings—such as the five sense qualities in the form of flowers, incense, and so on; the seven royal emblems; the eight modes such as grace; as well as the four continents and Supreme Mountain adorned by the sun and moon; and so forth—and offer them to the objects of refuge in front. Imagining that, do the meditation chant.[9]

Then you and all sentient beings with one voice recite, "The one who is kind . . ." (*gang gi drin gyis* . . .) and so on, doing the meditation liturgy while thinking of the praise.

## The Recitation

Visualize the white letter *hūṃ* sticking up like a pin in a cushion in the center of a coil and moon mandala in Machik's heart. Beginning from the front of it and turning to the right, the garland of the mantra *oṃ gate* . . . turns, shining[10] white like a pearl necklace. Then immeasurable light radiates from the mantra garland. It invokes the mindstreams of all the buddhas and bodhisattvas of the ten directions and gathers all the power and strength of their body, speech, and mind {211}, which then strikes the host of deities of the mandala. The blessings of the assembly of deities gather in the manner of various light rays and dissolve into Machik. They issue from Machik's big toe, like popping the stopper off a jug of *chang,* and enter through the tops of the heads of all the guests—you and the six kinds of beings that are gathered around. Imagine that as it strikes your bodies, voices, and minds, all the sickness, spirits, negativity, and obscurations that have accumulated since beginningless time are expelled in the form of soot and liquid charcoal from the pores and toes and lower orifices and dissolve into the great, powerful seat of golden ground.

If you want a further wrathful visualization, meditate that your own ignorant, dualistic delusion is embodied as the devil of coemergent ignorance with the head of a *makara,*[11] and the soot flows into its gaping maw, satisfying and pleasing it and clearing up all your debts and karmic obligations. That is called the black distribution (*nag 'gyed*).

## The Offering

The perceptions of your six senses appear in essence as outer perceived objects. Innumerable goddesses emanate from the heart of your own crystal-pure body and present various offering substances. The goddess of form holds a mirror, the goddess of sound holds a lute, the goddess of mind holds a dharma source, and so forth. Think that they make offerings to the refuge objects and their retinues, and say, "The worlds of the billionfold universe . . ." (*stong gsum rab byams 'jig rten . . .*).[12]

## IV. Separating Body and Mind and Offering the Mandala

Imagine that your own body, the form aggregate, has a pink complexion and is in the prime of youth. Inside the center of that body is the central channel with its four defining characteristics: white on the outside and red on the inside, clear and limpid, empty inside like a crystal tube, and very straight. The upper end reaches to the opening in the crown of the head, like the open end of a copper trumpet. {212} The lower end reaches to the perineum, where it forks into two and continues into the two thighs. The lower ends terminate at the bottoms of the two feet. Inside [the channel], at the right [foot], is the white vital drop (*thig le*) that came from the father, and inside the left is the red vital drop from the mother. On top of those two are black drops each marked with a black letter *tri*, the seed of hell. The seed of the hungry ghosts in the perineum is a yellow drop marked with a yellow *pre*. Similarly, the seed of the animals is a gray drop with *du* in the navel; the seed of humans is a green drop with *nṛi* at the heart; the seed of the demigods is a red drop with *a* in the throat; and the seed of the gods is a white drop marked with a white *oṃ* at the top of the head. Clearly visualize them.[13] Light rays emanate from the six letters. The individual realms of each of the six classes of beings along with their karmic causes and effects dissolve into the letters.

*phaṭ* The two white and red drops in the soles of the feet rise up and the sufferings of heat and cold of the hell realms along with their seeds dissolve into one drop, which has converged at the perineum and become the size of a new hen's egg. The seed of the hungry ghosts along with their hunger and thirst dissolves into the drop, and it ascends to the navel. The seed of the animals along with their dumbness dissolves into the drop, and it ascends to the heart. The seed of humans along with their poverty dissolves into the drop, and it ascends to the throat. The seed of the demigods along with their rivalry dissolves into the drop, and it ascends to the top of the head. The seed of the gods along with their [suffering from] transitioning and falling dissolves into the drop. At each of those stages, the drop becomes larger until it is the size of a large bird's egg, ready to fly up.[14] Uttering *phaṭ* with intensity, imagine that it quickly dissolves into Machik's heart. Then rest in equanimity.

In another system, you visualize your body and central channel with the white and red drops in the feet as before, [but] without meditating on the seeds of the six classes. {213} [When you utter] *phaṭ*, the two drops combine at the perineum. Then with another *phaṭ,* the drop of the consciousness goes up to the heart and then exits from the top of the head, dissolving into Machik's heart.

In a condensed version, where the heart is closed to the outside,[15] there is the form of an eight-petaled lotus. Meditate on the essence of consciousness as a drop in its center, and then with *phaṭ* it dissolves into Machik's heart, and so on. Do whichever of those three versions of transference (*'pho ba*) you can manage. This is called Opening the Sky Door (*nam mkha' sgo byed*).

Again, from Machik's heart the essence of your and others' intrinsic awareness becomes a red letter *hrīḥ*. As soon as it emanates, it instantly transforms into the form of Vajrayoginī, red in color, holding a hooked knife and blood-filled skull cup, with all ornaments and accessories complete and perfect. The form aggregate of the illusory body falls senseless on its back. With a mere gesture of the hooked knife, it is rendered from its housing, flayed of its casing, and spread out from the belly to become the skin of the great, powerful golden ground. The essence of the flesh and blood in the form of a mandala made of various jewels is placed upon it. The blood is no different from perfumed water sprinkled upon it. The front torso is Supreme Mountain in the middle; the upper right side with its arm is the eastern continent Majestic Body (Videha); the upper left side with its arm is the southern continent Land of Jambu (Jambudvīpa); the lower right side with its leg is the western continent Bountiful Cow (Godānīya); and the lower left side with its leg is the northern continent Unpleasant Sound (Kuru). The head is the Mansion of Complete Victory, the two eyes are the sun and the moon, the two ears are the parasol and banner, and the eight appendages are the eight islands. The heart is the wish-fulfilling gem, {214} the life channel is the wish-granting tree, the lungs are the clever horses, the liver is the *amalika* stone slab, the gallbladder is the white silk curtain, the kidneys are the god child and nāga child, the blood and phlegm are the seven circular lakes, the fat is the vase of great giving, the stomach is the uncultivated crop, the breasts are the bountiful cows, the teeth are the precious garland, the nails are the eight auspicious signs, the intestines are the iron mountains of the rim, the head and body hairs are all hills of sandalwood forests and saffron meadows, and all the insides are meadows and lawns.

Furthermore, innumerable worker ḍākinīs emanate from the heart and pores of you yourself appearing clearly as Jetsunma, carrying various offering substances such as forms, sounds, smells, tastes, and touches. Innumerable mandalas arrayed in that fashion are also emanated and individually offered in that arrangement to each of the objects of refuge. Then each one takes possession and partakes of it, and their dwelling places are supremely arrayed. The dharma protectors and guards also receive offering substances in harmony with their minds, and the powerful guards of the doctrine, such as the seventy[-five] glorious protectors of the outer tantras, also receive the seats and so forth according to their personal preferences. Their dwelling places become immeasurable excellent displays. As they take possession of them, imagine them sitting on their individual seats and enjoying themselves.

The merit of such an offering delights all the refuge objects—gurus, yidams, ḍākinīs, and so forth—in body, speech, and mind. Think that the two accumulations of the cause are perfected and the two obscurations of the path are purified and that supreme and common spiritual powers are granted. Imagine that because of your offering to all the dharma protector guards who protect virtue, they will guard the Buddha's doctrine {215} and accomplish without impediment all requested peaceful, enriching, controlling, and wrathful activities, and recite, "The skin is the golden ground . . ." (*pags pa gser gyi sa gzhi . . .*), and so on.[16] Then rest in equipoise.

## V. The Supplication and Descent of Blessings

This is described below [after the sequence of offering and giving].

## VI. The Sequence of Offering and Giving

Clearly visualize your own body aggregate of form as being huge and fat, rolled in oil, and white with a reddish hue. The consciousness leaves from its heart as above, and your own awareness arises from Machik's heart as

Vajrayoginī, as above. Within the state of that clarity, the skin of the butchered and flayed corpse becomes the golden ground. Upon that, the two arms and the right leg are planted in three directions and become three mountain-sized dry skulls for hearthstones. The kapāla is removed from the corpse with a slice of the knife and placed upon them, becoming as vast as the billionfold universe. The corpse's remains of flesh and blood are thrown inside. Imagine that you, as Vajrayoginī, butcher, pound, split, slice, heap, and knead it with the hooked knife in your hand, making an ocean of flesh and blood. Meditate on a green *yaṃ* and above it the mark of a red *raṃ* in the skull hearthstones. Meditate that there is a white *khaṃ* on the flesh-and-blood ocean, and upon that a white *oṃ*, red *āḥ*, and blue *hūṃ* are stacked up. Green light rays emanate from your heart as Vajrayoginī and strike the *yaṃ*, stirring up wind. As the wind strikes the *raṃ* above it, fire blazes up and heats the skull cup, boiling the ocean of flesh and blood. All the impure substances spill over like the foam of churned milk. The white *khaṃ* melts and becomes a liquid stream, cleansing all the impure defilements and purifying. Light rays from *oṃ āḥ hūṃ* radiate in all directions. {216} All the blessings of the body, speech, and mind of the victors in the ten directions take the form of white, red, and blue light rays and dissolve into the three letters. Those three melt by stages and dissolve into the elixir inside the skull, inseparably blending the awareness with the pledge being in a great ocean of elixir. Imagine it white in appearance with a red cast and a slightly bluish hue, possessing one hundred flavors and supreme power and ability, as big as the billionfold universe, swirling and swelling.

Worker ḍākinīs in an unimaginable variety of colors emanate from your heart and pores. They scoop up the elixir ocean with skull cups, filling them with the kapāla's elixir and with immeasurable offerings of form, sound, smell, taste, and so forth. They offer it before the Kagyu gurus, the roots of blessing.

### Specific [White Distributions]
### The Rare and Sublime Guests of Honor

For Vajradhara, the one hundred great adepts, the eighty great adepts, and so on, with their *heruka* gear, and similarly the root and lineage gurus who keep the mantric conduct of awareness-holders, imagine emanating and offering the five meats, the five elixirs, the six bone ornaments, the sigils of the five families, and a retinue of many knowledge women with excellent, young, beautiful bodies in a variety of colors. Imagine that the emanation forms (tulkus) with monastic attire are offered the three monastic robes, begging bowls, monk's staffs, and three white and three sweet foods by retinues of innumerable monastics with their attire. Furthermore, their individual dwelling places are arrayed with excellent enjoyments like the pure realms of Manifest Joy (Abhirati), Blissful (Sukhāvatī), and Richly Adorned (Ganavyūha). Even their houses are infinite palaces with two square and round stories and so forth, adorned with many doorway pediments. {217} Also mentally emanate and offer the seven royal emblems, the signs and objects of auspiciousness, and so forth. Make the connection by uttering *phaṭ*.

In the same way, offer to the deity hosts of the highest yoga tantras of the old and new traditions—such as these three: Chakrasaṃvara, Hevajra, and Guhyasamāja—the offering substances such as the five meats and five elixirs as before and the garments and body ornaments and so forth as before that are appropriate to the highest Mantra. To those of the lower tantras, such as yoga, kriyā, charyā, and so forth, emanate and offer unimaginable [quantities of the] three white and three sweet foods and divine elixir; various precious ornaments such as crowns, earring pairs, necklace sets, armbands, and rings for the fingers and toes; precious parasols and skirts and shirts of various silks; canopies, banners, pennants, tassels, fans, and bedding; lion thrones, lotus-and-sun seats, and other necessities; a variety of different palaces for their dwelling places; and entourages of divine boys and girls and such, carrying various desirables in their hands. Imagining that, make the connection by saying *phaṭ*.

To the ḍākinīs of the four families of Vajravārāhī and such, and the heroes and ḍākinīs of the three sites, offer pledge substances of the feast circle—the various meats, various liquors, various grains, and all the feast foodstuffs, leaving nothing incomplete; the attributes of splendor[17] and of the cemetery,[18] the six bone ornaments, and so forth; the sigils of the five families, such as the vajra, gem, lotus, crossed vajra, and crown; ḍāmarus, bells, knives, skulls, and khaṭvāṃkas made of various precious material; mirrors, flower garlands and ornaments, clothing, and accessories, with none left out; retinues according to their individual preferences, such as heroes and qualified knowledge women, all appropriate to their individual fortunes. Imagine that and make the connection with *phaṭ*. {218}

Especially for Machik Lapdrön and the other principal sources of refuge, imagine making the offerings again and again, an inconceivable number of times. It is taught that the practitioner's worker ḍākinīs are primarily white when offering to the host of gurus and primarily yellow when offering to the yidams and ḍākinīs.

Think that offering in that way to the rare and sublime guests of honor delights their body, speech, and mind and leads to the perfection of the accumulations of the cause, the purifications of the obscurations of the path, and the complete manifest buddhahood of the result, granting the supreme spiritual powers of mahāmudrā in this very lifetime.

### The Lordly Guests of Qualities

For the wisdom and worldly dharma protectors, the male classes, the female classes, the obedient ones, the haughty spirits, along with the further retinues and hosts of messengers, emanate and offer unimaginable oceans of human blood, flowers of the five sense organs, incense of burnt human flesh, and lamps of human fat; various victuals of flesh and bone; mountainous tormas of human blood; various musical instruments, such as the thighbone trumpet and the skull drum; flesh, blood, viscera, heart, skin, and so forth in accordance with their individual preferences; service substances, accomplishment substances, and fulfillment substances; various clothing such as black silk cloaks, felt skirts, human skins, tiger-skin skirts, and elephant-skin clothes; various ornaments such as dry or fresh skulls, the six ornaments, and snake and intestine lassos; various implements such as hooked knives, swords, dice, bullets, disease pouches, and powdered pigments; various attractive animals, such as black birds, black dogs, black horses, black yaks, and other kinds of creatures such as raptors, wild animals, and poisonous snakes; frightening and terrifically arrayed dwelling places such as arrayed cemeteries with fire, wind, red, black, blood lakes, skull hills, and so forth. All this is offered to the dharma protectors and guards. {219}

Also offer multitudes of offering clouds formed from all desirables—such as various jewels, fine silks, weapons, treasure chests, auspicious signs, seven gem pairs,[19] bountiful cows, and wish-granting trees—to the classes of wealth gods and harm-doers. Imagine offering immeasurable clouds of offerings that accord with their personal spheres of activity, such as flowers, fruit, grains, herbs, fine silks, ornamental garlands, divine palaces, bathing pools, and so on, to the guardians of the outer tantras, such as the seventy-five glorious lords of worldly protectors and direction protectors.

Think that by your offering in that way to the protectors, the guests of qualities, they are pleased and will guard the doctrine of the Buddha, protect the virtuous, and vanquish the negative through accomplishing whatever unimpeded activity is requested of them: peaceful, enriching, controlling, or wrathful.

## The Guests of Compassion: Six Classes of Beings

Again, emanate innumerable offering goddesses of various colors, but particularly white, carrying elixir-filled skull cups and unimaginable offering substances. They offer to each sentient being of the six types, headed up by your own parents. Imagine that they give them the multicolored elixir of the gods that calms all suffering: cooling those in the hot hells, warming those in the cold hells, ending the killing, cutting, chopping, and so forth. For the hungry ghosts, imagine that a rain of divine elixir falls with substances, food, and drink that quells their hunger and thirst and they gain excellent, fine forms. For the animals, imagine offering the multicolored elixir as a substance that generates intelligence, food, drink, and habitats appropriate to each one. Think that it purifies their obscurations of ignorance and they become endowed with excellent intelligence. For the humans, offer all the enjoyments that any of them desire, like opening the treasury of space—food; silk and clothes; gold, silver, and fine silks; treasuries, horses, mules, riches, cattle, and so forth {220}—and imagine their desires spontaneously fulfilled. For the demigods, imagine offering various enjoyments such as vajra weapons and the elixir of immortality. And for the gods, imagine offering multicolored elixir, the intelligent horse, bathing pools, crops needing no cultivation, various flower ornaments and garlands, playgrounds for the divine boys and girls, and so forth—the excellent pleasures of happiness and joy. In short, think that by your offering elixir and all the desired enjoyments to the six classes of beings, the guests of compassion, they will be liberated from whatever individual sufferings and problems they have and will attain buddhahood. Make the connection by saying *phaṭ*.

Furthermore, among those six classes of beings there are those with whom you have engaged in reciprocal killing and slaying during innumerable previous ages. That incurs the liability (*lan chags*) of a short life. Involvement with theft, robbery, and plunder incurs the liability of material poverty.[20] Hitting, beating, binding, depriving others of their faculties, and so forth carries the liability of much sickness and physical suffering. Stealing the body or life force of children and wives from the court of the kingdom creates a very huge liability of debt. Partaking of substances, items, flesh, and blood and so forth falls into the class of minor liabilities. Right now those beings all have thoughts and actions of pursuit and malice toward you over such [karmic] liabilities. For all those, imagine that the essence of the previous elixir is in the form of gleaming mountains of flesh, lakes of blood, riverbanks of bone, and rising vapors, better and more pleasing in essence than the flesh and blood of a seven-times-born brahmin that by a mere taste in the mouth or touch or whiff of its scent pacifies all suffering, temporary and ultimate, and brings about the attainment of supreme happiness. {221}

Furthermore, whatever you need to repay the debt—mansions, horses, gems, gold, silver, and precious items; men and women of excellent, beautiful form; various clothes and ornaments; in short, whatever stuff is needed to pay off those creditors—is all multiplied a hundred or a thousand times and emanated like a rainfall of desirables. Think that through that gift, all liabilities and debts of the flesh are cleared up and [those creditors] attain enlightenment. Make the connection by saying *phaṭ*.

This was the sequence for the White Feast in Three Cycles of Integration.

Again, innumerable white goddesses carrying skull cups filled with elixir emanate from your heart to each of the six realms, bringing the elixir. It relieves their [inhabitants'] individual sufferings, and they attain enlightenment. The places of the six classes of beings are emptied. Once again, light emanates from those goddesses and fills those empty realms. Imagine that the hell realm becomes pure as lapis, with the nature of vajra. Similarly, the hungry ghost realm becomes pure as ruby, with the nature of the lotus; the animal realm becomes pure as crystal, with the nature of the wheel; the human realm becomes pure as gold, with the nature of precious jewels; the demigods' realm becomes pure as emerald, with the nature of crossed vajras; and the gods' realm becomes pure with the essence of the five lights of lucid emptiness, the nature of great timeless awareness. In the end, the goddesses are gathered back into you and you rest without visualization.

Again, the leftover elixir itself becomes the three whites and three sweets, various medicines, fine silks and jewels, various grains, various domestic animals such as horses and cattle, various ungulates such as wild yaks and deer, fowl, carnivores, fish, aquatic mammals, turtles, and so on. The images of all those creatures are physically big and strong, and innumerable replicas emanate from each of their pores. {222} Many amazingly arrayed places, such as rocky and snowy mountains, grassy plains, forests, lakes, lawns, springs, and great groves of flowers; various select offerings, the "golden drink" of tea and beer in variously bejeweled vessels; arrows, spears, and weapons adorned with various silks; various colored yarns; and an array of innumerable desirables emanate as offerings to the ground masters (*gzhi bdag*). Their own sites, areas, adornments, clothes, food, drinks, and accouterments become excellent and abundant. The male ground masters ride on tigers, leopards, horses, and wolves, sit on thrones, and so forth, appearing in contented modes of behavior. The female ground masters wear silks and brocades and are adorned with jewels and garlands and so forth. They hold spindles of fine red and white thread balls in their hands and so on. Imagine they each are in possession of their particular preferred enjoyments, and make the connection by saying *phaṭ*.

Again, imagine the leftover elixir itself as many items that are pleasing to the nāgas: the three white substances of yogurt, milk, and butter; the three sweet substances of sugar, molasses, and honey; the bloods as a great lake of milk; the innards as various nāga medicine. The nāgas themselves have upper bodies like children of the gods and lower bodies of reptiles, and they may have five, seven, nine, or more hooded snake heads and copious precious ornaments. Imagine them enjoying all the pleasing items, while their malicious thoughts subside and they feel profuse joy and happiness.

Again, outside of the area separated by the variegated silk curtain at the outer circumference, the dark forces that delight in flesh and blood, such as outcaste nāgas, partake of an ocean of flesh and blood. Think that their noxious minds are pacified and the aspiration for enlightenment is born in their mindstreams. {223} Finally the offering goddesses are reabsorbed. Rest in equipoise.

Here, you must make special offerings to ground masters and nāgas separately. The special feature of Severance practice is to ascertain the inner state of conscious awareness of the one who is frightened based on external frightening objects. Therefore, a primary teaching is to wander in haunted mountain retreats. Also, you make those offerings for the purpose of commissioning whatever activities you desire under the circumstances. In fact, there is no being that is not included in the six classes of sentient beings. Ground masters are nonhumans [but are] included with the human migrators, and nāgas are included with animal migrators.

When making such offerings, in general the officiant's goddesses are of various colors. However, it is said that when doing mainly offerings to the dharma protectors they are red, and when it is the six classes of beings and so forth as in the outer tantras, they are white.

### Red Distribution

To do the red distribution, shoot the consciousness up as before. The essence of awareness is a blue-black *hūṃ*, which turns into [Vajrayoginī as] Krodhīkālī.[21] Generate her in accordance with the source texts, holding human skin in her right hand and human feet in the left, and so forth. The four female gatekeepers and innumerable fierce ones emanate from her heart. All those who were unsatisfied by the previous distribution—the male malicious spirits, female malicious spirits, nāga spirits, and so forth, who have wicked propensities—are drawn in. The flesh mountains and blood lakes of the corpse expand to equal the world realm. Imagine that those spirits eat the flesh, drink the blood, and suck the bones, enjoying them nonstop until cyclic existence is emptied. Make the connection by saying *phaṭ* and blow the thighbone, reciting, "Namo, [gods and demons living in this] haunted place . . ." (*namo / gnas gnyan sa . . .*).[22]

### Additional White Distributions

### The Vase of Elixir Distribution

There are also several different ways of distribution. Among them is the Vase of Elixir Distribution (*bdud rtsi bum 'gyed ma*). Do the transference of your own or another's consciousness as you wish. [The consciousness] flies into Machik's heart, {224} and from her heart the essence of awareness [emerges] as a white letter *ha*. From that, it transforms into a white worker ḍākinī carrying a curved knife in her right hand and an elixir-filled vase in her left hand, endowed with all the ornaments and attributes. Imagine that she pours the elixir from the vase into the corpse's cranial aperture and the corpse swells up like a belly bag full of milk. It is sliced open with the hooked knife in the right hand and becomes a great ocean of elixir. Light rays from your heart radiate to all the buddhas and bodhisattvas of the ten directions and gather in their blessings, which dissolve into the belly and melt into light, mixing with the elixir. Visualize it as multicolored offering clouds. Think that the ground foundation becomes as pure as a crystal vase full of elixir. Innumerable white goddesses emanate from your heart, carrying the vases of elixir in both hands and offering it to the gurus and yidams, the rare and sublime guests of honor.

Again that same elixir fills many fresh skulls and is offered to the lord protectors of the dharma, the guests of qualities. After that, the elixir is offered to the guardians, the six kinds of beings, creditors, the various types of obstructors, ground masters, and nāgas, and it satisfies them.[23]

## The Face Skull Cup

As before, the consciousness rises up and so forth. From Machik's heart, the essence of awareness as a white letter *hrīḥ* generates a single white worker ḍākinī carrying a hooked knife and blood-filled skull cup. [She slices off the skull] of the corpse above the eyebrows with the hooked knife and pours all of its flesh and blood inside it until it is full. Then, as before, the wind stirs and fire blazes, heating up the skull cup and boiling the elixir. Imagine that all the imperfections overflow. {225} Again, the quintessence of all the blessings of the buddhas and bodhisattvas of the ten directions as the timeless awareness elixir falls into the skull cup in your left hand [as the ḍākinī] and melts, filling it up. Elixir pours out of the cranial aperture in the skull cup as if from an unplugged beer barrel and melts into the elixir in the skull cup in front. The pledge elixir and awareness elixir blend inseparably. Imagine that the steam from the boiling emanates above in the form of white light rays, the liquid that is the nature of elixir endowed with one hundred sublime flavors swirls in the middle, and the dregs that have all desirable qualities stay below. A multitude of white worker ḍākinīs carrying skull cups offer it, starting from the rare and sublime guests of honor to the ground masters and nāgas. This is the Face Skull Cup [Feast] (*thod zhal ma*).

## The Five-Desirables Offering

Do [the next feast] from the ascent of the consciousness until the increase and processing of the white workers as in the Face Skull Cup. After that, emanate worker ḍākinīs in a variety of colors carrying various offering substances. They offer them to all of the guests, as in the previous Skull Hearthstones.[24] This is the Five-Desirables Offering (*'dod yon lnga mchod ma*).

In these kinds of distributions, essentially your flesh and body—in the form of whatever offering substances are desired, such as elixir—are increased and offered to the guests who are the recipients of the distribution: the rare and sublime guests of honor, the protectors with qualities, the six classes of beings [for whom one has] compassion, and the spirit, obstructor, and creditor guests. The results of such distributions are blessings of spiritual powers, strong effective activity, and [the knowledge that] whatever appearances of suffering arise, such as the suffering from karmic debt and so on, they are devoid of arising, ceasing, and abiding in the original dharmakāya. As you rest in the equipoise of the meaning of the Mother, free of thought and utterance, whatever temporary joys and sorrows occur, their very essence is by nature pure since forever, and in that state they are integrated onto the path.

The meanings of what are called the White Distribution for Four Guests (*dkar 'gyed mgron bzhi ma*) and the White Feast in Three Cycles of Integration (*dkar tshogs lam khyer skor gsum*) {226} are covered by these. Now there are some textbooks that are dissimilar, which explain seven [types of] distributions for this occasion or set forth an outline of subcategories for that occasion, and so forth. However, this one here was taught to me directly from the master, and so the transmission of exegesis is certain. Also, when Trungpa Rinpoche resided here, some of his trusted texts were the same as this. These two [reasons] are the proof.

### [Additional] Red Distributions
### The Excellent Stakeout

The consciousness flies up and awareness is generated as Vajrayoginī from the red letter *hrīḥ* as before. Imagine that she cuts off the four limbs of the corpse with the hooked knife and plants them in the four directions. Then she flays the skin and stretches it between [the limb stakes] and piles the corpse's blood, flesh, and bones in a great heap atop that. Four worker ḍākinīs—white, yellow, red, and green—emanate from your heart as Yoginī. They grasp the skin at the four corners and serve it up to all the guests. This is the Excellent Stakeout (*mchog phur ma*).

### The Flayed Skin

Again, your consciousness flies up and awareness is generated as Vajrayoginī. Without damage to the four limbs, the skin is spread out on the ground and the flesh, blood, and bones heaped up on top of it. The four worker ḍākinīs emanate from the heart as before and serve it up to the guests. This is the Flayed Skin (*g.yang gzhi ma*).

In this way, the flesh and blood itself is the means of performing the white or the red distribution and dedicating it to all types of guests. Think that as soon as it is offered, the special intentions of the rare and sublime guests of honor grow more and more complete. The guests who are the protectors with qualities accomplish various activities without hindrance. The guests of compassion, the six classes of beings, are freed from the three obscurations in the short term and will ultimately actualize buddhahood. {227} In particular, during the red distributions, the malicious spirits, obstructors, creditors, and elemental spirits are liberated from suffering just by smelling or tasting [the feast], and ultimately they too will attain the state of great awakening.

In general, whatever sequence of offering and giving of the illusory body you do, the most vital point is to understand it in this way: The original ground of lucid clarity, buddha nature (Skt. *sugatagarbha*), abides pervasively throughout all samsara and nirvana, in both the contained and the container. Until that itself is actualized, everything included in dualistic deluded thinking—good and bad, clean and dirty, hopes and fears for help and harm by gods and demons, and so forth—is the imputation (*kun btags*) of clinging to the mere superimposition of names. Everything included in dualistic appearance—birth, death, sickness, samsara, nirvana, and so forth—is the other-power (*gzhan dbang*) of clinging to the reification of subject-object appearances. All stains of conceptual patterns included in those two [categories] are pure in their own ground. Their own ground is empty lucid clarity, the buddha nature itself, which was never, ever covered by the stains of anything like permanence and nihilism, going and coming, arising and ceasing, one and many, and so forth—free of embellishment like the center of the sky. Moreover, this is not dead emptiness (*bem stong*) but the pure true identity (*bdag dam pa gtsang ba*) of the four kāyas and fivefold timeless awareness. You aspire to vajra-like absorption and its integration on the path until it is actualized. When this is put into practice, the power of fixation on the self [that results in] cherishing life and limb creates the feeling that sickness, suffering, and so forth are unbearable. This very self-fixation that clings to the reification of that experience arises as the material forms of the physical body, retinue, enjoyments, and so on. The idea that the various guests that are part of these dualistic appearances will appropriately enjoy [the feasts] and offering to them, and the reifying attachment to things, such as the illusory body that is held to be the self, {228} and the conceptual patterns with which you fixate on the duality of the recipients of generosity—

the guests of samsara and nirvana—and the giver of that generosity [are in fact] your own awareness: lucid clarity, dharmakāya, mahāmudrā, beyond the realm of the intellect, and devoid of thought or utterance. The necessity of the purity in that state of suchness is crucial. This seems to be the reason that the vital points of the Mother's Severance cycle—*The Great Bundle of Precepts, Another Bundle, the Appendices*, the root and commentaries of the *Heart Essence of Profound Meaning*, the *Secret Severance* of the great Drukpa renunciate,[25] and so forth—must be conclusively ascertained through the three means of understanding, experience, and realization.

If you do these visualization cycles more extensively, add them individually to each supplication and do the "Hundred *Phaṭ*" (*phaṭ brgya ma*). Also, at the beginning of reciting "Homage! [Gods and demons in this] site of haunted grounds . . ." (*namo/gnas gnyan sa . . .*), perform the extensive White Distribution for Four Guests (*mgron bzhi ma*) and the red distribution to the ground masters, nāgas, and malicious spirits, and so forth. Then, afterward, perform one or two of the distribution styles. Or, at the beginning of "site of haunted grounds," do an extensive practice of the Four Guests or whichever manner of distribution you prefer. After that, at the junctures of the supplications, do the descent of blessings and rest without visualization. Practice them according to how much spare time you have. These are the oral traditions of yore.

### The Supplication and the Descent of Blessings

During the supplications to the experiential precept lineage, the father lineage, the mother lineage, and the child lineage, pray for the instant reversal of all mental states of negativity and downfall that were the cause of cyclic existence in the three realms, which arose due to your own and all beings' ignorance. Pray that all the habitual patterns of deluded, dualistic appearance will subside in their own ground. Pray for the realization of the Great Mother's actual intention, the original dharmakāya, and your complete awakening. {229} For the sake of others, pray for the effortless, spontaneous arising of great and vast efficacy of the four enlightened activities by the two form kāyas for as long as samsara remains. It is important to think, with fierce devotion blazing from your heart, "All you sources of refuge: know this."

The visualization session on this occasion is as follows: The whole external environment is a precious vessel. The internal contents are all offered as various visual, auditory, olfactory, gustatory, and tactile offerings. When invoking the hundred thousand ḍakinīs, Machik and the five Vajravārāhī goddesses are essentially the same but appear separately. Vajravārāhī's physical adornments, hand implements, seats, surroundings, and such, and those of the hundred thousand ḍākinīs are as described in the meditation liturgy. In brief, imagine that when you supplicate ḍākinīs equal in number to the atoms of thirty-two supreme mountains, they bestow all common and supreme spiritual powers without hindrance. Then sprinkle the feast substances with purifying water (*bsang chu*). If you wish to recite the *Kagyu Feast Liturgy* (*tshogs las*), although its cycle of visualization is not clearly expounded in the ancient system of Zurmang, you can do it according to the explication tradition of the omniscient Situ Rinpoche. In the meditation chant, all of the gurus from the Great Mother down to your root guru take on the style of Glorious Heruka. You invoke them, along with their entourage of one hundred thousand heroes and heroines with their retinues, and they come to dwell in the sky in front of you along with the objects of refuge. Various colored light rays emanate from all their forms. As the light rays strike the outer dwelling area, it becomes the pure land of Oḍḍiyāna Kechara. As they strike the abode, it becomes the self-manifesting palace of Oḍḍiyāna made of wet and dry skulls. The whole container becomes a skull container, and all contents become the five meats and five elixirs. All the guests become exclusively heroes and ḍākinīs. {230}

### Mother Lineage Feast Activity

On the occasion of the mother lineage feast activities, the feast goddesses are invoked. In the descent of blessings, light radiates from the forms of the general objects of refuge and Machik undifferentiated from the five Vajravārāhī goddesses. From the Great Secret Graveyard in the center, it invokes innumerable black buddha ḍākinīs holding eight-spoked wheels in their right hands and vessels filled with various victuals in their left hands. They carry various offering substances and innumerable musical instruments. Imagine that they come to dwell in the sky around the objects of refuge. Instantly through your meditative absorption, innumerable offering goddesses emanate, and with your offering mudra light emanates from them. As it strikes the external world it becomes the graveyard of Oḍḍiyāna or the graveyard of Great Secret Play in the Center, where human and horse corpses are scattered about. The bushes are all arrows and spears. All the water is blood and pus. All sounds are the honking of geese. Fire blazes by day and winds howl by night. The mountains pound and sway like the dancing of male and female herukas. As the light strikes the interior, the place becomes a graveyard palace. Outside it is white, the nature of methods; inside it is red, the nature of wisdom; and in between [the walls] are made of chunks of flesh and bone fragments from the graveyard. Above there is a human-skin canopy fringed with garlands of wet human intestines and pennants of human fat. The floor is plastered with pus and blood. The chinks are all plastered with pus. {231} The skeletons of a variety of big and small humans form the various pillars and beams. It is frightening and horrible. Imagine that clouds of five-colored rainbows gather above, a rain of various flowers falls in between, and the ground emits the fragrance of incense.

Imagine that as the light strikes the male and female occupants inside and all the races of the phenomenal world, all the males appear as the naturally occurring originally pure forms of Glorious Heruka. All the females appear as Vajrayoginī—the original, naturally occurring forms of Yoginī now manifest as they really are. Imagine that all containers become various dry and wet skull cups and jewel-encrusted vessels. Imagine that all their contents become the five meats and five elixirs—the substances that conquer concepts of dualistic appearance. Similarly, any offering substances are all naturally occurring great bliss: appearing while nonexistent; empty while appearing. Imagine that it all becomes substance for the effortless, spontaneous enjoyment of the six consciousness groups of all the guests, and say *phaṭ*. Then, recite from "*Kye!* Mother, nonhuman ḍākinī of timeless awareness . . ." (*kye / ma mi min ye shes mkha' 'gro ma* . . .) up through ". . . bestow supreme and common spiritual powers" (. . . *mchog thun mong gnyis kyi dngos grub stsol*). The words in between are in the meditation liturgy.[26]

In this way, the vajra ḍākinīs of the east hold vajra skull cups (*pad snod*), the jewel ḍākinīs of the south hold jewel skull cups, the lotus ḍākinīs of the west hold lotus skull cups, and the karma ḍākinīs of the north hold crossed-vajra skull cups. Invoke innumerable attendant ḍākinīs as before and bless the ground. The benefactors, environment, contents, offering substances, and so forth are consecrated as was just explained. Also, everything in the east becomes the feast hall of White Great Bliss in the Savage Graveyard; {232} everything in the south becomes the feast hall of Yellow Accomplishment of Purpose in the Resounding Laughter Graveyard; everything in the west becomes the feast hall of Red Howlers in the Lotus Graveyard;

and everything in the north becomes the feast hall of Ultimate Variety in the Resounding Kīla Graveyard. Then do the blessing as before. These have the same meaning as the ḍākinīs of the four families, so it is very important to clearly visualize the descent of blessings.

Then sprinkle the feast substances with elixir and blend others' awareness with your own awareness. Blend your own awareness with space awareness. Blend the flesh and blood of the corpse with the feast. These should be done according to the Severance practitioner's own experience and realization, so it is suitable that there are several styles of explanation. Do not complicate matters with suspicions about the many texts.

In this way the essence is the combined corpse and feast torma, while the form is flesh and blood. A golden five-pronged vajra marked with a white *oṃ* at the top end, red *āḥ* at the center, and blue *hūṃ* at the bottom end stands in a sun disk. It is capped at the upper end by a moon mandala. Imagine that the feast tray itself is a kapāla, white on the outside and red on the inside, equal in size to the billionfold universe. Then recite, "*Oṃ* pray to Machikma . . ." and so on,[27] supplicating with the three syllables. As you visualize yourself as Vajrayoginī, a single white light ray emerges from your forehead and strikes the *oṃ* in Machik's forehead. White light from that *oṃ* radiates in the ten directions and strikes the forms of all buddhas and bodhisattvas. It gathers all the blessings of form and they dissolve into Machik's forehead. White light rays in the form of *oṃ* arise from that *oṃ* and strike the *oṃ* at the moon cover at the upper end of the vajra, dissolving it into light above the *āḥ*. {233} Similarly, by the application of the radiating and gathering to the *āḥ* at the throat and *hūṃ* at the heart as above, the sun, moon, vajra, and syllables all dissolve into light, filling the feast tray to the brim. Imagine that it becomes a great ocean of the undissipating elixir of the feast circle, white with a tinge of red and a bluish light, totally permeating the realms of the world.

## The Serving

Ḍākinīs of various colors come from your form as Vajrayoginī and from all your pores carrying various containers, such as skull cups and human skins. They emanate like swirling particles in the rays of the sun and scoop up the feast torma. It becomes immeasurable outer, inner, and secret offering substances that accord with [the recipients'] individual faculties. It is offered to the gurus, from Vajradhara down to your root guru. It is offered to the hosts of yidam deities, from the principal deity of the mandala, such as Chakrasaṃvara, down to the peripheral heroes and heroines. It is offered to all the ḍākinīs, from Vajravārāhī down to those belonging to the five families who move in space, move on the ground, and move beneath the ground. It is offered to the protectors, from the Glorious Awareness Protector and Goddess down to the male lineage and female lineage dharma guards and the fierce guards at the periphery of the mandala that are clustered like clouds. It is offered to the hosts of the six classes, from the Victor Shākyamuni down to the eighteen hell realms. It is offered to the spirits, from the ground masters of the billionfold universe down to your own embedded gods and demons. And it is served to the form and formless ones, from the guests of the six classes, especially the creditors.

Also, when performing the laying-on of hands for the sick and so on, visualize the five fingers of your right hand as the five ḍākinīs {234} and the five fingers of your left hand as the five powerful mover [ḍākinīs] (*shugs 'gro*). Imagine that innumerable ḍākinīs emanate from them, each eating [the patient] from head to toe themselves and giving it to other [beings], leaving not even a scrap of leftovers. Afterward, do some of the individual red distributions. Finally, rest without reference to the three spheres and seal it with the dedication of the accumulated virtue.

The offering to the guests of samsara and nirvana of exactly what they each want in their own ground without changing colors or shifting forms or fabricating looks is a banquet of offering and giving without discrimination in the equality of samsara and nirvana. It is called "the feast circle of the great being" (*bdag nyid chen po'i tshogs 'khor*). It is especially elevated over the offerings in the Sutra tradition, and not just in being similar to the style of feast circles in Mantra. It is not identical to that exactly, but it is said to belong to the domain of intelligent individuals. According to the former teaching tradition and to Mantra itself, those guests are originally coemergent since forever, as the timeless awareness of great bliss that is the actual Vajradhara. However, the stains of temporary dualistic delusions govern at this point, and various embodiments of that delusion appear. Nevertheless, since that original beginningless time itself, wishful forms, colors, implements, ornaments, and accoutrements of the principal and entourage, and so forth, are the embodiment of the timeless awareness of signs—the symbolic meaning. Thus, the triad of *Chakrasaṃvara*, *Hevajra*, and *Guhyasamāja*; the triad of *Māyājāla*, *Buddhakapāla*, and *Chatuḥpīṭhā*; *Kālachakra*, the *Eight Herukas*, and *Summary of the Intentions*,[28] and so forth *are* Glorious

Heruka. So it is a meditation on their forms in that sense of being. It is a meditation on the offering substance of the feast circle—all outer environment and inner contents, such as the five meats and the five elixirs—as the mandala of the original great bliss. This, then, is the actual feast circle of Unsurpassed Mantra, and it is especially distinguished from other common offering practices. {235}

When you offer the feast circle of whatever pleases whichever desires in that way, the outer feast consists of the items, adornments, clothes, dwellings, and palaces of the guests' own individual realms. The inner feast consists of food, drink, and the substances of physical sustenance. The secret feast engenders the bliss and joy of sexual intercourse. The suchness feast is to abide in the nondual great bliss of lucid clarity and reflexive awareness once the stains of dualistic delusion are purified in their own grounds. All of these are enjoyed. Lord Trungpa Rinpoche said:

> The outer [offering] is the extent of actual material things and such that are not at all grasped by an owner; the inner is fortune, fame, and so forth; the secret is the intercourse of father-mother and so forth; and suchness is mahāmudrā without reference to the three spheres.

In line with that, the feast substances of five meats and five elixirs and so forth—all the substances of various meats, various bloods, various alcohols, various grains, and so on—are gathered together into a single feast and consecrated.

The special priceless substances in the realms of the world increase for all kinds of guests of samsara and nirvana. For the highest ones dwelling on the stages and paths, timeless awareness grows greater and greater. For those who abide in sacred pledge, engaging [in the feast] without doubt purifies all the stains that come from imputing (*kun brtags*) good and bad, clean and dirty, and so on, regarding apparent things and the dependent nature (*gzhan dbang*) that fixates on samsara and nirvana as the pleasure and pain [that comes from] clinging to the reality [of these things]. The actualization of the embodiment of unity, great bliss, four kāyas, and fivefold awareness in the original absolute nature (*yongs grub*) is the intention of the unsurpassable feast circle. Therefore, persevere with understanding, experience, and realization.

Then, replenish the primary torma from the feast {236} and sprinkle it with elixir. If [the ritual is] extensive, do the inner torma of Secret Mantra or the "outer vessel of the world . . ." (*phyi snod 'jig rten . . .*) from the feast source text.[29] If extremely abbreviated, it is also sufficient to do a little "outer vessel of the world. . . ." Then sprinkle the fulfillment torma with elixir and visualize the fulfillment (*bskang ba*) in accordance with the meditation chant, and recite "Akaniṣhṭha . . ." (*'og min . . .*) and so on or whatever Severance fulfillment you want. Finally, the master and disciples enjoy the feast. Gather the leftovers on a plate and sprinkle them with elixir.

### Visualization for the Leftovers

As you appear clearly as Jetsunma, either four skeleton ḍākinīs or else just one emanates from your heart. Externally they have no flesh or skin. Internally they are without blood, organs, or hearts. Pale and jittery, they stand holding in their hands a skull vessel equal in size to the billionfold universe with the torma of leftovers inside—a fine and vast inexhaustible sea of flesh and blood possessing the qualities of the five sense desirables. They carry it and offer it to the ḍākinīs of the five families, who, although transcendent, take on the manner of the mundane, with hair of white, yellow, red, green, and dark blue. Their entourages, included by your mere thought, are ḍākinīs with sky-like bodies that can travel to whatever place they want, and powerful mover ḍākinīs that move like soaring vultures slicing swiftly through the sky to wherever they desire. In addition, there are the twenty-eight mighty ones (*dbang phyug*) that are empowered to receive leftovers, ground-protector heroes and ḍākinīs, haughty chieftains with their demon hordes gathered thick as clouds, the meek and powerless who were not able to obtain the former banquet, and so forth. In short, it is given to all those empowered to receive leftovers. Imagine them noisily consuming precisely what pleases them and put the leftovers outside.

All those who do the main practice of the Severance feast do not necessarily include the torma of leftovers at this point. {237} However, the lineage holders of the great adept Mase Rinpoche's[30] practice have been instructed to follow the sevenfold torma of leftovers done here, with Vajravārāhī and the realm ḍākinīs, the twenty-four sacred sites, and so forth.

## Offering the Torma of Severance

Think of the feast-leftovers torma as an ocean of elixir, the enjoyment of all needs. Invoke Machik's command guards (*bka' srung*), such as the five sets of worldly ḍākinīs, the three wolf-mounted siblings, night howlers, the Mountain God of Shampo, wild *tsen* spirits of Copper Mountain, and so forth. Imagine that they partake of the torma and accomplish all enlightened activity. Then recite from "*Kye!* Mother, nonhuman ḍākinī of timeless awareness . . ." (*kye / ma mi min ye shes mkha' 'gro ma . . .*) up through ". . . May flesh debts and liabilities . . . be cleared" (*. . . lan chags sha mkhon byang gyur cig*),[31] and throw it outside. On the occasion of performing wrathful actions, there is apparently a custom of doing the dance of Hayagrīva here, but that is not necessary for the feast activity.

Then replenish all the offerings and tormas, reciting *oṃ guru deva ḍākinī arghaṃ* . . . and so on. Offer with ". . . the Kagyu gurus, roots of blessing, . . ." (*byin rlabs kyi rtsa ba bka' brgyud bla ma rnams . . .*) and so on.[32] Praise with "Unutterable, unimaginable, inexpressible . . ." (*smra bsam brjod med . . .*). Recite from "Whatever I have not provided . . ." (*ma byor pa . . .)* through ". . . in the ritual of Great Mother dharmakāya . . ." (*. . . chos sku yum chen mo'i cho ga . . .*) and so on. Finally recite [the confession] from "*namo guru*, . . . [whatever] great happiness . . ." (*na mo gu ru / bde ba legs pa . . .*) until ". . . establish me in the state of irreversible great bliss" (*. . . mi ldog bde chen gyi sa la 'god gyur cig*).[33] Say the one-hundred-syllable mantra three times.

Then light rays radiate from your heart as Vajrayoginī and strike the Great Mother in the sky in front of you. Light rays radiate from the Great Mother's heart and strike the assembly of deities in the sky. Imagine the awareness beings returning to their own abodes. Recite the quatrain "*Oṃ* You [have performed] the welfare of beings . . ." (*oṃ / khyed kyi sems can don kun [mdzod] . . .*).[34] {238} After "*vajra mu*" conclude with *phaṭ*.

Then for the [visualized] pledge beings: the bodhisattvas to the right dissolve into the holy dharma, the holy dharma dissolves into the shrāvakas on the left, the shrāvakas dissolve into the buddhas of the ten directions, and they dissolve into the buddhas of the past, present, and future. Those three buddhas then dissolve into the Great Mother. The Kagyu lamas above and the host of yidam deities in between also all dissolve into the Great Mother. The Great Mother then dissolves into Machik in front. All other forms such as the ḍākinīs also dissolve into Machik. Machik, who is the embodiment of all the buddhas of the three times, inseparable and indivisible from your own root guru, dwells an arrow's length above your head. Imagine that and recite "*hūṃ* / Heart child emanated from the Great Mother's heart . . ." (*hūṃ / ma yum chen thugs las sprul pa'i thugs kyi sras* . . .) and so on.[35] And from "When you take three steps from the east . . ." (*shar nas gom gsum byon tsa na* . . .), continuing until after [three steps from] the center, through to the [request for] blessing.[36]

Imagine that light rays from your heart radiate to Machik and dissolve into light. The light rays become the size of a goose egg, which enters the top of your head and transforms all males into the form of noble Avalokiteshvara and all females into the form of noble Tārā. Repeat numerous six-syllable mantras. Say *phaṭ* and imagine that the guests, having been pacified and delighted, depart to their own places. You too transform into the white ḍākinī from before and enter into the ways of conduct, remaining in emptiness like the center of space.

Additionally, there is one tradition whereby during the meditation of Machik at the crown of the head, you imagine the five families—dark blue in the center, white in the east, yellow in the south, red in the west, and green in the north—and after supplicating them, the four dissolve into the principal one in the center. {239}

As your continuing practice goes well, you make a connection with the feast activities or other protection circles and so forth. When that time comes, there are two so-called esoteric instructions of the Round Lotus (*padma kha zlum*). First is the Peaceful Round. After the supplication described above, Machik dissolves into light. According to the former teaching tradition, Machik's form becomes extremely small, its face, hands, ornaments and accessories, and so forth, all clear and distinct, emanating light rays of the five colors. It enters your head through the cranial aperture and falls down the central channel. At the heart there is a white lotus with eight petals and stamens emanating five-colored light rays. Imagine that she comes to rest in its center in full lotus posture. The lotus petals in the directions are like closed flowers. Alternatively, meditate on Hevajra as a vase body. This is the Peaceful Round Lotus.

In the Wrathful Round, discard the previous lotus and [instead] in your heart there is an eight-spoked wheel of meteorite metal situated like a dome. Within it are souls (*bla*) and life forces of the enemies and obstructors, the essence of consciousness combined into the single essence of your own and others' intrinsic awareness. Think, "Until awakening I will not let go." That is the Wrathful Round Lotus. There is also the opinion that at this point one does not imagine the form described above but rather a drop. Afterward, do the dedication, aspiration, and prayers of auspiciousness extensively.

That is the end of the descriptions of the source feasts, body donations, and such, according to the oral tradition of Trungpa Rinpoche's intentions.

## [Wrathful Magnetizing and Red Distributions]

Second are the sequences for wrathful magnetizing and red distributions on the occasion of the body donation, wrathful activities, and so forth. After the three cycles of blending,[37] the consciousness transforms into the dark-blue letter *hūṃ*. Recite, "Instantly I [transform] into Krodhīkālī, the mistress of the graveyard . . ." (*skad cig bdag nyid dur khrod bdag mo khros ma nag mo . . .*) as in the meditation chant in the source text. In physical size, the head reaches as high as the gods' realm of Thirty-Three, and {240} likewise the upper body dominates the gods' realms—generate the pride of magnitude. The magnetizing action messengers are the worker ḍākinīs that emanate from your heart—white ones carrying hooks and so on—that cluster like dust particles in the rays of sunlight. Above, below, and all directions are completely cleared. Continue with the meditation chant. The spirits that are to be controlled are all the spirits from the enemy of self-fixating concepts and so on down to the spirits and their leaders from above, below, and in all directions. They are fastened by hooks, snared by lassos, bound by chains, and driven physically and mentally mad by bells. Additionally, they are trapped by the human skins held in the right hands of all the Krodhīs and terrorized unto trembling by the fierce blowing of the human-thighbone trumpets in their left hands. They are irresistibly drawn before you like husks in a great wind. Thinking about the great mountains of flesh, oceans of blood, and heaps of bones of the previous corpse, imagine that all those spirits consume the flesh like full-grown tigers, drink all the blood like calves suckling violently at the teat, chew all the bones like munching hares, and don all the skins however they fit. Imagine them totally delighted and recite, "*Kye!* Gather . . ." (*kye / dus shig . . .*) and so on from the meditation chant.

Also, if you want to do various red distributions at this point, do them as described below. Then imagine that in front of you as Krodhī are the mendicants (*bande*), mantrins, Severance practitioners, and so on who hold negative intentions such as malice toward you, each wearing their own garb. They carry instruments such as sickles for commissioning any of the four ele-

...ied by their curse-casting protector deities. Generate ...hat is awesome and menacing. To their right is the king of ...the form of a mendicant or minister, surrounded by infinite ...e hordes of yellow *gyalpo* spirits. To their left is Raivatī (Nam gru ...queen of the demonesses, with turquoise hair, yellow eyebrows, and ...nch-like fangs. She is surrounded by great demoness hosts of beautiful, seductive women like young maidens and by ugly, emaciated *senmo* spirits, some of them wearing clothes of human skin and such. In front is the king of earth lords with nine toad heads, surrounded by squadrons of earth lords and ground masters, such as the seventeen earth lord chiefs and ministers. In back is fish-headed Genyen carrying various weapons in his hands, together with an entourage similar to himself, and further surrounded by many more with various indefinite heads. Below the evildoers (*byad ma*) is the nāga devil with nine serpent heads, carrying a serpent lasso in his right hand and a bag of disease in the left, his lower body a writhing black serpent. He is surrounded by more black nāga devils like himself as well as those with various indefinite shapes. Meditate that they dwell inside the mists and clouds at the entrance to lakes. In the sky above the evildoers, amid black clouds and agitated rainbows, is the planet devil Rāhula, blue-black and just as described in the visualizations, surrounded by armies of planets and constellations. There are boundless legions of black devils with black horses to the right and left and to the front and back of all of those. Similarly, there are red *tsen* spirits and red horses with multicolored fetlocks and red birds and red dogs. There are male and female ghosts[38] wearing the bodies of young men and women with various beautiful or ugly forms; {242} small *si* ghosts in the form of naked boys; hosts of pledge perverters in the form of mendicants, mantrins, and Severance practitioners; and male and female *teurang* spirits in forms with a single foot, children in goat-fur coats, mounted on goats, and so on. In addition, generate gods and demons that are the embodiments of the habitual tendencies of deluded appearances of dualism that are included in apparent existence, [appearing with their appropriate] colors, shapes, and ornaments, carrying various weapons in their hands, with unimaginable retinues of their emanations, filling up all the realms of the worlds. Recite the "power of truth" with the pride of being Krodhī, as before. As you draw in all those spirits from before, they melt into those forms. Then imagine that with the pride of being Krodhī or Vajrayoginī, you grab the corpse, which equals the reaches of the billionfold universe in size, by the foot and throw it in the face of all those spirits. The flesh, blood, and bones become like a torrential onslaught of desired payback, and the spirits each consume their own food with great delight. Imagine that and recite, "*hūṃ*, mother, the great mendicant . . ." (*hūṃ / ma ban chen . . .*).

Alternatively, it is fine to do the Slapping, or Molten Human Skin[39] or Food Distribution and so forth. There is also the practice of doing the Corpse Distribution when throwing out the squeezed dough (*chang bu*) and ablution water (*khrus chu*).

Also, at this time and on the previous occasion of the gathering to eat flesh and such, while feeding the patient as described above, the five fingers of the right hand become five iron wolves and the five fingers of the left hand become five copper jackals. Innumerable identical forms emanate from them, and they themselves eat and dispatch the food to others. It is also fitting to do numerous accumulations [of the feeding] to whatever spirits are harming you. In the end, those malicious spirits consume the flesh, blood, and bones with the murmuring, smacking noises of meat eating; whistling, sucking noises of blood drinking; {243} and growling, gnawing noises of bone chewing. Visualize according to the source texts and do the meditation chant.

Then, as soon as you do the feast in the source text according to the previous explanation, after the visualization there of the leftovers when the worker skeletons emanate from the heart and so on, recite the meditation chant of "Skull cup of three existences . . ." (*srid gsum bhandha . . .*) and "Everything is the sky treasury . . ." (*thams cad nam mkha' mdzod . . .*), and do the dedication and aspiration with "Practicing Severance Object . . ." (*gcod yul nyams su len pa'i . . .*). In order to recall the sense of connection with the meaning lineage of Severance, conclude with *phaṭ*. Then, as in the source text of the feast, send off the awareness beings, dissolve the pledge beings, do whichever of the Peaceful Round and Wrathful Round you wish, and send off the guests. Finally, rest in the state of emptiness and so forth as above.

### [Additional Feasts]
### Casting Out the Corpse

Now, concerning the amended sequences mentioned before, one could elaborate a bit here on those ancient oral traditions that were not included above. During the red distributions, the corpse that is left after the separation of awareness and corpse is a large body with oily white fat, supple and soft, delightful and delicious. Its youthful flesh is corpulent and has a ruddy radiance. It is pleasing to behold, beautiful, and captivating and exudes a variety of excellent aromas. Visualize that it pervades the billion-fold universe with its abundant abilities: the quintessential flavors that have the power to alleviate all the suffering of hunger and thirst. Imagine that the gods and demons—creditors and so forth—gobble it up noisily like carnivores rushing the kill. For example, imagine it the way that vultures consume a horse's corpse left out on the empty plain. This is Casting Out the Corpse (*bem bskur ma*).

### The Four Continents

Or again, imagine all the gods and demons in all directions greedily consuming the corpse that you as Vajrayoginī cut into the four parts of the upper and lower torso and plant in the four directions. This is the Four Continents (*gling bzhi ma*). {244}

### The Banners

Or imagine yourself as Jetsunma flaying and chopping the corpse with hooked knife in hand, creating a great ocean of blood with bones stuck in it like stakes and all the flesh raised on the bone tips like banners or standards, with a mighty waterfall of flesh, blood, and bones coming out of it that the malicious spirits enjoy until the end of cyclic existence. This is the Banners (*ba dan ma*).

### The Bone Shaker

Again, imagine Krodhī or Vajrayoginī grabbing the corpse by the feet and swinging it over the space above the spirits. Like shaking up fish that are cooking, the flesh, blood, and bones fall in a vast and continuous stream down the mouths of the gods and demons. They each enjoy whatever they desire. This is the Bone Shaker (*rus sprugs ma*).

### The Corpse Distribution

Again, imagine that a whole host of dry, moist, and shriveled corpses of children, adults, elders, and so forth, as numerous as the atoms of the entire universe, emanate from the corpse, filling all the realms of appearance like objects and subjects. Unimaginable [numbers of] ḍākinīs distribute it to the spirits, who eat it and are satiated. This is the Corpse Distribution (*ro 'gyed ma*).

### The Slapping

Again Krodhī or Vajrayoginī grabs the corpse by the two feet and carries it up into the sky. Infinite gods and demons approach from below with their mouths opened upward, chomping as if on stony barley husks. The visualization of throwing it down into their mouths is "slapping." Alternatively, the severed head of the corpse in front becomes a boulder of molten lead as big as the billionfold universe and [the remaining corpse] is slapped upon that, breaking apart the flesh, blood, and bones and releasing them in a bloody mess that is consumed by the gods and demons. This visualization is the Slapping (*brdeb pa ma*).

### The Food Distribution

The root of all the red distributions is the Food Distribution (*gzan 'gyed ma*). {245} As in the blending, transference, and so forth from the source text, the essence of intrinsic awareness is Vajrayoginī, who butchers, cuts, and blends the corpse. It becomes a great ocean of flesh and blood inside a vast and wide kapāla. Identical yoginīs as numerous as the atoms of the four elements emanate from your [Vajrayoginī's] body and pores, bestowing the feast to the spirits and obstructors in their various regions. They eat the flesh, drink the blood, and suck the bones. Imagine that they don the skins, laughing in pleasure with the sound of *ha* and singing funny songs of satisfaction. Or imagine dispatching slightly fewer of those ḍākinīs just to the billionfold universe. Or imagine dispatching only hundreds of thousands from there, covering just a small extent of land. Or dispatch a mere hundred thousand to the ten directions, and say *phaṭ* ten times. Again, imagine that the flesh and blood completely fills up all the worlds, and those spirits greedily consume whatever they prefer. It is also appropriate to do such visualizations as an addendum to the white distribution, the variegated distribution, and the feast circle, after transforming it into an ocean of flesh and blood.

## Additions from the Oral Tradition of the Former Elders of Severance

In the segment of going for refuge, there are meditations in the style described in many of the notebooks, such as the stacking-up of Machik, Muni, and the Great Mother when going for refuge.

In the segment on generating the deities, there are the so-called ascending seats (*gdan mas rim*). Next to the lotus, sun, moon, and so forth, that is Machik's seat, but higher than that and to the right, there is the lotus-moon seat. Straight in front of that to the left is the dharma source–sun-corpse seat. In the center part of those two, at a much-elevated height, is the lion throne with six ornaments. Thus the meditation on one above the other four times is called the ascending seats.

There is also the meditation that in the center of the upper lion throne is a dark-blue *hūṃ*; {246} below that in the center on top of the throne is a white *oṃ* encircled by a blue *hūṃ*, a yellow *trāṃ*, a red *hrīḥ*, and a green *āḥ*; on the throne below that is an orange letter *mūṃ*; and on the throne below that there is a white or yellow *a*. Then below that on the lotus seat you meditate on a white *hūṃ*. This is said to be the ascending seed syllables (*sa bon mas rim*).

The meditation beginning with the visualization of Machik in the central *hūṃ* up through Vajradhara on the blue letter *hūṃ* above is taught as the descending deities (*lha yas rim*). All else is the same as before.

In the segment on the purification of negativities, there are also some styles of teaching traditions where the *gate* mantra string encircles Machik's heart-syllable *hūṃ* and likewise *gate* in the Great Mother, and so forth. The other deities also have their own mantras according to family mantras arranged and circling around [the seed syllables]. Some people have stopped this practice. But for me, without either rejecting or accepting a part of the teaching tradition, I visualize that way when I have the leisure and good health. I always do the visualizations that were described above primarily from the notes of Trungpa Rinpoche.

Also, in the segment on the distributions, there are six modes of distribution[40] presented in the teaching tradition. This also appears in Trungpa Rinpoche's notebooks. These two sources have the same vital points, so therefore I too will follow them.

The common denominators of the feast circle in Trungpa Rinpoche's notes and in the oral tradition are these:

1. Arousing the awakening mind and gathering the guests;
2. Meditation on the objects of refuge, mind training of the four immeasurables, and invocation of the field of accumulation;
3. Homage and offerings by means of the eight branches;
4. Separating mind from body and offering the mandala; {247}
5. The generosity of giving the body offering;
6. Supplication and descent of blessings; and
7. Conclusion with the dedication and aspiration, and the dissolution.[41]

With these, the presentation of all the ritual sequences of the three parts—preliminary, main part, and conclusion—is complete. The teaching tradition of seven modes of distribution and textbooks that are believable are difficult to find. Not only that, it is difficult to coordinate the outlines of the distribution modes in the segment on the White Distribution for Four Guests and the outlines of those aforementioned seven, and so on. That being the case, there is no clear identification. So rest with equanimity.

For the segment on the descent of the ḍākinīs, you invoke innumerable ḍākinīs of the five families that emanate from Vajravārāhī, the ḍākinīs of the four families, the forms and sigils and so on, and many hundreds of thousands of similar five-family emanations from the four directions and the center. They come to dwell around the objects of refuge. When you supplicate them with fierce faith and devotion, those vast hundreds of thousands of ḍākinīs land on the ground, bestowing blessings on the outer environment and the beings within. Visualize that after you dispatch a million ḍākinīs of the five families from Vajrayoginī's heart, they carry the skull cup full of elixir and offer it to those aforementioned ḍākinīs. Those million ḍākinīs then merge into one hundred thousand and become inseparable from you as Yoginī. In the segment of the offering and giving that follows, again there is the custom of emanating innumerable such masses for doing the offerings.

In the segment on the ascent and blending of consciousness, there is a teaching tradition [that advises when] not to do the blending: do not send up an insane consciousness or a pregnant woman's consciousness, and do not blend the consciousness of a leper or a person afflicted with a grave disease, and so forth. {248}

In that way, Trungpa Rinpoche's notes and the former printed explanatory guidebooks form the basis for the visualization sessions in the source feast activities. My master, the previous omniscient Situ Rinpoche, on the occasion of giving the scriptural transmissions (*lung*) of the various Severance cycle writings (*be bum*), the guidance transmission (*khrid lung*) of the Iron Vajra Mother mountain cycle,[42] and so forth, directly from the mouth of the great omniscient excellency, said, "In this Severance cycle, these teaching traditions and notes of Trungpa Kunga Namgyal are the main ones you need to release, study, and expound. Otherwise, there are many textbooks of notes on Severance, but mostly they are hard to grasp with certainty." Since the time that my master said that, I have acted accordingly and this [has been written] in that tradition. Thus, there are many other customs in the various red feasts, such as the teachings of Bangarwa[43] and some others. In the teaching traditions, moreover, in this segment of the wrathful activities in the body donations and so forth, there are other references. This is certainly the case. Also there seems to be a tradition of scriptural transmission, guidance, and so forth, of *The Extensive Explanation of the Manual on the Sublime Path of Severing Evil Object* (*Lam mchog bdud kyi gcod yul zin bris rgyas par bkral ba*). That tradition has been practiced unaltered and so is satisfactory, but otherwise you do not need any other references.

In general, this instruction on the profound Severance of Evil Object is itself the intended meaning of the Great Mother that gives birth to four kinds of noble ones. It gestures in the direction of the meaning of the nonself of the person that is the realization of those in the foundational approaches, such as shrāvakas and pratyekabuddhas. It reveals the meaning of profound emptiness and the awakening mind that is born in the hearts of the noble ones once the self-fixation of both the person and phenomena is refuted based on the Perfection of Wisdom sutras in the middle dharma wheel on the absence of characteristics. And it manifestly demonstrates the essence of timeless awareness, the buddha nature, which is free of any dissolution, destruction, or diminishment, from the sutras that ascertain the definitive meaning in the final dharma wheel. {249} In a similar way, it presents the meaning of the actualized embodiment of great bliss, the original union, in the four kāyas and five awarenesses from the tantras of both ancient and new Mantra, as well as their techniques, such as the secret conduct, engagement with awareness (*rig spyod*), and so forth. Thus the profound meaning of all of the aspects of the path of method and wisdom are perfectly presented right here. Knowing that to be the case, you must practice from the bottom of your heart.

When that is not the case, even if you do some bit of practice for the mere pacification of the sickness, spirits, and adverse conditions of this life, or for the self-aggrandizing purpose of gaining wealth, renown, and desirables, you will have gone down the path of the three deviations of Severance. The six gods and demons, such as the four devils of self-fixation, will not become part of your path.

Therefore, in contrast, from the outset cut out as much as possible the entanglements of attachment and clinging to the causes of the four devils, such as the pleasures and joys of this life. In the middle, sever as much as you can the karmic actions, afflictive emotions, and all the deluded concepts. In the end, once you have severed in space all inflation—the habitual patterns of dualistic deluded appearances—and then realized the real intention of the Great Mother, the lucid clarity of unborn dharmakāya, you will reach actual perfect buddhahood. In the meantime, you must achieve the immeasurable welfare of beings through the four enlightened actions. So it is taught, and you should practice accordingly.

## Colophon

This clarification of the notes on Severance was done by Bengen Tenzin Namdak, after donning as my crown the king of wish-fulfilling gems who commanded it, Garwang Chokgi Tulku,[44] the supreme leader and crown jewel of the Zurmang Kagyu practice lineage of essential meaning, that glorious holy lord of the doctrine and of beings. {250} Due to illness and poor eyesight, I dictated this in stages to Yeshe Wangden, a young Shākya monk, who wrote down the words and redacted them. May this virtue become the cause for the general doctrine of the victors and the doctrine of essential meaning to spread and the lotus feet of the doctrine holders to remain firm, and particularly may the immutable vajra throne of this sublime holy guru himself[45] remain steadfast for a hundred aeons; may the four kinds of enlightened activity increase effortlessly and spontaneously for the welfare of all beings throughout space; and may the doctrine of the essential practice lineage expand to the edges of space. Virtue!

# 18. Essence of the Vital Meaning

## *A Practice Manual of Profound Object Severance*[1]

### Tāranātha

In this practice instruction Tāranātha clearly lays out the main teachings of Severance and the order in which to practice them. To actually utilize this text as a practice, however, one would need the liturgy that should accompany these explanations, called *Supplication Liturgy for the Essence of the Vital Meaning: A Practice Manual of Profound Object Severance.** Kongtrul did not include that in this volume of the *Treasury,* perhaps because there were more recent liturgies from other lineage holders.

The *Record of Teachings Received* affirms that Kongtrul received the guidance or practice manual (*khrid yig*) "in the style of the transmission guidance (*lung khrid*) from the sacred writings of Venerable Kunga Drölchok and detailed guidance based on Venerable Jonang Tāranātha Rinpoche's *Essence of the Vital Meaning.*"†

As is typical of this particular lineage that originated with Machik via Samten Özer, through Kunga Drölchok, Tāranātha, and on to Kongtrul himself, the main practices have the specific designations of "the meaning of the Mother" (*yum don*) and "severing the four devils in basic space" (*bdud bzhi dbyings su gcod*). The first is the direct instruction on the nature of mind according to the perfection of wisdom (that is, the Mother), and the second is how to enact and enhance that realization through coping with the problematic experiences of existence, called the four devils. Everything beyond that is considered auxiliary practice to be done as postmeditation activity. This important fact was often lost as the demon-feeding

*Tāranātha, *Collected Works,* vol. 20, pp. 681–707.
†Tashi Chöpel, *Record of Teachings Received,* p. 773.

elements gained prominence, which is why Kongtrul emphasized it again and again.

---

*namo guru*

Source of spiritual powers, precious guru;
union of all places of refuge, precious lord of beings;
teacher of the abiding nature's meaning, precious dharma lord;
hero who conquers the four devils, grant your blessings.

A person who practices the profound Devil Severance
mentally gives up this life by recollecting capricious death,
has great fortitude and conviction devoid of nondharmic thoughts,
accomplishes the guru's advice entering haunted mountain retreats,
and blends bad circumstances in an expanse of equal value in whatever
occurs.

As stated, this is certainly what is needed. The required dharma practices are to cultivate devotion for the lineage and to have received the empowerment conferral that transfers the blessing. Then, the essence of the guiding instructions is [divided into] three: preliminaries, main practice, and conclusion.

## I. Preliminaries

This has four parts: refuge, arousing the aspiration, mandala, and guru yoga.

### A. Refuge

Imagine your root guru in the center of a lotus-and-sun seat on a lion throne in the sky in front of you. In front of the guru are the yidams and buddhas, to the right the volumes that are the essence of dharma, {187} to the left the sangha of the greater and lesser vehicles, and in back the ḍākinīs and dharma protectors. Thinking, "You know all the joy and sorrow, good and evil, of myself and all beings equal to the sky," say:

> All sentient beings equal to space, migrators such as myself,
> take refuge in Lord Buddha,
> take refuge in the holy dharma,
> take refuge in the sangha,
> take refuge in the guru, union of all.

And:

> I go for threefold refuge in the Buddha, dharma, and sangha.
> I go for threefold refuge in the guru, yidam, and ḍākinī.
> I go for threefold refuge in my own mind, emptiness, and dharmakāya.

Take refuge as much as you can. In the end, the objects of refuge dissolve into you.

### B. Arousing the Aspiration

In a state pained by love, compassion, and enlightening aspiration for all sentient beings that equal the reaches of space, reflect on this as you say this out loud:

> I will bring all these mother sentient beings happiness and all causes of happiness. {188}
> I will separate them from suffering and all causes of suffering.
> I will make them quickly attain unsurpassable enlightenment.

### C. Mandala

Imagine in front of you the guru inseparable from Machik Lapdrön, with the yidams in front of her and so forth, as in the refuge visualization. Offering substances, desirables, and luxuries of all world realms are piled high. Imagine offering that plus your own body, speech, and mind, along with your collection of virtue throughout the three times, to the guru and Jewels while offering any number of seven-heap mandalas. At the beginning and the end of each session, offer the extensive mandala. At the end of each mandala, say:

My body and possessions
and all virtue gathered in the three times
I offer to you, my guru and Jewels.
Please accept it with compassionate intent.

### D. Guru Yoga

Meditating on the guru and Machik inseparable above your head, arouse intense devotion from the bottom of your heart. If you want, do the lineage supplication of this practice. In particular, imagining that you and all sentient beings supplicate the guru with intense devotion, pray with single focus:

> Genuine Precious Guru, please bless me. You are my only hope; please bless me now. Bless me to relinquish ego-fixation. Bless me to decisively realize the unborn. Bless me to use obstacles as spiritual powers. Bless me that the devil hosts will be severed in their own ground. Bless me to achieve buddhahood in a single lifetime.

At the end of the session, the guru dissolves into light and absorbs into you. Recite prayers that you will be looked after by the guru, and then rest for a bit. {189}

Sometimes visualize each of those [separately] and meditate by training in each. Then [you could] meditate intensely on refuge in the morning, arousing the aspiration at midday, mandala in the evening, and guru yoga at night. Maintain that for a week or two or more. Whatever experiences are appropriate for those practices will come, and even a bit of experience[2] and realization related to the main practice might arise. In any case, those who have practiced them as individual meditations before should do each practice for seven days. Combining them all, it is important that the minimum time for the preliminaries be two and a half months.

### II. Main Practice

[This has two parts:] introducing the meaning of the Mother and severing the four devils in basic space.

## A. Introducing the Meaning of the Mother

[This has two parts:] instructions to apprehend the mind and the introduction.

### 1. Instructions to Apprehend the Mind

Place your body in the seven-point posture of Vairochana. Rest your speech in its natural condition. And for your mind, having cut off conceptual elaborations of the three times, rest in the immediacy of this instant of present consciousness when the previous thought has stopped and the next one has not arisen. If thoughts keep erupting, abruptly interrupt their trajectory and return to the previous way of maintaining. Since the biggest problem is the [unchecked] proliferation of an undercurrent [of subtle thoughts], make a powerful resolution that from now on this kind of thing won't occur, and remember it again and again. When you meditate as before, that [problem] will diminish.

For a while don't do any other method than just that. When you meditate for a long time, however, if only agitated thoughts arise, visualize a golden vajra the size of a barley grain in front of you, and concentrate by intensely focusing the awareness for the time it takes to eat three mouthfuls of food. Then right away return to maintaining a fresh state without contrivance. Again mentally focus on the vajra, and again maintain the state of freshness. [Again mentally focus on the vajra.][3] Alternating in this manner, meditate twenty-one times. If you do this every day, the force of the thoughts is broken {190} and they are completely clarified.[4]

In case that doesn't help, then in place of the vajra meditate on the form of the Bhagavān Buddha, Lord of Sages, about an inch high. Proceed as before with the other method. If even that doesn't work, then focus intently on the guru and Machik inseparable. A resounding *phaṭ* projects distinctly from her mouth, and from her body one-inch-high [miniatures] like blazing meteorites shoot out everywhere without obstruction, coming from everywhere and landing helter-skelter. They perforate your body, passing straight through from the top and bottom, and hither and thither. Then immediately meditate, maintaining a state of nonthought and so forth as before. This is the definite way to clear up all meandering thoughts and other obstacles to the arising of absorption.

With those kinds of techniques, when you rest in evenness as before, mind will abide however you want in clarity and vividness. You will be able to recall whatever you want, such as the needed frame of mind. Since this is not the unwanted mix of discursive thought, it approaches calm abiding.

At these times, if consciousness is not clear and there is a darkening gloom and in the breaks there is dullness with unclear recollection, it is the power of a gathering sinking. So go to a housetop or mountaintop or some other place that is cool and spacious. Gaze upward and intensify the awareness. If you meditate with concentration, that will certainly clear it up.

## 2. Introduction

Within that previous state, with the consciousness turned inward, look directly at the essence of that mind. External appearances with their variety will be vanquished just by your being unwavering. Since there is nothing at all, there is nothing to recognize—meditate again and again on just that. The guru needs to do the introduction in accordance with the way that your own experiences arise. Nonetheless, this is the way to put into practice the meaning that has been introduced:

When this mind itself is still, without any identification at all, self-appearance is lucid and clear, {191} but still arising and arising.[5] When it is moving, the essence of movement itself is empty of an objective object. Even though the appearance of movement is unhindered, there is not a single thing to identify. Even though various objective appearances arise, there is no identification from the first flashing-forth of the unimpeded appearing aspect arising and arising. Thus the essences of these three—objective appearance, conceptual thought, and the abiding mind—cannot be established as different. They are indivisible, yet not established as single: everything is empty of objective reality. This is precisely the meaning of the Great Mother Perfection of Wisdom. And one can certainly add any number of other designations: the intention of the buddhas of the three times, emptiness, free of elaboration, ineffability, the absolute, and so forth. Since the meaning is in the single moment of one's own mind, one rests in evenness without any fabrication through just recognizing that itself, whether there is abiding or movement or whatever.

### B. Severing the Four Devils in Basic Space

#### 1. Severing the Tangible Devil in Basic Space

The so-called tangible devil refers to the extent of the arising of fixating concepts in dependence on the objects of passion and aggression—enemies, friends, and so on—that are [perceived as] form, sound, smell, taste, or texture. The significance of "tangible" is that it is based on an external thing, such as form and so on—for instance, when you recall something like your supposed enemy and get worked up as aggressive thoughts gradually arise. To sever that, shout *phaṭ* that very instant without falling under its influence. Sever the concept abruptly as it emerges, without considering whether it has faults or qualities. Then rest freely there, as before, in the basic space of the meaning of the Mother. It is the same for mental attachment to friends, wealth, and other things, or attraction to pleasing forms and so forth, or disgust with what is unpleasant. You are afraid of some, upset at some, {192} and feel attachment or anger at anything in between, without discretion. Train as before with all emergence of intense conceptuality that fixates on those things. You will be carried off by the devil if you give in to the power of the sudden eruption of conceptual thought. Uttering *phaṭ* instantly and severing the flow of thought is Severance. Afterward, as the former meditation [on the meaning of the Mother] has been enhanced, there is the evidence of success and the evidence of severance. This applies in the same way to the following.

#### 2. Severing the Intangible Devil

The significance of the intangible devil is that it refers not to [events] based on external circumstances but to all conceptual thoughts such as joy or sorrow or excitement or regret or fear that arise even without [external] conditions. When those suddenly arise, sever their flow and rest in basic space.

#### 3. Severing the Devil of Exaltation

When [feelings of] exaltation and exhilaration arise based on pride and fixation on the greatness of having a good guru and dharma lineage, or on increasing spiritual practice, or conducive circumstances accruing to you, and so forth, it is the devil of exaltation. As above, sever it in basic space.

### 4. Severing the Devil of Inflation

Whatever concepts and fixations occur are all the devil of inflation. As before, *phaṭ* conveys all that arises to basic space to be cut off. This one includes the other three. Up to this point, it is worthless to wander in haunted retreats without experience with a well-established independent practice of your own. Foundational meditation must be established from this point on. Since doing it in haunted retreat is the enhancement and the reason for going, you need to understand it in this way.

## III. Conclusion: Maintaining Experience

This has three parts: peaceful severance; wrathful severance; and half-peaceful, half-wrathful severance.

### A. Peaceful Severance

In your own house, meditate intently for four sessions on love and compassion for all sentient beings. {193} At the end [of the fourth session][6] it is important to do the white distribution (*dkar 'gyed*) once. For that, imagine that three hearth skulls appear in front of you, and your own mind exits from between the eyebrows in the form of Vajravārāhī. The top of the skull is sliced off and placed upon the hearth skulls. The rest of the body is chopped up into pieces and poured into that. It becomes as vast as the reaches of the sky. As you utter *oṃ āḥ hūṃ* it turns it into an ocean of elixir. Root and lineage gurus, yidams, buddhas, bodhisattvas, heroes, ḍākinīs, and dharma guards and protectors are all invoked. As you offer it to all of them, they are satiated and pleased. As you donate it to all sentient beings of the six realms, they are temporarily satiated, and ultimately all of their negativity and obscuration will be purified. As you throw out the leftover elixir, innumerable offering goddesses arrive and offer it as unimaginable offerings. Understand that all of that is your own mind. Looking nakedly at its essence, utter *phaṭ* and blend space and awareness. Again all of that manifests vividly, and while recollecting it, say *phaṭ* again and blend space and awareness. Go through that process many times.

Once your visualization is somewhat trained by this meditation, you can go in person to a haunted place and there set your intention. Meditate with intense love and compassion for all sentient beings in general, and in particular for the local spirits, elementals, demons, malicious spirits, and such that live in that place. Then do the visualization of the white distribution as before, practicing it again and again for two or three days. When that is successful, again meditate by turns on love and compassion and blending space and awareness.

After arriving in that place, search for a power place to sit down. There, first send off a fragment torma (*sil gtor*) to the local spirit hosts, a general torma to the ḍākinīs, a local spirit host torma, {194} an obstructor torma, and whatever others you know about. It's very important to meditate intensely on love and compassion for them as well. Then for the preliminaries and so forth, dedicate yourself to the four parts of the preliminary practices for quite a long time. Afterward, meditate many times on the visualization of the white distribution as described above. Then again visualize sentient beings of the six realms and primarily the particular demons and malicious spirits of that haunted place and meditate with intense love and compassion. That area and the demons and spirits and so forth will appear vividly as sentient beings. Intently focus your consciousness directly upon them, blend awareness and space saying *phaṭ*, and rest without fixation. Again meditate on compassion. Again blend space and awareness and so forth—meditating on that alone. No matter what sights and apparitions occur, wrap yourself in these two [methods] of blending space and awareness and meditating on compassion. It is appropriate whether or not fierce apparitions occur. Ultimately, when the place feels quite pleasant and the spiritual practice is greatly enhanced, you are ready for evidence of success and evidence of severance. To give thanks for the enhancement of spiritual practice by means of visualization, do the white distribution many times and dedicate it to the yidams and ḍākinīs, and donate vast tormas to all the local spirit hosts. Recite whatever aspiration prayers you know. On the road, meditate as before, and when you arrive back home, offer as gratitude whatever offering tormas you know to the Three Jewels.

### B. Wrathful Severance

At first in your own home do the practice in sessions as with the peaceful severance, but at the final session do the visualization of the red distribution (*dmar 'gyed*) one time. For the red distribution, your mind goes out as before. Your body becomes an oily, greasy, juicy human corpse filling the billionfold universe. When you call out the summonses to the eight kinds of gods and spirits in the world realm, they all gather immediately. Imagine them pervading the earth and the sky. Then chop up the parts of your body into pieces, and say, "You all eat whatever you like, enjoy whatever you desire." {195} They eat, drink, and carry away the parts of flesh, blood, bones, innards, and limbs that they each prefer. Imagine that they are satisfied for the time being and that ultimately their afflictive emotions are pacified. Then meditate that they have all returned to their own places again. Then, while understanding that it is all your own mind, say *phaṭ* to blend space and awareness, and rest. Meditate in that way over and over again. When that becomes somewhat familiar, meditate for two or three days while visualizing a haunted place. The way to meditate on the road is the same as for the peaceful severance. When you arrive there, find a power spot to sit, and do the four preliminary practices and generally practice as before. Meditate on the guru and Machik inseparable and the five kinds of ḍākinīs with their entourages. During the guru yoga, guru-Machik inseparable dissolves into you and you imagine that you have become the ḍākinī of timeless awareness, blazing with the ferocious fire of timeless awareness, dancing with various wrathful stances, and resounding like thunder with various wrathful mantras. At this point you need to have the pride of actually being Machik and, without ever harboring ill will toward the demons and spirits, understand that they are all an illusory dream, blending more and more your own mind with the essence of whatever arises. [Say *phaṭ* and only do the blending of space and awareness. If turmoil and apparitions rise up,][7] run and jump with *phaṭ* and utter all the wrathful mantras you know.

Then, back in the place that you left, rest in the evenness of emptiness alone. Whatever lofty and lowly mind states or perceptual concepts occur, just say *phaṭ* and blend space and awareness. No matter what turmoil and apparitions rise up externally as visual appearances, internally as sickness, or secretly as afflictive emotions, wrong views, and so forth, know that they are delusions and just blend space and awareness. Don't do anything else. Just rest in the evenness of the meaning of the Mother. {196} Take up the practice with a promise and sincere oath never to say anything with the speech or move around with the body. At all times be without even an atom of cherishing body and mind. If it turns out that you have actually been transported by fierce gods and demons, imagine that you are still sitting in the previous vacated place [but stay where you are].

The actual practice is that in your current circumstances it is important that you do not succumb to requesting refuge of another, or succumb to a protection circle, or succumb to subduing demons, or succumb to hopes and fears. This is crucial no matter what occurs: cultivate an attitude of indifference and remain always in nonconceptuality by blending space and awareness.

As explained before, if the evidence of success and uprising are in order, do a few of the red distribution visualizations and then do the concluding practices as in the peaceful severance. Offer any number of tormas, such as water torma and nāga torma and so forth, and do many aspiration prayers. It is important to exert yourself at activities such as explaining the dharma and reciting sutras. When you do so, degeneration of [the spirits'] abodes, physical well-being, and wealth will be restored; they will become much more purified than before; and their thoughts will be endowed with dharma. Imagine that again and again, and do the concluding practices as before.

### C. Half-Peaceful, Half-Wrathful Severance

Do the preliminaries as before and then meditate on both white and red distributions. As soon as you arrive at a haunted retreat place, offer copious tormas as in the peaceful severance practice. For the four preliminary practices, do the first two sessions as in the peaceful severance and the last two sessions as in the wrathful severance. In the practice of the main part, for each session first do the peaceful severance visualization many times, and then, as in the wrathful severance, meditate only on emptiness. If uprisings do not occur for a long time, do the elaborate-style conduct for provoking uprisings described in the wrathful severance. Uprisings will certainly come. For a while, until they settle down, {197} meditate only on emptiness as in the wrathful severance. If it happens that gods and demons actually attack, tear out your whole living heart and give it to them or resolutely cut off your head, arms, and legs and give them away. Without even separating body and mind, without an atom of cherishing your body, this casting out the body as food is crucial. When the [evidence of] success and uprising are set, do the concluding activities as above.

A word about the required occasions for those [practices]: At first, go to practice peaceful severance in a retreat place with good, auspicious characteristics, where there are gentle local spirits sympathetic to dharma. It's very difficult to apply the practice in action if right from the start you do wrathful severance and stay in rough places and go to the abodes of malicious demons and spirits. Even if you can make your way there, it sets up bad interdependent connections with your dharma lineage, spiritual companions, and so forth. Therefore, for the first two or three times, do practice based upon peaceful severance in auspicious haunted places, and then after that meditate on peaceful severance in a few middling haunted retreats. Then meditate on peaceful severance in a few rough haunted places. In that way, when you have refined meditation in many haunted places, you can do the appropriate half-peaceful, half-wrathful severance in a few rough haunted places. In places of really malicious demons and spirits, the wrathful severance alone is only done on occasion. Generally, the ongoing practice is the combined peaceful-wrathful severance. Where the gods and demons are gentle and sympathetic to dharma, do mainly the actual peaceful severance, though it is appropriate to do the half-peaceful, half-wrathful as the occasion demands. It is not good to do wrathful severance alone.

Here the combined peaceful-wrathful as it was presented above is called "elaborate." The final practices of alternating meditation on love and compassion and blending space and awareness, as in the peaceful severance, are called "unelaborate." Afterward, entering into evenness on the meaning of the Mother alone is called "exceedingly unelaborate severance." {198} Therefore, you should meditate with that relationship to them.

When you set out to do Severance, if intense aggressive or passionate afflictive emotions arise, or devotion to the guru strays into fickleness, or your sacred pledges lapse due to arguing with spiritual companions and so forth, or seminal fluid is diminished, then the interdependent connections have deviated and wandering in haunted places will not be effective. In those cases it is important to fix the particular interdependent connections through supplications, compassion, confession, aspiration prayers, feast offerings, tormas, meditation on the energy channels and winds, and so forth before going.

Of three kinds of uprisings, outer uprisings are earthquakes, avalanches, and frightening visual and auditory perceptions that are certain to occur. Inner uprisings are sudden intense sickness such as depressive heart disease,[8] encephalitis, intestinal colic, and so forth. Secret uprisings occur in the mind. They are like the arising of unalterable feelings of happiness and sadness, fear, revulsion, thoughts of desirables, various impressions of the eight concerns, the increase of thoughts influenced by the three poisons, and so forth. When they occur, wrong views of the dharma and the guru come up. All of these sorts of things should be understood as being uprisings. Do not move physically. Except for your daily recitation routine and *phaṭ*, maintain the discipline of not uttering ordinary speech. Do not come under the influence of whatever perceptions occur in the mind. Blending space and awareness is important.

Also, when you need to stay in a place where many people gather or when you need to travel, persisting in spiritual practice in front of people is generally proscribed, and in particular shouting wrathful mantras [such as] *phaṭ* is inelegant. So it is important to keep *phaṭ* to a whisper and never deviate from your mode of practice.

In the case of local humans, demons, and spirits of a certain area {199} suddenly arising as visible objects or mental appearances, meditate with yearning compassion for all human and nonhuman beings, and set the intention of thinking that all of them are brought under your control. Then by your uttering *phaṭ* all of them are carried over to basic space. You can do this visualization at dawn or whenever, repeating it any number of times and then meditating. Finally, do extensive aspiration prayers. When you meditate without any attachment to anything, as if it is illusion, all the human and nonhuman beings in those areas will certainly come under your control. As this illustrates, this vital point of visualization should be applied in a similar fashion to whichever of the four actions you wish to accomplish.

Furthermore, when you convey devoted supplication to basic space, the guru accepts you with compassion and blessings enter. When you convey compassion to basic space, the welfare of migrators is accomplished and sentient beings are brought under control. When you convey revulsion and renunciation to basic space, your own individual spiritual practice gets to the point, and the mindstreams of others are greatly inspired in the dharma. When you convey the creation phase to basic space, abilities grow, and mundane and supramundane dharmas are brought under control. When you convey the yogas of energy channels, winds, and drops to basic space, realization grows greater and greater while the gathering of outer and inner ḍākinīs is continuous. If wandering in haunted retreats gets to the vital point, the fierce eight classes of spirits can all be compelled to serve. Furthermore, if desire is conveyed to basic space, you can subdue desirous beings, gathering them as your entourage. However, if you do not keep them with compassion, it will cause obstacles to arise for you and your close circle. Therefore, in conveying desire to basic space, it is important to convey that emptiness over to compassion. As that illustrates, the other thoughts of afflictive emotion can be applied similarly.

At the root of all of them is the importance of having no hopes or fears. Although Severance in general is a practice that clears away all obstacles and attains spiritual powers, {200} you must have absolutely no desires and hopes to gain such spiritual powers and benefits. You must have absolutely no fear about obstacles and troubles occurring and no hope of alleviating them. If the innermost flaws in your mind are not exposed, spiritual practice will not get to the point. Those with the wrong attitude about the guru, who judge the dharma, who are self-complacent and in denial, who grasp wealth and possessions with the clutch of death, and are so carried away by hopes and fears that they can't make up their minds—how could they possibly give rise to meditation by taking up the path of haunted retreats? Talk of pacifying the uprisings of malicious gods and demons and talk of achieving a bit of wealth and notoriety cause much confusion. So until there is great development of the mind of spiritual practice, do not trust in pseudo evidence of success. If spiritual practice is actually enhanced, it doesn't matter if the other things happen or not. That is the final point of good advice.

The essential meaning of all Object Severance
is summarized here in its intention.
Fortunate child, do the practice!
Don't be scatterbrained!

This *Essence of the Vital Meaning: A Practice Manual of Profound Object Severance* was taught by Tāranātha at the request of Jadralwa Rinchen Tashi and compiled at the dharma school of Taklung Tang.[9] Auspicious!

# 19. Rainfall of Desirables

## *A Profound Guide on Severance Instruction*[1]

Könchok Bang

Rainfall of Desirables is a supplement to the liturgy that immediately follows it, *The Body Donation and Feeding Ritual*. The two are listed under one heading in the Shechen edition and were apparently compiled together in this form by Karma Chakme Rinpoche, which may be why it is attributed to Karma Chakme in the Kundeling printing. However, they are listed separately in the *Catalog*.

This text is signed Könchok Bang (dKon mchog 'bang), the ordination name of the fifth Zhamar incarnation, Könchok Yenlak (dKon mchog yan lag, 1525–1583). He was the student and successor of the eighth Karmapa, Mikyö Dorje (Mi bskyod rdo rje, 1507–1554), himself a very important author in the Severance tradition. Könchok Yenlak was a prolific master whose commentaries on such works as the *Ornament of Clear Realization* (*Abhisamayālaṃkāra*) and *The Profound Inner Principles* (*Zab mo nang don*) are widely consulted. He authored several other texts on Severance that are listed in the Drepung Catalog, as well as providing the groundwork for a number of compositions on Severance by Karma Chakme.

*Rainfall of Desirables* contains some very practical instructions on the Severance practice that are not always found in other explanations: for example, what time of day or night to travel to and from the Severance practice locations; how to get there using various gaits; which apparitions are easy to deal with and which are difficult; how to prevent hail; and what to do in other specific challenging situations. The descriptions of the visualizations are quite brief, and many of the recitations are merely indicated by a few words. The full text of these can be found in *The Body Donation and Feeding Ritual*.

Aside from this useful information, what is most interesting about the text is that it appears to be based on a mysterious text called *Machik's Vajra Verses* (*Ma gchig gi rdo rje tshig rkang*). *Rainfall of Desirables* provides numerous intriguing quotations from that source, as does *The Body Donation and Feeding Ritual.* Other than these two texts and one brief mention in *Machik's Complete Explanation*,* this seemingly crucial source text has not surfaced.

---

I bow to the Great Mother Perfection of Wisdom,
the incomparable guru's body, speech, and mind,
the very essence of utter simplicity,
as I write this guide on the stages of Severance.

### I. Identification of What Is to Be Severed: The Devils

Machik stated:

> The tangible devil and the intangible devil,
> the devil of exaltation, and the devil of inflation.[2]

As taught there, the first of those four refers to appearing objects of the five senses, such as fire, water, poison, weapons, wild animals, and so forth. The intangible devil, from an external standpoint, is the gods and demons that appear in the person's field of vision moving through space. From an internal standpoint, it is afflictive emotion, sickness, suffering, and so forth. The devil of exaltation is to create the desire of hoping to attain the benefits and results of practice. The devil of inflation is the projection of various discursive thoughts.

### II. The Manner: How to Sever Them

### A. The Method to Raise What Has Not Risen Up {253}

### 1. Presentation of the Person Who Practices Severance

The superior individual is endowed with the four aspects of greatness that will be explained below.[3] The average individual is one who has great faith

*Harding, *Machik's Complete Explanation: Clarifying the Meaning of Chöd,* p. 101.

and does not lose the visualization sequence. The inferior individual must at least have diligence and little attachment.

## 2. Required Articles

These are the thighbone trumpet, skull cup, ḍamaru, *chokpu* tent,[4] small seat of human skin, and such, and an eye veil (*dom ra*) of four finger-widths.

## 3. Haunted Places and What Dwells There

Mountain ravines; valleys in great drought; glistening deserts; places in the shadow of mountain peaks; rocky peaks; charnel grounds; empty valleys; empty houses; lone trees; springs with nine, seven, five, or three outlets; springs, trickles, puddles, and so forth; wherever the sun does not penetrate {254}—in short, any place that is scary is a haunted place. There, a spring with nine outlets is a dwelling place for nāga outcastes, seven for priestly caste, five for warrior caste, and three for merchant and commoner castes. Minor nāgas dwell in water that is untouched by the sun. Pestilent spirits live by single juniper trees and bushes on the banks of lakes, and in all scary waters. Earth lords dwell in areas where there are things like boulders, tigers, snakes, toads, birds, and boars. Great pestilent nāga earth lords stay where there are things like rock faces, mountain hollows, frogs, scorpions, bears, yaks, camels, and water buffalo. *Tsen* spirits live among cliff faces that are like short swords,[5] and spurs and fissures in the rock face and lands with cliff cracks like braids.[6] Dense forests are places of devils. Oath breakers, *teurang,* and *sinmo* spirits live in overhangs, narrow defiles, crevice caves, and rock caves. *Serak* spirits, and male and female knife demons[7] dwell in the highland ruins, empty nomad camps, and market streets. *Mamo*s, death lords, and the masters of life force live in graveyards with crypts, *tsen* spirit houses, the remains of the dead, and the remains of those killed by warriors in battle. *Gyalpo* spirits and life-force master Pekar, and so on, live in shrine homes, storeroom homes, old monastery buildings, dilapidated practice houses, and isolated places.

## 4. The Way to Go There

Go there with a set gaze, as in [the phrase] "the yogin's gliding strut" (*rnal 'byor lding 'gros*). Go there dancing, as in "the ḍākinī's symbolic gait" (*mkha' 'gro'i brda' 'gros*). Go ambling back and forth, as in "the black mamba's undulation" (*sbrul nag 'kyugs 'gros*). Go there sometimes fast, sometimes slow, as in "the drunken elephant's gait" (*glang chen smyo 'gros*). The time to travel for staying in haunted places or taking off is midnight. The time to return is the coming of daybreak. That is said to be the practice.

### 5. Sequence of Visualization on How to Raise [the Spirits]

#### a. In General

In general, you must have the four great abilities of severance in haunted places: {255} the great vastness of emptiness realized as equal to the sky; the great natural liberality of magnanimity from great compassion and slight attachment; the great vast attainment of instructions by understanding all the vital points of the holy dharma; and the great perfect fidelity to practice due to diligence without laziness.

#### b. In Particular

##### i. The Visualization Sequence for Overwhelming

##### A) Actual

Before going, say *phaṭ*. From your heart a yellow vajra flies out like a bird and lands in the middle of the haunted ground. A bunch of hooks emanate from it and thoroughly draw in all the spirit hosts. Then flaming shackles bind them. When you set out to go, blow the thighbone, and say:

> *phaṭ*
> Right, left, front, back, above, below, and in ten directions,
> in mountains, springs, woods, and so forth,
> hosts of spirits of this place, come here for me.
> I will satisfy all your desires.

When you arrive at the haunted place and you dance in the four directions, blow the thighbone and say:

> *phaṭ*
> Today, in order to conquer the armies of the four devils,
> I, the yogin, dance for joy in the four directions.
> This dance of the four ḍākinī classes, swaying and swaying,
> conquers devils and thoughts, *a la la*!

### B) Supplement

When pitching the *chokpu* tent and laying out the seat, say:

> *phaṭ*
> The four kinds of ḍākinīs carry the tent stakes
> and plant them in the four continents and islands.
> This seat of flayed human skin covers the earth.
> Beneath it, all spirits and obstructors are suppressed.

These were a summary of the visualizations for the seven sets for overwhelming.[8] On this point, Machik's "Vajra Verses" states:

> Those that were not suppressed before,
> like bad enemies finding out top secrets, {256}
> need seven methods to overwhelm them.

### ii. The Actual Visualization of Uprisings

To do this according to the poem on Severance by the incomparable dharma lord,[9] visualize the three refuges and make the outer offerings. Then offer the body mandala and do the two supplications. First, arrange yourself on the seat with the vital points of the body posture and recite from "*namo guru* From now on the guru and Three Jewels . . ." (*na mo gu ru / deng nas bzung ste bla ma dkon mchog gsum* . . .) and so forth to ". . . within unembellished genuineness, directly expel" (. . . *spros bral ma bcos ngang der brjen par bud*). Do the meditation recitation intensely.

## 6. Evidence of Uprising and Evidence of Success

### a. Evidence of Uprising

Outer evidence of uprising includes the apparitions of gods and demons, displays of the forms of gods and demons, emission of sounds, repeated curses, and attempts at convincing you to reject the holy dharma. Inner uprising is physical sickness. Secret uprising is mental agony.

### b. Evidence of Success

Common evidence of success is the bestowal of things and food, other than of the red type [i.e., meat]. Uncommon evidence of success is to dream of the sun rising, wearing white clothes, washing the body, blood dripping, and expelling mucus. Furthermore, apparitions similar to evidence of success are dreaming of red clothes, giving blood, giving red meat, and so forth. Evidence of success similar to apparitions is when you or another attacks with weapons and draws blood. Those apparitions similar to evidence of success occur not only in dreams but also in visionary experience and such.

## B. Methods to Suppress Uprisings

### 1. Difficult- and Easy-to-Suppress Uprisings

In terms of place, charnel grounds, dilapidated temples, and the remains of dead men are frightening at the time but not ultimately frightening. {257} In terms of masters of place, *gyalpo* spirits, such as Pekar, and demonesses cause consciousness to be perturbed and awareness to fluctuate greatly between highs and lows. Though rough at the time, the uprising is easy and with little obscurity, so it is easy to suppress. Oath breakers and *sinmo* demonesses and mamos cause attachment to arise in the mind, loss of seminal drops, the desire to leave, and disenchantment. The uprisings are easy to suppress, but afterward there are unclean residues that make severance difficult later. Nāga devils and pestilent spirits and earth lords and *sin* spirits of the earth (*sa srin*) cause sleepiness, heavy consciousness, unclear awareness, and a drowsy dullness in which you cannot distinguish details. The suppression of uprisings of great drowsiness and so forth is difficult. Your confidence and mood will be very dark. *Tsen* spirits, *teurang,* and so forth show up as many turbulent dreams without focus. Uprisings whereby you are called by name, are bartered with, hear loud laments, or have a disturbed sense of being are difficult to suppress. In general, in all cases of nonarising and nonsuppression, it is important to keep trying.

### 2. The Actual Visualization

#### a. The Red Distribution to Do at Night, Summarizing the Meaning of the Sutra Tradition

Perform [the distribution] as the incomparable guru has done. There are two parts: giving in charity whatever kind of body is desired to all six kinds of migrators as the cause of perfect buddhahood, and giving it again to the meek. First, recite from "*phaṭ* My awareness arises as Vajrayoginī; my body's skin equals the size of the universe . . ." (*phaṭ / rang rig rdo rje rnal 'byor ma ru shar / rang lus g.yang gzhi stong gsum tshad du grub . . .*) to ". . . dedicate this virtue to the welfare of beings" (. . . *dge ba 'di sems can gyi don du bsngo*).

## b. The Variegated Distribution to Do in the Daytime, Summarizing the Meaning of the Mantra Tradition

According to the teachings of the incomparable dharma lord, after consecrating your body as the pledge substance of the feast circle, make the offering in order for all sentient beings to attain buddhahood. Maintain the intention and application of establishing, as much as you can, all grandmother beings in the state of buddhahood once their delusional madness of being deluded by harm-doers is cleared away. {258} For that first [principle] of mind training, recite from "*phaṭ* My awareness arises as the ḍākinī of timeless awareness . . ." (*phaṭ / rang rig ye shes mkha' 'gro ma ru shar . . .*) to ". . . may [this] become the cause of supreme awakening" (. . . *rgyud byang chub sems su 'gyur bar shog*).

## C. Giving in Charity after Suppressing

Those previous [practices] were certainly the generosity of material goods. But for the supreme [generosity], according to the works of the incomparable dharma lord, [recite] from "The harmed and the harmers are empty . . ." (*gnod bya gnod byed stong pa la . . .*) to ". . . may [this] become the cause of awakening. *phaṭ*" (. . . *byang chub mchog gi rgyur gyur cig / phaṭ*). Do the meditation liturgy up to this point intensely and often. Those [practices] concern the visualization of "snake binding" (*sbrul chings*), as referenced in Machik's "Vajra Verses":

> If the middle ones are not suppressed midway,
> it is like a hero who has lost his weapon.
> Then you need the vajra snake binding.

## D. Concluding Severance and Additional Practices

### 1. Concluding Severance

Once the haunted place has been severed and it is time to go, conceal the traces of your sleeping area and cooking place. Don't leave anything at all behind. Then say, "*phaṭ*. My own body becomes Avalokiteshvara. A continuous flow of undissipating elixir flows from it and completely fills the area. May beings be satisfied by undissipating elixir." Then when leaving the haunted place, make the forms of nine mounds of earthen hills, nine little flat plains between them, and nine streams between them. "Hey! The nine mountain passes and nine great rivers and nine great plains have already been severed, so don't you come after me. Stay here and enjoy that undissipating elixir." This is said in the "Vajra Verses":

> If later ones are not suppressed later,
> it is like pursuing lost bad wealth.
> Then you need a black garuḍa warlord.

## 2. Additional Practices

### a. Benefiting Others: Methods for Curing the Sick

{259} According to the works of the incomparable guru, you should lay a strong emphasis on the unity of emptiness and compassion to alleviate the torments of sickness and suffering that afflict grandmother sentient beings. Then do recollection meditation (*dran sgom*) and recite from "*phaṭ* Oppression by spirits of sickness in the world, and the experiences of ripening of former bad karma . . ." (*phaṭ / 'jigs rten na nad gdon gyis non pa dang / sngon las ngan gyi 'bras bur spyod pa yi . . .*) to ". . . May all beings become permanently free" (*. . . sems can kun gtan du thar gyur cig*). This alone is sufficient when you have brought someone such as a sick person to a haunted place. Diligently strive at this some fifteen times per session. Thus it was taught. The meaning is stated in Machik's "Vajra Verses":

> It is crucial to blend into a nondual unity
> these three: demons and disease and spirits.

### b. How to Protect from Lightning and Hail

The signs of the existence of lightning are the gathering of black clouds in the south [shaped] like clenched fists, with nine heads, sometimes dispersing and sometimes gathering; or dreaming of many blacksmiths pounding bullets and other ironworks in dreams; or [strikes like] iron stakes with no sound of thunder or flashing; or, in visionary experience, feeling the vibrant and aggressive sound of pounding metal. These are signs of severe lightning and hail. When the lightning and hail is upon you, clearly imagine yourself as the conqueror emanating golden vajras from your heart. They strike the lightning and lightning gods and dragons. Meditate that they all are sent far away to the mountains behind the ocean. Make the threatening pointer gestures and blow out and shout *phaṭ* at the sky.

### c. The Sequence of the Black Distribution

As it says in the "Vajra Verses":

> To wash away the stains of habitual patterns,
> the black distribution for purifying negativity is needed.

Visualize that inside your skull cup in front, Machik rises up and undissipating elixir falls from the skull cup in her hand and enters your cranial aperture. {260} It becomes the washing-water elixir that purifies all sickness spirits. Imagine that it is bestowed on the gods and demons. That was the gentle style. In the rough style, it is given without becoming elixir.

### d. Presentation of Needed Minor Visualizations

From the "Vajra Verses":

> If evidence of success occurs before
> and evidence of uprising occurs later,
> it is backward, so do this visualization.

*phaṭ* Instantly I generate myself as Jetsunma and transform. Jetsunma slices off the skull and puts the body into the skull. Imagine that it is given to all the gods and demons of that place and other places.

> If the guests run away somewhere,
> you need the visualization of red summons.

If you dream that many people get dispersed, it means that the guests have dispersed, so you should do this visualization. Imagine that immeasurable light rays emanate from your body and summon all those gods and demons irresistibly. It says:

> If the guests appear to be nauseated,
> you need the visualization of increase and cleansing.

If you dream that people and such are given food but they don't eat it, it is because they are nauseated. Transform it into charitable food that is abundant and delicious and savory, most excellent, and so forth, and then bestow it.

> If apparitions are great but evidence of success is scarce,
> you need to do the suppression of the wealthy.[10]

When evidence of success does not come but there are big apparitions, imagine Jetsuma carrying your corpse in her right hand. She brandishes it as far as the pinnacle of existence and throws it on the ground. The body, gods, demons, earth, and stones all mix, and [the gods and demons] irresistibly offer their very heart-life.

This composition [based on] the Severance practice by the incomparable guru was added due to immediate needs. The White Distribution for Four Guests (*dkar 'gyed mgron bzhi ma*) is not included here. In that, according to omniscient Rangjung Dorje, {261} you imagine the body possessing a hundred flavors, as white and round and big as Supreme Mountain, which is then given to the guests: the gurus and Jewels, the dharma protectors and guards, the eight classes of gods and spirits, and the creditors.

Composed by the Shākya monk Könchok Bang.

# 20. The Body Donation and Feeding Ritual Arranged as Convenient Liturgy

*Combining Lord Rangjung Dorje's Ninefold Spirit Feast and Six Earth Lord Application with Mikyö Dorje's Single-Seat Severance Poem*[1]

## Compiled by Karma Chakme

Karma Chakme, also known as Rāga Asya (1613–1678), cobbled together this ritual liturgy from writings attributed to Karmapa Rangjung Dorje (1284–1339) and Karmapa Mikyö Dorje (1507–1554). With some three hundred years of Karma Kagyu Severance masters behind him, the great Kamtsang master was free to borrow what he needed to form this practice, which he geared toward a healing ritual. Although such borrowing is widespread throughout Tibetan literature, it seems to be particularly common in the Severance tradition, whose prayers and liturgies would get recycled to align with the various traditions into which they were absorbed.

In this text, Mikyö Dorje's "poem" comes first. This is available in several other editions—for example, in a collection of recitation texts from Palpung Monastery (seat of the Karma Kagyu Tai Situ incarnations in Kham), where it is called simply *Profound Severance Guide* (*gCod khrid zab mo*).* All the liturgical sections in the first five pages in our text are from Mikyö Dorje, with Karma Chakme dividing it into parts and adding useful descriptions and instructions. The poem is reproduced accurately, with one notable exception: wherever Mikyö Dorje has the name of his own guru, Sangye Nyenpa (Sangs rgyas mnyan pa, 1445/57–1510/25), Karma Chakme has substituted the name of the second Karmapa, Karma Pakshi (1204–1283).

*Karma Chakme et al., *Collection of Mandala Rituals from Palpung. dPal spungs dpe rnying gsar bskrun las dkyil chog phyogs bsgrigs*. 14 vols. (Upper Bhattu, Himachal Pradesh, India: dPal spung gsung rab nyams gso khang, 2005). TBRC W1G4334.

Perhaps Karma Chakme preferred to identify the source of the lineage as the great master of the early days of the Karma Kagyu so that it would be more widely relevant and familiar to future practitioners. Karma Pakshi is legendary, though not known as a teacher of Severance.

Karma Chakme then adds a white and a black distribution that he attributes to Könchok Bang, but he renders them into verse to facilitate recitation. In the colophon he further states that these are the only parts of the liturgy that he has tampered with; all other sections remain true to the originals.

If that is so, then the rest of the liturgical sections until almost the end must be from Rangjung Dorje, although a separate text of those practices is not found in his extensive collected works. They are, however, found within many other Severance texts. For example, this Six Earth Lord Application liturgy can be found verbatim in *Source of All Qualities* in the present volume (see chapter 22), where it is identified as "Lord Rangjung Dorje's short calling of the pestilent spirits" (*gnyan 'bod thung*). Most of the Ninefold Spirit Feast is also found in Karma Chakme's *Pearl Rosary* (see chapter 21). According to Karma Chakme, the Ninefold Spirit Feast and Six Earth Lord Application are to be done for particularly severe illnesses. Therefore, one visualizes one's consciousness in the form of the black wrathful ḍākinī Krodhīkālī (Khros ma nag mo) rather than the usual form of Vajravārāhī. He also describes the six and nine sets of spirits (which overlap somewhat) and the specific ailments and problems that are cured by feeding each group.

After the dissolution, the text ends with the final prayers again from Mikyö Dorje's poem, including Karma Chakme's own pointing-out instructions, which will ultimately liberate the practitioner and the patient together.

---

*namo prajñāpāramitāyai*

Perform this ritual for your own sake from your sickbed, or for someone else far away who is sick. [The patient] should face toward you and lie down. If nearby, the patient should lie down on his or her right side in front of you. Remove protection circles, protection cords, weapons, and so forth, and set them aside. Without butter lamps or firelight, recite the meditation chant. Instantly all the spaces in the sky are filled with the Three Jewels like clouds. Go for refuge in them. After the four immeasurable sentiments for all sentient beings arise in your mindstream, think with deep conviction, "No matter what, I will quickly attain buddhahood."

> *namo gurave*
> From this time on, I seek certain refuge
> in the guru and Three Jewels.
> When the four immeasurable thoughts arise within me,
> I will establish the six kinds of beings in perfect enlightenment.

Say [those lines] three times.

> *phaṭ phaṭ phaṭ*

Meditate that Shākyamuni is in the sky in front and below him is Machik, surrounded by the gurus, yidams, buddhas, and bodhisattvas.

> From within the emptiness of all outer and inner phenomena,
> a lion throne appears in the sky in front with the Tathāgata,
> the Mighty Shākya, together with his children.
> Below him is Machik Lapdrön with a white body,
> one face, and three eyes gazing into the sky's expanse.
> She wears white silk cloth draped over her.
> In her right hand, a sandalwood ḍamaru resounds in the
> billionfold universe,
> and in her left hand a white silver bell touches her hip.
> Her hair partially falls down her back, with some tied up.
> The stance of half-vajra posture gestures to the space. {262}
> She plays in the midst of the Object Severance lineage adepts.
> The three seeds are in the three places of those deities.
> Light radiates, invoking the blessed ones from their natural abode,
> together with the Kagyu yidams and dharma protectors.
> They become inseparable with *jaḥ hūṃ baṃ hoḥ*.

In front of that clear visualization, all form appears as Form Vajra goddesses carrying mirrors, all sound as Sound Vajra goddesses carrying lutes, and so forth: offering goddesses emanate, filling the whole sky. Imagine that they make offerings to all those deities.

I offer pure form, sound, smell, taste, and texture
as an ocean of offering clouds of undissipating great bliss.

Say those two lines three times.

*phaṭ phaṭ phaṭ*

The essence of your life, merit, soul, and life force is a white sphere with a red tinge, the size of a thumb. It rises up the central channel and shoots straight out the cranial aperture. Your mind becomes the form of Vajravārāhī. With a mere gesture of her curved knife, the skin becomes the ground, and so forth; the body thus becomes a mandala. Meditate on offering it to the host of deities, and say:

*phaṭ*
My awareness exits my body and becomes
the ḍākinī of timeless awareness. My body's skin
becomes the mighty great ground, my head Supreme Mountain,
my four limbs the four continents, my two eyes the sun and moon,
and my flesh, blood, and bones the inexhaustible divine substances.
This arranged mandala without boundaries
I offer before the Great Sage, the Blessed One.
I offer before Mother Lapkyi Drönma.
Sublime lords of beings—hold me with compassion.

Do this three times, or one time is also acceptable. Say *phaṭ* until the visualization is finished.

*phaṭ phaṭ phaṭ*

Think, "I and the patient, along with the harmful spirit, pay homage with devotion to the deities in the sky. We offer, confess all negativity, rejoice in the vast roots of merit that you have performed, beseech you to teach the dharma to sentient beings, supplicate you not to pass into nirvana but to remain for the sake of beings, and dedicate the merit from those thoughts for all sentient beings to attain the state of the adept Karma Pakshi."[2]

I pay homage with body, speech, and mind; confess negativities;
rejoice in merit; request the turning of the dharma wheel; {263}
and supplicate you to remain without passing into nirvana.
By this merit, may we attain [the state of] the great adept Karma Pakshi.

Say *phaṭ* three times or until the visualization is finished.

*phaṭ phaṭ phaṭ* *phaṭ phaṭ phaṭ* *phaṭ*

Then, as you supplicate the hosts of deities and lineage gurus in the sky, a stream of elixir falls from their bodies and enters the cranial aperture of Machik's head. Machik's body fills up with elixir, and it comes flowing out of her left big toe. It enters the cranial apertures of the patient and yourself and fills your whole bodies. Negativities and obscurations are secreted out the soles of your feet and lower orifices like black liquid charcoal ooze. It falls beneath nine layers of earth and goes into the gaping jaws of Yamarāja, karmic lord of death. Meditate on Yamarāja satiated and satisfied by that foul liquid.

Upon sun-moon seats in the place above my head,
Great Mother Perfect Wisdom, Conqueror Shākyamuni,
Mañjushrī Lion of Speech, Āryadeva,
Indian Dampa, Mother Lapkyi Drön,
Khambuyale, great adept Jñānajvala,
Namtsowa, Rangjung, Venerable Yungtön,
Rolpai Dorje, Dargyal, Kachö Wangpo,
Dezhin Shekpa, Rinchen Zangpo,
Tongwa Dönden, omniscient Jampal Zang,
Sangye Nyenpa, fearless Mikyö Zang,
incomparable victor Könchok Yenlak,
Wangchuk Dorje, Chökyi Wangchuk,
[Kunga Namgyal, Karma Chakme,][3] and so forth—
all adepts of the Object Severance lineage with blessings,
Machik, guru of those blessed ones,
I supplicate you: Great Mother, bless me.

Recite all the sacred pledges, repeating the last one three times.

*phaṭ phaṭ phaṭ*

Keep saying *phaṭ* in a long and gentle fashion until the above visualization is finished. Then all the hosts of deities in the space dissolve into light, which melts into you as Vajrayoginī and the patient. Imagine that you receive all the blessings and empowerments of their Body, Speech, and Mind.

> Shākyamuni and Machik with entourage dissolve into Yoginī
> like water into water, nakedly exposing my awareness,
> uncontrived and free of embellishment. {264}

Then, as Vajrayoginī, you dissipate like a rainbow in space. The patient also dissipates into emptiness. Rest evenly in the state of emptiness for as long as you can remain. If experience and realization are not clear, and discursive thoughts proliferate, sharpen your attention by saying *phaṭ phaṭ*. Separate awareness from the material body. Meditate that, as Vārāhī, you flay the skin with a slice of the curved knife. It permeates the billionfold universe. Flesh and blood fills the world, and all gods and demons eat and drink voraciously and are satisfied.

> *phaṭ*
> My own awareness arises as Vajrayoginī.
> My body and skin extends to the billionfold universe.
> Mountains of flesh, oceans of blood, and heaps of bones
> are spontaneously present through *oṃ āḥ hūṃ*
> as the essence of undissipating elixir.

Say *phaṭ* many times until the visualization is complete. Then strike the thighbone three times on the palm of your left hand while saying, "Little spirits, fear not, be not afraid, do not run away." Imagine that and then blow the thighbone three times and say, "All you gods and demons from the pinnacle of existence down to the hell of incessant torment, listen up. All gather here. Gather quickly!" Think of this being vocalized as if calling with a loud voice from afar.

> *Ey ey*! From the pinnacle of existence down to the incessant hell,
> apparent existence's gods, demons, spirits of place,

body spirits, elementals, and those who lead us astray—
instantly gather here from far away.
I am a collected heap of elements, ever perishing.
All my bodies of beginningless birth and death
have been pointlessly exhausted in cyclic existence.
From now on, I will let go of this body for sure.
All you spirits that cause me harm
due to the fruition of my previous actions,
today take my body as one hundred or one thousand *changbu*.[4]
Eight kinds of gods above, take my upper corpse.
Eight kinds of nāga below, take my lower corpse.
Eight classes of gods and spirits, take this heart.
Gods and demons of existence, take the five sense organs.
Carry it to the midst of mountain peaks and great plains.
Carry it to crossroads and river channels,
to lake bottoms and into the cosmic fire to burn.
Now the flesh, bones, viscera, organs, innards,
skin, brains, fat, gristle, limbs, {265}
chunks of meat, globules of blood, tufts of hair—
hurry to take everything, leave nothing.

Say *phaṭ phaṭ phaṭ* intensely until the visualization is clear. At this juncture, meditate on whatever other visualization of red distributions you know while repeating *phaṭ*. Although not found elsewhere, [in this source text][5] it is appropriate to meditate multiple times. Donate all the leftovers of the corpse to the disempowered ones who did not get any before, and meditate that they are pleased and satisfied. Think that you dedicate this so that all sentient beings will attain buddhahood through the virtue of donating your body in this way.

*phaṭ*
At last you are empowered to get what you did not before.
Humble ones, watch intently, listen carefully, and wait.
Consume all that, be satisfied, and carry it off.
I dedicate this virtue to the welfare of beings.

Recite *phaṭ phaṭ phaṭ* until the visualization becomes clear.

## The Offering of the Body in the Feast Circle

Eject your consciousness and your mind becomes Vajravārāhī. Shear off the skull with a mere gesture of the curved knife. Put the corpse inside it and chop it into pieces. Beneath it, fire blazes up between the three hearth skulls, and the flesh and blood melts and boils. It becomes a hundred-flavored ocean of elixir of timeless awareness, the essence of the red and white bodhichitta from the syllables *a* and *haṃ*. From your heart, emanate innumerable ḍākinīs carrying skull scoops. They offer to all the guests throughout the sky and space: all the gurus, yidams, ḍākinīs, dharma protectors and worldly protectors, six kinds of living beings, harm-doers, creditors, and so forth. Meditate on them being pleased and satisfied.

*phaṭ*
My awareness arises as the awareness ḍākinī.
I chop this body into pieces
inside of my own skull.
It becomes the elixir of the short *a* and *haṃ* letters.
Buddha Vajradhara with the lineage of meaning,
lord of the unmistaken transmission of the Kagyu,
Karma Pakshi, I offer this to you.
Glorious Chakrasaṃvara and Yoginī,
deities of the four tantras, I offer to you.
Glorious Bernakchen and Four-Armed One,
guards who protect the dharma, I offer to you.
Host of shrāvakas, pratyekabuddhas, and bodhisattvas, {266}
lords of refuge, rare and sublime, I offer to you.
By this merit, may this body of mine
fulfill the inexhaustible wishes of hell beings,
hungry ghosts, animals, gods, humans, and so forth.
Eighty thousand obstructing forces,
eighteen[6] great malicious spirits of children,
*mamos* and masters of epidemic diseases,
male and female spirits, knife demons, *teurang*,
and whoever is karmically connected through debt,
even as this becomes the fulfillment of all your needs,
may you get inexhaustible enjoyment from it.

Keep saying *phaṭ phaṭ phaṭ* until the visualization is finished. Saying it without counting is called the "Hundred *Phaṭ*."

In the gentle severance (*'jam gcod*), with the thought of awakening, there is the actual visualization of giving and taking: When the body is offered as a feast in that way, there is an overwhelming love and compassion that regards all sentient beings as mothers and offspring. In particular, imagine that whatever sufferings, negativities, and obscurations afflict the harm-doers, malicious spirits, and obstructors all gradually collect and melt into you. They become free of all suffering. Your virtuous roots and all your happiness melt into all beings, mainly those harm-doers, and they gain immeasurable happiness.

> Once that is received, all crazy grandmothers
> give rise to love of the children as indeed children,
> and to unbearable compassion,
> with no display of evil deluded appearance:
> May your very being become the thought of awakening.
>
> Giving up victims and harm-doers,
> all sentient beings become the takers.
> In the mutual relationship of mothers and offspring,
> negativities, obscurations, and faults are reciprocally removed.
> May beings not remain in existence.
>
> Again, may any faults of the harm-doers
> all fall upon me, the harmed.
> May any of my happiness as the harmed
> all go over to you, the harm-doers.
>
> May that become the cause of supreme enlightenment.

Say *phaṭ phaṭ phaṭ* until the visualization is finished.

The white distribution that was taught loosely in prose by Könchok Bang[7] has been put into verse here for the sake of recitation.

*phaṭ*
My awareness exits my body as the white ḍākinī. {267}
My body becomes elixir with eight sublime flavors,
white and round and big as Supreme Mountain.
I offer it individually to Jewel guests of honor: gurus and yidams;
the guests of qualities: dharma protectors, guards, and lords;
guests of debt and liability: the eight classes of gods and spirits;
and guests of love and compassion: the six kinds of migrators.
May you be pleased.
May you be satisfied and relieved of suffering by this charity.
May all liability and the obscuration of misappropriation be purified.
May everyone attain omniscient buddhahood.
*phaṭ phaṭ phaṭ*

Say *phaṭ* in a long and gentle way until the visualization is finished. Similarly, the black distribution that purifies obscurations has been put into verse according to the teaching of the visualization in the source text.

*phaṭ*
Within the self-arising *bhandha* equal to the billionfold universe,
in the space where I or the patient dwells,
Machik Lapdrön stands upright,
a stream of undissipating elixir flowing from her body.
It enters the cranial aperture and purifies disease, spirits,
negativity, and obscurations.
The cleansing liquid fills the *bhandha* to the brim.

In the fierce style, [the body] is not changed to elixir.[8]

*oṃ āḥ hūṃ* transforms it into the elixir of timeless awareness.
All harmful and destructive gods and demons
drink and are quenched and satiated with pleasures.
*phaṭ phaṭ phaṭ*

Do the visualization many times. If this is done regularly up to here, then even if it is not completed in an uninterrupted way, it is suitable to do whenever you prefer in order to finish the accumulation. As for times, the night is best, any time after sunset. If you are practicing for signs to arise, then do it in six or four sessions.

Now, if you or another patient has a severe sickness spirit, perform the Six Earth Lord Application and the Ninefold Spirit Feast. First, bring spirits under control:

> *phaṭ*
> Instantly I become the ḍākinī of timeless awareness, blue-black in color, with one face, two hands, three eyes, and bared teeth. My right eye is the sun mandala, rolling around and red. The left is the moon mandala, a spinning and roving sphere. My central eye is the mixed sun-and-moon mandala, dark red and twitching with agitation. The black pig head on the top of my head grunts like thunder. {268} I am endowed with the eight graveyard accessories and the nine dance stances. I throw down a human skin with my right hand and piercingly blow the human thighbone with my left. All the eight classes of gods, demigods, and spirits of apparent existence are brought under control and subdued by splendor. The desire realm extends up to my navel. The form realm extends to my heart. The formless realm extends to my head. From my heart, which is totally victorious over the three realms, emanate immeasurable light rays, hooks, lassos, chains, and bells. All eight classes of gods, demigods, and spirits of apparent existence with orders to cause danger and harm immediately and irresistibly gather here.
> *hūṃ hūṃ hūṃ phaṭ phaṭ phaṭ*

Blow the thighbone trumpet fiercely three times. Your own consciousness and that of the patient in front of you rise up and blend inseparably with space. Meditate on the large, corpulent corpses as big as Supreme Mountain. The meditation of the Six Earth Lord Application in the six directions is like this.

> On the right the essence of the king is a *bande* with a *sakzhu* hat,[9] surrounded by an army of bandes.[10] To the left is the demoness, with turquoise hair, yellow eyebrows, and conch-like fangs, surrounded by a demoness army. In front is the king of earth lords, a nine-armed toad, surrounded by an army of earth lords. Behind is the great layman, with a fishhook mane, surrounded by an army of fish. Below is the nāga devil, with nine black serpent heads, surrounded by a billion kinds of nāgas. Above is Rāhula, the king

of planet devils, surrounded by an army of a billion planets. All around them are the gods and demons of apparent existence, the hosts of the eight classes of pledged gods, demigods, and spirits.
*phaṭ phaṭ phaṭ*

Blow the thighbone trumpet three times.

*namo*
Gods and demons living in this haunted place,
all the gods and demons of apparent existence
who show their apparitions to me, the fortunate one:
Come, massing here like cloud banks in the sky. {269}
Come, falling like rain from on high.
Come, swirling like whirlwinds over the ground.
I present this body as an offering to you all.
I offer you the six forms of my outer flesh:
May I attain Buddha's precepts of six perfections.
I offer you the nine inner organs with apertures:
May I attain the nine vehicles.
I offer you the five essential organs:[11]
May I attain the five kāyas and awarenesses.
To all of you gathered here, I offer this body:
You who are impatient, eat it raw.
You who are not hurried, eat it cooked.
Those who come early snatch the loot.
Latecomers gulp down the remains.[12]
Like lions relishing flesh,
take the first offering and leave nothing.
Like claiming the spoils of a great war,
take the first offering and leave nothing.[13]
Like a black bird diving in the water,
take the first offering and leave nothing.

As Krodhī, meditate on the five fingers of your right hand as Krodhī's in essence but appearing as five blue claws of the iron wolf. The five fingers on the left are five red claws of the copper jackal. With those you scoop up the corpses and hurl the gobs of raw flesh and blood into the open mouths of the gods and demons. They gobble it down with rapacious sounds and murmurs. Until the visualization becomes clear, hold your two hands in the gesture of grabbing up the corpse and make the motion of hurling it out with the revolving lotus mudra. Say *phaṭ phaṭ phaṭ,* strong and short.

> *hūṃ*
> A hundred great bandes and a thousand great *böns*,
> a hundred thousand knife-wielding butchers,
> minions beyond what the mind can grasp,
> sorcerers who would harm me or this person,
> gods and demons of apparent existence in general,
> and in particular, the gods and demons dwelling in this
> haunted ground—
> your needs and desires are satisfied by the dedication
> of these offerings and gifts of body, flesh, and blood.
> May you attain supreme spiritual power.
> *phaṭ phaṭ phaṭ*

This refers to all kinds of [Buddhist] bandes and Bön priests who send curses. "Butchers" means all of the bande protectors, Bön protectors, and workers of the calamities that they incite. Hurl the flesh and blood of the corpse into their mouths, and meditate that their needs and desires are satisfied and their vicious minds are pacified. Say *phaṭ phaṭ phaṭ* while stretching out the claw[14] and making the hurling gesture. If the curse is strong, it is important to do it as many times as necessary.

> *Gyalpo* spirits, white cloaked, black cloaked,
> gray dogs, red dogs, and old birds,
> nine demons of existence and so on, {270}
> ten malicious spirits of temples,
> *gyalgong* spirits who would harm this person,
> gods and demons of apparent existence in general,
> and in particular, the gods and demons dwelling in this haunted
> ground—
> your needs and desires are satisfied by the dedication
> of these offerings and gifts of body, flesh, and blood.
> May you attain supreme spiritual power.
> *phaṭ phaṭ phaṭ*

Clearly visualize the bande with the sakzhu hat with many bandes as essentially being all *gyalpo* spirits, and throw the flesh and blood into their mouths. Imagine that they are pleased and satisfied. This is done however many times for the madness of winds in the life channel, which is the harm caused by *gyalpo* spirits.

> Glorious black goddess Shrīdevī,
> twelve *tenma* sisters and so forth,
> mamos, ḍākinīs, powerful movers,
> oath breakers, black *tepur*,[15]
> demonesses who would harm this person,
> gods and demons of apparent existence in general,
> and in particular, the gods and demons dwelling in this haunted ground—
> your needs and desires are satisfied by the dedication
> of these offerings and gifts of body, flesh, and blood.
> May you attain supreme spiritual power.
> *phaṭ phaṭ phaṭ*

This is for semen-emission disease, crazed singing, distress at the inability to invoke the gods,[16] epidemics, plague, dysentery, and so forth. Do only this repeatedly for female evil spirits.

> Nine-headed black planet devil,
> eight planets such as the sun,
> twenty-eight constellations,
> four sibling [animal]-faced attendants,
> planetary devils who would harm this person,
> gods and demons of apparent existence in general,
> and in particular, the gods and demons dwelling in this haunted ground—
> your needs and desires are satisfied by the dedication
> of these offerings and gifts of body, flesh, and blood.
> May you attain supreme spiritual power.
> *phaṭ phaṭ phaṭ*

Repeat many times for the affliction of planetary diseases.

> Black nāga devils, consumers of vitality,[17]
> royal caste, merchant caste, brahmins,

commoners, servant caste nāgas, and so on;
Nanda, Takṣhaka, Shaṅkhapāla,
Upānanda, and so on of the nāga family;
nāga legions who would harm me;
gods and demons of apparent existence in general,
and in particular, the gods and demons dwelling in this haunted ground—
your needs and desires are satisfied by the dedication
of these offerings and gifts of body, flesh, and blood.
May you attain supreme spiritual power. {271}
*phaṭ phaṭ phaṭ*

Do this only for the harm and disease of nāgas and earth lords. For nāgas on the dark side, the flesh and blood is exactly that. For those on the side of virtue, visualize it as essentially elixir.

The ghastly black chief devil,
the devil Rete with a good head,[18]
[with a retinue of crow demons all around],[19]
brown human-flesh eaters and so on,[20]
[devil armies of hundreds of millions],[21]
devil armies who would harm this person,
gods and demons of apparent existence in general,
and in particular, the gods and demons dwelling in this haunted ground—
your needs and desires are satisfied by the dedication
of these offerings and gifts of body, flesh, and blood.
May you attain supreme spiritual power.
*phaṭ phaṭ phaṭ*

For all diseases of heaviness and torpor, do repeated visualizations of throwing flesh and blood into the mouths of black humans who are as tall as conifers and black horses, satisfying them.

Chief *tsen* spirit causing deadly skin disease;
four classes of quick, wild *tsen* spirits;
eight swift-footed spirits with harelips;
four mouths, eight faces, and so forth;

*tsen* legions who would harm this person;
gods and demons of apparent existence in general;
and in particular, the gods and demons dwelling in this haunted ground—
your needs and desires are satisfied by the dedication
of these offerings and gifts of body, flesh, and blood.
May you attain supreme spiritual power.
*phaṭ phaṭ phaṭ*

Donate the body to the legions of red humans, red horses, and tall red men carrying copper pipes. Meditate that they suck out all the pus and blood in the lungs with the copper pipes. Engage this many times for those harmed by *tsen* spirits and pulmonary disease.

Oath-breaker spirits with red fire sparks,
area demons, *gap* demons, and vagrant [demons],
harmful little spirits and darkening demons,
oath breakers who would harm this person,
gods and demons of apparent existence in general,
and in particular, the gods and demons dwelling in this haunted ground—
your needs and desires are satisfied by the dedication
of these offerings and gifts of body, flesh, and blood.
May you attain supreme spiritual power.
*phaṭ phaṭ phaṭ*

Give to the consuming demons who take the bodies of the deceased, the oath breakers in monastic bodies with shaved heads, and the little spirits with the bodies of naked children. Meditate that they disappear into the flesh and blood up to their necks.[22] Do this as much as possible for the killers and the dying and the little spirits that afflict children.

From Vajrasādhu down to
the least of the *teurang* spirits,
with retinues of various *uber* spirits,[23]
*telmo* spirits with round ears[24] and so on,
*teurang* spirits who would harm this person,
gods and demons of apparent existence in general,

and in particular, the gods and demons dwelling in this haunted ground—
your needs and desires are satisfied by the dedication
of these offerings and gifts of body, flesh, and blood.
May you attain supreme spiritual power.
*phaṭ phaṭ phaṭ*

Give it to the groups of boys and girls with goatskins and greenish complexions. Perform this multiple times for diseases of bloated stomach, abdominal cramps or dysentery, and accidental emission.

After donating the body in that way for three days, {272} do this visualization for the ultimate concluding severance: Stuffed full of flesh and blood, the gods and demons then turn aggressively on one another. The big ones eat all the small ones. The six chiefs swallow one another. The demonesses on the left are eaten by the *gyalpo* spirits on the right. The *gyalpo* spirits on the right are eaten by the rāhulas above. The rāhulas are eaten by the black fish-faced laymen from behind. The fish are eaten by the big toad earth lords in front. The earth lords are eaten by the nāga devils below. The nāgas disappear like rainbows in the sky. Meditate for a session on emptiness with no frame of reference. Meditate for a session on great compassion. Because this is quite fierce, it is very dangerous, so it is inappropriate to do it more than once at the end of the severance.

The feeding that is always appropriate is this: Visualize that disease demons, severing spirits,[25] and malicious spirits of the body all dissolve into the flesh and blood of the patient's corpse, which fills the world. Light rays emanated from your heart as Krodhīkālī invoke ḍākinīs from their natural abodes. They are white, yellow, red, and green, with hooked knives and blood-filled skull cups. Mostly they are the special wrathful females, the innumerable forms of Krodhīkālī, who serve the flesh and blood. Meditate that the many gods and demons with their retinues noisily consume the flesh and blood that is inseparable from the malicious spirits of disease, without leaving any remainders.

Mothers, great *ging* and lesser *ging*, with siblings:
Sounds of guzzling, sounds of *phaṭ—ti ri ri.*
Fierce palatal sounds—*chem se chem.*
Chomping sounds of eating flesh—*ti ri ri.*

Gulping sounds of drinking blood—*di ri ri.*
Breaking legs and slurping—*jip se jip.*
Grinding sounds of gnawing bones—*tra la la.*
Laughing in pleasure—*sha ra ra.*
Singing songs of gladness—*kyu ru ru.*
Mothers, come here for this bloody body offering.
Gods and demons of apparent existence, please partake.
While gods and demons of apparent existence partake,
may you be satisfied by the five desirables.
May you attain supreme spiritual power.
*phaṭ phaṭ phaṭ*

Intense meditation on this for the great malicious spirits of disease is extremely profound. After this kind of material offering of primarily the body, there is the gift of the dharma. You completely transform from Krodhī into the form of the Conqueror Shākyamuni, as large as Supreme Mountain. In front of you are all the gods, demons, elementals, and harm-doers, clasping their hands together in the gesture of faith and devotion. Meditate that they listen to this teaching:

*namo*
All things arise from a cause. {273}
That cause was taught by the Tathāgata.
Of that which stops that cause
the great shramaṇa also spoke.[26]

Do no negative action whatsoever;
practice abundant virtue.
Completely tame your own mind.
Do not disturb others' minds.
This is the Buddha's teaching.[27]

As the vows of body are good,
so are the vows of speech good.
As the vows of the mind are good,
so the vows of everything are good.
Ordained monastics who keep them all

> will certainly attain liberation from all suffering.[28]
> *phaṭ phaṭ phaṭ*

Now, present the path of awakening:

> *namo*
> Path of accumulation and path of application,
> path of seeing and path of meditation—
> traversing the paths without obstacles,
> may we attain the state of the Great Mother.
> *phaṭ phaṭ phaṭ*

White light emanates from your body. It strikes all the harmful gods and demons and it arouses their love, compassion, and awakening minds. They all are transformed into the forms of the Great Compassionate One, reciting the six-syllable mantra [with the sound of] *ti ri ri*. Meditate on them all around you, and repeat *phaṭ* until the visualization is complete. Persevere in this meditation for the afflicted.

### The Blending

As above, when the awareness is separated from the matter, your own body and that of the patient are blended. Then your consciousness and the patient's consciousness blend inseparably. The [unified consciousness] flies up, and the body is donated and so forth; if everything is done just as before, it will be of great benefit for the patient. If your realization is high, then just that is good. If your realization is just average, leave the bodies separate and eject the consciousnesses separately, and then blend them into one. Visualize making the body offering and donations separately. If your realization is no more than inferior, keep the bodies apart and separate out the consciousnesses individually. Your own consciousness changes into the ḍākinī. The patient's consciousness dissolves into space. It is fine to make the dual offering and donating of each body with the single recitation of the body gift. If you don't do that, you will be tainted by defilement and could become ill. Machik taught that if the visualization is clear, five hundred of your own body plus five hundred of the patient's body can become a thousand body donations at one time. After the above body donations,

{274} meditate on Pa Dampa Sangye, Machik, and Karma Pakshi clearly appearing in the expanse of space. Meditate on your own body, the patient's body, mental illness, and all malicious spirits inseparable as a single white letter *a*. It dissolves into Pa Dampa in space. Dampa dissolves into Machik. Machik dissolves into Karma Pakshi. That dissolves into space. Meditate that wherever space pervades, awareness pervades, and wherever awareness pervades, the dharmakāya pervades.

> *phaṭ*
> All who are oppressed by sickness and spirits in the world
> and experience the results of former bad actions—
> raise your gaze, and Indian Dampa is present;
> trust, and Machik Lapdrön is present;
> believe, and Karma Pakshi is present.
> Now, without doubts, be resolved.
> This inseparable body and mind of yours
> becomes unborn dharmakāya as the white letter *a*.
> It transfers to the heart of Black Dampa.
> Elixir flashes into light—*ya la la*.
> It transfers to Yeshe Lapma's heart.
> Brilliance billows into light—*pung se pung*.
> Whenever suffering arises in beings,
> Black Dampa changes it to bliss;
> Mother Lapma purifies it in space.

You and the patient combine inseparably with Dampa, Machik, and Karma Pakshi. Meditate on their compassion and blessing changing sickness into bliss-emptiness and discursive thought into dharmakāya.

> Great Mother's heart cannot bear it and stirs
> the unborn reality of dark compassion.
> From today onward, the sufferings of the six kinds of beings are relieved.
> From tonight onward, the spirits' river of suffering is blocked,
> sickness and pain fade away into space,
> and the basic roots of fear and panic are removed.
> Appearances with no attachment are wispy mists.

Look at the essence of your own mind without fixation on the object of looking or the act of looking. You cannot establish any sickness or spirits or suffering or fear whatsoever. It is like space. Gods and demons, happiness and suffering, are of equal flavor in emptiness. Until confident realization of that recognition occurs, you should continue to recite the liturgy and *phaṭ*. Intense compassion will arise spontaneously for all the sentient beings that do not have the realization that apparent existence is emptiness and great bliss. With that compassion as the catalyst, instantly the entire space of the sky is utterly filled with the essence of the Object Severance lineage gurus of the father lineage, {275} all in the form of Indian Dampa. The entire ground is utterly filled to the far reaches with the essence of the ḍākinīs of the mother lineage in the forms of Machik. All of them are dancing and rattling their drums and bells—*tro lo lo*; saying the sound of *phaṭ—di ri ri*; and making all apparent existence shake and tremble. The entire external world and all the sentient beings, primarily the gods and demons, dissolve into light and melt into the host of deities. They all melt into Pa Dampa, and he into Machik Lapdrön. They melt into you and the patient, which in turn disappear like a rainbow and become emptiness. Meditating on that, maintain the essence of the practice.

> The lineages of adepts of Object Severance
> do not fit into the realm of space above
> and cannot be put into the churning earth below.[29]
> All knowable objects resolve into Severance.
> Severance melts into the state of harming.
> Harming, in the play of emptiness,
> with nothing harmful, is empty of the harmed.
> From today onward, do not think there exists
> any fear on account of the body aggregate.
> By this miracle of the Kagyu gurus,
> we attain the realization that all beings' sufferings
> are liberated in their lack of a basis.
> May this be the cause of the permanent liberation of all beings.

Although it is taught that these words of blending are to be done five or ten times a session, three or seven or whatever is appropriate may be done, and it is important to do the visualization five or ten times. It states in the *Perfection of Wisdom in One Hundred Thousand Lines:*

> Whoever is without recollection and not mentally engaged is recollecting the Buddha, recollecting the dharma, and recollecting the sangha.[30]

And:

> There is the meditative absorption of completely pervading space and the meditative absorption of extensively filling space.

And in Machik's "Vajra Verses":

> It is crucial to blend into a nondual unity
> these three: the self, the patient, and the spirits.[31]

Since these sayings express the true meaning, there is certainly nothing more profound than resting within that state. However, in order to stop ordinary concepts, perform the dissolution of consciousness and blessings:

> *phaṭ*
> From the sky, a single white vital drop—the essence of spirit, vitality, life force, and breath—comes down and enters through the cranial aperture and melts in the center of the heart.
> *phaṭ phaṭ phaṭ*

Then place your prayer beads on top of your head and meditate on the lineage gurus and Machik sequentially on your head: {276}

> Dharmakāya Great Mother, Lady Perfection of Wisdom,
> [the Victor, Shākyamuni],[32]
> Mañjushrī Lion of Speech,
> Venerable Noble Tārā,
> Ḍākinī Sukhasiddhī,
> Āryadeva the Brahmin,
> One Father Dampa Sangye,
> Kyotön Sönam Lama,
> Machik Lapkyi Drönma,
> Dharmakāya Ḍākinī of Awareness,
> Saṃbhogakāya Ḍākinī of Awareness,

Nirmāṇakāya Ḍākinī of Awareness,
form emanation White Great Bliss Woman,
speech emanation Red Resounding Woman,
mind emanation Black Wrathful Woman,
quality emanation Yellow Accomplishing Woman,
activity emanation Variegated Consummation,
father lineage, the lineage of methods;
mother lineage, the lineage of wisdom;
child lineage, the lineage of experience: all gurus, grant your blessings.
Give rise to compassion and ability.
Grant your blessing to quickly pacify through this profound method
the causes: bad karma, negativities, obscurations; the conditions: spirits, obstructors, and elementals; and the results: all sickness and suffering.
Grant your blessing to pacify in their own ground the three poisons:
the three causal conditions of desire, hatred, and stupidity.
Grant your blessing to pacify in their own ground the three diseases:
diseases of the vital winds, bile, and phlegm.
Grant your blessing to pacify in their own ground the three malicious spirits:
malicious spirits of males, females, and nāgas.
Grant your blessing to cast out the body as food.
Grant your blessing to integrate the discarded food on the path.
Grant your blessing to cut off the single thing from the roots.
Grant your blessing to integrate the offering and charity of the body's flesh and blood on the path.
Grant your blessing to be able to benefit beings, the invisible gods and demons.
Grant your blessing to achieve common and supreme spiritual powers.
Grant your blessing to attain the deathless awareness holder of longevity.
Grant your blessing to obtain joyful health without sickness.
*phaṭ phaṭ phaṭ*

### The Dedication

> A mere taste in the mouth or mere a whiff of the smells
> of this offering and charity of the body's flesh and blood
> cures disease, revives death, and reverses age. {277}
> May all males attain the state of Avalokiteshvara.
> May all females attain the state of Venerable Tārā.
> May this Holy Dharma Severance of Evil Object
> fully pervade throughout all directions,
> like the sun rising in the sky.

Then the patient stands up and the protection circle and so forth are put on the patient to wear, and then the patient is sent away. Thus, it is good if, after three, five, seven, or some days, it happens that the empowerment is conferred and that there is a practice. It is also appropriate if that does not happen.

Other than just the white distribution and the black distribution that were put into verse, all other verses spoken by Lord Rangjung and Mikyö Dorje are uncorrupted and thus have great blessing. This arrangement of the practice is similar to the daily practice of the Severance practitioner Kunga Wangchuk, the nephew of Trungpa Kunga Namgyal.[33] The visualizations and so forth and the blessings are concordant with my own experiences and the intention of the great classic texts of Severance. In order to benefit all the retreatants and to keep my promise to my disciple, the novice Buddhist monk Jampa, the monk-yogin Rāga Asya wrote this during the Dragyal constellation of the Year of the Dragon, in the waxing moon of Ashvinī. May it be of vast benefit for migrating beings.

*maṅgalam*

# 21. Pearl Rosary

*A Liturgy for the Donation of the Body in Severance*[1]

## Karma Chakme

Karma Chakme, or Rāga Asya (1613–1678), was a remarkable scholar and yogin with an enormous literary output that covered a wide variety of topics from both the Karma Kagyu and Nyingma traditions. He founded the monastery of Nedo (mNas mdo dgon) in 1662, which became the locus of the Nedo Kagyu subsect and enabled the continuation of his teachings and practices (*gnas mdo* or *chags med lugs*). His Nyingma practices are continued by the Palyul tradition. Two entire volumes of his collected writings are devoted to Severance, and perhaps even more are not found there. It seems that the safest attribution of an unsigned Severance text is to Karma Chakme.

*Pearl Rosary* represents the now classical form of a Severance ritual to offer one's body, to be done as either a group or an individual practice. It is not particularly specified as a healing ritual for the sick, as the previous text is, yet it contains many of the same prayers and liturgies, including most of the Ninefold Spirit Feast (here attributed not to Rangjung Dorje but to his student Yakde Paṇchen). The general order of practice is similar to most later Severance practices, even in the very condensed sādhanas, and matches the descriptions in *Machik's Complete Explanation*. Authors of these rituals may expand any of the requisite sections almost indefinitely, adding the familiar prayers and praises that have become the classic fare of Severance. After the crucial separation of body and mind, the multiple transformations and offerings of the corpse that is left—as mandala, as ḍākinī feeding, as feast, and so on—can be confusing in their repetitiveness. Yet they reflect the many kinds of offering rituals to be found in Tibetan Buddhism, all of which are fulfilled by these offerings of one's own body.

*namaḥ śrī gurave*

Like the esoteric instructions of the lineage of the profound path, all the teachings of the Mahayana are completely contained in the process of Casting Out the Body as Food. In the stages of the liturgy for putting that into practice, first there is the arousing of the mind of awakening and the gathering of the guests.

> Enemies that antagonize, obstructors that harm, conditions that obstruct me and all other sentient beings: *namo,* malicious spirits of place and of body, masters and mistresses of debt, and sickness demons headed by the dual spirits of place and body—all of them must attain the state of the supreme Great Mother. To that end, I will practice the profound, sacred Severance of Evil Object.
> *phaṭ phaṭ phaṭ*

Do the visualizations while striking the open end of the thighbone trumpet [on your palm] and the visualization of summoning the guests by the sound of blowing it. Meditate on the abridged refuge in the "jewel style" (*nor bu lugs*), and while going for refuge, practice the mind training of the four immeasurables.

> Enemies that antagonize, obstructors that harm, conditions that obstruct me and all other sentient beings: *namo,* malicious spirits of place and of body, {281} masters and mistresses of debt, and sickness demons headed by the dual spirits of place and body—until all of them attain the state of the supreme Great Mother,
>
> We take refuge in the guru.
> We take refuge in the Buddha.
> We take refuge in the dharma.
> We take refuge in the sangha.
> (Repeat three times.)
> We take refuge in the glorious holy gurus of the Object Severance lineage, adepts of Buddha's Word.
> We take refuge in the mother ḍākinīs of the three places.

*namo*
We take refuge in the buddhas and bodhisattvas residing in the ten directions.
We take refuge in the sugatas of the five families.
We take refuge in the lords of the three families.
We take refuge in the gurus with their retinue of vajra ḍākinīs.
We take refuge in the Kagyu gurus with their retinues of ḍākinīs.
We take refuge in the kind root gurus with their retinues of ḍākinīs.
We take refuge in our own minds—empty, unborn dharmakāya. {282}
We supplicate for refuge.
We supplicate to be placed under your genuine protection.
I and all others rely on the Buddha.
We rely on the dharma.
We rely on the sangha.
May my body and those of all sentient beings become virtuous.
May our speech become virtuous.
May our minds become virtuous.
May the four hundred four kinds of illness be purified.
May we be free from the ninety-one kinds of mishaps.
May we not be afflicted by the three hundred sixty kinds of calamities.
May the eighty thousand kinds of obstructors subside in their own ground.
May they be purified in their own ground.
May they be empty in their own ground.

I pay homage to the Three Jewels.
I take refuge in the Three Jewels.
I make offerings to the Three Jewels.
I confess each negativity and nonvirtue.
I rejoice in the virtue of all beings.
I keep the buddhas and bodhisattvas in mind.
I take refuge until awakening

in the Buddha, dharma, and supreme assembly.
I arouse the mind of awakening
in order to fully accomplish my own and others' welfare.
Once the mind of supreme awakening is aroused,
I invite all sentient beings to be my guests.
I will engage in the good, pleasing conduct of bodhisattvas
and attain buddhahood for the benefit of beings.

Just as the lords of the three times
gave rise to the supreme mind of awakening
that definitely causes genuine awakening,
I too will give rise to that holy thought.
I will recall all that is generated
and expand on what I recall.

### Creating the Extensive Five-Tiered Refuge Source, the Field of Accumulation

*trāṃ ratna maṇḍala paṃ padma maṇḍala ma sūrya maṇḍala a candra maṇḍala.* The *hūṃ* syllable dissolves into light, and from it, in the sky in front, Machik Lapkyi Drönma is white like a polished conch shell. She has one face and two hands. {283} With her right hand she rattles a golden ḍamaru at the sky. She rests a silver bell in her left hand on her hip. Her three eyes gaze into space. Her hair is tied up into a topknot, with the rest flowing loosely down her back. To her right, at ear-level, dwells the one father, Dampa Sangye, surrounded by all the gurus of the method lineage of the father tantras. To the left are the five goddesses of venerable Vajrayoginī, surrounded by the gurus of the wisdom lineage of the mother tantras. Above her head is the Teacher, the genuine perfect Buddha Shākyamuni, surrounded by the buddhas of the past, the future, and the present, and hosts of bodhisattvas. Above his head is the dharmakāya Great Mother, surrounded by her children, the hosts of buddhas and bodhisattvas of the ten directions. Above them is the buddha Vairochana, with heroes to his right, heroines to his left, Tārā in front, and Vairochana Immense Ocean in back.[2] Behind her are the heroes and heroines, and behind them are the protectors and guards of the holy dharma all around. Below Machik Lapdrön's seat are the oath-bound gods and demons of apparent existence; the eight classes of oath-bound gods, demigods, and spirits; disease demons; and the masters and mistresses of debt. They are all physically prostrating with devotion, verbally supplicating with devotion, and mentally keeping faith and trust with devotion. They remain there in the mode of listening for commands and awaiting instructions. All of the deities have *oṃ* at the forehead, *āḥ* at the throat, and *hūṃ* at the heart.

Light radiates from *hūṃ* at the hearts and invokes Machik and the Great Mother from the palace of dharmadhātu in Akaniṣhṭha, surrounded by their retinue of glorious gurus of the Object Severance lineage, adepts of the Buddha's Word. They come to rest in the space in front.

*guru deva ḍākinī satva saparivāra vajra samaya jaḥ jaḥ* {284}

The awareness beings are invoked.

### Paying Homage and Making Offerings through the Eight-Branch Prayer

I bow and praise the mother of the victors,
who is beyond the realm of speech, thought, and expression.
I bow and praise the great sage,
all-knowing and supreme among the Shakyas.
I bow and praise the Indian Dampa,
who has helped beings for seven lifetimes.
I bow and praise Lapdrön,
nonhuman ḍākinī of timeless awareness.
I bow and praise the father gurus,
who show the timeless awareness of one's cognition.
I bow and praise the yidams,
who definitely grant spiritual powers.
I bow and praise the buddhas,
who have perfect renunciation and realization.
I bow and praise all the holy dharma
which pacifies and is free of desire.
I bow and praise the sangha,

offerings to whom are meaningful.
I bow and praise Mañjushrī,
who has qualities of youth and beauty.
I bow and praise Avalokiteshvara,
whose definite intentions are compassionate.
I bow and praise Vajrapāṇi,
who subdues evil with great power.
I bow and praise the dharma protectors,
who conquer obstructing and corrupting forces.

*namo*
By Buddha's Word, I take refuge in all of you
until cyclic existence is empty.
By Buddha's Word, I present offerings to you.
By Buddha's Word, I request you to turn the wheel of the dharma.
I request you to remain with us, not passing into nirvana.
I dedicate the roots of virtue to the welfare of all beings.

## Purification

Then purify negativities with the visualization of a stream of awareness water and the repetition of *tadyathā oṃ gate gate pāragate pārasaṃgate bodhi svāhā*

## Presenting the Four-Mudra Offering

*namo*
I offer all form that appears
in all the worlds of the billionfold universe
as the mudra of sublime Body.
Grant the spiritual power of immutable Body.

I offer all the sounds resounding
in all the worlds of the billionfold universe
as the mudra of sublime Speech.
Grant the spiritual power of unimpeded Speech. {285}

I offer all the memories and thoughts in the minds
in all the worlds of the billionfold universe

as the mudra of sublime Mind.
Grant the spiritual power of undeluded Mind.

I offer all the happiness and suffering
in all the worlds of the billionfold universe
as the mudra of auspiciousness.
[Grant the spiritual powers, both common and supreme.][3]

When happy, I dedicate it to collective happiness;
may great happiness pervade all space.
When suffering, I carry the suffering myself;
may the ocean of cyclic suffering dry up
and all beings of the three realms be happy.
*phaṭ*

### Separating Mind from Body and Offering It as a Mandala

On the golden ground of my skin,
centered in the iron mountain rings of my nails,
the Supreme Mountain palace of my head and torso
is adorned by the sun and moon of my eyes,
the four continents of my four limbs, and so on.
This complete and perfect mandala of my body
I offer to the guru, yidam, and host of ḍākinīs.
Please accept it and so grant your blessings.
*phaṭ*

### Offering and Donating the Body

At the end of the White Distribution for Four Guests:

*namo*
Gods and demons living in this haunted place,
all the gods and demons of apparent existence,
who show their apparitions to me, the fortunate one:
Come, massing here like cloud banks in the sky.
Come, falling like rain from on high.
Come, swirling like whirlwinds over the ground.

I present this body as an offering to you all.
I offer you the six forms of my outer flesh:
May I attain the Buddha's precepts of the six perfections.
I offer you the nine inner organs with apertures:
May I attain the nine vehicles.
I offer you the five sense organs:[4]
May I attain the five kāyas and awarenesses.
To all of you gathered here, I offer this body.
You who are impatient, eat it raw. {286}
You who are not hurried, eat it cooked.
All ravenous ones, gobble it up.
Like lions relishing flesh,
take the first offering and leave nothing.

At the end of the red distribution, do the visualization for purifying the places of the six kinds of beings.

## The Supplication

The abridged supplication of the father tantras and mother tantras together:

*namo guru*
Great Mother Perfection of Wisdom, Shākyamuni,
Mañjushrī Lion of Speech, Venerable Mother Tārā:
I supplicate you to bless my mindstream.
Sukhasiddhī, Āryadeva,
Dampa Sangye, Mother Lapdrön:
I supplicate you to bless my mindstream.
Khambuyale, Lord Jñānajvala,
Namtso Dopa, dharma lord Rangjung:
I supplicate you to bless my mindstream.
Senge Palwa, Wangdor, Ratnashrī,
Jampa Pal, Özer Tsenchen:
I supplicate you to bless my mindstream.
Buddharatna, Kunga Namgyal,
Karma Tenkyong, Gyurme Nyingpo:
I supplicate you to bless my mindstream.
Könchok Tenzin, Tenpa Namgyal,

Jamgön Rikzin, Sungrap Gyatso:
I supplicate you to bless my mindstream.
The blessings of all lineages gathered into one,
lord of the circle, Chökyi Jungne
and Venerable Dudtsok Dulwai Dorje:
I supplicate you to bless my mindstream.
Root guru, adepts of the Severance lineage,
with hosts of ḍākinīs and heroes of the three places:
I supplicate you to bless my mindstream.
Bless me to renounce self-fixation.
Bless me that contentment is born in my mindstream.
Bless me to cast out the body as food.
Bless me to wander in haunted places and mountain retreats.
Bless me to cut off the single thing at the roots.
Bless me to realize the unborn all at once.
Bless me to purify deluded perceptions in basic space.
Bless me to accomplish buddhahood in one lifetime.
Bless me to spontaneously achieve the two purposes.
May I master the unsurpassed state of the Great Mother.
*phaṭ*

Alternatively, {287} do the abridged supplication of the completely perfected tantras:

I pray to the method lineage of the father tantras.
I pray to the wisdom lineage of the mother tantras.
I pray to the meaning lineage of the nondual tantras.
I pray to the experiential lineage of the fortunate ones.
I pray to the Severance lineage of adepts.
I pray to the symbol lineage of ḍākinīs.
I pray to the powerful dharma protector lineage.
Bless me to overturn attachment
to worldly activities of deluded appearances.
Bless me to be released from cherishing this illusory body,
the confluence of the four elements.
Bless me with the ability to experience the equal flavor
of adverse circumstances, sickness, spirits, and obstacles.
Bless me to recognize as my own

the mental apparitions of apparent existence.
Bless me to attain mastery over my own awareness,
the spontaneous presence of the three kāyas.
In general, may I and the six kinds of beings
totally abandon the cause, the stains of dualistic fixation,
and quickly attain supreme awakening.
*phaṭ*

**Serving the Ḍākinīs of the Five Families**

*kye*
Nonhuman ḍākinī of timeless awareness,
the vajra-family ḍākinī of the east,
white one with wrathful implements,
holds a crystal hooked knife in the right hand
and a perfect kapāla in the left,
encircled by a retinue of a hundred thousand white ones.

Surrounded by a retinue of gods and demons of apparent existence,
Mother, come here! I present the body offering of flesh and blood.
Gods and demons of apparent existence, please partake.
Once the gods and demons of apparent existence have partaken,
may their five sense desires be satisfied
and they attain supreme spiritual power.
*phaṭ*

*kye*
Nonhuman ḍākinī of timeless awareness,
the jewel-family ḍākinī of the south,
yellow one with wrathful implements,
holds a yellow hooked knife in the right hand
and a perfect kapāla in the left,
encircled by a retinue of a hundred thousand yellow ones.

Surrounded by a retinue of gods and demons of apparent existence,
Mother, come here! I present the body offering of flesh and blood.
Gods and demons of apparent existence, please partake. {288}

Once the gods and demons of apparent existence have partaken,
may their five sense desires be satisfied
and they attain supreme spiritual power.
*phaṭ*

*kye*
Nonhuman ḍākinī of timeless awareness,
the lotus-family ḍākinī of the west,
red one with wrathful implements,
holds a coral hooked knife in the right hand
and a perfect kapāla in the left,
encircled by a retinue of a hundred thousand red ones.

Surrounded by a retinue of gods and demons of apparent existence,
Mother, come here! I present the body offering of flesh and blood.
Gods and demons of apparent existence, please partake.
Once the gods and demons of apparent existence have partaken,
may their five sense desires be satisfied
and they attain supreme spiritual power.
*phaṭ*

*kye*
Nonhuman ḍākinī of timeless awareness,
the action-family ḍākinī of the north,
green one with wrathful implements,
holds a turquoise hooked knife in the right hand
and a perfect kapāla in the left,
encircled by a retinue of a hundred thousand green ones.

Surrounded by a retinue of gods and demons of apparent existence,
Mother, come here! I present the body offering of flesh and blood.
Gods and demons of apparent existence, please partake.
Once the gods and demons of apparent existence have partaken,
may their five sense desires be satisfied
and they attain supreme spiritual power.
*phaṭ*

*kye*
Nonhuman ḍākinī of timeless awareness,
the tathāgata-family ḍākinī of the center,
black one with wrathful implements,
holds a meteorite hooked knife in the right hand
and a perfect kapāla in the left,
encircled by a retinue of a hundred thousand black ones.

Surrounded by a retinue of gods and demons of apparent existence,
Mother, come here! I present the body offering of flesh and blood.
Gods and demons of apparent existence, please partake.
Once the gods and demons of apparent existence have partaken,
may their five sense desires be satisfied
and they attain supreme spiritual power.
*phaṭ*

**Consecrating One's Body as the Feast**

*oṃ* pray to Machikma
*āḥ* pray to Machikma
*hūṃ* pray to Machikma
*kye*
Bless with white *oṃ*.
Bless with red *āḥ*.
Bless with blue *hūṃ*.
The blessing of the three letters
dissolves the flesh and blood into light,
filling the torma bowl of human skin. {289}
Through this feast offering of a blazing mass of light,
may I attain the mandala of the victors,
the lord gurus, yidams, and ḍākinīs.
May it fulfill the commitment with the dharma protectors,
Mahākāla, Shrīdevī, and oath-bound guards.
*phaṭ*

## The Feeding

*kye*
From the sixth lord, Vajradhara,
down to the kind root guru—
everyone, with your retinues, enjoy the feast.
Some enjoy the outer feast.
Some enjoy the inner feast.
Some enjoy the secret feast.
Some enjoy the suchness feast.
With no exception, including retinues, enjoy the feast.
*a la la*—joyfully enjoy!
Take the first offering and leave nothing.
*phaṭ*

*hūṃ*
From the hosts of deities of the mandala
down to the retinues of heroes and ḍākinīs—
everyone, with your retinues, enjoy the feast.
Some enjoy the outer feast.
Some enjoy the inner feast.
Some enjoy the secret feast.
Some enjoy the suchness feast.
With no exception, including retinues, enjoy the feast.
*a la la* —joyfully enjoy!
Take the first offering and leave nothing.
*phaṭ*

From the Mother Vajravārāhī
down to the mother ḍākinīs of the three places—
everyone, with your retinues, enjoy the feast.
Some enjoy the outer feast.
Some enjoy the inner feast.
Some enjoy the secret feast.
Some enjoy the suchness feast.
With no exception, including retinues, enjoy the feast.
*a la la*—joyfully enjoy!

Take the first offering and leave nothing.
*phaṭ*

From the dharma protectors Mahākāla and Mahākālī
down to the mandala-border protectors,
everyone, with your retinues, enjoy the feast.
Some enjoy the outer feast.
Some enjoy the inner feast.
Some enjoy the secret feast.
Some enjoy the suchness feast.
With no exception, including retinues, enjoy the feast.
*a la la*—joyfully enjoy!
Take the first offering and leave nothing.
*phaṭ*

From Shākyamuni
down to the eighteen hell realms—
everyone, with your retinues, enjoy the feast.
Some enjoy the outer feast.
Some enjoy the inner feast.
Some enjoy the secret feast.
Some enjoy the suchness feast.
With no exception, including retinues, enjoy the feast.
*a la la*—joyfully enjoy!
Take the first offering and leave nothing.
*phaṭ*

From the ground masters of the billionfold universe
down to the gods and demons dwelling here—
everyone, with your retinues, enjoy the feast.
Some enjoy the outer feast.
Some enjoy the inner feast.
Some enjoy the secret feast.
Some enjoy the suchness feast.
With no exception, including retinues, enjoy the feast.
*a la la*—joyfully enjoy!
Take the first offering and leave nothing.
*phaṭ*

From the guests of the six kinds of beings
down to the creditors and obstructing types—
everyone, with your retinues, enjoy the feast.
Some enjoy the outer feast.
Some enjoy the inner feast.
Some enjoy the secret feast.
Some enjoy the suchness feast.
With no exception, including retinues, enjoy the feast.
*a la la*—joyfully enjoy!
Take the first offering and leave nothing.
*phaṭ*

If it is necessary to do the hand feeding, as in the esoteric instruction for the sick and such,[5] make the connection with *phaṭ* at all the junctures. Then, if you choose to do the extended red distribution, first for the wrathful controlling, generate your own awareness as Krodhī, as in the instructions on blending and transferring.

*phaṭ*
Instantly I become the mistress of the charnel ground, Krodhīkālī, with one face, two hands, three eyes, and four totally bared fangs. My right eye is the sun mandala, rolling around and red. {290} My left is the moon mandala, a spinning, roving sphere. The central eye is the joined sun-moon sphere, dark red and twitching with agitation. Five dry skulls adorn my head. Fifty-one wet ones form a necklace. Meteorite-metal black hair falls down to the ground. A black pig's head protrudes from my hair, grunting upward and bringing the gods and demons of the three realms under control. The pig's bristles are blazing with the fire of timeless awareness, burning all the devil hosts. With my right hand I throw the pelt of human skin, red with blood, over the expanse of space, bringing the gods and demons of the three realms under control. Blowing the human thighbone in my left hand overwhelms the gods and demons of the three planes of existence. A khaṭvāṃka rests in the crook of my elbow. A wet elephant skin covers my torso, a human skin is tied around my waist, and a tiger skin forms the skirt. With right leg drawn in and left extended, I stand swaying upon the seat of lotus, sun, and corpse.

My head touches the god's realm of the Thirty-Three. My feet reach down to the *narak* vajra seat. My torso brings the god realm under control. My lower body brings the nāga realm under control. My waist brings the realm of pestilent spirits under control. Worker ḍākinīs emanate from the heart: white ones with hooks, yellow ones with lassos, red ones with shackles, green ones with bells. Furthermore, [emanated] krodhīkālīs flailing human skins with their right hands and blowing human thighbones in their left hands are totally visible above, below, and in all directions and in between, like dust motes in the rays of sunlight.

## Summoning the Malicious Spirits by the Power of Truth

*namo*

By the power of the True Word of the glorious holy gurus of the lineage of Object Severance, awareness holders, and adepts; and the True Word of the Three Jewels; {291} and the True Word of the dharmakāya ḍākinī of timeless awareness with a retinue of the gods of the Great Mother; and the True Word of the saṃbhogakāya ḍākinī of timeless awareness with a retinue of gods of foe-taming krodhīkālīs; and the True Word of the nirmāṇakāya ḍākinī of timeless awareness with the retinue of gods of Machik Lapkyi Drönma; and the True Word of the guardians of the Word of Object Severance with the retinue of gods of an ocean of oath-bound ones; and by the Great Truth:

All disease demons and disease masters, along with the leaders of malicious spirits—the nemesis that is concepts of self-fixation, male spirit kings, female spirit demonesses, nāga spirits, *teurang* spirits, consuming demons, executioners, corpse droppers, roving killers; those who lead away by disease at first, hold the full-fledged disease in the middle, and rob the life in the end; who ambush vitality, carry away the soul, bloat the mind, deceive and confuse, [cause beings to be] upside down; who leap around, wet, covered, and gone; who do not listen to commands or carry vows; who are out of control, not suppressed by splendor—all of you of whatever kind: Do not oppose the vows and commands of Machik Krodhīkālī and the five families of ḍākinīs. Gather here for this offering and donation of the body, flesh, and blood. Draw close. *hūṃ hūṃ hūṃ phaṭ phaṭ phaṭ*

### Calling the Pestilent Spirits

Blowing the thighbone, call the pestilent spirits by what is known as the "long call" (*'bod ring*) from the *Mind Training Wheel Weapon*[6] by the dharma lord Rangjung.

*kye*
Mothers gather, gather, gather to eat flesh.
All you who take away the breath, come gather here.
Come here for the butchered and stripped corpse.
Show up to help with divvying up the flesh.
You all are my fathers and mothers—
come to enjoy your child's flesh and blood.
All you kind fathers and mothers—
the good reward is available now; come take it.
Previously I held and cherished this body. {292}
I still wander in cyclic existence because of that.
Now I am not attached and dispense it as a banquet.
All types of guests from the peak of existence
down to the hell realms of the *narak*,
gods and demigods of the place,
male devils, karmic *sinpo* spirits—gather!
Female devils, karmic *sinmo* spirits—gather!
Male devils, *gyalgong* owners of vitality—gather!
Female devil demoness owners of vitality—gather!
Nine demons of existence—gather!
Ten malicious spirits of temples—gather!
Fifteen great malicious spirits of children—gather!
Eighteen great malicious spirit chiefs—gather!
One thousand eighty obstructing types—gather!
Three hundred sixty calamity causers—gather!
Ninety-one incidental spirits—gather!
Come hither! Gather here! Enjoy the flesh and blood!
From the crown of the head
down to the soles and toes of the feet,

I will not be attached and clingy,
so eat the flesh, drink the blood, suck the bones!
Carry out the head, limbs, and organs.
This whole body inside and out
is fit to eat and fit to have—eat what is there.
Everybody take it easy and be satisfied.
Be peaceful and get lost.
Let it go and cut from the roots.
Be tamed, be vanquished, be okay with me.
*phaṭ*

Employ the peaceful or wrathful visualization according to the circumstances. Then, once the visualization of the Six Earth Lord Application has been established as the basis, do the feeding known as the Ninefold Spirit Feast by Yakde Paṇchen.[7]

In front is the sorcerer spirit (*byad ma*) with gods and protectors. To her right, the essence of the *gyalpo* is a bande with a bow surrounded by an army of bandes. To her left is the demoness with turquoise hair, yellow eyebrows, and conch-shell fangs. In front is the king of earth lords, the nine-armed toad, surrounded by an army of earth lords. Behind is the one with the fishhook mane, surrounded by an army of fish. Below, the nāga devil with nine serpent heads is surrounded by a million armies of nāgas. {293} Above is the planet devil king Rāhula, surrounded by a million armies of planets. All around are the commanded gods and demons that appear in existence, the eight classes of commanded gods, demigods, and *sinpo* spirits, and the demons of disease and masters and mistresses of debt. All of these become completely clear.

Then do the meditation liturgy as before, from "the nemesis that is concepts of self-fixation . . ." to ". . . *hūṃ hūṃ hūṃ phaṭ phaṭ phaṭ*," and the conjuring and melting. Blow the thighbone. Repeat *phaṭ* while doing the visualization. Then:

*hūṃ*
A hundred great bandes and a hundred thousand races of men,
a thousand knife-wielding butchers,

minions beyond what the mind can grasp,
sorcerers that cause me harm,
gods and demons of apparent existence in general,
and in particular, the gods and demons dwelling in this haunted
ground—
your needs and desires are satisfied by the dedication
of these offerings and gifts of body, flesh, and blood.
May you attain supreme spiritual power.
*phaṭ*

*Gyalpo* spirits, white cloaked, black cloaked,
gray dogs, red dogs, and old birds,
nine demons of existence,
ten malicious spirits of temples,
*gyalgong* spirits that cause me harm,
gods and demons of apparent existence in general,
and in particular, the gods and demons dwelling in this haunted
ground—
your needs and desires are satisfied by the dedication
of these offerings and gifts of body, flesh, and blood.
May you attain supreme spiritual power.
*phaṭ*

Glorious black goddess Palden Lhamo,
mamos, ḍākinīs, powerful movers,
twelve *tenma* [sisters] and so forth,
oath breakers, black *temo* and such,
the demonesses that cause me harm,
gods and demons of apparent existence in general,
and in particular, the gods and demons dwelling in this
haunted ground—
your needs and desires are satisfied by the dedication
of these offerings and gifts of body, flesh, and blood.
May you attain supreme spiritual power.
*phaṭ*

Nine-headed black planet devil,
eight planets such as the sun,
twenty-eight constellations,

four sibling [animal]-faced attendants,
planet armies that cause me harm,
gods and demons of apparent existence in general,
and in particular, the gods and demons dwelling in this
haunted ground—
your needs and desires are satisfied by the dedication
of these offerings and gifts of body, flesh, and blood.
May you attain supreme spiritual power.
*phaṭ*

Black nāga devils, consumers of vitality,
royal caste, merchant caste, brahmins,
commoners, servant caste nāgas, and so on;
Nanda, Takṣhaka, Shaṅkhapāla,
Upānanda, and so on of the nāga family; {294}
nāga armies who would harm me,
gods and demons of apparent existence in general,
and in particular, the gods and demons dwelling in this
haunted ground—
your needs and desires are satisfied by the dedication
of these offerings and gifts of body, flesh, and blood.
May you attain supreme spiritual power.
*phaṭ*

The ghastly black chief devil,
the devil Rete with a good head,
with a retinue of crow demons all around,
devil armies of hundreds of millions,
devil armies who would harm me,
gods and demons of apparent existence in general,
and in particular, the gods and demons dwelling in this
haunted ground—
your needs and desires are satisfied by the dedication
of these offerings and gifts of body, flesh, and blood.
May you attain supreme spiritual power.
*phaṭ*

Chief *tsen* spirit causing deadly skin disease;
four classes of quick, wild *tsen* spirits;
eight swift-footed spirits with harelips;
four mouths, eight faces, and so forth;
*tsen* legions who would harm me;
gods and demons of apparent existence in general,
and in particular, gods and demons dwelling in this
haunted ground—
your needs and desires are satisfied by the dedication
of these offerings and gifts of body, flesh, and blood.
May you attain supreme spiritual power.
*phaṭ*

Oath-breaker spirits with red fire sparks,
area demons, *gap* demons, and vagrant [demons],
harmful little spirits and darkening demons,
oath breakers who would harm me,
gods and demons of apparent existence in general,
and in particular, the gods and demons dwelling in this
haunted ground—
your needs and desires are satisfied by the dedication
of these offerings and gifts of body, flesh, and blood.
May you attain supreme spiritual power.
*phaṭ*

From Vajrasādhu down to
the least of the *teurang* spirits,
with retinues of various *uber* spirits,
*telmo* spirits with round ears and so on,
*teurang* spirits who would harm me,
gods and demons of apparent existence in general,
and in particular, the gods and demons dwelling in this
haunted ground—
your needs and desires are satisfied by the dedication
of these offerings and gifts of body, flesh, and blood.
May you attain supreme spiritual power.
*phaṭ*[8]

Then do the visualization of the Banners[9] and so on with the well-known meditation liturgy.

*hūṃ*
Mothers, great *ging* and lesser *ging*, with siblings:
Sounds of *ha*, sounds of *phaṭ—di ri ri.*
Fierce palatal sounds—*chem se chem.*
Chomping sounds of eating flesh—*di ri ri.*
Gulping sounds of drinking blood—*kyu ru ru.*
Grinding sounds of gnawing bones—*jip se jip.*
Laughing in pleasure—*sha ra ra.*
Singing secret songs—*kyu ru ru.*
Mothers, come here for this flesh and blood body offering.

You flesh lovers, eat this flesh;
sounds of chewing flesh—*di ri ri.*
May all hungry ones be satiated.
Blood lovers, drink this blood;
gulping sounds of drinking blood—*kyu ru ru.*
May all the thirsty ones be satiated. {295}
Bone lovers, gnaw these bones;
grinding sounds of gnawing bones—*jip se jip.*
Skin lovers, wear this skin;
eating when wearing skin—*lhap se lhap.*
May all the hungry ones be satiated.
May all previous debts and liabilities
from beginningless existence be cleared.
May all the ties with grudge holders be severed.
May everyone be assuaged and satisfied.
May they attain supreme spiritual power.
*phaṭ*

### Collecting the Leftovers

In the torma trough of a blazing *bhañja* of three planes of existence,
the heap of leftovers is as big as Supreme Mountain and four continents.

Burning flesh of stupidity—*nyi li li.*
Blood oceans of desire—*me re re.*
Bone heaps of anger—*tra la la.*
The enjoyment of the five elixirs is unimaginable.
Ḍākinīs and protectors included in the entourage,
eight classes of helpful gods and spirits,
and eighty thousand types of outer and inner obstacles—
partake of this vast commanded legacy
and accomplish the yogins' requested activities.
*phaṭ*

## Concluding Dedication and Aspiration Prayers

By the power of this enormous generosity,
may all beings become naturally occurring buddhas.
May this generosity liberate all living beings
that were not liberated before by the victors.
*phaṭ*

May all enjoy continuous prosperity,
like the treasury of the sky.
May they enjoy independence
without conflict or misfortune.
*phaṭ*

May we who practice Object Severance
not view our own minds as devils
and cut through every conceit.
May we not get inflated
over any good qualities that arise.
May we remain without inflation
no matter what bad thoughts arise.

May this Holy Dharma Severance of Evil Object
spread throughout all times and directions
like the sun rising in the sky. {296}
*phaṭ*

At this juncture, do the visualization of the Peaceful Round Lotus or the Wrathful Round, whichever is appropriate.[10]

### Avalokiteshvara Meditation

Think of your own and everybody else's body as Avalokiteshvara:

> White body not clothed in flaws,
> head adorned by a perfect buddha,
> looking on beings with eyes of compassion:
> I bow to Avalokiteshvara.
> *oṃ maṇi padme hūṃ* (Recite as many as possible.)

Say *phaṭ* and imagine that all the guests return to their own places happy and satisfied. You become a white ḍākinī and say:

> By this merit, may I quickly attain
> Object Severance Mahāmudrā
> and establish in that state
> all beings without exception.
> *phaṭ*

Rest in emptiness like the center of space.

# 22. Source of All Qualities

*The Severance Feast Activities Arranged Unerringly According to the Teaching Tradition*[1]

Karmapa Tekchok Dorje

This text is the fourteenth Karmapa's arrangement of the prayers and practices traditionally used in the Severance feast activities of the Zurmang tradition. The first part of the title is nearly identical to that of *White Crystal Mirror* in this volume; most likely Karmapa Tekchok Dorje (Theg mchog rdo rje, (1798/9–1868/9) wished to enhance that earlier text. Also found here are many sections from *Pearl Rosary*. And it is clear from the internal comments (*yig chung*) that to practice it one must draw on the liturgies of these earlier compositions. What is distinctive in this text is the addition of a number of the ancient supplications to the gurus of the lineage, particularly the beautiful prayers to Machik by her son and grandson. The most unusual feature of all is that Tekchok Dorje provides the authorship for each of the added prayers, a rarity in this Tibetan tradition of recycled liturgy.

Karmapa Tekchok Dorje was a contemporary of Jamgön Kongtrul and similarly played an integral part in the nonsectarian (*ris med*) activities of the times in Kham. They exchanged transmissions and teachings, and both of them counted the great Situ Pema Nyinje Wangpo (Pad ma Nyin byed dbang po, 1774–1853) as a primary guru. Their close colleagues included Jamyang Khyentse Wangpo (1820–1892) and Tertön Chokgyur Lingpa (1829–1870), among many others.

In addition to this text, Tekchok Dorje is usually cited as the author of the most popular daily practice of Severance in the Kagyu tradition, *The Concise Charity of the Body for Daily Practice* (although the fifteenth Karmapa and Karma Chakme have also been credited with it). Despite their close connection, Kongtrul did not actually receive the transmission of *Source of All Qualities* directly from Tekchok Dorje but through the Chöwang Tulku, according to the *Catalog,* which also mentions that Tekchok Dorje himself received it from Situ Pema Nyinje.

---

Homage to the guru and the mother of the victors.

If you want to do the feast activity of Severance, arrange the tormas, offerings, and feast substances according to the source texts. First, the dedication of the white torma to the ground masters:

> *oṃ vajra yakṣa hūṃ*
>
> *oṃ vajra jola a na la ha na da ha pa tsa ma tha bhañja ra ṇa hūṃ phaṭ*
>
> *oṃ svabhāva śuddhāḥ sarvadharmāḥ svabhāva śuddho 'ham*

> All becomes emptiness.
> Out of emptiness, a vast and wide precious vessel arises from *oṃ*. Within it, infinite *oṃ āḥ hūṃ* syllables dissolve into light. The torma made from divine substances arises from that, its brilliance unhindered, generating special undissipating bliss, equal to the reaches of space.

> *oṃ akāro mukhaṃ sarvadharmāṇām ādyanutpannatvāt āḥ hūṃ phaṭ svāhā*

Repeat that three times for the consecration.

> *bhūmi pati saparivāra ākarṣaya jaḥ jaḥ / bhūmi pati saparivāra padma kamalāya stvaṃ / bhūmi pati saparivāra namaḥ sarva tathāgato bhyoḥ viśva mukhebhyaḥ / sarvathākham udgate / spharaṇa imaṃ gagana khaṃ gṛihṇedaṃ balyādi svāhā / bhūmi pati saparivāra arghaṃ / pādyaṃ / puṣpe / dhūpe / āloke / gandhe / naivedye / śabda pratīccha svāhā*

In that way the offered and donated tormas, endowed with the five sense desirables of form, sound, smell, taste, and texture, are dedicated and transmuted as offerings. {299}

*oṃ āḥ hūṃ* (three times)

Ground masters who dwell in the first thousand, second thousand, and third thousand [orders of the cosmos], high sky and low ground, big Supreme Mountain, seven golden mountains, and seven circular lapping lakes, four continents and eight islands; Jambudvīpa Sodor,[2] the set of four great kings, thirteen gods of Tibetan song, nine gods of creation, twelve *tenma* that protect Tibet and Kham; ground masters who dwell in the three districts in upper Tibet, the four districts of U and Tsang in the center, and the three or five ranges of Dokham in lower Tibet; masters of sites, masters of countries, masters of towns, indigenous inhabitants: into your mouths *oṃ āḥ hūṃ*.

Furthermore, the earth lord *tenma* goddess of earth, big-handed earth holder, eight trigrams (*spar kha*), nine magic-square numbers (*sme ba*), twelve-year animal cycle, sixty-year cycle, earth lord king of Tese and so forth, this year's animal sign, today's sun, planets, and constellations, all with the power of tracking time: into your mouths *oṃ āḥ hūṃ*. {300}

Ground masters of where we, the yogins, have been previously, where we will go henceforth, and where we are now: into your mouths *oṃ āḥ hūṃ*.

The far mountain to my right, near mountain to my left, traveled path, growing trees, falling water, solid cliffs, blowing wind, supported palace, and so forth—in the locations and areas, isolated sites, or this very practice site—ground masters who live here and who truly love virtue and have the mind of awakening: into your mouths *oṃ āḥ hūṃ*.

If we yogins and our retinues move, don't hold us back. If we stay, don't chase us out. Don't have bad thoughts and don't be rude. Supply provisions, be a patron, establish conducive conditions, clear away adverse circumstances, and totally pacify all circumstances of outer and inner obstacles *oṃ āḥ hūṃ*.

May ground masters in the three realms obtain without any

hindrance all their desires, all their wishes for whatever purpose, all of them of whatever kind, in all the realms of the world, without exception.

Say that and offer the torma in a clean place.

## The Consecration of the Inner Offering

Sprinkle with pure water.

*oṃ āḥ bighanānta kṛita hūṃ phaṭ*

*oṃ svabhāva śuddhāḥ sarva dharmaḥ svabhāva śuddho 'ham*

All becomes emptiness. Out of emptiness, from *yaṃ*, arises the blue wind mandala shaped like a bow with a *yaṃ* on the handle and marked by fluttering banners on the two ends. Upon that, from *raṃ*, is the mandala of fire, a blazing red triangle marked by *raṃ*. Upon that, from three *kaṃ*, are three complete skulls as hearthstones with the napes of the necks facing inward. Upon that, the syllable *a* completely transforms into a kapāla. It is a single piece, white outside and red inside, with the forehead facing you. It is equal in size to the realm of reality. In its center, from *mu*, is urine, like aquamarine. In the east, from *bi*, are feces, like crystal. In the south, from *ra*, is *rakta,* like refined gold. In the west, from *shu*, is white bodhichitta. In the north from *ma* are brains. {301} Again, from *na* in the center is human flesh. From *go* in the southeast is buffalo flesh. From *ku* in the southwest is dog flesh. From *da* in the northwest is elephant flesh. From *ha* in the northeast is horse flesh. All of those too are marked by their respective syllables. Breath in the shape of *hūṃ* is exhaled out of your left nostril. It strikes the wind mandala. The banners flutter, the wind stirs, the fire blazes, the skull heats up, and the substances boil. All the impurities spill out. Above it, light radiates from the three syllables *oṃ āḥ hūṃ* and draws the elixir of timeless awareness from the hearts of all the sugatas. It blends inseparably with the elixir of sacred pledge. It becomes a great ocean of elixir of timeless awareness.

*oṃ āḥ hūṃ* (three times)

Again, sprinkle the above torma with alcohol, wild water, and elixir, and do it one [more] time while visualizing the torma.

### The Consecration of the Offerings

Sprinkle with elixir.

> *oṃ karma ḍākinī hūṃ hūṃ phaṭ*
>
> *oṃ svabhāva śuddhāḥ sarva dharmaḥ svabhāva śuddho 'ham*
>
> All becomes emptiness. Out of that, from *a*, comes a vast and wide precious vessel. Within it, an infinite collection of *hūṃ* syllables dissolve into light. The actual offering items arise from that, made out of divine substances—vajra water for drinking, water for the feet, flowers, incense, light, perfume, food, music, and so forth. They are brilliant and unlimited masses of offering clouds, bigger and better than the masses of offering clouds in the life story of the bodhisattva, noble Samantabhadra. They expand and fill to the far reaches of the space of the universe, pleasing the noble ones. In duration, they have the nature of continual production until cyclic existence is vacated.
>
> *oṃ vajra arghaṃ* . . . (and likewise:) . . . *pādyaṃ* . . . *puṣpe* . . . *dhūpe* . . . *āloke* . . . *gandhe* . . . *naivedye* . . . *śabta āḥ hūṃ svāhā*

### Arousing the Awakening Mind and Summoning the Guests {302}

> Enemies that antagonize, obstructors that harm, conditions that obstruct me and all other sentient beings: *namo,* malicious spirits of place and of body, masters and mistresses of debt, and sickness demons headed by the dual spirits of place and body—all of them must attain the state of the supreme Great Mother. To that end, I will practice the profound, sacred Severance of Evil Object.
> *phaṭ phaṭ phaṭ*

Do the visualizations while striking the open side of the thighbone [on your palm] and imagine summoning the guests by the sound of blowing it.

## Going for Refuge

Enemies that antagonize, obstructors that harm, conditions that obstruct me and all other sentient beings: *namo,* malicious spirits of place and of body, masters and mistresses of debt, and sickness demons headed by the dual spirits of place and body—until all of them attain the state of the supreme Great Mother,

We take refuge in the guru.
We take refuge in the Buddha.
We take refuge in the dharma.
We take refuge in the sangha.
(Repeat three times.)

We go for refuge in the glorious holy gurus of the Object Severance lineage, adepts of Buddha's Word.
We take refuge in the mother ḍākinīs of the three places.
*namo*
We take refuge in the buddhas and bodhisattvas residing in the ten directions.
We take refuge in the sugatas of the five families.
We take refuge in the lords of the three families.
We take refuge in the gurus with their retinue of vajra ḍākinīs.
We take refuge in the Kagyu gurus with their retinues of ḍākinīs.
We take refuge in the kind root gurus with their retinues of ḍākinīs.
We take refuge in our own minds—empty, unborn dharmakāya.
We supplicate for refuge.
We supplicate to be placed under your genuine protection.
I and all others rely on the Buddha. {303}
We rely on the dharma.
We rely on the sangha.
May my body and those of all sentient beings become virtuous.
May our speech become virtuous.
May our minds become virtuous.

May the four hundred four kinds of illness be purified.
May we be free from the ninety-one kinds of mishaps.
May we not be afflicted by the three hundred sixty kinds of calamities.
May the eighty thousand kinds of obstructors subside in their own ground.
May they be purified in their own ground.
May they be empty in their own ground.

I pay homage to the Three Jewels.
I take refuge in the Three Jewels.
I make offerings to the Three Jewels.
I confess each negativity and nonvirtue.
I rejoice in the virtue of all beings.
I keep the buddhas and bodhisattvas in mind.
I take refuge until awakening
in the Buddha, dharma, and supreme assembly.
I arouse the mind of awakening
in order to fully accomplish my own and others' welfare.
Once the mind of supreme awakening is aroused,
I invite all sentient beings to be my guests.
I will engage in the good, pleasing conduct of bodhisattvas
and attain buddhahood for the benefit of beings.

## Arousing the Awakening Mind

Just as the lords of the three times
give rise to the supreme mind of awakening
that definitely causes genuine awakening,
I too will give rise to that holy thought.
I will recall all that is generated
and expand on what I recall.

## Creating the Field of Accumulation

*trāṃ ratna maṇḍala paṃ padma maṇḍala ma sūrya maṇḍala a candra maṇḍala*

The *hūṃ* syllable dissolves into light and from it, in the sky in front, Machik Lapkyi Drönma is white like a polished conch shell. She has one face and two hands. With her right hand she rattles a golden ḍāmaru at the sky. She rests a silver bell in her left hand on her hip. Her three eyes gaze into space. {304} Her hair is tied up into a topknot, with the rest flowing loosely down her back.

To her right at ear level dwells the one father, Dampa Sangye, black and glossy. He is charismatic, dressed as an āchārya. He has one face and two hands: the right one rattles a joined-skull drum (*bhandha*) at the sky, and with the left one he blows a human-bone flute. He dwells amid a veritable ocean of adepts. To Mother Jomo's left is venerable Vajrayoginī on a lotus-sun-corpse seat. She is red like the color of vermilion. She has one face and two hands, brandishing a hooked knife at the sky with the right and holding a blood-filled skull cup to her heart with the left. She has a khaṭvāṃka in the crook of her elbow. All her ornaments and accoutrements are perfect and complete. To her east, from *ha*, is the white vajra ḍākinī. To her south, from *ri*, is the yellow jewel ḍākinī. To the west, from *ni*, is the red lotus ḍākinī. To the north, from *sa*, is the green action ḍākinī. All of them have one face and two hands. In their right hands they hold hooked knives marked with, respectively, a vajra, a jewel, a lotus, and a sword. In their left hands they hold skull cups filled with elixir and have khaṭvāṃkas in the crooks of their elbows. Their ornaments and accoutrements are all the same as Jomo's.

Above Mother Jomo's head is Buddha Shākyamuni on a sun-moon-lotus seat. His body is the color of refined gold. He has one face and two arms. He makes the mudras of earth touching with his right hand and meditation equipoise with his left. His body is adorned by thirty-two excellent marks and eighty excellent minor marks. He is surrounded by a host of buddhas of the three times—past, future, and present—and the bodhisattvas. Above his head is the dharmakāya Great Mother on a sun-moon-lotus seat. She is brilliant orange, with one face and four arms. {305} One right hand holds a vajra, the other touches the ground; one left hand holds a volume of text, and the other makes the mudra of equipoise. Her body is adorned with silks and jewels. She sits with her legs in the vajra position, surrounded by her children—the assemblies of buddhas and bodhisattvas of the ten directions.

In the direction above her head is the buddha Vairochana, with heroes to his right, heroines to his left, Tārā in front, and [Vairochana] Immense Ocean behind him. Heroes and heroines are behind that, and the protector guards of the holy dharma are all around. Beneath Machik Lapkyi Drönma's seat are the oath-bound gods and demons of apparent existence; the eight classes of oath-bound gods, demigods, and spirits; disease demons; and the masters and mistresses of debt. They are all physically prostrating with devotion, verbally supplicating with devotion, and mentally keeping faith and trust with devotion. They remain there in the mode of listening for commands and awaiting instructions. All of the deities have *oṃ* at the forehead, *āḥ* at the throat, and *hūṃ* at the heart.

Light radiates from *hūṃ* in their hearts and invokes Machik and the Great Mother from the palace of dharmadhātu in Akaniṣhṭha, surrounded by their retinue of glorious gurus of the Object Severance lineage, adepts of the Buddha's Word. They come to rest in the space in front:

*guru deva ḍākinī satva saparivāra vajra samaya jaḥ jaḥ*

*hūṃ*
Protector of all sentient beings without exception,
deity who conquers unbearable devils with their hosts,
you who know all things just as they are,
Great Mother and entourage, please approach this place.

Great Mother, it is good you have come here.
We have merit and good fortune.
Please make yourself comfortable
on this lion-lotus-moon seat
in order to enjoy my offering delights.

After you do the extensive visualization of the invocation of the awareness beings as in the sources, they melt inseparably with the pledge beings. {306}

### The Bathing Ritual

Just as, as soon as he was born,
the gods bathed him,
just so, with pure divine water,
I bathe your body.[3]

### The Sequence of Offerings

I present offerings of drinking water,
washing water, incense, flowers, lamps,
scented water, food, and music
to the Great Mother and entourage.

I present the five desirable qualities—
form, sound, scent, taste,
and similarly texture—
to the Great Mother and entourage.

I present the seven royal treasures—
wheel, gem, queen, minister,
elephant, supreme horse, and general—
to the Great Mother and entourage.

I present the eight inner and outer goddesses—
grace, garlands, song, dance,
incense, flowers, lamps, and scents—
to the Great Mother and entourage.

This earth, anointed with perfume and strewn with flowers,
adorned by Supreme Mountain, four continents, sun, and moon,
visualized as a pure realm, is offered to the buddhas.
May all beings enjoy that perfectly pure realm.

Thus offer the mandala.

## The Sequence of Homages and Praises

I bow to the lotus feet of the vajra-endowed
body of the guru who is like a jewel
and through whose kindness
great bliss arises instantly.

I go for refuge in the master,
the natural kāya of all buddhas.
I bow to the deities of the mandala
and the deity where my flower first landed.

I bow and praise the mother of the victors of three times,
unutterable, unimaginable, inexpressible perfection of wisdom,
unborn, unceasing, the very essence of space,
the domain of individual reflexive awareness.

I bow and praise the mother of the victors,
on whom one can never gaze enough,
with her one face, four arms, and color of pure gold,
sitting in vajra posture, decked in precious ornaments. {307}

I bow and praise Mother Tārā.
Upon the golden ground of all pure realms,
numerous precious gems are laid out
and a rain of puṇḍarīka flowers falls.

I bow and praise the Tathāgata,
the protector endowed with great compassion,
the Teacher who knows everything,
the vast field of meritorious qualities.

I bow and praise the dharma that brings peace,
purity that is the cause of freedom from desire,
virtue that liberates from bad existences—
the sole sublime ultimate truth.

I bow and praise the sangha as well,
who, once liberated, show the way to liberation,
and have perfect devotion to the pure training—
a holy field with good qualities.

I bow and praise the yidams
of the outer, inner, and secret teachings
of whatever was said by the Teacher himself
in the four classes of tantra.

I bow and praise the dharma protectors
who promised before the Teacher himself
to undertake as commanded the protection
of the precious doctrine of the Teacher.

I praise with sublime faith
and bow with as many bodies
as there are atoms in the realm
to all that are worthy of worship.

In order to complete it with the confession of negativity, request to turn the dharma wheel, and dedication of the roots of virtue to awakening, do the single quatrain:

What little virtue I have gathered
through homage, offering, confession,
rejoicing, requesting, and supplication,
I dedicate to the awakening of all beings.[4]

Next, meditate that there is a silver-colored syllable *hūṃ* on a moon mandala in Machik's heart, with the *gate* mantra string situated in a clockwise direction around the edge, and repeat the mantra however many times:

*tadyathā oṃ gate gate pāragate pārasaṃgate bodhi svāhā*

With the emanation and reabsorption of light rays from the mantra string, imagine that a stream of elixir falls from Machik's body and washes away negativities and obscurations. Do the extensive visualization of the stream of timeless awareness for purification of negativity. If a wrathful visualization is required, you can also do the black distribution. Then, as in the source texts, the body becomes completely pure like a crystal ball. Offering goddesses emanate from the heart and present the [following] mudra offerings of body, speech, mind, and qualities:

> *namo*
> I offer all form that appears
> in all the worlds of the billionfold universe {308}
> as the mudra of sublime Body.
> Grant the spiritual power of immutable Body.
>
> I offer all the sounds resounding
> in all the worlds of the billionfold universe
> as the mudra of sublime Speech.
> Grant the spiritual power of unimpeded Speech.
>
> I offer all the memories and thoughts in the minds
> in all the worlds of the billionfold universe
> as the mudra of sublime Mind.
> Grant the spiritual power of undeluded Mind.
>
> I offer all the happiness and suffering
> in all the worlds of the billionfold universe
> as the mudra of auspiciousness.
> [Grant the spiritual powers, both common and supreme.][5]
>
> When happy, I dedicate it to collective happiness;
> may great happiness pervade all space.
> When suffering, I carry the suffering myself;
> may the ocean of cyclic suffering dry up
> and all beings of the three realms be happy.
> *phaṭ*

Machik composed this. The presentation of the mudra offerings on this occasion has the same intention as in the *Complete Explanation* source text.[6]

Then, do the middle-length transference, Opening the Sky Door, followed by the visualization of offering the body mandala as in the source text. Once that is clear, say:

On the golden ground of my skin,
centered in the iron mountain rings of my nails,
the Supreme Mountain palace of my head and torso
is adorned by the sun and moon of my eyes,
the four continents of my four limbs, and so on.
This complete and perfect mandala of my body
I offer to the guru, yidam, and host of ḍākinīs.
Please accept it and so grant your blessings.

This was also composed by Machik.[7] *phaṭ*

Then in the procedure for presenting the body offering and giving it away in charity, do the extensive transference [of consciousness and] summoning of the six kinds of beings from their places. Do the visualization process of the three cycles of integration in the white feast according to the source text. Do the extensive version, completing the series. During the red distribution for giving away the body, do what is known as the short call (*'bod thung*) from Lord Rangjung Dorje's long and short calling of the pestilent spirits.[8]

*namo*
Gods and demons living in this haunted place, {309}
all the gods and demons of apparent existence,
who show their apparitions to me, the fortunate one:
Come, massing here like cloud banks in the sky.
Come, falling like the rain from on high.
Come, swirling like whirlwinds over the ground.
I present this body as an offering to you all.

Recite this much, or continue:

I offer you the six parts of my outer flesh:
May I attain Buddha's precepts of the six perfections.
I offer you the nine inner organs with apertures:
may I attain the nine vehicles.
I offer you the five sense organs:
may I attain the five kāyas and awarenesses.
To all of you gathered here, I offer this body:
You who are impatient, eat it raw.
You who are not hurried, eat it cooked.

All ravenous ones, gobble it up
like lions relishing flesh.
Take the first offering and leave nothing.
*phaṭ*

Afterward, do the visualization of purifying the places of the six kinds of beings.

### The Supplications

Then, of the supplication and the descent of blessings to the feast, first are the general supplication to the Kagyu, the particular supplication to Father Dampa, the supplication to Machik and her children, and so forth. Of the many supplications to the lineage gurus of the father tantras, mother tantras, Sutra tradition, Mantra tradition, and so forth, first there is this supplication to the long lineage, written by Lord Rangjung's disciple Samten Rinchen of Lhapu.[9] Sing it with a melody:

I pray to the Great Mother Perfection of Wisdom
in the place of dharmadhātu's totally pure palace.

Bless me, your child disciple who supplicates you:
Pacify conditions of outer and inner obstacles,
grant the supreme and common spiritual powers,
and guide your child on the path to the unborn realm.

[You may add those four lines to the following couplets:]

I pray to the Lord, the Perfect Buddha,
in the place at Vulture Peak Mountain.

I pray to Mañjushrī, Lion of Speech,
on the throne of great curved lions. {310}

I pray to Brahmin Āryadeva
in the place of the thatched retreat hut in India.

I pray to the one father Dampa Sangye
in the place of Latö Dingri hermitage.

I pray to the lord scholar Kyochung[10]
in the place of Haunted Ground Retreat hermitage.

I pray to Machik Lapkyi Drönma
in the place of Red House of Copper Mountain hermitage.

I pray to the excellent son Gyalwa Döndrup
in the place of Tashi Langlung hermitage.

I pray to Lord Kyeme Zangtal,[11]
in the place of Anywhere in the Kingdom hermitage.

I pray to the adept Gyanak Cherbu
to the west of Chuwori Mountain.

I pray to Lord Sangye Raptön
in the place of Rapdrong Sewa hermitage.

I pray to Lord Tokden Gelong
at the place around Zalmo Gang.[12]

I pray to Lord Sumgom Chenpo
at the place of Tashi Lhundrup hermitage.

I pray to Lord Dringom Tokme
at the place of Tashi Chubar hermitage.

I pray to Lord Khepa Naljor
on the throne of mahāmudrā dharma.

I pray to Tokden Senge Palwa
at the place of Pomdrak Rinchen Hill.

I pray to Tsenden Wangchuk Dorje
at the Great Bliss hermitage in central province.

I pray to the adept Palden Rinchen
at the place of the hermitage upon spontaneous presence.

I pray to Tokden Jampa Palwa
at the place of Great Bliss Equanimity hermitage.

I pray to the lord Özer Tsenchen
at the place of Haunted Ground Retreat hermitage.

I pray to the lord Buddha Tsenchen
at the place of Great Bliss Retreat hermitage.

I pray to Lord Kunga Namgyal
at the place of Abundant Purity hermitage.

I pray to Lord Karma Tenkyong {311}
at the place of Definitive Essence palace.

I pray to the lord Gyurme Nyingpo
at the place of Single-Flavored Appearance hermitage.

I pray to Lord Könchok Tenzin
in the dharma of awareness manifesting great bliss.

I pray to Lord Tsoknyi Paljor
in the nature of finding supreme self-occurring awareness.

I pray to Lord Karma Tenkyong[13]
in the path of realizing the nature of profound ripening-liberation.

I pray to Lord Karma Tsultrim
in the meaning of nonaction in the state of unity.

I pray to Protector Tenzin Namdak
in the dharma of naturally manifested two truths.

I pray to Lord Jamyang Namgyal
in the supreme attainment of mahāmudrā spiritual powers.

I pray to the adepts of the Severance lineage
in the place of Anywhere Is Dharmadhātu hermitage.

I pray to the benevolent root guru
in the place upon the lotus-moon seat on my head.
Bless me, your child disciple who supplicates you:
Pacify conditions of outer and inner obstacles,
grant the supreme and common spiritual powers,
and guide your child on the path to the unborn realm.

## Abridged Supplication to the Father Tantras and Mother Tantras Together

*namo guru*
Great Mother Perfection of Wisdom, Shākyamuni,
Mañjushrī Lion of Speech, Venerable Mother Tārā:
I supplicate you to bless my mindstream.
Sukhasiddhī, Āryadeva,
Dampa Sangye, Mother Lapdrön:
I supplicate you to bless my mindstream.
Khambuyale, Lord Jñānajvala,
Namtso Dopa, dharma lord Rangjung:
I supplicate you to bless my mindstream.
Senge Palwa, Wangdor, Ratnashrī,
Jampa Palwa, Özer Tsenchen:
I supplicate you to bless my mindstream.
Buddharatna, Kunga Namgyal, {312}
Karma Tenkyong, Gyurme Nyingpo:
I supplicate you to bless my mindstream.
Könchok Tenzin, Tenpa Namgyal,
Jamgön Rikzin, Sungrap Gyatso:
I supplicate you to bless my mindstream.
The blessings of all lineages gathered into one,
lord of the circle, Chökyi Jungne
and Venerable Dutsok Dulwai Dorje:
I supplicate you to bless my mindstream.
Root guru, adepts of the Severance lineage,
with hosts of ḍākinīs and heroes of the three places:
I supplicate you to bless my mindstream.
Bless me to renounce self-fixation.
Bless me that contentment be born in my mindstream.

Bless me to cast out the body as food.
Bless me to wander in haunted places and mountain retreats.
Bless me to cut off the one thing at the roots.
Bless me to realize the unborn all at once.
Bless me to purify deluded perceptions in basic space.
Bless me to accomplish buddhahood in one lifetime.
Bless me to spontaneously achieve the two purposes.
May I master the unsurpassed state of the Great Mother.

This supplication of the lineage of Object Severance was written by the yogi of Minyak, Lodrö Rinchen. *phaṭ*

### Abridged Supplication of the Complete Lineages

I pray to the method lineage of the father tantras.
I pray to the wisdom lineage of the mother tantras.
I pray to the meaning lineage of the nondual tantras.
I pray to the experiential lineage of the fortunate ones.
I pray to the Severance lineage of adepts.
I pray to the symbol lineage of ḍākinīs.
I pray to the powerful dharma protector lineage.
Bless me to overturn attachment
to worldly activities of deluded appearances. {313}
Bless me to be released from cherishing this illusory body,
the confluence of the four elements.
Bless me with the ability to experience the equal flavor
of adverse circumstances, sickness, spirits, and obstacles.
Bless me to recognize as my own
the mental apparitions of apparent existence.
Bless me to attain mastery over my own awareness,
the spontaneous presence of the three kāyas.
In general, may I and the six kinds of beings
totally abandon the cause, the stains of dualistic fixation,
and quickly attain supreme awakening.
*phaṭ*

### Supplication to the Father Lineage

Homage to the lord guru.
I supplicate all the Kagyupas.
In particular, kindly grant your blessings.
Up in the excellent holy place are three circles:
outer circle, first circle, and second circle.
The outer circle is the surrounding iron mountain circumference.
The middle circle is the southern continent Jambudvīpa.
The inner circle is surrounding Dingri Lingkhor.[14]
In the pure land of fern hill retreat,
on the ḍākinī's lotus-moon seat,
who dwells in that place and who does not?
In that place, Dampa Sangye dwells.
His physical birthplace was in the land of India.
His resounding speech was heard in central Tibet.
Lord protector of beings, Vajradhara,
incomparable Lion of Speech,
glorious Virūpa with the warmth of realization,
Āryadeva, learned in grammar and logic,
Dampa Mutik, expert in the four tantra classes,
Lord Mipam Gönpo, conqueror,
the single ornament of Jambudvīpa:
I supplicate the lord protector of beings.
Protector of beings, grant blessings.
Lord Dampa Sangye Rinpoche,
above you hosts of gods amass,
to the right are the strong heroes,
to the left the radiant heroines,
in front the oath-bound protectors pile up,
in back the ḍākinīs move and sway,
below the malicious spirit hosts rove around.
Lord Dampa dwelling there, I pray. {314}
Lord Dampa dwelling there, bless me.

*hūṃ*
Great black father, brilliant and powerful,
your upper body is majestic like a great lion,
a sign of suppressing the four devils with your splendor.

Your lower body shudders like a peacock,
a sign that the five poisons are inherently pure.
Your waist is gathered in like a vajra,
a sign of cutting the basis of delusion from the roots.
Your two legs are like slender parallel canes,
a sign of traversing the dharmic path to awakening.
Your skin is black and glossy,
a sign of immutability in the nature of phenomena.
Your oily black hair is twisted upward,
a sign of leading the way to liberation and higher realms.
Your eyes are bloodshot and agitated,
a sign of subduing apparent existence with splendor.
Your teeth are white with sharp points,
a sign of severing the roots of birth and death.
Your fingers are long with sharp points,
a sign of drawing in fortunate ones with compassion.
Your toes are like lion cubs all set out,
a sign of severing the three poisons from the roots.
Lord, sometimes you sleep day and night,
a sign of continuous meditation in the native state.
Lord, sometimes you make various auspicious connections,
a sign of blessing the retinue and servants.
Lord, sometimes you enact crazy yogic conduct,
a sign of clearing away the retinue's obstacles.
I prostrate with respect when the lord is away or here.
I prostrate with devotion when you are before me.
Respectful, devoted prostration knows no distance.
I supplicate you from the center of my heart.
I receive blessings from the expanse of your heart.
Lord, the blessings of your Body enter my body.
Please heal the physical sufferings of sickness
and kindle bliss-warmth in my body.
Once the physical obscurations are purified,
may my body attain nirmāṇakāya.
Lord, the blessings of your Speech enter my speech.
Please heal verbal impediments and hoarseness
and raise the effectiveness of my speech.
Once the obscurations of speech are purified,
may my speech attain the saṃbhogakāya in Speech.

Lord, the blessings of your Mind enter my mind. {315}
Please pacify afflicted discursive thoughts
and cause the arising of realization in my mind.
Once the obscurations of mind are purified,
may my mind attain dharmakāya.
Three causes are desire, hatred, and stupidity—
please pacify the three poisons in their own ground.
Three conditions are male, female, and nāga malicious spirits—
please make mental concepts of spirits vanish.
Four disease types are winds, bile, phlegm, and their
combination—
please pacify the four hundred four in their own ground.
Three kāyas are nirmāṇakāya, saṃbhogakāya, and dharmakāya—
once the three kāyas have been actualized,
bless me with the arising of immeasurable benefit for others.

This was the praise to Lord Dampa Rinpoche by the ḍākinī of timeless awareness after being requested by Mara Serpo.[15] *phaṭ*

**Praise to Machik**

*hūṃ*
Mother, heart child emanated from Great Mother's heart,
One Mother Machik, Jomo Naljor.
Mother, adept of the perfections,
liberator of the mindstreams of fortunate ones—
please grant your blessings to me
and your respectful disciple-children.
Mother, small in stature while big in charisma,
white in color while blazing with light,
low in birth while high in enlightened intention,
with conduct that is harmonious with all,
heiress of the buddhas of the three times:
Please grant your blessings to me
and your respectful disciple-children.

Mother, you realize the meaning of no stinginess
and give away in all-pervasive generosity.

You realize the meaning of innate timeless awareness
and guard the morals without faults.
You realize the meaning of being without birth
and meditate patiently on the unborn.
You realize the meaning of effortless action
and undertake the diligence of nonaction.
You realize the meaning of no wavering
and meditate in concentration without distraction.
You realize the meaning of everything's nature
and are the yoginī who knows no self. {316}
Please grant your blessings to me
and your respectful disciple-children.

Mother, you are liberated from clinging by unbiased view,
liberated from reference point by meditating in equality,
liberated from cyclic existence by realizing the unborn,
and liberated from fear by nonconceptual conduct.
Please grant your blessings to me
and your respectful disciple-children.

Mother, when you just look within equality,
it means afflictions are cleared and awareness increased.
Surrounded by a hundred thousand buddha ḍākinīs,
your speech, the sweet songs of experience, resounds—*u ru ru*,
mists of blessings gather—*tip se tip*,
rains of spiritual power fall—*si li li*.
Please grant your blessings to me
and your respectful disciple-children.

Mother, when you just manifest within the unborn,
it means you have experience of postmeditation realization.
Surrounded by a hundred thousand awareness ḍākinīs,
your speech, the sweet songs of experience, resounds—*u ru ru*,
mists of blessing gather—*tip se tip*,
rains of spiritual power fall—*si li li*.
Please grant your blessings to me
and your respectful disciple-children.

Mother, when you just act on your intentions in the east,
it means you have experience of the immutable.
Surrounded by a hundred thousand vajra ḍākinīs,
[your speech, the sweet songs of experience, resounds—*u ru ru*,
mists of blessing gather—*tip se tip*,
rains of spiritual power fall—*si li li*.
Please grant your blessings to me
and your respectful disciple-children.]

Mother, when you just act on your intentions in the south,
it means you have experience of the perfection of qualities.
Surrounded by a hundred thousand jewel ḍākinīs,
[your speech, the sweet songs of experience, resounds—*u ru ru*,
mists of blessing gather—*tip se tip*,
rains of spiritual power fall—*si li li*.
Please grant your blessings to me
and your respectful disciple-children.]

Mother, when you just act on your intentions in the west,
it means you have experience of the unborn.
Surrounded by a hundred thousand lotus ḍākinīs,
[your speech, the sweet songs of experience, resounds—*u ru ru*,
mists of blessing gather—*tip se tip*,
rains of spiritual power fall—*si li li*.
Please grant your blessings to me
and your respectful disciple-children.]

Mother, when you just act on your intentions in the north,
it means you have experience of the unceasing.
Surrounded by a hundred thousand action ḍākinīs,
your speech, the sweet songs of experience, resounds—*u ru ru*,
mists of blessing gather—*tip se tip*,
rains of spiritual power fall—*si li li*.
Please grant your blessings to me
and your respectful disciple-children.

Mother, when you just act on your intentions above,
it means you have experience of no center or circumference. {317}

Intrinsic awareness in basic space flutters—*pu ru ru*,
unbiased view levels out—*cha la la*,
intention of evenness trembles—*tri li li*,
hosts of ḍākinīs gather—*tip se tip*.
Please grant your blessings to me
and your respectful disciple-children.

Mother, when you just roam in isolated, haunted places,
thoughts of inflation melt away—*nya la la*,
bliss-emptiness in your being trembles—*tri li li*,
hosts of ḍākinīs gather—*tip se tip*.
Please grant your blessings to me
and your respectful disciple-children.

Mother, when you just act for the benefit of beings,
vital instructions stream in—*sha ra ra*,
methods to sever devils rain down—*si li li*,
hosts of ḍākinīs gather—*tip se tip*.
Please grant your blessings to me
and your respectful disciple-children.

Mother, when you just go to unborn basic space,
knots of dualism release—*tro lo lo*,
mists of appearance vanish—*ya la la*,
thoughts of equality tremble—*tri li li*,
hosts of ḍākinīs gather—*tip se tip*.
Please grant your blessings to me
and your respectful disciple-children.

Mother, though you do not leave basic space,
it means that your unblocked compassion
[still arises for] me and all beings bewildered by ignorance.
It means surely holding us with compassion.
It means surely guiding us on the path.
It means surely removing obstacles.

This was the praise to Machik by Tönyön Samdrup.[16] *phaṭ*

### Praise to the Son [Gyalwa Döndrup]

Mother, Great Mother like the sky,
Son, born Gyalwa, like the sun and moon:
you are the heart son of that Great Mother.
Her Body's blessings entered your body, producing great charisma.
Her Speech's blessings entered your speech, producing great ability.
Her Mind's blessings entered your mind, producing great realization.
Her qualities' blessings entered and produced great compassion.
Her activity's blessings entered and produced great benefit for beings.
Lord of Langlung, endowed with all qualities,
please grant your blessings to me {318}
and your respectful disciple-children.

Lord, you realized the meaning of tangible devils
and understand actual phenomena to be like illusions.
You realized the meaning of intangible devils
and know liberation of affliction in its own ground.
You realized the meaning of the devil of exaltation
and know that qualities are equal in the mind.
You realized the meaning of the devil of inflation
and know samsara to be liberated in basic space.
Lord of Langlung who possesses all knowledge,
please grant your blessings to me
and your respectful disciple-children.

You have the family lineage of a child of the Great Mother.
You have the realization of view and meditation free of reference.
You have the knowledge of cutting through projections.
You have the influence of renown in India, Tibet, and Mongolia.
Lord of Langlung with widespread renown,
please grant your blessings to me
and your respectful disciple-children.
*phaṭ*

This praise to the son was reputedly composed by Nyenchung Lotsāwa.[17]

## Praise of the Mother's Four Bodies from the East Gate of the Casket[18]

*hūṃ*
Mother, perfection of wisdom adept,
liberator of all fortunate ones,
master of the intentions of Sutra and Tantra,
I bow and praise Lapkyi Drönma's Body.
Mother, you comprehend natural purity
and your mind pervades the reaches of space.
Beginning and end are both pure in place.
Fixation on self is liberated on its own.
Mother svābhāvakāya, I bow and praise you.

Mother, wisdom dawns in the expanse of space.
Your four daily activities are free from concept.
Inflation's despair is pure in basic ground.
Discursive thought is liberated in its own place.
Mother dharmakāya, I bow and praise you.

Mother, you know objects of knowledge through six clairvoyances.
Undissipating bliss-emptiness was born in you.
Fixating on meditation with characteristics is purified in basic ground.
Gods and demons of apparent existence are liberated in their own place.
Mother saṃbhogakāya, I bow and praise you.

Mother, emanated in the body of a woman, {319}
you enact the welfare of beings without good or bad.
Both desire and anger are pure in basic ground.
Both fraud and deception are liberated in their own place.
Mother nirmāṇakāya, I bow and praise you.

## Praise from the South Gate of the Casket

Mother, you purified obscurations and realized emptiness.
Mother with wisdom, I bow and praise you.
Mother, you separated body and mind and truly awakened.
Mother with instructions, I bow and praise you.
Mother, you kept to mountain retreats and were unafraid.
Mother with experience, I bow and praise you.
Mother, you cut off inflation and pacified the devils.
Mother with power, I bow and praise you.
Mother, you pacified the devils and increased awareness.
Mother with realization, I bow and praise you.
Mother, you realized emptiness and mastered the levels.
Mother who perfects the two accumulations, I bow and praise you.
Mother, you meditated on the unborn and reversed attachment.
Mother who renounces samsara, I bow and praise you.
Mother, you taught instructions in accordance with Buddha
Word.
Mother who understands scripture, I bow and praise you.
Mother, you composed songs and increased timeless awareness.
Mother with blessings, I bow and praise you.
Mother, even without being served you teach the instructions.
Mother with compassion, I bow and praise you.

## Praise from the West Gate of the Casket

Mother, not scared off by the three lower realms,
you cut off the inflation of the ten nonvirtues.
You are victorious over the devil of lower realms.
Mother who leads to higher realms, I bow and praise you.

Mother, you liberate in basic space the virtuous actions
that are contingent on going to the pleasant realms.
Free from the devil of samsaric gods and humans,
Mother who traverses freedom's path, I bow and praise you.

Mother, not frightened by birth and death,
you resolve inflation in the Great Mother's expanse.

There is no birth or death from the expanse of noninflation.
Mother who has gained the high ground, I bow and praise you.

Mother, not frightened by obstructing and misguiding spirits,
you resolve demons and spirits as mind's self-appearance. {320}
Liberated from the devils of male and female harmful spirits,
Mother who clears away obstacles, I bow and praise you.

### Praise from the North Gate of the Casket

Mother, first you were the mother who birthed body and mind.
In the middle you were the mother who enriched with material things.
In the end you are the mother who reveals the unborn.
Mother of great kindness, I bow and praise you.

Mother, you are the mother who casts out your life as food.
You are the mother who dwells in the basic ground of awareness.
Mother, in your mind of basic space there is no intention.
Your child has not yet resolved inflation.
Mother, while you stay here, do not feel happy.
When you depart, do not be cheerful.
Mother, staying here, grant your blessings.
The child supplicates the mother;
the mother blesses the child.
Please grant your blessings to me
and your respectful disciple-children.
Please generate bliss in the body.
Please ignite the power of speech.
Please arouse realization in the mind.
Grant the supreme and common spiritual powers.
Guide your child on the path of unborn basic space.
*phaṭ*

Mother, you practiced while roaming in mountain retreats.
One Mother, you dwell in emptiness.
In emptiness there is no miserliness.
Mother who has perfected generosity, I bow and praise you.

Mother, you practiced while roaming in mountain retreats.
One Mother, you dwell in emptiness.
In emptiness there is no violation.
Mother who has perfected morality, I bow and praise you.

Mother, you practiced while roaming in mountain retreats.
One Mother, you dwell in emptiness.
In emptiness there is no anger.
Mother who has perfected patience, I bow and praise you.

Mother, you practiced while roaming in mountain retreats.
One Mother, you dwell in emptiness.
In emptiness there is no laziness.
Mother who has perfected diligence, I bow and praise you.

Mother, you practiced while roaming in mountain retreats.
One Mother, you dwell in emptiness.
In emptiness there is no distraction.
Mother who has perfected meditative stability, I bow and praise you. {321}

Mother, you practiced while roaming in mountain retreats.
One Mother, you dwell in emptiness.
In emptiness there is no stupidity.
Mother who has perfected wisdom, I bow and praise you.

Mother, you hold the six perfections in your heart.
You realize the ultimate meaning and protect beings.
Machik, I bow and praise you.
To the form of Lapkyi Drönma I pay homage and praise.

These praises from the four directions of the casket were composed by the son Gyalwa Döndrup. *phaṭ*

### Summoning the Hundred Thousand Ḍākinīs

*kye*
Mothers, nonhuman ḍākinīs of timeless awareness,

a hundred thousand tathāgata-family ḍākinīs in the center,
ḍākis who give birth to genuine great bliss:
when I supplicate with the force of intense devotion,
heed me with unceasing compassion.
Bless the karmically linked men and women.
Grant sustenance to faithful disciples.

*kye*
Mothers, nonhuman ḍākinīs of timeless awareness,
a hundred thousand vajra-family ḍākinīs in the east,
ḍākis who give birth to genuine great bliss:
when I supplicate with the force of intense devotion,
heed me with unceasing compassion.
Bless the karmically linked men and women.
Grant sustenance to faithful disciples.

*kye*
Mothers, nonhuman ḍākinīs of timeless awareness,
a hundred thousand jewel-family ḍākinīs in the south,
ḍākis who give birth to genuine great bliss:
when I supplicate with the force of intense devotion,
heed me with unceasing compassion.
Bless the karmically linked men and women.
Grant sustenance to faithful disciples.

*kye*
Mothers, nonhuman ḍākinīs of timeless awareness,
a hundred thousand lotus-family ḍākinīs in the west,
ḍākis who give birth to genuine great bliss:
when I supplicate with the force of intense devotion,
heed me with unceasing compassion.
Bless the karmically linked men and women.
Grant sustenance to faithful disciples.

*kye*
Mothers, nonhuman ḍākinīs of timeless awareness,
a hundred thousand action-family ḍākinīs in the north,
ḍākis who give birth to genuine great bliss:

when I supplicate with the force of intense devotion,
heed me with unceasing compassion.
Bless the karmically linked men and women.
Grant sustenance to faithful disciples.

*kye*
Mothers, nonhuman ḍākinīs of timeless awareness;
a hundred thousand ḍākinīs of the five families helping beings
come from the five dry skulls that adorn the head.
A hundred thousand ḍākinīs who stop the fifty-one mental formations
come from the fifty-one wet skulls that form the necklace.
A hundred thousand ḍākinīs who establish beings in happiness
come from the strands of hair that cover the back.
A hundred thousand ḍākinīs with the experience of no-thought
come from the six bone ornaments that adorn the body. {322}
A hundred thousand ḍākinīs who dazzle the three planes of existence
come from the three-pronged khaṭvām that fully adorns.
A hundred thousand ḍākinīs with the meaning of the three kāyas
come from the three stacked human heads that fully adorn it.
A hundred thousand ḍākinīs who hold the ultimate aural tantra
come from the ḍaru drum and golden small drum.
A hundred thousand ḍākinīs proclaiming the dharma in the universe
come from the sweet sounding of the golden bells.
A hundred thousand ḍākinīs wander all over the country,
emanated from the silk ribbons that fully adorn.
A hundred thousand ḍākinīs who ravish the flesh in cemeteries
come from the posture of extended and bent legs on a huge seat.
Ḍākis who play in timeless awareness,
when I supplicate with the force of intense devotion,
heed me with unceasing compassion.
Bless the karmically linked men and women.
Grant sustenance to faithful disciples.

Machik composed this. *phaṭ*

### The Mother Tantra Feast Activities

*kye*
Mothers, nonhuman ḍākinīs of timeless awareness,
a host of tathāgata-family ḍākinīs in the center,
light rays blazing from their black bodies,
they hold wheels and lotus containers in their hands.
Sapphire topknots sway—*dem se dem.*
Precious ornaments jingle—*tra la la.*
Bracelets and anklets tinkle—*si li li.*
Silken headdress ribbons flutter—*pu ru ru.*
Bone ornaments jingle—*tra la la.*
Small hand drums rattle—*tro lo lo.*
Sounds of drums and long horns rumble—*ur ru ru.*
Lutes and flutes trill—*lang se lang.*
Mistress with your ḍākinī retinue, please approach
to bless the offerings and gifts of the graveyard feast.
Now that Ḍākinī and retinue have arrived,
sit upon the lotus-moon seat in order to sever the five poisons.
I pay homage with devotion to the completion of the six perfections.
I present the feast offerings of form, sound, smell, taste, and texture.
I pay homage with devotion to the dweller in eighteen emptinesses.

*kye*
Bless this shining palace of an assembly hall
as the sacred site of Oḍḍiyāna. {323}
Bless the men and women assembled here
as heroes and heroines.
Bless the various precious vessels
as *padma bhañja.*[19]
Bless all the nutritional ingredients
as undissipating elixir.
Make this mandala the support.
Draw out the radiance of this butter lamp.
Confer four empowerments on the disciples.

Imbue this feast torma with sustenance.
Pacify obstacles to the feast here,
and grant both supreme and common spiritual powers.
*phaṭ*

*kye*
Mothers, nonhuman ḍākinīs of timeless awareness,
a host of vajra-family ḍākinīs in the east,
light rays blazing from their white bodies,
they hold vajras and lotus vessels in their hands.
Crystal topknots sway—*dem se dem . . .*

(For the extensive recitation, fill in the rest. For an abridged version, omit it.)

*kye*
Mothers, nonhuman ḍākinīs of timeless awareness,
a host of jewel-family ḍākinīs in the south,
light rays blazing from their yellow bodies,
they hold jewels and lotus vessels in their hands.
Golden topknots sway—*dem se dem . . .*

*kye*
Mothers, nonhuman ḍākinīs of timeless awareness,
a host of lotus-family ḍākinīs in the west,
light rays blazing from their red bodies,
they hold lotuses and lotus vessels in their hands.
Coral topknots sway—*dem se dem . . .*

*kye*
Mothers, nonhuman ḍākinīs of timeless awareness,
a host of action-family ḍākinīs in the north,
light rays blazing from their green bodies,
they hold crossed vajras and lotus vessels in their hands.
Turquoise topknots sway—*dem se dem.*
Precious ornaments jingle—*tra la la.*
Bracelets and anklets tinkle—*si li li.*
Silken headdress ribbons flutter—*pu ru ru.*

Bone ornaments jingle—*tra la la.*
Small hand drums rattle—*tro lo lo.*
Sounds of drums and long horns rumble—*ur ru ru.*
Lutes and flutes trill—*lang se lang.*
Mistress with your ḍākinī retinue, please approach
to bless the offerings and gifts of the graveyard feast.
Now that Ḍākinī and entourage have arrived, {324}
sit upon the lotus-moon seat in order to sever the five poisons.
I pay homage with devotion to the completion of the six perfections.
I present the feast offerings of form, sound, smell, taste, and texture.
I pay homage with devotion to the dweller in eighteen emptinesses.

*kye*
Bless this shining palace of an assembly hall
as the sacred site of Oḍḍiyāna.
Bless the men and women assembled here
as heroes and heroines.
Bless the various precious vessels
as *padma bhañja.*
Bless all the nutritional ingredients
as undissipating elixir.
Make this mandala the support.
Draw out the radiance of this butter lamp.
Bestow four empowerments on the disciples.
Imbue this feast torma with sustenance.
Pacify obstacles to the feast here,
and grant both supreme and common spiritual powers.
*phaṭ*

Machik herself composed this, and it was amended somewhat by Rigongpa.[20]

## The Consecration of the Feast Torma

*oṃ* pray to Machikma
*āḥ* pray to Machikma
*hūṃ* pray to Machikma

*kye*
Bless with white *oṃ*.
The blessing of white *oṃ*
dissolves the feast into light,
filling the sun-moon torma basin.
May this feast offering of a blazing mass of light
please the lord guru, yidams, ḍākinīs,
and the mandala of the victors.
May it fulfill the commitments with dharma protectors
Mahākāla, Shrīdevī, and oath-bound guards.

Bless with red *āḥ*.
The blessing of red *āḥ*
dissolves the feast into light . . . (add the rest)

Bless with blue *hūṃ*.
The blessing of blue *hūṃ*
dissolves the feast into light . . . (add the rest)

## The Feeding

*kye*
From the sixth lord, Vajradhara,
down to the kind root guru— {325}
everyone, with your retinues, enjoy the feast.
Some enjoy the outer feast.
Some enjoy the inner feast.
Some enjoy the secret feast.
Some enjoy the suchness feast.
With no exception, including retinues, enjoy the feast.
*a la la*—joyfully enjoy!

Take the first offering and leave nothing.
*phaṭ*

*hūṃ*
From the hosts of deities of the mandala
down to the retinues of heroes and ḍākinīs—
everyone, with your retinues, enjoy the feast . . . (add the rest)

From the Mother Vajravārāhī
down to the mother ḍākinīs of the three places—
everyone, with your retinues, enjoy the feast . . .

From the dharma protectors Mahākāla and Mahākālī
down to the protectors of the mandala borders—
everyone, with your retinues, enjoy the feast . . .

From Shākyamuni
down to the eighteen hell realms—
everyone, with your retinues, enjoy the feast . . .

From the ground masters of the billionfold universe
down to the gods and demons dwelling here—
everyone, with your retinues, enjoy the feast . . .

From the guests of the six kinds of beings
down to the creditors and obstructing types—
everyone, with your retinues, enjoy the feast.
Some enjoy the outer feast.
Some enjoy the inner feast.
Some enjoy the secret feast.
Some enjoy the suchness feast.
With no exception, including retinues, enjoy the feast.
*a la la*—joyfully enjoy!
Take the first offering and leave nothing.
*phaṭ*

This was composed by Nyentön.[21]

### Feeding the Five Families of Ḍākinīs

Mothers, nonhuman ḍākinīs of timeless awareness,
vajra ḍākinīs in the east, enjoy the feast.
Jewel ḍākinīs in the south, enjoy the feast.
Lotus ḍākinīs in the west, enjoy the feast.
Action ḍākinīs in the north, enjoy the feast.
Celestial ḍākinīs above, enjoy the feast.
Terrestrial ḍākinīs below, enjoy the feast.
Worldly ḍākinīs on the border, enjoy the feast. {326}
Some enjoy the outer feast.
Some enjoy the inner feast.
Some enjoy the secret feast.
Some enjoy the suchness feast.
With no exception, including retinues, enjoy the feast.
*a la la*—joyfully enjoy!
Take the first offering and leave nothing.
*phaṭ*

Alternatively, do the nine lines beginning with "Mothers, great *ging* . . ." or "You flesh lovers . . . ," alternating between those two.[22] Follow that with "By the power of this enormous generosity . . ." or "May all enjoy continuous prosperity . . . ,"[23] alternating between them. *phaṭ*

### The Torma Dedication

Do the supplication for what you desire: "*oṃ*, the impure world and its inhabitants . . ." (*ma dag snod bcud* . . .). Alternatively, recite this by the fifth Zhamarpa:[24]

*oṃ āḥ hūṃ*
Inside the torma basin of the external world
is the *balingta* substance of the four elements.
I offer that to the host of peaceful and wrathful victors.
Bless me with accomplishing prolific activity.
Inside the torma basin of the human body's skin
is the *balingta* of flesh, blood, and bones.
I offer that to the vast host of guardians of the doctrine.

Bless me with life equal to the sun and moon.
Inside the torma basin of various mental perceptions
is the *balingta* of memory, awareness, and clarity.
I offer that to the dharmakāya pervading space.
Bless me with the five awarenesses in my mindstream.
*kha kha khāhi khāhi*

Recite from "Partake of this offering torma . . ." (*mchod sbyin gtor ma . . .*) through ". . . cause the achievement of all my desires" (*. . . yid la 'dod pa kun 'grub mdzod*).

**Another Torma Offering**

The outer torma basin of the world
is filled inside with the torma of its inhabitants.
Partake of the offering without birth or death.

The outer torma basin of the wide sky
is filled inside with the torma of the four elements.
Partake of the offering that is natural clarity with natural purity.

The outer torma basin of Buddha's Words of the perfections
is filled by the torma of the pure ten levels.
Partake of the torma without passing to nirvana.

The outer torma basin of the Buddha's Words of the Great
  Completion
is filled by the torma of the nine vehicles.
Partake of the offering that is unmixed and total perfection. {327}

The outer torma basin of the wide all-ground
is filled by the torma of the six consciousness groups.
Partake of the offering without increase or decrease.

The torma basin of my own mind's native state
is filled by the torma of body, speech, and mind.
Partake of the offering without expression.

The torma basin of birthlessness
is filled by the torma of awareness's felt experience.
Partake of the offering with self-liberated mental activity.

The torma basin of pure dharmakāya
is filled by the torma of the two form kāyas.
Partake of the offering with compassion and altruism.

The torma basin of emptiness
is filled by the torma of white and red appearances.
Partake of the offering in great nonappearance.

The torma basin of the purity of one's being
is filled by the torma of the master's instructions.
Partake of the offering in great bliss.

The torma basin of the pure nature of phenomena
is filled by the torma of mind's bliss and clarity.
Partake of the offering without a definable entity.

The torma basin of my own victor's body
is filled by the torma of respect and devotion.
Partake of the offering without hopes or fears.

The torma basin of the kapāla
is filled with the torma of flesh, blood, and organs.
Partake of the offering without attachment or clinging.

From the sixth lord, great Vajradhara,
down to the kind root guru,
may the dedication be received just so.
May the wishes come to pass just so.

From Samantabhadra
down to the bugs in the grass,
may the dedication be received just so.
May the wishes come to pass just so.

From Shākyamuni
down to the eighteen hell realms,
may the dedication be received just so.
May the wishes come to pass just so.

Through the qualities of this torma,
I pray that I and all beings of the six kinds
will engender well-being in body, {328}
enhance the power of speech,
and raise the realization of mind.

Machik composed this. Perform whatever fulfillment and leftovers torma liturgies are appropriate in turn. When doing the feeding multiple times,[25] do the above torma dedication and the renewal confession extensively. Then recite the long feeding as in the beginning of the body donation along with the Ninefold Spirit Feast. Then partake of the feast.

### The Dedication of Leftovers

*bhrūṃ akaro* . . . (etc.)
The first portion and leftovers torma become excellent, vast, and inexhaustible sense desirables with five qualities. *phaṭ*
*hūṃ*
From frightening graveyards in the four directions
come the five families of glorious, blazing ḍākinīs,
with white, yellow, red, green, and blue hair.
Although you are certainly ultimate ḍākinīs,
for my benefit as a practitioner,
assume the manner of a servant.
In partaking of this leftovers torma,
accomplish the activities I command.
Included in the retinues of those mothers
are ḍākinīs who move in the sky,
powerful mover ḍākinīs who move with power,
and, below them, the host of field-protector ḍākinīs,
all assuming the manner of servants.
In partaking of this leftovers torma—

consume, in amounts equal to this torma,
those who destroy the buddhadharma,
diminish the status of the Three Jewels,
harm the guru's body,
turn the disciples away from from the holy,
and interrupt the attainment of awakening.
Guard the retinue and avert [adverse] circumstances.
Accomplish the activities I command.

Rigongpa composed this. *phaṭ*

### Offering the Torma to the Ḍākinīs

*oṃ āḥ hūṃ*
This torma adorned by holy substances and sealed by the five meats and five elixirs is dedicated in this place of offering. Command guards of Severance with the retinue of five families of ḍākinīs, partake of the offering. In doing so, completely pacify all circumstantial outer and inner obstacles. {329} Please grant both the supreme and common spiritual powers without exception.

*kye*
Mother, nonhuman ḍākinī of timeless awareness,
buddha-family ḍākinī in the center,
with a million mother ḍākinīs,
surrounded by the gods and demons of apparent existence—
Mothers, come here for this adorned torma.
Gods and demons of apparent existence,
partake and be satisfied by the five sense desirables.
May we attain supreme spiritual power.

[Fill in the lines from above:]

*kye*
Mother, nonhuman ḍākinī of timeless awareness,
vajra-family ḍākinī in the east . . .

. . . jewel-family ḍākinī in the south . . .

. . . lotus-family ḍākinī in the west . . .

. . . action-family ḍākinī in the north,
with a million mother ḍākinīs,
surrounded by the gods and demons of apparent existence—
Mothers, come here for this adorned torma.
Gods and demons of apparent existence,
partake and be satisfied by the five sense desirables.
May we attain supreme spiritual power.

*kye*
Mother, nonhuman ḍākinī of timeless awareness,
celestial-family ḍākinī above,
terrestrial-family ḍākinī below,
worldly ḍākinī on the border,
with a million mother ḍākinīs,
surrounded by the gods and demons of apparent existence:
Mothers, come here for this adorned torma.
Gods and demons of apparent existence,
partake and be satisfied by the five sense desirables.
May we attain supreme spiritual power.

All types of guests of both samsara and nirvana,
above the earth, on the earth, and below the earth—
may you receive this torma of five desirables
in the way that it is dedicated.
May wishes be accomplished as wished.
May flesh debts and liabilities of lifetimes
in beginningless cyclic existence be cleared.

This was composed by Kyeme Gayen.[26]

## The Concluding Rites

*oṃ guru deva ḍākinī satva sapāriwāra vajra arghaṃ . . . śabda pratīccha svāhā* {330}

Into the mouths of the Kagyu gurus, roots of blessing—*oṃ āḥ hūṃ*.
Into the mouths of yidam deities, roots of power—*oṃ āḥ hūṃ*.
Into the mouths of dharma protectors and guards, roots of activity—*oṃ āḥ hūṃ*.

Unutterable, unimaginable, inexpressible perfection of wisdom . . . (etc.)

To all those worthy of worship . . . (etc.)

Whatever I have not provided . . . (etc., finish the verses.)

## The Confession

*namo guru*
I did not know that what happiness I found
was the root guru,
so I searched elsewhere for spiritual powers.
This I confess to Mother nirmāṇakāya.

I did not know that cutting through my mind's root
was the dharmakāya,
so I searched elsewhere for buddha.
This I confess to Mother nirmāṇakāya.

I did not know that knowing the nature of thought
was the unborn,
so I searched elsewhere for the antidote.
This I confess to Mother nirmāṇakāya.

I did not know that my own mind, the wish-fulfilling jewel,
was the source of all needs and desires,
so I exerted effort elsewhere.
This I confess to Mother nirmāṇakāya.

I did not know that to cut off the self's concepts
was the practice,

so I searched elsewhere for gods and demons.
This I confess to Mother nirmāṇakāya.

I did not know that all beings of the three realms
were my mothers,
so I inflicted harm on others.
This I confess to Mother nirmāṇakāya.

I did not know that the precious guru holding three vows
was the source of refuge,
so I had little faith, yearning, or devotion.
This I confess to Mother nirmāṇakāya.

I did not know that those loving, connected dharma friends
were the heroes and ḍākinīs,
so I felt jealousy and malice.
This I confess to Mother nirmāṇakāya.

I did not know that this Severance of Evil Object instruction
could be held by bad recipients,
so I spread it throughout the land.
This I confess to Mother nirmāṇakāya. {331}

I did not know that pure, unsullied moral discipline
was the way to freedom,
so I strayed into open and hidden immorality.
This I confess to Mother nirmāṇakāya.

I did not know that the actual and mentally emanated offerings
were the perfection of the two accumulations,
so I fell into arrogance and stinginess.
This I confess to Mother nirmāṇakāya.

I did not know that the lineup at the ḍākinīs' profound feast
was the secret sacred site,
so I mixed it with the debased and defiled.
This I confess to Mother nirmāṇakāya.

I did not know that the enjoyment of the feast food
was the source of spiritual powers,
so I spread it among those of negative conduct.
This I confess to Mother nirmāṇakāya.

I did not know that sending the gift of the body without attachment
was the way to purify the two obscurations,
so I held and cherished the body.
This I confess to Mother nirmāṇakāya.

Nonhuman ḍākinī of timeless awareness—I confess!
Adepts of the Severance lineage—I'm ashamed and regretful!
Absolved and pure, I request the powers of Body, Speech, and Mind.
Grant my desires: supreme and common spiritual powers.
Lead me on the unerring path to the dharmadhātu.
Please establish me in the state of irreversible great bliss.

Composed by Rigongpa Tsöndru Senge.

Dharmakāya Great Mother, I supplicate you to forgive all duplications and omissions, mistakes, meager supplies, damaged first offerings, and mantras, mudras, and concentrations that are incomplete, impure, or unclear, which I have committed in performing this ritual of the dharmakāya Great Mother.

*oṃ vajra satva . . .* (etc.)

Say the hundred-syllable mantra three times. Light rays from your heart [send off] each of the awareness beings. Alternatively:

*oṃ* Out of love for me and migrators,
[with your miraculous powers,
please remain here, Bhagavān,
for as long as I make offerings.][27]

or:

*oṃ*
You have performed the welfare of beings.
Grant your respective spiritual powers.
Even though you depart for the buddha realms,
please return again.
*vajra mūṃ* {332}

Whoever is left here at this place of offering and charity
[—elementals who move underground,
those who stay on the ground,
and those who move above the ground—
be satisfied and to your own places]
all of you return separately.[28]
*sarva bhūta gaccha*

Dedicate the virtue to awakening with:

Homage to the precious Three Jewels.
[Starting with this virtue established here,
all dissipating, nondissipating, and combined virtue
gathered in the three times by sentient beings
is dedicated to great, unsurpassable awakening.
May all migrators attain omniscience.][29]

## Prayers of Auspiciousness

Auspicious is the state of unborn awareness of basic space,
the space kāya free of all signs of reference to arising and cessation.
Bhagavatī, mother of all victorious ones in the universe,
may there be the auspiciousness of the Lady Perfection of Wisdom.

Auspicious is the sublime guide, incomparable Bhagavān;
the well-spoken, peaceful, unattached, unsurpassable holy dharma;
and the sublime, excellent field of merit, the precious sangha.
May there be the auspiciousness of the unsurpassable Three Jewels.

Auspicious are Mañjushrī and Mother Tārā;
sublime Dampa Sangye, who manifests the profound abiding nature;
and Lapkyi Drön, chief of all ḍākinīs of timeless awareness of basic space.
May there be the auspiciousness of the glorious root and lineage gurus.

Auspicious are the action, conduct, yoga, and highest tantras;
peaceful, joyful, and wrathful deities of the multitudinous mandalas;
and the manifold displays and heroes and ḍākinīs of the three places.
May there be the auspiciousness of the deity mandalas of pure apparent existence.

Auspicious are the wrathful forms from the space of phenomena's nature,
revealed as Mahākāla and Shrīdevī with their retinue of command guards;
the ocean of guards who protect the profound dharma of Word and treasure;
and virtuous local deities of place and ground: may there be auspiciousness.

Auspicious is seeing well the very face of the primordial
pure buddha nature and pacifying all dualistic delusion,
such that I and all others will be easily established in the state
of the victors' supreme mother: may there be the auspiciousness of good fortune.

Also recite whatever verses of auspiciousness are appropriate. This was added by the fourteenth Karmapa.

Then while making the connection through *phaṭ*, the bodhisattvas on the right {333} dissolve into the dharma behind, the dharma into the shrāvakas on the left, the shrāvakas into the pratyekabuddhas, the pratyekabuddhas into the Buddha, the Buddha into the Great Mother, the Great Mother into the teachers below—the buddhas of the three times—and they dissolve into Machik. Dampa, Vārāhī, and the dharma protectors all merge into Machik. As the essence of all the sources of refuge merged into one, Machik blazes with brilliance like one hundred thousand suns. Imagine that she comes to dwell above your head.

### The Descent of Blessings

*kye*
Mother, nonhuman ḍākinī of timeless awareness,
Mother, when you take just three steps from the east,
you are small in stature and white in color,
surrounded by a hundred thousand vajra ḍākinīs.
Mother, from the wide expanse of the space of phenomena's nature,
compassion's rain clouds cluster—*tip se tip*,
and a rain of blessings flows—*sil li li.*
Mother, please be seated here as my crown ornament.
Once you are seated, please confer blessings.
Machikma, I supplicate you.
Machikma, grant your blessing.
Machikma, confer supreme empowerment.
Machikma, clear away obstacles.
Machikma, turn back adverse conditions.
Machikma, grant spiritual powers.
Machikma, guide me on the path.
Machikma, engender realization.
Mother, bless me to recognize reflexive awareness.
Bless me with victory over the devil of ignorance.
Bless me to realize my own mind as buddha.
Bless me so that realization grows more and more.
Bless me so that it increases until I reach the end.

*kye*
Mother, nonhuman ḍākinī of timeless awareness,
Mother, when you take just three steps from the south,

you are small in stature and yellow in color,
surrounded by a hundred thousand jewel ḍākinīs.
Mother, from the wide expanse . . . (add the rest)

*kye*
Mother, nonhuman ḍākinī of timeless awareness,
Mother, when you take just three steps from the west,
you are small in stature and red in color,
surrounded by a hundred thousand lotus ḍākinīs . . .

*kye*
Mother, nonhuman ḍākinī of timeless awareness,
Mother, when you take just three steps from the north,
you are small in stature and green in color, {334}
surrounded by a hundred thousand action ḍākinīs . . .

*kye*
Mother, nonhuman ḍākinī of timeless awareness,
Mother, when you take just three steps from the center,
you are small in stature and black in color,
surrounded by a hundred thousand buddha ḍākinīs.
Mother, from the wide expanse of the space of phenomena's nature,
compassion's rain clouds cluster—*tip se tip*,
and a rain of blessings flows—*sil li li*.
Mother, please be seated here as my crown ornament.
Once you are seated, please confer blessings.
Machikma, I supplicate you.
Machikma, grant your blessing.
Machikma, confer supreme empowerment.
Machikma, clear away obstacles.
Machikma, turn back adverse conditions.
Machikma, grant spiritual powers.
Machikma, guide me on the path.
Machikma, engender realization.
Mother, bless me to recognize reflexive awareness.
Bless me with victory over the devil of ignorance.
Bless me to realize my own mind as buddha.

Bless me so that realization grows more and more.
Bless me so that it increases until I reach the end.
*phaṭ*

The liturgy is connected with the visualization of the Peaceful Round Lotus.[30] This descent of the ḍākinī's blessings is said to be by Machik herself, but it is also known that Langlungpa tried to dissuade Machik.

Imagine yourself and others as Avalokiteshvara, and recite from "White body not clothed in flaws . . ." (until) ". . . I bow to Avalokiteshvara." Repeat the six syllables. Saying *phaṭ,* imagine that the guests all return to their own places.

**The Dedication**

By this merit, may I quickly
attain Object Severance Mahāmudrā.
May every single being without exception,
everyone, be established in that state.
*phaṭ*

If you need a protection torma, then do that. Recite the accomplishment of the truth of one's virtue. Then enter into your activities as a white ḍākinī without ornaments. May virtue and goodness increase.

# 23. Supplication to the Long Lineage by Machik, Appended by Bengar Jampal Zangpo[1]

Bengar Jampal Zangpo

Lineage supplications are so informative—and so confusing. This one is not mentioned in Kongtrul's *Catalog*, except perhaps as one of the branches (*yan lag rnams bcas*) of *Source of All Qualities*, leading the editor of the table of contents of the Kundeling printing to assume that it belongs with the Zurmang feast activities. While that may be the case, it does not represent the Zurmang long lineage. That supplication can be found in *Source of All Qualities*, where it is attributed to Samten Rinchen of Lhapu. And the same one is used as the basis for the whole story of the lineage in the history of Zurmang, where it is also called the "supplication of the Severance lineage gurus by Bengar Jampal Zangpo."* That version and the one in *Source of All Qualities* are identical, despite the differing author identification. The version here may have been added to that liturgy to ensure that all relevant lineages were duly honored.

Here, the lineage is similar only up to Machik Lapdrön herself. It then veers over to Machik's grandson Khambuyale rather than coming through Machik's son Döndrup. Then it takes us the long way through a very Kamtsang line of lamas, including the purported author Bengar Jampal Zangpo, right up to Situ Pema Nyinje (1774–1853). This is where the lineage ends in this text as found in the Kundeling edition of the Palpung prints. However, at this point in the Shechen printing sponsored by Dilgo Khyentse Rinpoche (1910–1991), it continues from Pema Nyinje to Jamgön

*Tsewang Kunkhyap, *Clarifying the Awareness Ḍākinī's Intention: The History of the Profound Severance of Evil Object in the Precious Glorious Zurmang Kagyu Tradition*, pp. 533–85.

Kongtrul Lodrö Taye (1813–1900), then to the fifteenth Karmapa, Khakhyap Dorje (1871–1922), then to Kongtrul's disciple Tashi Özer (1836–1910), then to Khyentse Özer (1896–1945),* and ends in "my root guru."

How could Bengar Jampal Zangpo, who lived in the fifteenth century, have written such a contemporary addendum, let alone Machik Labdrön? One scenario is that Machik uttered a prayer to her lineage using the place-and-name format, beginning with, "In the palace of dharmadhātu in Akaniṣhṭa, the Great Mother Perfection of Wisdom has blessings" and ending with her teacher Kyotön Sönam Lama (who is in fact skipped over here, although he is named in the Zurmang version). Then the well-known author Bengar Jampal Zangpo picked up the trope and continued it up through his guru, the sixth Karmapa, Tongwa Dönden (1416–1453). After that, the prayer in all its various forms came to be known simply as Bengar's supplication. Jamgön Kongtrul himself must have continued the supplication style through to his teacher Pema Nyinje before the blocks were printed at Palpung. From Kongtrul on, the last stretch may have been added for the Shechen printing of the *Treasury*. Variations of this style can also be found in the *Kagyu Feast Liturgy* and Kongtrul's supplication *Essence of Auspicious Renown* in this volume, as well as in the popular Severance compilation known as *Precious Garland* (*Rin chen phreng ba*).

---

On the sun-moon seat at the crown of my head,
the root guru has blessings.
I pray to the one with blessings.
I supplicate the guru.
Great Mother, bless me.

In the palace of dharmadhātu in Akaniṣhṭa,
the Great Mother Perfection of Wisdom has blessings.
I pray to the one with blessings.
I supplicate the guru.
Great Mother, bless me.

*This is Karma mKhyen brtse 'od zer, the first Khyentse incarnation at Palpung, but it could just as well be 'Jam dbyangs mKhyen brtse 'od zer (1904–1953), the incarnation of Jamgön Kongtrul at Palpung and the son of Karmapa Khakhyap Dorje.

On Vulture Peak Mountain,
the Bhagavān Shākyamuni has blessings.
I pray to the one with blessings.
I supplicate the guru.
Great Mother, bless me.

On the throne of great curved lions,
Mañjushrī, Lion of Speech, has blessings.
I pray to the one with blessings.
I supplicate the guru.
Great Mother, bless me.

In the joined thatched hut in India,
Āryadeva has blessings.
I pray to the one with blessings.
I supplicate the guru.
Great Mother, bless me.

In Latö Dingri Langkor,
Dampa Sangye has blessings.
I pray to the one with blessings.
I supplicate the guru.
Great Mother, bless me.

In the Red House of Copper Mountain hermitage,
Machik Lapdrön has blessings.
I pray to the one with blessings.
I supplicate the guru.
Great Mother, bless me.

In the haunted mountain retreat hermitage,
Khambuyale[2] has blessings.
I pray to the one with blessings.
I supplicate the guru.
Great Mother, bless me.

In the pure land Array of Turquoise Petals,
Jñānajvala has blessings.

I pray to the one with blessings.
I supplicate the guru.
Great Mother, bless me.

In the island palace of Sky Lake,
the Great Namtso has blessings.
I pray to the one with blessings.
I supplicate the guru.
Great Mother, bless me.

In the sacred site of Tsurpu Valley,
Rangjung Dorje has blessings.
I pray to the one with blessings.
I supplicate the guru.
Great Mother, bless me.

In the display of self-occurring equality,
Great Yungtön has blessings.
I pray to the one with blessings.
I supplicate the guru.
Great Mother, bless me.

In the palace of unelaborated dharmadhātu,
Rolpai Dorje has blessings.
I pray to the one with blessings.
I supplicate the guru.
Great Mother, bless me.

In the mountain retreat of Nangyal place,
Lord of Hermits has blessings.[3]
I pray to the one with blessings.
I supplicate the guru.
Great Mother, bless me.

In the mandala of victory over apparent existence,
Kachö Wangpo has blessings.
I pray to the one with blessings.
I supplicate the guru.
Great Mother, bless me.

In the palace of nondual samsara-nirvana,
Dezhin Shekpa has blessings.
I pray to the one with blessings.
I supplicate the guru.
Great Mother, bless me.

In the mandala of profound emptiness,
Rinchen Zangpo has blessings.
I pray to the one with blessings.
I supplicate the guru.
Great Mother, bless me.

In the palace of inseparable bliss-emptiness,
Tongwa Dönden has blessings.
I pray to the one with blessings.
I supplicate the guru.
Great Mother, bless me.

In the palace of dharmakāya wherever one is,
Jampal Zangpo has blessings.
I pray to the one with blessings.
I supplicate the guru.
Great Mother, bless me.

In the palace of three realms completely liberated,
Chödrak Gyatso has blessings.
I pray to the one with blessings.
I supplicate the guru.
Great Mother, bless me.

In the palace of dharmadhātu of whatever arises,
Jampal Gyatso has blessings.
I pray to the one with blessings.
I supplicate the guru.
Great Mother, bless me.

In the boundless haunted mountain retreats,
Chökyi Gyatso has blessings.
I pray to the one with blessings.

I supplicate the guru.
Great Mother, bless me.

In the boundless vast mandalas, {336}
Yangpa Lode has blessings.
I pray to the one with blessings.
I supplicate the guru.
Great Mother, bless me.

In the palace of unchanging dharmakāya,
Paksam Wangpo has blessings.
I pray to the one with blessings.
I supplicate the guru.
Great Mother, bless me.

With cognition and liberation of the three trainings,
Puntsok Tenzin has blessings.
I pray to the one with blessings.
I supplicate the guru.
Great Mother, bless me.

With unity of creation and completion,
Tenzin Dargye has blessings.
I pray to the one with blessings.
I supplicate the guru.
Great Mother, bless me.

With skill in all sciences,
Rinchen Wangpo has blessings.
I pray to the one with blessings.
I supplicate the guru.
Great Mother, bless me.

With three doors to liberation,
Chökyi Wangpo has blessings.
I pray to the one with blessings.
I supplicate the guru.
Great Mother, bless me.

In the mandala of the indestructible drop,
Chökyi Döndrup has blessings.
I pray to the one with blessings.
I supplicate the guru.
Great Mother, bless me.

In the palace of absolute dharmadhātu,
Chökyi Jungne has blessings.
I pray to the one with blessings.
I supplicate the guru.
Great Mother, bless me.

Victorious over the four devils,
Dudul Dorje has blessings.
I pray to the one with blessings.
I supplicate the guru.
Great Mother, bless me.

In the sacred site of mahāmudrā,
Pema Nyinje has blessings.
I pray to the one with blessings.
I supplicate the guru.
Great Mother, bless me.

In the midst of the assembly of unbiased scholar-adepts,
Lodrö Taye has blessings.
I pray to the one with blessings.
I supplicate the guru.
Great Mother, bless me.

In the palace of unchanging bliss-emptiness,
Khakhyap Dorje has blessings.
I pray to the one with blessings.
I supplicate the guru.
Great Mother, bless me.

In the citadel of emptiness-compassion,
Tashi Özer has blessings.

I pray to the one with blessings.
I supplicate the guru.
Great Mother, bless me.

In the palace of controlling apparent existence,
Pema Wangchok has blessings.
I pray to the one with blessings.
I supplicate the guru.
Great Mother, bless me.

In the palace of boundless benefit for beings,
Khyentse Özer has blessings.
I pray to the one with blessings.
I supplicate the guru.
Great Mother, bless me.

In the citadel with threefold kindness,
my root guru has blessings.
I pray to the one with blessings.
I supplicate the guru.
Great Mother, bless me.

In the mountain retreat of boundless pure view,
friends and siblings practicing dharma have blessings.
I pray to the one with blessings.
I supplicate the guru.
Great Mother, bless me.

With unceasing compassion,
yidam deities have blessings.
I pray to the one with blessings.
I supplicate the guru.
Great Mother, bless me.

With unlimited pervasive activity,
heroes and ḍākinīs have blessings.
I pray to the one with blessings.

I supplicate the guru.
Great Mother, bless me.

Averting the hosts of enemies and obstacles,
dharma protectors and guards have blessings.
I pray to the one with blessings.
I supplicate the guru.
Great Mother, bless me.

By the power of supplicating you,
bless me and all grandmother sentient beings
to mentally discard self-fixation
and decisively cut through inflation.
Bless us to be free of inflation.
Bless us to realize the nature of phenomena.

# 24. Kagyu Feast Liturgy[1]

This feast liturgy is essentially the long lineage supplication found in the *Source of All Qualities* (pp. 309–11), the only difference being that the lines naming the place and the person are followed by "dwells in the midst of heroes and heroines: I supplicate with longing and devotion," rather than with the four lines requesting blessings. Then the short prayer requesting the consecration of the environs for the feast is added here after the supplication. This too is nearly the same as in the *Source of All Qualities*, where it is attributed to Machik and Rigongpa. It seems that this liturgy offers a short alternative, rather than an addition, to the extensive feast supplications in the longer liturgies.

In the place of the pure palace of dharmadhātu,
precious Great Mother Perfection of Wisdom
dwells in the midst of heroes and heroines:
I supplicate with longing and devotion.

In the place of Vulture Peak Mountain,
precious lord, perfect Buddha,
dwells in the midst of heroes and heroines:
I supplicate with longing and devotion.

In the place on the throne of great curved lions,
precious Mañjushrī, Lion of Speech,
dwells in the midst of heroes and heroines:
I supplicate with longing and devotion.

In the place of the joined thatched hut in India,
precious Brahmin Āryadeva
dwells in the midst of heroes and heroines:
I supplicate with longing and devotion.

In the place of Latö Dingri hermitage,
precious Father Dampa Sangye
dwells in the midst of heroes and heroines:
I supplicate with longing and devotion.

In the place of Haunted Ground Retreat hermitage,
precious lord, scholar Kyochung
dwells in the midst of heroes and heroines:
I supplicate with longing and devotion.

In the place of Red House of Copper Mountain hermitage,
precious Machik Lapkyi Drönma
dwells in the midst of heroes and heroines:
I supplicate with longing and devotion.

In the place of Tashi Langlung hermitage,
precious excellent son Gyalwa Döndrup
dwells in the midst of heroes and heroines:
I supplicate with longing and devotion.

In the place of Anywhere in the Kingdom hermitage,
precious lord Kyeme Zangtal
dwells in the midst of heroes and heroines:
I supplicate with longing and devotion.

To the west of glorious Chuwori Mountain,
precious adept Gyanak Cherbu
dwells in the midst of heroes and heroines:
I supplicate with longing and devotion.

In the place of Rapdrong Sewa hermitage,
precious lord Sangye Raptön

dwells in the midst of heroes and heroines:
I supplicate with longing and devotion.

In the place around Zalmo Gang,
precious lord Tokden Gelong
dwells in the midst of heroes and heroines:
I supplicate with longing and devotion.

In the place of Tashi Lhundrup hermitage,
precious lord Sumgom Chenpo
dwells in the midst of heroes and heroines:
I supplicate with longing and devotion.

In the place of Tashi Chubar hermitage,
precious lord Drigom Tokme
dwells in the midst of heroes and heroines:
I supplicate with longing and devotion.

On the throne of mahāmudrā dharma,
precious lord Khepa Naljor
dwells in the midst of heroes and heroines:
I supplicate with longing and devotion.

In the place of Pomdrak Rinchen Hill,
precious Tokden Senge Palwa
dwells in the midst of heroes and heroines:
I supplicate with longing and devotion.

In the place of Great Bliss hermitage in central province,
precious Tsenden Wangchuk Dorje
dwells in the midst of heroes and heroines:
I supplicate with longing and devotion.

In the place of the hermitage upon spontaneous presence,
precious adept Palden Rinchen
dwells in the midst of heroes and heroines:
I supplicate with longing and devotion.

In the place of Great Bliss Equanimity hermitage,
precious Tokden Jampa Palwa {338}
dwells in the midst of heroes and heroines:
I supplicate with longing and devotion.

In the place of Haunted Ground Retreat hermitage,
precious lord Özer Tsenchen
dwells in the midst of heroes and heroines:
I supplicate with longing and devotion.

In the place of Great Bliss Retreat hermitage,
precious lord Buddha Tsenchen
dwells in the midst of heroes and heroines:
I supplicate with longing and devotion.

In the place of Abundant Purity hermitage,
precious lord Kunga Namgyal
dwells in the midst of heroes and heroines:
I supplicate with longing and devotion.

In the place of Definitive Essence palace,
precious lord Karma Tenkyong
dwells in the midst of heroes and heroines:
I supplicate with longing and devotion.

In the place of Single-Flavored Appearance hermitage,
precious lord Gyurme Nyingpo
dwells in the midst of heroes and heroines:
I supplicate with longing and devotion.

In the dharma of awareness manifesting great bliss,
precious lord Könchok Tenzin
dwells in the midst of heroes and heroines:
I supplicate with longing and devotion.

In the nature of finding supreme self-occurring awareness,
precious lord Tsoknyi Paljor

dwells in the midst of heroes and heroines:
I supplicate with longing and devotion.

In the path of realizing the nature of profound ripening-liberation,
precious lord Karma Tenkyong
dwells in the midst of heroes and heroines:
I supplicate with longing and devotion.

In the meaning of nonaction in the state of unity,
precious lord Karma Tsultrim
dwells in the midst of heroes and heroines:
I supplicate with longing and devotion.

In the dharma of naturally manifested two truths,
precious protector Tenzin Namdak
dwells in the midst of heroes and heroines:
I supplicate with longing and devotion.

In the supreme attainment of mahāmudrā spiritual powers,
precious lord Jamyang Namgyal
dwells in the midst of heroes and heroines:
I supplicate with longing and devotion.

In the place of Anywhere Is Dharmadhātu hermitage,
precious adepts of the Severance lineage
dwell in the midst of heroes and heroines:
I supplicate with longing and devotion.

In the place upon the lotus-moon seat on my head,
precious benevolent root guru
dwells in the midst of heroes and heroines:
I supplicate with longing and devotion.

Lord, with your retinue of ḍākinīs, please approach.
Now that you have come with your ḍākinī retinue,
please bestow spiritual powers on me, the practitioner,
and bless this ground.

*kye*
Bless this shining palace of an assembly hall
as the sacred site of Oḍḍiyāna.
Bless the men and women assembled here
as heroes and heroines.
Bless the various precious vessels
as *padma bhañja*. {339}
Bless all the nutritional ingredients
as undissipating elixir.
Clear away adverse conditions and obstacles
and guide me on the conducive path to basic space.

# 25. Fulfillment Rituals of Profound Object Severance[1]

## Various Authors

An important function of vajrayāna ritual is to ensure that whatever offerings have been made will serve the purpose of fulfilling obligations as well as accumulating merit. This is the practice of *kangwa* (*bskang ba*), translated variously as fulfillment, renewal, amendment, appeasement, and so forth. The pledges or commitments or covenants (*dam tshig*) that are thereby fulfilled involve two levels: Secret Mantra practitioners have a special relationship with the buddhas, deities, ḍākinīs, and other holy beings who will bless and protect them as long as the practitioner keeps up his or her practice. The second level concerns the various worldly protectors, ground masters, and local spirits who pledged themselves to the dharma, usually under pressure during the time of Guru Padmasambhava, but who must be regularly appeased with offerings to remind them of that commitment. In both cases, the ritual also serves to emend any breaches or deficiencies in the mutual agreement, and thus it may also contain a confession of mistakes.

This text contains three rituals that utilize the offering of one's own body as a communal feast to renew those commitments. After the initial setup visualization, the first is "Mother Transformation" by Chökyi Drakpa of Tsalkar (mTshal dkar Chos kyi grags pa). This very common name might be the fourth Zhamar incarnation (1453–1524/5), but the Tsalkar designation is not identified. The title might suggest that it is a variation of a previous "mother" text. The text calls on the usual lineage gurus up through Karmapa Rangjung Dorje and continues with yet another line of masters coming through the Zurmang line. Then it focuses on the divine beings, such as the ḍākinīs of the charnel grounds, the buddhas of the ten directions, and the protectors, before going on to the local spirits.

The second text, "Gem Treasury," is attributed to Guru Dharmakīrti. This is the Sanskrit for the Tibetan name Chökyi Drakpa and could well indicate the author of the previous text. "Gem Treasury" is said to be an amendment of a composition by Situ Norbu Sampel (Si tu Nor bu bsam 'phel). Though this has been suggested as another name for the sixth Situ, Mipam Trinle Rapten (Mi pham phrin las rab brtan, 1658–1682), his dates do not line up with the statement in the colophon that it had been requested by Ratnashrī, or Palden Rinchen in Tibetan, the author of the third fulfillment liturgy and named here in the Zurmang lineage after [Rupa] Wangchuk Dorje, who is only two gurus after Rangjung Dorje (1284–1339). The lineage prayer ends with the fourth Trungpa, Kunga Namgyal (1567–1629).

The third text is called simply "Fulfillment Ritual" and is attributed to the adept of Runda, Palden Rinchen (Ru mda grub thob dPal ldan rin chen). His Sanskrit name, Ratnashrī, appears in many other Zurmang lineage prayers, and a brief account of his life can be found in the *Collected Histories of the Glorious Zurmang Kagyu.** This liturgy itself does not contain a lineage prayer but calls on the deities and ḍākinīs and then includes an extensive confession. It ends with a long list of the actual items that fulfill the pledges.

## Creating the Visualization

> *oṃ svabhāva . . .*
>
> From within emptiness come the fulfillment substances, support substances, accomplishment substances, outer offerings, inner offerings, secret offerings, and suchness offerings. They are higher than Supreme Mountain's heights, deeper than the ocean's depths, thicker than the southern clouds, and brighter than the sun and the moon. These are offered to the Kagyu gurus, yidam deities, all the glorious holy gurus of the lineage of adepts of the Object Severance precepts, and the assemblies of heroes, ḍākinīs, protectors, and guards. This fulfills again and again the continuity of our strict sacred pledge. Please fully pacify all con-

* *Collected Histories of the Glorious Zurmang Kagyu,* p. 578.

ditions of outer and inner obstacles and bestow all the supreme and common spiritual powers on my retinue and me.

### [1] Severance Renewal Ritual, "Mother Transformation" (*a ma gnas 'gyur*)

*hūṃ*
From the palace of Akaniṣhṭha dharmadhātu,
Vajradhara, epitome of the five kāyas,
Shākyamuni and Mañjushrī,
Āryadeva and [Dampa] Mipam Gönpo, {373}
lineage holders of the father lineage of method,
please come here with your retinues
in order to fulfill our strict sacred pledge.[2]

*hūṃ*
From the palace of totally pure great bliss,
mother of victors, perfection of wisdom,
Tārā and Sukhasiddhī,
the emanation Machik Lapdrön, and so forth,
lineage holders of the mother lineage of wisdom,
please come here with your retinues
in order to fulfill our strict sacred pledge.

*hūṃ*
From the palace of dharmakāya appearance,
Gangpa, Döndrup, Khugom,
Kyeme Gayen, and so forth,
lineage holders of the child lineage of experience,
please come here with your retinues
in order to fulfill our strict sacred pledge.

*hūṃ*
From the palace of the source of spiritual power,
deity assemblies of victorious yidams,
please come here with your retinues
in order to fulfill our strict sacred pledge.

*hūṃ*
From the Cool Grove Graveyard,
devil tamers Mahākāla and Shrīdevī,
please come here with your retinues
in order to fulfill our strict sacred pledge. {374}

*hūṃ*
The sacred substances of pledge renewal
here in this sublime site of offering
are particular outer and inner offerings:
victory banners of various forms,
human flesh incense and *rakta* medicine,
hero's beer and five elixirs,
torma of the five sense desirables,
skull drums and human-thighbone trumpets,
various feast circles,
sacred substances of union and release,
poignant songs and faithful thoughts.
Fulfill! Fulfill the sacred pledge of the ages.

*hūṃ*
From the infinite unborn dharmakāya,
unhindered compassion liberates beings.
All gurus, may our sacred pledge be fulfilled.

From the supreme site of Akaniṣhṭha dharmadhātu,
mother who gave birth to buddhas of the three times,
Great Mother Perfection of Wisdom, may our sacred pledge be fulfilled.

On Vulture Peak Mountain,
beings were liberated through twelve deeds.
Founder of the doctrine, may our sacred pledge be fulfilled.

On the lion throne in the east,
supreme in perfections and highest knowledge,
Lion of Speech, Mañjushrī, may our sacred pledge be fulfilled.

In the supreme site of the acacia forest,
mother of victors, protector from eight fears,
Venerable Tārā, may our sacred pledge be fulfilled.

In the supreme site of the great graveyard,
undissipating spiritual powers fall like rain.
Sukhasiddhī, may our sacred pledge be fulfilled.

At Vajra Seat in the south,
the debate with heretics was won as predicted.
Āryadeva, may our sacred pledge be fulfilled.

At the three circles of Dingri Langkor,
emanation body of the invincible mighty one,
Dampa Sangye, may our sacred pledge be fulfilled.

In glorious valleys of the border districts,
teacher of the essential meaning of the unborn,
Puṇya Guru, may our sacred pledge be fulfilled.

In the supreme site of glorious Copper Mountain,
nonhuman ḍākinī of timeless awareness, {375}
Lapkyi Drölma, may our sacred pledge be fulfilled.

In the mountain hermitage of Tashi Langlung,
you found supreme spiritual power in bad circumstances.
Lord of Langlung,[3] may our sacred pledge be fulfilled.

In the hermitage of glorious Gongma,
you overwhelmed four devils and released beings.
Jñānajvala,[4] may our sacred pledge be fulfilled.

In the supreme site of Tsāritra,
supreme blessings without effort,
Namtso Dopa, may our sacred pledge be fulfilled.

In the mountain hermitage of Dechenjong,
son of victors with amazing high knowledge,
Rangjung Dorje, may our sacred pledge be fulfilled.

In the mountain hermitage of Lhapuk Gang,
you found supreme powers by supreme conduct.
Samten Rinchen, may our sacred pledge be fulfilled.

In the supreme site of glorious Lhazhu,
the form of unchanging vajra of three times,
Gendun Gyaltsen, may our sacred pledge be fulfilled.

In the hermitage of Rinchen Ling,
yogin who has transcended characteristics,
Kunga Gyaltsen, may our sacred pledge be fulfilled.

In the haunted ground without divisions,
you perfect the paths and levels by integrating good and bad.
Yeshe Senge, may our sacred pledge be fulfilled.

Among the mountains of the three places,
lord of beings who attained power over winds and mind,
Rechen Chödar, may our sacred pledge be fulfilled.

In the palace of immeasurable devotion,
teacher of undissipating perfections,
Tsultrim Yeshe, may our sacred pledge be fulfilled.

In the mountain retreat of supreme pure appearance,
heart child of the buddhas of the three times,
Jetsun Repa, may our sacred pledge be fulfilled.

*hūṃ*
In the infinity of unborn dharmakāya,
all root and lineage gurus,
although without reference point for fulfilling sacred pledge,
in order to compassionately enact the welfare of beings,
fulfill sacred pledge in illusion-like nature
by outer, inner, and secret offerings
and unsurpassable excellence.
May we yogins and our retinues
not develop wrong views.

If wrong, renew them in the space of phenomena's nature. {376}
As for mistakes in meditation, meditation is not mistaken.
If mistaken, renew it through the meaning of mind itself.
As for deluded conduct, conduct is not deluded.
If deluded, renew it through profound interdependence.
As for failings of sacred pledge, sacred pledge has not failed.
If failed, renew it through the feast of great bliss.
I confess every failing and break.
Bestow supreme and common spiritual powers.

*hūṃ*
In the infinite self-arising dharma source,
upon the multicolored lotus, sun, and corpse,
mother who gives birth to buddhas of the three times,
Lapdrön, yoginī of great bliss,
be renewed! Be served! Sacred pledge fulfilled!

From the nature of unchanging dharmakāya,
in order to enact its purpose through unhindered compassion,
various continuous enlightened activities
bring beings under control in fierce ways.
Be renewed! Be served! Sacred pledge fulfilled!

The unchanging nature of phenomena is she of black body
who cuts off the four devils with the curved knife in her right hand
and controls ḍākinīs with the blood-filled skull cup in her left:
Be renewed! Be served! Sacred pledge fulfilled!

Three eyes to see the three realms,
bared fangs to cut off birth and death,
embracing in dance the khaṭvāṃka,
charming, youthful, *bhaga* engorged:
Be renewed! Be served! Sacred pledge fulfilled!

Loosed hair shows perfecting beings' welfare;
five dry skulls are the spontaneously present five kāyas;
fifty wet skulls show formations purified.

Adorned by bones indicating the six perfections,
be renewed! Be served! Sacred pledge fulfilled!

From the place of nondual bliss-emptiness,
in the midst of the bonfire of timeless awareness,
straight and bent legs bestride existence and peace.
Mudra of the buddha family,
be renewed! Be served! Sacred pledge fulfilled!

In the graveyard of the east,
white lady, mistress of peaceful activity,
your fierce body conquers hatred.
Mudra of the vajra family,
be renewed! Be served! Sacred pledge fulfilled!

In the graveyard of the south,
yellow lady, mistress of enriching activity,
your fierce body conquers pride.
Mudra of the jewel family,
be renewed! Be served! Sacred pledge fulfilled! {377}

In the graveyard of the west,
red lady, mistress of controlling activity,
your fierce body conquers desire.
Mudra of the lotus family,
be renewed! Be served! Sacred pledge fulfilled!

In the graveyard of the north,
green lady, mistress of wrathful activity,
your fierce body conquers jealousy.
Mudra of the action family,
be renewed! Be served! Sacred pledge fulfilled!

In the graveyard of the northeast border,
worldly ḍākinī with miraculous power,
perfectly pure body aggregate in a state of love,
in order to accomplish various activities,
be renewed! Be served! Sacred pledge fulfilled!

In the graveyard of the northwest border,
all-ḍākinī, sovereign of the three realms,
transforming formations in a state of equanimity,
you bring all beings under control.
Be renewed! Be served! Sacred pledge fulfilled!

In the graveyard of the southwest border,
variety ḍākinī, mistress of spiritual powers,
you transform formations in a state of joy
in order to enrich life and enjoyments.
Be renewed! Be served! Sacred pledge fulfilled!

In the graveyard of the southeast border,
pledge ḍākinī, mistress of great bliss,
with feelings perfectly pure in a state of compassion,
in order to expand undissipating experience,
be renewed! Be served! Sacred pledge fulfilled!

*hūṃ*
In the palace of timeless awareness space,
source of all spiritual powers,
mother of all sugatas, the space of empty clarity,
Machik and deity assemblies of ḍākinīs,
be renewed! Be served! Sacred pledge fulfilled!

Although there is no reference point for fulfilling sacred pledge,
sacred pledge is fulfilled in illusion-like nature
by outer, inner, and secret offerings
and unsurpassable excellence.

May we yogins and our retinues
not develop wrong views.
If wrong, renew them in the space of phenomena's nature.
As for mistakes in meditation, meditation is not mistaken.
If mistaken, renew it through the meaning of mind itself. {378}
As for deluded conduct, conduct is not deluded.
If deluded, renew it through profound interdependence.
As for failings of sacred pledge, sacred pledge has not failed.

If failed, renew it through the feast of great bliss.
I confess every failing and break.
Avert all outer and inner obstacles.
Bestow supreme and common spiritual powers.

*hūṃ*
From the supreme site of naturally pure Akaniṣhṭha,
without moving from the state of phenomena's empty nature,
you benefit beings through nonreferential compassion;
supreme emanation kāya, color of refined gold,
Great Mother Perfection of Wisdom, fulfill sacred pledge.

In the pure realm of the eastern world,
father who gives birth to all victors,
Buddha Precious Sublime Glorious Source
with your retinue, fulfill sacred pledge.

In the pure realm of the southern world,
pure protector of all sentient beings,
Buddha Glory without Misery
with your retinue, fulfill sacred pledge.

In the pure realm of the western world,
you appear as the fulfillment of beings' hopes.
Buddha Jewel Glory of Radiant Light
with your retinue, fulfill sacred pledge.

In the pure realm of the northern world,
supreme among boundless victors,
Buddha Glory of the Victors' Might
with your retinue, fulfill sacred pledge.

In the pure realm of the northeastern world,
the victor who liberates all in a state of peace,
Buddha Glory of the Elephant's Absorption
with your retinue, fulfill sacred pledge.

In the pure realm of the southeastern world,
stainless lotus eyes without attachment,
Buddha Glory of Sacred Lotus
with your retinue, fulfill sacred pledge.

In the pure realm of the southwestern world,
all-pervasive timeless awareness appearing as light,
Buddha Glory of Sacred Appearing Sun
with your retinue, fulfill sacred pledge.{379}

In the pure realm of the northwestern world,
unsurpassable, inalienable protector,
Buddha Glory of Sacred Parasol
with your retinue, fulfill sacred pledge.

In the pure realm of the world above,
lord of beings who protects with compassion,
Buddha Glory of Sacred Joy
with your retinue, fulfill sacred pledge.

In the pure realm of the world below,
clearing away the flaws of attachment,
Buddha Glory of Lotus
with your retinue, fulfill sacred pledge.[5]

*hūṃ*
In the palace of unborn dharmakāya,
Great Mother, unhindered giver of bliss,
with your sublime children, buddhas of ten directions,
be renewed! Be served! Sacred pledge fulfilled!

Although there is no reference point for fulfilling sacred pledge,
sacred pledge is fulfilled in illusion-like nature
by outer, inner, and secret offerings
and unsurpassable excellence.
May we yogins and our retinues
not develop wrong views.

If wrong, renew them in the space of phenomena's nature.
As for mistakes in meditation, meditation is not mistaken.
If mistaken, renew it through the meaning of mind itself.
As for deluded conduct, conduct is not deluded.
If deluded, renew it through profound interdependence.
As for failings of sacred pledge, sacred pledge has not failed.
If failed, renew it through the feast of great bliss.
I confess every failing and break.
Bestow supreme and common spiritual powers.
*hūṃ*

Further fulfillments of sacred pledge,

Obedient assemblies of glorious vajra holders,
Mahākāla and Shrīdevī, fulfill sacred pledge.

Glorious masters of the graveyard and so on,
Severance command guards, fulfill sacred pledge.

Three sister wolf-riders and so on,
field dākis, fulfill sacred pledge.

Mighty Indra and so on,
protectors of the outer tantras, fulfill sacred pledge. {380}

Nāga king Hand Protector[6] and so on,
Machik's command guards, fulfill sacred pledge.

Red Tsen of Copper Mountain and so on,
gods and demons of apparent existence, fulfill sacred pledge.

Ground masters of the universe and so on,
all inhabiting ground masters, fulfill sacred pledge.

I confess every failing and break.
Avert all outer and inner obstacles.
Bestow supreme and common spiritual powers.
Accomplish the requested enlightened activities.

The fulfillment ritual of the Object Severance lineage, the Mother Transformation, was composed in my personal retreat place, Kyongö, by Tsalkar Chökyi Drakpa.[7]

## [2] The Severance Fulfillment Ritual Called "Gem Treasury"

Beyond the objects of speech, imagination, and expression,
unborn realm of phenomena, the expanse of space,
you emanate a variety of guides for migrators.
Great Mother dharmakāya, fulfill sacred pledge.

Born in the Shākya family in this degenerate time,
you defeated the devil classes that others cannot
and discovered the awakened state.
Shākyamuni, fulfill sacred pledge.

Treasury of all victors' forms,
seated upon a throne held up by lions,
incomparable Lion of Speech,
Mañjushrī, fulfill sacred pledge.

Compassion's gift arising from emptiness,
mother of sugatas, exalted lady,
born from the green letter *tāṃ*,
Venerable Tārā, fulfill sacred pledge.

You realized the meaning of coemergence
and discovered undissipating great bliss.
Glory of beings, embodiment of four kāyas,
Sukhasiddhī, fulfill sacred pledge.

You achieved mastery of the essential meaning.
Glory of the doctrine, lord of dharma,
you enact beings' welfare in the degenerate age.
Āryadeva, fulfill sacred pledge.

Knower of all buddhas of the three times,
incomparable lord of migrators,
you brought India's teaching legacy to Tibet.
Dampa Sangye, fulfill sacred pledge.

The natural coemergent realm of phenomena
is displayed by your dance of unrestricted illusion
with unimaginable emanations from absorptions. {381}
Lapkyi Drölma, fulfill sacred pledge.

You saw the profound meaning and became an adept,
and the torch of dharma blazed in Tibet.
Skilled in the meaning of the perfections,
Khambuyale, fulfill sacred pledge.

You took into practice the quintessence
of the profound path of vajrayāna and became adept.
The patroness of Sky Lake offered spiritual powers.
Namtso Dopa, fulfill sacred pledge.

Lord of dharma in the degenerate age,
omniscient master of the doctrine,
glory of the doctrine in the world,
Rangjung Dorje, fulfill sacred pledge.

Firm root of love and compassion,
abundant leaves of bliss and emptiness,
giver of all desires, wish-fulfilling tree,
Senge Palwa, fulfill sacred pledge.

Emanation of the great Telo,
you single-pointedly practiced the essential meaning
and discovered all the spiritual powers.
Wangchuk Dorje, fulfill sacred pledge.

Grasping well the two oars of method and wisdom,
you liberate migrators with the boat of enlightened activity.
Incomparable captain of migrators,
Ratnashrī, fulfill sacred pledge.

You bestow both spiritual powers when served;
glory of accomplishing the two purposes of self and others,
lord guru, wish-fulfilling gem,
Jampa Pal, fulfill sacred pledge.

Your form is the nature of coemergence.
Master of knowing and knowledge
in nondual profundity and clarity,
Özer Gyaltsen, fulfill sacred pledge.

Satisfied by the taste of intransient bliss,
you attained the sublime undissipating joy
and manifest kāyas and timeless awareness.
Buddharatna, fulfill sacred pledge.

Holding signs of a teacher and perfected qualities,
knowledgeable in all sutra, tantra, and treatise,
you reveal the perfection of unborn wisdom.
You relentlessly guide all beings on freedom's path.
Kunga Namgyal, fulfill sacred pledge.

Deities of the outer, inner, and secret mandalas
of the four tantra classes, kriyā, charyā, yoga [and anuttara],
such as the supreme mother Vajravārāhī and so forth,
all yidams, fulfill sacred pledge.

Those who guard the Teacher's precious doctrine, {382}
assembly of dharma protectors and guards,
both Mahākāla and Mahākālī with minds like mothers;
outer and inner dharma protectors, fulfill sacred pledge.
Being fulfilled, grant empowerment and spiritual powers.

This amendment to the composition by Situ Norbu Sampel[8] requested by Ratnashrī was written by Guru Dharmakīrti, a yogin without clinging who respectfully follows the path of Object Severance, in the place of Dechen Lhundrup Ling.

### [3] "Fulfillment Ritual" by the Runda Adept Palden Rinchen

*oṃ svabhāva* . . . (etc.) From emptiness, these fulfillment substances, support substances, and accomplishment substances form a cloud of outer, inner, secret, and suchness offerings equal to the reaches of space. It renews again and again the continuum of the strict sacred pledges of the glorious, holy gurus of the lineage of Object Severance precept adepts.

*hūṃ*
From the palace of mahāmudrā,
Kagyu gurus and your retinues:
the feast and torma fulfill sacred pledge.
With sacred pledge fulfilled, grant Brahmā's supreme
spiritual power.

*hūṃ*
From the eight sites of secret graveyards,
male and female adepts with your retinues:
the feast and torma fulfill sacred pledge.
With sacred pledge fulfilled, grant Brahmā's supreme
spiritual power.

*hūṃ*
From the great bliss of the realm of phenomena,
Chakrasaṃvara with your retinue:
the feast and torma fulfill sacred pledge.
With sacred pledge fulfilled, grant Brahmā's supreme
spiritual power.

*hūṃ*
From the self-arisen graveyard of Oḍḍiyāna,
Guhyajñāna with your retinue:
the feast and torma fulfill sacred pledge.
With sacred pledge fulfilled, grant Brahmā's supreme
spiritual power.

*hūṃ*
From the secret graveyard in the east,
Vajra Ḍākinī with all your retinue:

the feast and torma fulfill sacred pledge.
With sacred pledge fulfilled, grant Brahmā's supreme
spiritual power.

*hūṃ*
From the secret graveyard in the south,
Jewel Ḍākinī with all your retinue:
the feast and torma fulfill sacred pledge.
With sacred pledge fulfilled, grant Brahmā's supreme
spiritual power.

*hūṃ*
From the secret graveyard in the west,
Lotus Ḍākinī with all your retinue: {383}
the feast and torma fulfill sacred pledge.
With sacred pledge fulfilled, grant Brahmā's supreme
spiritual power.

*hūṃ*
From the secret graveyard in the north,
Action Ḍākinī with all your retinue:
the feast and torma fulfill sacred pledge.
With sacred pledge fulfilled, grant Brahmā's supreme
spiritual power.

*hūṃ*
From the twenty-four supreme sacred sites,
heroes and ḍākinīs with your retinues:
the feast and torma fulfill sacred pledge.
With sacred pledge fulfilled, grant Brahmā's supreme
spiritual power.

*hūṃ*
From the various worldly graveyards,
various ḍākinīs with your retinues:
the feast and torma fulfill sacred pledge.
With sacred pledge fulfilled, grant Brahmā's supreme
spiritual power.

*hūṃ*
From the palace of great devil conqueror,

awareness dharma protectors and your retinues:
the feast and torma fulfill sacred pledge.
With sacred pledge fulfilled, grant Brahmā's supreme spiritual power.

For the confession, join your palms together.

*hūṃ*
From the palace of mahāmudrā,
Kagyu gurus and your retinues,
please listen and consider me.
Whatever physical, verbal, or mental transgressions
I have committed under the power of ignorance,
I admit and confess! Grant Brahmā's supreme spiritual power.

From the eight sites of secret graveyards,
male and female adepts with your retinues,
please listen and consider me.
Whatever physical, verbal, or mental transgressions
I have committed under the power of ignorance,
I admit and confess! Grant Brahmā's supreme spiritual power.

From the great bliss of the realm of phenomena,
Chakrasaṃvara with your retinue,
please listen and consider me.
Whatever physical, verbal, or mental transgressions
I have committed under the power of ignorance,
I admit and confess! Grant Brahmā's supreme spiritual power.

From the self-arisen graveyard of Oḍḍiyāna,
Guhyajñāna with your retinue,
please listen and consider me.
Whatever physical, verbal, or mental transgressions
I have committed under the power of ignorance,
I admit and confess! Grant Brahmā's supreme spiritual power.

From the secret graveyard in the east,
Vajra Ḍākinī with all your retinue,
please listen and consider me.

Whatever physical, verbal, or mental transgressions
I have committed under the power of ignorance,
I admit and confess! Grant Brahmā's supreme spiritual power.

From the secret graveyard in the south,
Jewel Ḍākinī with all your retinue,
please listen and consider me.
Whatever physical, verbal, or mental transgressions
I have committed under the power of ignorance,
I admit and confess! Grant Brahmā's supreme spiritual power.

From the secret graveyard in the west, {384}
Lotus Ḍākinī with all your retinue,
please listen and consider me.
Whatever physical, verbal, or mental transgressions
I have committed under the power of ignorance,
I admit and confess! Grant Brahmā's supreme spiritual power.

From the secret graveyard in the north,
Action Ḍākinī with all your retinue,
please listen and consider me.
Whatever physical, verbal, or mental transgressions
I have committed under the power of ignorance,
I admit and confess! Grant Brahmā's supreme spiritual power.

From the twenty-four supreme sacred sites,
heroes and ḍākinīs with your retinues,
please listen and consider me.
Whatever physical, verbal, or mental transgressions
I have committed under the power of ignorance,
I admit and confess! Grant Brahmā's supreme spiritual power.

From the various worldly graveyards,
various ḍākinīs with your retinues,
please listen and consider me.
Whatever physical, verbal, or mental transgressions
I have committed under the power of ignorance,
I admit and confess! Grant Brahmā's supreme spiritual power.

From the palace of the great devil conqueror,
awareness dharma protectors and your retinues,
please listen and consider me.
Whatever physical, verbal, or mental transgressions
I have committed under the power of ignorance,
I admit and confess! Grant Brahmā's supreme spiritual power.

*oṃ*
I admit and confess infractions of the Body sacred pledge.
I admit and confess infractions of the Speech sacred pledge.
I admit and confess infractions of the Mind sacred pledge.
I admit and confess infractions of the outer sacred pledge.
I admit and confess infractions of the inner sacred pledge.
I admit and confess infractions of the secret sacred pledge.
I admit and confess infractions of the root sacred pledge.
I admit and confess infractions of the branch sacred pledge.
I admit and confess infractions of the forbidden sacred pledge.
I admit and confess infractions of extrasufficient sacred pledge.
I admit! I admit! I admit it to the yidam deities.
I confess! I confess! I confess it to the strict guards.
Renew my promised sacred pledge that was damaged
and grant Brahmā's supreme spiritual power.

All-knowing, all-seeing gods, please heed me.
Since beginningless time I have transgressed {385}
the Victor's precepts—the three levels of vows—
with body, speech, and mind under the influence of the three poisons.
I admit and confess acts of faults, downfalls, and negativities.
It won't happen again—may I not experience [the consequences].
Please instantly clear away all the breaks and damages in the root and branch sacred pledges of Body, Speech, and Mind, the deluded appearances of the six kinds of beings, the seeds of habitual patterns, the tears in the three vows, and the whole mass of faults and downfalls and create vast purification.

From the place of the palace of the pure realm of phenomena,
Great Mother Perfection of Wisdom, dharmakāya,

you dwell in the midst of heroes and ḍākinīs.
Hosts of peaceful, enriching, controlling, and wrathful deities,
five families of ḍākinīs and vow holders,
heroes, heroines, and dharma protectors,
workers, meat eaters, blood drinkers,
messengers, murderers, butchers, and all:
as per the fulfillment of your previous sacred pledge,
this evening in this place, fulfill that sacred pledge.
Bestow the spiritual powers of Body, Speech, and Mind.
Accomplish the requested enlightened activities.

*hūṃ*
Fulfill! Fulfill the sacred pledge for the ages.
Fulfill the sacred pledge of gurus and yidams.
Fulfill the sacred pledge of heroes and heroines.
Fulfill the sacred pledge of dharma protectors, Mahākāla and Shrīdevī.
Fulfill the sacred pledge of the great kings and wealth gods.
Fulfill the sacred pledge of the eight spirit classes and local gods.
Fulfill the sacred pledge of nāgas, pestilent spirits, and earth lords.
Fulfill the sacred pledge of the six kinds of mothers and fathers.
Fulfill the sacred pledge of creditors and obstructing types.
Fulfill the sacred pledge of knife, infertility, and *gyalgong* demons.
Fulfill the sacred pledge of vow breakers, *sinmo*s, and demonesses.
All of you, take the sacred substances of pledge fulfillment
and fulfill the pledge with the edible feast of desirables.
Fulfill the sacred pledge with the precious gift of enjoyment.
Fulfill the sacred pledge with the liver of stupidity. {386}
Fulfill the sacred pledge with the heart-*chitta* of anger.
Fulfill the sacred pledge with the menstrual blood of desire.
Fulfill the sacred pledge with the torma of flesh, blood, and organs.
Fulfill the sacred pledge with the elixir of grains, essences, and first fruits.
Fulfill the sacred pledge with an ocean of blood and fat.
Fulfill the sacred pledge with a mountain of the five great meats.
Fulfill the sacred pledge with secret thighbone trumpets.
Fulfill the sacred pledge with the sound of joined-skull drums.

Fulfill the sacred pledge with drums, horns, cymbals, and guitars.
Fulfill the sacred pledge with the essence of *bhandha* elixir.
Fulfill the sacred pledge with human fat and bone marrow.
Fulfill the sacred pledge with garlands of six bone ornaments.
Fulfill the sacred pledge with the undulating dance of union.
Fulfill the sacred pledge with flowing silk garments.
Fulfill the sacred pledge with various poignant melodies.
Fulfill the sacred pledge with various beautiful gazes.
I fulfill your sacred pledge.
You restore my downfalls.
Accomplish this yogin's wishes.
Perform the requested activities.

This renewal ritual was written by the adept of Runda, Palden Rinchen.[9]

*sarva mangalam*

# 26. Offering Torma to All Ḍākimas[1]

This is the last of the addenda to the Severance feast activities in the Zurmang tradition that seem to be connected to Tekchok Dorje's compilation *Source of All Qualities*. It is a beautiful and quite graphic text, but unfortunately there is no author statement identifying the poet.

Torma (*gtor ma*) is literally "that which is thrown out or scattered," and it refers to the custom of creating sculpture out of flour or other malleable material that represents either the offerings in the ritual or the recipient of those offerings, such as the deities. The creation of torma is a vast and elaborate art form in vajrayāna practice. In particular, the torma at a feast offering may be represented by one or more feast torma sculptures and supplemented with many other edibles, or the edible offerings themselves may simply be designated as the feast torma. That seems to be the case here, where the "torma" is one's body that has been separated from consciousness and creatively prepared in imagination for the various recipients.

In this liturgy, those recipients are specifically all ḍākinīs—hundreds of thousands of them—affectionately called *ḍākimas* here. The principal one is Vajravārāhī, who always plays an important role in Severance. She is goddess, yidam, ḍākinī, lineage holder, and one's own consciousness. Designated here as "the birth mother of the buddhas," she is identical to the Great Mother, the perfection of wisdom. A hundred thousand ḍākinīs emanate from each aspect of her body and her accessories. But there are trillions more ḍākinīs of basic space, trillions more from the twenty-four sacred sites of India, and many, many others. All of them are invoked to receive the feast torma and then reminded about their sacred pledges. Finally, their powers are commandeered to avert all kinds of calamities, disease, and just plain bad luck.

## Invoking Hundreds of Thousands of Ḍākinīs

*oṃ āḥ hūṃ*

This torma adorned by holy substances and sealed by the five meats and five elixirs is dedicated in this place of offering. The yidam Vajravārāhī with the host of deities partake of the offering. Please completely pacify all circumstantial outer and inner obstacles. Please grant both the supreme and common spiritual powers without exception.

*hūṃ bhyo*
Over yonder in all directions,
over there, west of the sun,
on the northwest border of Vajra Seat,
in the graveyard of Oḍḍiyāna
all the mountains are bone mountains,
all the plants are arrows and spears,
all the waters are blood and pus,
all the sounds are grunts.
The terrifying land of Vajrapāṇi,
where the ten wrathful ones cannot move,
the place where five buddha families stay—
who dwells there and who does not?
The birth mother of the buddhas of three times,
Vajravārāhī, dwells there in that place.
Goddesses of her retinue dwell there.
A hundred thousand ḍākinīs of the changeless nature of phenomena
come from the fierce black pig's face on Mother's right. {343}
A hundred thousand ḍākinīs sent to do the Tathāgata's work
come from the awesome fierce red face on her left.
A hundred thousand ḍākinīs who sever the four devils at the roots
come from the fully bared fangs of her countenance.
A hundred thousand ḍākinīs with the six clairvoyances
come from her six intensely red twitching eyes.

A hundred thousand ḍākinīs of the five families helping beings
come from the five dry skulls that adorn her head.
A hundred thousand ḍākinīs who pour down compassion like rain
come from the strands of hair that cover her back.
A hundred thousand ḍākinīs who cut off life and take the breath
come from the curved knife brandished in her right hand.
A hundred thousand ḍākinīs who transmit blood disease and dysentery
come from the blood-filled skull cup in her left hand.
A hundred thousand ḍākinīs who control the three realms
come from her three-pronged khaṭvām that fully adorns.
A hundred thousand ḍākinīs victorious in the demigod battles
come from the straight white pounding poles. {344}
A hundred thousand ḍākinīs of the pure five kāyas and timeless awareness
come from the five-pronged vajra that fully adorns her.
A hundred thousand ḍākinīs who dazzle the three planes of existence
come from the three stacked heads that fully adorn.
A hundred thousand ḍākinīs who fell the devils' victory banner
come from the fluttering silk ribbons that fully adorn her.
A hundred thousand ḍākinīs who hold instructions of the aural lineage
come from the ḍaru and tiny golden bells.
A hundred thousand ḍākinīs with fully developed qualities
come from the vase of elixir that fully adorns.
A hundred thousand ḍākinīs with unhindered enlightened activity
come from the variegated crossed vajra that adorns.
A hundred thousand ḍākinīs with fifty pure mental formations
come from the necklace of fifty human heads.

A hundred thousand ḍākinīs who complete the six
perfections
come from the six bone ornaments that fully adorn her.
A hundred thousand ḍākinīs with experience of great bliss
come from the playful naked dance of stretching and
bending.
A hundred thousand ḍākinīs who lead beings out of their six
realms
come from sitting on the corpse seat without thought.
A hundred thousand ḍākinīs who unite method and wisdom
come from sitting on the seat of lotus and sun.
A hundred thousand ḍākinīs who burn discriminating
thoughts
come from the blazing mountain of fire at time's end.
A hundred thousand vajra ḍākinīs in the east.
A hundred thousand jewel ḍākinīs in the south.
A hundred thousand lotus ḍākinīs in the west.
A hundred thousand action ḍākinīs in the north.
A hundred thousand white ḍākinīs of the Body family.
A hundred thousand red ḍākinīs of the Speech family.
A hundred thousand black ḍākinīs of the Mind family.
A hundred thousand yellow ḍākinīs of qualities.
A hundred thousand green ḍākinīs of activities.
In accepting this elixir torma, {345}
perform activities of all kinds:
elevate awareness in the fortunate,
engender devotion in the unfortunate,
and punish detrimental foes and obstacles.[2]

## Invoking the Ḍākinīs of Basic Space

*oṃ āḥ hūṃ*

This torma adorned by holy substances and sealed by the five meats and five elixirs is dedicated in this place of offering. The trillion[3] ḍākinīs of basic space partake of the offering. Please completely pacify all circumstantial outer and inner obstacles. Please grant both the supreme and common spiritual powers without exception.

*hūṃ bhyo*
A trillion ḍākinīs of timeless awareness
come from the great bliss of the realm of space:
vajra ḍākinīs, Subduers of Devils;
jewel ḍākinīs, Glorious Spiritual Powers;
lotus ḍākinīs, Great Bliss;
action ḍākinīs, Embodiments of Activities.
They are all so irresistible.
Their colors are not one but indefinite:
white, yellow, red, and green.
Some are dark blue, the color of darkness,
and some are light blue, the color of sky.
Their implements are not of one kind but indefinite:
some hold curved knives and blood-filled skull cups,
some hold khaṭvāms and small drums,
some hold striking weapons,
some hold vases of elixir,
and some hold beautiful flowers.
Five graveyard ornaments beautify their bodies.
Sashes, bells, and bangles adorn them.
They make sweet sounds—*si li li.*
Their crowning jewels are silken diadems.
The breeze stirs—*pu ru ru.*
Their feet move in vajra gaits.
They are unconstrained in space—*bun ne bun.*
They have bracelets on their flexible arms.
They swiftly take various dance poses—*khyuk se khyuk.*
In accepting this elixir torma,
perform activities of all kinds:
elevate awareness in the fortunate,
engender devotion in the unfortunate, {346}
and punish detrimental foes and obstacles.

## Invoking the [Heroes and Ḍākinīs of] Twenty-Four Sacred Sites

*oṃ āḥ hūṃ*

This torma adorned by holy substances and sealed by the five meats and five elixirs is dedicated in this place of offering. The heroes and ḍākinīs of the twenty-four sacred sites partake of the offering. Please completely pacify all circumstantial outer and inner obstacles. Please grant both the supreme and common spiritual powers without exception.

*hūṃ bhyo*
From twenty-four sacred sites,
there are twenty-four main ḍākinīs
along with a host of millions of ḍākinīs.
The main ones are not manifest; they remain in basic space.
There are a trillion ḍākinīs in the entourage.

*bhyo*
Some are black women
wearing the old clothes of corpses,
adorned with drops of blood and grease,
gray with smeared human ashes.
Their yellow hair is bound in a topknot
with a faded flower as a crown jewel.
*Ha ha*—they laugh with their toothless mouths
and stagger on the ground with their feet.
Although they display such features,
they reveal the dharma of symbols to the fortunate.
Just encountering them is a blessing.
In accepting this elixir torma,
perform activities of all kinds:
engage in fearless yogic activity
and enhance the experience of nonthought.

*bhyo*
Some are youthful women
adorned by various ornaments.
Their individual family colors and
individual activities match their families.
Some are white and fine—
mudras of the vajra family
who evoke bodhichitta.
Some are light-yellow commanders—
mudras of the jewel family

who evoke supreme spiritual power.
Some are red and beautifully formed—
mudras of the lotus family
who evoke undissipating bliss. {347}
Some are light blue with wrinkled brows—
mudras of the action family
who evoke the welfare of beings.
Some are pure white like the sky—
mudras of the tathāgata family
who evoke the genuine meaning.
They are all so irresistible:
their beautiful faces radiant,
youthful bodies assuming poses,
and jeweled crowns on their heads.
Each embraces her hero consort.
Belts of tiny golden bells
jingle as their bodies move.
Their faces are lotuses with conch teeth,
their smiling speech sweetly sounding
the sweet language of godly melodies,
singing vajra songs that enchant.
In accepting this elixir torma,
perform activities of all kinds:
engender bliss in the dissipating body
and enhance experience in the undissipating mind.

*bhyo*
Some are women with ordinary forms,
doing various worldly activities:
there is nothing you would not do.
Some are dyers making alterations,
changing the colors of ordinary mind.
Some are intoxicating beer sellers,
intoxicating erring consciousness.
Some are fornicating whores,
uniting method and wisdom.
Some are scrubbing washerwomen,
cleaning the stains of habitual patterns.

Some are murderous butchers,
murdering discursive thought in basic space.
Some are dangerous robber women,
enjoying the freedom of others' minds.
Some are ascetic brāhmaṇīs,
severing the continuity of cyclic existence.
There are infinite more such as those.
From the twenty-four sacred sites of Jambudvīpa
to the south of Supreme Mountain,
all those come for the sake of migrators,
taming them by means of various actions
of many various methods. {348}
In accepting this elixir torma,
perform activities of all kinds:
for us yogins and so forth,
for all those doing practice,
level the eight worldly concerns
and spontaneously accomplish universal benefit.

### Invoking the Worldly Ḍākinīs

*oṃ āḥ hūṃ*

This torma adorned by holy substances and sealed by the five meats and five elixirs is dedicated in this place of offering. Carnivorous worldly ḍākinīs, partake of the offering. Please completely pacify all circumstantial outer and inner obstacles. Please grant both the supreme and common spiritual powers without exception.

*hūṃ bhyo*
The strong worldly ḍākinīs
from the graveyard of utter terror
are totally unbearable, with terrifying forms:
with various heads on women's bodies,
they grasp skulls and drink human blood,
eat human corpses and whistle tunes,[4]
spy on absorbed meditators and roam assembly halls.

All of you without exception,
accept this torma of command
and perform the activities to keep your sacred pledge
just as you promised before.

### Invoking the Ḍākinīs of the Eight Graveyards

*oṃ āḥ hūṃ*

This torma adorned by holy substances and sealed by the five meats and five elixirs is dedicated in this place of offering. Heroes and ḍākinīs of the eight emanated graveyards, partake of the offering. Please completely pacify all circumstantial outer and inner obstacles. Please grant both the supreme and common spiritual powers without exception.

*bhyo*
Charming women in the city of freedom,
within the encircling vajra fence,
outside of the infinite palace,
in the cities of the eight great graveyards:
Intensely Fierce and Dense Thicket,
Blazing Rumble and Terrifying,
Laughing *Ha Ha* and Sounding *Ki La*,
Unbearable Darkness and Great Forest. {349}
Eight *mamo*s are mistresses of the graveyards,
wrathful, holding curved knives and blood-filled skulls,
right legs bent and left outstretched in a scary way,
with hundreds of thousands of mamo retinues.
Accept this torma of command
and perform the activities requested.

### Invoking the Twenty-Eight Mighty Ones

*oṃ āḥ hūṃ*

This torma adorned by holy substances and sealed by the five meats and five elixirs is dedicated in this place of offering.

Twenty-eight mighty ones with your retinues, partake of the offering. Please completely pacify all circumstantial outer and inner obstacles. Please grant both the supreme and common spiritual powers without exception.

*bhyo*
Mothers—seven ḍākinīs come from the east.
Six dwell in the space of timeless awareness,
and one acts as gatekeeper of methods.
Ḍākinīs of the vajra family in the east,
come here to accept this adorned torma
and perform your peaceful activity.

*bhyo*
Mothers—seven ḍākinīs come from the south.
Six dwell in the space of timeless awareness,
and one acts as gatekeeper of methods.
Ḍākinīs of the jewel family in the south,
come here to accept this adorned torma
and perform your enriching activity.

*bhyo*
Mothers—seven ḍākinīs come from the west.
Six dwell in the space of timeless awareness,
and one acts as gatekeeper of methods.
Ḍākinīs of the lotus family in the west,
come here to accept this adorned torma
and perform your controlling activity.

*bhyo*
Mothers—seven ḍākinīs come from the north.
Six dwell in the space of timeless awareness,
and one acts as gatekeeper of methods.
Ḍākinīs of the accomplishment family in the north,
come here to accept this adorned torma
and perform your wrathful activity. {350}

You who obey Vajradhara's command,
twenty-eight mighty mamos,
partake of this torma of command

and perform peaceful, enriching, controlling, and wrathful activities.

## Invoking the *Tenma*

*oṃ āḥ hūṃ*

This torma adorned by holy substances and sealed by the five meats and five elixirs is dedicated in this place of offering. Twelve vajra *tenma*, twelve *kyongma*, and twelve *yama* who protect Tibet and Kham, along with retinues of vassals and servants, partake of the offering. Please avert all great craving, dread, calamities, plague, bad luck, famine, border wars, and quarrels and perform transforming activity.

*bhyo*
Along with the commanded assembly itself,
with sky forms just like blood drinkers,
all you protectors: come here, land here,
come here and perform activity to fulfill your pledge.

Great Mistress Dorje Kundrakma,[5]
Glorious Hari Dorje Yama Kyong,
Great Mother of the Snows Dorje Kuntuzang,
Great Nomad Taming Retinues Dorje Gekyitso:
you four great witches, with your excessive ornaments,
and retinues of many vassals and servants,
come here and perform activity to fulfill your pledge.

Pure Snow Mountain, Dorje Paldangden,
Kharak Garuḍa Dorje Palgyiyum,
Abundant Wound Mountain Dorje Drakmogyal,
Great Treasure Sky Soarer Dorje Lumogyal:
you four great yakṣhīs,
with your excessive ornaments,
and retinues of many vassals and servants,
come here and perform activity to fulfill your pledge.

Kongtsun Demo Dorje Bö Kham Kyong,
Playful Tsen Dorje Menchikma,

Lady Ukchö Dorje Yarmosil,
Turquoise Bell Dorje Zulema: {351}
you four great *mentsun*,[6]
with your excessive ornaments,
and retinues of many vassals and servants,
come here and perform activity to fulfill your pledge.

At first in the previous era,
when you were invited from India,
the master Padmakara and
spiritual guide Langchen Palseng[7]
presented to your hands the secret vajra
on the throne of overlapping human skins
and bestowed the name of your liberation.
In order to avert all future disease,
calamities, and plagues,
accept this torma of command
and perform the requested activities.

**Clapping [to Avert]**

*bhyo bhyo avert avert*
Avert disease,
avert calamity,
avert plague,
drought, frost, and hail three,
bad luck, famine,
daytime bad omens,
nighttime bad omens and all—
upon those sorcerers, harmers, and hateful enemies themselves:
*māraya bhyo bhyo avert avert*
Please perform the sacred activities of averting and transforming.

# 27. Distillation of the Profound

## *The Way to Practice the Essence of the Vast Object Severance in a Single Sitting*[1]

### Jamgön Kongtrul

This is Jamgön Kongtrul's own liturgy for the donation of the body as food; it is included in the collection of his compositions called *Treasury of Extensive Teachings* (*rGya chen bka' mdzod*). The idea of practice "in a single sitting"—literally, "on a single seat" (*stan thog gcig tu*)—basically indicates that the various extensive instructions, rituals, and postmeditation activities have been distilled into a manageable daily practice. Kongtrul stated his intention clearly in the colophon: the text was intended for use in the three-year retreat that he established in the upper hermitage at Palpung Monastery, Kunzang Dechen Ösal Ling. Although not specifically listed in the retreat curricula that he composed, the practice of Severance is a well-known integral part of the program. The successor of that retreat tradition, Kyapje Kalu Rinpoche, went on from Palpung to establish such retreats around the world. At some point, this composition of Kongtrul's was replaced in the retreats by the now popular version attributed to the fourteenth Karmapa, Tekchok Dorje, called *The Concise Charity of the Body for Daily Practice.*

Kongtrul also names his sources in the colophon: Samten Özer and Jamyang Gönpo, whose teachings from visionary experiences of Machik are called direct lineages (*nye brgyud*); and the composed teachings from Jonang Tāranātha and Minling Terchen Rinpoche. The Jonangpa tradition of Tāranātha's Severance coming from Kunga Drölchok was discussed in the introduction to chapter 14. Kongtrul regarded himself as an incarnation of Tāranātha, affirming his deep spiritual connection with that lineage.

Minling Terchen (sMin gling gter chen, 1646–1714), also known as Terdak Lingpa (gTer bdag gling pa) and Gyurme Dorje ('Gyur med rdo rje), was the great treasure revealer and founder of Mindroling Monastery, one of the six main Nyingma monastic complexes in Tibet. Jamgön Kongtrul relates many dreams of this master in his autobiography and mentions several great lamas who believed that Kongtrul himself was an incarnation of Minling Terchen.* Kongtrul's inspiration from these two masters is obviously much deeper than just an appreciation of their work.

There may be a direct connection here to Minling Terchen's brief composition (not a revealed text) bearing the similar name *Hero's Loud Laugh: Instructions on Object Severance in a Single Sitting* (as well as several supportive texts with the "single sitting" signature).† The basic procedure for the all-at-once practice in both texts is comparable, although by Minling Terchen's time this had become fairly standard. This text by Kongtrul, however, differs in several ways. The inclusion of the origin story based on the *Verse Summary* quotation and the classical definition of the term *gcod* is unusual for a short sādhana practice, though typical of Kongtrul. Kongtrul also makes the correlation between the three Buddhist meditative absorptions (Skt. *samādhi*) with the three phases of view, meditation, and conduct as applied to Severance practice.‡ Finally, the Samten Özer and Tāranātha connections are revealed in the inclusion of their two outstanding instructions: "the meaning of the Mother" and "severing the four devils in basic space." Thus it is truly a distillation of the many deep dharma streams of which Kongtrul was the beneficiary.

---

*namo guru*

I bow to the guru, sublime Great Mother,
who teaches many methods of severing deluded concepts

*See *Autobiography of Jamgön Kongtrul: A Gem of Many Colors*, pp. 88, 415.

†*gCod yul stan thog gcig ma'i gdams pa dpa' bo'i gad rgyangs* and *Zur 'debs* in *The Collected Works of Minling Terchen Rikzin Gyurme Dorje*, pp. 312–18. This may also be the inspiration for Jigme Lingpa's ('Jigs med gling pa, 1729/30–1798) discovered text on Severance, *The Ḍākinī's Loud Laugh* (*gCod yul mkha' 'gro'i gad rgyangs*).

‡The three absorptions as part of Opening the Sky Door instructions are found in a source text of Pacification (*zhi byed*) called the *Six Pieces* (*Brul tsho drug*), *DV*, vol. *ja*, pp. 71–4.

within the great purity of dharmakāya.
I shall explain the essential yoga.

It says in the *Summary of Precious Qualities*:[2]

> The powerful and wise bodhisattvas withstand four devils
> and remain undisturbed for four reasons:
> They dwell in emptiness, never abandon sentient beings,
> practice what they preach, and possess the blessing of
> the sugatas.

The instructions known as the Holy Dharma Severance of Evil Object, which are the heart of the esoteric instructions on the perfection of wisdom, are as vast as an ocean. Nevertheless, in order to effectively apply the instructions on the above four special points, it will promote good qualities on the path to correlate the three absorptions with the three [phases of] view, meditation, and conduct. Therefore, it should not be omitted from the body donation in a single sitting.

The term *severance* (*gcod*) means to totally abandon the clinging to "me" or "mine" within one's own mindstream and then to engage in illusion-like conduct regarding outer appearances without involving any notion whatsoever that fixates on attributes. With that as the basis, the actual practice has three parts: (1) the preliminaries, which implant the blessings of the sugatas; (2) the main practice of dwelling in emptiness and accomplishing the welfare of beings through the power of wisdom and compassion [respectively]; and (3) the subsequent activity of conduct that does not transgress one's sworn pledges. {355}

## I. Preliminaries, Which Implant the Blessings of the Sugatas

### A. Refuge and Awakening Mind

To enter the gate of the Great Vehicle, recollect the four mind-changers[3] and clearly visualize the objects of refuge:

> Guru Machik, Perfection of Wisdom,
> before me on a lion throne, lotus, and sun,
> surrounded by an ocean of refuge objects—Three Jewels and roots—
> looks compassionately upon beings throughout space.

Going for refuge:

I and all beings go for refuge with devotion
to the gurus, yidams, and ḍākinī hosts,
Buddha, dharma, and noble sangha,
who fill all space in the abode of space.

Arousing the awakening mind:

May sentient beings be happy.
May they be free from all suffering.
May they never be separated from happiness.
May they realize the equality of all phenomena.

### B. Descent of Blessings

To bring down blessings through devotion, first make those refuge objects the field of accumulation:

I offer respectfully to you
my body, wealth, and enjoyments
and all virtuous things in the three times
for the sake of all sentient beings.
You with all-seeing eyes,
holy abode of qualities,
consider me with kindness.
Accept this and grant your blessings. {356}

Supplication:

*namo guru*
Machik, Great Mother, queen of the ḍākinīs,
inseparable from the victors' mother, the perfection of wisdom,
and the root and lineage gurus of profound Object Severance,
I supplicate you: grant your blessings.

My body, enjoyments, and all things
I offer without attachment: please accept them.

For the sake of beings, bless me to abandon self-fixation
and instill contentment in my being.

Bless me to decisively realize my unborn mind
and take up adverse circumstances as the path.
Bless me to sever the duration of the three realms.
Bless me to count the six kinds of beings as friends.

Bless me to purify samsara and nirvana in basic space.
Bless me to cut the entanglements of dualistic fixation.
Bless me to realize the abiding nature of nonself.

Thus supplicate with single-pointed devotion. Then:

The retinue dissolves into the guru and from her three places
light from the three seed syllables enters my three places
and blesses my three doors as her three vajras.
The guru dissolves into light and we become inseparable.

### II. Main Practice

### A. Vajra-Like Meditative Absorption

### Blending Space and Awareness

First, in order to reach decisive resolution of the view through vajra-like absorption, do the practice of joining (*kha sbyor*) the vital winds, and:

Consciousness that pervades the body gathers together
and becomes shining white vital drops in my two soles.
*phaṭ*

They ascend the pathway from the feet and blend into one
at the juncture.
This exits out the head and becomes indivisible with space.
*phaṭ*

Recognize that wherever space pervades, there also awareness pervades, and rest.

### Recognizing the Mother's Meaning

Reflexive awareness is free of permanence and annihilation, arising and ceasing, and coming and going.
It does not come down on any side, such as existence or nonexistence.
Agent and action, benefit and harm, are not established.
Unidentifiable, it is free of any ground or root, like the sky.
*phaṭ*

Rest in equanimity for however long without any mental engagement whatsoever.

### Severing the Four Devils in Basic Space

Tangible devils arise from dualistic grasping of objects.
Intangible devils are spontaneous mental experiences. {357}
Devils of exaltation are diversions of manifold desires and favorable conditions.
Devils of inflation are fixating thoughts, the root of all.
Whatever arises, sever it in unborn basic space.
*phaṭ*

Thus abruptly cast out random conceptual thought.

### B. Illusion-Like Meditative Absorption

The lucid clarity of reflexive awareness free of all elaboration that comes from blending space and awareness is itself the meditation object and main practice. There are many formulations that reference calm abiding and higher insight to train in producing that realization. However, for our purposes here, there are two ways of casting out the body as food.

### 1. The White Distribution

*phaṭ*
My body, the radiant expression of emptiness, is big and brilliant.
It is youthful, beautiful, and appealing.

My mind projects out from its heart far into the space in front
as the knife- and skull-carrying Yoginī, endowed with bliss.
I completely sever the skull and put it on the self-arisen
hearthstones.
I cut up the corpse into sesame-size pieces and pour them in.
*oṃ āḥ hūṃ* transforms it into the elixir of timeless awareness.
It becomes unimaginable desirables and enjoyments.
*phaṭ*
All you included in the four kinds of guests of samsara and
nirvana
who have arisen from the energy of my reflexive awareness:
Come here! Gather here! Stay like clustered banks of clouds.
Emanated offering goddesses offer you the elixir of the skull.
*phaṭ*
Root and lineage gurus, precious Three Jewels,
victors of all times and directions, assemblies of bodhisattvas,
shrāvakas, and pratekyabuddhas,
mandala deities of the nine vehicles and four and six tantra classes,
ḍākinīs of sacred sites and areas, dharma protectors of three
tantras:
I present the unsurpassable offering clouds of Samantabhadra.
When your minds are satisfied by great undissipating bliss,
bless me and others to integrate adverse conditions onto the path
and reach the ultimate aim of Object Severance.
*phaṭ*
To pure classes, such as the seventy-five glorious protectors
and the guests of qualities, I offer goods to please your minds.
Nourish the whole world with happiness and
be allies for achieving our dharma goals.
*phaṭ* {358}
For all the guests of compassion, the six realms,
parents of the three times and three realms in four kinds of birth,[4]
may a rain of desired goods fall from the sky treasury
and everlasting bliss free of all suffering be attained.
*phaṭ*
To whomever I owe retribution for harm done
from beginningless lifetimes until now,
may this repay the debts and ransom of body, life, and wealth,

ending the blood grudge and enabling the awakening mind.
*phaṭ*

Optional prayer:

By the power of my aspirations
and the power of the tathāgatas' blessing
and the power of the realm of phenomena,
for the sake of offering to the noble ones
and the benefit all sentient beings,
may all my wishes, for whatever purposes,
all of them, in whatever way is appropriate,
come to pass without hindrance.

## 2. The Red Distribution

*phaṭ*
My mind in the form of Krodhī emerges into space
from my body, which pervades the whole universe.
I flay its skin and lay it out all at once.
I chop the limbs and body parts into pieces
and heap up the bits of the sense organs and innards.
Mountains of flesh, lakes of blood, mires of fatty brains,
and cluttered banks of bones fill the world.
Vapors of steaming grease waft upward,[5]
extremely potent and essential like that of a seven-times-born brahmin.
It becomes liberation upon tasting that never runs out.
*phaṭ*
You who dwell and move above, below, and on the ground,
gods and spirits of eight classes, fierce ones,
yamas, lords of death, malicious spirits of place and body,
particularly those whose wishes and actions
harm me and any sentient being,
along with your retinues, servants, and legions:
quickly gather here this minute!
*phaṭ*

The power of ignorance since the beginning
has brought about this body as the basis for suffering.
Up to now, clinging to it as a self has been disastrous.
Previously, my kind fathers and mothers,
I was deluded by fixating on you as demons.
Now I completely relinquish self-fixation.
Within the illusory state, whatever arises is false.
With no attachment, whatever you desire is granted.
Flesh, blood, bones, the five sense faculties, {359}
internal organs, skin, veins, ligaments, and the like,
boiled, burnt, or raw—eat whatever you like.
Don't worry—enjoy it with a happy mind.
Eat as much as you can and take the rest to go.
May debts be cleared and scores settled,
granting gratification and the mind of awakening.
May we all attain buddhahood together
once all afflictions, negativities, and obscurations are pacified.
*phaṭ*

## C. The Meditative Absorption of Heroic Conduct

Enhancement comes through the activity of the meditative absorption of heroic conduct. When you have cut through the inner inflated thoughts right in that sitting by having practiced those views and meditations, [generally] you get the special instructions to wander in haunted places in order to stabilize it through the ascertainment of evidence of uprisings and evidence of success. However, in this case, when practicing the view and meditations [in a single sitting], you should sever inflating thoughts by smashing them as soon as they rise up (*'bur 'joms*). Thus:

Mind is emptiness, like the sky.
Since it is blended, it is not seen by buddhas.
The body has already been donated.
There's no speck of an object of desire or attachment.
You all do whatever pleases you:
may self-fixation be demolished.
*phaṭ*

Thus, sever in the basic space of emptiness whatever inner and secret uprisings occur.

### III. Concluding Activities
### A. Acts of Love and Bestowal of Dharma

May all the negativities, obscurations, and sufferings of sentient beings,
who are my parents, and mainly of the harm-doers, ripen in me.
May all migrators be happy and free of suffering
once my happiness and virtue ripens in them.
*phaṭ*

All things arise from a cause.
That cause was taught by the Tathāgata.
Of that which stops that cause
the great shramaṇa also spoke.[6]

Do no negative action whatsoever;
practice abundant virtue.
Completely tame your own mind.
This is the Buddha's teaching.[7]

Regard all compounded things in this way:
as stars, hallucinations, and lamps,
illusions, dewdrops, and water bubbles,
dreams, lightning, and clouds.[8]

### B. Conveying That Which Is to Be Severed and That Which Severs to Basic Space

Gods are mind even as demons are your own mind.
Your mind is unborn since forever, free of elaboration. {360}
Without your clinging to unceasing appearances of interdependence,
the illusory mandala dissolves in basic space.
*phaṭ*

Thus, when you have looked directly at your own essence, mind's appearances dissolve into emptiness.

### C. Subsequent Attainment: Sealing with Dedication and Aspiration

> Through this merit, may all migrators throughout space
> purify the two obscurations and complete the two
> accumulations.
> May we forsake self-fixation and befriend adverse conditions.
> May we quickly attain the state of dharmakāya, the Great
> Mother.

Say this and whatever Mahayana dedications and aspirations are appropriate. Since this is a summary of the profound path of Object Severance, it is excellent if you can do this practice on a daily basis. To shorten it, you may eliminate the red distribution and its concluding practices. For a very abridged version, do the supplication from "*namo guru* . . ." and so forth, continuing through the three and a half verses and the entire white distribution, finishing with the loving-kindness and bestowal of dharma.

Just as in the Dakpo Kagyu mahāmudrā,
the view and conduct pervading Sutra and Mantra
are adorned by skillful methods of the instructions,
which are teachings appropriate for all capabilities.
Being so easy to implement, it does not require
scriptural citations and beautiful outlines.
But since nowadays mostly perverse Severance
is propagated just for some food and clothing,
this has been arranged with an altruistic attitude
to benefit those of similar inclinations to myself.
By this virtue, may the pure Object Severance
sever the self-fixation of all migrators.

Thinking mainly of the practices of those adepts in the upper hermitage of Kunzang Dechen Ösal Ling, I distilled the essence of the pure sublime teachings of the great Venerable Jonang [Tāranātha] and Minling Terchen

Rinpoche, within the oral tradition of the direct lineage of Gyaltangpa Samten Özer and Chöje Jamyang Gönpo. With the virtue and fortune of drinking from these many streams of instructions on Object Severance, Karma Ngawang Yönten Gyatso composed this at the heart of Tsādra Rinchen Drak. May it spread virtue and goodness.

# 28. Beloved Garden

## *Brief Notes on the Offering and Gift of the Body*[1]

### Jamgön Kongtrul

This is Jamgön Kongtrul's well-known and probably most useful instruction on the daily practice of Severance, written at the behest of Jamyang Khyentse Wangpo. It has been translated several times, with the title rendered variously as "Grove of Delights," "Garden of All Joy," "Garden of Pleasures," and so forth. It is also the basis of many oral commentaries by great contemporary masters such as Venerable Tenga Rinpoche, Khenchen Thrangu Rinpoche, and so on. Perhaps because it is so loved by practitioners, I have chosen "beloved" as the translation of *kunga* (*kun dga'*), which is in fact the short form of *kungyi gawa* (*kun gyis dga' ba*), "loved by all." Indeed, the text is concise and yet thoroughly informative; one might almost call it user-friendly. Each stage is laid out clearly, particularly the famous "feasts" or distributions of the body to the guests. By Kongtrul's time, many variations on the body-offering visualizations had developed. In this text, Kongtrul recommends a method to practice all of them by pairing up white (peaceful) and red (wrathful) visualizations and doing a few pairs at a time, thus cycling through all of them in a few evenings. (Nighttime is the recommended time for a daily practice.) These coupled sets and the rest of the commentary here have informed practitioners in their daily practice of Severance and provided the necessary references for its implementation.

Homage to the guru and Great Mother.

The practice called Object Severance Mahāmudrā presents the perspective and intention of the middle turning of the dharma wheel in conjunction with Mantra's vanquishing conduct for training in awareness. It is a radical method for cutting through the inflation of self-fixation through the willingness to accept what is undesirable, the direct subjugation of adverse circumstances, the realization that gods and demons are in your own mind, and the knowledge that you and everybody else are utterly equal.

Without such an understanding, [some people go around] repeating *hūṃ hūṃ phaṭ phaṭ* while seeing the enemy in their own deluded projections and engaging in all kinds of outrageous behavior in the hopes of defeating demons and bad spirits, or to gain fame, fortune, and food. This is known as perverted Severance (*gcod log*) and is an egregious distortion of this approach. So from the outset focus your mind in the right direction without confusion.

There are a great many systems [for the practice of Severance], as it is well known in all the Old and New [schools of Tibetan Buddhism]. However, in this Zurmang system it is considered a special legacy (*bka' babs*). {389} This means that there have been continual and extensive profound instructions that have never diminished and that the authority of realization, familiarization, assurance, and blessing has remained intact. Therefore it is especially elevated.

The cycle of visualizations for the feast activities and so forth in this tradition are elucidated elsewhere.[2] Here the daily practice of donating the body is roughly contained in a thirteen-point outline:

I. Preliminaries
    A. Arousing the awakening mind
    B. Going for refuge
    C. Gathering the accumulations
    D. Purifying the obscurations
    E. Presenting offerings
II. Main practice
    A. Transference of consciousness
    B. Body mandala
    C. Three cycles of white distributions
    D. Cycle of three red distributions together
    E. Feast activities

III. Concluding practice
   A. Dedication and aspiration
   B. Dissolution phase
   C. Integration

**I. Preliminaries**

**A. Arousing the Awakening Mind**

First, in the section for arousing the mind of awakening, you determine that you will practice Object Severance Mahāmudrā because you, by yourself, must establish in the state of the Great Mother, dharmakāya, all mother and father sentient beings that fill the reaches of space. Those beings are primarily represented by

- hateful enemies that have physical form;
- harmful obstructors that are without form;
- interfering conditions that are those who pervert your intentions;
- karmic spirits that are the four devils[3] arising due to coemergent ignorance;
- the devil of death, which robs you of life force;
- the spirits of place, which are gods and demons that live in those sites and haunted grounds [where you practice];
- the body spirits, which are the embodiments of the three poisons in equal measure that have been with you since the formation of this body from the confluence of sperm, egg, and vital winds. {390}

Thinking along those lines counts as the awakening mind and should be upheld throughout the practice from beginning to end.

**B. Going for Refuge**

First summon the guests. While striking the open end of the thighbone [on the palm of your hand] three times, say, "fear not," "be not afraid," "verily be not afraid." Then when blowing it three times, say, "listen" after the first blow, "gather here" with the second, and "gather quickly" with the third. Meditate that the sounds and words are heard from the peak of existence down to the deepest hell of incessant torment, and [the invited guests] gather densely like mists shrouding the great mountains.

On this occasion, the objects of refuge are visualized in the concise style.

The Great Mother sits upon a lion throne and lotus-moon seat in the space in front of you. She is golden with four arms; her first two hands rest in an equipoise earth-touching gesture.[4] The lower right hand holds a vajra and the left a volume of scripture. She is adorned by ornaments of saṃbhogakāya and surrounded by an entourage of all the victors and their heirs. In front of them, all sentient beings—predominantly the hateful enemies, harmful obstructors, and so forth—stand with their hands folded in respect, devotedly uttering the refuge formula with their speech, and with their minds in a state of one-pointed faith and devotion. Imagine them going for refuge, saying, "From now until I reach awakening, I place my complete trust and surrender in you. You know whatever I do." Repeat the refuge formula and so forth three times.

Continue with the aspiration prayer for virtue, offering the five branches, and taking the vows of awakening mind.[5] For the [latter], inspired by their previous promises and in the manner of learning from them, earnestly think, "The victorious ones of the past all gave rise to the heart of awakening and trained in the three kinds of ethical discipline.[6] Similarly, I too shall arouse the awakening mind and train in the trainings." {391}

### C. Visualizing the Field of Accumulation and Gathering the Accumulations

In this case, meditate on the middle-length version of the five-tiered objects of refuge. Meditate that the syllable *trāṃ* appears in the space in front and becomes a palatial jeweled [throne].[7] In its center is the lotus from *paṃ*, the sun from *ma*, and the moon from *a*. On that four-layered seat, the white syllable *hūṃ* dissolves into light and becomes Machik. Pa Dampa is on a lotus-moon seat to her right at the level of her ear. The Five Deities of Vārāhī are on a lotus-sun-corpse seat to her left at the level of her ear. Shākyamuni is above Machik's head. The buddhas are to his right, the holy dharma in back of him, and the sangha to his left. Vairochana is above his head, with the buddhas of the four families in the four directions around him. In front of them is Green Tārā and in back is Vairochana Immense Ocean.[8] This is the Zurmang tradition. In the oral tradition of the previous great omniscient lords, you meditate on the Great Mother in place of Vairochana.

They are all seated on lotus-moon seats on lion thrones, surrounded by their respective retinues of the father lineage, mother lineage, nondual lineage, and so on. The heroes and heroines are all around them, with the dharma protectors of male and female tantras in the spaces between. Below

Machik's seat are the protector guests of qualities, such as the seventy[-five] glorious lords of the pure abodes[9] and the worldly protectors; the guests of debt and liability of the obstructing type, such as the eight classes of gods and spirits, and the holders of debt and blood grudges; and the guests of compassion, the six classes of beings, such as gods and demigods. Meditate on them showing great respect in body, speech, and mind. Then meditate that light radiates from the three seed syllables in the three places of all the deities and instantly invokes the guests, who each dissolve into their [visualized forms], while you recite, "I and all sentient beings emanate as many bodies as there are atoms in the realm and pay homage . . . ." Thus offer the seven branches as usual, connecting the liturgy with the meditation.

### D. Purifying the Obscurations with a Stream of Timeless Awareness

{392} In Machik's heart is a white *hūṃ* on a lotus and moon. The string of letters of the *gate* mantra[10] is situated around it, starting from in front with the letters facing inward. Light radiates from it and strikes all those in the field of accumulation, inducing their compassionate blessings in the form of a stream, which dissolves back into the mantra string. A stream of light rays and white elixir falls from it. It fills Machik's body and pours out of her left big toe, flowing into the top of your head and that of all sentient beings. It washes away negativities, obscurations, faults, and downfalls accumulated since beginningless cyclic existence, as well as all current sickness, bad spirits, and obstacles. Think that the washing water in the form of liquid soot or coal sludge emerges from your bodies through the pores and lower orifices and dissolves into the mighty golden ground.

When pressuring a major spirit with a wrathful visualization, meditate on the lord of life and death with the head of a *makara* and gaping jaws right below you. The washing water changes into a substance with abundant color, smell, taste, ability, and power and disappears into his mouth, satisfying him. Debts are canceled and death is cheated. The mind of awakening is aroused in him and he disappears under the golden ground. This is known as the Black Poison Distribution (*ha la nag 'gyed*).

### E. Presenting Offerings

The whole extent of form appearing in the universe is appearance-emptiness; the action seal of Body (*karmamudrā*). The extent of sound resounding is sound-emptiness, the dharma seal of Speech (*dharmamudrā*). All mental thoughts and memories are awareness-emptiness, the great seal of Mind (*mahāmudrā*). All happiness and suffering are the seal of auspicious signs. That is how it has always been.

Maintain awareness of that and offer symbolically to all those in the field of accumulation by visualizing many goddesses emanating from the three places of your bright, crystal-like body—white goddesses of form carrying mirrors, red goddesses of sound carrying lutes, blue goddesses of mind carrying phenomena sources, and goddesses of indefinite colors carrying the seals of the five desirables and auspicious signs—and make the offerings. Imagine that the recipients are extremely delighted and satisfied. {393} Afterward, rest in the equipoise of the total purity of the three spheres [of agent, act, and recipient].

Dedicate your happiness and virtue to all sentient beings throughout space, and take upon yourself alone their negativities, obscurations, and sufferings. When this visualization of giving and taking (*gtong len*) is done sincerely, it becomes an excellent offering that pleases the four guests, and the supreme accumulation of merit. Through these methods, you accomplish the process of accumulation and purification that accords with the approach of the Common Vehicle.

## II. Main Practice

### A. Transference of Consciousness: Opening the Sky Door

The first part of the main practice, the transference of consciousness called Opening the Sky Door, has three parts: (1) transference with attributes and a support, for those of lesser capability; (2) transference with attributes but with no support, for those of average capability; and (3) transference without attributes or support, for those of superior capability. The first also has three versions: extensive, intermediate, and concise.

#### 1. Transference with Attributes and a Support, for Those of Lesser Capability

##### a. Extensive Version

In the center of your body is the central channel. It is white and clear and possesses four characteristics.[11] The upper end reaches the cranial aperture and the lower end reaches the perineum. Both ends are open. There is a white vital drop that was received from your father [at conception] in the sole of your right foot, and a red vital drop received from your mother in the left sole. They are the size of peas. On top of each of them is the seed syllable of the hell realms: black *du*. A yellow syllable *pre* of the hungry ghosts is at the perineum; gray *da* of the animals at the navel; green *nṛi* of humans at the heart; red *a* of the demigods at the throat; and white *oṃ*, seed syllable of the gods, is at the crown of the head. Light radiates from all the seed syllables and gathers all the karmic seeds for birth in each of the six realms that you and others have in your streams of consciousness. They dissolve into each [respective seed syllable].

Then say *phaṭ*. The white and red drops in the feet dissolve into the *du* syllables and they become two black drops. The causes and results of hell, including the places and sufferings, are all gathered up and dissolve [into the drops]. Say *phaṭ*—the two drops rise up and combine into one drop, the size of a new hen's egg, and then dissolve into the *pre* at the perineum. Then with *phaṭ* it moves to the navel; *phaṭ* to the heart; *phaṭ* to the throat; and *phaṭ* to the head. With each successive utterance of *phaṭ*, the drop flies up into [the next syllable] and the causes and results of the sufferings and places of each of those realms—animal, human, demigod, and god—are absorbed. {394} The drop becomes bigger and brighter with each ascent. Finally it becomes a vital drop with the nature of five-colored light, the size of a mature hen's egg, whereupon it ascends and dissolves into Machik's heart. Rest in equipoise.

### b. Intermediate Version

Visualize the central channel in your hollow body and the vital drops in the soles of your feet as before. When you say *phaṭ*, the two drops merge at the perineum. As the combined essence of vital drops, winds, and mind, it hovers there, ready to take off. With each utterance of *phaṭ* it flies up to the next place—the navel and so on—as before and finally dissolves into Machik's heart. Do this version for the daily practice of giving the body.

### c. Concise Version

The lower end of the central channel touches an eight-petaled lotus at the heart. In its center the essence of consciousness is a white drop with a red radiance. As you say *phaṭ* it shoots up into Machik's heart like an arrow and dissolves into it. Do this version in the subsequent distributions.

### 2. Transference with Attributes but with No Support, for Those of Average Capability

With attention to basic space and intrinsic awareness, blend them as follows: Say *phaṭ* and project consciousness into the sky. Wherever the sky pervades, awareness pervades. Wherever awareness pervades, dharmakāya pervades. Rest in great equanimity and the enlightened intention of dharmakāya, the absolute Machik. This is the regular practice, which has a continuous tradition of oral guidance.

### 3. Transference without Attributes or Support, for Those of Superior Capability

All phenomena subsumed in samsara and nirvana are none other than your own awareness, the awakening mind—forever inexpressible, unimaginable, and ineffable. It never went beyond the open expanse of the Great Mother, nor does it, nor will it ever. Those who are utterly convinced of that do not need transference or change from their perspective of emptiness-clarity endowed with essential awareness; they rest in that equipoise at all times. This great Opening the Sky Door is the sovereign of all transferences. It is the main practice of the intended meaning of the Mother. It is the ultimate sense of the doctrine of the Holy Dharma Severance of Evil Object. This resting in equipoise is concordant with the uncommon vehicle {395} and is the breakthrough into the realm of reality.

## B. Offering the Body Mandala

The practices from the offering of the body as a mandala through the branches of the conduct to enhance subsequent attainment are concordant with the vanquishing conduct to [enhance] awareness and so on found in the Mantra vehicle.

Your mind, in the form of the red letter *hrīḥ* in Machik's heart, projects out and becomes Vajravārāhī. You gesture toward your corpse with the curved knife in your right hand. The skin of the corpse is flayed whole and spread out, and the corpse is piled on top of it. The skin is the golden foundation of the ground; the blood and pus are an ocean of scented water; the fingers and toes are the iron mountain rings; the torso is Supreme Mountain; the four limbs are the four continents and islands; the head is the gods' abode; the eyes are the sun and moon; the heart is the wish-fulfilling gem; and the inner organs are the eight auspicious signs, the seven emblems of royalty, the precious treasure, the five desirable qualities, and so forth. All of this is arranged in great abundance with nothing left out, like Samantabhadra's offering cloud. In extent, it totally fills the sky. In terms of time, it lasts as long as cyclic existence. It transcends number and measure. When you offer it, meditate on all sentient beings perfecting the accumulations and purifying obscurations. Afterward, rest within the state of the total purity of the three spheres.

### C. White Distribution

Of the many types of white distribution, for this occasion do what is known as the White Feast in Three Cycles of Integration or [White Distribution for] Four Guests.[12] After you have done the appropriate extensive or concise Opening the Sky Door, proceed through to the awareness projecting outside as Vajrayoginī as before.

Then, visualize that the syllable *yaṃ* from your heart emanates in front of you and becomes wind, and *raṃ* becomes fire. In the midst of that, three human-skull hearthstones as big as three Supreme Mountains appear spontaneously. By a mere gesture to the corpse with the curved knife, the top of the skull is separated and lifted up.[13] It becomes equal to the billionfold universe and is placed on the hearthstones. The corpse is lifted up by the point of the curved knife, and with a mere gesture the flesh and bones are chopped into pieces and poured into the skull.

The syllables *khaṃ*[14] and *oṃ āḥ hūṃ* emanate from Vajravārāhī's heart and stack up above the open end of the skull. {396} Again light emanates and the wind stirs, the fire blazes, and the flesh and bones in the skull melt into elixir and boil. Elixir streams out from *khaṃ* and washes away all its flaws and defects. Light emanates from the three syllables and invokes the blessings of the Body, Speech, and Mind of the victors as awareness elixir, which absorbs [back into them]. The three letters then melt into light and dissolve [into the contents of the skull], becoming an ocean of blended white, red, and blue elixir. Various offering substances manifest from the steam and fill the realm of space. The liquid becomes an elixir of one hundred flavors and the dregs become an unimaginable wealth of whatever is needed.

A variety of offering goddesses emanated from your heart fill the space and offer all of this to the root and lineage gurus as offering clouds of pleasing delights; to the yidams of the four tantra classes as outer, inner, and secret offerings; to the heroes and ḍākinīs as the feast supplies; to the oath-bound guardians as offering substances of support and fulfillment; to the glorious protectors of the pure abodes as objects of delight; to the obstructors and creditors as desirable sense pleasures; to the ground masters of the billionfold universe as smoke offerings and rewarding substances; to the virtuous types of nāgas as nāga medicine[15] and the three white substances; to the negative nāga spirits as oceans of flesh and blood; and to the six kinds of migrators as whatever they each desire. The four kinds of guests are extremely pleased and satisfied by the gift of these offerings. It repays the debts and liabilities to the creditors, and the mind of awakening arises in their mindstreams. The sufferings of each of the six realms are quelled, and those beings develop an interest in liberation and the practice of the holy dharma. Repeat *phaṭ* [during this visualization].

### D. Red Distribution

The leftover elixir instantly becomes mountains of flesh, oceans of blood, and stacks of bones—bloody, greasy, and steaming. In essence it is undissipating elixir and in form it is like the flesh of a seven-times-born brahmin that has the power to pacify physical and mental afflictions when seen, heard, or tasted. Then blow the thighbone three times. {397} Imagine that all kinds of obstructors gather around—primarily the eight kinds of malicious spirits, such as spirits of place and body spirits—to whom you owe karmic debts of life, merit, and power. Recite, "*namo*, [gods and demons] living in this haunted place . . ." (*namo / gnas gnyan sa 'dir gnas . . .*)[16] and, as the words suggest, think that those gods and demons, experiencing each moment as an aeon, enjoy the flesh and blood. They relish it and are satisfied. Flesh debts are cleared away, debts canceled, and the trajectory of karmic ripening is interrupted.

These two—the white distribution and the red distribution—are the root of all the distributions. The pairs of white and red distributions from here on have no definite order; they can be applied however you like.[17] For instance, by rotating through them in the daily practice of the body donation, you will complete them in a few evenings.

All the versions [of white and red pairs of distributions] that follow should be added on to the previous visualizations up through the consciousness flying up and your awareness transforming into Yoginī.

### The Face Skull Cup

Once the corpse is flayed and the skin spread out, the three limbs[18] are severed and stuck on top of it. They become the three human-head hearthstones. Place the skull bowl upon them and cut up your body inside of that. Stir the contents three times with the curved knife, transforming it into pure elixir. The blessings of the buddhas and bodhisattvas of the ten directions are gathered into the elixir in the skull cup in your (Vajrayoginī's) left hand. It pours out of the cranial aperture into the skull bowl in front and melts into it. The contents become an ocean of inseparable pledge and awareness elixir. Imagine that numerous white ḍākinīs emanate from your heart carrying skull cups, scoop it up, and serve it to the four kinds of guests, pleasing them. This is the Face Skull Cup (*thod zhal ma*) [a white distribution].

### The Excellent Stakeout

Cut off the four limbs with the curved knife and stake them in the four directions. Flay the skin and impale it on them. The flesh and blood are contained within it. Imagine that ḍākinīs of four colors—white, yellow, red, and green—emanate from your heart and grasp the flayed skin by the four corners and present it to the guests. This is the Excellent Stakeout (*mchog phur ma*) [a red distribution].

### The Vase of Elixir Distribution

Your consciousness projects out from Machik's heart as the letter *ha* {398} and becomes a white ḍākinī carrying a curved knife in the right hand and a vase filled with elixir in the left. She pours the elixir from the vase into the corpse's cranial aperture, and the corpse becomes like a belly bag full of milk. With a gesture of the curved knife, it suddenly bursts open and spills on the ground, which is pure as crystal, and the ocean of elixir pervades everywhere from the peak of existence down to the deepest hell. You invoke the awareness elixir and dissolve it into the ocean of elixir. Then numerous white goddesses carrying vases emanate from your heart and serve the elixir to the four kinds of guests. Imagine that the dharma protectors are offered fresh skulls full of flesh. This is the Vase of Elixir Distribution (*bdud rtsi bum 'gyed ma*) [a white distribution].

### The Flayed Skin Distribution

Again, your awareness as Yoginī spreads the skin on the ground and piles up the flesh, blood, and bones upon it. Four worker ḍākinīs raise it up and feed it to the guests. This is the Flayed Skin (*g.yang gzhi ma*) [a red distribution].

### The Five Desirables Offering

The basis of this visualization is the Face Skull Cup. Then, variously colored worker ḍākinīs carry a variety of offering articles that include form, sound, smell, taste, and texture and offer them to the guests. This is the Five Desirables Offering (*'dod yon lnga mchod ma*) [a white distribution].

### The Food Distribution

Yoginī chops up the corpse and it becomes an ocean of flesh and blood within the vast and wide kapāla. Ḍākinīs emanate from your (yoginī's) form in numbers equal to the atoms of Supreme Mountain. They give it to the eight great malicious spirits, and so forth. Imagine the spirits satisfied—laughing in delight and singing songs of joy. This is the Food Distribution (*gzan 'gyed ma*) [a red distribution].

### Emptying the Six Realms

This is similar to the Vase Distribution, but then the offering goddesses go to the individual abodes of the six classes of beings and give them [the elixir]. It eases their specific sufferings. Light shines on them and the six realms become empty. Meditate that the hell realm transforms into the pure land of Abhirati ("Manifest Joy"); the hungry ghost realm becomes Sukhāvatī ("Blissful"); the animal realm becomes Gaṇḍavyūha ("Richly Adorned"); the human realm becomes Shrīmat ("Glorious"); the demigod realm becomes Karmaprasiddhi ("Consummate Activity"); and the god realm becomes the pure land of Akaniṣhṭa Dharmadhātu ("Unexcelled Realm of Reality"). This is Emptying the Six Realms (*rigs drug gnas stong ma*) [a white distribution].[19]

### Casting Out the Corpse

The corpse becomes huge {399}, lustrous, attractive, and alluring, with excellent color, smell, flavor, ability, and power filling the billionfold universe. Imagine that the gods and demons all gobble it up noisily with satisfied sounds of *ha*. This is Casting Out the Corpse (*bem bskyur ma*) [a red distribution].

### Assorted Distribution

Yoginī flays the skin of the corpse and spreads it out. She draws a checkered pattern on it with the curved knife. Each square contains whatever pleases the particular types of guests, such as the five meats and the five elixirs; the five desirable sense pleasures; the auspicious articles and signs; the substances of support, fulfillment, and accomplishment; the three whites and three sweets; elixir, flesh, blood, human wealth, lands, dwellings, and so forth. Imagine that each of them enjoys their particular favorites and are delighted. This is the Assorted Distribution (*khra 'gyed*) [counted as a white distribution].

### The Banners

As Jetsunma, you chop up the corpse with the curved knife. The blood collects in a huge lake and the bones are stuck in it like stakes. The flesh is raised on the tips [of the bones] like standards. A waterfall of flesh, blood, and bones falls continuously from them. Imagine that the malicious spirits and obstructors enjoy it for aeons. This is the Banners (*ba dan ma*) [a red distribution].

That completes the white distributions and red distributions presented as pairs.

### Additional Red Distributions

### The Four Continents

Vajravārāhī cuts off the corpse's limbs and throws them in the four directions. Imagine that all the spirits—primarily the scent-eaters, death lords, nāgas, and harm-doers—greedily gobble them up. This is the Four Continents (*gling bzhi ma*).

### The Corpse Distribution

The corpse turns into dry, fresh, and putrid corpses in the shapes of children, elders, youths, and so forth, as numerous as atoms. Imagine that the gods and demons partake of them according to their individual desires. This is the Corpse Distribution (*ro 'gyed ma*).

These two may be joined with any of the white distributions described above.

### The Bone Shaker

Visualize your mind as Krodhī. She grabs the corpse by the feet and swings it around, scattering little pieces of flesh, blood, and bones, {400}, which fall into the spirits' wide-open mouths in an uninterrupted flow. Imagine that they are thus satisfied. This is the Bone Shaker (*rus sprugs ma*), a slightly wrathful visualization.

### The Slapping

Krodhī grabs the corpse's two feet with her two hands and carries it up into the sky. Imagine the gods and demons below holding up their red mouths, opening and closing them. She gives them the corpse by slapping it [on their mouths].

Alternatively, the severed head of the corpse in front becomes a huge boulder of molten lead and [the remaining corpse] is slapped upon that, whereupon the red flesh and blood scatters and is consumed by the gods and demons. These visualizations are the Slapping (*rdeb pa ma*). They are intense wrathful visualizations customarily done during the Ninefold Spirit Feast.[20] In between the visualizations, pray to the lineage gurus with intense devotion from the bottom of your heart. Make the aspiration to stop self-fixation and hopes and fears. Rest for a while without thought in the purity of the three spheres.

### E. The Communal Feast Offering of the Bodies of Self and Others

First perform the three cycles of blending: the blending of your own and others' awareness, the blending of awareness and the realm of phenomena, and the blending of your own and others' corpses in the feast. The container is the *padma bhañja* (lotus skull cup): white outside, the nature of the moon, and red inside, the nature of the sun. In its center, the essence of the corpses is the feast substance. In appearance, it is a vertical golden vajra marked with *āḥ* at the hub, *oṃ* on the upper tip, and *hūṃ* on the lower end. Above it is the lid of the moon and below it the seat of the sun.

Light radiates from the *oṃ* in your forehead and strikes the *oṃ* in Machik's forehead. Light then radiates from that and gathers all the Body blessings of the buddhas and bodhisattvas in all directions and times in the form of white light rays, which dissolve into Machik's forehead and immediately emanate as white light rays from the *oṃ* and strike the *oṃ* of the marked vajra. The moon lid along with the upper part of the vajra and the *oṃ* dissolve into light, filling the kapāla with white elixir. Follow the same pattern {401} with the red *āḥ* and the gathering of the Speech blessings, which dissolves the middle part of the vajra and fills the skull with red elixir, and the dark blue *hūṃ* and the gathering of the Mind blessings, which dissolves the lower part of the vajra and fills the skull with blue elixir. The white, red, and blue mixture of elixir becomes an abundance of excellent color, scent, taste, ability, and power. In essence it is the elixir of timeless awareness and in appearance it becomes immeasurable, inexhaustible outer, inner, and secret feast offerings.

Unimaginably numerous offering goddesses emanate from your (Vajrayoginī's) heart and offer it to all who are included in the four kinds of guests, from the gracious root and lineage gurus down to the sentient beings of the six realms. It is offered as an outer feast of all the glory and wealth there is in all existence that belongs to no one. It is offered as an inner feast of personal possessions such as life force, merit, good fortune, and dominion. It is offered as a secret feast of the pleasure of male and female union. And it is offered as a suchness feast of mahāmudrā's lucid clarity without referencing the three spheres. Meditate that the guests are extremely pleased by this exquisite offering and they each grant their particular spiritual powers.

You may perform the Ninefold Spirit Feast for the occasion of a particular malicious spirit or sick person and so forth. Certainly there are some traditions of the daily practice in which this is done. However, since this is merely a particularly wrathful visualization of the red distribution, it does not warrant separate mention in the outline. There are a variety of special visualization procedures that can be found in the major manuals.

The Leftovers is a branch of the communal feast activities. All the leftovers from the offering and giving of the body in this way become mountains of flesh, lakes of blood, and banks of bones inside a kapāla that extends throughout the three existences. A skeleton ḍākinī emanates from you and distributes it to the powerful mover ḍākinīs who partake of leftovers, the eight classes of gods and spirits who have power to take [only] leftovers, those who did not come before and just arrived, and {402} the humble and meek ones who have dominion over nothing but leftovers. Meditate that they are satisfied and rejoice, promising to accomplish activities for you.

### III. Concluding Practices

### A. Dedication and Aspiration

Following the example of the dedications by the previous victors and their heirs, dedicate all the virtue that you and others have accumulated in the three times, and especially the virtuous roots of making this donation of your body on this occasion, in order that all sentient beings realize the intention of the unborn Mother once they have totally severed the inflation of self-fixation.

### B. Dissolution Phase

The entire field of refuge gradually dissolves into light, clockwise and downward, melting into Machik.[21] Machik's form becomes a thumb-sized figure radiating five-colored lights. She enters through your cranial aperture and descends, coming to rest in vajra posture in the center of the eight-petaled lotus in your heart. Imagine that the petals of the heart lotus close around her. However, there is also a customary practice when doing the daily body donation of meditating that Machik becomes [an orb of] light the size of a duck's egg and melts into the top of your head.

### C. Integration

Visualize that you instantly become four-armed Avalokiteshvara, Tamer of Beings. The gods, demons, and six classes of beings make prostrations, circumambulate, and pay homage to you. Light rays emanate from your heart and turn all males into Avalokiteshvara and all females into Venerable Tārā. Meditate on them reciting the six syllables with a great humming sound. After you repeat the six syllables, meditate that all the guests joyfully return whence they came. Then maintain the view and intention of the uncontrived, native state of mahāmudrā.

## [Clarification][22]

This is a very rough presentation of the preliminaries, main part, and concluding practices just in the context of the body donation. In terms of the general Holy Dharma Severance of Evil Object, in the preliminaries one would develop definite resolution, the heart pangs of impermanence, {403} the utter certitude in infallible karmic cause and effect, and a sense of urgency and focused attention. Then one goes for refuge, develops the awakening mind, purifies obscurations, accumulates merit, and cultivates guru yoga. Once those general practices are done, the main practice is the introduction to the meaning of the Mother and severing the four devils in basic space. The concluding practice is to integrate vanquishing conduct into one's life through peaceful severance, wrathful severance, and half-peaceful, half-wrathful severance in order to maintain the experience.

Therefore, in short, with regard to the two practices of the body donation and the feast activities, there are extensive explicit instructions on the preliminaries and concluding practices, while the main practice must be realized in an implicit manner.[23] Nevertheless, nowadays it appears that those known as Severance practitioners for the most part do not stick to the root but only chase after the branches.

## Introducing the Meaning of the Mother

First, you need to turn your muddled concepts into bright clarity by implementing the instructions on focusing the mind. With your body in the sevenfold posture of Vairochana, speech in the natural state of breathing, and mind divested of past, present, and future thoughts, rest in wonder (*hed de*) directly upon ever-fresh consciousness. If you cannot remain within that, focus your attention in front of you on a golden vajra the size of a barley grain; the essence of the Mother. When that also cannot hold your attention, focus your mind on the figure of Shākyamuni. Adjust [your meditation] if dullness or agitation occurs so that faultless meditative stability is born in your being.

Then, with inward-facing consciousness, look at the essence of the one that abides and the one that moves. In essence, these three—external appearances, the movement of discursive thought, and the one who cognizes them—do not exist separately. Since nothing can be identified, anything at all may arise. The unimpeded experience of clarity-emptiness is beyond description and expression. Free of all conceptual elaboration, it is the very characteristic of space—the perfection of wisdom. Since it is the enlightened perspective of the victors of the three times, do not ever leave this meditative absorption.

### Severing the Four Devils in Basic Space

Insofar as external things, such as form and so forth, provide support [for perception], they are tangible. {404} When thoughts of attachment or aversion arise toward them, it is a devil. When you fall under its power, it is an obstacle. Therefore, whenever those thoughts of attachment or aversion, or acceptance or rejection, arise, in that very instant utter *phaṭ* and convey them to basic space. That is the severance of the tangible devil. When you progress in the meditation without falling under the power of that thought, the evidence of success (*tshar tshad*) and degree of uprising (*lhongs tshad*) will be sufficient. This applies to other devils as well: when your mind is not under your control, the five toxic emotions, happiness, sadness, fear, and terror will arise. This is the intangible devil. Fixating on your own excellence, pride, or exuberance over the signs [of successful meditation] on the path and so forth is the devil of exaltation. The clinging of self-fixation is itself the devil of inflation.

Therefore, without letting the sentinel of mindful knowing deteriorate or knowing awareness leave its post, convey all that arises to basic space with *phaṭ*. If you can utterly sever the ties of inflated thoughts and self-fixation, you will become the most sublime and superior practitioner of Severance.

### [Enhancement]

For the sake of enhancing such a view and meditation, there are concluding activities such as the white distributions of peaceful severance, the red distributions of wrathful severance, and the assorted distributions of half-peaceful, half-wrathful severance. Those are what is known as elaborate severance. Alternating meditation on love and compassion with the blending of awareness and basic space is unelaborate severance. To rest in equipoise in the meaning of the Mother alone is highly unelaborate severance. When you put all three of those into practice, it will be complete from beginning to end.

In raising the spirits, if you become attached to visions of gods and demons or frightening dreams, you will not feel secret arisings in the mind. You must cut through [that fixation] by holding your seat in the haunted retreats. There is much that is not severed. Therefore, it is crucial to remain physically unmoving, verbally silent, and mentally unyielding to whatever perceptions occur by conveying them to basic space with *phaṭ*.

Even though you understand that you must sever the three poisons and other negative thoughts in basic space {405}, when you are bound by the knots of fixation on the goodness of your good thoughts, gods will deteriorate into devils. This is very common. So if you also practice devotion, compassion, creation phase with characteristics, completion phase, and so forth, while conveying them into basic space with *phaṭ*, your practice of virtue will increase and you will get very close to the supreme spiritual power. In short, the basis of Severance is to be without hope and fear.

Since discursive thought is conditioned,
we are bound by the bonds of four devils;
the Mother's meaning, severing in basic space,
and unifying view and conduct are supreme.

When the manifestation of virtue thus obtained
conquers the whole web of discursive thought,
may we quickly attain the state of the Mother,
unborn and free of inflation.

Merely in order not to disobey the command of Jampal Khyentse,[24] who is the embodiment of the perfection of wisdom, Yönten Gyatso wrote this at the seat of Palpung. May virtue and goodness increase.

# 29. Essence of Auspicious Renown

## *A Ritual of Offering and Supplication to All the Gurus of the Holy Dharmas of Pacification and Object Severance Together*[1]

Jamgön Kongtrul

Styled as an offering and supplication to all the gurus of both Severance and Pacification, this text provides a great example of how such a liturgy can be so much more. Here is Jamgön Kongtrul at his creative best, with nearly all the prayers being original compositions. Within the refrains of supplication and service, not only are all the relevant lineage gurus worshipped, but the various practices are as well, if one knows where to look. The text could serve as a communal ritual or "guru pūja" covering all the bases, and would be both inspirational and informative.

The text was placed at the end of the previous volume on Pacification (*zhi byed*) in the Palpung blocks, but it was appropriately moved in the Shechen printing to the end of this volume on Severance. In Jamgön Kongtrul's scheme of the Eight Great Chariots of the practice lineages that entered Tibet from India—the organizational framework for this *Treasury of Precious Instructions*—Pacification is listed as the sixth, with Severance considered a subsidiary of that. Both lineages connect back to the Indian saint Pa Dampa Sangye. This liturgical ritual is the grand finale covering all the gurus and practices of both Pacification and Severance.

*namo guru sarva buddha ḍākiniyai*
Lord Dampa Sangye, who saw the meaning of the unborn,
Machik Lapdrön, who severed the inflation of self-fixation,

manifesting as the forms of spiritual mentors for migrators—
until awakening, I offer to you as my crowning jewel.

I faithfully set forth this method of offering and supplication
to the adepts of the Pacification and Severance lineages
in order to simultaneously accomplish
the accumulations of both merit and timeless awareness.

A practitioner with excellent devotion and virtue who wishes to take up this practice [should do the following:] Choose a special time, such as the great holy date of Dampa Sangye's union with the realm of dharmakāya: the fourteenth day of the middle winter month. Clean your dwelling place and decorate it with ornaments such as canopies, banners, and parasols. In the shrine alcove, arrange whatever painted or relief images you have of the Jewels in general and the gurus of the Pacification and Severance lineages, such as Dampa and Machik, in particular. Cover the shrine stand with fine fabric, and in the center of it place a precious mandala anointed with saffron water and an eight-petaled lotus made of colored powders. Behind that, place a drawing of a sixteen-petaled lotus and array it with heaps of flowers—two in the center and one on each of the petals. If you cannot produce a drawing of the lotus, it is sufficient to put just the heaps directly on a table. In the front, place a round offering torma with all sorts of edibles. All around this arrange the offerings of twofold waters: one hundred or more if possible, or if not, then a single line [of seven bowls]. Set out any other offering items that you may have collected, such as images, deity cards (*tsakli*), and so forth. Assemble the offering mandala and necessary pledge substances of the feast. {427}

The actual ritual has three sections: preliminaries, main practice, and conclusion.

## I. Preliminaries

### Going for Refuge

> With the desire to liberate all beings,
> I constantly go for refuge
> in the Buddha, dharma, and sangha
> until reaching the heart of awakening.
> (Repeat three times.)

## Arousing the Thought of Awakening

With wisdom, love, and kindness,
I take my place before the buddhas
and vow to attain perfect buddhahood
diligently for the sake of beings.
(Repeat three times.)

I pay homage to the Three Jewels.
I take refuge in the Three Jewels.
I make offerings to the Three Jewels.
I confess each negativity and nonvirtue.
I rejoice in the virtue of all beings.
I keep the buddhas and bodhisattvas in mind.
I take refuge until awakening
in the Buddha, dharma, and supreme assembly.
I arouse the mind of awakening
in order to fully accomplish my own and others' welfare.
Once the mind of supreme awakening is aroused,
I invite all sentient beings to be my guests.
I will engage in the good, pleasing conduct of bodhisattvas
and attain buddhahood for the benefit of beings.

Just as the lords of the three times
gave rise to the supreme mind of awakening
that definitely causes genuine awakening,
I too will give rise to that holy thought.
I will recall all that is generated
and expand on what I recall. {428}

## Meditation on the Four Immeasurables

May all beings have happiness and [the causes of happiness.
May they be free from suffering and the causes of suffering.
May they never be separated from joy that is without suffering.
May they rest in great equanimity, free from attachment and
aversion to those close or distant.]

*oṃ hrīḥ ha ha hūṃ hūṃ phaṭ*
In an instant I become the form of Chakrasaṃvara in union.

### Consecration of the Offering Substances

Cleanse with:

*oṃ vajra amṛita [kuṇḍalī hana hana hūṃ phaṭ]*

Purify with:

*oṃ svabhāva [śuddhāḥ sarva dharmāḥ svabhāva śuddho 'haṃ]*

From within emptiness, the abode appears as the vast and spacious palace. Inside, arising from *oṃ*, are splendid vessels of jewels and *padma bhañja* and so forth. Offering articles come from *āḥ*. Their nature is bliss-emptiness, their form is offering substance, and their function is to satisfy through undissipating bliss. *Hūṃ* increases [the offerings] to pervade space, expanding them to completely fill all outer and inner space.

Consecrate with:

*oṃ vajra arghaṃ aḥ hūṃ (similarly:) . . . pādyaṃ . . . puṣpe . . . dhūpe . . . āloke . . . gandhe . . . naivedye . . . śabta āḥ hūṃ*

*oṃ vajra spharaṇa khaṃ*

### II. Main Practice
### Visualization of the Accumulation Supports

*oṃ svabhāva śuddhāḥ sarva dharmāḥ svabhāva śuddho 'haṃ*

All phenomena are without reference. Out of that, all directions of the earth arise as an amazing, pure buddha field, attractively arrayed with unimaginable decorations. In the center of it is a vast and wide palace of great liberation, completely perfect with all the characteristics. Within that there is a variegated eight-petaled lotus with innumerable petals around the outer rim. On the fully blossomed stamen in the center is the lion throne of fearlessness, the lotus seat of nonattachment, the sun seat of compassion, and the *kṛishṇasara* antelope skin of awakening mind. Upon that sits the great sage, Venerable Indian Dampa, the color of smoke. His eyes are red and his hair is in dreadlocks. His right hand bestows refuge and his left holds an auspicious *parbu*[2] at his heart. His upper body is naked with his chest extended, and his lower body is covered with a white wool skirt. The six bone ornaments adorn him. He makes the gaze of suppressing samsara and nirvana with splendor. He has the illusion-like body that manifests an unimpeded display of the three kāyas for whoever is to be tamed.

There are four fully blossomed lotus seats above the crown of his head. In the east [or front] are the eleven gurus of mahāmudrā symbol, such as Saraha and so forth.[3] To the right are the eleven gurus of the moving winds of the father tantras, such as Buddhaguhya.[4] To the left are the eleven gurus of blissful experience of the mother tantras, such as Saroruhavajra.[5] {429} In back are the eleven gurus of dialectics, philology, and logic, such as Nāgārjunagarbha.[6] In between are the ten gurus who introduce one's own intrinsic awareness, such as the ḍākinī Sukhasiddhī.[7] Above all of them are the thirty-six glorious gurus of the wonderful celestial realm.[8] Above them are the twenty-four gurus of ḍākinī blessings who move above, on, and below the ground.[9] Above them are the gurus of the twelve sugatas of [Dampa's] spiritual practice.[10] Above them are the gurus of the four buddha kāyas: dharmakāya Vajradhara in the east; saṃbhogakāya Vairochana in the south; nirmāṇakāya Shākyamuni in the west; and svabhāvakāya Vajrapāṇi in the north.

To the left of Dampa Sangye, on a lotus-and-moon seat, is Machik Lapkyi Drönma. She is as white as a polished conch shell, with one face and two arms. She rattles a golden ḍamaru at the sky with her right hand and holds a silver-white bell at her hip with the left. Her three eyes gaze into space. Her hair is tied up in a bun on her head, with some of it loose down her back. Bone and jewel ornaments adorn her naked body. She stands with her right leg drawn in and left one straight in a dance pose.

On the eight petals of the lotus are Dampa Charchen in the

east; Vajrakrodha in the south; Dampa Charchung in the west; Bodhisattva Kunga in the north;[11] Kashmiri Jñānaguhya in the southeast;[12] Ma Chökyi Sherap as a monk in the southwest; So Gendun Bar in the northwest; and Kam Yeshe Gyaltsen as a monk in the northeast.[13] All the others are in the style of yogins and make various mudras such as that of equipoise.

The lineage gurus on the outer lotus petals are principally Patsap Gompa, Gyalwa Tenne, Rok Sherap Ö, Zhikpo Nyima Senge, and Nyedo Mawai Senge.[14] Thus, the lineage gurus of the three spiritual legacies of Pacification—early, middle, and later—[are all represented]. Also the gurus of the adept lineage of Object Severance are all around, principally the sixteen great children of the transmissions, such as [Machik's] son Gyalwa Döndrup, Tönyön Samdrup, Khugom Chöseng, and so forth. {430}

In addition, all directions and in-between places are filled with hosts of yidam deities, buddhas, bodhisattvas, heroes and ḍākinīs, and an ocean of oath-bound dharma protectors, such as the glorious lord of awareness Aghora. They are as thick as clouds. Light radiates from the three syllables that mark their three places. Splendid throngs of root and lineage gurus, buddhas, bodhisattvas, yidams, ḍākinīs, and dharma protectors and guards arrive directly in front.

*vajra sa mā jaḥ*

Ho! Though you never leave the natural realm of phenomena,
the illusory dynamic play of your unimpeded compassion
manifests the loving intent of compassion for your devoted children.
Please come, be a field of merit for the faithful.

From Tuṣhita above, the meeting place of the hundred gods,
Reverend Sangye Dampa, the Indian,
assembly of male and female adepts of the Pacification lineage,
please come, looking with your vajra gazes.

From the mystic city of blissful Kechara,
Great Mother Perfection of Wisdom, Lapkyi Drön,

assembly of female and male adepts of the Object Severance lineage,
please come, dancing with your vajra songs.

Though everything is one flavor to the dharmakāya guru,
you show up for those to be tamed in various forms of display.
Buddhas with your heirs, hosts of ḍākinīs and dharma protectors,
please come, displaying your many apparitions.

*oṃ guru kamalaśīla deva ḍākinī saparivāra e hye hi*
*samaya hoḥ samaya stvaṃ jaḥ hūṃ baṃ hoḥ*

Within dharmakāya, going or staying has no reference point.
For the sake of clearing the obscuration of migrators' dualistic thinking
and increasing the great accumulations of merit and awareness,
please steadfastly stay here as an object for offerings.

*jñāna samaya tiṣṭha vajra*
The awareness beings dwell inseparable from the pledge beings.

## Homage

*namo*
Homage to all gurus of the four kāyas,
supreme heads of all families,
who display the svabhāvakāya,
dharmakāya, saṃbhogakāya, and nirmāṇakāya.

Homage to all gurus,
the twelve sugatas of spiritual practice:
three family lords, Mother Tārā,
Yamāntaka, Nīviraṇaviṣhkambhin, and so on. {431}

Homage to the twenty-four
blessed ḍākinī gurus,
ḍākinīs of Body, Speech, and Mind,
acting below the ground, on the ground, and above.

Homage to the thirty-six:
six kings, queens, and seers,
six brahmins, householders, and captains,
sublime gurus enjoying wonderful celestial realms.

Homage to the group of fifty-four[15]
popular male and female adepts
who introduced intrinsic awareness,
mahāmudrā, father and mother tantras, and sutra dialectics.[16]

Homage to the Great Mother Perfection of Wisdom,
to Shākyamuni, to Lion of Speech,
Venerable Tārā, Ḍāki Sukhasiddhī,
and Āryadeva [the Brahmin].

Homage to the mighty yogin
Mipam Gön, master of the tenth level,
Dampa Sangye, lord of migrators,
who turned the dharma wheel in three transmissions.

Homage to Lapkyi Drönma,
nonhuman ḍākinī of timeless awareness,
who fully integrated Sutra and Tantra,
beings' protector who realized the genuine meaning.

Homage to the four yogins:
Dampa Charchen and Charchung,
Vajrakrodha and Bodhisattva Kunga,
auspiciously connected with the four directions.

Homage to the gurus of the first lineage:
the Kashmiri [Jñānaguhya],
translator Puhrang the younger,
Martön Chögyal, Yolmo Shen, Chupa, and all.

Homage to the lineage of the Ma tradition:
Chökyi Sherap, Gangwar Shen,

Shubu Lotsā, Lama Sheu,
Sokpo Dode, and Zhang Gaden.

Homage to the lineage of the So tradition:
Sochung, Shami, Dartsönpa,
Sangye Gompa, Yeshe Zhön,
sublime being Samten Palwa, and all.

Homage to Malgyi Kawachenpa,
Gyergom Chenpo, Sangye Wön,
Rinchen Bum, Riwache,
and Gyaltsen Palzang.

Homage to the lineage of the Kam tradition:
Yeshe Gyaltsen, Drakmarwa,
Indian Jose, Lharipa, and
the two upper lineages and two lower lineages.

Homage to the later lineage:
Patsap, Gyalwa, Tennepa,
omniscient emanations of the three families,
the [three] bodhisattva brothers, and so forth.

Homage to the Jangpa [lineage]:
Mara Serpo of Yarlung,
Trotsang, Druk Lhaling Khawa,
Drapa Ngönshe, Che father and son.

Homage to disciples of Dampa, the Lord of Beings: {432}
the specially elevated one hundred eight great heirs,
holders of the twenty-six seats of Trulshik,
the thirteen disciples, and so forth.

Homage to the lineage of Object Severance:
followers of Lapdrön, Perfection of Wisdom,
mighty adepts who sever in basic space
all inflation of dualistic clinging.

Homage to the sixteen great heirs of the transmission legacy:
the excellent son Gyalwa Döndrup and so on,
the four heart sons and four heart daughters,
along with the eight who were equal to herself.

Homage to the lineage of disciples, male and female adepts
of Object Severance such as the one hundred eight,
and to the lineage holders of Sutra
whose activity pervaded Tibet and Kham.

Homage to the lineage holders of Mantra:
the incomparable Tönyön Samdrup,
the twenty-one daughters, spiritual adepts,
the eighteen, and so forth, called Gangpa.

Homage to the lineage holders of the union [of Sutra and Mantra]:
Khugom Chökyi Senge,
Sangye Tönpa, Zhönnu Drup,
and omniscient Rangjung Dorje.

Homage to all those who uphold
the special lineages of precept and treasure:
Lacham, Samten Özer,
Tsöndru Senge, and Dorje Drön.

Homage to the yidams, deities of the four tantras,
buddhas and bodhisattvas of the ten directions,
heroes and ḍākinīs of the three places,
and the dharma protectors and guards.

For an abbreviated homage it is sufficient to end here.

Homage to the glorious guru,
the one who grants all qualities,
whose mere name recalled
soothes the agitation of my mind.

Homage at the feet of the guru
with fully developed immaculate qualities,
the crown jewel of all migrators,
precious source of needs and desires.

Homage at the feet of the guru,
who clears up the darkness of unknowing
with the light of realizing what to accept or reject,
the supreme mandala of the stainless sun.

Homage at the feet of the guru,
who grows the grove of benefit and happiness
with the cool rays of merit and awareness,
the supreme mandala of the pure moon.

Homage at the feet of the guru,
who cures the suffering of afflictions
with the supreme medicine of holy dharma's elixir,
the supreme skilled physician of migrators.

Homage at the feet of the guru, {433}
who transports to the far shore of the ocean of existence and peace
on the great ship of methods and wisdom,
the supreme and powerful guide of migrators.

Homage at the feet of the guru,
who affords refuge from all harm
and accomplishes immeasurable benefit,
loving protector, the only friend of migrators.

I pay homage with excellent faith
to all who are worthy of prostration
and bow down to all of you
with as many bodies as atoms in the realm.

## Presentation of Offerings
## Accumulation of Merit by Means of the Mandala

Perform it according to the general prose formula of the continued practice of this tradition, which is that of the Seven Heaps (*tshom bu bdun ma*) arrangement.

> Precious Supreme Mountain adorned by golden seas of
>   enjoyment,
> the eastern island of Majestic Body, beautified by fine vases,
> the island of Unpleasant Sound with the wish-granting tree,
> Bountiful Cow adorned by all one's desires,
> Land of Jambu, well adorned by wish-fulfilling gems,
> circled by the pair of illuminators—the sun and moon—
> with the seven precious items and so forth in all the spaces,
> filled with the offering substances of gods, nāgas, and humans.
> I offer this to the gurus, Three Jewels, yidam deities,
> and hosts of ḍākinīs and dharma protectors.
> Please accept it with compassion for the sake of migrators.
>
> *oṃ namo guru deva ḍākinī dharmapāla ratna maṇḍala pūjā*
> *megha samudra spharaṇa samaye hūṃ.*

Offer as many times as you can.

## Accumulation of Merit by Means of Offering Your Own Body

> A yellow letter *trāṃ* on my head
> dissolves into light and melts into my body,
> which becomes a precious corpse, a wish-fulfilling gem.
> Glorious guru and all your retinue,
> I offer a variety of whatever pleases you
> as an inexhaustible sky treasure to enjoy.
> Please accept it with great loving-kindness.
>
> *oṃ namo guru trāṃ ratna maṇḍala pūjā megha samudra*
> *spharaṇa samaye hūṃ* (three times)

### Accumulation of Merit by Various Means

If you want the extensive version, imagine that innumerable offering goddesses emerge from the tips of the light rays from the seed syllable in your heart and produce clouds of various offering substances.

The whole billionfold universe of pure realms
is entirely filled with the eightfold elixir of sense offerings.
I graciously offer this to the excellent guru {434}
so all beings will master the ocean of meditative stability.

*oṃ ratna guru kamalaśīla ḍākinī saparivāra vajra arghaṃ
pratīccha hūṃ svāhā*

I offer a grove of thousand-petaled fully bloomed lotuses,
bright and resplendent as a rainbow,
filling the whole ground and the sky,
so all beings will master supreme diligence.

*oṃ ratna guru kamalaśīla ḍākinī saparivāra vajra puṣpe
pratīccha hūṃ svāhā*

I offer a pile of incense powder equal to Supreme Mountain
and appealing, fragrant clouds of incense
infusing a million miles with sublime perfume
so all beings will preserve pure morality.

*oṃ ratna guru kamalaśīla ḍākinī saparivāra vajra dhūpe
pratīccha hūṃ svāhā*

I offer light shining from gems not obscured by anything,
the total luminaries of day and night, and the supreme oil lamp,
light that illuminates the far reaches of the world,
so all beings will blaze with the light of wisdom.

*oṃ ratna guru kamalaśīla ḍākinī saparivāra vajra āloke pratīccha
hūṃ svāhā*

I offer perfumed water soothing the burns of cyclic existence,
alleviating the thick dullness of ignorance,
generating great bliss of definite goodness in the higher realms,
so all beings are endowed with the armor of patience.

*oṃ ratna guru kamalaśīla ḍākinī saparivāra vajra gandhe pratīccha hūṃ svāhā*

I offer to the lord guru the qualities of the hundred flavors of divine food,
sublime fare that opens a hundred doors of absorption,
completely filling the billionfold universe,
so all beings enjoy the glory of generosity.

*oṃ ratna guru kamalaśīla ḍākinī saparivāra vajra naivedye pratīccha hūṃ svāhā*

I offer sounds resonating from the animate and inanimate world,
rousing the sleep of stupidity and the fear of hordes of wrong view,
a symphony that spreads the words of dharma throughout the world,
so all beings may attain the melody of dharma.

*oṃ ratna guru kamalaśīla ḍākinī saparivāra vajra śabda pratīccha hūṃ svāhā*

## The Inner Offering

Whatever forms appear in the world,
whether labeled beautiful or not, are mind's deception.
I offer the emptiness of whatever appears
so the stupidity of all beings is liberated as Vairochana's Body.

*oṃ ratna guru kamalaśīla ḍākinī saparivāra vajra rūpa pratīccha hūṃ svāhā*

Whatever sounds are heard resounding,
whether grasped as pleasant or unpleasant, are mere categories.
I offer all as self-liberated sound-emptiness
so the anger of all beings is liberated as Akṣhobhya's Body.

*oṃ ratna guru kamalaśīla ḍākinī saparivāra vajra śabda pratīccha hūṃ svāhā*

Whatever odors are grasped as good or bad feelings
are all designations of discursive thought.
I offer the emptiness of feeling that is uncorrupted by intellect
so the pride of all beings is liberated as Ratnasambhava's Body.

*oṃ ratna guru kamalaśīla ḍākinī saparivāra vajra gandhe pratīccha hūṃ svāhā*

Sweet, delicious flavors fashioned from beginningless habits—
rejecting or accepting any of them is the wheel of delusion. {435}
I offer the equal flavor of taste-emptiness, interrupting its turning,
so that the desire of all beings is liberated as Amitābha's Body.

*oṃ ratna guru kamalaśīla ḍākinī saparivāra vajra rasa pratīccha hūṃ svāhā*

All denial or indulgence of good or bad touch sensations
is the reification of not knowing that whatever arises is illusion.
I offer the breakthrough to the expanse of phenomena's nature
so that the jealousy of all beings is liberated as Amoghasiddhi's Body.

*oṃ ratna guru kamalaśīla ḍākinī saparivāra vajra sparśe pratīccha hūṃ svāhā*

### The Secret Offering

Whoever realizes that the fundamental root of cyclic existence
is in fact the characteristic of the production of all afflictive emotion
resulting from causes and conditions of attachment and aversion
offers the sixteen pleasures of coemergence as the best of all.

The union of method and wisdom is supreme, changeless bliss.
Gurus who have mastered undissipating absorption,
enjoy this offering, a grand celebration of bliss-emptiness awareness,
and pacify the sufferings of sentient beings.

### The Absolute Offering of Suchness

The nature of all phenomena is uncontrived,
without beginning, end, or middle, not bound by the name
"samsara" or "nirvana," free of change, increase, or decrease.
This is the greatest offering among all offerings.

The object of offering is the primordial guru, dharmakāya.
The offerer is the yogin of reflexive awareness and clarity.
The offering substances are the magical illusion of self-manifestation.
The whole is the primordially genuine offering.
*sarva dharmāḥ mahāśūnyatā pūjā hoḥ*

If that much is not enough, or to offer a condensed version of everything:

I present to the guru and host of ḍākinīs
drinking water, ablution water, incense,
flowers, butter lamps, perfumed water,
food, and music offerings.

I present to the guru and host of ḍākinīs
the qualities of the five senses:
form, sound, smell, taste,
and also texture offerings.

I present to the guru and host of ḍākinīs
the seven royal treasures:
wheels, gems, queens, ministers,
elephants, and fine horses.

I present to the guru and host of ḍākinīs
the eight outer and inner goddesses:
goddesses of charm, garlands, song, dance,
incense, flowers, lamps, and perfume.

### The Offerings of the Mudras of Body, Speech, Mind, Qualities, and Activities

I offer all form that appears
in all the worlds of the billionfold universe
as the mudra of sublime Body.
Grant the spiritual power of immutable Body.

I offer all the sounds resounding
in all the worlds of the billionfold universe
as the mudra of sublime Speech.
Grant the spiritual power of unimpeded Speech. {436}

I offer all the memories and thoughts in the minds
in all the worlds of the billionfold universe
as the mudra of sublime Mind.
Grant the spiritual power of undeluded Mind.

I offer all the happiness and suffering
in all the worlds of the billionfold universe
as the mudra of auspiciousness.
[Grant the spiritual powers, both common and supreme.][17]

When happy, I dedicate it to collective happiness;
may great happiness pervade all space.
When suffering, I carry the suffering myself;
may the ocean of cyclic suffering dry up
and all beings of the three realms be happy.

## Remaining Branches of Confession, [Rejoicing, Supplicating, Requesting, and Dedicating]

The general confession is to repeat the Guru Vajrasattva [mantra] three times, then:

I confess with shame, regret, and a promise [not to repeat]
all negative actions accruing naturally through the three doors
that I have committed, requested, or celebrated
under the influence of afflictive emotions since beginningless
time.

I rejoice with an utterly joyful mind
in the life stories of sublime beings and their heirs,
as well as in the virtue accumulated by all beings
that they have done, will do, or are doing now.

I supplicate the sovereigns of the dharma and their heirs
to continuously turn the wheel of the dharma,
whether profound or vast, for whoever is to be tamed,
in order to benefit all migrators and inspire virtue.

I request you to remain here a long time,
out of love for helpless beings of the degenerate times,
not passing into nirvana nor leaving for the sake of other
nirmāṇakāya realms,
although the dharmakāya is without birth or destruction.

For the sake of all beings attaining unsurpassable awakening,
I forever go for refuge in you, the supreme refuge.
From this day forward I will assume and properly maintain
all the common and special sacred pledges and vows.

By the power of my virtue accumulated in the three times,
may all beings be released from the bonds of existence,
be cared for by the glorious, supreme guru,
and quickly attain the spiritual power of supreme omniscience.

## Reliance on the Path

I pay homage and go for refuge to all the holy gurus.
Please bless me to quickly attain genuine, complete
enlightenment.
Until I awaken, please bless me with the generation
of unimaginable respect and devotion for the holy gurus.

I pay homage and go for refuge to all the hosts of yidam deities.
Please bless me to quickly attain genuine, complete
enlightenment. {437}
Until I awaken, please bless me with the generation
of unimaginable respect and devotion for the yidam deities.

I pay homage and go for refuge to all the hosts of ḍākinīs.
Please bless me to quickly attain genuine, complete
enlightenment.
Until I awaken, please bless me with the generation
of unimaginable respect and devotion for the hosts of ḍākinīs.

Gurus, yidams, and ḍākinīs, please consider me. I offer to the guru all the roots of virtue gathered together from the past, the present, and the future. By having offered this to the guru, may the special intentions of all the precious gurus be completely realized. And may the virtuous roots that come from that produce various offerings equaling space, offered before the eyes of the sugatas. And may the virtuous roots that come from that be dedicated to all sentient beings in common. With that kind of dedication, may all sentient beings be liberated from the ocean of suffering that is cyclic existence and quickly attain unsurpassable, genuine, complete, precious enlightenment. Until they attain that, may I quickly attain manifest, complete buddhahood and become the guru of all beings without exception. May just that be accomplished.

Thus, the excellent going for refuge, supreme arousal of the mind of awakening, making of amazing offerings, dedicating to ensure the benefit to others, and aspirations that are not disconnected from sentient beings—these five, if taken as your spiritual practice, will give rise to all meditative experience and realization on the five spiritual paths, according to the teachings of Lord Dampa Rinpoche.

### Supplications

Place your palms together and repeat with intense feeling:

> I supplicate the guru, buddha dharmakāya;
> bless me to quickly realize suchness.
> I supplicate the guru saṃbhogakāya;
> bless me that all appearances arise as the pure universe.
> I supplicate the guru, buddha nirmāṇakāya;
> bless me to accomplish immense altruism.

Do that as much as you can, and:

> I supplicate Kamalashīla,
> who realized the literal meaning of *āli kāli*
> through the blessing of Mañjushrī, Lion of Speech,
> such that the intentions of all Sutra and Tantra arose in his mind
> and every instruction lineage became his domain.

Dampa himself gave this to Sochung, so repeat it many times. {438} You may also recite the supplication of the three transmissions of Pacification with the places included.[18]

> Mother, heart child emanated from Great Mother's heart,
> One Mother Machik, Jomo Naljorma,
> adept of the perfection precepts,
> liberator of the mindstreams of fortunate ones—
> please grant your blessings to me
> and your respectful disciple-children.[19]

Abridged supplication of the complete Object Severance:

> I pray to the method lineage of the father tantras.
> I pray to the wisdom lineage of the mother tantras.

I pray to the meaning lineage of the nondual tantras.
I pray to the experiential lineage of the fortunate ones.
I pray to the Severance lineage of adepts.
[I pray to the symbol lineage of ḍākinīs.][20]
I pray to the powerful dharma protector lineage.
Bless me to overturn attachment
to worldly activities of deluded appearances.
Bless me to be released from cherishing this illusory body,
the confluence of four elements.
Bless me with the ability to experience the equal flavor
of adverse circumstances, sickness, spirits, and obstacles.
Bless me to recognize as my own
the mental apparitions of apparent existence.
Bless me to attain mastery over my own awareness,
the spontaneous presence of the three kāyas.
In general, may I and the six kinds of beings
totally abandon the cause, the stains of dualistic fixation,
and quickly attain supreme awakening.[21]

Repeat this many times. Additionally, if you are able and willing, it is a very great blessing to do the praises and supplications to Dampa and Machik found in the *Severance Feast Activities* (*gCod kyi tshogs las*). In any case, at the conclusion of the [supplications, recite]:

All venerable, holy gurus; three precious Jewels; hosts of yidam deities of the mandala; hosts of ḍākinīs, dharma protectors, and guards—please arouse the supreme realization in me. Please help me to develop an altruistic mind without intense attachment and give birth to great compassion in my mindstream. Please cause the arising of various pure appearances.

Just that much or, if you like:

All victorious ones of space and time, lords of compassion rolled
into one,
the venerable gurus, all positioned in a direct line,
tamers of those to be tamed—myself and so on—in the
degenerate times,
your vision of timeless awareness, knowledge, and love is unobscured.

Although out of stupidity we did not seek encouragement from you,
the natural condition at the end times of the five-hundred-year cycle
and the manifest mode of practicing a [mere] reflection of the precious doctrine
[have created] a horrible and intolerable situation. {439}

As you all look at this with eyes of knowledge,
do not leave in equanimity the powerful capacity of compassion.
Do not give up on the obtuse savages to be tamed.
The time has come for activity that tames those difficult to tame.

Living beings are tormented by the unbearable sufferings
of shifting waves of animate and inanimate elements in turmoil.
Grant your blessings to quickly pacify
all disease, famine, war, and elemental danger.

Followers of the doctrine, disturbed by impulses of attachment and aversion,
engage in careless behavior, casting the three vows far away.
It's too late to exert effort in hearing, contemplating, and meditating.
Bless us so everyone behaves according to the dharma.

We avoid cause and effect and the two levels of pledges and vows
while distracted by misdeeds of conduct and food;
dharma fakes who burn ourselves and others with our three poisons ablaze.
Bless us to convert to the genuine dharma.

To all people who practice the yoga of the practice lineage,
undeceived by the dissipating path and empty sights,
grant your blessings to actualize without mistake
the timeless awareness of bliss-emptiness union, mahāmudrā.

Without inflaming the tumor of egotistical anger or desire
over the minor signs on the path, a semblance of qualities,

bless me with the ultimate fruition of the yogic ground,
the attainment of the four kāyas inseparable.

Minor powers for the sake of this life's desires,
and a grip on the eight worldly concerns for the sake of beings—
bless me to achieve genuine, supreme spiritual power
without being deceived by the devil of simulating the two benefits.

In particular, bless me to uphold the spirit of the first transmission
of Pacification, the ultimate five instructions
whose meaning is indicated by the five analogies:
sky, vajra, lotus, elixir, and wheel.[22]

Bless me to master the instructions of the Ma system
of the middle transmission, once I have taken into experience
the sixteen direct guides that introduce the meaning lineage
and the sixteen vital points to sever misconceptions.

Bless me in the So system to see naked intrinsic awareness
by finding timeless awareness through the vital points of body,
  winds, and mind,
to see the very face of dharmakāya through three introductions,
and possess the clinchers of clearing obstructors and enhancing
  practice.[23] {440}

Bless me in the Kam system with liberation through the
  instructions
and guides to the meaning of the perfection of wisdom
by uncontrived altruistic compassion, the forceful severance of
  concepts in meditative equipoise,
and the integration of the nature of phenomena in the subsequent
  attainment.

Bless me in Bodhisattva Kunga's system of the last transmission,
the instructions on the perfection of wisdom consistent with
  Mantra,
the practice of the Immaculate Drop, in which all the teachings
are practiced upon a single seat at one time.

Bless me to ripen body, speech, mind, and mentation
through possessing the four vital points, having properly received
the vase, secret, wisdom-awareness, and word empowerments,
which are sufficient to behold, grasp, know, and meet.

Bless me to reach the ultimate fruition of accomplishment in this life
through the white-guidance mind training, the red-guidance five paths,
and reliance on letters in the black guidance,
all of which emerge from the straight path of asceticism.

Bless me to cut attachment to cyclic existence in the outer preliminaries,
establish the foundation of the path by the special preliminaries
of completing the accumulations and purification,
and receive personal blessings through devotion to the guru.

Bless me to possess the foundations of yoga:
the three vows as support—the shrāvaka's sacred discipline,
the bodhisattva's vast training, and the unsullied pledges of Mantra—
and yoga's own six restraints undamaged.[24]

Bless me to arrive at the culmination of yoga's five paths:
mind training on the path of accumulation, austerity on the path of application,
subsequent conduct on the path of seeing, equal flavor on the path of meditation,
and freedom from action on the ultimate path.

Bless me to achieve the fruitional yoga of nonaction,
the three examples, individuals, times, and systems of conferral,
which will turn out well from the straight path of three austerities,
the consummation of the promise to accomplish.

Bless me to practice the profound path of Object Severance Mahāmudrā,

the ḍākinī's life essence, combining the intentions of Sutra and
Tantra,
befriending adversity, and taking bad omens as wealth,
like a wish-fulfilling gem.

Bless me to cut off from the root the four devils—
tangible, intangible, exaltation, and inflation—
and pacify in their own place the obstacles of three sickness spirits
that come from the causal three poisons and resultant three faulty
[humors].

Bless me to roam in haunted grounds and cast out my body as
food,
to give up self-fixation by cutting off its roots all at once,
and to actualize the fruitional three kāyas
for the immeasurable welfare of others. {441}

**Offering of the Communal Feast**

Cleanse and purify the pledge substances.

> From within emptiness, wind comes from *yaṃ*, fire from *raṃ*, and three hearth skulls from *kaṃ*. Upon that, from *a*, the vast and wide kapāla is white outside and red inside. Inside it, the five meats arise from *go ku da ha na* and the five elixirs from *mi mu ma ra shū*, and each are marked by those respective letters. *Hūṃ* from my nostrils emanates and fans the wind. Fire blazes and the skull substances melt. Steam from the boiling takes the shape of the three seed syllables: *hūṃ āḥ oṃ*. The three syllables melt by stages and dissolve [into the skull]. The ingredients become an ocean of blue, red, and white elixir that is the nature of Mind, Speech, and Body. Immeasurable goddesses of sense pleasure emanate.

Repeat the three seed syllables three times.

### Descent of Blessings[25]

In the place of the pure palace of dharmadhātu,
the precious Buddha, four-kāya lord.

In the place of the heavenly realm pure palace,
precious gurus, the Kagyu lords.

In the place of Latö Dingri hermitage,
precious Father Dampa Sangye.

In the place of Red House of Copper Mountain hermitage,
precious Mother Lapkyi Drönma.

In the place of Anywhere Is Dharmadhātu hermitage,
precious adepts of the Severance lineage.

In the place upon the lotus-moon seat on my head,
precious benevolent root guru
dwells in the midst of heroes and heroines.
I supplicate with longing and devotion.

Lord, with your retinue of ḍākinīs, please approach.
Now that you have come with your ḍākinī retinue,
please bestow spiritual powers on me, the practitioner,
and bless this ground.

*kye*
Bless this shining palace of an assembly hall
as the sacred site of Oḍḍiyāna.
Bless the men and women assembled here
as heroes and heroines.
Bless the various precious vessels
as *padma bhañja.*
Bless all the nutritional ingredients
as undissipating elixir.
Clear away adverse conditions and obstacles
and guide me on the conducive path to basic space.

### Offering

*hūṃ*

From the sixth lord, Vajradhara, {442}
down to the kind root guru—
everyone, with your retinues, enjoy the feast.
Some enjoy the outer feast.
Some enjoy the inner feast.
Some enjoy the secret feast.
Some enjoy the suchness feast.
Enjoy, enjoy! Enjoy the feast.
Consume, consume! Consume the feast.
*a la la*—joyfully enjoy!
Partake of the offering without first cuts or remains.

From the hosts of deities of the mandala
down to the retinues of heroes and ḍākinīs—
everyone, with your retinues, enjoy the feast.
Some enjoy the outer feast.
Some enjoy the inner feast.
Some enjoy the secret feast.
Some enjoy the suchness feast.
Enjoy, enjoy! Enjoy the feast.
Consume, consume! Consume the feast.
*a la la* —joyfully enjoy!
Partake of the offering without first cuts or remains.

From the Mother Vajravārāhī
down to mother ḍākinīs of the four families—
everyone, with your retinues, enjoy the feast.
Some enjoy the outer feast.
Some enjoy the inner feast.
Some enjoy the secret feast.
Some enjoy the suchness feast.
Enjoy, enjoy! Enjoy the feast.
Consume, consume! Consume the feast.
*a la la*—joyfully enjoy!
Partake of the offering without first cuts or remains.

From the dharma protectors Mahākāla and Mahākālī
down to the mandala border protectors—
everyone, with your retinues, enjoy the feast.
Some enjoy the outer feast.
Some enjoy the inner feast.
Some enjoy the secret feast.
Some enjoy the suchness feast.
Enjoy, enjoy! Enjoy the feast.
Consume, consume! Consume the feast.
*a la la*—joyfully enjoy!
Partake of the offering without first cuts or remains.

From Shākyamuni
down to the eighteen hell realms—
everyone, with your retinues, enjoy the feast.
Some enjoy the outer feast.
Some enjoy the inner feast.
Some enjoy the secret feast.
Some enjoy the suchness feast.
Enjoy, enjoy! Enjoy the feast.
Consume, consume! Consume the feast.
*a la la*—joyfully enjoy!
Partake of the offering without first cuts or remains.

From the ground masters of the billionfold universe
down to the gods and demons dwelling here—
everyone, with your retinues, enjoy the feast.
Some enjoy the outer feast.
Some enjoy the inner feast.
Some enjoy the secret feast.
Some enjoy the suchness feast.
Enjoy, enjoy! Enjoy the feast.
Consume, consume! Consume the feast.
*a la la*—joyfully enjoy!
Partake of the offering without first cuts or remains.

From the guests of the six kinds of beings
down to the creditors and obstructing types—

everyone, with your retinues, enjoy the feast.
Some enjoy the outer feast.
Some enjoy the inner feast.
Some enjoy the secret feast.
Some enjoy the suchness feast.
With no exception, including retinues, enjoy the feast.
*a la la*—joyfully enjoy!
Partake of the offering without first cuts or remains.[26]

**Fulfillment**

In the palace of unborn dharmadhātu,
Dampa Sangye, Lapdrön, and so on,
root and lineage gurus,
yidams, peaceful and wrathful victors and deities,
buddhas and bodhisattvas in ten directions,
heroes, ḍākinīs, and dharma protectors,
although without reference point for fulfilling sacred pledge,
in order to compassionately enact the welfare of beings,
fulfill sacred pledge in illusion-like nature
through outer, inner, and secret offerings
and unsurpassable excellence.
May we yogins and our retinues
not develop wrong views.
If wrong, renew them in the space of phenomena's nature.
As for mistakes in meditation, meditation is not mistaken.
If mistaken, renew it through beings' welfare.[27]
As for deluded conduct, conduct is not deluded.
If deluded, renew it through profound interdependence.
As for failings of sacred pledge, sacred pledge has not failed.
If failed, renew it through the feast of great bliss.
I confess every failing and break.
Please generate bliss of the body.
Please ignite the power of speech.
Please arouse realization in the mind.
Grant the supreme and common spiritual powers. {443}

Then partake of the feast using the inner yoga. Then bless the leftovers with the three seed syllables and dedicate them:

> In the torma trough of a blazing *bhañja* of three planes of existence,
> the heap of leftovers is as big as Supreme Mountain and four continents.
> Burning flesh of stupidity—*nyi li li.*
> Blood oceans of desire—*me re re.*
> Bone heaps of anger—*tra la la.*
> The enjoyment of the five elixirs is unimaginable.
> Ḍākinīs and protectors included in the entourage,
> eight classes of helpful gods and spirits,
> and eighty thousand types of outer and inner obstacles—
> partake of this vast commanded legacy
> and accomplish the yogins' requested activities.[28]

## III. Concluding Activities

Offer the concise seven branches and then the aspiration prayers:

### Thirtyfold Prayer by Dampa[29]

> *namo guru*
> May the blessings of lineage gurus enter our mindstreams.
> May the vital point of introducing the meaning be assimilated.
> May the realization of things as they are be born in my mindstream.
> May I obtain the ten powers, fearlessness, and prophecy.
> May false appearance diminish and interdependence arise.[30]
> May I gain the ability to place all migrators on the path of ripening and liberation.
> May I gain the ability to traverse the stages and paths in a single sitting. {444}
> May I see the truth of phenomena's nature with the eyes of wisdom.
> May qualities spread like foliage.
> May the fruit ripen like the wish-fulfilling tree.

May devotion be steadfast like Supreme Mountain.
May true conviction arise free of doubt.
May karmic propensities awaken and prayers be perfectly pure.
May the armor of worldly stains be purified.[31]
May practice be uninterrupted and austerity undertaken.
May channels, winds, and drops become practicable.
May thoughts always be perfectly pure.
May awakening mind be undiminished.
May the Mahayana view and meditation be experienced.
May dualistic appearances be liberated in their own ground.
May I be born in the exceptional family.
May I be accepted by a guru with lineage.
May I not regress into extreme actions.
May I be trained in the three wisdoms.
May the blessings of empowerment enter.
May bliss become like a vajra.
May I gain control of consciousness, channels, and winds.
May my body achieve the rūpakāya.
May I realize actual dharmakāya.
May I achieve the ultimate welfare of others through the activities of the nirmāṇakāya.

## Kunga's Thirteenfold Prayer

May the holy guru's blessings enter my heart.
May I obtain the yidam deity's prophecy.
May mamos and ḍākinīs gather like clouds.
May dharma protectors and guards clear up obstacles.
May I attain dharmakāya, the equality of existence and peace.
May I attain saṃbhogakāya of perfectly pure realms.
May I attain nirmāṇakāya with unrestricted activity.
May I attain svabhāvakāya, the inseparability of the three kāyas.
May my mindstream be liberated through realization.
May others' mindstreams be ripened through compassion.
May I be skilled in methods of interdependence.
May all relationships be meaningful.
May these things be accomplished just so.

### Confession of Mistakes

> Whatever has been insufficient [or damaged,
> whatever I have done or caused to be done
> through a mind afflicted by stupidity,
> lord, be patient with all of that.][32]
> (Repeat the hundred syllables.)

### Request for Empowerment and Blessings

> I supplicate the guru, buddha dharmakāya;
> [bless me to quickly realize suchness.
> I supplicate the guru saṃbhogakāya;
> bless me that all appearances arise as the pure universe.
> I supplicate the guru, buddha nirmāṇakāya;
> bless me to accomplish immense altruism.]

Repeat three times this prayer from before and: {445}

> *oṃ āḥ hūṃ hrīḥ* manifest clearly in the four places of the principal figures. My intense devotion evokes their mindstreams and supplicates them. With this, the lower ones supplicate the higher ones, and they dissolve into one another until all are gathered into the main figure.

With that visualization, repeat *oṃ āḥ hūṃ hrīh guru siddhi hūṃ* as much as you can. Again with intense devotion repeat the mantra with a melody three times.

> The guru comes to the crown of my head. Immeasurable compassion and great blessings arise from the guru's four places in the form of white, red, blue, and variegated light rays and dissolve into my four places like water poured into water. The obscurations of [each of] the three doors and those created in equal measure [by body, speech, and mind] are purified. The blessings of Body, Speech, and Mind—form-emptiness, sound-emptiness, and thought-emptiness inseparable—enter me. Experience and realization blaze vigorously. Finally, the guru buddha melts into

light and dissolves into me. The guru's three vajras and my body, speech, and mind become inseparably blended.

With that visualization, rest in equipoise for however long. When you arise from that, do the Six Vajra-Line Prayer:

*namo*
May I, the lord of my family, and so forth—
all beings included in the boundless continuum—
when we pass on from here to the precious pure land,
due to our aspiration prayers of awakening mind,
be born in the perfectly pure infinite palace,
the beautiful citadel of the ornamental wheel.

Do many aspiration prayers, such as the Prayer of Samantabhadra, those that are common to the Mahayana, and those not held in common. Perform extensive lines of auspicious verse, principally those that were spoken [by the Buddha], such as, "Holy, supreme teacher, worthy of offerings by gods and humans . . ." and so forth. Play gentle music and toss a shower of flowers.

May whatever virtue was obtained by writing this synthesis
of the means to offer to the gurus of the lineages of the Holy Dharmas
of Pacification of Suffering and Object Severance
become the cause for all migrators to consummate the five paths.

May the river of quintessential elixir of essential instructions,
flowing unceasingly until the end of existence,
transfer limitless embodied creatures, equaling the *preta*s,
to the life force of liberation and everlasting happiness.

[Colophon]
*The Treasury of Precious Instructions* contains the deep meaning of the essence of the Eight Great Chariots of the practice lineages unified like a priceless gem. {446} Here, the focus was the branches of the Teachings of Pacification and Severance. It was written by Karma Ngawang Yönten Gyatso, or Gyalse Lodrö Taye, who practices the yoga of being nobody, in the retreat place Kunzang Dechen Ösal Ling at the heart of Devīkoṭi Tsādra Rinchen Drak in the upper hermitage of Palpung. May virtue increase.

# Abbreviations

ACIP Electronic files of the Asian Classics Input Project. www.acip.org.

ATG Acharya Tenpa Gyaltsen

*BD* *Big Tibetan-Chinese Dictionary. Bod rgya tshig mdzod chen mo.* Edited by Zhang Yisun. 2 vols. (Beijing: Mi rigs dpe skrun khang, 1985, 1987).

*CDC* Khamnyön Dharma Senge, *The Religious History of Pacification and Severance: A Precious Garland Ornament of Liberation. Zhi byed dang gcod yul gyi chos 'byung rin po che'i phreng ba thar pa'i rgyan.* In *A Cycle of Teachings on Severance. Gcod kyi chos skor* (Delhi: Tibet House, 1974), pp. 411–597.

Dg.K. Derge Kangyur (sDe dge bka' 'gyur): Derge edition of the Tibetan canonical collection of sutras and tantras.

Dg.T. Derge Tengyur (sDe dge bstan 'gyur): Derge edition of the Tibetan canonical collection of commentarial treatises.

*DNZ* Jamgön Kongtrul Lodrö Taye, *The Treasury of Precious Instructions. gDams ngag rin po che'i mdzod.* 18 vols. (Shechen printing) (Delhi: Shechen Publications, 1999).

*DNZ-K* Jamgön Kongtrul Lodrö Taye, *The Treasury of Precious Instructions. gDams ngag rin po che'i mdzod.* 12 vols. (Kundeling printing) (Delhi: N. Lungtok and N. Gyaltsan, 1971–1972).

*DV* *The Volumes of the Root Teachings of the Sacred Dharma Pacification of Suffering, and the Subsidiary, Severance of Evil Object. Dam chos sdug bsngal zhi byed rtsa ba'i chos sde dang yan lag bdud kyi gcod yul gyi glegs bam.* (*Dingri Volumes*) (New Delhi: Dingri Langkor Tsuglag Khang, 2013).

GTR Gangteng Tulku Rinpoche

Limi *Practices of the Severance Collection and So Forth. gCod tshogs kyi lag len sogs. A Collection of Gcod Texts Representing the Ancient Practices of the Adepts of the Tradition.* Reproduced directly from a rare manuscript collection from Limi, Nepal (Bir, Himachal Pradesh, India: D. Tsondu Senghe, Bir Tibetan Society, 1985). TBRC W23390.

*MCE* Sarah Harding, *Machik's Complete Explanation: Clarifying the Meaning of Chöd,* expanded ed. (Boston and London: Snow Lion Publications, 2013).

| | |
|---|---|
| rKTs | Universität Wien, Resources for Kanjur and Tanjur Studies. www.istb .univie.ac.at/kanjur/xml4/xml |
| RT | Ringu Tulku |
| TBRC | Tibetan Buddhist Research Center. www.tbrc.org. |
| Toh. | *A Complete Catalogue of the Tibetan Buddhist Canons.* Edited by Hakuju Ui et al. (Sendai, Japan: Tohoku University, 1934). |
| *TOK* | Jamgön Kongtrul Lodrö Taye, *The Treasury of Knowledge. Shes bya kun khyab (theg pa'i sgo kun las btus pa gsung rab rin po che'i mdzod bslab pa gsum legs par ston pa'i bstan bcos shes bya kun khyab) The Treasury of Knowledge.* 3 vols. (Lhasa: Mi rigs dpe skrun khang, 1982). |
| *TSB* | Tāranātha, *Collected Works. rJe btsun Tā ra nā tha'i gsung 'bum.* 23 vols. (Dzamthang edition, 2000?). |
| ch. | chapter |
| f., ff. | folio, folios |
| p., pp. | page, pages |
| vol., vols. | volume, volumes |

# NOTES

*Chapter numbers refer to the translations in this volume. Where reference is made to a text in this volume, page numbers are those of the Tibetan edition* (DNZ), *which are embedded in the translation in curly brackets { }.*

## TRANSLATOR'S INTRODUCTION

1. 'Jam dbyangs mkhyen brtse dbang po (1820–1892), mChog 'gyur bDe chen gling pa (1829–1870), Mi pham rgya mtsho (1846–1912), and many more masters were involved in this movement, such as Kongtrul's guru Si tu Pad ma nyin byed (1774–1853), and some authors in this collection, such as Karmapa Theg mchog rdo rje (1798/9–1868/9). See E. Gene Smith, "'Jam mgon Kong sprul and His Friends," in *Among Tibetan Texts*, pp. 247–50; Jamgön Kongtrul, *Treasury of Knowledge: Esoteric Instructions*, pp. 25–48; Ringu Tulku, *The Ri-me Philosophy of Jamgön Kongtrul the Great*, and so forth.
2. The specific text by Shes rab 'od zer that expounds the eight chariots is *Meditation's Ambrosia of Immortality* (*sGom pa 'chi med kyi bdud rtsi*). A study of this has been done by Marc-Henri Deroche: "'Phreng po gter ston Shes rab 'od zer (1518–1584) on the Eight Lineages of Attainment." According to Deroche, "This text may be considered as an (if not the) original source of the '*ris med* paradigm' of the eight lineages of attainment" (p. 17). It is interesting to note that the eight lineages are arranged in a different sequence in that text—Nyingma, Kadampa, Shangpa Kagyu, Lamdre, Marpa Kagyu, Zhije, Jordruk, Dorje Sumgyi Nyendrup—which may have been more chronological than Kongtrul's preferred order.
3. One finds this idea developed in the volume on esoteric instructions in *The Treasury of Knowledge*, where Kongtrul describes in incredibly condensed detail the basic principles and sources of these eight lineages. It is expounded in the catalog of *The Treasury of Precious Instructions* (*DNZ*, vol. 18), published in English as *The Catalog of The Treasury of Precious Instructions*, trans. Richard Barron (Chökyi Nyima). Also see Stearns, *Luminous Lives*, pp. 3–8, where the verse from Prajñārasmi was first brought to my attention.

4. Jamgön Kongtrul Lodrö Taye, *Catalog*, p. 21. Translation by Richard Barron.
5. *The Treasury of Precious Instructions. gDams ngag rin po che'i mdzod* (*DNZ*) 12 vols. (Delhi: N. Lungtok and N. Gyaltsan, 1971–1972). Known as the Kundeling printing.
6. *The Treasury of Precious Instructions. gDams ngag rin po che'i mdzod* (*DNZ*) 18 vols. (Delhi: Shechen Publications, 1998). Known as the Shechen printing.
7. From Jamgön Kongtrul's final aspiration prayer in the *Catalog* (*DNZ,* vol. 18, p. 546).
8. Since confusion abounds regarding Machik's birthplace, I will pursue it a bit here. For instance, a mistake in Roerich's translation of *The Blue Annals* (p. 124) gives her birthplace as "Khe'u gang," which in the Tibetan text (Gö Lotsāwa, *Deb ther sngon po,* p. 1142) is actually her paternal clan name (*rus*), while her birthplace is given as *g.ye labs*, which would be phoneticized as Yelap (not Gyelab), leading to repeated errors in some Western sources. This is just one example. According to *MCE*, she was born in "a town called Tsomer, in the lower part of so-called Tamshö in Ei Gangwa in the Lapchi region" (*yul lab phyi e'i gang bar tam shod bya ba'i smad du / grong khyer mtsho mer bya ba*) (p. 59). In Khamnyön Dharma Senge's *Religious History of Pacification and Severance,* we find "the town called Tsomer in the lower area of Ei Damshe in Tibet" (*bod yul e'i dam shed kyi smad yul grong mtsho mer*) (f. 21a). The spelling variations are quite confusing. I tentatively propose that the town is present-day Tsome (mtsho smad, in "lower Tso" county), which is administered from the capital at Tamzhol ("Tamshö"?), according to Gyurme Dorje's *Footprint Tibet* (pp. 215–16). This is in south central Tibet, below Samye and the Yarlung valley, close to the Bhutanese border. The snow peak Yarlha Shampo is visible from here (ibid.), a sacred site that plays an important role in Machik's biographies. Drapa Ngönshe, one of Machik's early teachers, is also known to be from this area (ibid., p. 173). Not far to the north is Eyul (*e yul*, "the area of E"), which might be the E in Ei Gang (*e'i gang*, "the mountain of E"?) and *e'i dam shed* (?) and pronounced the same as in *g.ye labs*. The name E refers to the place where three rivers come together to form a shape similar to the Tibetan letter *E* (ཨེ) (*BD*, p. 3140–41). Lapchi, or just Lap, the most important word of all, is more confusing, especially as spelled unusually in *The Blue Annals* as *labs*. A spelling of *la phyi* ("other side of the pass") might be pronounced as "lapchi" and is an important mountain range that was also frequented by Milarepa. But a separate district called "Lap" has not been located. "The Light of Lap" needs to be shown more brightly by future scholars.
9. For example, *MCE* and Edou, *Machig Labdrön and the Foundations of Chöd.*
10. *Khrid brgya'i brgyud pa'i lo rgyus,* in *DNZ,* vol. 18, pp. 74–75. Kun dga' grol mchog (1507–1566) was an eclectic master of Sakya, Shangpa Kagyu, and other systems but mainly associated with the Jonang monastery.
11. Tashi Chöpel, *Record of Teachings Received*, pp. 772–78.
12. I have pursued this subject in some detail in a paper delivered at the Thirteenth Seminar of the International Association for Tibetan Studies: "Did Machik Lap-

drön Really Teach Chöd? A Survey of the Early Sources." http://wordpress.tsadra.org/?cat=75.

13. In Sanskrit, *māra* is a nominalized form of the verbal root *mṛ-*, "to die," and can be associated with actual death or spiritual death. It was personified in the Perfection of Wisdom scriptures and elsewhere as the familiar figure of the Buddha's antagonist, who played a role similar to the "devil," which is the term I have chosen. The Tibetan translation of *māra* as *bdud* complicated matters, since there were already hordes of spirits called *bdud* in Tibet before the advent of Buddhism. Whatever the specific referent, it gestures to negative or obstructing forces, so I have also used "evil." Some examples from the early texts in this volume are the devil of belief in intrinsic existence, of merely mental emptiness, of making dharma a big project, of clinging to the reality of accomplishing enlightenment, of actual things, of depression and despair, of obstinate reification, etc. For further discussion, see *MCE,* pp. 33–42.
14. *Treasury of Knowledge: Esoteric Instructions*, p. 278.
15. *MCE*, pp. 69–71.
16. *Treasury of Knowledge: Esoteric Instructions,* pp. 276–88.
17. Ch. 29, pp. 445–46.

## 1. Esoteric Instructions on the Noble Perfection of Wisdom

1. Also called *Grand Poem* (*Tshigs bcad chen mo*) and *Fifty-Verse Poem* (*Tshigs su bcad pa lnga bcu pa*), in *DNZ,* vol. 14 (*pha*), pp. 1–7. Other sources: Narthang Tengyur, mdo, *nyo*, ff. 396b–399a (pp. 793–97); Golden Tengyur, *nyo*, ff. 517a–520a; and Khamnyön Dharma Senge, *The Religious History of Pacification and Severance*, ff. 1–5.
2. This entire verse is not found in the Narthang or Golden Tengyur editions.
3. An interlinear note here says, "This is not in order." See the commentary for more on this.
4. *nyams can*, but in all other editions it is *nyams tshad* (degree of experience).
5. This line is absent from the Tengyur editions.
6. The Tengyur editions have an additional line after this one: *nyon mongs dgra las rgyal bar 'gyur* ("You will be victorious over the enemy, afflictive emotions").
7. In the Tengyurs the colophon reads: *paṇḍita chen po mi pham mgon pos sgra rang 'gyur du mdzad pa'o* ("The great paṇḍita Mipam Gönpo translated this himself"). Mipam Gönpo (Ajitanātha) is a name for Dampa Sangye. Zha ma (or Zhwa ma) lo tsā ba sTon pa seng ge rgyal po is the translator of many of the texts transmitted by Dampa Sangye/Kamalashīla in the Tengyur.

## 2. The Great Bundle of Precepts

1. *Shes rab kyi pha rol tu phyin pa zab mo gcod kyi man ngag gi gzhung bka' tshoms chen mo,* in *Source Texts of Severance of Evil Object, The Profound Meaning of the*

*Perfection of Wisdom (Shes rab kyi pha rol tu phyin pa zab don bdud kyi gcod yul gyi gzhung)*, in *DNZ*, vol. 14 (*pha*), pp. 7–17. Other editions consulted: *Ma gcig gi bka' tshoms (Machik's Bundle of Precepts)*, in *The Collected Works of Omniscient Longchen Rabjam (Kun mkhyen klong chen rab 'byams kyi gsung 'bum)*, vol. 26, pp. 291–300 (hereafter cited as Longchenpa edition); *Shes rab kyi pha rol tu phyin pa zab mo gcod kyi man ngag gi gzhung bka' tshoms chen mo*, in *The Complete Writings of Padampa Sangye and Machik Labdron*, in *DV*, pp. 97–113. This translation previously appeared in Harding, *Machik's Complete Explanation: Clarifying the Meaning of Chöd*, expanded ed.

2. According to Rangjung Dorje's commentary (see ch. 5), this line is actually part of the following quatrain. In the poem here it seems better to include it with the statement of the title. Also, in the Longchenpa edition these two lines are in a four-line verse as follows: "[In] this Great Testament of Severance, 'severance' (*gcod*) is to naturally sever discursive thought; 'word' (*bka'*) is explained as a collection of explanations. It has been written in order to benefit beings" (p. 292).
3. Interlinear note: "based on the outer object."
4. Interlinear note: "based on inner mental designation."
5. Interlinear note: "based on attachment to the reality of qualities."
6. Additional line in the Longchenpa edition: *gzugs la dngos por ma bzungs bas* ("by not grasping form as definite").
7. For an explanation of this unusual statement, see Rangjung Dorje's commentary.
8. Taking *byung tshul* here as *byung tshor* based on Rangjung Dorje's commentary and the Longchenpa edition.
9. *rang byung sems las ma gtogs pa*, but in Longchenpa edition: *rang byung sems nyid ma rtogs pas* ("By not realizing that they come from naturally arising mind").
10. *chos dbyings klong chen ngang gsal la[s]*. Longchenpa edition: *sems nyid klong chen dang gsal la* ("The mind itself's great expanse and clarity").
11. *DNZ* and *DV* read *rigs 'khrul* ("deluded types"), which might have been understood as confusing the two types of devil, common and supreme. However, the Longchenpa edition has *rig 'khrul* ("deluded cognition or awareness"), which corresponds better with Rangjung Dorje's commentary as *rang rig 'khrul pa las byung pa yin* ("it comes from one's own deluded cognition").
12. *dgra gnyen* ("friends [and] foes"). Longchenpa: *snyan grag* ("reputation").
13. Insertion based on the Longchenpa edition: *yon tan bdag* (rather than *dag*) *tu med gzung bar*.
14. *'dzin med rang lugs spyod mchog 'di.* Longchenpa: *'dzin med rang grol gcod mchog yin* ("self-liberated nonfixation is supreme severance").
15. *dbyings su skyur* rather than *bsgyur* here. Also, I have followed the Longchenpa edition with *nyams shar* ("experience arising") rather than *DNZ mnyam shar* ("equipoise arising"), although this might be a possibility.
16. *Mi lta ba ni gcod kyi mchog.* Longchenpa: *mi lta ba ni lta ba'i mchog* ("no view is the best view").

17. *lhan ne lhang nge lham me*, alliterative words with variable experience-based meanings.
18. *ched du byas nas spyad du med*. Longchenpa: *ched du byas nas spang du med* ("doing it purposefully is not abandoning"), but this does not correspond to the commentary.
19. Here *mnyam shar gnyen pos bzung du med*, but Longchenpa: *nyams shar gnyen pos bcos su med*. Rangjung Dorje's gloss also indicates that the use of *mnyam shar* ("arising equanimity") should be understood as *nyams shar* ("arising experience").
20. *gcud* ("forsaken, rejected"). An interlinear note on this word reads, "In some texts this is said to be 'devil' (*dpe la lar bdud zer ba 'dug*)." However, in the Longchenpa edition it is totally different as *ci yang rang byung yin shes na* ("If you know that anything is self-occurring"). Then again, Rangjung Dorje's commentary on this line glosses *gcud* as *bcug*, which makes much more sense as "Even if [the antidote] is applied (*bcug*), when you know it is self-occurring . . ."
21. Longchenpa: *bla ma'i byin rlabs* ("blessings of the guru").
22. Longchenpa: *gcod yul kun las khyad par 'phags* ("is especially elevated above all severance objects").
23. Longchenpa: *mi gcod spyod pa mchog tu gsungs* ("is said to be the supreme conduct of no severance"). *Spyod* ("conduct") and *gcod* ("severance") sound the same and are often used interchangeably. Etymological explanations of the practice called *gcod*, severance or cutting through, traditionally give both words as sources.
24. The text appears to read *blo snang yul du bcad pas bos*, but *DV* has corrected *bos* ("call out") to *blos* ("by mind or intellect"; here, "attitude"). Longchenpa has the even stranger *blo snang yul du spyad pa'o*.
25. A corruption in the *DNZ* (and *DV*) text here is cleared up by comparison to the Longchenpa edition and the commentary by Rangjung Dorje. Two consecutive lines (*'bras bu yid bzhin nor bu bzhin* and *mchog gi bdud ni 'di bzhin no*) have been combined as *'bras bu bdud ni 'di bzhin no*. This mistake is confirmed by the commentary, which says this section should have ten lines, and that the next one should begin with *mchog*. I have restored the line to its correct reading.
26. The word *gdeng* ("confidence") is missing in the *DNZ* edition but added in *DV*. This verse is quoted somewhat differently in a commentary of *Heart Essence of Profound Meaning* called *The Big General Guide to Severance*, from a collection associated with Padma Lingpa: *re dogs med par gcod gyur na / spangs blang gnyis kyi mtha' dang bral / bzung 'dzin thag pa chad gyur pas / nges par sangs rgyas sa la 'gro* ("If [one practices] severance without hopes and fears, free of the extremes of both accepting and rejecting, decisively cutting off dualistic fixation, one will certainly go to buddhahood"), p. 291.
27. This verse quoted in Jamyang Gönpo, *Big General Guide:* "Fears about unreal demons, hopes about invisible gods, formless devils and so on—cut off hope-and-fear doubts about mental objects," p. 258.
28. Longchenpa: *'thab rtsod sdug bsngal bdud las thar* ("released from the devil of the suffering of dispute").

29. Longchenpa: *snyems thag ma chod sdug bsngal rgyu* ("inflation not decisively cut off is the cause of suffering").
30. A different version of this last line is found in Jamyang Gönpo, *Big General Guide: nad gdon kun gyis gnod mi nus* ("disease spirits cannot harm"), p. 249.
31. Longchenpa: *rang shar rtogs pas gcod pa yin* ("by realizing [that it is] self-arising, it is severance").
32. *nyam ngas 'ching*, but Longchenpa: *nyams kyis 'chings* ("bound by experience").
33. *rang thang* ("unaffected") or possibly *rang thad* ("directly [on] oneself") as in *DV.* Longchenpa: *rang dwangs* ("one's own refined essence").
34. Longchenpa: *myang 'das log nas sgrub mi dgos* ("no need to accomplish nirvana apart from that").
35. Instead of *dwangs ma* ("refined essence"), the Longchenpa edition has *rang sa* ("own ground"). More significantly, instead of *ngos bzung med*, it has *ngos gzung nas* ("having recognized").
36. *sems can*, but in Longchenpa: *sems nyid* ("mind itself"), which seems preferable here since the next line covers the benefit for others.
37. *rgyu 'bras med pa'i don du blta*, with an interlinear note that reads *dpe la lar med* ("not in some texts"). In Longchenpa the sentence reads *'du 'bral med pa'i don la lta* ("see the meaning of indivisibility/beyond meeting and parting").
38. Longchenpa: *bsam pa'i yul ni de nyid min* ("the object of thought; no such thing").
39. Quoted in Jamyang Gönpo, *Big General Guide* (pp. 318–19), with the last line quite different: *byung tshor dran rtogs rjes mi bcad / mkha' la glog 'gyu klog* [*sic*] *rang bzhin / dran rtogs byung yang de ni yal / rgya mtsho'i rdzings la bya phur bzhin* ("Don't cut off sensations and thoughts after the fact. As lightning bolts in the sky are the nature of lightning, even though conceptual thoughts occur, they dissipate. It is like the bird who flies [back] to the ship in the sea").
40. This text in *DNZ* (and *DV*) has *mdze gnas* ("leprosy places"), but I have followed the Longchenpa version of *'jigs gnas* ("frightful places").
41. *sems nyid*, but in Longchenpa: *rig pa*.
42. Longchenpa: *yum sras* ("mother's children").
43. This line is missing from the Longchenpa edition.
44. *king dang kang* is corrected in *DV* to *kin ka ra*, Sanskrit for *pho nya* ("emissary"). Longchenpa: *khro bo khro mo* ("wrathful male and female").
45. Longchenpa: *'dzin bya med par nya la la* ("without something to be attached to, *nyalala*").
46. Longchenpa: *zhe sdang zhen med* ("without anger [and] clinging").
47. *rang la gcod pa* here is *rang la gnod pa* ("harm oneself") in Longchenpa, which is perhaps more consistent with the commentary.
48. This line is not in the Longchenpa edition.
49. The widespread term *rig pa* is often used to indicate nondual awareness, but in this section it is used in the sense of being aware of something, so I have used "cognition" to distinguish it.

50. I have followed Longchenpa: *dbyer med gcig las* (rather than *la*).
51. *ltos chos* or *bltos chos*, but in Longchenpa: *lha chos* ("divine dharma"), meaning Buddhism.
52. Here *chad pas cad med yul du rig* is better understood in the Longchenpa edition: *chad pa cang med yul du rig.*
53. Longchenpa: *rlung du rig* ("cognize vital winds").
54. This line is missing in Longchenpa.
55. Longchenpa: *'khrul pa'i sems* ("deluded mind").
56. Longchenpa: *gzhi ru byung* ("occurs as ground").
57. Longchenpa: *ma byas 'dus ma byas pa yin* ("the unmade is unconditioned"). The Longchenpa version fits with Rangjung Dorje's outline and commentary, which lists this verse as beginning with "unmade" (*ma byas*) rather than "buddha" (*sangs rgyas*).
58. *gnyis med*, but in Longchenpa: *gnyis 'dzin* ("dualistic fixation"), which makes more sense here.
59. Longchenpa: *'khor ba snang bar mi 'gyur ro* ("not become the appearance [of] samsara"). Neither reading is particularly clarified in the commentary.
60. Here ends the correspondence with the Longchenpa edition. From here onward, another text has been mistakenly attached to that edition.
61. There is an interlinear note here that says that these two lines do not appear in most editions (*'di nas tshig rkang gnyis dpe phal cher du med*). That accords with Rangjung Dorje's commentary that attributes only thirteen lines to this section, rather than fifteen.
62. *'khor ba'i pha rol 'das pa yin*, should be *min*, as in the commentary: *'khor ba'i pha rol 'da' bar mi nus te* ("there would be no ability to pass over samsara").
63. *rma byung. DV: rmad byung* ("wonderful"). Quoted in Jamyang Gönpo, *Big General Guide: mes tshig me yi bdug pa dang / ma byung gtar sreg byed pa bzhin / slar gcod log non gdams pa'i gnad / rkyen rnams khal du bkal bar gyis*, p. 240. Or again differently: *ji ltar me yis tshig pa la / me nyid gyis ni 'dug pa bzhin / rma byung gtar bsreg byed pa ltar / slar gnod log non gdams pa'i gnad*, p. 269.
64. Interlinear note here: "Note 109: this is not in the source text, but since it is especially illuminating it seems to have been added on."
65. The monk Haktön (Grwa pa Hag ston) is mentioned in Gö Lotsāwa, *The Blue Annals* (vol. 2, p. 1143), in the female *gcod* lineage among the "great children" (*bu chen*) who received instructions from Machik Lapdrön.

## 3. Heart Essence of Profound Meaning

1. *Shes rab kyi pha rol tu phyin pa gcod kyi gzhung dang man ngag mtha' dag gi yang bcud zab don thugs kyi snying po*, in *Shes rab kyi pha rol tu phyin pa'i zab don bdud kyi gcod yul gyi gzhung*, in *DNZ*, vol. 14 (*pha*), pp. 17–22. Also found in *The Collected Works of Longchen Rabjam* (Longchenpa), under the title *Zab don gyi gzhung*, vol. 26, pp. 124–30, with the misleading colophon "Severance

Object Created by the Omniscient Stainless One, Obtained from the Awareness Holder Padma Lingpa" (*Kun mkhyen dri med pas mdzad pa'i gcod yul rig 'dzin Padma gling pa las thob pa'o*). Apparently this means that the text was found in the collection of works in the Padma Lingpa tradition, since Longchen Rabjam (1308–1364) predates Padma Lingpa (1450–1521), who in fact considered himself an incarnation of Longchenpa (who did not create this text). I also referenced *The Complete Writings of Padampa Sangye and Machik Labdron* (*DV*, vol. *ja*, pp. 115–20). Another edition is found in *gCod tshogs kyi lag len sogs: A Collection of Gcod Texts Representing the Ancient Practices of the Adepts of the Tradition*. Reproduced directly from a rare manuscript collection from Limi, Nepal (Bir, Himachal Pradesh, India: D. Tsondu Senghe, Bir Tibetan Society, 1985). TBRC W23390 (hereafter cited as Limi). An extensive commentary, also by Jamyang Gönpo, is *The Big General Guide to Severance*, pp. 47–339. This is also in Limi, pp. 105–97.

2. A ma Jo mo: this refers to Machik Lapdrön (Ma gcig Lab sgron, 1055–1153), who was often called simply Jomo, an honorific title for women. *Ama* is "mother," usually shortened to *ma*.
3. A slightly different version of this verse is found in Jamgön Kongtrul, *Treasury of Knowledge: Esoteric Instructions*, p. 277.
4. This and other inserts are based on Kongtrul's helpful dissection of this section; ibid., pp. 280–81.
5. Jamyang Gönpo, *Big General Guide*, f. 7–7b (59–60), lists six skills, apparently counting realization and loving-kindness as the other two. The six are (1) skill in casting out the body as food after definitely distinguishing samsara and nirvana through the view; (2) skill in maintaining undistracted mindfulness after understanding mental nonaction in meditation; (3) skill in discerning the boundary of samsara and nirvana once the meaning of the lack of validity of appearance and emptiness of tenets is actualized; (4) skill in teaching the support of the word-guides without acceptance and rejection; (5) skill in teaching the esoteric instructions on "carrying flesh, carrying blood" of the meaning-guides; and (6) skill in the enhancements of practice. But note that Limi has only "endowed with special skills" (*mkhas khyad ldan*).
6. See Kongtrul's description of the types of empowerment in *Treasury of Knowledge: Esoteric Instructions*, p. 281.
7. In most editions and instances of quoting this text or commenting on it, this is rendered as *log rtogs* ("perverse realization"), which I have followed here rather than *DNZ: log rtog* ("perverse thoughts"). In Jamyang Gönpo, *Big General Guide* (f. 13b/72), these four flaws to be severed are explained by examples.
8. In Limi (*gCod tshogs kyi lag len),* the sentence reads: "With the integration of circumstances on the path, adverse circumstances arise as glory" (*lam 'khyer rkyen la byas pas 'gal rkyen dpal du 'char*).
9. Limi: "one is freed of hopes and fears" (*re dogs gnyis dang bral*).
10. *mkhan po* (khenpo) functions as a personifier, though in other contexts it is an

abbot or scholar or even "wise guy." In this case, other editions have instead *dngos po* ("things"), such as in Limi (p. 97) and *Big General Guide* (f. 32b).

11. A Sanskrit and Pāli (*dukkha*) term equivalent to the Tibetan *sdug bsngal*, and usually translated (some say mistranslated) as "suffering" in English. This edition keeps the Sanskrit, perhaps only as shorthand, so I followed suit.
12. *log rtog*, but in Limi it is *log rtags* ("mistaken" or "perverse signs").
13. *DNZ: skar chen thibs 'og bcug pas 'khor 'das rdzun phug[s] gtib* (or *stibs*). This idiom is also used in Āryadeva's *Grand Poem*. It is explained in *Big General Guide:* "When [something] has been put under thumb (*thebs*), it cannot rise up. For example, in the sky the light of the sun overwhelms the moon by its brilliance. When all the constellations are put under the thumb of the sun, they become incapacitated. Similarly, for the yogin who realizes the view, the external obstacles of devils and subtle or gross internal thoughts of attachment, aggression, eight concerns, and so forth are like the stars: however many arise, the view of mental nonengagement in the unminding mind is like the sun that overwhelms them with brilliance so that they cannot rise up" (f. 60a–b).
14. The letters appear to be corrupted in all copies. Here it appears to be *gnyan sar gnyan yog dbang pas lha 'dre sgyu mar zhig;* in *DNZ-K,* the first part appears to be *gnyan sar* (unclear) *srog dbab pas.* In *Big General Guide* it is explained in this way: "Overpowering pestilence directly with pestilence (*gnyan thog tu gnyan dbab pa*) means that while outwardly it [seems to be] the pestilent palace of nāgas, the mind that realizes emptiness is more pestilent (or powerful) than that."

    All of these obscure variations would seem to indicate that the original spellings were lost. Perhaps the original is the distinctively different version found in the *Six Pieces* (*Brul tsho drug*), surely one of the earliest attested source texts of both Pacification and Severance. The four phrases and their explanations from that source are offered here in full for comparison:

    > The four vital points of the view: burning the morning star in the hearth (*skar chen thab su sreg pa*); cornering the great mistake (*log chen mtha' la gtad pa*); going to gamble on a great pestilence (*gnyan chen skugs su gcar ba*); and overwhelming with the brilliance of Mahayana (*theg chen zil gyis gnon pa*). (1) Just as the morning star rises in the empty sky, thoughts of the four devils rise within the empty mind. [In the phrase] "burning in the hearth," the hearth is the nature of phenomena, and "burning" is to conquer it in naturally occurring self-pacification. For example, when the great sun rises in the sky, the morning star is suppressed by its splendor. In that way, whatever thoughts of the four devils or apparitions arise, by knowing that they are the mind's apparitions, you rest in their natural occurrence and they will naturally subside. (2) The "great mistake" is thoughts of the four devils, by which you enter into a mistaken path. To "corner that" means that whatever thoughts of four devils arise, you immediately corner [them with] awareness. That cuts the roots and [those thoughts] subside naturally.

(3) "Going to gamble on a great pestilence" can cause great harm if [that pestilence] is not recognized. But if it is recognized, mantras and substances can beat it and render it harmless. Just so, if you stray into your own thoughts, you will wander in samsara. Here, once you recognize the devil, it becomes the spiritual path and thoughts cannot harm you. They do not transcend the nature of phenomena. (4) The great vehicle is the perfection of wisdom, unutterable, inconceivable, inexpressible. It "overwhelms by brilliance" through realizing its meaning, which overwhelms all thoughts of the four devils by its brilliance. All thought becomes the essence of the unutterable, inconceivable inexpressible perfection of wisdom.

15. *sar la mnan. Big General Guide*: *ar la mnan. DV: slar la mnan.* Limi: *ur la gnan.*
16. *da rung cho 'phrul ston na na dga' di skyid gyis* should be *shi skyid bya* as in *Big General Guide.* Note that in the Limi edition this quatrain precedes the previous one, which might make more sense according to content.
17. Here *rdug* and in *DV, brdugs* ("conquer"), but *rtags* ("signs") in *Big General Guide* makes more sense. It explains the three kinds of evidence of termination or success: in time or duration; through outer, inner and secret signs; and the consummate realization, which is the resting in emptiness.
18. *Zung 'jug 'khor 'das 'khrul shan chod par the tshom med. Big General Guide: Zung 'jug 'khor 'das kun gyis 'khrug shan 'byed par the tshom med.*
19. *mngon du. Big General Guide* (f. 190): *sngon du* ("previously"). Also *dbang dang ngo sprod* ("empowerment *and* introduction") with the comment that the yogin is ripened first (i.e., "previously") by the empowerment and then given the introduction, which is specifically from *Opening the Sky Door,* quoting Machik's *Yang tshom* (*Another Bundle*) (ch. 7). This may be a preferable reading. Finally, note that in Limi, the yogin is not mentioned and the sentence reads "by the nature of phenomena actualized [by] empowerment and introduction" (*dbang dang ngo sprod mngon du gyur pa'i chos nyid kyis*).
20. *Big General Guide* comments: "The thoughts are ascertained on the ground, path, and result; [what is] not realized, that stained aspect, is conquered by view, meditation, and conduct."
21. *rang bzhin mi rtog* ("natural nonconceptuality"), but in Limi it is *rang bzhin med rtogs* ("realizing intrinsic nonexistence"). Also *bsgyur mkhas* ("skillful or wise [about] transformation") but in Limi it is *sgyur mkhan*, "transformer" or "ruler." *Big General Guide* quotes this as *sgyu mkhan* ("the one who deceives") but then glosses as *nyon mongs pa ye shes su bsgyur nus* ("able to transform afflictions into timeless awareness").
22. *mchod par bzhes. Big General Guide: mchod par shes* ("know offerings") and glosses as *tha mas bde bar gshegs pa la mchod par shes shing* ("the lowest know to make offerings to the Tathāgata"). This verse is analyzed according to three levels of applying remedy: the highest that needs no remedy because of natural

nonconceptuality, the average remedy of transformation, and the least remedy of making offerings.

23. *lus sems gnyis kyi de nyid shes na grol bar nges.* This is clarified by the *Big General Guide* version: *lus sems gnyis su yin de nyid bral na grol bar nges* ("body and mind are two, and if those are separated, liberation is assured"). It describes the process of transference, the separation of the mind or consciousness from the body (f. 101a).

24. *lam,* but in Limi and in *Big General Guide* (f. 105b) it is *rbad khams,* glossed as *lta ba'i rbad khams* ("great boasting of view"), one in the list of these eight characteristics necessary for a Severance practitioner who can cut off all adverse conditions in the daytime.

25. In place of this last paragraph, Limi ends with the following colophon: "This completes the Profound Heart Essence, the source text of Severance instructions, made by the Shākya monk, holder of the vajra, Prajñāsambhava."

## 4. Pure Honey

1. *Shes rab kyi pha rol tu phyin pa'i man ngag gcod kyi gzhung 'grel zag med sbrang rtsi,* in *DNZ,* vol. 14 (*pha*), pp. 23–51. Author's name in colophon: Kun dga' dpal 'byor. Kongtrul's catalog (*DNZ,* vol. 18) names Drung Sa ru pa Kun dga' dpal 'byor (possibly also known as Drung pa Ru pa).

2. 'Jam dpal smra ba'i seng ge, Mañjushrīvādasiṃha. This probably refers to both the bodhisattva and to the human master. He is listed along with Āryadeva the Brahmin and Virūpa as one of the three main Indian teachers of Dampa Sangye (Dam pa sangs rgyas).

3. *rtsis 'go yan lag lnga: rtsom pa gang gis mdzad pa, khungs gang las btus pa, phyogs gang du gtogs pa, dgos ched gang yin pa, dbu nas zhabs su bsdu ba'i don gang yin bcas lnga'i sgo nas 'chad pa'o.* Kongtrul: "the resident scholars of Vikramashīla Monastery expounded treatises by making five kinds of essential observations: (1) who the author is; (2) what its scriptural sources are; (3) how it is classified; (4) for whose benefit it is written; and (5) what is the import of the work as a whole" (*Treasury of Knowledge: Myriad Worlds,* p. 81). But in this case, (2) and (3) are combined, and the new (4) is how it is named.

4. There was most likely a spelling error in the Tibetan: the original *rtogs* ("to realize") should be *gtogs* ("to belong, include"), as the author does not discuss realization in this part at all.

5. Seventeen of the *Prajñāpāramitā* sutras are referred to as mothers and sons: six as mothers because they teach the complete subject matter of the eight *abhisamaya* (Tib. *mngon par rtogs pa,* "clear realization"), which are the subject matter of Maitreya's *Ornament of Clear Realization,* and eleven as sons because they do not teach the complete eight *abhisamaya.* The six mothers are *Sutra in One Hundred Thousand Lines, in Twenty-Five Thousand Lines, in Eighteen Thousand Lines,*

*in Ten Thousand Lines, in Eight Thousand Lines,* and the *Verse Summary.* The eleven sons are *Seven Hundred Lines, Five Hundred Lines, Three Hundred Lines, One Hundred Fifty Modes, Fifty Lines, Twenty-Five Doors, Questions of Suvikrāntavikrami, Questions of Kaushika, Few Letters, Single Letter,* and *The Heart of Wisdom.*

See Hopkins, *Meditation on Emptiness,* p. 862n514; and Brunnhölzl, *Gone Beyond: The Prajñāpāramitā Sūtras, The Ornament of Clear Realization, and Its Commentaries in the Tibetan Kagyü Tradition,* vol. 1, pp. 34–35.

6. Maitreya, *Abhisamayālaṃkāra. mNgon rtogs rgyan* (Toh. 3786), Dg.T., shes phyin, *ka.*
7. *gsung rab yan lag bcu gnyis,* included in the Tripiṭaka (sDe snod gsum): (1) general teachings; (2) hymns and praises; (3) prophecies; (4) teaching in verse; (5) aphorisms; (6) pragmatic narratives; (7) biographical narratives; (8) narratives of former events as examples; (9) narratives of former births; (10) extensive teachings; (11) narratives of marvels; and (12) teachings on profound doctrines.
8. *Root Verses on the Middle Called Wisdom. Prajñānāmamūlamadhyamakakārikā. dBu ma rtsa ba'i tshig le'ur byas pa shes rab ces bya ba,* dedicatory verse (Toh. 3824), Dg.T., dbu ma, *tsa,* f. 1a.
9. Master Dignāga (sLob dpon Phyogs kyi glang po, c. 480–540 C.E.) the great Indian logician. This is from *Condensed Verses on the Perfection of Wisdom. Prajñāpāramitāpiṇḍārthaḥ. 'Phags pa shes rab kyi pha rol tu phyin ma bsdus pa'i tshig le'ur byas pa* (Toh. 3809), Dg.T., shes phyin, *pha,* f. 292b4–5. (Skt: *prajñāpāramitā jñānam advayaṃ sā tathāgataḥ / sādhyā tādarthyayogena tācchabdyaṃ granthamārgayoḥ*).
10. *khyad chos bzhi.* Four special attributes of the treatises: the attribute of motivation (*kun slong gi khyad par*), the attribute of expressive words (*rjod bya tshig gyi khyad par*), the attribute of expressed meaning (*brjod bya don gyi khyad par*), and the attribute of purposeful composition (*dgos pa byed las kyi khyad par*).
11. *rnam thar sgo gsum*: the essence: emptiness; the cause: absence of characteristics; and the result: wishlessness (*ngo bo stong pa nyid, rgyu mtshan ma med pa, 'bras bu smon pa med pa*).
12. Note that these syllables have varied over time. For instance, in Jamgön Kongtrul's *Beloved Garden* (ch. 28), they are black *du,* yellow *pre,* gray *da,* green *nṛi,* red *a,* and white *oṃ* in the five places, respectively (p. 393).
13. Although the text actually says "arousing the mind [of awakening]" (*sems bskyed*), that is not borne out by the commentary, which concerns the nature of mind itself.
14. This oft-quoted verse is from Saraha's *Treasury of Dohā Songs, Dohakoṣagīti. Do ha mdzod kyi glu* (Toh. 2224), Dg.T., rgyud, *wi,* f. 72b5. The same text is also known as "People's Dohā" in Saraha's *dohā* trilogy. For translations, see Jackson, *Tantric Treasures;* and Schaeffer, *Dreaming the Great Brahmin.*
15. In this commentary the line reads *bla ma'i bslab bya mig ltar bsrung* ("guard the guru's precepts like your eyes"), but the root text appears to be correct as *blangs pa'i bslab bya mig ltar bsrung.*

16. This entire verse is not found in the Tengyur editions.
17. Shāntideva, *Entering the Way of the Bodhisattva. Bodhisattvacaryāvatāra. Byang chub sems dpa'i spyod pa la 'jug pa*, ch. 4, v. 1 (Toh. 3871), Dg.T., dbu ma, *la*, f. 8a2–3.
18. Ibid., f. 8b2.
19. Asaṅga, *Bodhisattvabhūmi. rNal 'byor spyod pa'i sa las byang chub sems dpa'i sa.* (Toh. 4037), Dg.T., sems tsam, *wi*.
20. Chandragomin, *Bodhisattvasaṃvaraviṃśaka. Byang chub sems dpa'i sdom pa nyi shu pa* (Toh. 4081) Dg.T., sems tsam, *hi*, ff. 166b–167a. Chandragomin was a seventh-century Indian Buddhist lay master, a disciple of Sthiramati. Of the two main lineages of bodhisattva vows that entered Tibet, he received and passed on the one from Maitreya and Asaṅga. See Jamgön Kongtrul, *Treasury of Knowledge: Buddhist Ethics*, pp. 172–73.
21. The fifth part corresponding below is actually labeled "elimination of adversities on the path."
22. The text here has *drug* ("six") but that is not borne out by the following sections.
23. Words in parentheses have been added from the interlinear notes in the original, p. 32.
24. *dbang 'bras sam / skyes bus byed pa'i 'bras bu.* More commonly *bdag po'i 'bras bu* ("dominant result").
25. Here *mthu chung ba* ("little power"), more commonly *gzi chung ba ("little charisma")*.
26. *kha zhing chung ba*, it is also sometimes *rtsub pa* ("coarse").
27. The four formless realms are the four perception-spheres of Infinite Space, Infinite Consciousness, Nothing Whatsoever, and Neither Presence Nor Absence [of Perception] (*gzugs med pa'i khams bzhi: nam mkha' mtha' yas, rnam shes mtha' yas, ci yang med pa, yod min med min te skye mched mu bzhi'o*).
28. Nontransferring actions (*mi g.yo ba'i las*) are the virtues that make one attain the two higher realms. They are so called since, apart from ripening in their respective abodes, they do not transfer one to other abodes.
29. This may be a reference to the eight topics of the perfection of wisdom found in *Ornament of Clear Realization*: the knowledge of all aspects, the knowledge of paths, the all-knowledge, the full realization of all aspects, the attainment of culmination, the serial one, the full realization in a single instant, and the dharmakāya. Brunnhölzl, *Gone Beyond*, vol. 2, p. 475 (vv. 1.3–4). Or it may simply refer to the eight parts in section ii below.
30. Nāgārjuna, *Root Verses on the Middle Called Wisdom. Prajñānāmamūlamadhyamakakārikā. dBu ma rtsa ba'i tshig le'ur byas pa shes rab ces bya ba,* ch. 24, v. 18 (Toh. 3824), Dg.T., dbu ma, *tsa*, f. 15a6. Garfield, *The Fundamental Wisdom of the Middle Way*, p. 69.
31. Shāntideva, *Entering the Way of the Bodhisattva,* ch. 9, v. 32.
32. A substantial cause (*upādānahetu, nyer len gyi rgyu*) is a direct cause (*dngos rgyu*), which produces its own particular result. For example, a sunflower seed is the substantial cause for a sunflower sprout. Substantial causes by definition must

precede their results. (Note that substantial cause is also translated as "primary cause" or "perpetuating cause.") See Jamgön Kongtrul, *Treasury of Knowledge: Frameworks of Buddhist Philosophy*, pp. 390–91n766.

33. This is most confusing. There is a note in the *DNZ* edition of the root text, placed after the following verse (i.e., "Meditate on recollecting the Buddha, / naturally clear of thoughts and memories, / free of all mental engagement") that says "this is out of order" (*'di dkyus su med*). Apparently this part of the commentary is an attempt to explain that note, using the same terms: *tshig rkang 'di mchan dkyus la shor ba yin pa 'dra*. This interlinear note, however, is not found in any other edition of the root text, which would seem to make this commentary contemporary with or later than the publication of the *DNZ*. More confusing still, this line "The meaning of the perfection of wisdom" (*shes rab pha rol phyin pa'i don*) itself is not found in the Tengyur editions but *is* found in the *CDC* (but without the note). The Tengyur editions instead have a line that follows "Do not seek elsewhere, you have it yourself," which reads, "The coemergent timeless awareness is . . ." (*lhan cig skyes pa'i ye shes ni*). Thus in both editions, the number of lines ends up the same: two hundred lines, or exactly fifty quatrains (Skt. *śloka*). Āryadeva's root text is widely known as "The Fifty-Shloka." Our commentator appears to be explaining an additional line.

34. *Perfection of Wisdom in Eight Thousand Lines. Āṣṭasāhasrikāprajñāpāramitā. Shes rab kyi pha rol tu phyin pa brgyad stong pa* (Toh. 12), Dg.K., shes phyin, *ka*, f. 3a3. A similar statement is found in the *Perfection of Wisdom in One Hundred Thousand Lines. Śatasāhasrikāprajñāpāramitā. Shes rab kyi pha rol tu phyin pa stong phrag brgya pa* (Toh. 8), Dg.K., f. 326a5 (p. 651): *'di ltar sems de sems ma yin te / sems kyi rang bzhin 'od gsal ba'i phyir ro.*

35. Maitreya, *Highest Continuum. Mahāyānottaratantraśāstra. Theg pa chen po rgyud bla ma'i bstan bcos*, ch. 4, v. 63 (Toh. 4024), Dg.T., sems tsam, *phi*, f. 57b1–2 (p. 114).

36. *sangs* in all copies of the root text, although the commentary reproduces it as *spang* ("abandoned").

37. A much-condensed gloss of a tract in the *Perfection of Wisdom in One Hundred Thousand Lines. Śatasāhasrikāprajñāpāramitā. Shes rab kyi pha rol tu phyin pa stong phrag brgya pa*, Lhasa Kangyur (rKTs–K8), shes phyin, *da*, ff. 365b–372a (and on). Also in the *Perfection of Wisdom in Twenty-Five Thousand Lines* (rKTs–K9), shes phyin, *ga*, ff. 260b–263a.

38. The sentence is a contextual explanation for the Tibetan word *sangs rgyas*, which translates "buddha." *Sangs* means "to clear away or purify [faults]," and *rgyas* means "to expand or develop [qualities]."

39. All other editions of the root text have "fresh awareness" rather than "empty awareness" (*rig pa so mas gar khyab pa*).

40. The text actually is in the negative, *chos sku <u>mi</u> khyab*, but I think this must be a mistake for *chos sku khyab*.

41. *nam mkha' sgo 'byed*, the name of a practice of mahāmudrā consciousness transference in Machik's tradition. See other texts in this volume, such as Rinchen Senge's *Opening the Sky Door: Instructions on Severance Mahāmudrā (Phyag rgya chen po gcod kyi gdams pa nam mkha' sgo 'byed)* (ch. 13).
42. *Heart of the Perfection of Wisdom (Heart Sutra). Bhagavatīprajñāpāramitāhṛdaya. bCom ldan 'das ma shes rab kyi pha rol tu phyin pa'i snying po* (Toh. 21), Dg.K., shes phyin, *ka,* f. 145a7 (p. 289).
43. *DNZ* root and commentary and Golden Tengyur: *g.ya' khang*, Narthang Tengyur: *g.yang khang*, *CDC*: *g.ya' gangs*. *g.ya'* most commonly means rust oxide or other extraneous exuded matter, or slate rock.
44. The Tengyurs have *phyugs gnas* (cattle grounds) rather than *dben phug* (secluded caverns).
45. *stong pa nyid la stong nyid kyis / glags rnyed pa lta* (or *yang*) *ga la srid*. But in the Tengyurs it reads *stong pa nyid kyis stong nyid las / glags rnyed pa yang ga la 'gyur.*
46. *Verse Summary on the Perfection of Wisdom. Prajñāpāramitāsaṃcayagāthā. Shes rab kyi pha rol tu phyin pa sdud pa tshigs su bcad pa,* (Toh. 13), Dg.K., shes phyin, *ka* f. 8a3–4 (p.15).
47. Ibid., f. 14b1–2 (p. 28).
48. Paraphrased from large sections of both the *Perfection of Wisdom in One Hundred Thousand Lines* and *Twenty-Five Hundred Thousand Lines.* In the former, for instance, in one place the discussion of emptiness not taking advantage of emptiness, signlessness, or wishlessness extends from 315b to 319b, Lhasa Kangyur (rKTs–K8), shes phyin, *ca.* The statements concerning outer space and inner space appear in *na*, f. 205b.
49. Rather than *rtags sam mtshan ma pha rol tu* (*DNZ* and *CDC*), the Tengyurs have *brtags sam 'bras bu phyir rol na* ("examination or results [are] outwardly . . .").
50. Here *gnyis med rang grol*, Tengyurs: *rang snang rang grol* ("self-appearing self-liberated").
51. *Sutra of Skill in the Methods of the Great Secret. Sarvabuddhamahārahasyopāyakauśalya Sūtra. gSang chen thabs la mkhas pa'i mdo* (Toh. 82), Dg.K., dkon brtsegs, *cha*, f. 39a2–4.
52. Machik Lapdrön, *The Great Bundle of Precepts* (*bKa' tshoms chen mo),* the other major source text of Severance. A reference to: "Not fixating on body is the Victor's Body, / not fixating on speech is the Victor's Speech, / not fixating on mind is the Victor's Mind. /Other than lucid clarity without fixation, / do not seek elsewhere for the Victor's intent" (ch. 2, p. 16).
53. *lta mtha' sgom pa'i 'du byed dang*, but in the Tengyurs and *CDC* it is *lta mtha' sgom pa'i 'gyu byed dang* ("extreme views, [thought] movements in meditation"), and more interestingly, *TOK* (vol. 3, p. 420) reads *lta mthar sgom pa'i rgyu byed dang* ("that which causes meditation in extreme views"). In *The Religious History of Pacification and Severance* of the *CDC* and other sources, this verse is attributed directly to Machik (*ma cig gi zhal nas*) (3a3).

54. *snyems byed thams cad gcod pa'i phyir*, but in the Tengyurs: *shes pa'i snyems byed gcod pa'i phyir* ("Since it severs inflation of knowing").
55. *Verse Summary* (Toh. 13), f. 2b7. The whole verse reads: "Why are these heroes called great? They are the sublime ones of many assemblies of beings, and they have greatly severed the views of all sentient beings. Therefore they are well spoken of as great heroes."
56. Not found in the same text, which is all in verse.
57. Source not identified.
58. *chod pa'i rtags*, but the actual heading below is "evidence of severing" (*chod tshad*).
59. Here and in *CDC* this is *de la ji ltar bcad zhe na*, but the Tengyur editions have *de ltar ji ltar spyod zhe na* ("How should one engage with that?").
60. The Tibetan term for "devil" is *bdud*, which translates the Sanskrit *māra*, which in turn derives from the root *mṛ-*, to die. The *māra*s represent spiritual death or impediments in spiritual development. The explanation here seems to hark back to this etymology.
61. *gnyan* refers to pestilent diseases and to the spirits that cause them. The "fierce types" (*gnyan rigs*) are one class of spirits included in the eight classes (*sde brgyad*). Also described as "a god of Tibetan culture and the patron of rulers and all patriots. He is associated with the mountains." Chögyam Trungpa, "The Pön Way of Life," in *The Heart of the Buddha*. The dictionary definition is of an earth lord (*sa bdag*) who brings epidemic. The same word with "ground" or "place" (*gnyan sa*) is being translated as "haunted place," since it refers to an area infested with such spirits.
62. Tengyurs: *me tsha* (not *btsa'*): geomantic center, focal point, or meridian. Apparently a reference to the practice of applying moxibustion to infected wounds, i.e., using fierce methods for fierce circumstances.
63. *ri skor*, a cycle of teaching for secluded retreat practice.
64. *skar chen thibs 'og dag tu gzhug*, but the root text has *skar chen thims* ("dissolve"), and *CDC*: *skar chen thig* ("line," "drop"). Both Tengyurs have *skar chen thib 'og dbang du bzhugs* ("keep the morning star [or great constellations] powerfully under thickness"). *Heart Essence of Profound Meaning* contains a similar reference in *skar chen thibs 'og bcug pas 'khor 'das rdzun phug gtib* ("putting the morning star under thumb collapses the false cave of samsara and nirvana"), p. 18. Its commentary, where it is *skar chen 'theb* (or *theb* or *thebs*) *'og bcug pa*, explains the aphorism by reference to the analogy of the sun outshining the stars so that they cannot even appear (pp. 166–67). (Also see ch. 3, notes 13–14.)
65. The following quote from *MCE* (p. 109) elaborates:

    Mere realization of the inherent nature of mind
    Overwhelms the outer haunted places.
    Freedom from fixation on anger, desire, or cherishing
    Overwhelms inner sickness and spirits.
    Freedom from calculating what is or isn't
    Overwhelms secret discursive thinking.

Freedom from prejudice
Overwhelms cyclic existence.

66. *gcod na*, but in root text and *CDC*: *gcod ni*, and in Tengyurs *gcod kyi*.
67. *de dag kun la nyams rab kyi*; *CDC*: *rab rnams kyis*; Golden: *de dag kun byung la nyams len gyis*.
68. *tha mas phung po gzan du bskyur*. The Tengyurs have instead: *tha mas de la brtag dpyad bya* ("the inferior should examine and analyze them"). Our text might represent a later change to bring it more into line with the current practice of Severance, while the Tengyur suggests a more Mahayana approach for the perfection of wisdom.
69. The text mistakenly has "secondly."
70. The Tengyurs have a line that is omitted before these two lines, which reads *des kyang zhi bar ma gyur na* ("if that does not pacify them"). It makes more sense without it, since this couplet describes the situation of having separated awareness and body in doing *powa* (*'pho ba*, consciousness ejection), not what to do if it doesn't work.
71. *dByings kyi rdo rje pha lam*. Text not identified.
72. In the original outline, this section was called simply "Results."
73. The text says "three" (*gsum*), but the text bears out that there are in fact five parts.
74. This could refer to the two obscurations and the realization of abiding mind, or to the three immediately previous sections (which is about the same), or to the purity of the three spheres (i.e., subject, object, and action).
75. Here *phyag chag* or *chag chag* in the root text, *phyag chags* ("hand-sprinkle"), but in all other editions it is *phyag byab[s]* ("hand cleanse"). Khenchen Thrangu Rinpoche confirms the meaning as "to pat." (Personal communication, August 2011).
76. This line is absent from the Tengyur editions.
77. *'khyam gcod*. Two texts are found in the volumes of the *Zur lugs* collected by Drung pa Kun dga' rnam rgyal: {wa} *'Khyam gcod bar cad kun sel gyi pa shin tu zab pa* and {zha} *'Khyam gcod bar cad kun sel gyi dmigs rim dang / gzer bu drug pa'i las tshogs*. (Tashi Chöpel, *Record of Teachings Received*, p. 776).
78. Khenchen Thrangu Rinpoche comments that this refers to sending the blessed sticks and stones to wherever the sick person is living. (Personal communication, August 2011).
79. *gnod sbyin, yakṣha*. This text reads *gdon gnod spyin pho mo dam la thogs* ("evil spirits, male and female *yakṣhas* will be held under oath"), which is one too many syllables; the other editions are probably correct without *gdon*. *CDC* replaces *gnod sbyin* with the more general *gnod byed* ("harm-doers").
80. The Tengyur editions have an additional line after this one: *nyon mongs dgra las rgyal bar 'gyur* ("one will be victorious over the enemy, afflictive emotions").
81. Here the word is *yan lag* ("branches"), but all other editions have *phan yon* ("benefits"), which seems correct. Also, in the root text, it reads *dpag tu med pa 'byung bar gsungs*, rather than *'byung bar 'gyur*, as here and elsewhere.

82. *mtho ris kyi yon tan bdun*. The seven qualities of a high rebirth are noble family, beautiful bodily form, long life span, no illness, good fortune, abundant wealth, and great intelligence.
83. The Tengyur editions contain two extra lines of dedication: "By the virtue of arranging this unborn single cut / May all beings realize the Mother's meaning" (*skye med gcig chod bkod pa'i dge ba des / 'gro ba kun gyis yum gyi don rtogs shog*).
84. The colophons of the Golden and Narthang Tengyurs state only that the great paṇḍita Mipam Gönpo (Mi pham mgon po) translated it. This is another name for Dampa Sangye.
85. Zhwa ma lo tsā ba ("Translator in the Zhwa [family line]"). His personal name was Seng ge rgyal po, also known as Zhwa ma Seng ge or Seng ge rgyal mtshan. According to Roerich, *The Blue Annals* (p. 220), he studied translation under rMa lo tsā ba (b. 1044) and others and was a student of Dampa Sangye. The colophon in the *CDC* edition adds that it was edited in the fern forest retreat at Dingri (*Zha ma lo tsās ding ri mkhan pa'i nags khrod du zhus te gtan la phab pa'o*) (5a1).
86. Vajrāsanapāda, *Grub chen brgyad cu'i bstod pa*, actually entitled *Supplication to the Eighty-Four Great Adepts, Grub thob brgyad cu rtsa bzhi'i gsol 'debs* (Toh. 3758), Dg.T., rgyud, *tshu*, f. 111b3–4. The spelling of his name as Kāmāla follows the Tibetan transliteration in this text; more usually it is Kamalashīla. The identification of Dampa Sangye with the famous Indian scholar Kamalashīla (fl. 713–733) is based on an elaborate Tibetan legend that requires the suspension of belief in historical time, among other things.
87. rTing ri or Ding ri, also called Dingri Langkor, in Latö.
88. sKyo ston sku mched, also known as bSod nams bla ma, the primary teacher of Machik Lapdrön.
89. *Ma jo mo Ganga'i lha mo'i sprul pa*, a reference to Machik Lapdrön.
90. Khu sgom chos seng (Khu sgom chen chos kyi seng ge) from sNye mo khu, one of Machik's disciples and lineage holders. There is a brief history of him in Roerich, *The Blue Annals* (pp. 988–89), where it is said he received the transmission of the Meaning Lineage and was supposed to pass it on to Machik's son Döndrup, but the latter did not want it. Chöseng is featured as the interlocutor in *MCE*, ch. 7.
91. Zal mo brag pa, mentioned in Tashi Chöpel, *Record of Teachings Received* (p. 773), in the lineage of Machik's root texts. His full name and epithet there is Zal mo brag gi mtha' rtsar rTogs ldan dge slong (possibly the same as rTogs ldan dge slong Chos ston bzang po, thirteenth century) (TBRC).
92. Nyang gi jo sras Rin chen gsal.
93. The four underlined words indicate the name Kunga Paljor (Kun dga' dpal 'byor: "All-joy glorious wealth"), the name of the author of this text. According to Tashi Chöpel, *Record of Teachings Received* (p. 778), he was known as Drung Sarupa Kunga Paljor (Drung sa ru pa Kun dga' dpal 'byor) and he received all the transmissions directly from Machik in visions. This may be the Kunga Paljor mentioned in Roerich, *The Blue Annals* (p. 672), who lived from 1428 to 1476 and

was later abbot of sGam po. Or possibly it was the Ralung abbot by that name mentioned in the *Treasury of Names* (*Ming mdzod,* p. 581). Khenchen Thrangu Rinpoche believes it must be the name of a lama from Zurmang Monastery. (Personal communication, August 2011).

## 5. The Great Bundle of Precepts on Severance

1. *gCod bka' tshoms chen mo'i sa bcad,* in *DNZ,* vol. 14 (*pha*), pp. 53–79 (including commentary). Second source: *Collected Works of Karmapa Rangjung Dorje,* vol. 11, pp. 265–98.
2. Although the outline in both of my editions has *rig pa rang lugs* ("intrinsic awareness's own style"), in all copies of the root text this line begins with *rig pas rang lus,* so I believe it is a mistake.
3. The outline here has *'jig rten mi rtogs* ("not realized by the world"), but the outline given within the commentary is *'dzin pas mi rtogs,* which I have used here.
4. *spros pa'i mtha' brgyad.* These are views concerning birth, cessation, eternalism, nihilism, going, coming, singularity, and differentiation.
5. Attributed to Nāgārjuna's (or Rāhulabhadra's) *Eulogy to the Perfection of Wisdom. Prajñāpāramitāstotra. Sher phyin bstod pa* (Toh. 1127), Dg.T. Although Tibetan scholars attribute this famous verse to Rāhulabhadra, it does not appear in the three versions of the *Prajñāpāramitāstotra,* which is commonly said to be by Rāhulabhadra, but the Tibetan Tengyur attributes to Nāgārjuna. (See Karma Phuntsho, *Mipham's Dialectics and the Debates on Emptiness,* p. 229n28.) It does, however, appear in Ratnakīrti's *Eulogy to the Deities of the Four Yogas. Yogacaturdevastotra. sByor ba bzhi'i lha la bstod pa* (Toh. 1170), Dg.T., f. 247b.
6. Called simply 'Phags pa ("Noble") when cited, this seems to refer to any of the longer Perfection of Wisdom sutras. In this case, the closest quotation may be found in *Perfection of Wisdom in Eighteen Thousand Lines* (*Aṣṭadaśasāhasrikāprajñāpāramitā. Shes rab kyi pha rol tu phyin pa khri brgyad stong pa*) (Toh. 10), Dg.K., *kha,* f. 175b7, with the one difference of "empty of the essence of form" rather than "free of the essence of form."
7. Note that the Longchenpa edition of the *bKa' tshoms chen mo* actually has *sems nyid* ("mind itself" or "nature of mind") here instead of *chos dbyings* ("realm of phenomena"), in line with this commentary.
8. *rGyas pa,* the *Perfection of Wisdom in One Hundred Thousand Lines* (*sTong phrags brgya pa*), found in ACIP, vol. *tha* (bam po 254), 532b–538a, although due to the repetitive nature of the sutra the ending of *rnam pa thams cad mkhyen pa nyid* could be almost anywhere. In other words, a large section of this huge sutra is devoted to the idea of mental nonengagement.
9. The text says "six lines."
10. *dngos 'dzin,* but actually the root text in both copies begins with *dngos po'i yul* ("objective things"), which is also indicated by Rangjung Dorje's outline above.
11. *de yang,* but actually it is *des na* in both editions.

12. *Verse Summary on the Perfection of Wisdom. Prajñāpāramitāsaṃcayagāthā. Shes rab kyi pha rol tu phyin pa sdud pa tshigs su bcad pa,* ch. 20, v. 2 (Toh. 13), Dg.K., f. 11b2–4 (p. 22). Translated in Conze, *The Perfection of Wisdom in Eight Thousand Lines and Its Verse Summary,* p. 45.
13. Although the text here says "three lines," there are in fact four in all copies of the root text.
14. *Verse Summary,* ch. 3, v. 5, f. 4b2–3 (p. 8); Conze, *Perfection of Wisdom,* p. 15.
15. *Verse Summary,* f. 12a2–4 (p. 23); Conze, *Perfection of Wisdom,* p. 46. The simile of the miracle that precedes this verse reads: "For example, a monk who has excellent powers of miraculous emanation stays in the sky and simultaneously emanates apparitions that display coming and going, lying down and sitting, yet does not regret them nor feel fatigue."
16. *'khor ba rang grol.* However, the line in the root text begins with *'khor ba rang sar grol ba* ("samsara is liberated on its own ground").
17. *Verse Summary,* ch. 1, v. 25, f. 3a6 (p. 5); Conze, *Perfection of Wisdom,* p. 12.
18. *Verse Summary,* ch. 1, v. 26, f. 3a6–7 (p. 5); Conze, *Perfection of Wisdom,* p. 12.
19. In fact there are seven lines in the root text. In these cases, lines may have accrued over time.
20. *Verse Summary,* ch. 2, v. 9, f. 4a2 (p. 7); Conze, *Perfection of Wisdom,* p. 14. There are variances in the second line of this quotation as it appears in both editions of the commentary. The translation here is based on the Tibetan as it appears in the Derge edition of the Tengyur: *gzugs ni shes rab ma yin gzugs la shes rab med / rnam shes 'du shes tshor dang sems pa 'di dag ni / shes rab ma yin 'di dag la yang shes rab med / 'di ni nam mkha'i khams dang mtshungs te tha dad med.*
21. *bsam pa dran ldan* should be *bsam pa drag ldan*, as in the Kangyur.
22. *Verse Summary,* ch. 24, vv. 1–2, f. 14b1–2 (p. 28); Conze, *Perfection of Wisdom,* p. 54.
23. *Perfection of Wisdom in Eight Thousand Lines. Aṣṭasāhasrikāprajñāpāramitā. Shes rab kyi pha rol tu phyin pa brgyad stong pa* (Toh. 12), Dg.K., f. 3a3. Conze, *Perfection of Wisdom,* p. 84.
24. Butter that is not dyed yellow is white, as everyone used to know.
25. The two editions of this commentary both say here that the verse begins with *snyems grol,* while in fact it begins in both my editions with *snyems sangs.* The meaning is very similar.
26. References to examples of the essential pure nature temporarily obscured, as found in Maitreya, *Highest Continuum* (*rGyud bla ma*) (ATG).
27. *sems tsam rnam bden pa.* Skt. *satyākāravādin.* Also called true aspectarians.
28. *sems tsam rnam rdzun pa.* Skt. *alīkākāravādin.* Also called false aspectarians.
29. Telopa, *Mahāmudrā Esoteric Instructions. Mahāmudropadeśa. Phyag rgya chen po'i man ngag* (Toh. 2303), Dg.T., f. 243b7. This instruction is better known as the *Ganges Mahāmudrā* (*Phyag chen ganga ma*), as it was said to be Telopa's instructions to Nāropa while on the banks of the Ganges River. The version in the Derge Tengyur is slightly different; the second line there reads: *'dul ba'i sde snod la sogs*

*chos rnams dang* ("the vinayapiṭaka and all such dharmas"). Also the last line here is not present in the Tengyur at all. Another version is in the *Collected Works of Marpa* (who originally translated it from the Sanskrit). There the second line is *'dul ba'i sde snod mdo sde'i sde snod la sogs dang* ("the vinayapiṭaka, sūtrapiṭaka, and so on"), and again the fifth line is missing (vol. 1, p. 369). Finally, this instruction is also found in *DNZ*, vol. 7 (pp. 33–36). In this edition, the verse quoted here has the same second line as in the Tengyur; however, it does include the missing fifth line (*zhe 'dod byung bas 'od gsal ma mthong bsgribs*), f. 17b3–4 (p. 34), which is also attested in Rangjung Dorje's commentary (*DNZ*, vol. 7, p. 41). Many English translations of this famous instruction can be found on http://www.naturalawareness.net/ganges.html.

30. *Verse Summary*, ch. 3, vv. 5–6, f. 4b2–4 (p. 8); Conze, *Perfection of Wisdom*, p. 15.
31. The root text in *DNZ* begins with *sangs rgyas 'dus ma byas yin pas* ("since buddha is unconditioned"), although in the Longchenpa edition it is *ma byas 'dus ma byas pa yin* ("the unmade is unconditioned").
32. This refers to "four perception spheres" (*skye mched mu bzhi*) in the root text, which are four kinds of absorption of the formless realms. See ch. 4, note 27.
33. There are actually fifteen lines in this section, but an interlinear note in the root text explains that two of the lines are not found in most editions.
34. *Noble Sutra*: partially found in *Perfection of Wisdom in Eighteen Thousand Lines*, f. 177a.
35. Maitreya, *Mahāyānottaratantraśāstra. Theg pa chen po rgyud bla ma'i bstan bcos*, ch. 5, v. 219 (Toh. 4024), f. 61b2 (p. 128).
36. *Verse Summary*, ch. 2, two lines of v. 10 and two lines of v. 11, f. 4a2 (p. 7); Conze, *Perfection of Wisdom*, p. 14. In the right order, the verses read: "This [inherent nature] is indivisible like space. That inherent nature of all reference has no outer limit. Whatever is the inherent nature of sentient beings has no outer limit. The inherent nature of the space of the sky has no outer limit. The wisdom of worldly knowledge also has no outer limit. The guides have completely proclaimed 'perceptions are on this side.' Once perception is totally annihilated, renunciation goes to the other side."

## 6. A Hair's Tip of Wisdom

1. *Shes rab kyi pha rol tu phyin pa'i man ngag gcod kyi gzhung shes rab skra rtse'i sa gzhung spel ba rin po che'i gter mdzod*, in *DNZ*, vol. 14 (*pha*), pp. 81–99; *DNZ-K*, vol. 9, pp. 528–46.
2. Condensed from *Perfection of Wisdom in One Hundred Thousand Lines. Śatasāhasrikāprajñāpāramitā. Shes rab kyi pha rol tu phyin pa stong phrag brgya pa*, Lhasa Kangyur (rKTs–K8), shes phyin, *ka*, f. 460a. Also found in *Perfection of Wisdom in Twenty-Five Thousand Lines. Pañcaviṃśatisāhasrikāprājñāpāramitā. Shes rab kyi pha rol tu phyin pa stong phrag nyi shu lnga pa*, Lhasa Kangyur (rKTs–K9), shes phyin, *ka*, f. 171a.

3. Maitreya, *Ornament of Clear Realization. Abhisamayālaṃkāra. mNgon rtogs rgyan,* opening verse (Toh. 3786), Dg.T., shes phyin, *ka,* f. 1a.
4. *bud med sgyu ma'i gzugs*, but in the tantra it is *bud med sgyu ma'i spros pa yis* ("by the emanations of woman illusions").
5. *Ḍākinī Vajra Tent Tantra. Ḍākinīvajrapañjarātantra. mKha' 'gro ma rdo rje gur zhes bya ba'i rgyud kyi rgyal po chen po'i brtag pa rgyud* (Toh. 419), Dg.K., rgyud 'bum, *nga,* f. 50a1–2.
6. *Chakrasaṃvara Ḍākinī Illusion Later Tantra. Śrīsarvabuddhasamayogaḍākinījāl asaṃvara-nāmottaratantra. dPal sangs rgyas thams cad dang mnyam par sbyor ba mkha' 'gro ma sgyu ma bde ba'i mchog ces bya ba'i rgyud bla ma* (Toh. 366), Dg.K., rgyud 'bum, *ka,* f. 151a (Lhasa Kangyur, f. 246b).
7. Presumably the *Udānavarga*, though not found there but in its commentary by Prajñāvarman, *Commentary on the Udānavarga. Udānavargavivaraṇa. Ched du brjod pa'i tshoms kyi rnam par 'grel pa* (Toh. 4100), Dg.T., f. 72b5.
8. *spang blang thabs kyis*, literally "by means of rejecting and accepting."
9. The commentary here seems to advise the exact opposite of the root text.
10. That is, listening to important people (ATG).
11. *las mtha'* (*las kyi mtha'*), literally, the end or result of action.
12. Here and below, "thought" (*rtog pa*) is mistakenly written as *rtogs pa* ("realization"), which is not borne out by the Tengyur version. The eightfold path of the noble ones, or eightfold noble path (*'phags lam yan lag brgyad*), is the authentic way of seeing (*lta ba*); the authentic way of expressing that vision in thoughts (*rtog pa*) and in words (*ngag*); the authentic way of exerting oneself in that vision (*rtsol ba*); the authentic livelihood (*'tsho ba*); the authentic mindfulness in attending that vision (*dran pa*); the authentic absorption in the vision (*ting nge 'dzin*); and the authentic way of expressing the vision in actions (*las kyi mtha'*).
13. Nāgārjuna, *Letter to a Friend. Suhṛllekha. bShes pa'i spring yig,* v. 113 (Toh. 4182) Dg.T., spring yig, *ngi,* f. 46a1–2. Translated in Nagarjuna, *Nagarjuna's Letter to a Friend: With Commentary by Kangyur Rinpoche.*
14. *Perfection of Wisdom in Twenty-Five Thousand Lines,* Lhasa Kangyur (rKTs–K9), f. 391b. Note that in the Kangyur, the second sentence is reversed.
15. The source of this verse is unclear.
16. The line itself does not appear but seems to be a condensation of the line beginning with "form has the support of space" and ending several folios later with "it does not transcend that support," repeated many times for each phenomenon, from the *Perfection of Wisdom in Eight Thousand Lines. Aṣṭasāhasrikā-prajñāpāramitā. Shes rab kyi pha rol tu phyin pa brgyad stong pa* Lhasa Kangyur (rKTs–K12), shes phyin, ff. 262b–264a.
17. *Perfection of Wisdom in One Hundred Thousand Lines,* Lhasa Kangyur (rKTs–K8), f. 384a and again on f. 385b. Also found in *Perfection of Wisdom in Twenty-Five Thousand Lines,* Lhasa Kangyur (rKTs–K9), f. 434b.
18. *gter du spos,* an obscure term meaning literally "transfer to the treasury."

19. *dmigs pa'i 'du shes*, same as *yod pa'i 'du shes*, where *'du shes* equals *'dzin pa* (ATG).
20. *Perfection of Wisdom in Twenty-Five Thousand Lines*, Lhasa Kangyur (rKTs-K9), f. 268a–b.
21. Although both the editions have *lus* ("body"), it seems that it must be *las* ("karma") (ATG). The following line—*'du byed med cing mkhyen pa med* in *DNZ*— is *'du kyang med cing* in the earlier *DNZ-K*.
22. Maitreya, *Highest Continuum. Mahāyānottaratantraśāstra. Theg pa chen po rgyud bla ma'i bstan bcos*, fifth vajra point (Toh. 4024), Dg.T., sems tsam, *phi*, ff. 10b7–11a1. See Kongtrul's commentary in Rosemarie Fuchs, trans., *Buddha Nature: The Mahayana Uttaratantra Shastra with Commentary*, p. 200.
23. Machik Lapdrön, *bKa' tshoms chen mo*, ch. 5, p. 12. The analogy there refers to the chicks who will die in the autumn if not nourished properly.
24. *gos ngan* ("bad clothes") *rgyal mtshan rtse la phyar*. This refers to displaying or promoting bad qualities or actions as being good, similar to the English idiom "airing one's dirty laundry."
25. *chos spyod bcu*. The ten dharma-related activities: copying scriptures, making offerings, giving alms, listening to discourses, memorizing, reading, expounding, reciting, and reflecting upon and training in the meaning of the dharma.

### 7. Another Bundle

1. *Shes rab kyi pha rol tu phyin pa'i man ngag yang tshom zhus len ma*, in *DNZ*, vol. 14 (*pha*), pp. 101–13; *DNZ-K*, vol. 9, pp. 547–59. Another edition entitled *Another Bundle of Twenty-Five* (*yang tshoms nyer lnga pa*) found in *Practices of the Severance Collection and So Forth* (*gCod tshogs kyi lag len sogs*) from Limi Monastery, pp. 33–43.
2. The three lines *rtsol dang bral ba de yis ni / dus gsum sangs rgyas gdung zin nas / skye med sa la gnas par 'gyur* in the Limi edition are just the one line: *rtsol dang bral ba'i chos nyid de /* continuing directly into *dmigs med* ("nonreferential . . .").
3. This line added from the Limi edition for clarity. In general, I have added lines from Limi or mentioned variances in the endnotes only when the meaning would be enhanced or changed.
4. In Limi, this is counted as two questions.
5. *srin [bu]*. It was believed that after the silkworm spins its cocoon from its saliva it dies. Actually, in the wild it eats its way out and becomes a moth. Domesticated silkworms are boiled alive in their cocoons for the sake of the silk. In any case, the analogy could still work, whether the metamorphosis is considered a death or the production of silk its ultimate demise.
6. Literally "obstructed" (*thogs*).
7. In *DNZ*, there is the added "according to precepts" (*bka' dang mthun*). Since this makes too many syllables for the verse and is not included in Limi, I have left it out. Note, however, that in the Limi edition from here through to the next

paragraph, which is introduced as "internal devil," the verse lapses into prose as follows: "In this way apply the above teaching to the ear organs and so forth. You should understand that the tangible devil lacks intrinsic existence. Those are what are known as the external devils."

8. *zhar la rang re mthong ba dang*, but translated according to Limi: *zhe la rang re mtho ba dang* (p. 36).
9. *rang [b]zhin tsam na bdud kyang gnas*. Limi: *rang zhi tsam na bdud kyang zhi / rang gnas tsam na bdud kyang gnas* ("if oneself is just pacified, the devil is also pacified; if one is just abiding, the devil also abides") (ibid.).
10. *bdag nyid chos sku yin*. Limi: *bdud nyid chos sku yin* ("the devil itself is dharmakāya").
11. *snyems chas*. Limi: *sems tsam* ("mere mind").
12. *Sems dang lus la 'phongs pa*. Limi: *sems can lus la phang ba* ("losing the body to beings") (p. 37).
13. *brtson pas nyams su len pa 'byung*, added from Limi (ibid.).
14. *g.yas med* is being tentatively taken to be *g.ya' med*. The same word occurs repeatedly in these texts.
15. Limi: *rigs kyi bu de bzhin bzhag na sangs rgyas rnams kyi zhal mthong bar 'gyur ro* ("Noble child, if you rest like that you will see the faces of the buddhas").
16. Limi: *rkyen snang 'phral gyi rang spyod* ("The appearance of circumstances is its own spontaneous conduct").
17. *byis pa mgo thug byed pa bzhin*. Limi (*rko dug byed pa*) makes even less sense.
18. *sems la sa zin mi bdog pas*. Limi: *sems la ma zin mi dgos pas* ("since there is no need to not grasp in mind") (p. 39).
19. This answer, which is obviously of importance as a definition of this practice, seems to be recorded in a variety of ways. In Limi, every instance of the word *severance* (*gcod*) in this question is instead "conduct" or "action" (*spyod*). These are often said to be equivalents in the *gcod* tradition, but it does lend a slightly different sense. The metaphor of the thief is also absent. In *CDC*, the passage is quoted very differently and corresponds exactly to a text in the Limi edition called *bKa' tshom* but in fact is closer to this *Yang tshom*. In those two places, it translates as: "Trampling upon the unbearable is explained as severance. If you realize everything as mind, there is no other object to sever. If you realize mind itself as empty, there is no duality of severing and that which is severed. If you experience nonduality, there is no severance: all devils are already cut off, like, for example, a thief in an empty house" (f. 3b). Usually, the thief in an empty house refers to there being no harm to be done.
20. In Limi, the last three lines read instead, "Blessing that is possessed of a self is not blessing and has little efficacy. Even if it benefits others, it has little power. There is no blessing in that which possesses desire and craving."
21. The first line (only) can be found in *Chos thams cad rdzogs pa chen po byang chub kyi sems kun byed rgyal po*, Lhasa Kangyur (rKTs–K822), f. 43A.

22. Four lines added from Limi (p. 42).
23. Line added from Limi (ibid.).
24. Following Limi's *rkyen gyis ded pa*, rather than *DNZ*'s *rkyen gyis dad pa*, according to Ringu Tulku.
25. This difficult section is translated based on three very different versions: the *DNZ*, and the Limi editions of *Yang tshom* and *bKa' tshom*, with clarifications from Ringu Tulku.
26. *Zhus lan gyi gdams pa yang tshom nyi shu rtsa lnga pa*. This alternative title given in the colophon here and as the main title of the text in Limi reveals a discrepancy in the counting.

## 8. Vajra Play

1. *Zhus len rdo rje rol pa*, in *DNZ*, vol. 14 (*pha*), pp. 113–15; *DNZ-K*, vol. 9, pp. 559–61; *DV*, vol. *ja*, pp. 209–14. The title of this prose set of questions and answers that is usually included at the end of *Yang tshom* (*Another Bundle*) is not given until its colophon and not mentioned in the catalog of the *DNZ*, nor is it included at all in the Limi edition of *Yang tshom*. However, in following the example set by the new *DV*, I have set it apart as a discrete text and taken the full title from there.
2. *glor 'dug*. Although this might be a spelling mistake for *blor 'dug* ("in the mind"), that would not explain the harsh answer, which would be elicited only by a silly question.
3. *dmigs pa gcig* in both *DNZ* and *DNZ-K* is not clear, so I have interpolated one possibility. Another option appears in *DV*, where it has been changed to *dmigs pa zhig*, which could be interpreted as "[So one should] destroy the reference points[?]"

## 9. The Essential Bundle

1. *Shes rab kyi pha rol tu phyin pa'i man ngag bdud kyi gcod yul las nying tshom*, in *DNZ*, vol. 14 (*pha*), pp. 116–30; *DNZ-K*, vol. 9, pp. 562–76. This text is not mentioned in Tashi Chöpel's *Record of Teachings Received*.
2. The phrase "just as there is no changing nor discursive thought in mind" (*ji ltar sems la 'gyur ba med cing rnam par rtog pa med*) is found dozens of times in *Perfection of Wisdom in One Hundred Thousand Lines. Śatasāhasrikāprajñāpāramitā. Shes rab kyi pha rol tu phyin pa stong phrag brgya pa*, Lhasa Kangyur (rKTs–K8), *ka*, ff. 451b–459b; and in *Perfection of Wisdom in Twenty-Five Thousand Lines. Pañcaviṃśatisāhasrikāprajñāpāramitā. Shes rab kyi pha rol tu phyin pa stong phrag nyi shu lnga pa*, Lhasa Kangyur (rKTs–K9), *ka*, f. 169b.
3. *Perfection of Wisdom in Eight Thousand Lines. Aṣṭasāhasrikāprajñāpāramitā. Shes rab kyi pha rol tu phyin pa brgyad stong pa*, Lhasa Kangyur (rKTs–K12),

f. 4b: "In this way that mind is not mind, the nature of mind is certainly lucid clarity" (*'di ltar sems de ni / sems ma mchis pa ste / sems kyi rang bzhin ni / 'od gsal ba lags so*).

4. The text appears to be *rig med* ("no awareness"), but in context *ris med* seems more likely.
5. Paraphrasing from *Perfection of Wisdom in Twenty-Five Thousand Lines,* Lhasa Kangyur (rKTs–K9), ff. 143a–146a.
6. *Heart of the Perfection of Wisdom* (*Heart Sutra*). *Bhagavatīprajñāpāramitā-hṛdaya. bCom ldan 'das ma shes rab kyi pha rol tu phyin pa'i snying po,* Lhasa Kangyur (rKTs–K529), f. 260a.
7. Attributed to the *Extensive Mother* in *A Hair's Tip of Wisdom: A Precious Treasure Trove to Enhance the Original Source* (ch. 6, pp. 81–99), where the line reads "form" rather than "all phenomena." However, the line itself does not appear but seems to be a condensation of the line beginning with "form has the support of space" and ending several folios later with "it does not transcend that support," repeated many times for each phenomenon, from *Perfection of Wisdom in Eight Thousand Lines,* Lhasa Kangyur (rKTs–K12), ff. 262b–264a.
8. The phrase as it is here does not appear in any wisdom sutra, but in reverse form—"since all phenomena are equal, the perfection of wisdom is equality" (*chos thams cad mnyam pa nyid pas shes rab kyi pha rol tu phyin pa mnyam pa nyid do*)—it is found repeatedly in nearly all of them, including *Perfection of Wisdom in Eight Thousand Lines,* ibid., f. 445b.
9. *Verse Summary on the Perfection of Wisdom. Prajñapāramitāsaṃcayagāthā. Shes rab kyi pha rol tu phyin pa sdud pa tshigs su bcad pa,* Lhasa Kangyur (rKTs–K13), f. 196a. The phrase there is *nam mkha'i khams dang mtshungs te dbyer med gcad du med* ("Inseparable, indivisible, just as the element of space").
10. *krim gyis bsgrim la lhod kyis glod / shigs kyis bshigs la phyal gyis thong / lhugs kyis klug la cog gis zhog / bsgom pa'i bzhag sa de na yod.* Perhaps the most famous saying attributed to Machik, quoted frequently and variously.
11. While the first parts of this citation appear in various forms innumerable times in the sutras, it does not appear in conjunction with this ending.
12. *Perfection of Wisdom in One Hundred Thousand Lines,* Lhasa Kangyur (rKTs–K8), f. 157a. There it is *phyi stong pa nyid sgom pa'i tshe mi dmigs pa'i tshul gyis phyi stong pa nyid bsgom par bya'o* ("When meditating on external emptiness, meditate on external emptiness in a nonreferential way").
13. Again, the reverse of this line, "To meditate on the perfection of wisdom is to meditate on space," is found in *Perfection of Wisdom in Twenty-Five Thousand Lines,* Lhasa Kangyur (rKTs–K9), f. 444a. It is quite common for authors who have memorized many scriptures to misquote them slightly. The previous two citations were not found.
14. *Verse Summary,* Lhasa Kangyur (rKTs–K13), f. 191b.

## 10. The Eight Common Appendices

1. *Thun mong gi le lag brgyad pa,* in *DNZ,* vol. 14 (*pha*), pp. 130–40; *DNZ-K,* vol. 9, pp. 576–86. *Le lag brgyad pa* in *Practices of the Severance Collection and So Forth* (*gCod tshogs kyi lag len sogs*) from Limi Monastery, pp. 57–66. *DV,* vol. *cha,* pp. 239–53.
2. In Limi, this first appendix is called "the appendix on sublime instruction" (*gdam[s] ngag dam pa'i le lag rdzogs sho*).
3. *bsdigs mor che.* Limi: *gzigs mor che* ("a great spectacle").
4. *thog bab gdams ngag bstan par bya.* Limi: *brtson la thags bcas gdam[s] ngag bstan* ("Give the instructions to those of definite diligence").
5. Limi: *ci phyir rang snang sems yin pas / de nas sems med lhug par zhog* ("Because self-appearance is mind, so rest serenely with no mind").
6. *sdug.* Limi: *rdung* ("beat").
7. *sems kyis bkra lag bgyi ba las.* But I have used the Limi version: *sems kyi spra lag. BD*: *spra lag: g.yo khram gyi spyod tshul* ("a deceptive behavior").
8. *phur pa btson pas dbyings su sleb.* Limi: *phung po stong pa'i dbyings su slob* ("The aggregate[s] is trained in empty space").
9. *rtsol ba dang bcas pa'i le lag.* Limi: *rtsol med kyi le lag* ("appendix on effortlessness").
10. *mkhas pa rnams.* Limi: *mkha' 'gro rnams* ("ḍākinīs"). Also, this is the fourth appendix in Limi (pp. 60–61), the third and fourth being reversed.
11. *'phrig pa* here understood as in Limi: *'khrigs pa.*
12. *de ni don med sgom pas stong.* Limi: *de ni don med sgom pas bcings* (". . . and binding").
13. "thought of emptiness" added from Limi for clarification.
14. *btags par shes pas rtogs 'gyur bsgom.* Limi: *btags pas rnam par rtog 'gyur sgom* ("by designating [it] becomes conceptual; meditate").
15. In Limi, this appendix is called, again, "appendix on effortlessness" (p. 62). The next section in Limi is totally different, but then seems to pick up some of this appendix on p. 66, ending with *rgya skad gyi le lag rdzogs so.* It appears that *rgya skad* ("Indian language") is a mistake for *rgya gad* ("scolding"), as in the title for the sixth appendix here.
16. *rnal ma 'byor,* literally, "does not connect to the natural state," the negation of *rnal 'byor,* the Tibetan translation of *yoga.*
17. *nga rgyal chags pa,* but here I'm following Limi: *nga rgyal 'chag pa.* I have interpreted the phrases ending simply in *na* ("if") as rhetorical questions.
18. In *DNZ* and *DNZ-K,* there is an added sentence ("By relaxing and resting in being and fullness of clarity and bliss . . .") that is broken up by spaces and an *x* (*glod dang yin gyis zhog dang gsal / gyis / x dol dang bde yis / e ma ho*). In Limi (p. 62), it is a continuous sentence: *glod dang yin gyis zhog dang bsam gyis bdol dang bde ba yis* and not followed by *e ma ho.* Finally, in *DV,* the sentence and the extra *e ma ho* are deleted, which seems to be the best solution.

19. *bsam pa'i yul las sangs rgyas med*. But perhaps better in Limi: *bsam pa'i yul na bud dha med* ("buddha is not an object of thought").
20. *tshi re chad*. The meaning of this phrase is not clear.
21. *skyel med* ("no escort"), but I have used Limi: *skyel ma* ("escort").
22. *sangs rgyas sems can yin*. Limi: *sangs rgyas sems yin* ("buddha is mind").
23. These are the three techniques for the three levels of practitioners: superior, average, and inferior, respectively.

## 11. The Eight Uncommon Appendices

1. *Thun mong ma yin pa'i le lag brgyad pa*, in *DNZ*, vol. 14 (*pha*), pp. 140–55; *DNZ-K*, vol. 9, pp. 586–601. *DV*, vol. *ja*, pp. 255–77.
2. *gnyan khrod*. The word *gnyan* has a wide range of meanings, starting with "pestilence" or "pestilent" (*Merriam-Webster*: "1. destructive of life: deadly; 2. injuring or endangering society: pernicious; 4. infectious") and the spirits that cause pestilence, which are basically fierce or malignant. I have termed the places (*sa*) or retreats (*khrod*) that are inhabited by such spirits "haunted" or "fierce" places throughout the text.
3. The phrase appears in the *Perfection of Wisdom in Eight Thousand Lines* (Lhasa Kangyur, rKTs–K8, f. 445B), as well as in the twenty-five-thousand-line and hundred-thousand-line versions.
4. According to the explanation of Venerable Geshe Champa Lodro Rinpoche in Savvas, "A Study of the Profound Path of Gcod: The Mahāyāna Buddhist Meditation Tradition of Tibet's Great Woman Saint Machig Labdron," this refers to obstacles that start up and then dissappear. This technique is meant to make the obstructing spirits remain put so that the yogin gets the benefit of the practice (p. 161n1).
5. *yas stags*: the articles needed, such as hair or clothing of the patient, in ransoming ceremonies and averting rituals such as the thread-cross rite. See *MCE*, p. 347n21.
6. *thab gzhob*: in the Bön tradition, the idea of burning a foul object to repel spirits.
7. *lhog pa*: generally, ulcers, swellings, cancer, but: "muscular spasms (inflammation in muscular tissues)" in Drungtso and Drungtso, *Tibetan-English Dictionary of Tibetan Medicine and Astrology*.
8. *Thog brdzis*, "direct subjugation," explained by Ringu Tulku as overcoming problems by doing the exact opposite of what is usually done, confronting the problem itself, and using "like to cure like." In this example, it is to cure pollution by partaking of mixed food (*kha bsres*) or using a bowl that has been used for holding polluted substances like corpses (*ro bag*) and leprous parts (*mdzes can*).
9. *stebs* here should be *stengs pa*, as in the heading.
10. *Verse Summary on the Perfection of Wisdom. Prajñāpāramitāsaṃcayagāthā. Shes rab kyi ph rol tu phyin pa sdud pa tshigs su bcad pa*. Lhasa Kangyur (rKTs–K13), f. 205A, line 2.

11. Explained by Ringu Tulku, this refers to a kind of bad luck that occurs when a child dies and the propensity to die carries over to the next born. To remove this jinx (*sri'u*), one has to do a ritual or ceremony using either the actual child or clothing and so forth.
12. *gos tshul bkrus* should be *gos chu las krus* as in *DNZ-K.*
13. *ril ma*: tiny balls of dirt, grease, or skin rolled from the child's body (RT).
14. *mdze can gyi kha 'phro blud*: According to Ringu Tulku, this means something like water from a cup that has been used by a leper or other contaminated or contagious person.
15. These activities again are applying seemingly contradictory or normally harmful methods. According to Ringu Tulku, they are called *tho cho spyod pa* ("nonsensical conduct") and were generally not recommended by Machik Lapdrön.
16. *ba su ki*: (Skt. Vāsukī). Vāsukī is the name of one of the great nāga kings but seems also to refer to a kind of ritual offering to nāgas and to a kind of nāga medicine. Here, the torma is made of (or as in the) Vāsukī along with the three whites and three sweets.
17. *bras* should be *brus* ("gouge," "dig") as in *DNZ-K.*

## 12. The Eight Special Appendices

1. *Khyad par gyi le lag brgyad,* in *DNZ,* vol. 14 (*pha*), pp. 155–64; *DNZ-K,* vol. 9, pp. 601–10. *DV,* vol. *ja*, pp. 279–93.
2. This is highly unusual and may be a simple mistake. Most images of the four-armed Great Mother (*yum chen mo*) depict her holding either a vajra or a rosary in the upper right hand and a volume of the perfection of wisdom (usually resting on a lotus) in the upper left hand, with the two remaining hands either in the equipoise mudra in her lap or in the teaching mudra at her chest.
3. *'phang lo 'bring po'i mig gi tshad tsam*: Ringu Tulku describes this as being about the thickness of a pencil.
4. From the *Perfection of Wisdom in Eighteen Thousand Lines. Aṣṭadaśasāhasrikāprajñāpāramitā. Shes rab kyi pha rol tu phyin pa khri brgyad stong pa,* Lhasa Kangyur (rKTs–K10), shes phyin, *ga*, f. 260b; and in *Verse Summary on the Perfection of Wisdom. Prajñāpāramitāsaṃcayagāthā. Shes rab kyi pha rol tu phyin pa sdud pa tshigs su bcad pa* (rKTs–K13), f. 196a. Note the difference, however, in the *DNZ* (*dbyer med dpyad du med*) and the sutras (*dbyer med gcad du med,* "inseparable and unseverable").
5. This well-known quote from Machik has not surfaced in her works, though a similar quote is found in *Essential Bundle*, with the first line the same.
6. The phrase appears eight times in the *Perfection of Wisdom in One Hundred Thousand Lines. Śatasāhasrikāprajñāpāramitā. Shes rab kyi pha rol tu phyin pa stong phrag brgya pa,* Lhasa Kangyur (rKTs–K8), shes phyin, *da*, ff. 365a–366b and *ga*, ff. 260b–261a.
7. Paraphrasing from *Perfection of Wisdom in Twenty-Five Thousand Lines.*

*Pañcaviṃśatisāhasrikā-prajñāpāramitā. Shes rab kyi pha rol tu phyin pa stong phrag nyi shu lnga pa*, Lhasa Kangyur (rKTs–K9), shes phyin, *ka*, ff. 143a–146a.

8. Quoted this way in *The Essential Bundle* as well, the phrase as it is here does not appear in any Perfection of Wisdom sutra except in reverse form, i.e.: "Since all phenomena are equality, the perfection of wisdom is equality" (*chos thams cad mnyam pa nyid pas shes rab kyi pha rol tu phyin pa mnyam pa nyid do*). In this form, it is found repeatedly in nearly all the sutras, including the *Perfection of Wisdom in Eight Thousand Lines. Aṣṭasāhasrikāprajñāpāramitā. Shes rab kyi pha rol tu phyin pa brgyad stong pa,* Lhasa Kangyur (rKTs–K12), f. 445b. Similarly, most of the other statements here are found in reverse form.
9. From the *Perfection of Wisdom in Eighteen Thousand Lines,* Lhasa Kangyur (rKTs–K10), f. 279a, and in *Verse Summary,* Lhasa Kangyur (rKTs–K13), f. 213b.

## 13. Opening the Sky Door

1. *Phyag rgya chen po gcod kyi gdams pa nam mkha' sgo 'byed,* in *DNZ,* vol. 14 (*pha*), pp. 407–23; *DNZ-K,* vol. 9, pp. 848–64. *DV,* vol. *ja*, pp. 757–82. By Rin chen seng ge, signing with the Sanskrit Ratnasiṃha.
2. The mantra of the perfection of wisdom: *oṃ gate gate pāragate pārasaṃgate bodhi svāhā.*
3. This prayer of invocation is completed here from *Source of All Qualities* (ch. 22, p. 305).
4. I was not able to find this line, which begins only with *'di nyid*. It was reconstructed from Āchārya Lama Tenpa's memory as *'di nyid du ni bzhugs su gsol.*
5. *Source of All Qualities*, ch. 22, p. 306.
6. *Rab 'byams ma.* This refers to the prayer attributed to Machik that begins with *stong gsum rab 'byams 'jig rten thams cad du*, as found in most Severance liturgies, such as *Source of All Qualities*, ibid., pp. 308–9.
7. All these prayers are filled in from *Source of All Qualities*, ibid., pp. 306–7.
8. This prayer was not located.
9. This prayer seems to be from the same source as the homage in *Pearl Rosary* (ch. 21, p. 284), but with significant differences, primarily omissions. I have pieced it together from there, following the indications here.
10. *rjes gnang.* This is often translated as "permission blessing," a kind of condensed empowerment that is given to permit the disciple to do a practice. Here, since the text is also drawing on authoritative scriptural sources to verify the practice, "authorization" seems to capture both senses of authorizing the disciple and citing the scriptural sources.
11. In Kongtrul's *Treasury of Knowledge: Esoteric Instructions*, this verse is quoted and attributed to *Another Bundle* (*yang tshoms*), but it is not found there or in any of Machik's works in this volume.
12. *brTags gnyis. Hevajratantrarājanāma.* Lhasa Kangyur (rKTs–H378a), rgyud,

f. 342b. Farrow and Menon, *The Concealed Essence of the Hevajra Tantra*, part 1, ch. 6, v. 5, p. 63.

13. *Another Bundle*, ch. 7, p. 107.
14. These are all experiential words with no fixed meaning: *bol le / shig ge / had de / cam me*.
15. Source not found. Again, this includes words of experience, the translation of which is uncertain: *thal le ba, 'bol le ba, zings se ba, had de*.
16. *Another Bundle*, ch. 7, p. 107. This is a continuation of the quote "Rest the body in the way of a corpse . . . ." The one difference here is "an ocean unmoved by ships," rather than "an ocean unmoved by wind."
17. This was *not* found in the *Two-Part Hevajra Tantra*, but in the *Kālachakra Tantra That Issued from the Supreme Original Buddha*, known generally as the *Condensed Tantra. Laghutantra. bsDus pa'i rgyud*. Lhasa Kangyur (rKTs–K362), rgyud, K362, f. 360b. (Toh. 362). The last line there is slightly different and I have followed that: *'dod pas rnal 'byor mas shes kyis*. In context, the statement is referring to the eighteen dhātus.
18. The third Karmapa (thus the second incarnation), Rangjung Dorje, *Complete Explanation [of Severance]* (*gCod kyi ṭīkā*). See ch. 5, pp. 57–79.

## 14. Object Severance Empowerment Known as Opening the Sky Door

1. *gCod yul gyi dbang nam mkha' sgo 'byed du grags pa*, in *DNZ*, vol. 14 (*pha*), pp. 361–70. By Tāranātha. *DV*, vol. *ja*, pp. 691–703. Thank you to Gangteng Tulku Rinpoche (GTR) of Bhutan for his help with this text.
2. Tāranātha's story of this empowerment (*gCod dbang nam mkha' sgo 'byed kyi lo rgyus mu tig phreng ba*), which must be read when it is conferred, can be found in his *Collected Works* (Dzamthang edition, 2000?), vol. 20, pp. 715–26.
3. *manydzi*: usually a tripod, although any kind of stand can be used (GTR).
4. *mdo sgrub*, here equivalent of *mdo 'dun*, would be recitation of the *Heart Sutra* (*Sher snying*), according to GTR.
5. *Ḍākinī Vajra Tent Tantra. Ḍākinīvajrapañjarātantra. mKha' 'gro ma rdo rje gur zhes bya ba'i rgyud kyi rgyal po chen po'i brtag pa* (Toh. 419), Dg.K., rgyud 'bum, *nga*.
6. *gSol 'debs dgongs bskyod ma*, sometimes spelled as *dgongs bskyed ma* ("arousing the intention"). This prayer is included in *The Required Liturgies on the Occasion of Venerable Tāranātha's Severance Empowerment of Opening the Sky Door* (ch. 15, pp. 169–71). It is also found in Tāranātha's *Collected Works* (vol. 20, pp. 775–77), with considerable variation. The colophon there states that it must be read before the torma empowerment when conferring the empowerment on disciples. Note that it is very similar to the "Praise of Machik" in *Source of All Qualities* (ch. 22, pp. 315–17, there attributed to Tönyön Samdrup rather than

Machik's son Gyalwa Döndrup), as well as to the "Descent of Blessings" (ibid., pp. 333–34), a good example of the mix-and-match nature of Severance texts.

7. *chos dbang sems la bskur ba.* This is a reference to the empowerment that Machik received from her guru, Kyotön Sönam Lama (see *MCE*, pp. 69–72). It is distinguished from "the deity empowerment conferred on the body" (*lha dbang lus la bskur ba*). "Opening the sky door" is related to "opening the dharma door." See also the reference by Kongtrul in *Treasury of Knowledge: Esoteric Instructions*, p. 281, or Tāranātha's story of this empowerment (see note 2 above).

## 15. The Required Liturgies on the Occasion of Venerable Tāranātha's Severance Empowerment

1. *rGyal thang lugs kyi gcod dbang nam mkha' sgo 'byed kyi cho ga rje btsun tā ra nā thas mdzad pa'i skabs su nye bar mkho ba'i 'don cha,* in *DNZ*, vol. 14 (*pha*), pp. 165–71; *DNZ-K*, vol. 9, pp. 611–17. *DV*, vol. *ta*, pp. 587–600.
2. Added from *DV*.
3. *Ra sa spang lhung* or more commonly *spang lung* (but mistaken in *DV* as *spang lhud*), literally "grassy valley goat land." Sönam Lama was Machik Lapdrön's principal guru.
4. *gSol 'debs dgongs bskyod ma,* sometimes spelled as *dgongs bskyed ma* ("arousing the intention"). See ch. 14, note 5.

## 16. Practice Manual on the Profound Severance of Evil Object

1. *Zab mo bdud kyi gcod yul gyi khrid yig bzhugs / Karma pa rang byung rdo rjes mdzad,* in *DNZ*, vol. 14 (*pha*), pp. 173–84; *DNZ-K*, vol. 9, pp. 618–28. Second source: *Collected Works of Karmapa Rangjung Dorje*, vol. 11, pp. 299–312.
2. *dran pa,* often translated as "mindfulness."
3. This is both a reference to the forms of peaceful activity, white color and round shape, as well as possibly the visualization of it as a lake of elixir.
4. *Verse Summary on the Perfection of Wisdom. Prajñāpāramitāsaṃcayagāthā. Shes rab kyi pha rol tu phyin pa sdud pa tshigs su bcad pa.* Lhasa Kangyur (rKTs–K13), f. 312b. Also found in *Perfection of Wisdom in Eight Thousand Lines*, Lhasa Kangyur (rKTs–K12), *ga*, f. 279a. There is an additional line and other minor differences in the sutra:

   > [The bodhisattva] would give up the head and limbs without hesitating, / giving up all possessions always without attachment. / Knowing the nature of all phenomena is without self and hollow, / if one would even give up one's own flesh without hesitation, / what need to mention giving up external things at that time?

   Also see Conze, *The Perfection of Wisdom in Eight Thousand Lines and Its Verse Summary*, p. 69.

5. *gnad them[s] bdun*, mentioned as *The Steps of Vital Points* (*gnad them*) in *MCE*, p. 98. One of the ten teachings brought to India from Tibet. The text has not been located.
6. *DNZ-K* has *log non*, while the other two have *lag non*. As well as a suppression practice, the words literally pick up the "mistake" (*log*) from the previous paragraph and indicate a way to suppress or counteract mistaken practice.
7. In all copies this is written as either *lan tsha* or *lan tshwa*, "sea salt." Lama Tenpa Gyaltsen suggested that it must be *na tsha* ("sickness").
8. *Verse Summary*, Lhasa Kangyur (rKTs–K13), H17, f. 192b.
9. Here Kham bu ya le, but in the *History of Pacification and Severance* (f. 44a) it is Kham bu yag[s] legs, so named at birth because he was as good (*yag*) and fine (*legs*) as a peach (*kham bu*). His ordination name was bSod nams rin chen. He is said to have been the sole lineage holder of the practice lineage (*sgrub brgyud*) of Machik's son Gyalwa Döndrup (rGyal ba don grub). Janet Gyatso suggests that Kham bu ya le may have been Gyalwa Döndrup's son ("The Development of the gCod Tradition," in *Soundings in Tibetan Civilization*).
10. gNam tsho ba, a teacher at Tsurpu Monastery, postdating Karma Pakshi (1204–1283) in the lineage succession of the Karmapas. His full name was gNam tsho do pa Mi bskyod rdo rje, and he was also known as Ras pa Sangs rgyas nyi ma. He spent many years at the sacred sites of Namtso (Sky Lake) and Tsari Mountain.

## 17. White Crystal Mirror

1. *gCod kyi tshogs las yon tan kun ldan gyi dmigs rim bla ma'i gsung rgyun gyi zin bris shel dkar me long*, in *DNZ*, vol. 14 (*pha*), pp. 201–50, by Old Monk Tenzin Namdak (Ban rgan bsTan 'dzin rnam dag); *DNZ-K*, vol. 9, pp. 646–95. *DV*, vol. *ja*, pp. 333–98. Also found in Kunga Namgyal's *Explanations of Severance: Lamp of Clarity, and Others (gCod kyi bshad pa gsal ba'i sgron me sogs)*, pp. 275–409 (TBRC W27477) and in Karma Chakme's *Collection of Mandala Rituals from Palpung (dPal spungs dpe rnying gsar bskrun las dkyil chog phyogs bsgrigs)*, vol. 8, pp. 109–80 (TBRC W1G4334).
2. rJe btsun Kun dga' rnam rgyal (1567–1629), the fourth Trungpa incarnation in the Karma Kagyu lineage, associated with the Zurmang monasteries in eastern Tibet. The sequence of practice (*phyag bzhes kyi rim pa*) referenced here is probably in Kunga Namgyal's *Explanations of Severance* (see note 1).
3. Literally, "above." I'm not sure what this refers to.
4. In Tekchok Dorje, *Source of All Qualities* (*yon tan kun 'byung*), ch. 22, p. 302. Most of the liturgy indicated in the present text is written out in full in *Source of All Qualities*, although it is not certain that this is the original source. Page numbers are added for convenience.
5. This is not found in the sādhana *Source of All Qualities*.
6. *Source of All Qualities*, ch. 22, p. 303.

7. The texts say "two" (*gnyis pa*), apparently a miscount. There is no precise structural outline imposed on this text, and the occasional enumeration is confusing.
8. *Source of All Qualities*, ch. 22, p. 305.
9. Ibid., p. 306.
10. *hram mer* (in all copies), taken to be the equivalent of *lham mer* and *lam mer*.
11. *chu srin*, a crocodile-like sea monster.
12. *Source of All Qualities*, ch. 22, p. 307.
13. ཏྲི་སྲེ་དུ་ཧྲི་ཨ་ཨོཾ་
14. *yar la khad pa* in the *DNZ* editions has been changed in *DV* to *yal la khad pa* ("about to vanish"). Note that Kongtrul's *Beloved Garden* (ch. 28) uses a similar phrase, *phar la khad* ("about to take off").
15. In this visualization, the central channel extends from the cranium to the heart center, without continuing further down.
16. *Source of All Qualities*, ch. 22, p. 308.
17. The ten glorious ornaments of a wrathful deity: the fresh elephant skin to show the meaning of the supreme vehicle; the "basis for prosperity" human skin to show that samsara need not be abandoned; the garland of black vipers to show that anger has been defeated; the leopard skirt to show that the four activities are spontaneously accomplished; the grease smears to show the extracted essence of samsara; the *rakta* spots to show that desire has been mastered; the triple skull garlands to show that the three kāyas are spontaneously present; the vajra armor to show being totally indestructible; the wisdom flames to show that the darkness is burned away; and the attire of flaming and subjugating wings.
18. The eight charnel ground ornaments: human-head ornament, human-head garland, elephant-skin upper garment, human-skin shawl, tiger-skin skirt, smeared human fat, blood drops, and cemetery ash clots.
19. *nor bu cha bdun*: king's earrings, queen's earrings, rhinoceros horns, coral stalks, elephant tusks, minister's earrings, and three-eyed gems.
20. *nor dbul*, mistakenly copied in the Shechen edition as *nor 'bul*.
21. Khros ma nag mo ("Fierce Black Lady"). Sanskrit alternatives: Krodhakālī, Kālikā, Krodheshvarī, Krishma Krodhinī.
22. *Source of All Qualities*, ch. 22, p. 308. This "short call" and a "long call" are attributed there to Karmapa Rangjung Dorje.
23. This last section is the red distribution, called by Kongtrul the "Flayed Skin Distribution" (*g.yang gzhi ma*). *Beloved Garden*, ch. 28, p. 397.
24. *thod sgyed ma*: this may be an alternative for *thod zhal ma*, Face Skull Cup.
25. 'Brug pa Kun spangs chen po, probably Pema Karpo (1527–1592), for his works on *gcod* found in the cycle called *Nā ro gsang spyod*, *Nāro's Secret Conduct* (*spyod* is used interchangeably with *gcod*).
26. *Source of All Qualities*, ch. 22, p. 321.
27. Ibid., p. 324.
28. This is a list of tantras, abbreviated here in the Tibetan, as indicated by the parentheses. Each of the tantras features deities of the same name, which seems to be the sense here.

29. *Source of All Qualities*, ch. 22, p. 326.
30. Drung rMa se rtogs ldan, or bLo gros rin chen (1386–1423), a disciple of the fifth Karmapa, De bzhin gshegs pa (1384–1415), and the founder of Zurmang Monastery.
31. *Source of All Qualities*, ch. 22, p. 329.
32. Ibid.
33. Ibid., p. 330.
34. Ibid., p. 331.
35. Ibid., p. 315.
36. Ibid., pp. 333–34.
37. *bsre ba skor gsum*: As above, blend others' awareness with your own awareness, blend your own awareness with space awareness, and blend the flesh and blood of the corpse with the feast.
38. *dar sri*: spirits who neither mature nor die (*mi dar ma shi ba'i sri*).
39. *khro chu zhing lpags*: the alternative visualization in the Slapping (see below, p. 244).
40. *'gyed tshul drug*: just below there are "seven modes," so I am not sure if this is a mistake.
41. This basic general outline is not followed exactly in this text. The supplication and descent of blessings is mentioned as part V but then is put in the appropriate order after the body offerings (with no number). The concluding practices (number 7) are omitted.
42. *lcags rdor ma ri skor*: reference unknown.
43. Ban sgar ba 'Jam dpal bzang po, fifteenth-century Karma Kamtsang master, author of the famous prayer called the Short Vajradhara (*rDo rje 'chang thung ma*).
44. Gar dbang mchog gi sprul ku ("supreme emanation Garwang"), or Zurmang Garwang, a line of incarnate lamas connected with the Zurmang monasteries. The first Garwang is identified as the rebirth of Drung Mase (see note 29). The Garwang here is apparently Gar dbang Chos skyong rnam rgyal, according to the lineage list in Jamgön Kongtrul, *Catalog* (p. 161).
45. *'gyur med rdo rje'i khri*. I've interpreted this literally as "immutable vajra throne," but it may also be a reference to the lineage holders coming from Yongs dge gter ston Mi 'gyur rdo rje (1628/41–1708), a disciple of Kun dga' rnam rgyal (see note 2).

## 18. Essence of the Vital Meaning

1. *gCod yul zab mo'i khrid yig gnad don snying po*, in *DNZ*, vol. 14 (*pha*), pp. 185–200; *DNZ-K*, vol. 9, pp. 630–45. Second source: Tāranātha's *Collected Works* (*TSB*) (Dzamtang printing, 2000?), vol. 20, pp. 661–79.
2. *DNZ* has *sems rtogs* ("mental experience"), but *TSB* has *nyams rtogs*, which I have preferred.
3. This additional line from *TSB*.

4. *sal ding gi 'gro* from *TSB* is correct, rather than *dal deng gi 'gro* in *DNZ*, according to Ringu Tulku (personal communication, April 2013).
5. Following *TSB: ces kyang 'char 'char du btub pa* rather than *DNZ*: *ci yang 'chag tu btub pa btub.*
6. *thun bzhi khar* inserted from *TSB*, vol. 20, p. 670.
7. Added lines from *TSB*, vol. 20, p. 673, line 3.
8. *snying rlung*: literally "heart-wind," a kind of wind disorder (*rlung nad*) of the heart that causes sadness and depression for no reason.
9. [dPal] stag lung thang is the seat of the Taklung Kagyu subsect in central Tibet.

## 19. Rainfall of Desirables

1. *gCod khrid zab mo 'dod dgu'i char 'bebs*, in *DNZ*, vol. 14 (*pha*), pp. 251–61; *DNZ-K*, vol. 9, pp. 696–706. *DV*, vol. *ja*, pp. 399–412. The author is dKon mchog 'bangs, also known as dKon mchog yan lag, the fifth Zhamarpa (*DNZ*, vol. 18, p. 456).
2. *The Great Bundle of Precepts* (*bKa' tshoms chen mo*) (ch. 2).
3. *'og nas 'byung ba*: These are the four great abilities of severance in haunted places from section five *DNZ* p. 255.
4. *tsog pu* or *cog pu*, a single-person tent just big enough to sit in.
5. *brag gdong mi ring ral gri 'dra ba*: this phrase is not clear to me.
6. The word spelled *khrag zer* (a type of symptom of hearing disorder) perhaps should be *brag ser*, "crevices or cracks in the cliff side." Thanks to Dolmakyab for the clarification.
7. Ghosts of those murdered by knife. Thanks to Dolmakyab for that information.
8. *zil gnon sde bdun*: the seven are not clearly enumerated here.
9. *gCod tshigs bcad ma*: This seems like a reference to *Esoteric Instructions on the Noble Perfection of Wisdom*, which is usually called the *Grand Poem* (*Tshigs bcad chen mo*), by Āryadeva the Brahmin (ch. 1). However, the references to "incomparable dharma lord" and "incomparable guru" throughout the text may instead refer to one of the gurus in Könchok Bang's lineage.
10. *phyugs po* in both printings of the *DNZ* has no referent, but in *DV* it has been corrected to *phyug po*, "the wealthy." It could also be a misspelling of *'phyugs po*, "blunderer" (RT).

## 20. The Body Donation and Feeding Ritual

1. *rJe rang byung rdo rjes mdzad pa'i gdon tshogs dgu ma sa bdag drug sbyor dang / mi bskyod rdo rjes mdzad pa'i gdan thog gcig ma gcod tshigs bcad ma dang gnyis gab sprad nas lus byin dang bsngo ba [*or *bstab pa] bya tshul bltas chog 'don 'grigs*, in *DNZ*, vol. 14 (*pha*), pp. 261–77. Second source: *Collected Works of Karma Chakme* (*Karma chags med gsung 'bum* ), vol. 52, pp. 248–80 (TBRC W1KG8321). Third source: *rJe Rang byung rdo rjes mdzad pa'i gcod kyi tshogs las*

*rin po che'i phreng ba 'don sgrigs bltas chog tu bkod pa gcod kyi lugs sor* (Paro, Bhutan: Lama Ngodrub and Sherab Drimey, 1981), pp. 255–93. Note: most editions and lists use *bstab pa* rather than *bsngo ba* in the title. Note also that in the *DNZ,* this text is found within the previous text, *Rainfall of Desirables.*

"Mikyö Dorje's Poem" can also be found as a separate text arranged by Karma Chakme, in the latter's *Collected Works*, entitled *Mi bskyod rdo rjes mdzad pa'i gcod tshigs bcad ma'i dmigs rim mdor bsdus dang dmigs pa nyer mkho 'ga' zhig*, vol. 53, pp. 337–58 (TBRC W1KG8321). The verses in Mikyö Dorje's text starting with *namo guru . . .* are actually from Rangjung Dorje.

2. Karma Pag shi (1204–1283), considered the incarnation of the renowned meditator Dus gsum mkhyen pa (1110–1193), and thus the second Karmapa and the first tulku of Tibet.
3. Added from the Rangjung Dorje and Karma Chakme editions.
4. Here spelled *kham bu*, a variant of *chang bu* (ATG). *Changbu* are bits of dough that are squeezed out between the fingers and offered to spirits, or offerings of small bits of food.
5. Added from the *gDon tshogs dgu ma* and the Rangjung Dorje versions.
6. *gDon tshogs dgu ma* and the Rangjung Dorje edition have "fifteen."
7. dKon mchog 'bangs, better known as dKon mchog yan lag, the fifth Zhamar (1525–1583), author of the text immediately preceding this one.
8. *bdud rtsir mi bsgyur rtsub lugs yin.* Rangjung Dorje edition: *bdud rtsir ma bsgyur btsub lugs lan.*
9. *sag zhu* or *swag zhu*, described as a hat with holes in it (Dolmakyab), possibly a Mongolian-style hat.
10. *bande* (*ban de*, Skt. *bandi*), a word for a Buddhist monk or mendicant, possibly connected to the honorific word for monastics, *bhante*, as used in modern-day Sri Lanka. There is also a type of earth lord known as "king" (*gyalpo*). The edition in Karma Chakme's *Collected Works* has an army of kings surrounding the bande (p. 255).
11. *don snying lnga*: the five essential organs are the heart, lungs, liver, spleen, and kidneys. Other versions of this prayer have, instead, the five sense organs (*dbang po rnam lnga*).
12. In Karma Chakme's collection, the descriptions are reversed and make more sense: "those who come early swallow it whole (*snga ma rnams kyis jur mid gyis)* and those who come late scavenge [the rest] (*rjes ma rnams kyis hab thob gyis*)." Also note that these two lines are not in the well-known short daily practice (*rGyun khyer gyi lus sbyin bsdus pa*), though most of this prayer is familiar from there. In the *gcod* collection by Rangjung Dorje, the first of these two lines is similar to the one above, and the second line is omitted (p. 273).
13. *dmag chen gyis gnang chen chod pa bzhin*; Rangjung Dorje text: *dmag chen mnog chen chod pa bzhin* (p. 273).
14. *spar* (or *sbar*) *snyob* (but *spar sgom* in *rJe Rang byung rdo rjes mdzad pa'i gcod kyi tshogs las rin po che'i phreng ba 'don sgrigs bltas chog tu bkod pa gcod kyi lugs sor.*

15. *lte phur nag mo*, unknown female spirit, possibly shaped like a dagger (*phur ba*) from the navel (*lte ba*) down.
16. *DNZ* editions: *lha 'bab ma thub par skyo ba*. But in Chakme edition: *lha bab ma thub pa sogs snyon pa'i rigs*, and Rangjung Dorje edition: *lha bab ma thub pa smyo ba'i rigs*, both meaning "types of insanity such as inability to bring down the gods."
17. *DNZ: klu bdud nag po mgo dgu* ("nine-headed black nāga devil"), but this appears to be a mistaken transfer from "nine-headed black planet devil" above. The Chakme and Rangjung Dorje editions and the same liturgy in *Pearl Rosary* (ch. 21) all have *klu bdud nag po srog gzan dang*, as translated here.
18. *DNZ* has *yag* but in *Pearl Rosary, nyag* ("scales, measure, single, dented, notched").
19. *kwa ta 'dre yug 'khor dang bcas*. This is added from the Chakme edition and from the same liturgy in *Pearl Rosary* (ch. 21).
20. *DNZ: khams pa mi zan la sogs pa*. This line is unclear to me and is not found in the same prayer in *Pearl Rosary* (ch. 21). In the Chakme edition it is not clarified by the alternate spelling of *kham pa*.
21. With these two lines added from *Pearl Rosary*, the pattern of this section remains consistent.
22. *DNZ: sha khrag gi nang du ske tshags nub pa*; *DNZ-K: sha khrag gi nang (nad?) du[g] tshigs (tshags) nus pa* (p. 716); Chakme: *sha khrag nang du sked tshigs nub pa*; Rangjung Dorje: *sha khrag nang du ske tshud de nub pa*.
23. *u ber* or *u wer* or *ur wer*: unidentified.
24. *thel mo* (or *thel ma*) *rna zlum*: According to Ringu Tulku, these are female *teurang* spirits who have only one leg and move by hopping.
25. *gcod phyi* should be *gcod sri*, as in the earlier *DNZ-K* edition and others.
26. *Supreme Dharma of the Application of Attention. Saddharmasmṛtyupasthāna. 'Phags pa dam pa'i chos dran pa nye bar gzhag pa*. Lhasa Kangyur (rKTs-K287), mdo sde, *ra*, f. 353a. This was the reply that the arhat Asvajit gave when asked by Shāriputra what his master taught. Shāriputra thereupon gained the first stage of an arhat.
27. *Individual Liberation Sutra. Prātimokṣasūtra. So sor thar ba'i mdo*. Lhasa Kangyur (rKTs-K2), 'dul ba, f. 29b. The first line there is *sdig pa thams cad mi bya ste*, rather than here *sdig pa ci yang mi bya zhing*. Also, the line "Do not disturb others' minds" does not appear in any of the sutras that contain this quotation or in the other editions of this text.
28. Ibid.
29. Following *'og dong mo'i sa ru ma tshud par* from the Chakme and Rangjung Dorje editions, rather than *'og dogs mo'i sa la ma chud par* as in the *DNZ* editions.
30. This is greatly abridged from ten folios covering just the application to the Three Jewels. The text continues from there to apply the concept to the perfections, and so forth. *Perfection of Wisdom in One Hundred Thousand Lines. Śatasāha-*

*srikāprajñāpāramitā. Shes rab kyi pha rol tu phyin pa stong phrag brgya pa*. Lhasa Kangyur (rKTs-K8), shes phyin, vol. *da.*, ff. 365a–75a.

31. A specific text called "Vajra Verses" attributed to Machik has not been found, although it has been quoted elsewhere. For example, this line was quoted in *Rainfall of Desirables* by Könchok Bang (ch. 19), although there the three are demons, disease, and spirits. However, there are many similar statements, such as this one in Machik's *Another Bundle*: "For the inner blessing power, / resting within the nondual unity / of one's mind and demons and sickness / brings about the blessing of pacifying suffering" (ch. 7, p. 109).
32. This line added from the Chakme and Rangjung Dorje editions.
33. Kun dga' rnam rgyal (1567–1629) was the fourth incarnation of the Trungpa tulkus of the Zurmang monasteries. He wrote extensively on *gcod*. Karma Chakme (Rāga Asya) is listed among his students.

### 21. Pearl Rosary

1. *gCod kyi lus sbyin gyi ngag 'don mu tig phreng ba,* in *DNZ,* vol. 14 (*pha*), pp. 279–96; *DNZ-K,* vol. 9, pp. 723–40. *DV,* vol. *ja*, pp. 559–85. This *Pearl Rosary* should not be confused with Samten Özer's *Pearl Rosary: An Account of the Lineage* (*brGyud gtam mu tig phreng ba*).
2. Immense Ocean (Gang chen mtsho) is an epithet for Vairochana. In *Beloved Garden* (ch. 28, p. 391), Jamgön Kongtrul explains that this comes from the Zurmang tradition, and that in his own oral tradition one should substitute the Great Mother in place of Vairochana.
3. This line has been added from the same prayer in *MCE*, pp. 155–56, because it seems to make sense and so that it is not lost. However, it may have been dropped in later liturgies to accommodate the music and meter of the quatrains.
4. *dbang po rnam lnga*: the five sense faculties are sight, hearing, smelling, tasting, and feeling. Other versions of this prayer have, instead, the five essential inner organs (*don snying lnga*).
5. See the visualization for this in *White Crystal Mirror* (ch. 17, pp. 233–34).
6. *bLo sbyong mtshon cha 'khor lo* is a well-known text by Dharmarakṣhita, given by him to Atisha. I have not found a work so named that was authored by Rangjung Dorje. However, there is no "long call" (*'bod ring*) in the Dharmarakṣhita text, so it may be that the wrong title is given here.
7. g.Yag sde paṇ chen brTson 'grus dar rgyas (1299–1378) studied with Rangjung Dorje. Note that in a previous text arranged by Karma Chakme, the Ninefold Spirit Feast is apparently attributed directly to Rangjung Dorje in the title: *The Body Donation and Feeding Ritual Arranged as Convenient Liturgy, Combining Lord Rangjung Dorje's Ninefold Spirit Feast and Six Earth Lord Application with Mikyö Dorje's Single-Seat Severance Poem.*
8. This liturgy, but with brief descriptions and recommendations, is also found in

*The Body Donation and Feeding Ritual Arranged as Convenient Liturgy, Combining Lord Rangjung Dorje's Ninefold Spirit Feast and Six Earth Lord Application with Mikyö Dorje's Single-Seat Severance Poem* (ch. 20).

9. *ba dan ma*. See brief descriptions of the various distribution visualizations, including this one, in *White Crystal Mirror* (ch. 17).
10. For a description, see ibid., p. 239.

## 22. Source of All Qualities

1. *gCod kyi tshogs las yon tan kun 'byung gsungs rgyun 'khrul med ltar bkod pa bzhugs pa'i dbu phyogs lags so*, from the Zurmang tradition. According to the *Catalog*, compiled and arranged by the fourteenth Karmapa, Tekchok Dorje (Theg mchog rdo rje, 1798/9–1868/9). *DNZ*, vol. 14 (*pha*), pp. 297–334; *DNZ-K*, vol. 9, pp. 741–78. *DV*, vol. *ja*, pp. 587–647.
2. bSo dor, the main earth lord (*sa bdag*) of the Earth (Ringu Tulku).
3. This famous verse is found in tantras such as the *Chakrasaṃvarābhidhānottaratantra*. *mNgon par brjod pa'i rgyud bla ma* Lhasa Kangyur (rKTs–K369), rgyud, f. 167a. (Toh. 369)
4. From "The King of Aspiration Prayers: Samantabhadra's Aspiration to Good Actions" from the *Gaṇḍhavyūha* chapter of the *Flower Ornament Sutra* (*Avataṃsakasūtra*).
5. This line has been added from the same prayer in *MCE* because it seems to make sense and so that it is not lost. However, it may have been dropped in later liturgies to accommodate the music and meter of the quatrains.
6. Machik spoke the first three verses to Dampa Sangye (ibid., p. 84). All five verses appear later in the same text (pp. 155–56). The one difference is in the fourth verse, where it is "the mudra of nonduality" rather than "auspiciousness."
7. See ibid., p. 162.
8. This was also mentioned in *Pearl Rosary* (ch. 21, p. 291), which contains the "long call." There, it is sourced in the *Mind Training Wheel Weapon*.
9. Lha phu ba bSam gtan rin chen. This prayer, with minor variations, is usually attributed to Rangjung Dorje himself, as in *Tshogs las rin chen 'phreng ba*. It does seem strange that this lineage supplication does not even include Rangjung Dorje, Samten Rinchen's guru. And the question must be asked—who continued this prayer after his time?
10. sKyo chung, or Kyo the Younger, would be Kyotön Sönam Lama (sKyo ston bSod nams bla ma), Machik's main teacher. Kyotön Shakya Yeshe would be the elder.
11. sKye med zang thal, also Dol pa zang thal, according to TBRC.
12. Although the text here says *zab mo brag* (literally, "profound cliff"), in the *Kagyu Feast Liturgy* (ch. 24), the nearly identical prayer has *zal mo sgang*, which is one of the six ranges of Dokham and makes more sense.
13. Karma bsTan skyong, repeated here for the second time. The lineage here is the

same as in *Pearl Rosary* up through Könchok Tenzin and then branches off. There, it continues to Tenpa Namgyal, which possibly could be meant here, or perhaps there was actually a second Tenkyong.

14. Ding ri gling 'khor. This might be a mistake for Dingri Langkor (ding ri glang skor), the place of Dampa Sangye's monastery, or else a double entendre, with *gling* serving to indicate the islands around (*gling 'khor skor*) this world of Jambudvīpa.
15. sMa ra ser po, a disciple of Dampa Sangye. See Gö Lotsāwa, *The Blue Annals (Deb ther sngon po)*, vol. 2, p. 997.
16. Thod smyon bsam grub, Machik's son according to *MCE*, although some sources indicate a person of the same name as either her grandson, great-grandson, or grandnephew. See *MCE*, p. 287n7.
17. gNyan chung Lotsāwa (Dar ma grags), thirteenth century; worked with the Indian translator Vajrapāṇi.
18. *gdung sgrom*, the structure that holds the body of an important master for cremation.
19. Written here as *padma bhanydza* and elsewhere as *padma bhanda*, it seems to mean "lotus vessel," as in the Tibetan *pad snod* that shows up below, and refers to a ritual skull cup. A possible Sanskrit reconstruction might be *bhagāla,* which equals *kapāla*, or *bhanya*, "bone." This doesn't explain the connection with the lotus.
20. Ri gong pa, later identified in this text as brTson 'grus seng ge (1207–1278), which was the ordination name of Sangs rgyas ston pa. He was the seventh or last of the Shangpa single-transmission lineage from Niguma. His master, Chos kyi shes rab (1175–1255), is also known as Rigongpa, both of them associated with the Shangpa monastery Ri gong (or Ri gung) dgon pa. Although he is best known in the Shangpa lineage, he is also mentioned in Severance lineages. He met Machik as a boy in 1216 and received a single-transmission lineage from her. He authored a life story of Machik, which includes many liturgies, entitled *Ma gcig lab kyi sgron ma'i rnam thar dang gcod kyi chos skor ma 'ongs lung bstan bcas pa* (TBRC W1KG1646).
21. gNyan ston, probably Sangs rgyas gnyan ston Chos kyi shes rab (1175–1255), the Shangpa master who founded Rigong Gönpa.
22. These liturgies can be found in *Pearl Rosary* (ch. 21, pp. 294–95).
23. Ibid., p. 295.
24. dKon mchog yan lag, also known as dKon mchog 'bangs (1525–1583), author of *Rainfall of Desirables* (ch. 19).
25. *tshar rgyab ma*. This refers to the practice of repeating a portion of a ritual for more merit. *DV* has changed this to *chang bu brgya rtsa ma*, "One Hundred Changbu" ritual, which is a short liturgy by Rangjung Dorje that is repeated 108 times for offering 108 small pieces of torma (*changbu*). This may be a correct assumption, but I am not sure.
26. sKye med dga' yan, one of the eight disciples of Machik's sixteen heart disciples,

called "equal to herself" (*rang dang mnyam pa*). See *TOK,* vol. 1 of 3, p. 545; Jamgön Kongtrul, *Treasury of Knowledge: Buddhism's Journey to Tibet*, pp. 363–64.

27. *bdag dang 'gro la thugs brtse'i phyir / nyid kyi rdzu 'phrul mthu yis ni / ji srid mchod pa bdag bgyid pa / de srid bcom ldan bzhugs su gsol /*
28. *mchod sbyin gnas 'dir gang lhag pa'i / 'byung po sa 'og rgyu ba dang / gang yang sa steng 'god pa dang / sa blar rgyu ba gang yin pa / mgu bar gyis la rang gnas su / thams cad tha dad 'gro bar gyis /*
29. *dkon mchog rin chen gsum la phyag 'tshal lo / dge ba 'di yis nye bar mtshon nas ni / sems can rnams kyis dus gsum bsags pa yi / zag bcas zag med zung 'jug dge ba rnams / bla med byang chub chen por bsngo bar bgyi / 'gro kun thams cad mkhyen pa thob par shog /*
30. *Padma zhi zlum*, a brief description of this is found in *White Crystal Mirror* by Tenzin Namdak (ch. 17, p. 239).

## 23. Supplication to the Long Lineage by Machik, Appended by Bengar Jampal Zangpo

1. *Ring brgyud kyi gsol 'debs ma gcig gis mdzad par ban sgar 'jam dpal bzang pos kha bskang ba,* in *DNZ,* vol. 14 (*pha*), pp. 335–36; *DNZ-K,* vol. 9, pp. 779–80. *DV,* vol. *ja*, pp. 649–57. Bengar Jampal Zangpo (Ban sgar 'Jam dpal bzang po, fifteenth century) was a famous Kaṃtsang master who transmitted the teachings from the sixth Karmapa (mThong ba don ldan, 1416–1453) to the seventh Karmapa (Chos grags rgya mtsho, 1454–1506). He wrote a number of texts on *gcod*, acc. Drepung Catalog (*Tibskrit Philology*). This text comes from the Zurmang tradition and is not mentioned separately in the *Catalog*.
2. Here Kham bu la ye should be Kham bu yag legs. He is said to be the younger son of Gyalwa Döndrup and hence Machik's grandson. See ch. 16, note 9, and *MCE*, p. 102.
3. Ri khrod dbang phyug, usually a name associated with Shavari, here probably Seng ge ye shes (1181–1255) (Roberts, *The Biographies of Rechungpa*, p. 10).

## 24. Kagyu Feast Liturgy

1. *bKa' brgyud tshogs las,* in *DNZ,* vol. 14 (*pha*), pp. 337–39; *DNZ-K,* vol. 9, pp. 781–83. *DV,* vol. *ja*, pp. 659–63.

## 25. Fulfillment Rituals of Profound Object Severance

1. *gCod kyi skong ba rnams bzhugs pa'i dbu phyogs lags so*. Grub thob dPal ldan rin chen, in *DNZ,* vol. 14 (*pha*), pp. 371–86. Second source: *Zab mo bdud kyi gcod yul gyi bskang ba*, in *DV,* vol. *ja*, pp. 705–30.

2. *thugs dam bskang*. From Sanskrit *paripūraṇa*, "to fill": (1) to please (*dgyes pa*), to satisfy (*tshim pa*), or to gratify through offerings; (2) to restore or renew vows, either one's own or those of the deity. I use either "fulfill" or "renew," since both meanings seem to be implied.
3. Machik's son, Gyalwa Döndrup.
4. Tibetan would be *ye shes 'bar ba*, which is the name of a tantra.
5. These are one version of the names of the buddhas of the ten directions. (1) dKon mchog 'byung gnas; (2) Mya ngan med pa'i dpal; (3) Rin chen 'od 'phro'i dpal; (4) rGyal ba'i dbang po'i dpal; (5) Ting 'dzin glang po dpal; (6) Padmo'i dam pa'i dpal; (7) Nyi snang dam pa'i dpal; (8) gDugs kyi dam pa'i dpal; (9) dGa' ba dam pa'i dpal (sometimes Padmo'i dpal nyid); (10) Padmo dpal (sometimes dka' ba'i dpal can).
6. *lag skyong*, changed to *zla skyong* ("moon protector") in *DV.*
7. mTshal dkar Chos kyi grags pa. Perhaps the fourth Zhwa dmar (1453–1524) or Mi bskyod rdo rje (1507–1554). sKyo ngos rang gi ri khrod apparently refers to the name of his retreat, according to Ringu Tulku.
8. Si tu Nor bu bsam 'phel, b. 1566 (TBRC). But *Tibskrit Philology* (p. 254) gives Nor bu bsam 'phel as the fourth Situ, Mi pham phrin las rab brtan, 1658–1682.
9. Ru mda' grub thob dPal ldan rin chen.

## 26. Offering Torma to All Ḍākimas

1. *mKha' 'gro ma rnams la gtor ma 'bul ba*, in *DNZ*, vol. 14 (*pha*), pp. 341–51; *DNZ-K*, vol. 9, pp. 784–94. *DV*, vol. *ja*, pp. 665–78. Though without colophon and not mentioned in the *Catalog*, the table of contents in *DNZ-K* subtitles this *Zur lugs gcod tshogs gtor 'bul*: "Torma Offering of the Severance Feast in the Zurmang tradition." However, it is not mentioned in the long list of teachings received in the Zurmang tradition.
2. A variation of this prayer in *Source of All Qualities* (ch. 22) is attributed there to Machik.
3. *bye ba 'bum*: ten million (*bye ba*) times one hundred thousand (*'bum*) is a trillion.
4. Taking *bshud glu len* for *shu glu len*.
5. In these lists of the twelve *tenma* (short for *bstan srung ma bcu gnyis*, "twelve female protectors of the doctrine"), the first two words represent either their title or their location—tentatively translated where possible. The proper names are next, each one beginning with Dorje. See Nebesky-Wojkowitz, *Oracles and Demons of Tibet*, pp. 182–202, for alternatives.
6. *sman btsun*, alternative of *sman mo* ("*menmo* spirit"). These three sets of four represent the twelve *tenma*. The twelve *kyongma* (*skyong ma*) and the twelve *yama* are not named individually here.
7. rLangs chen dPal gyi seng ge, one of the twenty-five main disciples of Padmasambhava, who employed the eight classes of gods and demons as his servants.

## 27. Distillation of the Profound

1. *gCod yul rgya mtsho'i snying po stan thog gcig tu nyams su len pa'i tshul zab mo'i yang zhun,* in *DNZ,* vol. 14 (*pha*), pp. 353–60. Shangpa Texts (Samdrup Darje Ling Monastery, n.d.), vol. 4, pp. 579–97. *DV,* vol. *ja,* pp. 679–90. Also in Jamgön Kongtrul, *Treasury of Extensive Teachings* (*rGya chen bka' mdzod*), vol. 12, pp. 449–59.
2. *Yon tan rin po che sdud pa,* known also as *Verse Summary on the Perfection of Wisdom. Prajñāpāramitāsaṃcayagāthā. Shes rab kyi pha rol du phyin pa'i sdud pa tshigs su bcad pa* Lhasa Kangyur (rKTs–K13), shes phyin, f. 209A. Also in *Perfection of Wisdom in Eighteen Thousand Lines* (*khri brgyad stong pa*) Lhasa Kangyur, GA-274B. See Roerich, *The Blue Annals,* p. 981, or in Tibetan, vol. 2, p. 1140. Conze states the whole name as *Prajñāpāramitāratnaguṇasaṃcayagāthā.*
3. *blo ldog rnam bzhi:* four contemplations that turn the mind toward the practice of dharma: (1) the precious human birth; (2) impermanence and death; (3) karmic cause and effect; and (4) the shortcomings of samsara.
4. Birth from a womb, from an egg, from warmth and moisture, and miraculous birth.
5. *sbre snum rlangs pa ma yal ba,* literally, this seems to say "undissipating steam of monkey grease."
6. *Supreme Dharma of the Application of Attention. Saddharmasmṛtyupasthāna. 'Phags pa dam pa'i chos dran pa nye bar gzhag pa,* Lhasa Kangyur (rKTs-K287), mdo sde, *ra,* f. 353a. This was the reply that the arhat Asvajit gave when asked by Shāriputra what his master taught. Shāriputra thereupon gained the first stage of an arhat.
7. *Individual Liberation Sutra. Prātimokṣasūtra. So sor thar ba'i mdo,* Lhasa Kangyur (rKTs–K2), 'dul ba, f. 29b. The first line there is *sdig pa thams cad mi bya ste,* rather than here *sdig pa ci yang mi bya zhing.*
8. *Diamond Cutter Sutra. Vajracchedikāprajñāpāramitasūtra. Shes rab kyi pha rol tu phyin pa rdo rje gcod pa.* Lhasa Kangyur (rKTs–K16), shes phyin, *ka,* f. 235b.

## 28. Beloved Garden

1. *Lus mchod sbyin gyi zin bris mdor bsdus kun dga'i skyed tshal,* in *DNZ,* vol. 14 (*pha*), pp. 387–405; *DNZ-K,* vol. 9, pp. 829–47. *DV,* vol. *ja,* pp. 731–55.
2. For example, see *White Crystal Mirror* (ch. 17).
3. *bdud bzhi*: The four devils here seem to refer to the traditional *māra* from the sutras: the devil of the aggregates, of afflictive emotions, of death, and of divine progeny. The same is more clearly elucidated by Tenzin Namdak in *White Crystal Mirror* (ch. 17), where the karmic spirits are directly equated with the essence of the four devils as the habits of dualistic projections. It is odd that Kongtrul here specifically mentions one of them, the devil of death, while the rest of the list follows the normal enumeration of the six spirits (*gdon*), plus two parents. Additionally, Kongtrul seems to be making a correlation between the first four

spirits in this list—hateful enemies, harmful obstructors, interfering conditions, and karmic spirits—with the four devils in the Severance tradition: the tangible devil, intangible devil, devil of exaltation, and devil of inflation.

4. The text here (all copies) says *sa gnon mnyam bzhags*, which would appear to mean "earth-touching [and] equipoise [mudras]." Generally, all depictions of the Great Mother show her two hands either in equipoise mudra or dharma-teaching mudra. However, several of the other texts in this collection also describe this unusual position, so apparently it was once an alternative that never made it into the tangkha iconography.
5. These refer to the prayers that follow the refuge in the daily practices, such as Tekchok Dorje's *Concise Charity of the Body for Daily Practice* (*rGyun khyer gyi lus sbyin bsdus pa*).
6. *tshul khrims rnam pa gsum*. The three divisions of the bodhisattva vows: to abandon nonvirtue, practice the virtue of the six perfections, and benefit sentient beings.
7. *trāṃ las rin po che'i gzhal yas khang*. Although this appears to say "a jeweled palace from *trāṃ*," other commentaries specify a jeweled throne, which makes more sense in terms of the "four-layered seat" (*gdan bzhi*) that is mentioned.
8. Immense Ocean (Gangs chen mtsho) is an epithet for Vairochana and refers to the Buddhist cosmological presentation of existence as issuing forth from the scented water that flows from the bodies of these buddhas, manifesting the pure realms and all universes.
9. One version consists of ten guardians of the directions (*phyogs skyong bcu*), eight great gods (*lha chen po brgyad),* eight great nāgas (*glu chen po brgyad*), eight great planets (*gza' chen po brgyad*), four worldly guardians (*'jig rten skyong ba bzhi*), twenty-eight constellations (*rgyu skar gnyis shu tsa brgyad*), and nine great bhairavas (*'jigs byed chen po dgu*). http://www.himalayanart.org/search/set.cfm?setID=2130.
10. The mantra of the prajñāpāramitā sutras: *tadyathā oṃ gate gate pāragate pārasaṃgate bodhi svāhā.*
11. Traditionally these are (1) straight as an arrow; (2) white colored with a red tinge; (3) glistening or oily; and (4) hollow.
12. See *White Crystal Mirror* (ch. 17, pp. 219 and 225–26) for descriptions of these two distributions.
13. *thod bskar gyis 'phar ba*: This spelling is from *DNZ-K.* I believe it has been miscopied everywhere, even in the *DNZ* printing from the same woodblocks, as *thod pa sgar gyis 'phar ba.*
14. The seed syllable of water.
15. An extensive list of nāga "medicines," including their scientific names and the diseases they cure, can be found in "The Splendor of Generosity: An Elaborate Torma Offering to the Nāgas" (*klu gtor rgyas pa sbyin pe* [sic] *lang tsho Nāga Menaka*), available from www.drikung.org/texts.
16. Tekchok Dorje, *Source of All Qualities*, ch. 22, p. 308. This "short call" and a "long call" are attributed there to Karmapa Rangjung Dorje.

17. For instance, in *White Crystal Mirror* (ch. 17), which resembles this commentary in many ways, the distributions are ordered differently.
18. *rkang lag gsum*. Other translations, apparently benefiting from oral commentaries, specify two arms and a leg.
19. These are the buddha fields of the five buddha families plus Gaṇḍavyūha: a variation of this feast can be found in *White Crystal Mirror* as an extension of the White Feast in Three Cycles of Integration (ch. 17, p. 221). There, the six realms become the nature of the six families, represented as precious jewels and metals.
20. *gDon tshogs dgu ma*, usually attributed to Rangjung Dorje, but in *Pearl Rosary* it is attributed to his disciple Yakde Paṇchen (ch. 21, p. 292).
21. For the exact sequence, see *MCE*, p. 182.
22. The following is not included in the outline.
23. *zhar byung gi tshul*: for instance, from oral instruction (ATG).
24. 'Jam dpal mkhyen brtse: this would be Kongtrul's friend, teacher, and disciple Jamyang Khyentse Wangpo (1820–1892). 'Jam dpal and 'Jam dbyangs are both Tibetan names for Mañjushrī.

## 29. Essence of Auspicious Renown

1. *Dam chos sdug bsngal zhi byed dang gcod yul brgyud pa'i bla ma rnams chab gcig tu mchod cing gsol ba 'debs pa'i cho ga bkra shis grags pa'i snying po,* in *DNZ,* vol. 14 (*pha*), pp. 425–56; *DNZ-K,* vol. 9, pp. 865–86 (placed at the end of the *zhi byed* volume). *DV,* vol. *cha*, pp. 609–48.
2. *rten 'brel gyi spar bu*. This is unclear, but may be *par bu*, a small vessel or box, or fresh skull.
3. With Saraha, these are Caryāpa, Guṇati (Guṇari?), Kuddāla, Koṣhapa?, Shabari?, Maitripā, Sāgarsiddhi, Ravigupta, Ākarasiddhi, and Ratnavajra. (These Sanskrit names and those through note 7 are mainly from Dan Martin, "Padampa Portrait, Part Two" on tibeto-logic.blogspot.com/2011/06/padampa-portrait-part-two.html, cross-checked with Dampa Sangye's biography.
4. Buddhaguhya, Padmavajra, Vāgīshvara, Godhari (or Gu bha ri, Ghu da ri), Karmavajra, Jabaripa, Jñānapāda, Nāgabodhi, Ānanda, Kṛṣhṇapa, and Vasudhārin.
5. Saroruhavajra, Indrabhūti, Ḍombipa, Vajraghaṇṭapa, Telopa, Kṛṣhṇapa, Lalitavajra, Lūyipa, Virūpa, Ānandagarbha, and Kukkuripa.
6. Nāgārjunagarbha or Nāgārjunasāra, Prajñābhadra, Guṇaprabha, Dharmakīrti, Ākarasiddhi, Shaṅkara, Jñānagarbha, Asaṅga, Āryadeva, Shāntideva, and Suvarṇadvīpin.
7. Sukhasiddhī, Shabarī, Padmopāda?, Kumudā, Sukhākara, Gaṅgābhadrī, Cintā, Lakṣhmi, Parṇa, and Vimalā. All together, these constitute Dampa Sangye's fifty-four common male and female adepts (*thun mong ba'i bla ma grub thob pho mo lnga bcu rtas bzhi*).
8. Dampa Sangye's thirty-six uncommon awareness-holder celestial (Kechari) gurus (*thun mong ma yin pa rig 'dzin mkha' spyod kyi bla ma sum cu rtsa drug*), who dwelled in the twenty-four sacred places of India. See Dampa's biography:

Khamnyön Dharma Senge, *The Life Story of the Great Mighty Adept, Venerable Dampa Sangye (Grub pa'i dbang phyug chen po rje btsun dam pa sangs rgyas kyi rnam par thar pa ngos grub 'od stong 'bar ba'i nyi ma)*, p. 27. Translation in Molk, *Lion of Siddhas*, pp. 45–46.

9. Dampa Sangye's twenty-four spiritual power–bestowing ḍākinī gurus (*dngos grub ster ba mkha' 'gro ma'i bla ma nyi shu rtsa bzhi*). Khamnyön, *Life Story*, p. 25; Molk, *Lion of Siddhas*, p. 45.
10. Tārā, Mañjushrī, Avalokiteshvara, Vajrapāṇi, Yamāntaka, Kharsapāṇi, Sarvanivāraṇavishkhambhin, Svabhutarajñī, Mārīchī, Samantabhadra, Vajravārāhī, and Achalā. See Khamnyön, *Life Story*, p. 27. See also Roerich, *The Blue Annals*, p. 870.
11. Dam pa phyar chen, Vajra kro dha, Dam pa phyar chung, and Byang chub sems dpa' Kun dga', known as the four gatekeeper yogins (*sgo ba'i rnal 'byor bzhi*), were disciples of Dampa Sangye from his final visit to Tibet when he was in residence at Dingri. They are always associated with these four directions, which may reflect their origins. Though not in one of the three main transmission lines, Bodhisattva Kunga had an enormous impact on the lineage through his writings.
12. Kha che Jñānaguhya, Dampa Sangye's principal disciple from the first transmission (of three), who held the lineage of Dampa's teachings called the *Three Cycles of the Lamp of Pacification*.
13. rMa Chos kyi shes rab, So [chung] dGe 'dun 'bar, and sKam Ye shes rgyal mtshan, representing the three systems established during Dampa's middle transmission in Tibet, called, respectively, the Ma system, the So system, and the Kam system.
14. These are all in the direct line of Dampa's final transmission to Bodhisattva Kunga. Pa tshab sgom pa was Bodhisattva Kunga's principal disciple. rGyal ba Ten ne was Patsap's principal dharma heir. He was the seventh and last in line under the seal of secrecy. Rog shes rab 'od was the first of three Rok brothers who received the dharma lineage from Gyalwa Tenne and spread it widely to many disciples. He also held all lineages of Pacification. Zhig po Nyi ma seng ge and sNye mdo sMra ba'i seng ge were his younger brothers and lineage holders. For more on these figures, see the life of Rok Sherap Ö in Cabeźon, *The Buddha's Doctrine and the Nine Vehicles*, pp. 39–51.
15. Dampa Sangye's fifty-four popular or "common" male and female adepts (*thun mong ba'i bla ma grub thob pho mo lnga bcu rtsa bzhi*). They are "common" (*thun mong*) in that they taught other disciples. See notes 3 through 7 for the complete list. Also see Khamnyön, *Life Story*, p. 24; Molk, *Lion of Siddhas*, pp. 45–46; or Roerich, *The Blue Annals*, pp. 868–69.
16. *mtshan nyid*. In Roerich, *The Blue Annals* (p. 869): *phyi mtshan nyid*, "sutras of the outer doctrine."
17. This line has been added from the same prayer in *MCE* because it seems to make sense and so that it is not lost. However, it may have been dropped in later liturgies to accommodate the music and meter of the quatrains.
18. *Supplication to the Lineage of Gurus of the Three Transmissions of Pacification*

*Known as Golden Rosary* (*Zhi byed bka' babs rnam gsum gyi bla brgyud gsol 'debs gser phreng mar grags pa*), *DNZ*, vol. 13, pp. 300–9.

19. This is nearly the same as the first verse of the Praise to Machik by Tönyön Samdrup that can be found in *Source of All Qualities* (ch. 22, pp. 315–17). It is unclear whether Kongtrul intends for one to recite the whole praise here.
20. Missing line added from *Pearl Rosary* (ch. 21, p. 287) and *Source of All Qualities* (ch. 22, p. 312).
21. This supplication is found in *Pearl Rosary* (ch. 21, p. 287) and *Source of All Qualities* (ch. 22, p. 312), as well as in the *Concise Charity of the Body for Daily Practice* by Karmapa Tekchok Dorje.
22. The text gives "sky, vajra, lotus, vajra, wheel" in all editions, but in other sources, such as Jamgön Kongtrul, *Treasury of Knowledge: Esoteric Instructions*, the fourth one should be "elixir" (*bdud rtsi*).
23. For a brief description of the ten clinchers (*chings ba bcu*) see ibid., p. 267, or Lochen Dharmashrī, *Distilled Elixir* (*DNZ*, vol. 13, p. 336).
24. *rnal 'byor rang sa drug*. These are (1) not to supplicate worldly deities; (2) not to request attainments from demons; (3) not to expend vigor on this life; (4) not to give one's nose rope to others (i.e., give away one's freedom); (5) not to let secrets pass through the door of the lips (i.e., speak of attainments); and (6) not to brandish the tip of the victory banner of acclaim (i.e., exult proudly in attainments), written alternatively as "not to brandish dirty clothes on the tip of the victory banner." Jamgön Kongtrul, *Treasury of Knowledge: Esoteric Instructions*, p. 272.
25. This is a concise version of the *Kagyu Feast Liturgy* (ch. 24, pp. 337–39). In the extensive version, two lines are added to each couplet: "dwells in the midst of heroes and heroines: / I supplicate with longing and devotion." It is unclear if this is meant to be repeated here.
26. From *Pearl Rosary* (ch. 21, p. 289), with slight variations.
27. The line in the *Fulfillment Rituals of Profound Object Severance* (ch. 25, p. 376) reads "renew it through the meaning of mind itself."
28. From *Pearl Rosary* (ch. 21, p. 295).
29. This prayer appears in several prayer collections as *Pha dam pa sangs rgyas kyis mdzad pa'i smon lam sum cu pa*. See TBRC W4CZ1042 and W23685.
30. The texts in *DNZ* and *DV* say, "May I accomplish the gazes and may interdependence arise" (*lta stang grub cing rten 'brel 'char bar gyur cig*), but other copies make more sense as *ltar snang 'grib cing . . .*, especially since *ltar snang* ("false appearance" or "semblance") contrasts with *ci lta ba bzhin du* ("things as they are") two lines above.
31. Here it is *go chas 'jig rten gyi dri ma dag par gyur cig*, which would be "May worldly stains be purified by armor." Armor is often associated with patience, so this is also a possible interpretation. However, in other sources it is *go cha'i 'jig rten gyi dri ma*, which I have preferred.
32. *ma 'byor ba dang nyams pa dang / gang yang bdag rmongs blo yis ni / gyis pa dang ni bgyis stsal ba / de kun mgon pos bzod par gsol.*

# Bibliography

The bibliography comprises three main sections, each separately alphabetized: (1) the texts translated in this volume; (2) works cited in the texts (subdivided into scriptures and treatises); and (3) a reference bibliography (subdivided into Tibetan works and English-language translations and other works).

## 1. The Present Texts

### *The Source Volumes*

Jamgön Kongtrul Lodrö Taye, comp. *The Treasury of Precious Instructions. gDams ngag rin po che'i mdzod.* Vol. 14 (*pha*). Delhi: Shechen Publications, 1999. (Shechen printing).

Jamgön Kongtrul Lodrö Taye, comp. *The Treasury of Precious Instructions. gDams ngag rin po che'i mdzod.* Vol. 9. Delhi: N. Lungtok and N. Gyaltsan, 1971–1972. (Kundeling printing).

### *The Translated Texts*

Āryadeva the Brahmin. *Esoteric Instructions on the Noble Perfection of Wisdom. *Āryaprajñāpāramitopadeśa. 'Phags pa shes rab kyi pha rol tu phyin pa'i man ngag.* Also called *Grand Poem (Tshigs bcad chen mo)* and *Fifty-Verse Poem (Tshigs su bcad pa lnga bcu pa).* In *Source Texts of Severance of Evil Objects: Profound Meaning of the Perfection of Wisdom (Shes rab kyi pha rol tu phyin pa'i zab don bdud kyi gcod yul gyi gzhung).* In *DNZ*: Shechen printing. Vol. 14 (*pha*), pp. 1–7. Second source: *Āryaprajñāpāramitāmahāparipṛccha. 'Phags pa shes rab kyi pha rol tu phyin pa tshigs su bcad pa chen po.* Narthang Tengyur, mdo, *nyo,* ff. 396b4–399a4 (pp. 793–97). Third source: *Āryaprajñāpāramitāmahāparamatamahāparipṛccha. 'Phags pa shes rab kyi pha rol tu phyin pa tshigs su bcad pa chen po.* (Title page: *gCod kyi rgya gzhung Ārya de bas mdzad pa'o).* Golden Tengyur, *nyo,* ff. 517a–520a.

Bengar Jampal Zangpo (Ban sgar 'Jam dpal bzang po). *Supplication to the Long Lineage by Machik, Appended by Bengar Jampal Zangpo. Ring brgyud kyi gsol 'debs ma gcig gis mdzad par ban sgar 'jam dpal bzang pos kha bskang ba.* In *DNZ*: Shechen printing. Vol. 14 (*pha*), pp. 335–36; Kundeling printing. Vol. 9, pp. 779–80. Second source: *Dingri Volumes.* Vol. *ja*, pp. 649–57.

*Fulfillment Rituals of Profound Object Severance. gCod kyi skong ba rnams bzhugs pa'i dbu phyogs lags so.* In *DNZ*: Shechen printing. Vol. 14, pp. 371–86. Second source: *Zab mo bdud kyi gcod yul gyi bskang ba.* In *Dingri Volumes.* Vol. *ja*, pp. 705–30.

Jamgön Kongtrul Lodrö Taye ('Jam mgon kong sprul bLo gros mtha' yas, a.k.a. Yon tan rgya mtsho). *Beloved Garden: Brief Notes on the Offering and Gift of the Body. Lus mchod sbyin gyi zin bris mdor bsdus kun dga'i skyed tshal.* In *DNZ*: Shechen printing. Vol. 14 (*pha*), pp. 387–405; Kundeling printing. Vol. 9, pp. 829–47. Second source: *Dingri Volumes.* Vol. *ja*, pp. 731–55.

———. *Distillation of the Profound: The Way to Practice the Essence of the Vast Object Severance in a Single Sitting. gCod yul rgya mtsho'i snying po stan thog gcig tu nyams su len pa'i tshul zab mo'i yang zhun.* In *DNZ*: Shechen printing. Vol. 14 (*pha*), pp. 353–60. Second source: In *Shangpa Texts.* Vol. 4, pp. 579–97. Samdrup Darje Ling Monastery, n.d. Third source: *Dingri Volumes.* Vol. *ja*, pp. 679–90.

———. *Essence of Auspicious Renown: A Ritual of Offering and Supplication to All the Gurus of the Holy Dharmas of Pacification and Object Severance Together. Dam chos sdug bsngal zhi byed dang gcod yul brgyud pa'i bla ma rnams chab gcig tu mchod cing gsol ba 'debs pa'i cho ga bkra shis grags pa'i snying po.* In *DNZ*: Shechen printing. Vol. 14 (*pha*), pp. 425–56; Kundeling printing. Vol. 9, pp. 865–86. Second source: *Dingri Volumes.* Vol. *cha*, pp. 609–48.

Jamyang Gönpo ('Jam dbyangs mgon po). *Heart Essence of Profound Meaning: The Quintessence of All Source Texts and Esoteric Instructions of Severance, the Perfection of Wisdom. Shes rab kyi pha rol tu phyin pa gcod kyi gzhung dang man ngag mtha' dag gi yang bcud zab don thugs kyi snying po.* In *DNZ*: Shechen printing. Vol. 14 (*pha*), pp. 17–22. Second source: *Source Text of Profound Meaning. Zab don gyi gzhung.* In *The Collected Works of Longchen Rabjam.* Vol. 26, pp. 124–30. Third source: *Dingri Volumes.* Vol. *ja*, pp. 115–26. Fourth source: In *Practices of the Severance Collection and So Forth. gCod tshogs kyi lag len sogs.* TBRC W23390, pp. 96–101.

*Kagyu Feast Liturgy. bKa' brgyud tshogs las.* In *DNZ*: Shechen printing. Vol. 14 (*pha*) 337–39; Kundeling printing. Vol. 9, pp. 781–3.
Second source: *Dingri Volumes.* Vol. *ja*, pp. 659–63.

Karma Chakme (Karma chags med, a.k.a. Rāga Asya). *The Body Donation and Feeding Ritual Arranged as Convenient Liturgy, Combining Lord Rangjung Dorje's Ninefold Spirit Feast and Six Earth Lord Application with Mikyö Dorje's Single Seat Severance Poem. rJe rang byung rdo rjes mdzad pa'i gdon tshogs dgu ma sa bdag drug sbyor dang / mi bskyod rdo rjes mdzad pa'i gdan thog gcig ma gcod tshigs bcad ma dang gnyis gab sprad nas lus byin dang bsngo ba [*or *bstab pa] bya tshul bltas chog 'don 'grigs.* In *DNZ*: Shechen printing. Vol. 14 (*pha*), pp. 261–77. Second source: In *Collected Works of Karma Chakme. Karma chags med gsung 'bum.* Vol. 52, pp. 248–80. TBRC W1KG8321. Third source: *rJe Rang byung rdo rjes mdzad* *pa'i gcod kyi tshogs las rin po che'i phreng ba 'don sgrigs bltas chog tu bkod pa gcod kyi lugs sor*, pp. 255–93. Paro, Bhutan: Lama Ngodrub and Sherab Drimey, 1981.

———. *Pearl Rosary: A Liturgy for the Donation of the Body in Severance. gCod kyi lus sbyin gyi ngag 'don mu tig phreng ba.* In *DNZ*: Shechen printing. Vol. 14 (*pha*), pp. 279–96; Kundeling printing. Vol. 9, pp. 723–40. Second source: *Dingri Volumes.* Vol. *ja*, pp. 559–85.

Könchok Bang (Zha dmar dKon mchog 'bang). *Rainfall of Desirables: A Profound Guide on Severance Instruction. gCod khrid zab mo 'dod dgu'i char 'bebs.* In *DNZ*: Shechen printing. Vol. 14 (*pha*), pp. 251–61; Kundeling printing. Vol. 9, pp. 696–706. Second source: *Dingri Volumes.* Vol. *ja*, pp. 399–412.

Kunga Paljor (Kun dga' dpal 'byor). *Pure Honey: A Commentary on the Source Text of Severance, "Esoteric Instructions on the Perfection of Wisdom." Shes rab kyi pha rol tu phyin pa'i man ngag gcod kyi gzhung 'grel zag med sbrang rtsi.* In *DNZ*: Shechen printing. Vol. 14 (*pha*), pp. 23–51.

Machik Lapdrön (Ma gcig lab sgron). *Another Bundle: Answers to Questions on the Esoteric Instructions of the Perfection of Wisdom. Shes rab kyi pha rol tu phyin pa'i man ngag yang tshom zhus len ma.* In *DNZ*: Shechen printing. Vol. 14 (*pha*), pp. 101–13; Kundeling printing. Vol. 9, pp. 547–59. Second source: *Dingri Volumes.* Vol. *ja*, pp. 191–208. Third source: *Another Bundle of Twenty-Five. Yang tshoms nyer lnga pa.* In *Practices of the Severance Collection and So Forth. Gcod tshogs kyi lag len sogs*, pp. 33–43.

———. *The Eight Common Appendices. Thun mong gi le lag brgyad pa.* In *DNZ*: Shechen printing. Vol. 14 (*pha*), pp. 130–40; Kundeling printing, Vol. 9, pp. 576–86. Second source: *Le lag brgyad pa.* In *Practices of the Severance Collection and So Forth* (*gCod tshogs kyi lag len sogs*), pp. 57–66. Third source: *Dingri Volumes.* Vol. *cha*, pp. 239–53.

———. *The Eight Special Appendices. Khyad par gyi le lag brgyad.* In *DNZ*: Shechen printing. Vol. 14 (*pha*), pp. 155–64; Kundeling printing. Vol. 9, pp. 601–10.

———. *The Eight Uncommon Appendices. Thun mong ma yin pa'i le lag brgyad pa.* In *DNZ*: Shechen printing. Vol. 14 (*pha*), pp. 140–55; Kundeling printing. Vol. 9, pp. 586–601. Second source: *Dingri Volumes.* Vol. *ja*, pp. 255–77.

———. *The Essential Bundle from the Severance of Evil Object, Esoteric Instructions on the Perfection of Wisdom. Shes rab kyi pha rol tu phyin pa'i man ngag bdud kyi gcod yul las nying tshom.* In *DNZ*: Shechen printing. Vol. 14 (*pha*), pp. 116–30; Kundeling printing. Vol. 9, pp. 562–76.

———. *The Great Bundle of Precepts: The Source Text of Esoteric Instructions on Severance, the Profound Perfection of Wisdom. Shes rab kyi pha rol tu phyin pa zab mo gcod kyi man ngag gi gzhung bka' tshoms chen mo.* In *DNZ*: Shechen Printing. Vol. 14 (*pha*), pp. 7–17. Second source: *Machik's Bundle of Precepts. Ma gcig gi bka' tshoms.* In *The Collected Works of Omniscient Longchen Rabjam. Kun mkhyen klong chen rab 'byams kyi gsung 'bum.* Beijing: dPal brtsegs bod yig dpe rnying zhib 'jug khang, 2009. Vol. 26, pp. 291–300 (partial). Third source: *Dingri Volumes.* Vol. *ja*, pp. 97–114.

———. *Vajra Play: Questions and Answers on the Profound Severance of Evil Object. Zhus len rdo rje rol pa.* In *DNZ*: Shechen printing. Vol. 14 (*pha*), pp. 113–15; Kundeling printing. Vol. 9, pp. 559–61. Second source: *Zab mo bdud kyi gcod yul gyi zhus lan rdo rje'i rol pa.* In *Dingri Volumes.* Vol. *ja*, pp. 209–14.

Machik Lapdrön and Kunga Paljor (?). *A Hair's Tip of Wisdom: A Precious Treasure Trove to Enhance the Original Source Text of Severance, the Esoteric Instructions on the Perfection of Wisdom. Shes rab kyi pha rol tu phyin pa'i man ngag gcod kyi gzhung shes rab skra rtse'i sa gzhung spel ba rin po che'i gter mdzod.* In *DNZ*: Shechen printing. Vol. 14 (*pha*), pp. 81–99; Kundeling printing. Vol. 9, pp. 528–46.

*Offering Torma to All Ḍākimas. mKha' 'gro ma rnams la gtor ma 'bul ba.* In *DNZ*: Shechen printing. Vol. 14 (*pha*), pp. 341–51. Second source: *Dingri Volumes.* Vol. *ja*, pp. 665–78.

Rangjung Dorje, Karmapa (Rang byung rdo rje). *The Great Bundle of Precepts on Severance Outline (gCod bka' tshoms chen mo'i sa bcad)* and *Complete Explanation of Severance (gCod kyi ṭīkā)* In *DNZ*: Shechen printing. Vol. 14 (*pha*), pp. 53–79. Second source: *gCod bka' tshoms chen mo'i sa bcad* and *gCod kyi ṭīkā*. In *Collected Works of Karmapa Rangjung Dorje (Karma pa rang byung rdo rje gsung 'bum).* Vol. 11, pp. 265–98.

———. *Practice Manual on the Profound Severance of Evil Object. Zab mo dud kyi gcod yul gyi khrid yig bzhugs/ Karma pa rang byung rdo rjes mdzad.* In *DNZ*: Shechen printing. Vol. 14 (*pha*), pp. 173–84; Kundeling printing. Vol. 9, pp. 618–28. Second source: *Collected Works of Karmapa Rangjung Dorje.* Vol. 11, pp. 299–312.

Ratnasiṃha/Rinchen Senge (Rin chen seng ge). *Opening the Sky Door: Instructions on Severance Mahāmudrā . Phyag rgya chen po gcod kyi gdams pa nam mkha' sgo 'byed.* In *DNZ*: Shechen printing. Vol. 14 (*pha*), pp. 407–23; Kundeling printing. Vol. 9, pp. 848–64. Second source: *Dingri Volumes.* Vol. *ja*, pp. 757–82.

*The Required Liturgies on the Occasion of Venerable Tāranātha's Severance Empowerment of Opening the Sky Door in the Gyaltang Tradition. rGyal thang lugs kyi gcod dbang nam mkha' sgo 'byed kyi cho ga rje btsun tā ra nā thas mdzad pa'i skabs su nye bar mkho ba'i 'don cha.* In *DNZ*: Shechen printing. Vol. 14 (*pha*), pp. 165–71; Kundeling printing. Vol. 9, pp. 611–17. Second source: *Dingri Volumes.* Vol. *ta*, pp. 587–600.

Tāranātha. *Essence of the Vital Meaning: A Practice Manual of Profound Object Severance. gCod yul zab mo'i khrid yig gnad don snying po.* In *DNZ*: Shechen printing. Vol. 14 (*pha*), pp. 185–200; Kundeling printing. Vol. 9, pp. 630–45.
Second source: *Collected Works. rJe btsun Tā ra nā tha'i gsung 'bum.* Vol. 20, pp. 661–79. Dzamtang printing, [2000?].

———. *Object Severance Empowerment Known as Opening the Sky Door. gCod yul gyi dbang nam mkha' sgo 'byed du grags pa.* In *DNZ*: Shechen printing. Vol. 14, pp. 361–70. Second source: *Dingri Volumes.* Vol. *ja*, pp. 691–703.

Tekchok Dorje, Karmapa (Theg mchog rdo rje), comp. *Source of All Qualities: The Severance Feast Activities Arranged Unerringly According to the Teaching Tradition. gCod kyi tshogs las yon tan kun 'byung gsungs rgyun 'khrul med ltar bkod pa bzhugs pa'i dbu phyogs lags so*. In *DNZ*: Shechen printing. Vol. 14 (*pha*), pp. 297–334; Kundeling printing. Vol. 9, pp. 741–78. Second source: *Dingri Volumes*. Vol. *ja*, pp. 587–647.

Tenzin Namdak ([Ban rgan] bsTan 'dzin rnam dag). *White Crystal Mirror: Notes on the Guru's Teaching Tradition of the Visualization Sequence for Severance Feast Activities "Endowed with All Qualities." gCod kyi tshogs las yon tan kun ldan gyi dmigs rim bla ma'i gsung rgyun gyi zin bris shel dkar me long*. In *DNZ*: Shechen printing. Vol. 14 (*pha*), pp. 201–50; Kundeling printing. Vol. 9, pp. 646–95. Second source: *Dingri Volumes*. Vol. *ja*, pp. 333–98.

## 2. Works Cited in the Texts

### *Scriptures (Kangyur)*

*Chakrasaṃvara Ḍākinī Illusion Later Tantra. Śrīsarvabuddhasamayogaḍākinījālasaṃvaranāmottaratantra. dPal sangs rgyas thams cad dang mnyam par sbyor ba mkha' 'gro ma sgyu ma bde ba'i mchog ces bya ba'i rgyud bla ma*, Dg.K. rgyud 'bum, *ka* (Toh. 366).

*Chakrasaṃvara Explanatory Later Tantra. Cakrasaṃvarābhidhānottaratantra. mNgon par brjod pa'i rgyud bla ma*. Dg.K. rgyud 'bum, *ka* (Toh. 369). Lhasa Kangyur (rKTs-K369).

*Ḍākinī Vajra Tent Tantra. Ḍākinīvajrapañjarātantra. mKha' 'gro ma rdo rje gur zhes bya ba'i rgyud kyi rgyal po chen po'i brtag pa rgyud*. Dg.K. rgyud 'bum, *nga* (Toh. 419).

*Diamond Cutter Sutra. Vajracchedikāprajñāpāramitāsūtra. Shes rab kyi pha rol tu phyin pa rdo rje gcod pa*. Dg.K. shes phyin, *ka* (Toh. 16). Lhasa Kangyur (rKTs-K16).

*Flower Ornament Sutra. Avataṃsakasūtra. Sangs rgyas phal po che'i mdo*. Dg.K. phal chen, *ka, kha, ga, a* (Toh. 44).

*Heart of the Perfection of Wisdom (Heart Sutra). Bhagavatīprajñāpāramitāhṛdaya. bCom ldan 'das ma shes rab kyi pha rol tu phyin pa'i snying po*. Dg.K. shes phyin, *ka* (Toh. 21). Lhasa Kangyur (rKTs-K529).

*Individual Liberation Sutra. Prātimokṣasūtra. So sor thar ba'i mdo*. Dg.K. 'dul ba, *ca* (Toh. 2). Lhasa Kangyur (rKTs-K2).

*Kālachakra Tantra That Issued from the Supreme Original Buddha (Kālachakra Condensed Tantra). Laghutantra/Paramādhibuddhoddhṛtaśrīkālacakranāmatantrarāja. dsDus pa'i rgyud/mChog gi dang po sangs rgyas las phyung ba rgyud kyi rgyal pod dpal dus kyi 'khor lo*. (Authored by Mañjushrī Yashas). Dg.K. rgyud 'bum, vol. *ka* (Toh. 362). Lhasa Kangyur (rKTS-K362).

*Perfection of Wisdom in Eight Thousand Lines. Aṣṭasāhasrikāprajñāpāramitā. Shes rab kyi pha rol tu phyin pa brgyad stong pa*. Dg.K. shes phyin, *ka* (Toh. 12). Lhasa Kangyur (rKTs-K12).

*Perfection of Wisdom in Eighteen Thousand Lines. Aṣṭādaśasāhasrikāprajñāpāramitā. Shes rab kyi pha rol tu phyin pa khri brgyad stong pa*. Dg.K. shes phyin, *kha* (Toh. 10). Lhasa Kangyur (rKTs-K10).

*Perfection of Wisdom in One Hundred Thousand Lines. Śatasāhasrikāprajñāpāramitā.*

*Shes rab kyi pha rol tu phyin pa stong phrag brgya pa.* Dg.K. shes phyin, *ka–a* (Toh. 8). Lhasa Kangyur (rKTs–K8). ACIP, vol. *tha.*

*Perfection of Wisdom in Twenty-Five Thousand Lines. Pañcaviṃśatisāhasrikā-prajñāpāramitā. Shes rab kyi pha rol tu phyin pa stong phrag nyi shu lnga pa.* Dg.K. shes phyin, *ka–ga* (Toh. 9). Lhasa Kangyur (rKTs–K9).

*Supreme Dharma of the Application of Attention. Saddharmasmṛtyupasthāna. 'Phags pa dam pa'i chos dran pa nye bar gzhag pa.* Dg.K. mdo sde, *ya* (Toh. 287). Lhasa Kangyur (rKTs–K287).

*Sutra of Skill in the Methods of the Great Secret [of All Buddhas: The Chapter on the Questions of the Bodhisattva Jñānottara]. Sarvabuddhamahārahasyopāyakauśa-lyajñānottarabodhisattvaparipṛcchāparivartanāmamahāyānasūtra. gSang chen thabs la mkhas pa'i mdo (Sangs rgyas thams cad kyi gsang chen thabs la mkhas pa/ byang chub sems dpa' ye shes dam pas zhus pa'i le'u zhes bya ba theg pa chen po'i mdo).* Dg.K. dkon brtsegs, *cha* (Toh. 82).

*Two-Part Hevajra Tantra.* (part 1) *Hevajratantrarājanāma.* Kye'i rdo rje zhes bya ba rgyud kyi rgyal po. Dg.K. rgyud, *nga* (Toh. 417). Lhasa Kangyur (rKTs–K378a).

*Verse Summary on the Perfection of Wisdom. Prajñāpāramitāsaṃcayagāthā. Shes rab kyi pha rol tu phyin pa sdud pa tshigs su bcad pa.* Dg.K. shes phyin, *ka* (Toh. 13). Lhasa Kangyur (rKTs–K13).

### *Treatises (Tengyur)*

Āsaṅga. *Bodhisattva Stages. Bodhisattvabhūmi. rNal 'byor spyod pa'i sa las byang chub sems dpa'i sa.* Dg.T. sems tsam, *wi* (Toh. 4037).

Chandragomin (Go mi dge bsnyen). *The Twenty Verses on Bodhisattva Vows. Bodhi-sattvasaṃvaraviṃśaka. Byang chub sems dpa'i sdom pa nyi shu pa.* Dg.T. sems tsam, *hi* (Toh. 4081).

Dignāga (sLob dpon Phyogs kyi glang po). *Condensed Verses on the Perfection of Wisdom. Prajñāpāramitāpiṇḍārtha. Shes rab kyi pha rol tu phyin ma sdus pa'i tshig le'ur byas pa.* Dg.T. sher phyin, *pha* (Toh. 3809).

Maitreya (Byams pa). *Highest Continuum. Mahāyānottaratantraśāstra. Theg pa chen po rgyud bla ma'i bstan bcos.* Dg.T. sems tsam, *phi* (Toh. 4024).

———. *Ornament of Clear Realization. Abhisamayālaṃkāra. Shes rab kyi pha rol tu phyin pa'i man ngag gi bstan bcos mngon par rtogs pa'i rgyan zhes bya ba'i tshig le'ur byas pa (mNgon rtogs rgyan).* Dg.T. shes phyin, *ka* (Toh. 3786).

Nāgārjuna (Klu sgrub). *Letter to a Friend. Suhṛllekha. bShes pa'i spring yig.* Dg.T. spring yig, *ngi* (Toh. 4182).

———. *Root Verses on the Middle Called Wisdom. Prajñānāmamūlamadhyamaka-kārika. dBu ma rtsa ba'i tshig le'ur byas pa shes rab ces bya ba.* Dg.T. dbu ma, *tsa* (Toh. 3824).

Nāgārjuna (or Rāhulabhadra). *Eulogy to the Perfection of Wisdom. Prajñāpāramitā-stotra. Sher phyin bstod pa.* Dg.T. bstod tshogs, *ka* (Toh. 1127).

Prajñāvarman. *Commentary on the Udānavarga. Udānavargavivaraṇa. Ched du brjod pa'i tshoms kyi rnam par 'grel pa.* Dg.T. mngon pa, *tu* (Toh. 4100).

Ratnakīrti. *Eulogy to the Deities of the Four Yogas. Yogacaturdevastotra. sByor ba bzhi'i lha la bstod pa.* Dg.T. bstod tshogs, *ka* (Toh. 1170).

Saraha. *Treasury of Dohā Songs. Dohākoṣagīti. Do ha mdzod kyi glu.* Dg.T. rgyud, *wi* (Toh. 2224). (Also known as "People's Dohā" in Saraha's *dohā* trilogy)

Shāntideva. *Entering the Way of the Bodhisattva. Bodhisattvacaryāvatāra. Byang chub sems dpa'i spyod pa la 'jug pa.* Dg.T. dbu ma, *la* (Toh. 3871).

Telopa. *Mahāmudrā Esoteric Instructions. Mahāmudropadeśa. Phyag rgya chen po'i man ngag (Ganges Mahāmudrā: Phyag chen ganga ma)* Dg.T. rgyud, *shi* (Toh. 2303). Also in *Collected Works of Marpa.* Vol. 1, p. 369. Also in *DNZ*: Shechen printing. Vol. 7, pp. 33–36.

Vajrāsanapāda (rDo rje gdan pa). *Supplication to the Eighty-Four Great Adepts. Grub thob brgyad cu rtsa bzhi'i gsol 'debs.* Dg.T. rgyud, *tshu* (Toh. 3758).

## 3. Reference Bibliography

### *Tibetan Texts*

*Big Tibetan-Chinese Dictionary. Bod rgya tshig mdzod chen mo.* Edited by Zhang Yisun. 2 vols. Beijing: Mi rigs dpe skrun khang, 1985, 1987.

*Collected Histories of the Glorious Zurmang Kagyu: Pearl Necklace That Fulfills Desires. dPal zur mang bka' brgyud kyi chos 'byung phyogs bsgrigs 'dod 'byung nor bu'i phreng ba.* rdo dgon gna' deb srung skyob tshogs pa, n.d. TBRC W4CZ48435.

Dampa Sangye. *Six Pieces. Brul tsho drug.* In *Dingri Volumes.* Vol. *ja,* pp. 53–95.

*Dingri Volumes (The Volumes of the Root Teachings of the Sacred Dharma Pacification of Suffering, and the Subsidiary, Severance of Evil Object). Dam chos sdug bsngal zhi byed rtsa ba'i chos sde dang / yan lag bdud kyi gcod yul gyi glegs bam.* New Delhi: Dingri Langkor Tsuglag Khang, 2013.

Drakpa Jungne (Grags pa 'byung gnas). *Treasury of Names. Ming mdzod.* Lan kro'u: Kan su'u mi rigs dpe skrun khang, 1992.

Gö Lotsāwa Zhönnu Pal ('Gos lo tsā ba gZhon nu dpal). *The Blue Annals. Deb ther sngon po.* 2 vols. Chengdu: Si khron mi rigs dpe skrun khang, 1984.

Jamgön Kongtrul Lodrö Taye ('Jam mgon kong sprul bLo gros mtha' yas). *An Ocean of Auspicious Renown: A Catalog of the Treasury of Precious Instructions, A Collection of the Ripening and Liberating Essence of the Eight Great Chariots of the Practice Lineages. sGrub brgyud shing rta chen po brgyad kyi smin grol snying po phyogs gcig bstus pa gdams ngag rin po che'i mdzod kyi dkar chag bkra shis grags pa'i rgya mtsho. DNZ,* Vol. 18, ff. 381–547. Delhi: Shechen Publications, 1999.

———. *The Sword That Severs Deluded Thoughts in the Daily Practice of Body Donation. rGyun khyer lus sbyin 'khrul rtog gcod pa'i ral gri.* In *Treasury of Extensive Teachings* (*rGya chen bka' mdzod*). Vol. 12, pp. 17–21. Paro, Bhutan: Ngodup, Kyichu Temple, 1976.

———. *The Treasury of Knowledge. Shes bya kun khyab (Theg pa'i sgo kun las btus pa gsung rab rin po che'i mdzod bslab pa gsum legs par ston pa'i bstan bcos shes bya kun khyab)* 3 vols. Lhasa: Mi rigs dpe skrun khang, 1982.

Jamyang Gönpo (Mañjughoṣanatha). *The Big General Guide to Severance. gCod kyi spyi khrid chen mo.* In *A Collection of Gcod Texts Reflecting the Teachings of Padma-ling-pa (Zab don thugs kyi snying po bdud kyi gcod yul gyi skor)*, pp. 47–339. New Delhi: P. K. Tashi, 1981. Also found in *The Collected Works of Omniscient Longchen Rabjam.* Vol. 26, pp. 131–272.

Jigme Lingpa ('Jigs med gling pa). *The Ḍākinī's Loud Laugh on Object Severance. gCod yul mkha' 'gro'i gad rgyangs.* TBRC W8LS16235.

Karma Chakme (Karma Chags med, Rāga Asya). *Collected Works of Karma Chakme. mKhas grub karma chags med kyi gsung 'bum.* 60 vols. Yushu, Tibetan Autonomous Prefecture: gNas mdo dpe rnying nyams gso khang, 2010. TBRC W1KG8321.

——— et al. *Collection of Mandala Rituals from Palpung. dPal spungs dpe rnying gsar bskrun las dkyil chog phyogs bsgrigs.* 14 vols. Upper Bhattu, Himachal Pradesh, India: dPal spung gsung rab nyams gso khang, 2005. TBRC W1G4334.

Karma Damchö. *Festival of Fortunate Faith: The Life of the Hidden Buddha Tenzin Namdak. sBas pa'i sangs rgyas bstan 'dzin rnam dag gi rnam thar skal bzang dad pa'i dga' ston.* In *Collected Histories of the Glorious Zurmang Kagyu*, pp. 635–52.

Khamnyön Dharma Senge (Khams smyon Dharma seng ge, also known as 'Jig 'bral Chos kyi seng ge). *The Religious History of Pacification and Severance: A Precious Garland Ornament of Liberation. Zhi byed dang gcod yul gyi chos 'byung rin po che'i phreng ba thar pa'i rgyan.* In *A Cycle of Teachings on Severance. Gcod kyi chos skor*, pp. 411–597. Delhi: Tibet House, 1974.

———. *The Life Story of the Great Mighty Adept, Venerable Dampa Sangye: A Sun Ablaze with Thousandfold Rays of Attainment. Grub pa'i dbang phyug chen po rje btsun dam pa sangs rgyas kyi rnam par thar pa dngos grub 'od stong 'bar ba'i nyi ma.* Darjeeling: rdor gling dpe mdzod khang, 200-?. TBRC W23755.

Khetsun Sangpo. *Biographical Dictionary of Tibet and Tibetan Buddhism. Bod du sgrub brgyud shing rta mched brgyad las / shangs pa bka' brgyud / zhi gcod / sbyor drug / rdor bzlas bcas kyi bla ma brgyud pa'i rnam thar bzhugs.* Vol. 12. Kathmandu: Nyingmapa Wishfulfilling Centre for Study and Practice, 1990.

Kunga Namgyal (Kun dga' rnam rgyal. *Explanations of Severance: Lamp of Clarity, and Others. gCod kyi bshad pa gsal ba'i sgron me sogs.* Thimphu, Bhutan: Kunsang Topgay, 1978. TBRC W27477.

Kunga Paljor (Kun dga' dpal 'byor). *Space Diamond. dByings kyi rdo rje pha lam.* Unknown.

Machik Lapdrön. *Bundle of Precepts. bKa' tshom.* In *Practices of the Severance Collection and So Forth. Gcod tshogs kyi lag len sogs*, pp. 15–31.

Mikyö Dorje, Karmapa (Mi bskyod rdo rje). *Profound Severance Guide. gCod khrid zab mo.* In *dPal spungs dpe rnying gsar bskrun las khrid yig phyogs bsgrigs.* Vol. 2, pp. 578–84. dPal spungs dgon pa'i par khang, 2006. TBRC W1KG4336.

Minling Terchen (sMin gling gter chen). *The Collected Works of Minling Terchen Rikzin Gyurme Dorje. sMin gling gter chen rig 'dzin 'gyur med rdo rje'i gsung 'bum.* Dehra Dun, India: D. G. Khochhen Tulku, 1998. TBRC W22096.

———. *Esoteric Instruction That Severs Deluded Duality (from Vajrasattva's Heart Practice). rDor sems thugs kyi sgrub pa las / gNyis 'dzin 'khrul gcod man ngag.* In *The Collected Works of Minling Terchen Rikzin Gyurme Dorje.* Vol. 12 (*na*), p. 61.

———. *Hero's Loud Laugh: Instructions on Object Severance in a Single Sitting. gCod yul stan thog gcig ma'i gdams pa dpa' bo'i gad rgyangs* and *Addendum* (*zur 'debs*). In *The Collected Works of Minling Terchen Rikzin Gyurme Dorje.* Vol. 6 (*cha*), pp. 312–18.

*Practices of the Severance Collection and So Forth. gCod tshogs kyi lag len sogs: A Collection of Gcod Texts Representing the ancient Practices of the Adepts of the Tradition.* Bir, Himachal Pradesh, India: D. Tsondu Senghe, Bir Tibetan Society, 1985. TBRC W23390.

Rangjung Dorje (Rang byung rdo rje). *Lord Rangjung Dorje's Severance Feast Activities: Precious Garland. rJe rang byung rdo rjes mdzad pa'i gcod kyi tshogs las rin po che'i phreng ba 'don bsgrigs bltas chog tu bkod pa gcod kyi lugs sor bzhag.* Paro, Bhutan: Lama Ngodrub and Sherab Drimey, 1981.

Samten Özer (rGyal thang pa bSam gtan 'od zer). *Cycle of Profound Severance of Evil: A Collection of gCod Texts Chiefly Connected with the Tradition Transmitted by bSam gtan 'od zer. bDud gcod zab mo'i skor.* Darjeeling: Lama Dawa and Chopal Lama, 1974. TBRC W27506.

———. *Nectar of Meaning of the Profound Severance of Evil. bDud gcod zab mo don gyi nying khu.* In his *Cycle of Profound Severance of Evil. bDud gcod zab mo'i skor,* pp. 122.

———. *Pearl Rosary: An Account of the Lineage. brGyud gtam mu tig phreng ba.* In his *Cycle of Profound Severance of Evil. bDud gcod zab mo'i skor*, pp. 23–69.

*Shangpa Texts. Shangs chos. (Indian Source Texts of the Dharma Cycle of Five Golden Dharmas of the Glorious Shangpa. dPal ldan shangs pa'i chos 'khor gser chos rnam lnga'i rgya gzhung).* Edited by Karma Rangjung Kunkhyab (Kalu Rinpoche). 11 vols. Sonada, India: Samdrup Darje Ling Monastery, n.d.

Tāranātha. *Collected Works. rJe btsun Tā ra nā tha'i gsung 'bum.* 23 vols. Dzamthang edition, [2000?].

———. *Supplication for the Liturgy for Essence of the Vital Meaning: A Practice Manual of Profound Object Severance. gCod yul zab mo'i khrid yig gnad don snying po'i ngag 'don gsol 'debs.* In his *Collected Works.* Vol. 20, pp. 681–707.

Tashi Chöpel (bKra shis chos 'phel. *Record of Teachings Received ("Record of How Jamgön Kongtrul Yönten Gyatso Received the Precious Teachings of Sutra, Tantra, and Classical Studies with Their Source Lineages"). 'Jam mgon kong sprul yon tan rgya mtshos dam pa'i chos rin po che mdo sngags rig gnas dang bcas pa ji ltar thos shing de dag gang las brgyud pa'i yi ge dgos 'dod kun 'byung nor bu'i bang mdzod.* Beijing: Mi rigs dpe skrun khang, 2008.

Tekchok Dorje (Theg mchog rdo rje) or Khakhyap Dorje (mKha' khyab rdo rje). *The Concise Charity of the Body for Daily Practice. rGyun khyer gyi lus sbyin bsdus pa.* In *Karmapa's Collection of Instructions for Ritual Offerings. Karma pa sgar bsangs chen mo.* Delhi: Karma Chophel, 1977. TBRC W00EGS101623.

Tsewang Kunkhyap (Tshe dbang kun khyab). *Clarifying the Awareness Ḍākinī's Intention: The History of the Profound Severance of Evil Object in the Precious Glorious Zurmang Kagyu Tradition. Dpal ldan zur mang bka' brgyud rin po che'i bka' srol las byung ba'i zab mo bdud kyi gcod yul gyi chos 'byung ye shes mkha' 'gro'i dgongs pa gsal byed.* In *Collected Histories of the Glorious Zurmang Kagyu,* pp. 533–95.

***Translations and Other Works in English***

Batchelor, Stephen, trans. *A Guide to the Bodhisattva's Way of Life.* Dharamsala: Library of Tibetan Works and Archives, 1979.

Brunnhölzl, Karl. *Gone Beyond: The Prajñāpāramitā Sūtras, The Ornament of Clear Realization, and Its Commentaries in the Tibetan Kagyü Tradition.* 2 vols. Ithaca, NY: Snow Lion Publications, 2011.

Cabeźon, José Ignacio. *The Buddha's Doctrine and the Nine Vehicles: Rog Bande Sherab's "Lamp of the Teachings."* New York: Oxford University Press, 2013.

Chögyam Trungpa. "The Pön Way of Life." In *The Heart of the Buddha.* Boston: Shambhala Publications, 1991.

Conze, Edward. *The Perfection of Wisdom in Eight Thousand Lines and Its Verse Summary.* San Francisco: Four Seasons Foundation, 1973/1983.

Deroche, Marc-Henri. "'Phreng po gter ston Shes rab 'od zer (1518–1584) on the Eight Lineages of Attainment: Research on a Ris med Paradigm." In *Contemporary Visions in Tibetan Studies. Proceedings of the First International Seminar of Young Tibetologists.* Chicago: Serindia Publications, 2009.

de Rossi-Filibeck, E. "The Transmission Lineage of the Gcod Teaching According to the 2nd Dalai-Lama." In *Contributions on Tibetan and Buddhist Religion and Philosophy.* Proceedings of the Csoma De Körös Symposium Held at Velm–Vienna, Austria, 13–19 September 1981. Edited by Ernst Steinkellner and Helmut Tauscher. Vol. 2. Delhi: Motilal Banarsidass, 1995.

Dorje, Gyurme. *Footprint Tibet.* 3rd ed. Bath, U.K.: Footprint, n.d.

Drungtso, Tsering Thakchoe, and Tsering D. Drungtso. *Tibetan-English Dictionary of Tibetan Medicine and Astrology.* Dharamsala, India: Drungtso Publications, 1999.

Edou, Jérôme. *Machig Labdrön and the Foundations of Chöd.* Ithaca, NY: Snow Lion Publications, 1996.

Farrow, G. W., and I. Menon. *The Concealed Essence of the Hevajra Tantra.* Delhi: Motilal Banarsidass, 1992.

Fuchs, Rosemarie, trans. *Buddha Nature: The Mahayana Uttaratantra Shastra with Commentary.* Ithaca, NY: Snow Lion Publications, 2000.

Garfield, Jay L., trans. *The Fundamental Wisdom of the Middle Way: Nāgārjuna's Mūlamadhyamakakārikā.* New York: Oxford University Press, 1995.

Gyatso, Janet. "The Development of the gCod Tradition." In *Soundings in Tibetan Civilization,* edited by Barbara Aziz and Matthew Kapstein. New Delhi: Manohar, 1985.

Harding, Sarah. "Did Machik Lapdrön Really Teach Chöd? A Survey of the Early

Sources." Unpublished manuscript, 2013. Available at http://wordpress.tsadra.org/?cat=75

———. *Machik's Complete Explanation: Clarifying the Meaning of Chöd,* expanded ed. Boston and London: Snow Lion Publications, 2013.

———. *T'hröma Nagmo: A Practice Cycle for Realization of the Wrathful Black Ḍākinī, A Treasure of Dudjom Lingpa.* Junction City, CA: Padma Publishing, 1990.

Holmes, Ken and Katia. *The Changeless Nature.* Eskdalemuir, Scotland: Karma Drubgyud Darjay Ling, 1985.

Hopkins, Jeffrey. *Meditation on Emptiness.* London: Wisdom Publications, 1983.

Jackson, Roger R. *Tantric Treasures: Three Collections of Mystical Verse from Buddhist India.* New York: Oxford University Press, 2004.

Jamgön Kongtrul Lodrö Tayé. *The Autobiography of Jamgön Kongtrul: A Gem of Many Colors.* Translated by Richard Barron. Ithaca, NY: Snow Lion Publications, 2003.

———. *The Catalog of The Treasury of Precious Instructions.* Translated by Richard Barron (Chökyi Nyima). New York: Tsadra Foundation, 2013.

———. *The Treasury of Knowledge, Book 1: Myriad Worlds.* Translated by the Kalu Rinpoché Translation Group. Ithaca, NY: Snow Lion Publications, 1995/2003.

———. *The Treasury of Knowledge, Books 2, 3, and 4: Buddhism's Journey to Tibet.* Translated by the Kalu Rinpoché Translation Group (Ngawang Zangpo). Ithaca, NY: Snow Lion Publications, 2010.

———. *The Treasury of Knowledge, Book 5: Buddhist Ethics.* Translated by the Kalu Rinpoché Translation Group. Ithaca, NY: Snow Lion Publications, 1998/2003.

———. *The Treasury of Knowledge, Book 6, Part 3: Frameworks of Buddhist Philosophy.* Translated by the Kalu Rinpoché Translation Group (Elizabeth M. Callahan). Ithaca, NY: Snow Lion Publications, 2007.

———. *The Treasury of Knowledge, Book 8, Part 4: Esoteric Instructions.* Translated by the Kalu Rinpoché Translation Group (Sarah Harding). Ithaca, NY: Snow Lion Publications, 2007.

Kalupahana, David J. *Mūlamadhyamakakārikā of Nāgārjuna.* Albany: State University of New York Press, 1986.

Nebesky-Wojkowitz, René de. *Oracles and Demons of Tibet: The Cult and Iconography of the Tibetan Protective Deities.* The Hague: Mouton, 1956.

Martin, Dan. *Tibskrit Philology: A Bibliography of Tibetan Philology.* Edited by Alexander Cherniak. Online only: 2006, revised 2014. http://rywiki.tsadra.org/index.php/A_Bibliography_of_Tibetan_Philology_by_Dan_Martin

Molk, David, trans. *Lion of Siddhas: The Life and Teachings of Padampa Sangye.* Ithaca, NY: Snow Lion Publications, 2008.

Nāgārjuna. *Nagarjuna's Letter to a Friend: With Commentary by Kyabje Kangyur Rinpoche.* Translated by the Padmakara Translation Group. Ithaca, NY: Snow Lion Publications, 2006.

Orofino, Giacomella. "The Great Wisdom Mother and the Gcod Tradition." In *Tantra in Practice,* edited by David Gordon White. Princeton, NJ: Princeton University Press, 2000.

Palmo, Anila Rinchen, trans. *Cutting Through Ego-Clinging: Commentary on the Practice of Tchod.* Montignac, France: Dzambala, 1988.

Phuntsho, Karma. *Mipham's Dialectics and the Debates on Emptiness.* London and New York: RoutledgeCurzon, 2005.

Ringu Tulku. *The Ri-me Philosophy of Jamgön Kongtrul the Great: A Study of the Buddhist Lineages of Tibet.* Boston: Shambhala Publications, 2006.

Roberts, Peter Alan. *The Biographies of Rechungpa: The Evolution of a Tibetan Hagiography.* London: Routledge Taylor and Francis Group, 2007.

Roerich, George N., trans. *The Blue Annals.* Calcutta, 1949. 2nd ed., Delhi: Motilal Banarsidass, 1976/1988.

Savvas, Carol Diane. "A Study of the Profound Path of Gcod: The Mahāyāna Buddhist Meditation Tradition of Tibet's Great Woman Saint Machig Labdron." PhD diss., University of Wisconsin–Madison, 1990.

Schaeffer, Kurtis R. *Dreaming the Great Brahmin: Tibetan Traditions of the Buddhist Poet-Saint Saraha.* Oxford: Oxford University Press, 2005.

Shantideva. *The Way of the Bodhisattva.* Translated by the Padmakara Translation Group. Boston: Shambhala Publications, 1997.

Sheehy, Michael R. "Severing the Source of Fear: Contemplative Dynamics of the Tibetan Buddhist GCod Tradition." *Contemporary Buddhism: An Interdisciplinary Journal* 6, no. 1 (2005): 37–52. http://dx.doi.org/10.1080/14639940500129504

Smith, E. Gene. *Among Tibetan Texts: History and Literature of the Himalayan Plateau.* Boston: Wisdom Publications, 2001.

Sorensen, Michelle J. "Mahāmudrā Chöd? Rangjung Dorje's Commentary on the Great Speech Chapter of Machik Labdrön." In *Wading into the Stream of Wisdom: Essays in Honor of Leslie Kawamura,* edited by Sarah F. Haynes and Michelle J. Sorensen. Berkeley, CA: Institute of Buddhist Studies and BDK America, Inc., 2013.

———. "Making the Old New Again and Again: Legitimation and Innovation in the Tibetan Buddhist Chöd Tradition." PhD diss., Columbia University, 2013.

Stearns, Cyrus. *Luminous Lives: The Story of the Early Masters of the Lam 'bras Tradition in Tibet.* Boston: Wisdom Publications, 2001.

Tatz, Mark. "Twenty Verses on the Bodhisattva Vow." In *Difficult Beginnings: Three Works on the Bodhisattva Path.* Boston: Shambhala Publications, 1985.

Tenga Rinpoche. *Chö: The Garden of All Joy and Generosity of the Body.* Auckland, N.Z.: Zhyisil Chokyi Ghatsal Charitable Trust Publications, 2008.

Thekchok Dorje and Jamgön Kongtrül Lodö Taye. *Chöd Practice Manual and Commentary.* Translated by Lama Lodö Rinpoche. Ithaca, NY: Snow Lion Publications, 2007.

Thinley, Karma. *The History of the Sixteen Karmapas of Tibet.* Boulder: Prajñā Press, 1980.

Wallace, Vesna A., and B. Alan Wallace. *A Guide to the Bodhisattva Way of Life.* Ithaca, NY: Snow Lion Publications, 1997.

# Index


abiding nature of mind
  as buddha, 80
  equality in, 184
  introducing directly, 226–27
    (*see also* introduction [*ngo sprod*])
  as lucid clarity, 53–54
  recognizing, 45, 550n13
  resting in, 118, 147–54, 178, 193, 251
  revealing, 10, 69
  in between sessions, 169
Absence of Characteristics, Wheel of, 41
absorptions, meditative
  authentic, 108
  blessing of, 164
  of completely pervading space, 342
  cornering with, 177, 180, 181
  of extensively filling space, 342
  of heroic conduct, 479–80
  of higher realms, 96, 559n32
  illusion-like, 476–79
  in perfection of wisdom, 44–45
  of suchness, 56
  three, 472, 473
  vajra-like, 278, 475–76
acceptance and rejection, 115, 117, 119–20, 133, 172, 174, 249–50
accoutrements
  of ḍākinīs, 270, 463
  eight charnel ground, 572n18
  to eliminate stagnancy, 177
  of Machik, 376, 572n18
  in mother lineage feast offering, 401
  required, 313, 574n4
accumulation, field of, 348–49, 375–77, 486–87, 508–9, 583n9
accumulations, two, 115, 169, 186, 268, 413
Āchārya Āryadeva, 3, 584n6
action, authentic results of, 107
Action Ḍākinī, 453, 455
adepts, Severance lineage of, 353, 385, 387, 414, 435, 438, 508, 509, 512
Adro Chöpa Sangye Tashi, 257
adventitious stains, 34, 54
adverse conditions/circumstances
  direct subjugation of, 484
  in haunted places, 130
  leftover offerings to avert, 409–10
  as samsara's conduct, 131–32
  sufferings of, 35, 36
  *See also* integration (*lam 'khyer*)
afflictive emotions
  antidotes for, 140
  ceasing from within, 137
  conduct free of, 22–23, 78, 92
  controlling, 72
  as delusions, 306
  as devils, 31, 154, 250
  as intangible devil, 18, 62, 77, 312
  interdependent connections, role of in, 308
  lack of reference to, 141
  purification of, 216
  remedy for, 35
  results of purifying, 72
  as self-liberated, 7, 59, 93, 151
  severing, 296
  sickness and, 37
  subtle spirits of, 34
  and timeless awareness, single basis of, 167

aggregates, five, 25, 31, 96, 111, 154, 250, 255
aggression/anger
  acting presumptuously with, 110
  antidotes, 105, 192
  finishing off, 37
  heart-*chitta* of, 457
  liberated on own ground, 19, 77, 86–87, 167
  mental nonengagement of, 127
  purity of, 212–213
  in between sessions, 169
  tangible devil and, 303
  *See also* aversion
Aghora, 508
Akaniṣhṭha, 236, 264, 349, 377, 422, 439, 440, 446
Akṣhobhya, 201, 212, 263, 517
altruism, 136, 408, 522, 534
Amitābha, 201, 214, 263, 517
Amoghasiddhi, 201, 214, 263, 517
analogies, examples, and metaphors
  for aggregates, 255
  beasts and boulder, 110
  beetles tangled in wood, 165
  for body, 146–47
  butter, 16, 23, 93, 558n24
  cauterizing wounds by fire, 26
  chicks in autumn, 21, 89, 115, 561n23
  for compounded things, 480
  cornering deer, 174, 566n4
  cows, 21, 77, 89
  crop cultivation and harvest, 52
  deceiving thieves, 110
  door frame, 8, 65
  embers covered with ashes, 167
  empty house with dead owner, 217
  on faith, 125–26
  fierce gatekeepers, 22
  fish in sea, 23, 92
  garuḍa, 21, 90
  ice in summer, 136
  illusionist, 18, 86, 255
  island of gold, 7, 59–60
  lightning bolts, 22, 91
  lions, 19, 87
  miracles, 88, 558n15
  mirages, 159
  moon reflected in water, 189, 218, 250
  morning star under thumb, 8, 32, 64, 547nn13–14, 554n64
  mothers with sick children, 58
  ocean and waves, 22, 91, 160
  parents, 173
  poisonous food, 35
  poisonous snakes, 23, 93, 161
  rainbows, 86
  for resting mind, 217
  rope, cutting, 148
  rope on camel's nose, 160
  sharp weapons, 20, 87
  shrine-room statue, 21, 91
  silkworm saliva, 127, 561n5
  simpleton with full belly, 22, 91
  skilled warriors, 87
  sky, 6, 9, 56, 67
  smoke in wall, 18, 86
  snakes, 36
  sovereign, sea captain, shepherd, 259
  sun/sunlight, 34, 173
  thick forest and sharp axe, 8, 34, 63
  thief in empty house, 132, 526n19
  tree trunk, cutting root of, 4, 21, 45–46, 60, 90
  uḍumbara flowers, 125
  vultures, 166
  water, gold, and sky, 94, 558n26
  water moon, 198
  for ways of resting, 131
  wild horse, 167
analysis, 8, 34, 62, 63, 167
animals, 19, 87, 175, 273
*Another Bundle* (Machik), xvi, 279, 548n18, 577n31
  titles and variants, 123–24, 138, 561n1, 563n26
  *Vajra Play* and, 139, 563n1
antidotes, 412
  lack of, 17, 84, 89
  not using, 159–61
  obstacles and, 10, 70
  and problems, inseparability of, 90
anxiety
  of beginners, 251

conduct, 8, 60, 61
as felt experience, 252
as one's own mind, 116, 150–51
practices for, 32, 99, 118, 251
of superior practitioners, 155
apparitions (*cho 'phrul*)
by capability, 252
cutting, 177
engaging, 137
external devils, 128, 561–62n7
fear and ideas arising from, 169
in haunted places, 305
introduced in oneself, 111
manner of occurrence, 252–53
as one's mind, 150–51
as ornaments, 174
as projections, 116
without evidence of success, 320
appearances
annihilating, 96
applying enhancements to, 169
applying seal of invalidity to, 83–84
attachment to, 162
changing to path of awakening, 106
as delusions, 306
emptiness and, 218, 481, 487
as energy and allies, 151
fixation on, 160–61
lack of clinging to, 141
mental inflation over, 158
not evaluating, 161
during resting evenly, 32
resting in, 108
rootlessness of, 18, 86
severing, 183–84
as support, 168
as timeless awareness, 95
torma of red and white, 408
as unblocked perceptions, 227
without fixation, 149–50
*See also* dualistic appearances
*Appendices*, xvi, 79. See also *Eight Common Appendices, The*; *Eight Special Appendices, The*; *Eight Uncommon Appendices, The*
arrogance, 5, 15, 16, 50–51, 83, 111, 112, 413
Āryadeva the Brahmin. *See* Brahmin Āryadeva
*Āryaprajñāpāramitā Upadeśa*. See *Esoteric Instructions on the Noble Perfection of Wisdom* (Brahmin Āryadeva)
Asaṅga, 40, 47, 584n6
aspirations, 144
in *Body Donation and Feeding Ritual*, 341
for daily practice, 478, 481, 498
in *Hair's Tip of Wisdom*, 121
for helpers and harmers, 33
Kunga's Thirteenfold Prayer, 533
in ongoing meditation, 186
in *Pearl Rosary*, 367
in preliminary practices, 248–49, 299
purpose of, 176
for rousing consciousness, 188
Six Vajra-Line Prayer, 535
Thirtyfold Prayer by Dampa, 532–33
at time of death, 153
timeless awareness and, 105
for virtue, 486
Assorted Distribution, 495
attachment
to appearing objects, 14, 80, 278–79
to body, 188–89
to conduct, 92
cutting by casting out the body, 251, 479
to dharma, 167
due to spirit uprisings, 316
to enjoyment, 112
finishing off, 37
to gods and demons, 500–501
as inflation, 18, 85
lack of in meditation, 309
lack of in separating body from mind, 147
to mere designations, 160–61
to phenomena arising from oneself, 159
practicing without, 17
to qualities, 15–16, 76, 82
reifying, 162
to spirit powers, 20, 77, 88
as tangible devil, 8, 109, 127–28

attachment (*continued*)
to tenets, 10, 69
to worldly things, 104–5, 296
attraction, four methods of, 50
auspicious symbols, eight, 203, 491
auspiciousness
mudra of, 351, 381, 488, 519, 578n6
prayers of, 415–16
verses of, 535
authorization ritual, xvii, 197, 220
*Autobiography of Jamgön Kongtrul*, xi
Avalokiteshvara, 287, 318, 339, 368, 419, 498, 585n10
*Avataṃsakasūtra*. See *Flower Ornament Sutra*
aversion
in dreams, 150
in inferior practitioners, 63
as inflation, 18
severing, 36, 500
as tangible devil, 109
as traceless, 23
*See also* aggression/anger
averting, 225, 429, 470, 566n5
awakening, path of, 49, 50–51, 72–73, 106, 339
awakening mind, arousing
*Appendices*, instructions in, 186–88
in Āryadeva's instructions, 5, 46–47, 50, 52, 70
in casting out body, 346, 348
in daily practice, 473, 474, 485
in empowerments, 200, 207–8, 225–26
in *Essence of Auspicious Renown*, 505
gift of, 108
in six perfections practice, 50
in Zurmang instructions, 259–61, 262, 373, 375
awareness
agitation as, 152
as ḍākinī, 328, 330
direct, 9, 67
emptiness and clarity of, 149–50
engagement with (*rig spyod*), 295
free of basis or root, 7, 56, 150
free of inflation, 163
guarding, 130
knowing, 500
letting go of, 147
and matter, separating from, 9, 67
mindful, 57, 108
not wasting, 164
pervasiveness of, 6, 56
and quintessence, differentiating, 176
recognizing, 4, 45
reflexive, 24, 204, 284, 379, 417, 418, 476, 477, 518
space and, 189
strengthening, 169
of thoughts as Great Mother, 22
unclear, 316
unsupported and naked, 175
*See also* intrinsic awareness
awareness beings
in confession, 414
departure of, 218, 286, 290
descent of, 228–29
inviting, 264–66
invoking, 202, 348–49, 375–77, 568n3
*See also under* pledge beings
awareness protectors, 215, 283
awareness-holders, 73, 120, 269
*See also* thirty-six uncommon awareness-holders

*bandes*, 331, 333–34, 362, 575n10
Bangarwa, 295, 573n43
Banners feast, 291, 366, 495
*bardo* practice, 37
bathing ritual, 378, 578n3
begging, 107, 175
*Beloved Garden*, xviii, 483, 550n12, 577n2
benefiting beings, 164
aspiration for, 106
not hoping to, 180
potential to, 158
through realization, 21, 77, 89–90
teachings as, 4, 43
*See also* healing rituals
Bengar Jampal Zangpo, 421–22, 580n1
Bengen Tenzin Namdak, 258, 296, 385, 435
Bhagavān. *See* Buddha Shākyamuni

*Big General Guide to Severance* (Jamyang Gönpo), 30, 545n1, 546n5
"Billionfold Universe," 203, 568n6
birth, four kinds, 477, 582n4
Black Cloaked (Bernakchen), 264, 328
black distributions, 266, 319, 322, 330, 381
  Black Poison Distribution, 487
"black mamba's undulation," 313–14
Blazing Graveyard, 223
blending, three cycles of, 288, 496, 573n37
blending space and awareness, 64, 258, 500
  in daily practice, 475–76, 490
  disdaining, 176
  in healing rituals, 339–41
  method of, 6–7, 54, 55–56
  in mother lineage feast offerings, 282
  in Opening the Sky Door, 229
  in peaceful severance, 304, 305
  profundity of, 46
  to purify habitual patterns, 45
  purpose of, 7, 56
  during uprisings, 309
  in wrathful severance, 306
blessing-empowerment lineage, 79, 507, 509, 585n9
blessings
  conduct of, 92
  conferring, 156
  creating for others, 133, 526n20
  in curing others, 180
  descent of, 383–86, 417–19, 474–75, 527, 586n25
  as devil of exaltation, 112
  devotion, importance of to, 182–83
  as distractions, 15
  losing, 177
  in mother lineage feasts, 280
  for oneself, 136–37
  realization and, 17
  requesting, 287, 534–35
  of resting, 148
  from words, lack of, 27
  *See also* supplications
bliss
  as bondage, 139
  of buddhahood, 141
  in dissipating body, 465
  everlasting, 167
  of lack of contrivance, 217
  in mother and father tantra, differentiated, 94
  resting consciousness in, 145–46, 147–53, 155, 174–75
  of secret feast, 284
  undissipating, 370, 506
  of union of method and wisdom, 518
  *See also* great bliss
bliss-emptiness, 24
  awareness within, 150–51
  of offering substances, 506
  in secret offering, 518
  sickness, changing into, 340
  timeless awareness of, 94, 524
Blissful (Sukhāvatī), 270, 494
*Blue Annals, The* (Roerich), 556n85, 556n90, 540n8
bodhichitta (seminal fluid), 179, 328, 372, 464
Bodhidharma, 3
Bodhisattva Kunga, 508, 510, 525, 585n11, 585n14
bodhisattva path, 50. *See also* perfections, six; ten stages
*Bodhisattva Stages* (Asaṅga), 47
*Bodhisattvacaryāvatāra*. See *Entering the Way of the Bodhisattva* (Shāntideva)
bodhisattvas, 135
  afflictive emotions of, 59
  benefit to others, 90
  casting out body by, 251, 570n4
  conduct of, 375
  display of deeds of, 88
  dissolution of, 416
  elaboration of, 153
  offering body to, 328
  perfection of wisdom, training in, 102, 103
  qualities of, 108, 473
  skill of, 87
body
  in blending space and awareness, 6, 56
  as charnel ground, 34

body (*continued*)
cherishing, 414
fear of losing, 130, 341
fixation on, 31, 60, 116, 227, 479
impurity of, 146–47
like a stone, 9, 67, 163
in meaning of Mother, 301, 499
nonfixation on, 26, 78, 98
in overwhelming devils, 128
purifying, 205, 381, 534–35
rarity of human, 124–25
during resting method, 21, 22, 44–45, 118, 131, 148, 163, 164
severing clinging to, 172
severing inflation of, 67
signs of warmth in, 153, 389
in ten perfections, 105
in torma blessing, 215, 216
as torma offering, 459, 460–70
vital point of, 216, 217, 226, 315, 525
vows of, 338
when sick or curing others, 178–80, 339–40
*See also* body-offering practice; illusory body; mandalas; separating body from mind
Body (*kāya/sku*)
blessings and empowerments of, 326, 491, 497, 534
family, 462
as liberated, 21, 90
mandala of, 267–68
mudra of, 228, 350, 381, 487, 519
nonfixation as, 60, 78, 98, 198, 553n52
pledge substances as, 527
representations of, 199
sacred pledge of, 456
timeless awareness of, 98
*Body Donation and Feeding Ritual*, 311, 312, 321–22, 574n1
body-offering practice, 187–88
development of, xvi, xvii, 483, 555n68
to free self-fixation, 31
fulfillment rituals of, 437–38
in healing ritual, 324, 326–37
liturgies for, 351–52, 472–82
in peaceful severance, 304
place in Severance tradition, 345
practitioners suited to, 9, 67
in red distribution, 316–17
texts emphasizing, xviii
at time of death, 153
as uncommon preliminary, 249
*See also* casting out body as food
Bön tradition, 193, 333, 566n6
bondage, 161
by bliss and clarity, 139
by cognition, 24
of craving dharma, 26, 98
origin of, 250
practice as, 21, 77, 89, 165
bone ornaments
empowerment of, 228
in fulfillment, 458
offering, 269
six perfections and, 228, 444, 462
Bone Shaker feast, 291, 496
Bountiful Cow (Godānīya), 267
Brahmin Āryadeva, xiv, xvi, 40, 43
identity of, 3
Mañjushrī and, 41, 549n2
in Severance lineage, 256
supplications to, 237, 342, 352, 383, 386, 388, 423, 432
See also *Esoteric Instructions on the Noble Perfection of Wisdom* (Brahmin Āryadeva)
branch offerings
eight, 208–9
five, 486, 520–22
prayers for, 248, 349–50
seven, 262, 487, 532–35
breath
in blending, 342
dullness indicated by, 152
during inner warmth, 153
in meaning of Mother, 499
in Opening Sky Door, 226
as seed syllable, 372
at time of death, 154
*Brief Synopsis of Visualization Sequence for Severance Feast Activities "Endowed with All Qualities,"* 257–58
Buddha Ḍākinī, 211
buddha nature, 39, 278, 295, 416

Buddharatna, 352, 386, 451
Buddha Shākyamuni
body offering to, 324
dissolution of, 326
feeding, 358, 405
in gift of dharma, 338
as Golden One, 208
as meditation object, 499
praise to, 43, 379
on referential notions, 112–13
requesting to remain, 414–15
in Severance lineages, 13, 256, 342, 510
in torma blessing, 215
visualizations of, 201, 301, 323, 348, 376, 417, 507
Buddha Tsenchen, 385, 434
Buddha Vairochana. *See* Vairochana
buddha/buddhas
becoming, 88
meaning and purpose of, 134–35
as one's mind, 23, 417, 418
perfection of wisdom and, 102, 103
recognizing in one lifetime, 164–65, 565n15
sentient beings and, 94
Severance view of, 95
timeless awareness of, 80, 113
as unconditioned, 25, 78, 95–96
without fixating concepts, 141
*See also* five buddhas; ten directions, buddhas of
Buddhaguhya, 507, 584n4
Buddhaguptanātha, 221
buddhahood, 9, 68
aspiration for, 479
hoping for as devil, 168
meaning of, 131
as mental nonengagement, 96–97
no-mind and, 93
in one lifetime, 169
for self and other, 33
Severance view of, 17–18, 85, 296
unconditioned, 26, 98
without fixating concepts, 141
*Buddhakapāla*, 283
butchers, 333, 362–63, 457, 466
Butön Rinchendrup, 198
calm abiding, 114, 160, 167, 302, 476
capability, 41, 83, 122, 134
in blending consciousness, 339
in dealing with obstacles, 193, 253
in integrating devils, 155–56
meditative experiences by, 189
practices by, 8, 9, 62–63, 91, 99, 169, 174–75, 249–50, 566n23
in severing devils, 66–68
in transference, 488–90
in understanding apparitions, 252
carrying the load, 27, 78, 99
casting out body as food, 133, 168
authorization for, 216–18
capability for, 91, 99, 169, 193, 250, 252
instructions, 169, 191–92, 251
results of, 175
skill of, 546n5
*See also* body-offering practice; daily practice (body donation); distributions
Casting Out the Body as Food
scope of practice, 346
in Zurmang tradition, 257, 259, 266–69, 307, 382–83
*See also* body-offering practice; feasts
Casting Out the Corpse feast, 290–91, 494–95
*Catalog of The Treasury of Precious Instructions, The*, 197, 311, 370, 421, 580n1, 581n1
cause and effect, 21, 37, 115–16, 338, 480, 576n26, 582n6
causes
substantial, 52, 551n32
without conditions, 126
celestial realm, thirty-six gurus of, 507, 510, 584n8
central channel, 266, 267, 268, 324, 488, 489, 572n15, 583n11
Chakrasaṃvara, 263, 270, 283, 328, 425, 452, 454, 506
*Chakrasaṃvara*, 283
*Chakrasaṃvara Ḍākinī Illusion Later Tantra*, 103
*Chakrasaṃvarābhidhānottaratantra*, 578n3

Chandragomin, 47, 551n20
*changbu* offerings, 327, 575n4
channels, energy, 34, 37, 94, 216, 308, 309, 533. *See also* central channel
charnel grounds/graveyards/cemeteries
  attributes of, 270, 572n18
  eight great, 239, 280–81, 444–45, 452–54, 467
  of one's body, 33, 34
  ornaments of, 270, 572n18
  as place of practice, 31, 147, 313
  for suppressing uprisings, 316
*Chatuḥpīṭhā*, 283
child lineage, 279, 343, 439
Chime Drupa, 238
chittamātrins, 24, 94, 558nn27–28
Chöd. *See* Severance (*gcod*)
*chöd,* use of term, xvii
Chödrak Gyatso, seventh Karmapa, 425, 580n1
Chöje Jamyang Gönpo, 482
Chokgyur Dechen Lingpa, xi, 369
*chokpu* tent, 313, 315, 573n4
Chöku Lhawang, 238
Chökyi Döndrup, 427
Chökyi Drakpa, 437, 438, 439–49
Chökyi Gyatso, 425
Chökyi Jungne, 353, 386, 427
Chökyi Sherap, 510
Chökyi Wangpo, 426
Chökyong Gyurme, 258
Chökyong Namgyal, 258
Chölung Demchok, 238
Chölung Jangtse, 238
Chöpel Gyatso, 238
Chöwang Tulku, 370
Chöying Dorje, 238
Chupa, 510
Chuwori Mountain, 384, 432
circles, three, 388
clapping, 470
clarity
  as bondage, 139
  emptiness and, 118
  in father tantra, 24, 94
  of mind, 218
  not blocking, 140
  of phenomena, 15, 150, 153
  resting in, 131, 147, 217–18, 302
clarity-emptiness, 153, 211, 490, 499–500
clinging
  reversing, 165
  reverting from within, 140, 142
  to words, 137
clouds, offering, 271, 275, 373, 477, 491
cognition, 23–24, 78
  clinging to/fixating on, 14, 16, 95
  deluded, 15, 82, 113, 542n11
  as haunted place, 91
  naturally deluded, 23, 94
  reflexive, 80
  in tenet systems, 24, 94
  use of term, 544n49
  vital wind and, 108
cognitive obscuration, 25, 42, 69, 72, 96, 114
*Collected Histories of the Glorious Zurmang Kagyu*, 39, 257, 438
*Collected Works of Longchen Rabjam* (Longchenpa), 545n1
command guards (*bka' srung*), 286, 448
*Common Appendices, The*, xvi
Common Vehicle, 171, 488
Communal Feast Offering of the Bodies of Self and Others, 496–98
compassion
  abiding nature and, 169
  arousing, 299
  benefits of, 501
  in conduct, 96
  of ḍākinīs, 229
  emptiness and, 10, 70–71
  as enemy, 115
  as enhancement, 38, 181–82
  as evidence of success, 253
  in fulfillment, 440, 443, 446, 449
  in gentle severance, 329
  guests of, 272–74
  holding apparitions with, 32
  importance of, 175
  meditation on, 181–82, 191, 192, 304, 305, 308, 309, 337, 500

spontaneous, 341
completion phase, 501
conceptual thoughts
emptiness of, 129
mental nonengagement in, 145
no-mind and, 93
obscuration of, 80
resting and, 22
as root of samsara and nirvana, 89
severing, 79, 87, 98, 303
trampling, 100
as without basis, 86
*Concise Charity of the Body for Daily Practice* (attributed to Tekchok Dorje), 369, 471, 522–23, 583n5, 586n22
concluding practices, 121–22, 498, 499, 500
for empowerments, 218–20, 231
for haunted places, 317–18
for healing rituals, 337–39
liturgies for, 367–68, 411–12, 480–81, 532–34
in peaceful and wrathful severance, 305, 307
*Condensed Verses on the Perfection of Wisdom* (Dignāga), 44
conduct
analogies for, 22–23, 92
carefree, 25
with compassion, 96
as conceit, 16, 83
as conquering fear, 56
correcting deluded, 443, 445, 448
displaying, 100
elaborate-style, 307
enhancing practice through, 183–84
meditative absorption of, 479–80
as natural occurrences, 95
negative, 414
of no conduct, 17, 76, 84, 543n23
of nonfixation, 16
nonsensical, 180, 567n15
obstruction of, 176
resting in, 148
secret, 295
in separating body from mind, 147
to subdue helpers and harmers, 33
supreme, 161
three absorptions and, 473
toward oneself, 23
of unity, 168
view and, 20, 36, 87, 99, 117
without reference points, 131–32
*See also* yogic discipline/vanquishing conduct
confession, 144, 209, 226, 286, 380, 409
in fulfillment rituals, 437, 443, 446, 448, 454–57
liturgies for, 412–15, 520, 534
confidence
of being without hope, 18, 543n26
creating, 144
devotion and, 183
in guru's instruction, 100, 134
necessity of, 17
in severing, 109
in view and conduct, 36
without inflation, 19, 104, 112, 116–17, 164
consciousness
ascent and blending of, 294
collecting scattered, 178
dissolution of, 342
keeping unbounded, 158
letting go of, 147
of mental apparitions, 253
relaxing, 145
resting, 131
resting in, 140, 301
of self and patient, blending, 331, 339–41
as self-liberated, 217
consciousness groups
enjoyment of, 281
resting in, 22, 78, 91, 119, 145, 148
torma of, 407
transforming, 55
conventional reality, not opposing, 180
Cool Grove Graveyard, 440
Copper Mountain, 286, 441, 448
Corpse Distribution, 290, 291–92, 495–96

creation phase, 309, 501
creditors
  body, offering to, 249, 251, 283, 291, 320, 328, 359, 405, 530
  in daily practice, 261
  desirables, offering to, 273
  elixir, offering to, 276
  fulfillment of, 457
  as good fortune, 200
  in red distribution, 278
  in white distribution, 492
*Cycle of Profound Severance of Evil* (Samten Özer), 29
cyclic existence, 134–35, 154, 164, 165, 209, 279

daily activities, four, 7, 57, 147, 183, 250
daily practice (body donation), 471, 472, 483
  concluding activities for, 480–81, 498
  enhancement practice in, 479–80
  meditative absorptions in, 475–79
  offering body mandala in, 490–91
  outline of, 484–85
  preliminaries, 473–75, 485–88, 583n5
  transference for, 489
  variations in, 481
  See also *Concise Charity of the Body for Daily Practice*
ḍākimas, use of term, 459. *See also* ḍākinīs
*Ḍākinī Vajra Tent Tantra*, 103, 226
ḍākinīs
  attendant, 281
  auspiciousness of, 416
  of basic space, 462–63
  binding, 10, 71–72
  black buddha, 280
  descent of, 294
  eight graveyard, 444–45, 467
  feeding, 357, 363, 367, 405
  field, 448
  in five-tiered refuge, 263–64
  four, 201, 215, 270, 281–82, 453, 455, 463, 468–69
  mover, 285
  one hundred thousand, 216, 398–400, 460–62, 581n2
  role in feasts, 459
  secret awareness, 263
  skeleton, 285, 498
  supplications to, 280, 342–43
  symbol lineage of, 353, 387
  of timeless awareness, 124, 331
  white, 287, 330, 368, 419, 493
  worker, 215, 268, 269, 270–71, 275, 276, 277, 288
  worldly, 286, 406, 411, 444, 466–67
  wrathful, 337
  *See also* five-family ḍākinīs
"ḍākinī's symbolic gait," 313
Dakpo Kagyu, 481
Dampa Charchen, 507–8, 510, 585n11
Dampa Charchung, 508, 510, 585n11
Dampa Mutik. *See* Dampa Sangye
Dampa Sangye, 11, 73, 376, 504
  aspiration prayer by, 532–33
  fifty-four common adepts of, 507, 510, 584nn3–7, 585n15
  lineage of, xiii–xiv, 3–4, 198, 247, 256
  Machik and, xiv, 578n6
  names of, 388, 541n7, 556n84
  praises to, 208, 349
  on self-liberation, 217–18
  students of, 511, 556n85, 585nn11–15
  supplications to, 237, 342, 352, 383, 386, 388–90, 423, 432, 508, 510
  teachers of, 549n2
  thirty-six uncommon awareness-holders of, 507, 510, 584n8
  twenty-four spiritual power-bestowing ḍākinī gurus, 79, 507, 509, 585n9
  visualizations of, 201, 263, 340, 341, 348, 417, 507
dance
  of ḍākinīs, 223, 314, 462, 463
  desiring to, 149
  of Hayagrīva, 286
  nine stances, 331
  offering, 203, 378, 519
  of union, 458
Dartsönpa, 511
death, 162
  devils of, 31, 154, 250, 485

practice for moment of, 153–54
spiritual, 554n60
willingness for, 32, 65, 179–80
death lords, 313, 478, 495
debt
karmic, 272–73, 328, 492
masters and mistresses of, 346, 349, 362, 373, 374, 377
Dechen Lundrup Ling, 451
Dechenjong, 441
dedication
after casting out body, 192
in daily practice, 481, 498
in eight branch vows, 209
general instructions for, 218–19
in healing ritual, 327
prayers, 342–43, 367, 415, 419
in preliminary practices, 144, 488
in torma offering, 408–10
deities
descending, 293
dissolution of, 326
feeding, 357, 405
fulfillment of, 457
as hosts, 270
mandala, homage to, 379
offerings to, 206
ten ornaments of wrathful, 572n17
torma offerings to, 459
unbearable, 133
*See also* gods; yidams
deity empowerment conferred on body, 570n7
Delek Gyaltsen, 237
delusion, 24, 93, 108, 142, 184, 283, 284. *See also* cognition
demigods
as guests, 361, 362
offerings for, 272
as pledge beings, 202, 331–32, 349, 362, 377
realm of, 273
seed syllable of, 266, 267, 489
timeless awareness of equality and, 87
demonesses, 289, 316, 334, 337, 360, 363, 457
demons, 313, 326–27, 328, 335, 336, 457, 574n7
dependent arising, 51–52
desire
acting presumptuously with, 110
as adventitious stain, 54
blood oceans of, 367, 532
clinging, 113
conveying to basic space, 309, 310
as devil of conceit, 17
as devil of exaltation, 312, 476
as devil of result, 77, 85
freedom from, 554n65
of gods, 72
of hungry ghosts, 87
as leftovers, 367
liberated on own ground, 19, 87
menstrual blood of, 457
mental without object, 128
purity of, 214, 395
for severance, 165
severing, 61
subsidiary devil of, 155
turning one's back on, 33
desire realm, 49, 145, 331
devils
armies of, 335, 364
of being god's child, 250
of conceit, 17
constituents as, 255
of creation, 22
cutting in nature of phenomena, 148
of death lord, 154, 250
domain/sphere of, not getting lost in/straying into, 154–56, 192–93
dwelling places of, 313
identifying, 31, 35, 66, 67, 150
liberated on own ground, 17, 84, 137
mind as root, 14
not identifying, 166
as obstacles to meditation, 32
of path, 15, 76, 82, 83
planetary, 334, 363–64
root, 31, 154
secret, 134
self-occurring self-pacification of, 23, 93
spiritual powers from, 162

devils (*continued*)
  subsidiary, 155
  uses of term, 541n13, 554n60
devils, four, 14, 30, 31, 76, 542nn3–5
  bodhisattva's ability to withstand, 473
  clinging to, 296
  in fulfillment rituals, 443
  habitual patterns as, 260
  identifying, 127, 312
  overwhelming, 128, 129
  pacification of, 194
  results of severing, 72
  rootlessness of, 21, 77, 90
  severing method, 61
  traditional *māras*, 485, 582n3
  *See also* individual devils
devotion, 175, 298, 501
  confessing lack of, 413
  in descent of blessings, 474–75
  as enhancement, 38, 182–83, 184
  as evidence of success, 253
  interdependent connections, role of in, 308
  in invoking awareness beings, 377
  of sangha, 380
Dezhin Shekpa, fifth Karmapa, 257, 425
dharma
  afflictive emotions toward, 35
  being trapped by, 165
  blending with mind, 109
  bondage of craving, 26, 98
  enjoyment of, 136
  gift of, 338–39
  giving up, 166
  inflation and, 129
  inspiration for, 130
  melody of, 516
  as notion of mind, 160
  prayer for bestowal of, 480
  protection rites for, 181
  rarity of practicing, 125
  rejecting, 256
  and Severance, connection with, 142
  spreading, 132
  ten activities of, 122, 561n25
  without realization, limits of, 168
dharma doors, 165, 186, 570n7
dharma empowerment conferred on mind, xvii, 231, 570n7
dharma protectors
  binding, 10, 71–72, 380
  body-offering to, 328
  feeding leftovers, 367
  inviting, 235
  offerings to, 205–6, 268, 271–72
  in refuge, 262, 264
  tormas for, 224, 236
  visualizations of, 182, 201–2, 348
dharmadhātu, 238, 414
  palace of, 236, 349, 377, 383, 422, 424, 425, 427, 431, 439, 528, 531
dharmakāya, 279
  arising as form kāya, 114
  attainment of, 52
  as cutting mind's root, 412
  inflation and noninflation in, 160
  of inseparable ground and result, 218
  mind as, 81, 137, 174
  as oneself, 129
  pervasiveness of, 56
  self-arising as adornment of, 20
  self-liberated delusion as, 169
  as white *a*, 340
  without inflation, 162
Dhūmāvatī. *See* Smoky Lady (Dud sol ma)
*Diamond Cutter Sutra*, 480, 582n8
Dignāga, 44, 550n9
Dilgo Khyentse Rinpoche, 421
diligence, 105, 126, 144, 515
Dingri Langkor (Latö), 11, 73, 237, 383, 388, 423, 432, 441, 556n87, 579n14
*Dingri Volumes*, 139, 258, 563n1
direct lineages (*nye brgyud*), 471, 482
direct subjugation, 176, 566n8
disciples and practitioners
  appropriateness of, 104
  eight characteristics of, 36, 549n24
  in empowerments, 225, 230
  errors and mistaken views of, 110, 113, 115, 117, 255–56, 310, 499

faults of, 165–66, 484
four great abilities of, 312–13, 314, 573n3
qualities of, 30, 36, 168, 298, 500, 549n24
worthy and unworthy, 120–21
*See also* capability
discipline, moral, 105, 413, 486, 515, 583n6
discriminating wisdom, 193
disease
on application path, 153
averting, 470
from blessing of absorptions, 164
causes of, 37
controlling, 177
curing with hot needle, 10, 64, 172, 554n62
demons of, 349, 360–61, 362, 377
helping others with, 70–71, 156, 175–76, 180, 566n7
lack of real existence of, 116
masters of, 360–61
as metaphor, 19, 22, 91, 126, 166, 168
setting disease on, 179–80
treating, 192, 334–37
dissolution
after daily practice, 498
of consciousness, 342
fierce, 337
of guru buddha, 534–35
in healing rituals, 326, 337, 341
order of, 416–17
of pledge beings, 286–87, 290
*Distillation of the Profound*, 471–72
distributions (*'gyed*), 276–77, 278, 279
Corpse Distribution, 290, 291–92, 495–96
in daily practice, 492
Food Distribution, 290, 292, 494
red and white as pairs, 493–95, 496
six modes of, 293
subsequent, 489
variegated, 292, 317
Vase of Elixir Distribution, 275–76
white, 269–71, 275–77, 292, 294, 307
*See also* black distributions; feasts; red distributions; white distributions
divination, curative, 176–77
divine substances, 224, 324, 370, 373
doctrine. *See* dharma
Dolpopa, 221
Dorje Drön, 512
Dorje Sumgyi Nyendrup, xiii
doubt, 31, 32, 35, 37, 109, 136, 137, 163, 183, 340
Drakmarwa, 511
Drapa Haktön, 27, 545n64
Drapa Ngönshe, 511, 540n8
dreams
apparitions in, 149–50, 193, 252, 253
appearances in, 32, 159
as dualistic fixation, 23, 93
evidence of success in, 316
indicating guests have gone, 319–20
intermediate state of, 153
of nauseated guests, 320
phenomena as, 250
recognizing, 37
spiritual powers as, 112
treating objects as, 16, 76, 83
Drepung Catalog, 311, 580n1
Dringom Tokme, 384, 433
Drogön Tonyön Samdrup, 187
Drölchok. *See* Kunga Drölchok
drops, vital
in blending space and awareness, 475
dissolution of, 342
in separating body from mind, 147, 210, 250, 266–67, 488–89
in Wrathful Round Lotus, 288
yogas of, 309
Druk Lhaling Khawa, 511
Drung Mase, 257, 285, 573n30, 573n44
Drung Sarupa Kunga Paljor. *See* Kunga Paljor
"drunken elephant's gait," 314
dualistic appearances, 6, 54, 150, 278, 281, 289–90, 296
dualistic fixation, 6, 7, 43, 54, 55, 56, 59, 86, 93, 94, 117, 127–28
Dudtsok Dulwai Dorje, 353, 386
Dudul Dorje, 427
duḥkha, 32, 33, 34, 35–36, 37, 547n11

earth lords (*sa bdag*), 289, 313, 316, 331, 335, 337, 362, 371, 457, 554n61, 575n10, 578n2. *See also* Six Earth Lord Application liturgy
eclectic movement. *See* nonsectarian movement (*ris med*)
effort, 107, 118, 129, 131, 132, 133, 161–62, 168
*Eight Common Appendices, The*, 157–58, 171
Eight Great Chariots, xii–xiv, 503, 535, 539n1
*Eight Herukas*, 283
*Eight Special Appendices, The*, 185
*Eight Uncommon Appendices, The*, 171
eightfold noble path, 106–8, 121, 560n12
eight-spoked wheel, meteorite metal, 287
eighty excellent minor signs, 25, 97
eighty-four thousand dharmas, 160, 167
Ekajaṭī, 264
elemental spirits (*'byung po*), 227, 278, 305, 327, 338, 343, 415
elements, 35, 151–52, 179, 407
elixir (*bdud rtsi*), 40
  in body offering, 269
  consecration of, 259
  with eight flavors, 330
  in empowerments, 206
  five, 367, 440
  in fulfillment rituals, 458
  of gods, multicolored, 272
  in healing ritual, 325
  leftover, 273–74
  pledge and awareness, blending, 276, 493
  of sacred pledge, 372
  for six classes of beings, 273
  of timeless awareness, 218, 276, 328, 330, 372, 380
  undissipating, 282, 318, 319, 326, 330, 401, 403, 436
  Vase of Elixir Distribution, 275–76
  white, red, blue, 491, 497
  *See also* five meats and five elixirs
emotional obscurations, 42–43, 69, 72
emotions. *See* afflictive emotions
empowerments
  actualizing meaning of, 33, 548n19
  and authorization, similarity between, 197
  blessing, 222
  conferred on mind and body, differences in, 231, 570n7
  door-opening, xvii
  life-force for gods and demons, 71
  of meaning, 198
  in mother lineage feast offering, 401, 403
  necessity of, 298, 343
  requesting, 534
  ritual form of, 198
  of six bone ornaments, 228
  supreme, 30
emptiness
  appearing, 25, 218
  in curing sickness, 178
  of ḍākinīs, 229
  dead, 278
  desiring, 163
  dharma traditions of, 219
  as enemy, 115
  equal flavor of, 341
  from form to omniscience, 81
  four factors as, 10, 70–71
  of four mudras, 487–88
  importance of, 175
  inherent nature as, 56
  meditation on, 36, 37, 151, 307, 337
  mental inflation over, 158
  mental nonengagement with, 161
  merely mental, 134, 162
  of mind, 80
  not meditating on, 160, 162–63
  obstacles and, 31
  realization as remedy, 35
  resting in, 33, 290, 326, 368
  as single cut, 4, 45
  as unborn, 137
  without reference points, 51–52
emptiness-clarity, 490. *See also* clarity-emptiness
Emptying the Six Realms distribution, 494

encouragement, teachings of, 118–19
*Endowed with All Qualities*, 258
enemies, 168, 303, 429
  of dharma, 181
  hateful, 259, 261, 470, 485, 486, 582–83n3
  in refuge and aspiration, 200, 346, 373, 374
  as result of nonvirtue, 48–49
  three that rise up, 115–16
  trampling, 184
  in Wrathful Round, 287–88
energy channels. *See* channels, energy
enhancement practices, 89, 93, 99–100, 169, 181–84, 252–54, 479–80, 500–1
enjoyments, 104–5, 112, 136, 177, 203, 457, 477
enlightened activities, four, 279, 296, 457, 468–69
enlightenment, 31, 112–13, 129, 167, 329
*Entering the Way of the Bodhisattva* (Shāntideva), 47, 52
equal taste/flavor, 35, 133, 341
equality, 484
  dharmakāya as, 533
  expanse of, 262
  meditating in, 391
  of phenomena, 146, 174, 190, 474, 564n8, 568n8
  of samsara and nirvana, 283
  self-occurring, 424
equanimity
  abiding in, 155–56
  compassion and, 524
  resting in, 108–9, 111, 133, 267, 294, 476, 490
  timeless awareness of, 213
  towards all migrators, 186
equipoise
  abiding in meaning of, 156
  in daily activities, 57
  nonconceptual, 150, 155
  practitioners in mudra of, 190, 210, 211, 248
  of purity of three spheres, 488
  resting in, 44–46, 114, 218, 249, 251, 268, 274, 489, 535
  superior capability for, 490
  as supreme, 83
  trusting, 140
  as vital point of mind, 217–18
escorts, 31, 168, 183
*Esoteric Instructions on the Noble Perfection of Wisdom* (Brahmin Āryadeva), xvi, 315, 574n9
  additional line in, 53, 552n33
  classification of, 41
  colophon of, 11, 541n7
  commentaries on, 39–40
    (see also *Pure Honey* [Kunga Paljor])
  composition of, 40, 41
  as foundational instruction of Severance, 27
  homage in, 4, 42–43
  title of, 4, 41, 42, 541n1
  transmission of, 3–4, 39
*Essence of Auspicious Renown*, xviii, 503
*Essence of the Vital Meaning* (Tāranātha), 297, 310
*Essential Bundle*, xvi, 124, 143, 567n5, 568n8
eternalism, 24, 25, 94, 96, 161
ethical discipline. *See* discipline, moral
*Eulogy to the Deities of the Four Yogas* (Ratnakīrti), 80, 557n5
*Eulogy to the Eighty Great Adepts*. See *Supplication to the Eighty-Four Great Adepts* (Vajrāsanapāda)
*Eulogy to the Perfection of Wisdom* (Rāhulabhadra or Nāgārjuna), 80, 557n5
evil, use of term, 541n13
exaltation, devil of, 14, 76, 542n4
  arrogance as, 51
  causes of, 175
  common and supreme, 15–16, 76, 82–83
  in devil of inflation, 20, 77, 88–89
  identifying and severing, 112, 303
  purity of, 129
  standing firm to, 132
examples. *See* analogies, examples, and metaphors
Excellent Stakeout feast, 277, 493
exorcism, 222, 235

expedient meaning/method, 25, 78, 97
experiential lineage, 353, 387
experiential precept lineage, 279
*Explanations of Severance* (Kunga Namgyal), 572nn1–2
*Extensive Explanation of the Manual on the Sublime Path of Severing Evil Object, The*, 295
extremes
  eight, 43, 79, 94, 557n4
  freedom from, 5, 51, 68, 80, 99, 165, 247
  three, 96
  two, 4, 8, 60–61
Eyul, 540n8

Face Skull Cup, 276, 493, 494, 572n24
faith
  fierce, 243–44, 294
  inspiration of, 144
  one-pointed, 486
  of practitioners, 30, 35, 40, 138, 139, 168, 312–13
  qualities of, 125–26
  of visualized beings, 206, 349, 377
father lineage, 279, 341, 343, 439
father spirits, 260, 261
father tantras, 24, 94, 263, 353, 387, 507, 510, 584n4
fear
  conduct and, 56
  of cyclic existence, 165
  as demon, 168
  emptiness of, 341
  freedom from, 8–9, 65
  in haunted places, 130, 163
  as intangible devil, 303
  letting go of, 164
  liberating on own ground, 31
  during meditation, 32
  practices for, 251, 253
  realization and, 20
fearlessness, 77, 87, 141, 507
"feast circle of the great being," 283
feast substances, 218, 224, 280, 282, 284, 370, 495, 496
feasts (*tshogs*)
  Banners, 291
  body-offering in, 205–6, 328–37
  Bone Shaker, 291
  Casting Out the Corpse, 290–91
  communal, 496–98, 527–32
  in empowerments, 218, 224–25, 231, 244
  Excellent Stakeout, 277
  Face Skull Cup, 276, 527n24
  feeding liturgies, 357–59, 404–6, 529–31, 579n25, 586n26
  Five-Desirables Offering, 276, 494
  Four Continents, 291
  general outline, 293–94, 573n41
  of great bliss, 443, 446
  during illness, 133–34, 497
  inner offering consecration in, 372–73
  Kagyu liturgy, 431–36
  liturgy for consecrating body, 356
  in mother lineage, 279, 280–88, 401–3
  *Offering Torma to All Ḍākimas*, 460–70
  outer, inner, secret, suchness meanings, 284
  in removal rite, 71
  Slapping, 290, 292, 573n39
  in Sutra and Mantra, compared, 283
  torma offering in, 206, 285, 370–72, 402, 403, 459
  White Feast, 269–73
  in Zurmang tradition, 369
  *See also* distributions; leftovers
Ferocious Lady (Rab gtum ma), 263
*Festival of Fortunate Faith: The Life of the Hidden Buddha Tenzin Namdak*, 258
*Fifty-Verse Poem*. See *Esoteric Instructions on the Noble Perfection of Wisdom* (Brahmin Āryadeva)
fish-faced laymen, 337
five buddhas, 201, 224, 263, 494, 516–17, 584n19. *See also* individual buddhas
five desirable objects, 62
five desirable qualities, 203, 378, 409, 491
Five-Desirables Offering, 276, 494
five families, 224, 269, 270, 287, 444,

464–65. *See also* five buddhas; five-family ḍākinīs
five great treasuries, xi–xii
five meats and five elixirs
in descent of blessings, 280
in fulfillment rituals, 458
mother lineage feasts, 281, 284
seed syllables of, 527
in white distributions, 269, 270, 495
five paths, 339, 526
accumulation, path of, 31, 37, 83
application, path of, 89, 153
completion of, 96
meditation, path of, 96–97, 108
perfection of wisdom and, 126
seeing, path of, 72, 93
six perfections and, 98
five-family ḍākinīs
descent of, 229–30, 294
fulfillment of, 444, 457
inviting, 235
leftovers, visualization for, 285
in mother lineage feast, 401–3
offering liturgies, 354–56, 406, 409–11
summoning, 398–400
supplication to, 241–42, 243–44
visualizations of, 223, 306
fixation (*'dzin pa*)
afflictive emotions and, 140
clearing away four types, 114
cutting, importance of, 18, 85
as devil, 168
freedom from, 52, 119
liberated on own ground, 129, 134
on permanence, 14, 81
to phenomena arising from oneself, 159
relinquishing, 116, 118
Flayed Skin Distribution, 276, 277, 494, 572n23
*Flower Ornament Sutra*, 380, 578n4
Food Distribution, 290, 292, 494
*Footprint Tibet* (Gyurme Dorje), 540n8
forbearance, requesting, 218, 231
form realm, 49, 145, 331
Form Vajra goddesses, 323
formless realms, 50, 145, 331, 551n27, 559n32
Four Armed (Phyag bzhi pa), 264, 328
four continents, 265, 267, 324, 351, 366, 378, 382, 490
Four Continents feast, 291, 495
four immeasurables, 323, 346, 505
four mind-changers, 473, 582n3
fulfillment rituals (*bskang ba*), 409, 581n2
"Fulfillment Ritual" (Palden Rinchen), 438, 452–58
"Gem Treasury" (Guru Dharmakīrti), 438
initial visualization, 438–39
in mother lineage feast, 282
"Mother Transformation" (Chökyi Drakpa), 437, 438, 439–49
prayers for, 531, 532
purpose of, 437

gaits, 313–14, 463
*Ganges Mahāmudrā*. See *Mahāmudrā Esoteric Instructions* (Telopa)
Gangpa, 439, 512
Gangwar Shen, 510
*gap* demons (*gab 'dre*), 365
garuḍa warlord, black, 318
Garwang Chokgi Namgyal, 296, 573n44
Garwang incarnations, 258, 296, 573n44
gatekeeper yogins, four, 507–8, 510, 585n11
Gelukpa lineage, xv, 221
gem pairs, seven, 271, 572n19
"Gem Treasury" (Guru Dharmakīrti), 438
Gendun Gyaltsen, 442
generosity, 251, 278–79, 294, 317, 516. *See also* perfections, six
genuine meaning, 24–25, 56, 78, 113–14
Genyen, fish-headed, 289
ghosts, 289, 573n38, 574n7
*ging* spirits, 337, 366, 406
giving and taking (*gtong len*), 329, 488
Glorious Awareness Protector, 283
Glorious Heruka, 280, 283–84
goddesses. *See* offering goddesses
gods
directly relinquishing, 159
eight classes of, 320, 330

gods (*continued*)
  fulfillment of, 457
  as guests, 361
  oath bound, 10, 71–72, 349, 362
  as projections, 116
  realm of, 19, 87, 273
  as root devil, 31, 154
gods and demons
  of apparent existence, 326–27, 332–37, 351, 354–56, 363, 377, 382, 410, 411
  arousing compassion of, 339
  attachment to, 500–1
  being attacked or transported by, 9, 32, 68, 306–7
  common basis of, 159
  emptiness of, 341
  engaging, 128, 137
  in field of merit, 349
  fixating on, 15
  four kinds, 192–93
  freedom from, 142
  giving thanks to, 149
  as illusions, 32
  as inflation, 129
  as intangible devils, 8, 63, 312
  life-force empowerment for, 71
  as mind and beyond mind, 163
  nonarising of, 19
  nonduality of, 64
  as one's mind, 480, 484
  overwhelming, 173
  rejecting closeness and distance of, 8, 64, 173–74
  as self-appearance of mind, 148
  self-liberated, 193
  as symbols for training, 116
  as totally gathered, 162
  turning on themselves (wrathful dissolution), 337
  as without established essence, 158
  worldly, 9, 66
  in wrathful magnetizing, 289
gods and humans, path of, 49, 72
*Grand Poem*. See *Esoteric Instructions on the Noble Perfection of Wisdom* (Brahmin Āryadeva)
graveyards. *See* charnel grounds/graveyards/cemeteries
great bliss
  actualized embodiment of, 284, 295
  of definite goodness, 516
  emptiness and, 341
  in father tantra, 94
  feast of, 443, 446, 531
  of Great Mother Perfection of Wisdom, 216
  as intent of feast circle, 284
  of lack of contrivance, 163
  offering substances as, 281
  on path of application, 153
  of self-liberation, 169
*Great Bundle of Precepts, The* (Machik), xvi, 13, 80, 279, 312, 574n2
  *Another Bundle* and, 123, 124
  commentaries on, 75
  in *Hair's Tip of Wisdom*, 115, 121–22, 561n23
  oral explanation of, 27
  in *Pure Honey*, 60, 553n52
  title of, 26, 78, 80, 98
  topics of, 79
Great Compassionate One. *See* Avalokiteshvara
Great Completion (*rdzogs chen*), 24, 95
Great Madhyamaka (*zhentong*), 22, 221
Great Mother/Great Mother Perfection of Wisdom
  as all phenomena, 490
  as mother of the buddhas, 102-4
  benefits of, 126–27
  dark compassion of, 340
  designations for, 302
  as dharmakāya, 102, 216, 268, 342, 376–77, 485
  five paths and, 339
  as ground, 24
  hand mudras of, 486, 583n4
  invoking, 202
  offerings to, 202, 206
  refuge in, 187–88, 261–63, 293, 567n2
  resting in, 22, 91
  substituting in accumulation field, 486, 577n2

texts. *See* Mother (texts)
in torma blessing, 215, 216
traditions of, 219–20
Vajravārāhī as, 459, 460, 529
visualizations of, 46, 187, 200–202, 286–87, 348–49, 376–77, 417, 486
great pervasive expanse/great pervasiveness, 6, 56, 108, 146, 147, 173, 216
Great Vehicle. *See* Mahayana
ground
of appearances, 278
golden, 204, 265, 267, 268–69, 351, 379, 382, 487
severing distinctions in, 172
skin as, 324, 351, 382, 490
unconditioned, 25, 78, 96
as unity of two truths, 52
ground masters (*gzhi bdag*)
offerings to, 274, 283, 358, 405
tormas for, 206, 222, 224, 234–35, 371–72
in wrathful magnetizing, 289
guests
all sentient beings as, 375
as coemergent, 283
departure of, 287, 290, 368, 498
in empowerments, 234–35
gathering, 261, 346, 373, 485–86
in healing rites, 261
and hosts as one, 31
liturgy for feeding, 357–59
offering body to, 249, 258, 328, 330
of samsara and nirvana, 283–84, 411, 477
torma offerings to outer, 206
types of, 276–77, 278
Guests of Compassion distribution, 272–73
Guhyajñāna, 452, 454
Guhyasamāja, 263, 270
*Guhyasamāja*, 283
Guru Dharmakīrti, 438, 451. *See also* Chökyi Drakpa
guru yoga, 182–83, 300, 306, 499
gurus
acceptance by, 309
binding, 10, 71–72
errors of, 219–20
inviting, 235
Kongtrul's extended prayer to, 512–13
of Pacification and Severance, lineage lists, 507–8, 509–12, 584–85nn3–15
qualities of, 30, 546n5
relying on, 84
root, meditations on, 172–73, 182–83
*gyalgong* spirits, 333, 361, 363, 457
*gyalpo* spirits, 162, 289, 313, 316, 333–34, 337, 362, 363, 575n10
Gyaltang tradition, 29, 222, 233, 244, 482
Gyaltsen Palzang, 511
Gyalwa Döndrup, 123, 419, 556n90, 580n2, 581n3
lineages of, 421, 508, 571n9
prayers by, 395–98
refuge and visualization of, 187–88, 567n2
supplications to, 239, 384, 394, 432, 512, 569–70n6
Gyalwa Tenne, 508, 511, 585n14
Gyanak Cherbu, 384, 432
Gyergom Chenpo, 511
Gyurme Dorje. *See* Minling Terchen
Gyurme Nyingpo, 352, 385, 386, 434

habitual patterns (*bag chags*)
of buddhas, lack of, 113
in dreams, 149
dualistic clinging and, 247
duḥkha and, 33
embodiments of, 260
liberating, 132
nonarising of, 25
purifying, 45
seed of, 108
severing, 118, 296
in wrathful magnetizing rites, 289–90
hail, rites for, 181, 318–19, 470
*Hair's Tip of Wisdom, A*, xvi, 39, 101–2, 119, 121
hand feeding, 359–60, 577n5
Hand Protector (nāga king), 448, 581n6

hands, laying-on, 283, 290, 332–33
happiness
  as auspicious sign, 488
  collective, 351, 381, 519
  emptiness of, 341
  lack of, 132
  meditating for, 168
  negativity and, 125
  offering, 381
  root gurus as, 412
  source of, 96
harm-doers (*yakṣha; gnod sbyin*), 180, 191, 227, 261, 264, 271, 317, 328, 329, 338, 480, 495, 555n79
haunted places (*gnyan sa*)
  analogy of practicing in, 26–27, 99
  arrogance in, 15
  as conceptual thinking, 22, 91
  healing rites in, 318
  meaning of terms, 566n2
  obstacles in, 10, 70, 174, 566n4
  practices for, 9, 67, 305, 307, 314–15
  pride in, 165
  purposes of, 129–30, 172, 274, 309
  for renunciation, 104
  resting in mind in, 130–31
  subtle body as, 34
  suitability for, 253, 304–5, 308, 310
  traveling to and from, 313–14, 318
  types of, 313
  visualization of, 306
  when sick, 178
Hayagrīva, 286
healing rituals, 171, 178, 180, 321
  arrangement of spirits in, 261
  dedication in, 343
  dissolution in, 326, 337, 341
  hand feeding in, 359–60, 577n5
  instructions on, 318
  liberation of practitioner and patient, 322
  in mother lineage, 283
  preparation for, 322–23
  in red distributions, 290
  supplication in, 325
heart essence, 166–68
*Heart Essence of Profound Meaning* (Jamyang Gönpo), xvi, 29, 38, 279, 545n1, 549n25
*Heart of the Perfection of Wisdom* (*Heart Sutra*), 56, 86, 145, 222, 225, 235, 569n4
hearth contamination, 174, 566n6
hell
  devil of, 19, 87
  fear of, 168
  purifying, 273, 494
  realm, 48, 87, 220, 272
  seed syllable of, 266, 489
  spirits of, 361
heroes
  feast practitioners as, 401, 403
  feeding, 357, 405
  fulfillment of, 438
  offerings to, 270, 283
  supplication to, 239, 428
  visualization of, 187, 262, 263, 348, 377
heroines (*dpa' mo*), 280, 377, 388, 401, 403, 431–36, 528. *See also* ḍākinīs
*Hero's Loud Laugh* (Minling Terchen), 472
Hevajra, 263, 270, 287
*Hevajra*, 283
higher insight, 114, 476
*Highest Continuum* (Maitreya), 54, 97, 114, 558n26
highest yoga tantras, 235, 236, 270
hooked knives, 267, 269, 275, 276, 277, 291, 354–56, 376
hope and fear
  buddha and, 135
  destruction of, 142
  devils of, 168
  five poisons and, 18, 86
  freedom from, 136, 161
  harboring, 89
  importance of being without, 310, 501
  lack of, 18, 148, 543nn26–27
  liberation from, 18, 32, 85
  practices to cut, 253
  rejecting, 33
  resting without, 111
  severing, 118, 172
  succumbing to, 307

host and guest, mixing as one, 31
hot needle, sticking precisely, 8, 10, 64, 172, 554n62
humans
  birth as, 48–49, 124–25, 582n3
  migrators, 174
  purpose of life, 126
  realm of, 19, 87, 273, 494
*Hundred Guides of Jonang, The* (Kunga Drölchok), 221
"Hundred *Phaṭ*," 279, 329
hungry ghosts, 19, 87, 152, 273

ignorance
  abiding, 255
  coemergent, 94, 265–66
  karmic spirits and, 260
  suffering and, 479
  supplicating for reversal of, 279, 417, 418
  timeless awareness, banished by, 34
  without objects, 24, 78, 95
illness. *See* sickness
illusions, 103, 112, 169, 309
illusory body, 267, 278, 353, 387, 523
illusory state, 479
Immaculate Drop, 525
impermanence, 137, 146–47, 210
increase and cleansing, visualization of, 320
India, xii, xiv–xv, xvi, 3–4, 388, 459, 470, 503, 571n5, 584n8
Indian Jose, 511
*Individual Liberation Sutra*, 338–39, 480, 576n27, 582n7
Indra, 448
inflation (*snyem*)
  as all one's own, 129
  awakening and, 20, 77, 88
  of cherishing body, 227
  conduct without, 23, 92–93
  discarding concepts of, 132
  emptiness from, 163
  of fixation on gender, 166–67
  freedom from, 23, 93, 116–17, 141, 184, 429
  in healing, 179
  of helping and harming, 110
  as including everything, 19
  as intangible devil, 111
  liberated on own ground, 19, 21, 87, 90, 93
  as momentary, 167
  and noninflation, indivisibility, 160
  resting without, 145, 159
  reviving by cutting, 161
  of self-fixation, 484
  severing, 8, 9, 60–61, 67, 128–29, 132, 296, 479–80, 526n19
  without object, 24
inflation, devil of, 14, 77
  deluded thought as, 68
  intangible devil in, 63
  others devils in, 18, 86, 158
  severing, 112–16, 118, 304
inseparability
  of appearance, thought, and abiding, 302
  of appearance and mind, 117
  of body and phenomena, 116
  of ground and result, 218
  of guru and Great Mother, 208, 261
  of guru and Machik, 299–300, 301, 306
  of guru and yidam, 224
  of patient, guru, and self, 340–41
  of pledge and awareness beings, 203
  of problem and antidote, 90
  of space and awareness, 56, 59, 210
  of space and phenomena, 146
  of vital wind and cognition, 108
intangible devils, 8, 162
  after severing, 10, 72
  descriptions of, 14–15, 62, 63, 76, 82, 128, 542n4
  in devil of inflation, 18, 77, 86–88
  direction action for, 110–12
  identifying and severing, 109–10, 158, 303
  overwhelming, 128
  severing, 8, 63–65
  training with, 116
integration (*lam 'khyer*), 30, 38, 56, 60, 67, 70, 110, 134, 162, 168, 183–84, 477

interdependence, 37, 51–52, 260, 338, 443, 445, 448, 480
interdependent connections, 308
intermediate state, 37, 153, 161
intrinsic awareness, 78, 557n2
  bliss and, 153
  introduction to, 210–11
  methods of resting in, 145
  seed syllable of (*hrīḥ*), 267
  ten gurus who introduce, 507, 510, 584n7
  timeless wisdom of, 179
  in transference, 205
intrinsic nature, 36, 63, 127, 129, 131, 163, 189, 190, 250
introduction (*ngo sprod*), 104, 189
  on cutting root, 108
  in Gyaltang tradition, 244
  in meaning of Mother, 302, 499–501
  by separating body and mind, 210–11
  single, goal after, 176
  without elaboration, 226–27
isolation, importance of to practice, 27, 99, 216

Jadralwa Rinchen Tashi, 310
Jambu, Land of (Jambudvīpa), 267, 388, 466, 579n14
Jambudvīpa Sodor, 371, 578n2
Jamgön Kongtrul Lodrö Taye
  biographical information, xi
  lineages of, 422
  Minling Terchen and, 472
  source for Zurmang Severance, 258
  Tāranātha and, 222, 233, 471
  Tekchok Dorje and, 369, 370
  visionary experiences of, 39
  See also *Autobiography of Jamgön Kongtrul*; *Beloved Garden*; *Catalog of The Treasury of Precious Instructions, The*; *Essence of Auspicious Renown*; *Treasury of Knowledge, The*; *Treasury of Precious Hidden Teachings, The*; *Treasury of Precious Instructions, The*
Jamgön Rikzin, 353, 386
Jampa Pal, 352, 386, 451
Jampal Gyatso, 425
Jampal Khyentse Wangpo. *See* Jamyang Khyentse Wangpo
Jampal Zangpo, 425
Jamyang Gönpo, 29–30, 124, 143, 471. See also *Big General Guide to Severance* (Jamyang Gönpo)
Jamyang Khyentse Wangpo, xi, 369, 483, 501, 584n24
Jamyang Namgyal, 385, 435
Jangchup Ling, 237
Jangpa lineage, 511
Jetsun Repa, 442
Jetsunma. *See* Vajravārāhī
Jewel Ḍākinī, 453, 455
Jikme Wangpo, 239
Jñānajvala, 247, 256, 352, 386, 423, 441, 581n4
Jomo Lapkyi Drönma. *See* Machik Lapkyi Drönma
Jonang lineage, xv, 221, 233, 471
Jordruk, xiii

Kachö Wangpo, 424
Kadampa, xiii
*Kagyu Feast Liturgy*, 280, 422, 431, 527, 578n12, 586n25
Kagyu traditions, xiii, xv, 75, 233, 328, 345. *See also* Karma Kagyu lineage; Karma Kamtsang tradition; Shangpa Kagyu; Zurmang Kagyu lineage
*Kālachakra Tantra That Issued from the Supreme Original Buddha*, 283, 569n17
Kalu Rinpoche, xiv, xviii, 471
Kam system, 511, 525, 585n13
Kam Yeshe Gyaltsen, 508, 585n13
Kamalashīla, 3, 73, 522, 541n7, 556n86
kapālas. *See* skull cups (*kapāla*)
karma
  action of, 9, 50, 69, 296, 551n28
  liability of, 272–73
  negativity and, 125
  not accumulating, 59
  recognizing, 36
  of rejecting dharma, 256
  seeds of, 489

sickness and, 37
spirits of, 260, 261, 485, 582n3
*See also* cause and effect
Karma Chakme, 311, 321–22, 345, 369, 574–75n1, 577n33
Karma Ḍākinī, 201, 214
Karma Kagyu lineage, xv, 247, 257, 321–22, 345
Karma Kamtsang tradition, 295, 321, 412, 573n43, 580n1
Karma Ngawang Yönten Gyatso. *See* Jamgön Kongtrul Lodrö Taye
Karma Pakshi, second Karmapa, 321–22, 324, 325, 328, 340, 575n2
Karma Tekchok Tenpel, 258
Karma Tenkyong, 352, 385, 386, 434, 435, 578n13
Karma Tsultrim, 385, 435
Kashmiri Jñānaguhya, 508, 510, 585n12
kāyas
five, 332, 352, 382, 443
four, 278, 284, 295, 395–98, 507, 509, 522, 525
two, 52, 154, 279
kāyas, three
attaining, 55
as expedient, 25, 97–98
homage to, 30
as one's own body, speech, mind, 17, 20, 77, 85, 89
as result, 194
Kechara, 508
Khakhyap Dorje, fifteenth Karmapa, 369, 422, 427
Kham, 369
Khambuyale, 247, 256, 352, 386, 421, 423, 450, 571n9, 580n2
Khamnyön Dharma Senge, 198. See also *Religious History of Pacification and Severance* (Khamnyön)
Kharak Samling, 238
khaṭvāṃkas, 201, 270, 359, 376, 443
Khedrup Gyatso, 239
Khepa Naljor, 384, 433
Khugom Chöseng, 74, 439, 508, 512, 556n90
Khyentse Özer, 422, 428
"King of Aspiration Prayers: Samantabhadra's Aspiration to Good Actions," 380, 578n4
Könchok Tenchö, 239
Könchok Tenzin, 352, 385, 386, 434
Könchok Yenlak, fifth Zhamarpa (Könchok Bang), 311, 320, 329, 406, 574n9, 575n7, 579n24
Krodhīkālī, 275, 527n21
in feast offerings, 288–89, 291, 292, 478, 496
in healing rituals, 322, 332, 337, 359–60
supporting rituals of, 231
Kukkuripa, 584n5
Kundeling printing, xii–xiii, xvi, xxi, 233, 311, 421, 540n5. See also *Treasury of Precious Instructions, The*
Kunga Döndrup, 247
Kunga Drölchok, xiv, 221, 233, 238, 297, 471, 540n10
Kunga Gyaltsen, 442
Kunga Lhundrup, 238
Kunga Namgyal, fourth Trungpa, 571n2, 577n33
lineage of, 352, 385, 386, 434, 438
on offerings, 284
Severance tradition, role in, 257–58, 259, 277, 294–95
See also *Explanations of Severance* (Kunga Namgyal)
Kunga Nyingpo, 238
Kunga Paljor, xvi, 39, 74, 101, 556n93. See also *Pure Honey* (Kunga Paljor)
Kunga Sönam, 238
Kunga Wangchuk, 343
Kunga Yeshe, 238
Kunga's Thirteenfold Prayer, 533
Kunzang Dechen Ösal Ling, 471, 481, 535
Kyeme Gayen, 411, 439, 579n26
Kyeme Zangtal, 384, 432, 578n11
Kyochung. *See* Sönam Lama
*kyongma*, twelve, 469
Kyongö retreat place, 449
Kyotön Kuche, 73
Kyotön Shākya Yeshe, 3–4, 197, 198, 578n10
Kyotön Sönam Lama. *See* Sönam Lama

Lacham, 512
Lama Martön, 30
Lama Sheu, 511
Lamdre, xiii
Langchen Palseng, 470, 581n7
Langlungpa/Lord of Langlung. *See* Döndrup, Gyalwa
Lap/Lapchi, 540n8
Latö Dingri Langkor. *See* Dingri Langkor (Latö)
leaping over (*thod rgal*), 189, 210
leftovers, 409
  collecting, 366–67
  in communal feasts, 497–98
  dedication liturgies, 409–10, 532
  visualizations, 285–87, 290
*Letter to a Friend* (Nāgārjuna), 106–7
levels. *See* ten stages
Lhaden Gazhi, 239
Lhalung Karma Desal, 258
Lharipa, 511
Lhateng, 254
liberation
  certainty of, 163
  at death, 179–80
  by leaving well alone, 160
  natural, 76, 82, 151
  of resting in one's ground, 159
  since forever, 9, 69
  as symbolic, 76, 83–84
life force, 7, 35, 60, 62, 260, 272, 287, 324, 342, 485, 497
*Life Story of the Great Mighty Adept, Venerable Dampa Sangye* (Khamnyön), 198
life-force masters (*srog bdag*), 313
light rays, 34
  in communal feast, 497
  in confession, 414
  in descent of awareness deities, 229, 264, 265, 377
  in empowerments, 227–28
  in field of accumulation, 486–87
  five-colored, 218
  in healing ritual, 339
  in invoking ḍākinīs, 337
  in mandala offerings, 205
  from mantra string, 380
  in offering leftovers, 286
  in refuge visualization, 262–63
  from seed syllables, 269, 282
  of six realms, 266–67, 273, 489
  in summoning gods and demons, 320
  in supplications, 280
  in torma blessing, 215
lightening, protection from, 318–19
Limi Monastery manuscripts, 29, 123–24, 561n7, 563n1
*Lineage Stories from the Hundred Guides* (Kunga Drölchok), xiv–xv
livelihood, authentic, 107
Lobsang Gyatso, Fifth Dalai Lama, 221
Lodrö Rinchen, 387
Longchen Rabjam, 545–46n1
Lord of Hermits, 424, 580n3
lord of life and death, 487
Lordly Guests of Qualities distribution, 271–72
Lorepa Wangchuk Tsöndru, 30
Lotus Ḍākinī, 453, 455
love
  arousing, 299
  aspiration prayer for, 480
  in gentle severance, 329
  meditation on, 191, 192, 304, 305, 308, 500
Lower Drukpa lineage, 29
lucid clarity (*'od gsal*), 284
  apparitions as, 150–51
  in body offerings, 278–79
  of dharmakāya, 296
  as intrinsic nature, 127
  of mahāmudrā, 95, 497
  meditating on, 37, 476
  of mind, 53–54, 80, 93, 144, 147
  path to, 54
  without characteristics, 6, 53–54
  without fixation, 26, 98, 553n52
Lungrik Gyatso, 238

Ma Chökyi Sherap, 508, 585n13
Ma system, 510–11, 525, 585n13
Machik Lapkyi Drönma, 79
  absolute, 490

biographical information, xiv, xvii, 540n8
in black distribution, 319
on body donation, multiplying, 339
in descent of blessings, 417–19
feast composed by, 401–3
in gentle severance, 330
as Jomo/Mother Jomo, 200–201, 205–7, 215, 216, 218, 219, 546n2
as Lady Mother, xiv–xv, 73, 143, 187–88, 556n89, 567n2
liberation of, 197
as Lord Mother, 30, 546n2
as Mother, 121, 205–6, 207–8, 211–16, 248–49, 263–65, 395–98
offerings to, 270–71
as One Mother, xiii, xiv, 236, 390, 397–98, 522
in Peaceful Round Lotus, 287
praises to, 390–93, 395–98, 522, 579n18, 586n19
prayers composed by, 381–82, 398–400, 406–9, 431, 578n6
in Severance lineage, 256
supplications to, 474–75, 508–9, 510
texts and verses attributed to, xvi, 39, 101, 148, 157, 189, 422, 553n53, 564n10, 567n5
on title of *Great Bundle*, 13
transmissions and empowerments received, 4, 124, 570n7
visionary encounters with, 233
visualizations of, 223, 224, 263, 293, 299–300, 323–27, 340, 341, 348–49, 376, 377, 486–87, 498, 507
See also *Another Bundle*; *Great Bundle of Precepts, The*; *Vajra Play*
*Machik's Complete Explanation*, 13, 312, 345, 381, 578n6
*Machik's Vajra Verses*, 312, 315, 317, 318, 319, 342, 577n31
madhyamaka, 24, 94, 114
mādhyamikas. *See* madhyamaka
Mahākāla, 201, 356, 358, 404, 405, 416, 440, 448, 451, 457
Mahākālī, 201, 334, 358, 405, 440, 451
mahāmudrā, 279, 488
aspiration for, 220, 271
consciousness transference in, 553n41 (*see also* Opening the Sky Door)
deluded cognition of, 24, 94–95
eleven gurus of, 507, 510, 584n3
maintaining, 498
Severance and, 75, 247, 481
as suchness feast, 284, 497
*Mahāmudrā Esoteric Instructions* (Telopa), 95, 558n29
Mahayana
affinity/disposition, 104, 186
brilliance of, 32
entering, 472
perfection of wisdom in, 30, 547–48n14
Severance and, 41, 61, 79, 346
Maitreya, 551n20. See also *Highest Continuum*; *Ornament of Clear Realization*
Majestic Body (Videha), 267
*makaras*, 265, 572n11
"male Severance," 3–4
Malgyi Kawachenpa, 511
*mamos*, 216, 313, 316, 328, 334, 363, 467, 468–69, 533
Man of the Charnel Ground. *See* Samten Özer
mandala-border protectors, 358, 405
mandalas
body, 315, 324, 351, 382, 490–91
illusory, 480
moon, 282
offering prayer, 514
offerings, 203–4, 211, 225, 230–31, 268, 299–300, 378
of original great bliss, 284
from seed syllables, 372
as support in feast offering, 401, 403
Manifest Joy (Abhirati), 270
Mañjughoṣhanatha. *See* Jamyang Gönpo
Mañjushrī, 350, 416, 585n10
Mañjushrī Vādasiṃha (Lion of Speech), 4, 41, 42–43
identity of, 549n2
lineage of, 237, 256, 342, 388, 510

Mansion of Complete Victory, 267
Mantra tradition
feasts in, 283–84, 317
fulfillment in, 437
great bliss in, 295
ground, path, result in, 55
seed syllables in, 45
Severance in, xvii, 41, 171, 484, 490
tantras of, 270
tenets of, 94–95
three requirements for, xvii
vows in, 60
mantras
to avert, 470
common, 236
for concluding rites, 411–12
for confession, 414–15
for consecrating offerings, 373, 506
for creating field of accumulation, 375, 506, 508, 509
for deity generation, 224, 229–30, 377
for dissolution, 534–35
of five ḍākinīs, 223
garland/string, 265, 487
*gate*, 199, 205, 265, 293, 350, 380, 487, 568n2, 583n10
for inner offerings, 372, 516–17
for mandala offering, 514
one-hundred-syllable, 286, 414, 534
for six perfections, offering, 515
six-syllable, 287, 339, 368, 419, 498
of "sky treasure," 234
of Speech, 228
*sumbha*, 234
*svabhāva*, 222
for torma offering, 370
Vajrasattva, 520
wrathful, 177, 306
Mara Serpo, 390, 511, 579n15
Marpa Kagyu, xiii
Martön Chögyal, 510
Mase Rinpoche. *See* Drung Mase
*Māyājāla*, 283
meaning of the Mother, 41, 136–37, 258, 295, 500, 556n83
apprehending the mind, 301–2
introduction to mind, 302, 499–501
Opening the Sky Door in, 490
resting in, 277, 303–4, 306, 308
for single sitting, 476
sources for, 297
medical examination, pledging not to perform, 193
medicine turning to poison, 252
meditation
for all times, 190
as conceit, 16, 83
correcting mistakes in, 443, 445, 448
disturbances in, 9, 32, 36–37, 66
on emptiness, 14, 81–82
on Great Heruka, 284
inspiration for, 149
of letting thoughts stop, 82
locations for, 7, 57
methods of, 77–78, 91–92, 140
nonreferential, 127
of not meditating, 16, 83–84, 179
purpose of, 34
referential, limits of, 84
refuge and awakening mind in ongoing, 186–88
resting place of, 148, 564n10
self-arising thought in, 20
and severance, compared, 19, 87
three absorptions and, 473
three kinds of experience in, 189
unmistaken, 135
view and, 20, 87, 109
without fixation, 131
without recollection, 249–50, 570n2
*Meditation's Ambrosia of Immortality* (Sherap Özer), 539n2
meditative stability (*bsam gtan*), 49–50, 84, 105, 106, 499, 515
memories, 15, 21, 22, 33, 78, 91
mental disorders, 334, 576n16
mental nonaction, resting within, 155–56
mental nonactivity, 83–84
mental nonengagement
in appearance and nonappearance, 96
of characteristics, 126–27
difficulty of, 165
in emptiness, 81
evenly resting in, 91

in healing, 179
in *Perfection of Wisdom in One Hundred Thousand Lines*, 84, 557n8
in recollection of Buddha, 6, 54
resting in, 132
as supreme path, 25, 96
mental problems, 37
mentation (*yid*), 14, 16, 82, 136, 148, 152, 526
*mentsun*, four great, 470, 581n6
merit
accumulating without bias, 105
of body offering, 188, 268, 514
enjoyment of, 177
from fulfillment ritual, 437
limits of accumulating, 53
as obstacle, 107
offering tormas for, 177
prayers for accumulating, 514–16
from rejoicing in others actions, 49
from repetition, 409, 579n25
supreme accumulation of, 488
method and wisdom, 24, 35, 36, 52, 94, 295
Mikyö Dorje, eighth Karmapa, 311, 321, 322, 343
"Mikyö Dorje's Poem," 321, 322, 323–27, 574–75n1
mind (*sems, yid*)
abiding in space, 152
altering of disciples, 207
apprehending, 301–2
cutting root, 412
and dharma, blending, 109
emptiness and clarity of, 80
everything as one's own, 108
grasping as object, 14, 80
nonduality of, 130
as nonreferential, 112–13
not engaging in, 141
not meddling with, 137
as object, delusion of, 159
as phenomena's root, 85, 110
purity of, 160
recognizing, 32, 144
resolution of, 129
as root of samsara and nirvana, 4, 45
self-occurring, 16
seven ways of resting, 148
severing inflation of, 68, 132, 526n19
severing root of, 7–8, 60, 172
as space, 168
taming demons of, 32
torma of bliss and clarity of, 408
uncontrived, 56
vital point of, 216, 217–18
and vital wind, combined, 190
as vital wind and cognition, 108
as without cause, 144
without established essence, 158
without intrinsic nature, 163
*See also* introduction (*ngo sprod*); separating body from mind
Mind (*thugs*)
blessings and empowerments of, 326
as liberated, 21, 90
mudra of, 350–51, 381, 488, 519
nonfixation on, 26, 78, 98
pledge substances as, 527
sacred pledge of, 456
timeless awareness of, 98
*Mind Training Wheel Weapon* (Dharmarakṣhita), 361, 577n6, 578n8
mindfulness, 107, 129, 500, 546n5, 560n12, 570n2. *See also* recollection
Mindroling Monastery, 472
Minling Terchen, 471, 472, 481–82
Mipam Gönpo. *See* Dampa Sangye
Mipam Gyatso, xi
Mipam Trinle Rapten, sixth Situ, 438, 451, 581n8
miracles, 88, 558n15
mistakes, cornering great, 32, 547n14
Molten Human Skin, 290, 573n39
monasticism, xv, 338–39
monkey grease, 478, 582n5
Mother
traditions of, 219
women as, 103
*See also* Great Mother/Great Mother Perfection of Wisdom; Machik Lapkyi Drönma; meaning of the Mother practice

Mother (texts), 41, 44, 54. See also *Perfection of Wisdom in Eight Thousand Lines*; *Perfection of Wisdom in Eighteen Thousand Lines*; *Perfection of Wisdom in One Hundred Thousand Lines*; *Perfection of Wisdom in Twenty-Five Hundred Thousand Lines*; *Perfection of Wisdom in Twenty-Five Thousand Lines*; Perfection of Wisdom sutras
mother lineage, 279, 280–88, 341, 343, 439
mother of buddhas/victors
  homages to, 102, 259, 349, 370, 379
  as lucid clarity, 127
  offering to, 204
  praising, 208
  realization of, 103–4
mother spirits, 260, 261, 337, 338, 361, 366, 406
Mother Tantra Feast Activities, 401–3
mother tantras, 24, 94, 263, 353, 387, 507, 510, 584n5
"Mother Transformation" (Chökyi Drakpa), 437, 438, 439–49
mountain cycles, 64, 68, 261, 295, 554n63
Mountain God of Shampo, 286
mountain retreats, 27, 71, 78, 99, 104, 175
mudras
  of Body, Speech, Mind, 228, 350–51, 381, 487–88, 519
  dharma-teaching, 583n4
  earth touching, 376, 486, 583n4
  of equipoise, 187, 190, 201, 210, 211, 248, 261, 376, 508, 567n2, 583n4
  of five families, 444, 464–65
  four offering, 350–51, 381, 487–88, 519, 578n6
  offering, 280–81
  revolving lotus, 333
  vajra-binding, 228

Nāgārjuna, 3, 40, 80, 106–7, 557n5. See also *Root Verses on the Middle Called Wisdom* (Nāgārjuna)
Nāgārjunagarbha, 507, 584n6
nāgas
  binding, 10, 71–72
  body-offering to, 327
  as devils, 289, 316, 334–35, 337, 364
  directly relinquishing, 159
  diseases of, treating, 335
  fulfillment of, 457
  haunted abodes of, 172, 313
  from inflation, 164
  medicine of, 492, 583n15
  offerings to, 274, 276
  pacifying, 192
  pestilent palace of, 547n14
  as projections, 116
  rites with, 180, 567n16
  spiritual powers from, 162
  in wrathful magnetizing, 289
Nairātmyā, 263
Namkha Özer, 237
Namtso Dopa Mikyö Dorje (Namtsowa), 247, 256, 257, 352, 386, 424, 441, 450, 571n10
Nanda, 335, 364
Nāropa, 85, 264, 558n29
*Nāro's Secret Conduct*, 572n25
native state, 144, 146, 389, 407, 498
nature of mind. *See* abiding nature of mind
nature of phenomena (*dharmatā; chos nyid*)
  abiding in, 152, 154
  apparitions as support for, 193
  as beyond misery, 147
  empowerment of meaning of, 229
  hiding concepts in, 133
  integrating devils into, 155–56
  play of, 227
  realizing, 429
  renewing pledge in, 443, 445, 448
  resting in, 131, 146
  stains of, 34
  view and, 130
*Nectar of Meaning of the Profound Severance of Evil* (Samten Özer), 233
Nedo Kagyu lineage, xv, 345
negative companions, 58

negativity (*sdig pa*)
decreasing, 69
definition of, 125
in gentle severance, 329
as liquid charcoal ooze, 325
pledge to abandon, 193, 480
purifying, 182, 205, 215, 293, 319
purity of, 9, 69
Ngawang Trinle, 238
Ngedön Nyingpo, 238
nihilism, 14, 24, 25, 81, 94, 96, 161
nine vehicles, 160, 332, 352, 382, 407
Ninefold Spirit Feast (Rangjung Dorje), 331, 409, 496, 497, 574–75n1, 577nn7–8, 584n20
in *Body Donation and Feeding Ritual*, 333–37
in *Pearl Rosary*, 322, 345, 362–65
nirmāṇakāya, 201, 412–14
nirvana
accepting and rejecting, 250
certainty of, 22, 91
Great Mother as ground of, 24, 78, 95
liberated on own ground, 89
mind as root, 4, 45, 60
neither inhibiting nor indulging, 30
as one's mind, 129
setting aside, 174
Severance view of, 20
Nīviraṇaviṣhkambhin, 509, 585n10
no making, path of, 25, 78, 96
no-mind, 53, 93
nonaction, 167, 526
nonconceptuality, 34, 111, 548n22
nondual tantras, 353, 387
nonduality
of acceptance and rejection, 117
of base and based, 163
of male and female, 167
method and wisdom cognizing, 24
of mind and object, 83, 108
no need for severance of, 562n19
of object and mind, 83, 108
of problem and remedy, 10, 57, 64, 70
of samsara and nirvana, 135, 137
of severing and objects of severance, 526n19
two obscurations self-liberated in, 7, 59
as unconditioned, 25
of virtue and negativity, 162
of yogins and apparitions, 57, 67
noninflation, 160, 164, 248, 397
nonreferentiality, 106, 126, 127, 146, 219
nonreturners, 21, 90
nonsectarian movement (*ris med*), xi–xii, xv, 222, 369, 539nn1–3
nonself, 89–90, 92–93, 95, 100
nonthought, 161
in daily activities, 250
examples for, 21–22, 77, 91
maintaining, 301
meaning of, 141
meditating on, 165
resting in, 169
nonvirtues, ten, 5, 48–49, 49–59, 255
no-thought, 8, 62, 63
Nyamtok Tarchin, 238
Nyedo Mawai Senge, 508, 585n14
Nyen, Lama, 217
Nyenchung Lotsāwa, 394, 579n17
Nyentön, 405, 579n21
Nyingma tradition, xiii, xv, 224, 345, 472

oath-breaker spirits (*dam sri*), 313, 316, 334, 336, 363, 365
*Object Severance Empowerment Known as Opening the Sky Door* (Tāranātha), 221–22, 233, 569n2
obscurations (*sgrib*)
from blessings, 133
clearing, 175–76
in gentle severance, 329
as liquid charcoal ooze, 325
purifying, 182, 205, 215, 487
two, 7, 59, 69, 80, 96, 268, 414, 555n74
obstacles (*bar chad*)
to absorption, 301–2
antidotes and, 10, 70
clearing, 70–71
cornering deer technique for, 174, 566n4
dullness from, 151, 152
as good fortune, 199
incidental, 193

obstacles (*continued*)
instructions on, 153, 252–53
letting go of, 155
protection from, 7, 58
regarding as mothers, 149
subsiding in emptiness, 31
three kinds, 70
as training, 19, 87
obstructors (*gegs*), 260–261
eighty thousand, 191, 192, 328, 375
one thousand eighty, 361
Oḍḍiyāna, 237, 401, 403, 436, 452, 454, 460
Oḍḍiyāna Kechara, 280
offering goddesses, 266
colors of, 273, 274
in communal feasts, 497, 527
eight, 203, 378, 519
four-mudra offering by, 381, 488
for inviting awareness beings, 265
in mother lineage, 280
reabsorption of, 274
for six classes of beings, 272
in white distributions, 275, 491–92, 494
offering substances, 281, 282, 284
*Offering Torma to All Ḍākimas*, 459, 581n1
offerings, 144
actual and mental, 209
blessings of, 235
common, 248–49
consecrating, 259, 372–73
covetousness toward, 175
in daily practice, 487–88
in fulfillment, 440, 452
by gods and goddesses, 150
in healing ritual, 323–24
as perfection of two accumulations, 413
prayers, 516–17, 518–19
promising, mandala, qualities, 230–31
as remedy, 34, 35, 548n22
of six senses, 266
suchness, prayer for, 518
three kinds, 5, 46
*See also under* mandalas; mudras, four offerings; tormas
omens, bad, 148, 470
omniscience, 30, 31, 104, 145, 153
omniscient ones. *See* buddha/buddhas
"One Hundred Changbu Ritual" (Rangjung Dorje), 579n25
Önse Chölek, 237
Opening the Sky Door, 56, 250, 381, 553n41, 569–70nn6–7
altering disciples' minds, refuge, awakening mind, 207–8
authorization in, 216–18
awareness beings, invoking, 202
capability for, 488–90
concluding activities, 218–20, 231, 244
eight branch vows, 208–9
introduction in, 210–11, 226–30
invitation liturgy, 235
meanings of, 197–98
offerings in, 202–6
pledge beings, generating, 199–202
preliminaries, 199, 222–26, 234–35
as sovereign among transferences, 490
torma blessing in, 211–16
white distributions and, 491
*See also* separating body from mind
*Opening the Sky Door* (Rinchen Senge), 197–98, 548n19
organs, 332, 352, 382, 491, 575n11
*Ornament of Clear Realization* (Maitreya), 41, 73, 103, 311, 549n5, 551n29
Özer Gyaltsen, 451
Özer Tsenchen, 352, 385, 386, 434

Pacification (*zhi byed*)
Dampa Sangye, role of in, 3
five analogies for instructions, 525, 586n22
lineages of, 507–8, 509–11, 522
and Severance, synthesis of, xviii, 503
source texts for, 547n14
in *Treasury of Precious Instructions, The*, xiii, xiv, xviii
pacification of elaboration, 79, 80
Padma Ḍākinī, 201, 214
Padma Lingpa tradition, 545–46n1
Padmasambhava (Padmakara), 470, 581n7

Paksam Wangpo, 426
Palden Lhamo, 363
Palden Rinchen (Ratnashrī), 352, 384, 386, 433, 438, 450, 451, 452, 458
Palpung Monastery, xii, xviii, 321, 471, 501, 535
  text collection of, 197, 421, 422, 503
Palyul tradition, 345
pāramitās, six. *See* perfections, six
passion, 127, 167, 169, 192, 303. *See also* desire
paths
  to basic space, 436
  devil of exaltation of, 16, 17, 76, 83
  five, 34, 51, 52, 53, 69, 70, 72, 116, 522
  genuine, 186
  nondoing as, 25
  severing deviations of, 84
  threefold integration on, 56, 60, 67, 70
  as unity of two accumulations, 52
  as unmistaken, 254
  *See also* adverse conditions/circumstances; awakening, path of; gods and humans, path of; integration (*lam 'khyer*)
Patsap Gompa, 508, 511, 585n14
peace
  existence and, 247, 259, 444, 513, 533
  limits of, 27, 42, 99
  of pacification of elaboration, 43, 79
  practices that bring, 107, 175
  of shrāvakas (hearers), 86, 103
Peaceful Round Lotus, 287, 290, 368, 419
*Pearl Rosary* (Karma Chakme), 205, 345, 369, 568n9, 577n1
  leftover dedication in, 532
  lineage supplication in, 522–23, 578–79n13, 586n22
  Ninefold Spirit Feast in, 322, 578n8
*Pearl Rosary: An Account of the Lineage* (Samten Özer), 577n1
Pekar, 313, 316
Pema Wangchok, 428
perception spheres, four, 25, 78, 96, 559n32
perfection of wisdom, 98
  blessings of, 7, 57, 58, 110–11
  brilliance of, 547–48n14
  eight topics of, 551n29
  equality of, 146, 174, 190, 564n8, 566n3, 568n8
  homages to, 79, 80, 247–48, 379
  Machik's realization of, xiv
  mantra of, 199, 205, 265, 293, 350, 380, 487, 568n2, 583n10
  meditation on, 152
  not object of intellect, 26, 97
  and phenomena, indivisibility, 114
  as protector, 254
  qualities of practitioners of, 151
  realization of, 58–59
  as self-liberated inflation, 87
  in Severance, importance of, xvi–xvii, 79, 473
  as source of *Fifty-Verse Poem*, 3
  as space, 500
  in Sutra and Mantra, importance of, 41
  temporary results of, 71–72
  three usages of term, 43–44
  ultimate, 226
  unmade ground of, 78, 95–96
  without root, 4, 6
*Perfection of Wisdom, Severance of Evil Object, The,* 121, 156, 185
*Perfection of Wisdom in Eight Thousand Lines*
  on casting body by bodhisattvas, 570n4
  on equality, 174, 566n3
  on meditation on perfection of wisdom, 190
  on nature of mind, 144
  on no-mind, 53, 93, 552n34
  on phenomena and space, 111, 145, 564n7
*Perfection of Wisdom in Eighteen Thousand Lines*
  on aggregates, emptiness of, 81–82, 557n6
  on bodhisattva qualities, 473, 582n2
  on casting out body, 191
  on mental nonengagement, 96–97
  on space, 189, 567n4

*Perfection of Wisdom in One Hundred Thousand Lines*
on equality, 174, 566n3
on meditating on external emptiness, 151
mental nonengagement in, 84, 557n8
on mind, 144, 563n2
on protection from obstacles, 58, 553n48
on recollection, 54, 190, 341–42, 552n37, 576n30
refuge in, 263
as source of *Fifty Verses*, 73
on space, 111
on training, 102–3
*Perfection of Wisdom in Twenty-Five Hundred Thousand Lines*, 58, 553n48
*Perfection of Wisdom in Twenty-Five Thousand Lines*
on doing nothing, 190
on equality, 174, 566n3
on meditation on space, 152
mental nonengagement in, 145
on mind, 144, 563n2
on referential notions, 112–13
on space, 110–11
Perfection of Wisdom sutras, 568n8
as mothers and sons, 41, 549n5
"Noble," 557n6
as source of Severance, xvi–xvii, 185, 295, 541n13
*See also* Mother (texts)
perfections, six, 5, 50–51
as antidotes, 104–5
benefits from, 72–73
in body offering, 192, 332, 352, 382
eight topics, 50, 551n29
five paths and, 98
nothing to accomplish in, 135–36
as offering, 515–16
severing what is inconsistent with, 61
six bone ornaments and, 228, 444, 462
and wisdom, importance of to, 6, 50, 53
perfections, ten, 104–5, 105–6, 121
permission blessings, 216, 228, 568n10
pestilence, 8, 32, 64–65, 172, 547n14, 554n61, 554n65. *See also under* spirits
*phaṭ*, empowerment of, 228
phenomena (*chos*)
as beyond intellect, 161
brought into mind, 140
carrying the load of, 27, 78, 99
cutting root of, 137
as dependently arisen, 5, 51
equality of, 146, 147, 174, 190, 474, 564n8, 568n8
experiencing nature of, 17
inherent nature of, 114
mental, 113
as mental nonengagement, 97, 190
mind as root of, 85
nature of mind and, 4, 45
as nonreferential, 112–13, 114
as not truly existent, 80
as one's own awareness, 56, 490
realizing empty nature of, 7, 57–60
space and, 111, 145, 564n7
*See also* nature of phenomena
places, 31, 36, 106
by capabilities, 252
for clearing obstacles, 302
delightful, 119
discretion in, 309
of ground masters, 371
isolated places, 106, 175, 199, 313
length of stay at, 175
masters of, 235, 316
for meditation, 147
sacred, 236–39
spirits of, 260, 261, 326, 346, 374, 485
twenty-four sacred, 239, 453, 455, 459, 463–66
vital point of (place), 216–17
*See also* haunted places
planetary diseases, 334–35
pledge beings
dissolution of, 286–87, 290
generating in empowerments, 199–202
inseparable with awareness beings, 203, 265, 269, 377
pledge substances, 270, 317, 527
pointing-out instructions, 79, 157, 168, 169, 322, 341. *See also* introduction (*ngo sprod*)

poisons
five, 18–19, 62, 86–87, 148, 163, 166
three, 48, 62, 72, 501
postmeditation, xvii, 297, 304–7, 308
*See also* subsequent attainment (*rjes thob*)
postures
in empowerments, 210, 211, 228
half-vajra, 323
in preliminary practices, 248
for separating body and mind, 250
seven-point Vairochana, 301, 499
vital points, 315
*powa* (consciousness ejection), 555n70
power of truth recitation, 289, 360–61
practice lineages, eight, xii–xiii, xv, 539n3
*Practices of the Severance Collection and So Forth*, 29, 123–24, 157
Praise to Machik, 390–93, 522, 586n19
Prajñāsambhava, 29, 549n25. *See also* Jamyang Gönpo
*Prātimokṣhasūtra*. See *Individual Liberation Sutra*
pratyekabuddhas, 24, 94, 102, 263, 295, 328, 416–17
Prayer of Samantabhadra, 535
*Precious Garland*, 422
preliminaries, 10, 70, 168
for daily practice, 473–75
for empowerments, 199, 222–26, 234–35
in *Essence of Auspicious Renown*, 504–6
five perfections of method as, 52
instructions on, 143, 248–49, 298–300
purpose of, 499
times and sessions of, 300, 305, 307
presumption, resting without, 105, 110
pride, 19, 87, 112, 130, 213, 260, 289, 303, 306
*Profound Inner Principles, The* (Rangjung Dorje), 311
*Profound Severance Guide*, 321
prophecy lineage, 79
prostrations, 4, 46–47, 144, 248, 377
protection circles, 234, 287–88, 307, 322, 343
Puhrang the younger, 510
Puntsok Tenzin, 426
Puṇya Guru, 441
*Pure Honey* (Kunga Paljor), 39, 73–74, 556nn83–93
pure lands/realms, 270, 379
of five buddha families, 494, 584n19
in mandala offerings, 378
in supplications, 237
of ten directions, 446–47
pure true identity, 278
purposes, two, 4, 33, 42, 69, 73, 74, 106, 353, 387, 451

qualities
attachment to, 77, 82–83
of benefiting self and other, 43, 106
enhancing, 38
equality in, 133
expression of, 146
as faults, 162
of higher realms, 72, 556n82
increasing, 36, 37
nondissipating, 183
not grasping at, 15–16
offering, 230–31
of practice, 150
of realization, 60
of stages and paths, 52, 69, 108
support for, 35

radiance, unimpeded, 115–16
Rāga Asya. *See* Karma Chakme
Rāhula, 289, 331–32, 362
Rāhulabhadra, 80, 557n5
rāhulas, 337
rainbows, five-colored, 281
*Rainfall of Desirables* (Könchok Bang), 311, 342, 574–75n1, 577n31
rain-making, 180, 181
Raivatī, 289
Rangjung Dorje, third Karmapa, xvi, 219, 254, 321, 322, 343, 569n18, 574–75n1
classification of *Appendices*, 157
"long call" of, 361–62, 577n6, 578n8
names of, 247
"One Hundred Changbu Ritual," 579n25

Rangdung Dorje, third Karmapa (*continued*)
Severance, importance of to tradition, xv, 75, 247
in Severance lineage, 256, 257, 352, 386, 424, 437, 438, 512
"short calling," 322, 492, 583n16
students of, 383, 578n9
supplication attributed to, 577n7
on White Distribution for Four Guests, 320
ransom, ritual objects as, 174, 566n5
Rare and Sublime Guests of Honor distribution, 269–71
Rasa Panglung, 237, 570n3
Ratna Ḍākinī, 201, 213
Ratnakīrti, 80, 557n5
Ratnasambhava, 201, 213, 263, 517
Ratnashrī. *See* Palden Rinchen
Ratnasiṃha. *See* Rinchen Senge
realization
as bondage, 20, 77, 87
conduct, necessity of for, 17, 84
courage of, 34
through examination, 167
four flaws, 31
as nontransferable, 104
qualities of persons with, 15
realm of phenomena (*dharmadhātu; chos dbyings*)
as free of dualistic appearances, 54
lack of delusion in, 113
liberation in, 18
nonduality of samsara and nirvana in, 137
objective cognition in, 23, 544n49
resting in, 153
as suchness, 114
thoughts as nature of, 22
realm of Thirty-Three, 288
realms, three, visualization of, 331
rebirth, 48–49, 124–25, 556n82
Rechen Chödar, 442
recollection (*dran pa*), 570n2
agitation and, 152
of Buddha, 6, 54, 64
in healing rites, 318
hollowness of, 162
meditation without, 249–50
for not regressing, 253
unwavering, 169
upholding, 200
without mental engagement, 190
*Record of Teachings Received* (Tashi Chöpel), 39, 222, 257–58, 297
*Red Annals* (Dampa Sangye), 247
red distributions, 305–7, 500
Banners, 291, 366, 495
Bone Shaker, 291, 496
Casting Out the Corpse, 290–91, 494–95
Corpse Distribution, 290, 291–92, 495–96
in daily practice, 478–79, 492
with evidence of success and uprising, 307
Excellent Stakeout, 277, 493
Flayed Skin Distribution, 276, 277, 494, 572n23
Food Distribution, 290, 292, 494
Four Continents, 291, 495
guests suited to, 279
in healing rites, 283, 327, 359
instructions for, 275, 277–78, 290–92, 352
short call in, 382–83, 578n8
Slapping feast, 290, 292, 496, 573n39
summarizing meaning of Sutra, 316–17
wrathful magnetizing and, 288–92, 305
Red House of Copper Mountain, 384, 423, 432
Red Howlers feast hall, 281
red summons visualization, 319
Red Tsen, 448
reference points, 5, 6, 26, 51–52, 55, 99, 112–14, 140, 145, 563n3
refined essence, resting in, 20
refuge, 5, 31, 46–47
conferring, 207, 225
in daily practice, 473–74, 485–86
in empowerments, 200
for entering Severance, 186

in *Essence of Auspicious Renown*, 504
five-tiered, 262–64, 348–49, 486–87, 583n7
in guru, 413
in healing ritual, 323
instructions for, 248–49, 298–99
"jewel style," 346–48
Machik as one, 417
within the nature of phenomena, 10, 70
offerings to objects of, 268
precepts, purpose of, 49
stacking-up in, 293
succumbing to, 306
at time of death, 153
ultimate, 70, 249
visualization for, 261–62
in visualizing uprisings, 315
in Zurmang feasts, 374–75
*See also* preliminaries; Three Jewels
regressing, instructions on not, 253–54
rejoicing, 5, 49, 128–29, 144
reliance on path, prayer for, 521–22
*Religious History of Pacification and Severance* (Khamnyön), 13, 101, 123, 124, 197
removal rite, 71, 555n78
renunciation, 104, 109, 163, 165, 309
Resounding Kīla Graveyard, 282
Resounding Laughter Graveyard, 281
restraints, yoga's own six, 526, 586n24
results, 78
analogy for, 23
of blending space and awareness, 6, 55, 56
common, 69–71
conforming with cause, 48–49
as devil of exaltation, 17, 85
of distributions, 277, 278
for guests of feast offerings, 284
immediate and ultimate, 194
of inseparable three kāyas, 184
obstruction of, 176
of offering body, 271, 272
supreme, 69
three, 69, 555n74
ultimate, 72–73
as unity of two kāyas, 52
as unreal, 25–26, 97
Rete, 335, 364
Retī sisters, four, 264
retinues, four, 72
rhetoric, 43, 550n7
Richly Adorned (Ganavyūha), 270
Rigong Gönpa, 579nn20–21
Rigonpa Tsöndru Senge, 403, 410, 414, 431, 579n20
Rikdröl Dupa, 239
Rinchen Bum, 511
Rinchen Senge, xvii, 197–98, 548n18
Rinchen Wangpo, 426
Rinchen Zangpo, 425
Ringu Tulku, xviii–xix
Riwache, 511
Rok Sherap Ö, 508, 511, 585n14
root letters, 45, 550n12
*Root Verses on the Middle Called Wisdom* (Nāgārjuna), 43, 51
rootlessness, 18, 19, 20, 21, 23, 77, 86, 90, 127–28
Round Lotus, 287–88, 290
royalty, seven articles of, 203, 265, 378, 491, 519
Runda, adept of. *See* Palden Rinchen (Ratnashrī)

sacred pledge, 254
blessings of, 239
breaking, 161
elixir of, 372
fulfilling/renewing, 439, 443, 445, 447, 581n2 (*see also* fulfillment rituals)
illusion-like nature of, 442, 445, 447
interdependent connections, role of in, 308
reciting, 325
of Severance, 60, 193
for those with faith, 139
types of, 456
*Saddharmasmṛtyupasthāna*. See *Supreme Dharma of the Application of Attention*
sakzhu hat, 331, 333, 575n9
Samantabhadra, 373, 408, 477, 491, 535, 585n10

samsara
  abandoning, 22, 91
  accepting and rejecting, 250
  bondage of, 255
  buddhahood and, 9, 68
  causes of, 21, 144
  confusion of, 55
  emancipation due to faith, 139
  grasping tangible devils in, 14, 81
  Great Mother as ground of, 24, 78, 95
  lack of real in, 26, 97
  liberated on own ground, 20, 77, 89
  liberation by realizing meaning, 78, 96–97
  mind as root, 4, 45, 60
  neither inhibiting nor indulging, 30
  as one's mind, 129
  setting aside, 174
  *See also* cyclic existence
Samten Özer, xv, 29, 222, 233, 237, 297, 471, 472, 482, 512, 577n1
Samten Palwa, 511
Samten Rinchen, 383, 421, 442, 578n9
sanctimony, 175, 183
*sangs rgyas* (buddha), use of term, 55, 552n38
Sangye Dorje, 238
Sangye Dudul Dorje, thirteenth Karmapa, 258
Sangye Gompa, 511
Sangye Nyenpa, 321
Sangye Raptön, 384, 432
Sangye Tönpa, 512
Sangye Wön, 511
Saraha, 45, 507, 550n14, 584n3
Saroruhavajra, 507, 584n5
Saru, 39
Savage Graveyard, 281
seal of invalidity, 83–84
seats
  ascending, 293
  corpse, 462
  crowning sun and moon, 239
  in five-tiered refuge, 262–64
  of flayed skin, 315
  jeweled, 486, 583n7
  lion throne, 323, 486
  lion-lotus-moon, 377
  lotus-moon, 386, 388, 401, 435
  lotus-sun-corpse, 376
  offering, 202
  sun-moon, 422
  sun-moon-lotus, 376
  symbolism of, 507
  vajra throne, 296, 573n45
secrecy, 112, 230
Secret Mantra. *See* Mantra tradition
*Secret Severance* (attributed to Pema Karpo), 279, 572n25
seed syllables
  ascending, 293
  of awareness beings, 264, 265
  body offering, 269
  in body-offering feasts, 328, 356, 477, 491, 497
  in communal feasts, 527
  in consecrating offerings, 372, 373
  in consecrating torma, 404
  in descent of blessings, 475
  in Face Skull Cup feast, 276
  in field of accumulation, 486–87
  in healing ritual, 340
  of heart, 223, 265, 275
  in invoking awareness beings, 348–49, 377
  for leftovers, 532
  in refuge visualization, 262–63
  of six classes, 266–67, 489
  in torma offering, 370
  on vajras, 282
seeker as not established, 159
self, 16, 90, 412
self-appearance, 14, 148, 302, 397
self-arising, 16, 19, 20, 330, 443, 544n31
Self-Arising Queen (Rang byung rgyal mo), 264
self-empowerment, 236–40
self-entrance, 224, 225
self-fixation, xiii, 60–61
  eliminating through body-offering, 31, 479
  freedom from, 142
  guests as, 278–79
  letting go of, 111

from objects, 32
of person and phenomena, 295
purified on own ground, 98
severing, 118
spirits of, 360–61
tangible devils and, 109
self-liberation, 14, 17, 84, 116, 169, 174, 184
seminal fluid loss, 308, 316, 334, 337
Senge Palwa, 352, 386, 450
Senge Yeshe, 580n3
sensations, 15, 16, 76, 82, 108, 128, 250
sense desirables, 150, 411, 440
sense doors, five, 7, 14, 59, 167
sense objects, 14, 56, 250, 312, 518
sense organs, 56, 131, 352, 382, 577n4
sense perceptions, 14, 150
sentient beings
as buddhas, 159–60, 163, 164, 168
controlling, 309
as deluded cognition, 94
emptiness as basis of helping, 10, 70–71
emptiness of, 341
grandmother, 429
as guests, 375
inherent nature of, 97
as kind parents, 181–82
lack of true existence of, 90
liberating, 21
maturing, 50, 105
meaning of, 161
as mothers and offspring, 329
types of, 485
separating body from mind, 31, 35–36, 549n23
capability for, 174–75, 193
in eliminating stagnancy, 177
four experiences in, 210–11
instructions on, 146–47, 188–90, 250
introducing intrinsic awareness in, 210
liturgy for, 351
offering as feast, 205–6
sequence of, 268–78
when sick, 178
in Zurmang instructions, 266–67
*See also* Opening the Sky Door
*serak* spirits, 313
Serding monastery, 29–30
Seven Heaps mandala arrangement, 514
Severance (*gcod*)
articles for (*See* accoutrements)
befriending adversity in, 30
benefits of, 10, 38, 72–73
*chöd*, use of term, xvii
classifications of, xiii, 39, 503
combined peaceful-wrathful, 307, 308, 499, 500
conduct of, 23, 92–93
connecting ritual with meaning, 290
definitions, 132, 137–38, 526n19
demon-feeding, role of in, 297–98
development of, 185, 258
distinctiveness of, 117, 164
elevation of, 19, 87, 142, 484
empowerments in, xvii
fear, special role in, 274
foundational instructions on, 27
founding of, 13
four vital points of, 216, 568n11
as heart-blood of wise, 161
Indian source of, xiv, xvi, 3–4
indigenous practices in, 171
Karma Chakme's role in, 345
lineages of, 256, 257–58, 297, 421–22
Mahāmudrā tradition of, 197–98, 483, 526–27
Mikyö Dorje, role of in, 311
Mother's cycle of, 279
outer, inner, secret meanings of, 255
and Pacification, synthesis, xviii, 503
peaceful, 304–5, 306–7, 308, 499, 500
perversions and deviations in, 176–77, 219–20, 296, 481, 484
place in Eight Great Chariots schema, xiv
poem condensing meaning of, 254–56
purpose of, 35
Rangjung Dorje's role in, xv, 75, 247
signature phrase of, xvii
sixteen great children of transmission, 508
source scriptures and commentaries of, xiv–xvii, 295, 322, 345, 547n14, 569–70n6

Severance (*continued*)
suitability for, 137, 158, 186, 413
suspicions about, 282
Tāranātha's connection with, 221
in three-year retreat, 471
topics of instruction in, 79
twofold approach of, 139–40
vital points of, 109
as without view, 16, 84
wrathful, 305–7, 308, 499, 500
yogic emphasis of, xv
severance
desiring, 164
evidence of, 8–9, 65, 305
fierce style, 330
gentle, 329–30
meanings of term, 8, 60–61, 172, 473, 543n23, 562n19
when to apply, 140
*Severance Feast Activities*, 523
severing four devils in basic space, 499, 500
in daily practice, 476
instructions, 303–4
sources for, 297
sexual intercourse, 284
Shākya Özer, 237
Shami, 511
Shangpa Kagyu, xiii, 221, 233, 579nn20–21
Shaṅkhapāla, 335, 364
Shāntideva, 47, 52, 584n6
Shavari, 424, 580n3
Shechen editions, 197, 311, 421, 422, 503
Sherap Özer, xii, 539n2
shrāvakas
deluded cognition of, 24, 94
nirvana of, 86
offering body to, 328
perfection of wisdom, training of in, 102, 103
realization of, 295
in refuge visualization, 187, 263
visualization of, 416
Shrīdevī. *See* Mahākālī
shrines, instructions for setting up, 504
Shubu Lotsā, 511
sickness
attachment to, 147
bliss-emptiness, transforming to, 340–41
causes of, 37
of children, 180, 567nn13–15
cutting by casting out body, 251
delighting in, 32
as delusion, 306
demons of, 346
from elements, 179
emptiness of, 341
feasts for, 133–34, 497
as inner uprising, 308–9
as intangible devil, 312
as karmic liability, 272
practices during, 178–80
practices for, 133–34, 252
as projections, 116
purifying, 215, 375
release from, 194
support for, 35–36
as unbearable, 133
*See also* healing rituals
"single seat," 471, 525. *See also* daily practice (body donation)
*Single-Seat Severance Poem* (Mikyö Dorje), 321, 322, 323–27, 574–75n1
*sinmo* spirits, 313, 316, 361, 457
*sinpo* spirits, 361, 362
Situ Norbu Sampel, 438, 451, 581n8
Situ Pema Nyinje Wangpo, 369, 370, 421, 422, 427
Situ Rinpoche, 280, 295
*siu*, 180, 567nn13–15
Six Armed [Mahākāla] (Phyag drug pa), 264
six classes of beings
aspirations for, 323, 340
feeding, 359, 405
as guests, 272–74, 382
habitual patterns of, 45
in haunted places, 305
karmic liabilities to, 272–73
karmic spirits of, 260
in mantra visualizations, 265
mothers and fathers of, 457

offerings to, 276, 283, 328, 330
purifying places of, 352, 383
purifying sufferings of, 19, 86–87
*See also* sentient beings
six continuums, 144
Six Earth Lord Application liturgy, 322, 331, 361–62
*Six Pieces*, 4, 197, 547n14
six realms
controlling, 360
guests of, 261
pure lands, transformation into, 494, 584n19
qualities of higher, 72, 556n82
rebirth in, 48–49
tormas for, 224
vital drops of, 266–67
Six Vajra-Line Prayer, 535
skull cups (*kapāla*), 313, 408
of ḍākinīs, 282
of elixir, 269, 272, 273, 294, 319, 497
feast tray as, 282
of five-family ḍākinīs, 354–56
of four ḍākinīs, 201, 281, 376, 463
for leftovers, 497–98
lotus (*padma bhañja*), 401, 436, 496–97, 579n19
of Machik, 205–6, 443, 461
from syllable *a*, 372, 527
of three existences, 290
of Vajrayoginī, 267, 269, 292, 376, 494
of wrathful ḍākinīs, 337
*See also* Face Skull Cup feast
Skull Fragment (Thod pa'i dum bu), 263
Skull Hearthstones, 276, 572n24
sky, blending with consciousness, 147
sky door, opening, xvii. *See also* Opening the Sky Door
Sky Lake (Namtso), 424, 450, 571n10
sky-like nature/sky-like realm, 145, 154
Slapping feast, 290, 292, 496, 573n39
Smoky Lady (Dud sol ma), 264
snake binding, vajra, 317
So Gendun Bar, 508, 585n13
So system, 511, 525, 585n13
Sochung, 511
Sokpo Dode, 511
Sönam Lama
as Kyochung, supplication to, 384, 432, 578n10
lineage of, 198, 237, 342, 422
Machik and, xiv, 4, 570n3, 570n7
Sönam Paljor, 39
songs of meditative experience. *See* vajra songs
Sound Vajra goddesses, 323
sounds
as apparitions, 32
of ḍākinīs, 228, 229
of Great Mother, 261
in invoking awareness beings, 264
*Source of All Qualities* (Tekchok Dorje), xvii, 258, 369–70, 578n1
invocation prayer, 202, 568n3
Kagyu feast liturgies and, 431, 459
lineage supplication in, 421, 522–23, 586n22
Praise of Machik in, 569n6
recitations in *White Crystal Mirror*, 262, 264–65, 266, 268, 275, 281, 282, 285, 286, 287, 571n4, 572n22
Six Earth Lord Application liturgy in, 322
space
abiding nowhere, 152
awareness and, 189
basic, 160
Buddha's intent as, 6, 54
homages to, 14, 76, 80
path to basic, 436
resting in, 108, 111
unbiased experience of, 16
waves rising from, 82
*See also under* inseparability; severing four devils in basic space
speech (*ngag*), 107, 216, 217, 309
Speech (*gsung*)
blessings and empowerments of, 326
as liberated, 21, 90
mantra of, 228
mudra of, 350, 381, 487, 519
nonfixation on, 26, 78, 98
pledge substances as, 527
sacred pledge of, 456

Speech (*continued*)
  timeless awareness of, 98
spike-like suppression, 8, 65–66
spirits
  appearance of, 37
  applications specific to female, 334
  of body, 260, 261, 327, 337, 346, 374, 485, 492
  casting away, 227
  child, 328, 336
  controlling, 177, 331
  cornering, 174, 177, 566n4
  of disease, 337–38
  eights kinds, 259–60, 261, 309
  evil, 10, 31, 70–71
  oath bound, 349
  pestilent, 313, 316, 322, 360, 361–62, 382, 457
  in pre-Buddhist Tibet, 541n13
  purifying, 215, 307
  raising, 314–15
  spiritual powers from, 162
  summoning malicious, 360–61
  sympathetic to dharma, 307–8
  in wrathful magnetizing, 288, 289–90
  and yogins, nonduality of, 57
spiritual masters. *See* gurus
spiritual powers (*siddhi*; *dngos grub*), 162–64
  attachment to, 20, 88
  as buddha quality, 136
  circumstances as, 252
  as devil of exaltation, 15, 112
  granting of, 268
  requesting, 402, 403, 410, 411
  source of, 414
  torma empowerment for, 230
spiritual practice
  alone, 162, 166
  applied to faculties, 174–75
  beyond referential objects, 26, 99
  continuous, 105
  devil of exaltation in, 312
  diligence in, 107
  effect of haunted places on, 130
  guidelines for, 168–69
  integrating, 109
  locations for, 31
  pride in, 303
  progressive presentation of, 185
  required occasions for, 307–8
  sessions and times for, 188, 191, 300, 301, 304, 309, 318, 327, 330, 337, 341
  uninterrupted, 166
splendor, attributes of, 270, 572n17
spontaneous presence, 164
stains, incidental, 34, 548n20
*Steps of Vital Points, The*, 79, 252, 571n5
Sthiramati, 551n20
stupidity
  antidote to, 192
  dullness as, 152
  inseparable great, 14
  as leftovers, 367
  liberated on own ground, 19, 87
  liver of, 457
  of negative actions, 125
  noncognizant, 23–24, 78
  purity of, 211, 212
Subhuti, 112–13
subject-object dualism, 5, 6, 51, 55, 95, 166, 217, 278
subsequent attainment (*rjes thob*), 57, 154, 481, 490–91, 525
  *See also* postmeditation
success, evidence of, 253, 305, 310, 316, 319, 320, 479
suchness
  bodhisattva's warmth and, 153
  of feast offering, 284
  resting in, 118, 146, 158–59, 565n2
  understanding, 110
suffering
  abandoning, limits of, 165
  attachment to, 147
  as auspicious sign, 488
  of body, 146–47
  carrying alone, 351, 381, 519
  as devoid of arising, ceasing, abiding, 277
  emptiness of, 341
  in gentle severance, 329
  as intangible devil, 312
  meditating on, 182

negativity and, 125
pacifying, 133
as resolved in bliss, 153
severing, 83
of six classes, 19, 86–87
sugatas
precept lineage of, 79, 157
twelve, 507, 509, 585n10
*See also* buddha/buddhas
Sukhasiddhī, 3, 237, 342, 352, 386, 507, 510, 584n7
Sumgom Chenpo, 384, 433
*Summary of the Intentions*, 283
Sungrap Gyatso, 353, 386
*Supplication Liturgy for the Essence of the Vital Meaning* (Tāranātha), 297
*Supplication Stirring the Intention*, 230, 240–43, 569n6
*Supplication to the Eighty-Four Great Adepts* (Vajrāsanapāda), 73, 556n86
*Supplication to the Lineage of Gurus of the Three Transmissions of Pacification Known as Golden Rosary* (Lochen Dharmashrī), 522, 585n18
supplications, 144, 279–80
additional Zurmang variations, 294
to basic space, 309
casket, praises from four directions of, 395–98, 579n18
of complete lineages, abridged, 353–54, 387
for descent of blessings, 474–75
*Essence of Auspicious Renown* as, 503
of father and mother tantra, abridged, 352–53, 386–87
to father lineage, 388–90
in guru yoga, 182–83
in healing ritual, 325
long lineage, 383–86, 422–29, 523–27, 578n9, 578n13
by Mikyö Dorje, 342–43
place-and-name format, 422
Praise of Machik, 390–93
Praise to the Son, 394
preliminary, 224
to Severance lineage, abridged, 522–23, 586n21
Summoning the Hundred Thousand Ḍākinīs, 398–400
at time of death, 153
in torma offerings, 234, 235, 236
two, 315
suppression practices, 33, 254, 320, 571n6, 574n10
*Supreme Dharma of the Application of Attention*, 338, 480, 576n26, 582n6
Supreme Mountain, 260
in body mandala, 351, 382, 490
in body-offering, 205, 249, 267, 324, 330
in gift of dharma, 338
in healing rites, 178, 331
leftovers as, 366, 532
in mandala offering, 378
offering, 265
in White Distribution for Four Guests, 320, 491
*Sutra of Skill in the Methods of the Great Secret*, 59
Sutra tradition, 4, 41, 79
svabhāvakāya, 97. *See also* kāyas, two
svabhāvika-dharmakāya, 184
"swift foot" practice, 13
symbolic meaning, 79, 107, 113, 116, 283, 464

Tai Situ incarnations, 321
Taklung Kagyu, 574n9
Taklung Tang monastery, 310, 574n9
Takṣhaka, 335, 364
tangible devils, 8
after severing, 10, 72
descriptions of, 14, 62, 76, 81–82, 542n3
in devil of inflation, 18, 77, 85–86
identifying and severing, 109, 116, 127–28, 158, 303
tantra tradition. *See* Mantra tradition
tantras, classes of, 270, 380, 451
Tārā, 287, 585n10
Green, 486
homages to, 102, 204, 379
in integration practice, 498
Khadiravaṇī, 263
lineage of, 3, 342, 509, 510

Tārā (*continued*)
  Machik's direct experience of, xiv
  visualizations of, 201, 263, 348
Tāranātha, xv, xvii, 221–22, 297, 310, 471, 481
Tashi Chöpel, 39, 222, 257
Tashi Chubar, 384, 433
Tashi Lhundrup, 384, 433
Tashi Özer, 422, 427
Tathāgata. *See* Buddha Shākyamuni
Tekchok Dorje, fourteenth Karmapa, 258, 369, 370, 416, 471, 578n1. See also *Source of All Qualities* (Tekchok Dorje)
*telmo* spirits, 336, 365, 576n24
Telopa, 95, 257, 264, 450, 558n29, 584n5
ten directions, buddhas of, 185, 249, 263, 286, 437, 446–47, 581n5
ten stages, 25, 34, 52, 69, 72, 96, 126, 407
tenet systems
  attachment to, 10, 69
  avoiding bad, 139
  deluded cognitions of, 24, 78, 94–95, 219
Tenga Rinpoche, 483
*tenma* (protector goddesses), 334, 363, 371, 469–70, 581nn5–6
Tenpa Namgyal, 352, 386
Tent Protector (mGur mgon), 264
Tenzin Dargye, 426
Tenzin Namdak. *See* Bengen Tenzin Namdak
*tepur*, black, 334, 576n15
Terdak Lingpa. *See* Minling Terchen
termination, evidence of, 8, 33, 65, 67, 548n17
Tertön Chokgyur Lingpa. *See* Chokgyur Dechen Lingpa
*teurang* spirits, 289, 313, 316, 328, 336, 360, 365, 576n24
thighbone, human, 199, 242, 313
  empowerment of, 229
  in empowerments, 241
  in fulfillment, 440, 458
  in gathering guests, 177, 261, 271, 275, 314, 346, 373, 485
  in healing rituals, 326, 331–32
  visualizing, 201, 288
*Thirty-Five Questions and Answers on the Bundle of Precepts, the Quintessence of the Mother's Super Secret Heart-Mind* (Jamyang Gönpo?), 123–24
Thirtyfold Prayer by Dampa, 532–33
thirty-six uncommon awareness-holders, 507, 510, 584n8
thirty-two marks, 25, 97
thoughts, 78
  authentic, 107
  ceasing from within, 137
  cutting root, 4, 45–46, 161
  deluded, 113
  as devils, 9, 68, 150, 312
  dharmakāya, transforming to, 340–41
  freedom from, 142
  as Great Mother, 22, 91
  lack of as buddha, 141
  mistaken, 32
  as naturally liberated, 15, 59–60
  observing, 227
  regarding as dreams, 83
  resting between, 301
  rootlessness of, 21
  as self-arising, 19
  severing, 33, 172, 479–80
  signs of warmth and, 153
  stamping down, 17
  as timeless awareness, 148, 150
Thrangu Rinpoche, Khenchen, 483
thread-cross rite, 174, 566n5
three bases, 4, 44–45, 56
*Three Cycles of the Lamp of Pacification* (Dampa Sangye), 585n12
three doors to liberation, 44, 58, 104–5, 550n11
Three Jewels, 8, 64
  auspiciousness of, 415
  in healing rituals, 322–23
  mandala offerings to, 204, 205
  offering body to, 187–88, 249, 320, 330
  recollection of, 342
  refuge in, 8, 64, 225, 235, 299, 375, 505
  root guru as, 172–73

torma offerings to, 305
Three Precious Collections (Tripiṭaka), 43, 550n7
three roots, 72, 224, 299
three spheres, 72, 488, 491
three whites and three sweets, 180, 273, 495, 567n16
Tibetan Buddhism
textual preservation in, xi–xii, 539n1
variety of practices in, 345
Tibetan literature, features of, 321, 369
time
for beginning practice, 504
for body donation, 337
for body-mandala offering, 491
for daily practice, 483
for distributions, 492
for practice, 31, 36, 252, 279, 300, 301, 309
for red distribution, 316
for severance, 330
for traveling to haunted places, 314
as uncontrived, 167
for variegated distribution, 317
timeless awareness (*ye shes*)
of accomplishing action, 215
and afflictive emotions, single basis of, 167
discriminating, 214
of equality/equanimity, 213
expansion of, 34
five kinds, 19, 86–87, 278, 284, 295, 332, 352, 382 (*see also* individual awareness)
as five lights, 273
form as, 128
fourfold, 55, 105
of great bliss, 283
mirror-like, 212, 213
not established as real, 97–98
of phenomena, 24, 78, 93, 95
purification by, 216
realization of, 106
of realm of phenomena, 82, 95, 211, 212
for removing flaws, 34
of signs, 283
unborn, 117
Tokden Gelong, 384, 433
Tokden Jampa Palwa, 385, 434
Tokden Senge Palwa, 384, 433
Tokden Tenzin Namdak. *See* Bengen Tenzin Namdak
Tongwa Dönden, sixth Karmapa, 422, 425, 580n1
Tönyön Samdrup, 393, 508, 512, 569n6, 579n16
torma-blessing authorization (Opening the Sky Door), 197–98
authorization in, 216–18, 568n10
concise offerings and homages, 203, 205, 568n9
concluding practices, 218–20
eight branches in, 208–9
generating pledge beings, 199–202
invoking awareness beings in, 202
offerings in, 202–4
preliminaries, 199
purifying disciples' mindstreams in, 207–8
separating body and mind in, 209–10
torma blessing in, 211–16
torma offering in, 206
tormas
in accumulating merit, 177
adorned, 468
blessing, 236
of command, 467, 468–69, 470
in concluding practices, 307
in consecrating body as feast, 356
corpse and feast, combined, 282–83
elixir, 463, 466
in empowerments, 222, 224, 225, 230–31, 240–43
in enhancing practices, 181
in feasts, 285, 370–72, 402, 403
in fulfillment ritual, 457
in haunted places, 305, 307
of leftovers, 285–86, 366–67
liturgies for, 404, 406–9, 410–11
for obstructors, 199, 222, 225, 230, 234–35
in preliminaries, 259

tormas (*continued*)
  protection, 419
  purpose of, 199, 459
trampling upon the unbearable, 132–33, 526n19
transference
  path of, 37
  in Vase of Elixir Distribution, 275
  *See also* Opening the Sky Door
transformation, remedy of, 34, 35, 548–49n22
transitory collection, 255. *See also* aggregates, five
treasure tradition, 472
*Treasury of Dohā Songs* (Saraha), 45, 550n14
*Treasury of Extensive Teachings*, 470
*Treasury of Kagyu Mantra, The*, xii
*Treasury of Knowledge, The*, xi, xviii, 568n11
*Treasury of Precious Hidden Teachings, The*, xii, xv
*Treasury of Precious Instructions, The*, xi, 503, 535
  *Another Bundle* in, 123
  editions of, xii–xiii, 422
  *Hair's Tip of Wisdom* in, 101
  "Heart Essence of Profound Meaning" in, 29, 545n1
  *Hundred Guides of Jonang, The*, 221
  "male" Severance lineage in, 3–4
  omissions from, 297
  organization of, xii–xiii, xv–xvi
  Rangjung Dorje in, 75, 247
  *Vajra Play* in, 139
treatises
  five rubrics of composition, 40, 549n3
  four special attributes of, 44, 550n10
  separating outline from commentary, 75
  twelve divisions of, 43, 550n7
  vehicles of, 79
Tropu Monastery, 198
Trotsang, 511
True Word. *See* power of truth recitation
Trungpa lineage, 39. *See also* Kunga Namgyal, fourth Trungpa
truths, two, 52
Tsādra Rinchen Drak, 482, 535
Tsang, 221
Tsari Mountain, 571n10
Tsāritra, 441
*tsen* spirits, 286, 289, 313, 316, 335–36, 365, 448, 469
Tsenden Wangchuk Dorje, 384, 433
Tsoknyi Paljor, 385, 434
Tsomer, xiv, 540n8
Tsöndru Senge, 512
Tsultrim Yeshe, 442
Tsurpu Monastery, 247, 571n10
Tsurpu Valley, 424
Tuṣhita, 508
*Twenty Verses on Bodhisattva Vows* (Chandragomin), 47
twenty-eight mighty ones (*dbang phyug*), 285, 467–69
*Two-Part Hevajra Tantra*, 216–17, 218, 569n17

*Udānavarga*, 104, 560n7
*Udānavargavivaraṇa* (Prajñāvarman), 560n7
Ultimate Variety feast hall, 282
unborn, 17
  abiding in, 137
  buddha as, 134–35
  emptiness, 137
  ground, 25, 127, 129
  inherent nature as, 56
  innate disposition as, 115–16
  lack of intention within, 138
  nature of thought, 412
  practicing, 7, 57
  single cut, 4, 45, 60, 556n83
  that cannot be asserted, 113
uncommon vehicle, 490
union, of male and female, 497
unity
  actualized embodiment of, 284, 295
  of clarity and emptiness, 118
  of emptiness and compassion, 96, 100, 318
  in healing rites, 318
  of samsara and nirvana, 33
  of self, patient, and spirits, 342, 577n31

of view and conduct, 20, 87, 99, 501
Unpleasant Sound (Kuru), 267
Upānanda, 335, 364
uprisings (*lhongs ba*)
difficult and easy, distinctions in, 316
evidence of, 315, 319, 479
provoking, 307
signs of, 33, 67
three kinds, 308–9
visualization of, 315
Urepa, 29
Uttara, 263
*Uttaratantra*. See *Highest Continuum* (Maitreya)

Vairochana
in empowerments, 201, 211
Immense Ocean, 348, 377, 486, 538n8, 577n2
in inner offering, 516
posture of, 301, 499
in refuge field, 263, 348
visualization of, 377, 507
Vajra Ḍākinī, 201, 212, 452, 455
*Vajra Play* (Machik), xvi, 139
Vajra Seat, 441, 460
vajra siblings, 239
vajra songs, 217, 465, 509
vajra straws, 206
*Vajracchedikāprajñāpāramitasūtra*. See *Diamond Cutter Sutra*
Vajradhara, 172
dedication to, 408
as guest, 269, 328, 357, 404
supplications to, 225, 388
as timeless awareness of great bliss, 283
visualizations of, 263, 507
Vajrakrodha, 508, 510, 585n11
Vajrapāṇi, 350, 460, 507, 579n17, 585n10
vajras
analogy for mind, 198
golden, visualization of, 301, 319, 496–97, 499
in mother lineage feasts, 282
Vajrasādhu, 336, 365
Vajrāsanapāda, 73, 556n86
Vajravārāhī, 237, 322, 417, 585n10
feeding, 357, 405
five deities of, 263, 280, 348
in healing ritual, 324, 326, 328
in offering body mandala, 490–91
in peaceful severance, 304
in red distributions, 495
self-visualization as Jetsunma, 268, 285, 291, 319, 495
in Severance, importance of, 459
in suppression of wealthy, 320
torma offering to, 460
in white distributions, 491
vajrayāna. *See* Mantra tradition
Vajrayoginī
all women as, 281, 282
in body offering, 269, 328
as Krodhīkālī, 275, 527n21
in offering leftovers, 286
in red distributions, 277, 291, 292, 494
in separating mind from body, 267
visualizations of, 326, 376
in white distributions, 491
in wrathful magnetizing, 289
vanquishing conduct, 32, 484, 490, 499
vase body, 287
Vase of Elixir Distribution, 275–76, 493, 494
Vāsukī (*ba su ki*), 180, 567n16
*Verse Summary on the Perfection of Wisdom*
on becoming buddha, 88
on benefiting others, 89–90
on blessings, 58, 180
on casting body by bodhisattvas, 251, 570n4
on conduct, 92
in *Distillation of the Profound*, 472, 473, 582n2
on equanimity, 155
*Great Bundle of Precepts* and, 27
on limitlessness, 97–98, 559n36
miracle simile in, 88, 558n15
on self and other, 90
on severing view, 60–61, 554n55
on skilled bodhisattvas, 87
on space and awareness, 189, 567n4

*Verse Summary on the Perfection of Wisdom (continued)*
on space and phenomena, 146
on unmade ground, 95–96
on wisdom and five aggregates, 91–92
view, 77, 90
authentic, 107
as carrying load, 78, 99
as conceit, 16, 83
conduct and, 17, 76, 84
conduct and meditation, unity of, 20, 87
confidence of, 116–17
conviction in, 140
cutting doubts about, 109
decisive resolution of, 475
four vital points of, 547n14
generating heightened, 184
of inherent nature, 56
of integrating devils, 154–56
lack of frame of reference of, 52
limits of, 20, 87
looking with, 130
obstruction of, 176
preventing straying from, 192–93
realizing, 165
in separating body from mind, 147
three absorptions and, 473
unmistaken, 135
*See also* wrong views
Vikramashīla Monastery, 549n3
violation contamination, 159
virtue
aspiring to, 480
conditioned, limits of, 5, 51, 106, 127
increasing, 69, 165, 501
inspiration for, 148
purity of, 9, 69
strength of, 106
virtuous roots, 115, 209, 329
Virūpa, 388, 549n2, 584n5
visionary experiences, 233, 316, 319, 471
visualizations
dissolution of, 341, 416–17
for fulfillment, 438–39
of giving and taking, 329
in guru yoga, 182, 183
of increasing and cleansing, 320
for order of evidences, 319
of red summons, 319–20
for self-entrance, 224, 225
sequence for overwhelming spirits, 314–15
of "snake binding," 317
training of, 304–5
wrathful, 265–66, 380–81, 487, 496
yogic, 37
*See also* dissolution
vows, 47, 144
of awakening mind, 486, 583n5
bodhisattva, 5, 47, 50, 486, 551n20, 583n6
of body, speech, mind, 338–39
breakers of, 457
confessing transgressions, 456–57
of eight branches, 208–9
importance of, 115
of individual liberation, 49
not contravening, 254
*See also* sacred pledge
Vulture Peak Mountain, 236, 383, 423, 431, 440

Wandering Severance, 71
Wangchuk Dorje, 438, 450
Wangdor, 352, 386
warmth, 59–60, 85, 88, 146, 150, 153, 177
wealth gods, 264, 271, 457
wheel-wielding monarch, 125, 263
White Ablution Water (Khrus chab ma dkar mo), 265
*White Crystal Mirror* (Tenzin Namdak), 257–58, 295, 369, 571n1, 571n4, 582n3
white distributions, 304–5, 307, 491–92, 500
Assorted Distribution, 495
attributed to Könchok Bang, 322
in daily practice, 476–78
Emptying the Six Realms, 494
Face Skull Cup, 276, 493, 494, 527n24
Five Desirables Offering, 494
Guests of Compassion, 272–73
in healing ritual, 329–30
Lordly Guests of Qualities, 271–72

Rare and Sublime Guests of Honor, 269–71
Vase of Elixir Distribution, 275–76, 493, 494
White Distribution for Four Guests, 277, 279, 294, 320, 351–52
White Feast in Three Cycles of Integration, 269–73, 277, 382, 491, 584n19
White Great Bliss feast hall, 281
winds, vital, 147, 189, 190, 309, 334, 475
wisdom (*prājña; shes rab*)
to eliminate stagnancy, 177
experiential practice of, 96–97
and method, relationship of, 5–6, 52
offering, 515
Severance for practitioners with, 139–40
*See also* timeless awareness
wisdom protectors, 264
wish-fulfilling gems, 17, 267, 412, 491, 514
wish-granting trees, 267, 271
wolf-riders, three sister, 448
wonder, resting in, 499
word continuum instructions, 124
words
and meaning, instructions for, 256
as method, 137
in Severance, place of, 140, 162
worldly protectors, 234, 271, 328, 437, 487
wrathful actions, 286, 288–90, 295, 305–7, 308, 443, 499, 500
Wrathful Round Lotus, 287–88, 290, 368
wrong views, 94–95
correcting by fulfillment, 442–43, 445, 447–48
cutting, 149
dangers of, 161
as delusions, 306
types of, 255–56
as uprisings, 308–9

Yakde Paṇchen, 322, 345, 577n7
yakṣhīs, four great, 469
*yama*, twelve, 469
Yamāntaka, 509, 585n10
Yamarāja, 325
Yangpa Lode, 426
Yarlha Shampo, 540n8
Yarlung Mara Serpo, 4
Yellow Accomplishment of Purpose feast hall, 281
Yeshe Gyaltsen, 511
Yeshe Senge, 442
Yeshe Wangden, 296
Yeshe Zhön, 511
yidams
binding, 10, 71–72
fulfillment of, 439
offerings to, 205, 206, 275, 283, 328, 330
as oneself, 23
prophecies of, 150
torma of, 224, 236
Yikdruk Shepal, 238
yoga
absence of afflictive emotions in, 22–23, 78, 92
of being nobody, xviii
crazy, 32
nonduality in, 57
not wasting awareness in, 165, 565n16
yogāchāra, 117
yogic discipline/vanquishing conduct, 32, 484, 490, 499
yogins, meaning of term, 141–42
"yogin's gliding strut," 313
Yolmo Shen, 510
Yönten Gönpo, 238
Yönten Gyatso. *See* Jamgön Kongtrul Lodrö Taye
Yungtön, 424

Zalmo Drakpa, 74, 556n91
Zalmo Gang, 384, 433, 578n12
Zangri Karmar, 237
Zhama Lotsā, 3, 11, 73, 541n7, 556n85
Zhamar incarnations, 311
Zhang Gaden, 511
*zhentong*. *See* Great Madhyamaka
Zhije (*zhi byed*). *See* Pacification
Zhikpo Kunseng, 29
Zhikpo Nyima Senge, 508, 585n14
Zhönnu Drup, 512

Zurmang Kagyu tradition, 197, 296, 577n2
feasts of, 369–70, 459, 581n1
field of accumulation in, 486
lineages of, 421, 437, 438
in Severance tradition, xv, 257–58, 484, 580n1
Zurmang Khenchen Pema Namgyal, 198
Zurmang Monastery, 257, 556–57n93